CANADIAN HISTORY SINCE CONFEDERATION

EIGHTH EDITION

Destinies

CANADIAN HISTORY SINCE CONFEDERATION

EIGHTH EDITION

ROBERT A. WARDHAUGH
University of Western Ontario

ALAN MACEACHERN
University of Western Ontario

and
R. DOUGLAS FRANCIS
RICHARD JONES
DONALD B. SMITH

NELSON

NELSON

Destinies: Canadian History since Confederation, Eighth Edition

by Robert A. Wardhaugh and Alan MacEachern

VP, Product and Partnership Solutions:
Anne Williams

Publisher, Digital and Print Content:
Alexis Hood

Managing Editor, Content Development, and Acquisitions Editor:
Mark Grzeskowiak

Marketing Manager:
Ann Byford

Content Development Manager:
Linda Sparks

Photo and Permissions Researcher:
Indu Arora

Senior Production Project Manager:
Natalia Denesiuk Harris

Production Service:
Cenveo Publisher Services

Copy Editor:
June Trusty

Proofreader:
Manikandan N

Indexer:
BIM Creatives, LLC

Design Director:
Ken Phipps

Managing Designer:
Franca Amore

Interior Design:
Dianna Little

Cover Design:
Courtney Hellam

Cover Image:
Shaunl/Getty Images

Compositor:
Cenveo Publisher Services

Library and Archives Canada Cataloguing in Publication Data

Wardhaugh, Robert A. (Robert Alexander), 1967–, author
  Destinies : Canadian history since Confederation / Robert A. Wardhaugh, University of Western Ontario, Alan MacEachern, University of Western Ontario, and R. Douglas Francis, Richard Jones, Donald R. Smith. — Eighth edition.

First published: Destinies : Canadian history since Confederation / R. Douglas Francis, Richard Jones, Donald B. Smith.
Includes bibliographical references and index.
Issued in print and electronic formats.
ISBN 978-0-17-659308-7 (paperback).—ISBN 978-0-17-676782-2 (pdf)

  1. Canada—History—1867— — Textbooks. I. MacEachern, Alan Andrew, 1966–, author II. Francis, R. D. (R. Douglas), 1944–, author III. Jones, Richard, 1943–, author IV. Smith, Donald B., 1946–, author V. Title. VI. Title: Canadian history since Confederation.

FC164.F73 2016   971.05
C2016-903476-3
C2016-903477-1

ISBN-13: 978-0-17-659308-7
ISBN-10: 0-17-659308-X

Brief Contents

PART FOUR   Modern Canada, 1945 to the Present

Contents

PART THREE War and Depression, 1914–45

PART FOUR   Modern Canada, 1945 to the Present

List of Maps

Preface

The Nature of History

History changes. It changes because new sources about the past become available, and because individuals and societies themselves change and so see the past from new perspectives. The forces that shape the writing of all history have certainly shaped the writing of *Origins* and *Destinies*. These textbooks were first written by R. Douglas Francis, Richard Jones, and Donald B. Smith in 1988. Robert Wardhaugh came on board for the seventh editions in 2013. Alan MacEachern has joined the team for this, the books' eighth editions.

Origins and *Destinies* have undergone constant revision throughout the eight editions. There is more "past" all the time to write about, new sources have become available, and our understanding of the past has changed greatly. In fact, Canadian historiography (the history of history) has likely changed more in the past few decades than in any previous time period. From the earliest development of professional history in Canada at the beginning of the twentieth century, the field was dominated by a small group of male historians located at a few select universities. Canadian history relied on a nation-building narrative that emphasized the connection to Britain and the Empire. It was based on politics, economics, and geography. From the 1960s to the 1980s, a historical revolution took hold, a reorientation that focused on social history. It sought to include previously ignored groups, such as women and ethnic minorities, and to tell the story of Canada "from the bottom up."

But in recent decades, even as explorations of class, gender, and ethnicity gained ascendancy in Canadian historiography, these paradigms themselves began to be challenged. Postmodernism and poststructuralism questioned the possibility of objective knowledge, and postcolonialism interpreted nations such as Canada through the lens of imperialism. New paradigms such as age and the environment gained favour, and the profession witnessed a return to the narrative. *Origins* and *Destinies* have constantly evolved, both to discuss the changes in Canadian historical scholarship and to incorporate the new findings of the scholars employing these changes.

The Structure of These Books

Origins and *Destinies* cover the study of Canada's past from the beginnings of human settlement to the present. *Origins* tells the story from the last Ice Age to Confederation in 1867; *Destinies* brings the story to the present. Students should note that even such a "commonsense" structure as this is itself a decision, even an argument. For example, we might have hinged the two volumes at 1885 or 1914 or some other year important to Canada's development; we might likewise have ended our history at 1995 or 2001 or 2015. But we chose 1867 as the transition point because it is a key moment in Canadian nation building, and we see nation building as a key theme to the story we tell. Similarly, we end the book at the present (or as close to the reader's present as we possibly can) so as to demonstrate contingency: that contemporary Canada is tied to, even dependent on, the past for its existence and its character.

The textbooks are divided first into large thematic sections, each introduced by a brief overview of topics highlighted in the section's chapters. Each chapter treats a period (or region or theme) and begins with a "Time Line" listing the key events discussed. The history is principally told in chronological fashion, to help students understand how events developed over time. Exceptions in *Origins* occur when the colonies were developing independently, in which case their histories are presented regionally; exceptions in *Destinies* occur when some important issues are presented thematically. To assist students' understanding, chapter material is further divided into sections and subsections.

Each chapter contains a "Where Historians Disagree" boxed feature, which highlights some of the most contentious debates in Canadian history. In doing so, they explore how historians using different sources and methodologies quite often interpret history in radically different ways. The "A Historical Portrait" features highlight the lives of well-known and lesser-known people and communities whose lives and experiences reflect the important issues and trends of the era. The textbooks also seek to reflect and incorporate current trends in historical writing. As such, we include the most up-to-date research by Canadian historians and expose students to the most innovative approaches presently being employed. An annotated "Bibliography" appears at the end of each chapter to identify the major historical writings on the period and the themes covered.

What Is New in the Eighth Editions?

We have made many changes to the eighth editions. As historians have increasingly moved beyond study of the nation state to consider history in transnational and international terms, we have devoted more attention to Canada's position in the Atlantic world, tied as it has historically been to Western Europe and the United States. In keeping with a greater awareness of the nation's settler colonial past, we have incorporated more history of the First Nations and of Canada's treatment of them. Because environmental issues such as oil sands extraction and climate change have grown in prominence, we have expanded coverage of environmental history.

The most innovative addition to the eighth editions of *Origins* and *Destinies* is MindTap™. A fully online learning solution, MindTap combines all student learning tools—readings, multimedia, activities, and assessments—into a single Learning Path that guides the student through the curriculum. The Learning Path for each chapter of *Origins* and *Destinies* in MindTap begins with a short "Setting the Scene" video that summarizes the chapter's main themes. "Think Like a Historian" activities explore how historians use primary and secondary sources, visual sources, and maps to interpret topics discussed in the chapter. "History in Your Neighbourhood" activities introduce a national historic site relevant to the period and place under discussion. Instructors will appreciate each chapter's "Discussion Activity," which has students write an online post about a historical issue of contemporary concern, and "Polling Question," which can be used in class to survey students' opinions on a matter of historical debate. "Check Your Understanding" quizzes allow the student and instructor to ensure that the content and ideas underlying the material are being understood.

Acknowledgments

In preparing the eighth editions of *Origins* and *Destinies*, we benefited enormously from the knowledge and wisdom of countless Canadian historians from across the past century, whose research and analysis at the coal face of history made it possible for us to write the synthesis we have. Above all, we want to thank R. Douglas Francis, Richard Jones, and Donald B. Smith for having written the original *Origins* and *Destinies* almost thirty years ago, and having shepherded the volumes through many editions since then, constantly finding ways to update and reinvent what were already fine textbooks.

At Nelson, we benefited enormously from a dedicated and enthusiastic editorial team. In particular, we thank Mark Grzeskowiak, publisher; Natalia Denesiuk Harris, senior production project manager; Linda Sparks, content development manager; Lindsay Shipman, learning solutions consultant; Ezhilsolai Periasamy, project manager at Cenveo; and June Trusty, copy editor. Thank you for making the process such a smooth one.

We want to thank a number of Ph.D. candidates who assisted in the production of this and the previous edition. Tim Compeau, Michael Del Vecchio, Craig Greenham, Daniel Heidt, Michelle Hutchinson-Grondin, Jeremy Marks, and Carly Simpson worked on the "Where Historians Disagree" boxes. Adrian Ciani assisted with editing work. Jonathan Scotland deserves special thanks for his work with bibliographies, photos, maps, and captions, as does Elliot Worsfold, for his work with bibliographies.

Finally, we want to express thanks for the advice and assistance we receive year-in and year-out from our teaching assistants in History 2201, the Canadian history survey course at the University of Western Ontario, on matters historical, Canadian, pedagogical, academic, authorial, editorial, historiographical—you name it. You keep teaching us so much.

Robert Wardhaugh
Alan MacEachern

Instructor Resources

 The **Nelson Education Teaching Advantage (NETA)** program delivers research-based instructor resources that promote student engagement and higher-order thinking to enable the success of Canadian students and educators. Visit Nelson Education's **Inspired Instruction** website at www.nelson.com/inspired to find out more about NETA.

The following instructor resources have been created for *Destinies*, Eighth Edition. Access these ultimate tools for customizing lectures and presentations at www.nelson.com/instructor.

PowerPoint

Microsoft® PowerPoint® lecture slides have been created for every chapter. Some 15 slides per chapter have been provided, many featuring key figures, tables, and photographs from *Destinies*, Eighth Edition. NETA principles of clear design and engaging content have been incorporated throughout, making it simple for instructors to customize the deck for their courses.

Image Library

This resource consists of digital copies of figures, short tables, and photographs used in the book. Instructors can use these jpegs to customize the PowerPoint slides or create their own PowerPoint presentations.

MindTap

MindTap® Offering personalized paths of dynamic assignments and applications, MindTap is a digital learning solution that turns cookie-cutter into cutting-edge, apathy into engagement, and memorizers into higher-level thinkers. MindTap enables students to analyze and apply chapter concepts within relevant assignments, and allows instructors to measure skills and promote better outcomes with ease. A fully online learning solution, MindTap combines all student learning tools—readings, multimedia, activities, and assessments—into a single Learning Path that guides the student through the curriculum. Instructors personalize the experience by customizing the presentation of these learning tools to their students, even seamlessly introducing their own content into the Learning Path.

Visions: The Canadian History Modules Project

Choose the material that best fits your course.

Visions: The Canadian History Modules Project combines a traditional peer-reviewed resource with the newest production techniques to address key issues that history instructors told us they were facing in the classroom. Each module is organized around a theme or question that is frequently taught in the tutorial or seminar portion of your course. The modules combine carefully chosen primary and secondary sources with a contextual introduction, questions to help you guide your students through the material, annotations for unfamiliar material, and suggestions for further readings.

The complete table of contents and a preview of each of the Visions modules are available at visions.nelson.com.

Available are two Editor's Choice editions, covering twelve key modules for the pre- and the post-confederation periods.

ISBN 978-0-17-666939-3
Visions: Editor's Choice Pre-Confederation,
Second Edition
Editorial Board: Bryden, Coates, Lux, Marks, Martel, Samson

ISBN 978-0-17-666940-9
Visions: Editor's Choice Post-Confederation,
Second Edition
Editorial Board: Bryden, Coates, Lux, Marks, Martel, Samson

Compose

COⅢPOSE Search, build, review, and publish your own custom textbook on our new custom publishing platform, Compose! Compose is a database of Nelson Education and Cengage Learning published materials, from which you can easily build, chapter by chapter, a resource that suits the unique needs of your course. Compose allows you to build your custom resources yourself or with the help of your Learning Solutions Consultant (LSC), to review all content, to choose from our cover gallery, to upload and incorporate your own original materials, to preview price quotes, and, ultimately, to have control over the resource you want to create. To sign up for Compose, please go to http://compose.nelson.com/content/home, click Register, and complete the required information fields. You will be granted immediate access to the site, with an administrator confirming your status as an instructor and linking you to your Learning Solutions Consultant within 24 hours. If you need a walkthrough of Compose, or help signing up, please contact your LSC or the Custom Team by going to http://compose.nelson.com/help/contact, or email us at nelson.custompublishing@nelson.com.

ISBN 978-0-17-650282-9
Module 1   *First Nations in Their Own Words: The Early History of Canada to 1500*
Maureen Lux

ISBN 978-0-17-650287-4
Module 2   *Contact Zones from the Sixteenth to Eighteenth Centuries: How Did Aboriginal People Perceive European Newcomers?*
Colin Coates

ISBN 978-0-17-650288-1
Module 3   *Fur Traders and Their Prey, Seventeenth to Nineteenth Centuries: Why Did Aboriginals Participate in the Fur Trade?*
Colin Coates

ISBN 978-0-17-650289-8
Module 4   *Seigneurial Tenure in Early Québec, Seventeenth to the Nineteenth Centuries: What Was the Meaning of Land Ownership?*
Colin Coates

ISBN 978-0-17-650290-4
Module 5   *On the Edge of Empires: Acadians and Mi'kmaq in the Eighteenth Century*
Daniel Samson

ISBN 978-0-17-650291-1
Module 6   *The Fourteenth Colony: Nova Scotia and the American Revolution*
Daniel Samson

ISBN 978-0-17-650292-8
Module 7   *Gender, Sexuality, and Evangelical Protestantism in Early Upper Canada, 1795–1855*
Lynne Marks

ISBN 978-0-17-650293-5
Module 8   *Worlds of Work: Pre-Industrial Work, 1860–1880*
Daniel Samson

ISBN 978-0-17-650294-2
Module 9   *The Rebellions of 1837–38 in Lower and Upper Canada: Why Did People Take Up Arms against the Government?*
Colin Coates

ISBN 978-0-17-650295-9
Module 10   *Race, Class, and Gender: The Limits of Victorian Liberalism, 1830–1860*
Daniel Samson

ISBN 978-0-17-650305-5
Module 11   *The Métis and Red River Society: Change, Adaptation, and Resistance—1830s to 1870s*
Maureen Lux

ISBN 978-0-17-650296-6
Module 12   *Schools, Prisons, and Asylums in Mid-Nineteenth-Century British North America: What Did Institutional Reforms Have in Common?*
Colin Coates

ISBN 978-0-17-650297-3
Module 13   *Gender, Race, and Sexuality in Colonial British Columbia, 1849–1871*
Lynne Marks

ISBN 978-0-17-650298-0
Module 14   *Immigrants and Immigration: The Case of the Irish, 1830–1860*
Daniel Samson

ISBN 978-0-17-650299-7
Module 15   *Confederation: What Kind of Country Are We to Have?*
P.E. Bryden

ISBN 978-0-17-650300-0
Module 16   *Industrialization and Women's Work, 1870s–1920s*
Lynne Marks

ISBN 978-0-17-650301-7
Module 17   *Secularization in Late Nineteenth- and Early Twentieth-Century English Canada*
Lynne Marks

ISBN 978-0-17-650302-4
Module 18   *Immigration in the Late Nineteenth- and Early Twentieth-Century Canada*
Lynne Marks

ISBN 978-0-17-650303-1
Module 19   *As Long as the Sun Shines and the Waters Flow: Treaties and Treaty-Making in the 1870s*
Maureen Lux

ISBN 978-0-17-650304-8
Module 20   *What Did It Mean to Be Canadian? Conflicting Views on Nationalism and Identity (1880s–1920s)*
Marcel Martel

ISBN 978-0-17-650316-1
Module 21   *The Early Canadian Women's Movement and the Struggle for the Vote, 1870s–1918*
Lynne Marks

ISBN 978-0-17-650306-2
Module 22   *The Great War: Leaders, Followers, and Record-Keepers*
P.E. Bryden

ISBN 978-0-17-650307-9
Module 23   *Protest, Parties, and Politics between the Wars, 1919–1939*
P.E. Bryden

ISBN 978-0-17-650308-6
Module 24   *Canada in the 1930s: Surviving Canada's Great Depression*
P.E. Bryden

ISBN 978-0-17-650309-3
Module 25   *A National Crime: Residential Schools in Canada, 1880s to 1960s*
Maureen Lux

ISBN 978-0-17-650310-9
Module 26   *World War II and the Internment of Enemy Aliens: Circumscribing Personal Freedoms*
Marcel Martel

ISBN 978-0-17-658443-6
Module 48 *Age Matters: Growing Up in the Interwar Years*
Cynthia Comacchio

ISBN 978-0-17-658444-3
Module 49 *Medium and Message: Popular Culture, Mass Media, and National Identity, 1960s–2000s*
Cynthia Comacchio

ISBN 978-0-17-658445-0
Module 50 *Sporting Identities: "Race," Gender, Nation and Sport in Late Nineteenth- to Early Twentieth-Century Canada*
Cynthia Comacchio

Student Ancillaries

MindTap

MindTap® Stay organized and efficient with MindTap—a single destination with all the course material and study aids you need to succeed. Built-in apps leverage social media and the latest learning technology. For example:

- ReadSpeaker will read the text to you.
- You can highlight text and make notes in your MindTap Reader. Your notes will flow into Evernote, the electronic notebook app that you can access anywhere when it's time to study for the exam.
- Setting the Scene videos provide a multimedia introduction to the chapter.
- Check Your Understanding quizzes allow you to assess your understanding.
- Polling Questions provide the opportunity to state your opinion on a matter of historical debate.

Visit www.nelson.com/student to start using MindTap. Enter the online access code from the card included with your textbook. If a code card is not provided, you can purchase instant access at NELSONbrain.com.

Source: Library and Archives Canada/RG84, C-4, vol. 2377.

Chapter One

CONFEDERATION

TIME LINE	
1841	Union of the Canadas
1846	Britain adopts free trade and ends colonial timber and wheat preferences
1848	Responsible government achieved
1854	British North America (BNA) enters into reciprocity agreement with the United States
1857	Queen Victoria chooses Ottawa as future capital of Canada Economic recession begins
1861	Beginning of American Civil War
1864	Confederate raid on St. Albans, Vermont, from BNA Formation of "Great Coalition" to work toward BNA federation Maritime and Canadian delegates discuss union at Charlottetown and Quebec conferences
1865	Canadian Legislature approves Quebec Resolutions
1866	United States government terminates Reciprocity Agreement of 1854 Pro-Confederation party wins election in New Brunswick Westminster Conference in London, England, prepares passage of BNA Act through Parliament
1867	BNA Act is passed, creating the Dominion of Canada, consisting of Nova Scotia, New Brunswick, Canada East (Quebec), and Canada West (Ontario) John A. Macdonald becomes Canada's first prime minister

The union of the British North American colonies had long been discussed, but by the 1860s both internal and external forces turned talk into reality, and a new nation was born. Fear of another American invasion after the Civil War, pressure from Britain for unification of the colonies, internal problems such as heavy public debt from extensive railway building and political deadlock in the Canadas, and the desire to acquire the Northwest led politicians from both the Canadas and the Maritime colonies to consider union. These circumstances, more than a spirit of nationalism, prepared the way for Confederation.

Yet despite the results, there was no assurance in 1867 that this experiment in nation building would succeed. Even before the ink was dry on the new BNA Act, a movement was already developing in the Maritimes to "repeal" Confederation. Considerable opposition also existed in Quebec. Confederation was only the first step in a process that would continue well into the twentieth century. The next decade in particular would witness continued growth and expansion at a frantic rate. Indeed, the pace of expansion would be so rapid that severe growing pains would strain the new dominion to the breaking point. In addition, Canada faced a number of immediate issues that threatened its fragile existence, including relations between the new federal and provincial governments, French and English, and Catholics and Protestants, and relations with a reunified and expansionist United States.

The Impact of the **American Civil War**

The Alabama *and* Trent *Affairs*

Union: North
Confederate: South
(advocated to uphold slavery)
Result: The Confederacy collapsed + slavery was abolished

Fear of American annexation during the Civil War was a major factor contributing to Canada becoming a nation. Although Britain—and therefore BNA—was officially neutral during the American Civil War, there was widespread support for the Confederacy. While Britain supported the North's opposition to slavery (the British Empire abolished slavery completely by the 1840s), that issue was overshadowed by more strategic ones. The North was, like Britain, a manufacturing region that competed with many British exports, and Britain depended on Southern cotton for the textile industry. As well, many Britons wanted to see the American experiment in "republicanism" break up on the shoals of its own independence. The embarrassment faced by "the greatest empire on Earth" at having the American colonies successfully break away still simmered beneath the surface of popular sentiment. British politicians also recognized that having two American nations rather than one would pose less of a threat to British supremacy. In the early stages of the war, marked by Confederate victories, it seemed the British (and BNA by extension) were backing the winning side.

The international rules of neutrality forbade the construction of Confederate warships in British shipyards. Regardless, the South secretly built the CSS *Alabama*, a swift and powerful cruiser, in a shipyard near Liverpool. During its 22-month rampage on three oceans, the *Alabama* burned or captured 64 Northern merchant vessels and a Union warship before being itself sunk in June 1864. Not surprisingly, the North held Britain responsible for the damage caused by the *Alabama* and other British-built Confederate vessels. Some American politicians demanded the annexation of British North America as compensation. While this demand was voiced by a minority in the Northern states and never became a serious possibility, it fit into a larger American aspiration to eventually absorb all of North America. But regardless of its likelihood, the threat was perceived as real to Canadian politicians.

Another incident, the *Trent* affair, added to Anglo–American antagonism. In November 1861, an American warship stopped the British steamer *Trent* and forcibly removed two Confederate envoys on their way to England to secure assistance for the Southern cause. Tempers flared on both sides. Britain threatened retaliation if the North did not free the Confederate agents, seized in neutral waters; the North denounced Britain for aiding the Southern cause. In the end, President Abraham Lincoln released the prisoners on Christmas Day, 1861, to avoid war with Britain.

The St. Albans Raid

By 1864, the Confederacy was using the sanctuary provided by the Canadian border to launch attacks against the North. The largest of these attacks occurred at St. Albans, Vermont, on October 19, 1864, during which 26 Confederate sympathizers terrorized the town, robbed three banks of $200,000, set several fires, wounded two men and killed another, and then fled north to Canada. The Canadian authorities arrested them but a Montreal magistrate released them on a legal technicality. This act of leniency infuriated Northerners and was viewed as another example of British and Canadian support for the South. The colonial government condemned the judge's decision and passed legislation to deport aliens involved in acts against a friendly foreign state. Nevertheless, Canada remained suspect in American eyes.

The ensuing tension led Britain to send 14,000 troops to BNA to protect her colonies. Many of the soldiers had to reach their destination by sled, since no rail link existed into the interior. Britain therefore came to view a union of the colonies as a means both to get the colonies to assume responsibility for their own defence and to achieve a railway link to the Atlantic by providing a larger financial base for railway construction. Britain believed such a union inevitable. But a union in no way meant that the colonies were breaking away from Britain and becoming independent or that the mother country no longer wanted them. The Empire's colonies around the world, or at least the white self-governing colonies, were treated much like children "growing up" within a family. In this sense, Canada would come to be viewed as "the eldest daughter of Empire." Confederation, while occurring under pressure, was seen as a natural evolution.

Negotiating Confederation

The Great Coalition

The external forces pushing for the union of the BNA colonies were strong but there was also pressure coming from within the main colony of the United Canadas. To an extent, the process of union had already commenced in 1841, in the aftermath of the Rebellions in Upper and Lower Canada and Lord Durham's *Report*. But while the Act of Union was passed to solve the problem of "two nations warring in the bosom of a single state" by returning to the design of assimilating the French Catholics in Lower Canada, it had again failed, and instead produced another more immediate crisis: political deadlock. The colonial politicians might celebrate the winning of responsible government in 1848 when Lord Elgin refused to intervene with the passage of the Rebellion Losses Bill, but the principle meant little if the colonial legislature for the United Canadas became paralyzed whenever a contentious issue came before the Assembly.

Neither the Conservatives nor the Reformers—the two political parties that had taken shape on the basis of the British system—could form and maintain a stable government. The problem was that in uniting Upper and Lower Canada, the two provinces of Canada East and Canada West were represented in the Legislature by 42 seats each. While this seemed fair, the result was deadlock when the Assembly split along religious or ethnic lines. In the brief period between 1861 and 1864, for example, the Canadas experienced two elections and three changes in government. The administrations even reflected the divided nature of the united colony in the names of their coalitions, representing the leader of the party in Canada West and Canada East. On June 14, 1864, the Conservative Macdonald–Taché coalition went down in defeat. Governor General Monck urged John A. Macdonald, leader of the Tories in Canada West, to negotiate with George Brown, leader of

1840 Act of Union united colonies of Upper Canada; Canada West (ON) ENGL / Lower Canada; Canada East (QC) FR > under) gov't, creating the Province of Canada

the province's Reform Party, to form a larger coalition that cut across party lines. Despite Brown and Macdonald's mutual antagonism, the two men agreed to work together to resolve the deadlock. On June 30, a jubilant Assembly heard Brown announce that he and two other Reformers would enter a coalition cabinet to work for federation. Thus was born the "Great Coalition" of 1864.

Brown made three demands of the coalition in return for the support of his party. It must seek a federation of *all* of the British North American colonies, the federation must employ representation by population (or "rep by pop," as it became popularly known), and Rupert's Land—the vast territory to the west of the Canadas and owned by the Hudson's Bay Company— must be incorporated into Confederation. Each of these demands reflected the particular desires and ambitions of Canada West. A larger union of BNA would reconfigure the government and break the political deadlock; "rep by pop" would work to the advantage of the more numerous English Protestants in overpowering and assimilating the French Catholics; and the purchase of the vast Northwest would serve as a logical extension of Canada West. The ambitious plan was suitably couched in the language of nation building and empire. On January 22, 1863, Brown, the Toronto newspaper editor of the *Globe*, outlined his vision:

> *If Canada acquires this territory it will rise in a few years from a position of a small and weak province to be the greatest colony any country has ever possessed, able to take its place among the empires of the earth. The wealth of 400,000 square miles of territory will flow through our waters and be gathered by our merchants, manufacturers and agriculturists. Our sons will occupy the chief places of this vast territory, we will form its institutions, supply its rulers, teach its schools, fill its stores, run its mills, navigate its streams.*

The Charlottetown Conference (P.E.I: 1864)

But Brown and Macdonald's dream of nation was not shared by all. In the early 1860s, the Maritime colonies of Nova Scotia, New Brunswick, and Prince Edward Island considered union among them- selves as the best path forward. Newfoundland was not included, because the more remote colony was not viewed as politically advanced or ready for federation. But even this less ambitious scheme had its detractors. Many in the Maritime colonies viewed any form of union as undesirable and ultimately as distancing them from Britain. Union with Canada was seen as particularly distasteful, because it would inevitably draw the Maritime colonies into the ethnic and religious struggles between Canada East and Canada West. Despite the reservations, the leaders of the three colonies agreed to meet. But before a date or place had been decided, the government of the Canadas asked permission, through the Governor-General to the Colonial Office, to attend such a meeting to present a proposal for a wider British North American federal union. The Maritimers agreed to hear what the Canadians had to say. The meeting was set for September 1, 1864, in Charlottetown, Prince Edward Island.

Maritime Colonies / NS — NB ~ PEI

At the Charlottetown Conference, the Canadian delegation gave an impressive presentation. John A. Macdonald, along with George-Étienne Cartier, the main leader from Canada East, set out the general terms of the Canadian proposal, particularly those aspects dealing with the divi- sion of powers between the central and local governments. Alexander Tilloch Galt, the minister of finance in the Canadas, dealt with economic issues, while George Brown handled constitu- tional concerns. The main features of their proposal included continued loyalty to the British Crown through membership in the British Empire; a strong central government within a federal union in which the provinces retained control over their own local affairs; and representation in a lower house based on population and an upper house based on regional representation. Thomas D'Arcy McGee, the poet–politician who had cultivated his oratorical skills as a young Irish activist, spoke eloquently in terms of the need for a common British North American vision.

John A. Macdonald appears seated in the centre of this photo, taken on the first day of the Charlottetown Conference, September 1, 1864. Immediately to the left of Macdonald stands his old political enemy George Brown, with D'Arcy McGee, the orator and Irish activist, standing directly behind Brown. McGee was assassinated on April 7, 1868, before the dominion was one year old.

Source: Library and Archives Canada/C-733.

Within seven days, the delegates agreed to meet again on October 10 in Quebec City to explore in greater detail the nature of a federation.

The Quebec Conference

In Quebec City, the Canadian delegates presented the broad general principles set out in Charlottetown in the form of the seventy-two resolutions. Within a two-week period, these resolutions were debated and accepted to become the political framework for a union of the colonies and the constitution of a new nation. But the conference discussions indicated significant differences of opinion. While these differences were officially worked out in the resulting agreement, they would continue to simmer beneath the surface and become sources of contention for the young dominion.

At the conference, Macdonald clearly favoured a legislative union, or if this was not possible, a strong central government. He believed that the Civil War in the United States was the result of overly powerful local governments, and he was intent on not allowing the same to occur in Canada. The Maritime delegates feared a loss of their identity in a legislative union and favoured instead a federal union with powerful local governments. Some representatives for Canada West, most notably Oliver Mowat, were also concerned by the prospect of a powerful central government. George-Étienne Cartier favoured a federal union, with a local government in Quebec strong enough to protect the religion, language, civil law, and customs of French Canadians. As one Colonial Office official astutely noted of the challenges facing the

"Fathers" of Confederation: "The great difficulty is to arrange for a real union of the five provinces ... on terms which shall make the central or federal legislation really dominant, so as to make one body politic of the whole, and yet to provide security to French Canadians that this dominancy would not be used to swamp their religion and habits."

The delegates reached a compromise. They granted powers to the provincial governments but gave the federal government residual powers (those not specifically assigned to the provinces). As well, they provided the federal government the power "to make laws for the peace, order and good government of Canada"—a highly open-ended provision. The federal government also gained the right to disallow provincial laws if they went against the national interest. While a compromise had been reached, it is debatable whether the Fathers of Confederation realized just how much power had been handed to the federal government.

The political structure of the new nation followed British precedent but with a uniquely Canadian character. The delegates agreed on a federal lower house (the House of Commons) based on representation by population and an upper house (the Senate) based on regional representation. They disagreed, however, over the number of representatives from each region in the upper house. The smaller Maritime provinces viewed the Senate as a means of strengthening their regional representation to offset their numerical weakness in the House of Commons. In the end, the delegates agreed that the Maritimes would have a total of 24 seats, the same number given to each of Canada East and Canada West.

The delegates also agreed, after much debate, that the new federal government would assume the public debts, up to a specified maximum amount, of each of the provinces that joined. In addition, the federal government would finance the Intercolonial Railway, linking the Maritimes to the Canadas. To cover these costs, the federal government was provided unlimited taxing powers, including not only the collection of direct taxes, but also of indirect taxes such as customs and excise duties, one of the main sources of revenue at the time. In contrast, the provinces could levy only direct taxes. To compensate the provinces for the cost of education, roads, and other local obligations under their jurisdiction, it was agreed that the federal government would pay annual subsidies to the provinces based on 80 cents for each member of their populations.

The Debate over Confederation

The Canadas

After the Quebec Conference, the delegates returned to their respective colonies to secure approval for the resolutions. The Fathers of Confederation considered submitting the draft constitution for popular approval but decided to follow the British procedure of ratification by the colonial legislatures.

The proposals led to considerable debate in the volatile legislature of the United Canadas. George Brown and his Reformers from Canada West had concerns, but they accepted the agreement mainly because its electoral system was based on the principles of "rep by pop." The politicians in Canada West were most in favour because they had the most to gain from Confederation. Aside from breaking the political deadlock and solving the immediate problem in the Canadas, the lure of western expansion served as a powerful impetus in advancing union.

In Canada East, however, members of the Parti rouge, under the leadership of Antoine-Aimé Dorion, had serious reservations. Even though the French Canadians would finally be provided a local legislature to handle local concerns, the specified and unspecified powers of the federal government remained a concern. In particular Dorion remained distrustful of Macdonald's ulterior motives. "It is not at all a confederation that is proposed to us, but quite simply a Legislative Union disguised under the name of a confederation," Dorion argued. "How could one accept as a federation a scheme … that provided for disallowance of local legislation?" In the new House of Commons, he pointed out, English-Canadian representation from Canada West and the Maritimes would greatly outnumber French-Canadian representation. Dorion was also concerned that by allowing the united legislature of the Canadas to decide the question, there was no way for the French-Canadian population to voice its own opinion.

George-Étienne Cartier was the voice of Confederation in Canada East and he attempted to counter Dorion's criticisms. Cartier argued that in the new federal union, French Canadians would control their own provincial government, have their own local administration, and retain the Civil Code. Through Confederation, they were finally achieving what they had sought since the Conquest in 1763. The British design of assimilation that reared its head in the Royal Proclamation of 1763 and more recently in Durham's *Report* and the Act of Union of 1840–41 would finally be laid to rest. The French language would be official in the province of Quebec as well as in the federal administration. The rights of religious minorities (meaning Catholics) for separate denominational schools would have limited recognition in all the provinces. Quebec would have two school systems—one Protestant and one Catholic. Cartier attempted to assure detractors that the "new nationality" of Confederation would be political, not cultural. He also reminded them of the importance of the British connection in allowing the survival of the French-Canadian identity up to this point in time and in offsetting the threat of American annexation that posed an even greater threat to that identity. For French Canadians, union with the United States would be the worst possible fate. The existing union, crippled by deadlock, could not go on. Only a larger federation of British North American colonies offered French Canadians control of their own affairs within their own province. Confederation was the best hope for cultural survival.

Cartier turned to the influential Catholic clergy for support, despite his personal concerns about mixing politics and religion. Bishop Ignace Bourget of Montreal, the most powerful French-Canadian bishop, feared for the future of the church in the new political union with English-speaking colonies that had large Protestant populations. He kept silent about his misgivings, however, since the other Quebec bishops were more favourably disposed, at least in principle. They realized that the alternative to Confederation was support of their arch-enemies, the *rouges*, who were strongly anticlerical.

In the final vote on Confederation in the Legislature of the United Canadas, 91 were in favour and 33 opposed. In all, 54 of the 62 members from Canada West favoured the proposal, as did 37 of the 62 members from Canada East. But of the 48 French-Canadian members, only 27 voted for and 21 against. Confederation won overall, but among French Canadians the victory was narrow, indicating serious reservations.

Atlantic Canada

In New Brunswick, Samuel Leonard Tilley, premier since 1857 and the representative at both the Charlottetown and the Quebec conferences, pushed the economic advantages of Confederation. The city of Saint John would serve as a year-round, ice-free port for the export of Canadian goods. A lucrative market would be created in central Canada for Maritime coal and manufactured goods. The promised Intercolonial Railway would make trade a reality.

But strong opposition to Confederation continued in New Brunswick. A.J. Smith, the opposition leader, led the anti-Confederation forces. He argued that no guarantee was being offered to ensure that the Intercolonial Railway would even be constructed. If it were built, there was no indication of where it would run and, as a result, whether it would benefit the north shore or the southern Saint John River valley. He also pointed out that New Brunswick's economic trade pattern, especially since the Reciprocity Treaty of 1854, ran north–south rather than east–west. Commercial interests in the province had no significant economic ties with the Canadas; instead, these links existed with the New England states. Furthermore, union with Canada would likely lead to the New Brunswick market being flooded by Canadian imports. The Canadas would seek to construct a high tariff structure that would ensure east–west trade and cut off the lucrative American market to the south. To make matters worse, New Brunswickers would be forced to assume a portion of the heavy Canadian debt from canal and railway building. Smith added political weight to this opposition by arguing that Confederation would diminish New Brunswick's power by giving the province only 15 members of Parliament in a House of Commons with 194 members. The Catholic clergy also opposed Confederation, believing that a Canada dominated by Protestant "extremists" in Upper Canada could threaten Roman Catholic schools. They would soon be proved correct.

Confederation was debated in the election campaign of early 1865. New Brunswickers responded clearly and decisively: the Tilley pro-Confederation government was handed a humiliating defeat.

In Nova Scotia, Charles Tupper, the pro-Confederation premier, also faced challenges. In particular, opposition came in the form of Joseph Howe, "Father of Responsible Government." Although he was no longer a member of the Assembly, Howe was still the most powerful political figure in the colony. He argued that Nova Scotia would lose its identity in the proposed Confederation and cease to be an important colony in the British Empire. Furthermore, Howe pointed out that Nova Scotia looked eastward to the Atlantic Ocean and Britain, rather than westward to the continent and the Canadas. "Take a Nova Scotian to Ottawa," he vividly noted, "away above tidewater, freeze him up for five months, where he cannot view the Atlantic, smell salt water, or see the sail of a ship, and the man will pine and die." Howe favoured maintaining colonial ties to Britain. He asked Nova Scotians why they would want to entangle the colony in the often bitter and divisive ethnic and religious quagmire that had long bogged down the Canadas. In the winter of 1866–67, Howe went to England to present his case for Nova Scotia staying out of Confederation.

On Prince Edward Island, support for Confederation was also questionable. At the Charlottetown and the Quebec conferences, the island's representatives had driven a hard bargain, pressing for better terms on representation in the Senate and in the House of Commons, and for better economic terms. But when they returned home, their enthusiasm and interest waned even further when they realized that the populace opposed Confederation for a number of reasons. The problem of absentee landlordism was of serious concern. For over a century, British landlords controlled the island, much to the resentment of the local population. In 1860, a British commission appointed to investigate the question issued a report favourable to the islanders, only to have it rejected by the proprietors and the Colonial Office. Thus, when the Colonial Office pressured Prince Edward Islanders to adopt Confederation, it met with widespread resistance. Many islanders saw Confederation as simply replacing one set of distant landlords in Britain with another in Ottawa. In addition, they believed that Confederation offered Prince Edward Island very little of substance. It would mean higher taxes to support the costs of the Intercolonial Railway and higher tariffs to create interprovincial trade—neither of which would greatly benefit Prince Edward Island. They also disliked the proposed form of representation in the Senate and House of Commons, which would deny them a strong voice in distant Ottawa.

[handwritten margin note: little economic benefit, Lack of political power]

The colony of Newfoundland failed to support Confederation as much out of apathy as opposition. The island did not participate in the Charlottetown Conference, although it did send two representatives to the Quebec Conference, both of whom endorsed Confederation. They returned to a colony that was initially mildly interested as a result of Newfoundland's declining fishing industry, agriculture, and timber trade. But if Newfoundland's politicians initially hoped that joining Confederation might solve their economic ills, they soon came to believe that Canada was too distant. R. J. Pinsent, a member of the Legislative Council, summed up the prevailing opinion: "There is little community of interest between Newfoundland and the Canadas. This is

[handwritten note: Colonial mindset = distant from the rest of Canada]

not a Continental Colony." As with the Maritime region, the island continued to look eastward to Britain rather than westward to Canada.

External Pressures

By the end of 1865, public support for Confederation had waned in all but Canada West. It certainly did not portend well for creating a new nation. All four of the Atlantic colonies opposed the scheme, while Canada East had serious reservations. Two external developments, however, altered the situation: British pressure and the American threat.

British Support for Confederation

By the mid-1860s the British Empire was at the height of its power. The Empire adopted a policy of free trade in the 1840s, indicating confidence in its global economic power. Its position on the world stage was unrivalled. Britain sought to maintain and expand its influence through informal empire. This meant empire through trade and political arrangement rather than through direct military means. Britain's position and policies obviously affected Canada. The move to free trade in the 1840s, for example, had serious implications by diminishing BNA's preferred access to imperial markets. But Britain also looked to reduce its expensive role in defending the colonies. The first step in this process involved some sort of colonial amalgamation; the second necessitated good relations with the United States.

The British intended to pressure the colonial governments to cooperate. Thus, when in the autumn of 1865 a pro-Confederation delegation from the Canadas arrived in London, it was warmly welcomed; a counter-delegation from Nova Scotia under Joseph Howe was not. Instead, the British government replaced the anti-Confederation governor of Nova Scotia with one more supportive. The Colonial Office also ordered New Brunswick Governor Arthur Gordon to intervene in his colony's politics to ensure the success of Confederation. Finally, Britain guaranteed the loan interest for the proposed Intercolonial Railway on the assumption that the Maritimes would join Confederation.

The American Contribution to Confederation

While Britain applied direct pressure, the United States did so indirectly. When the Civil War ended in 1865, some American politicians from the Northern States advocated using their experienced army to annex the BNA colonies in retaliation for British sympathy with the Confederacy. Influential politicians in the American Midwest, meanwhile, advocated taking possession of Rupert's Land as part of the United States' manifest destiny. Other American politicians, including Hamilton Fish, the secretary of state in Ulysses S. Grant's administration, urged possession of all the British territory in North America.

Amid such annexationist appeals, the American government announced that the Reciprocity Treaty of 1854 would be terminated in 1866. It was reasoned that the treaty's abrogation would cause such economic hardships for the British North American colonies that they would be forced to join the United States. Instead, the announced abrogation of reciprocity, while a devastating blow, encouraged the colonies to consider an alternative commercial union among themselves.

But it was the Fenian raids that served as the most visible example of the American threat. While these raids were minor from a military standpoint, and while the actual nature of the threat was overblown and exaggerated, they caught the popular imagination and fuelled the fires of paranoia. The Fenians, republican Irish in the United States, were committed to fighting for the independence of their homeland. For these Irish Americans, many of whom were Union veterans from the Civil War, the proximity of BNA posed an attractive target of British imperialism. One scheme they devised was to capture the British North American colonies and use them as ransom to liberate Ireland from British rule. Their marching song explicitly set out their goals:

> We are the Fenian Brotherhood, skilled in the art of war,
> And we're going to fight for Ireland, the land that we adore.
> Many battles we have won, along with the boys in blue,
> And we'll go and capture Canada for we've nothing else to do.

The Fenians expected the support of Irish Catholics in the British colonies, but they received relatively little. Some prominent Irish individuals, such as Thomas D'Arcy McGee, spoke out strongly against the Fenians. He paid for this opposition in 1868 when he was assassinated by a suspected Fenian, P. James Whelan.

The Fenians posed little threat until the end of the Civil War. The movement had the support of the American government, which sympathized with their anti-British sentiments. Many American politicians also feared that if they failed to support the Fenians, they would alienate the large number of American Irish Catholic voters.

But the threat was more psychological than real. Military skirmishes were few and restricted to border areas. The two most important took place in New Brunswick and in the Niagara Peninsula. In April 1866, a small band of Fenians crossed into New Brunswick, where they stole the flag from

The funeral cortege in Montreal, April 13, 1868, of Thomas D'Arcy McGee, the victim of Canada's first political assassination, believed to be the work of Irish revolutionaries. McGee strongly opposed the Fenians, the Irish Americans who wanted to end British rule in Ireland. He had been assassinated in Ottawa six days earlier.

Source: George Martin/Library and Archives Canada/PA-165260.

a customs house before the local militia and British regulars forced them back across the border. Although the raid was insignificant in military terms, it helped to turn the tide in favour of Confederation in the New Brunswick election taking place at the time. Then in May, 1500 Fenians crossed the Niagara River into Canada West. At Ridgeway on June 2, the Fenians defeated the Canadian militia, but then withdrew—never to return, although they continued to pose a threat until 1870.

Turning the Tide in New Brunswick

The colonial government in New Brunswick resigned in April 1866. In the ensuing election campaign, Samuel Leonard Tilley resurrected his arguments for Confederation. He promised lower taxes, the Intercolonial Railway, a fair share in the running of the nation, and a market for the colony's raw materials and manufactured goods—in other words, material progress and modernization.

During the campaign, both parties benefited from external funds. The anti-Confederates received money from Nova Scotia (and possibly, it has been asserted, the United States), while the pro-Confederates obtained financial support from the government of the Canadas. "Give us funds," a desperate Tilley cabled John A. Macdonald. "It will require some $40,000 or $50,000 to do the work in all our counties." Macdonald gave it. He did not want Confederation to go down to defeat in New Brunswick simply for lack of money. Direct British pressure and threatened Fenian raids also assisted Tilley's cause. After his resounding electoral victory, Tilley had the New Brunswick legislature quickly endorse Confederation.

The Final Negotiations   The London Conference

In the autumn and winter of 1866, delegates from Nova Scotia, New Brunswick, and the United Canadas met in London to prepare the passage of the British North America Act through the British Parliament. Although the Maritime delegates pressed for modifications of those aspects of the seventy-two resolutions that provided for a strong central government, in the end the resolutions were accepted with only a few minor but significant changes. Subsidies to the provinces would be increased beyond the agreed 80 cents per person by a fixed grant from the federal government. The contentious issue of separate schools was settled by applying the Quebec clause on education, which safeguarded the Protestant separate schools in Quebec, to all other provinces in the union, or to new provinces that had separate schools "by law" at the time they joined Confederation. Furthermore, provisions were included for religious minorities to appeal to the federal government if a provincial government threatened their school system as they existed before Confederation. The "school issue" as it became known would indeed remain contentious well into the future.

While the delegates were meeting in London to finalize the terms of Confederation, Joseph Howe continued his opposition to Nova Scotia joining. He urged British officials to reject union. But the British government refused to retract its support. When the British North America Act was signed on March 29, 1867, Howe returned to Nova Scotia cured "of a good deal of loyal enthusiasm" and embittered against the Canadians. He was not alone. Many Nova Scotians saw Confederation as the end and not the beginning of a vibrant Nova Scotia. Elsewhere, Confederation was accepted, although not with enthusiasm, except in Ontario. The foundation of the new nation was shaky at best.

Naming the Nation

John A. Macdonald wanted to call the new nation the "Kingdom of Canada," but the British government objected because it feared that the term would further offend the Americans, implying as it did a more autonomous country. Instead, the word "dominion" was chosen. It was a word Britain had long used for possessions under its sovereignty. The term would soon become associated with a verse from the Bible, Psalms 72:8, "He shall have dominion also from sea to sea, and from the river unto the ends of the earth," and so gave Canada a motto: *A Mari Usque Ad Mare*—From Sea to Sea. On July 1, 1867, the Dominion of Canada was born. It consisted of the four provinces of Nova Scotia, New Brunswick, Quebec, and Ontario.

Politics in the New Dominion

As intended, Confederation ushered in a new era in politics. The various political factions and parties that existed before Confederation—the Tories and the Clear Grits (or Reformers) in Canada West, the *Parti bleu* and the *Parti rouge* in Canada East, the conservative and reform factions in New Brunswick and Nova Scotia—coalesced into two major parties: the Conservatives and the Liberals. These two parties had representation and eventually a federal party machinery throughout the dominion. They also had distinct platforms. The Conservatives generally favoured the establishment of a strong central government, a policy of tariff protection, and close association with Britain. In contrast, the Liberals championed provincial autonomy, free trade, and closer association with the United States.

The Conservative Party was the more unified and organized party, and it won the first federal election in November 1867 with 100 of the 180 seats. Whereas the Liberals remained divided along ethnic lines (and were without a leader until 1873), the Conservatives used their powerful commercial interests to unite across the French–English divide. John A. Macdonald became Canada's first prime minister. A man of marked wit and intelligence with personal charm and a sense of humour as well as a masterful politician, he preferred practical politics to philosophical debate. He remained in the prime minister's office—with the exception of a five-year Liberal interlude in the mid-1870s—from 1867 until his death in 1891. Thus the late nineteenth century is often referred to politically as the Macdonald era. To win essential support in Quebec, Macdonald relied on George-Étienne Cartier, particularly as he himself did not speak French. Macdonald once referred to Cartier as "my second self." From 1867 until his death in 1873, Cartier came second only to Macdonald in the Conservative Party. The relationship between the two men commenced a tradition that became a mainstay of Canadian politics: an English-Canadian prime minister and a French-Canadian lieutenant. Such an alliance ensured Quebec an influential voice in federal politics while providing the governing party with a base in the province.

Until 1874, voting in federal elections was restricted to males who owned property, constituting only 20 percent of the Canadian population. As well, there was no secret ballot; voters had to declare their party preference openly. This system of open voting led to abuse. Street brawls often occurred at election time. Candidates openly bribed voters. Employers sometimes coerced their employees to vote "the right way." Elections were also held at different times in different areas of the country, greatly influencing electoral results. It would be the Liberal Party under Alexander Mackenzie that would reform the electoral system in the 1870s.

The Nature of Confederation

Confederation did not come easily. The divisive deadlock that plagued the Canadas was one of the causes of Confederation, but these divisions did not disappear with the signing of the BNA Act. In fact, they were added to a host of new divisions—including a simmering bitterness in the Maritime provinces, who felt they had been manipulated into joining the new nation. Ethnic, religious, and regional divisions remained thorns in the side of Canada. These problems would play out in the new political arena and they would test the federal structure, in particular the division between provincial and federal jurisdictions. The new nation would have to find a way forward on the basis of a political rather than a cultural nationality. As Cartier noted during the Confederation debates: "Now, when we were united together, if union were attained, we

Sir John A. Macdonald addressing a meeting in Toronto. From the Canadian Illustrated News, *April 31, 1878. "One thinks of those audiences, dead and gone now, the noise, the whisky, the laughter, the tobacco, the smell of unwashed humanity: political meetings were entertainment, the translation of newspapers into life" (P.B. Waite, "Reflections on an Un-Victorian Society," in D. Swainson, ed.,* Oliver Mowat's Ontario *[Toronto: Macmillan, 1972], p. 26). Note that all those in attendance are male; women would have to wait over a third of a century until they gained the federal franchise.*

Source: Library and Archives Canada/C-68193.

would form a political nationality with which neither the national origin, nor the religion of any individual, would interfere." The Fathers of Confederation hoped that this nationalism would serve as a source of strength. Despite their laudable intentions, however, Canada's founders built disunity into the political structure. The new Canadian system, by combining aspects of the American federal and the British parliamentary forms of government, resembled a carriage pulled by two horses moving in different directions.

WHERE HISTORIANS DISAGREE

The Meaning of the BNA Act

Since the passage of the British North America Act in 1867, historians have disagreed as to its meaning and indeed as to the original intentions of the Fathers of Confederation. Some commentators view it as an act of the British Parliament , while others interpret it as a political *contract* among four British North American colonies to establish a new country. Still others see Confederation as a cultural *compact* between "the two founding peoples," English and French Canadians. (The First Nations are pushed to the background in either interpretation. Unfortunately, this is a reasonable reading of the role they played, and were given, in how Confederation came about.) Some historians view the BNA Act as establishing a centralizing nation, while others see it as emphasizing the role of provincial autonomy. The debate goes to the core of Canada's identity as a nation.

A.R.M. Lower, writing in the "colony to nation" tradition of the 1940s, viewed the BNA Act as an act of the British Parliament, imposed from above and with authority emanating from the Crown: "What happened in 1867 was that the Crown, in the fullness of its wisdom, decided to rearrange its administrative areas in British North America. . . . All were cast into the crucible of Imperial omnicompetence and came out remelted, shining, new, and fused."[1] This interpretation implies that the central government—the new Canadian equivalent of the old imperial authority—alone inherited the sweeping powers of the central authority, including the sole right to change the constitution. Donald Creighton (biographer of John A. Macdonald) supported this view.[2] This centralist (and Tory) interpretation privileged a strong federal government in Canada. While it emerged out of the 1930s, 1940s, and 1950s, an era in which the federal government was at its strongest and most centralized, it continues to wield considerable influence.

Those who oppose this interpretation question the centralizing nature of the BNA Act as well as the intentions of its architects. They argue that the Constitution was the result of a "compact." But there is disagreement as to the nature of the compact. Some claim it was an agreement among the provinces, while others argue it was between English and French Canadians.

These historians agree, however, that strong support for local control existed in all four colonies that made up Confederation in 1867. This support was made clear in the battles waged by Oliver Mowat, one of the original "Fathers" who then became premier of Ontario and was dubbed the "Father of Provincial Rights." Historian Paul Romney

reinforces this perspective. He argues that Ontarians fought for strong local control at the time of Confederation and provincial rights after 1867 as much as Quebeckers and Maritimers did, even though Ontario had the most to gain from a strong central government in Ottawa since it had the largest representation. Romney goes so far as to argue that in allowing a stronger national state to develop, Canadians (including centralizing historians) have "forgotten their past and imperiled Confederation."[3]

Historians who argue that the BNA Act constituted a compact between Canada's founding groups take a more positive approach to Confederation and emphasize the role of compromise. The compact was not, in their eyes, a legal or even a political commitment so much as it was a moral one, an unwritten understanding that underlay the negotiations of the BNA Act. In the 1950s, George F.G. Stanley claimed that "the idea of a compact between races was not a new one in 1865; it had already become a vital thing in our history. It influenced both the political thinking and the political vocabulary of the day; and it was already on the way to becoming a tradition and a convention of our constitution."[4]

More recently, John Ralston Saul has emphasized Canada's flexible identity that had its roots in Confederation but also earlier in the foundations of compromise laid by Louis-Hippolyte Lafontaine and Robert Baldwin in the struggle for responsible government of the 1840s. Saul expanded the concept of two founding peoples into a "triangular reality" that included the equal role of First Nations.[5]

Historians and political scientists of late have debated the ideological underpinnings of Confederation. The traditional interpretation presented by Peter Waite argued that Confederation was based on compromise and driven by pragmatism. In 1987, Peter J. Smith argued that the BNA Act reflected a contest between classical republican values and a new pro-capitalist ideology based around centralizing power. In 2000, Ian McKay published an article that became the basis for a new historiographical paradigm in Canada. He argues that the "liberal order framework"—that is, the privileging of the well-being of the individual over that of the community–has long served as the dominant ideological basis for the nation, including Confederation.[6]

Janet Ajzenstat reinforced the role of individualist liberal ideology with roots in the writings of John Locke and the enlightenment. In 2008, Andrew Smith disagreed and claimed that 1867 highlighted a struggle between an individualistic economic philosophy and a collectivist view of the state's role, with the latter emerging triumphant.[7]

1   A.R.M. Lower, *Colony to Nation* (Toronto: Longmans, Green, 1946), p. 328.

2   Donald Creighton, *Dominion of the North* (Toronto: Macmillan, 1957).

3   Paul Romney, *Getting It Wrong: How Canadians Forgot Their Past and Imperiled Confederation* (Toronto: University of Toronto Press, 1999).

4   George F.G. Stanley, "Act or Pact: Another Look at Confederation," *Canadian Historical Association Report*, 1956, p. 13.

5   John Ralston Saul, *Reflections of a Siamese Twin* (Toronto: Penguin, 1998); *Louis-Hippolyte Lafontaine & Robert Baldwin* (Toronto: Penguin, 2011).

6   Peter Waite, *The Life and Times of Confederation, 1864–1867: Politics, Newspapers, and the Union of British North America* (Toronto: University of Toronto Press, 1962); Peter J. Smith, "The Ideological Origins of Canadian Confederation," *Canadian Journal of Political Science* 20 (1): pp. 3–29; Ian McKay, "The Liberal Order Framework: A Prospectus for a Reconnaissance of Canadian History," *Canadian Historical Review* 81: pp. 617–645.

7   Janet Ajzenstat, *The Canadian Founding: John Locke and Parliament* (Montreal: McGill-Queen's University Press, 2007); Andrew Smith, "Toryism, Classical Liberalism, and Capitalism: The Politics of Taxation and the Struggle for Canadian Confederation" *Canadian Historical Review* 89 (1): pp. 1–25.

Dominion–Provincial Relations

For a century and a half, historians, political scientists, and legal experts have debated the intentions of the Fathers of Confederation. Those who believe they sought to build a strong central government point out that the BNA Act delegated only precise and very circumscribed powers to the provincial governments. In contrast, the federal government gained the important economic and taxation powers, including the right to grant subsidies to the individual provinces. Ottawa received the right to make laws for the "peace, order and good government of Canada" in relation to all matters not exclusively assigned to the provincial legislatures. This phrase "peace, order and good government of Canada" and the phrase "regulation of trade and commerce" incorporated all powers not exclusively given to the provinces. Furthermore, centralists point out that the lieutenant governors of the provinces, appointees of the dominion government, could reserve and disallow provincial legislation.

In contrast, provincial-rights advocates argue that since the colonies established the union, Confederation constituted a deal made among them: a provincial compact. Furthermore, they point to the general phrase "property and civil rights in the province" in section 92 of the BNA Act, which deals with the constitutional rights of the provinces, as evidence. They note that the provinces received a structure of government parallel to that of the federal government, implying that provincial association with the Crown was similar, not subordinate, to that of the dominion. Finally, they direct attention to legal tradition: in the late nineteenth and early twentieth centuries, the Judicial Committee of the Privy Council, the highest court of appeal in the British Empire, consistently interpreted the BNA Act in favour of the provinces.

The third quarter of the nineteenth century marked the high point of Maritime-built sailing ships, to be replaced by iron and steel vessels. The image shows sailing ships in Courtenay Bay, New Brunswick, about 1860.

Source: Provincial Archives of New Brunswick/P5-360: Sailing Ships, Courtenay Bay, 1860.

Relations with Britain and the United States

Nationhood did not mean independence. By law and by desire, Canada remained a British colony, with the British Parliament controlling Canada's external affairs. In 1867, Canadians, particularly English Canadians, considered the imperial connection the best means for Canada of fulfilling its destiny. Much like a child maturing within a family, Canada would grow up within the Empire, and while increasingly exercising its own autonomy it would remain loyal. The alternatives were possible annexation by the United States or existence as an insignificant and isolated nation on the northern half of the North American continent. The question and the source of future contention was not whether Canada would remain part of the British Empire, but rather what Canada's role would be within it.

The Economy

One of the reasons behind the push for Confederation was the need to create a more unified economic structure. But the economy faced serious challenges that would require more than simply uniting the colonies. An internal trade system was necessary but Canada also needed to establish external trade links. In addition, the economy had been slow to industrialize and diversify away from a reliance on natural resource staples. More than 80 percent of the Canadian labour force in 1867 worked in the primary industries—farming, fishing, and lumbering—to produce what had become the dominion's staple products of trade. The fur trade, while continuing in the more remote "north country," had declined steadily since the early nineteenth century.

But as the economy developed, the same regional divisions that posed political barriers emerged again. The Maritimes were the centre of the shipbuilding industry. In 1865 alone, for example, the region built more than 600 vessels. The ports of Saint John, Halifax, and Yarmouth were the major shipbuilding centres in the Maritimes, along with Quebec City and Montreal in the Canadas. But as steel ships replaced wooden ones and as steam replaced sails as the source of energy, the era of wood, wind, and sails came to an end. Some Maritimers equated the decline of their "golden age" with Confederation and they resented union.

The vast majority of Canadians in 1867 lived on farms. Agriculture was important in Nova Scotia, especially in the Annapolis valley, while in New Brunswick, farmers made up more than half the labour force. In southern Quebec, dairy farming predominated. Some Quebec farmers, with the encouragement of the Catholic Church and the Quebec government, colonized further north in the Saguenay Lac-Saint-Jean region, in the Laurentians, or in Témiscamingue in the upper Ottawa Valley. These "colonist farmers" had to clear the land of forests before breaking ground. Even then, farming in these northern reaches was marginal because of poor soil, short frost-free periods, and long distances from market centres. As the joke went, northern farmers raised two crops: one stone, the other snow. For every Quebecker who went north to farm, ten went south into the New England states in search of work, a movement known as "la Grande Hémorragie": the Great Hemorrhage.

In Ontario, wheat farming served as "the engine of economic growth,"[1] according to economic historian John McCallum. At the time of Confederation, the best agricultural land lay within the province, where 60 percent of the working population farmed. Coarse grain or flour made up half of all exports at mid-century. By the time of Confederation, the peak of wheat production was reached, with most of the good farmland occupied and some of the older districts exhausted. Fortunately for Ontarians, just as they faced an agricultural crisis, the Canadian government acquired the vast prairie lands to the west, which served as an outlet for aspiring young farmers.

The Canadian economy relied on the exporting of raw materials to either Britain or the United States in return for manufactured goods: textiles, textile fibres, agricultural products, consumer goods, and iron products. But Confederation coincided with the rudimentary beginnings of the production of manufactured goods within Canada itself. Historian O.J. Firestone notes that in the decade of the 1860s, over 20 percent of Canada's gross national product (GNP) came from manufacturing—a dramatic increase from the preceding decade. Manufacturing employed nearly 200,000 Canadians in roughly 40,000 establishments. Most of these were small family businesses attached to the owner's residence and employing only a few people doing jobs by hand.

Mechanization developed swiftly in some fields. In the agricultural-implements industry, Daniel Massey, a farmer at Newcastle, east of Toronto, manufactured ploughs, harrows, reapers, and other simple horse-drawn implements in machine-based factories. Canadian shops and factories in the large urban centres of Montreal, Quebec City, Toronto, Hamilton, Saint John, and Halifax began to specialize and to break production tasks down into smaller components. Already there was evidence that manufacturing would be concentrated predominantly in the Montreal area, in the vicinity of Toronto, and at the western end of Lake Ontario, from Hamilton westward to Brantford.

Urbanization

In 1867, only one in five Canadians lived in urban centres—communities with a population over 1000. Canada had only three large cities: Montreal with 105,000 people; Quebec City with 60,000; and Toronto with 50,000. Six other cities had populations greater than 10,000: Saint John and Halifax in the Maritimes, and Hamilton, Ottawa, Kingston, and London in Ontario. A host of smaller towns in the 1000–5000 range dotted the Canadian landscape. The larger metropolitan centres serviced a hinterland region that went beyond the adjacent rural area, due to their extensive rail connections. Montreal's hinterland, for example, included the rural areas of southwestern Quebec as well as eastern Ontario.

The Maritime cities of Saint John and Halifax grew slowly, compared with cities in central Canada. Many of the manufacturers in these two port cities faced difficult times because they lacked a large local market and faced competition from wealthier entrepreneurs in central Canada. In 1867, industrialists in the Maritimes looked forward to the promised completion of the Intercolonial Railway, which would, they hoped, make Ontario and Quebec economic hinterlands of Halifax and Saint John.

Canadian cities in 1867 were, with the exception of Montreal, preindustrial. In Montreal, however, there already existed predominantly working-class districts in the city core and along the St. Lawrence River and Lachine Canal. Wealthy families were leaving the inner city to live in the spacious, clean, airy suburban districts of the west end, with its numerous parks and good public services. Thus, in the case of Montreal, the modern industrial segregated city made an appearance by 1867. By 1914, such segregated cities would be commonplace throughout the country.

Population

In 1867, the total population of the new Dominion of Canada was 3.5 million. The First Nations in the four original provinces numbered approximately 30,000, or roughly 1 percent. The three largest groups were the Anishinaabeg, in Ontario; the Iroquois, in Ontario and Quebec; and the

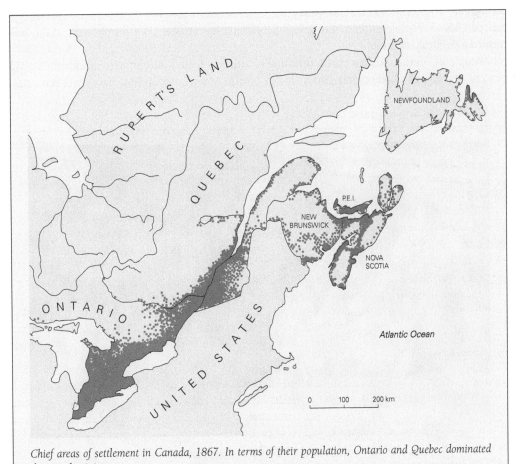

Chief areas of settlement in Canada, 1867. In terms of their population, Ontario and Quebec dominated the new dominion.

Source: Based on John Warkentin, *Canada: A Geographical Interpretation* (Toronto: Methuen 1968), p. 45.

Mi'kmaq, in Nova Scotia and New Brunswick. Legally, they were considered "wards of the state." Crown responsibility for "Indians" as indicated in the Royal Proclamation of 1763 was transferred to the federal government through Confederation. Section 91 (subsection 24) of the British North America Act assigned responsibility for "Indians and lands reserved for Indians" to Ottawa.

But the plight of the First Nations had deteriorated, particularly after the War of 1812. The crude reality was that white society felt it no longer needed the Aboriginal population. Their important roles as fur trade partners and military allies were no longer required. Increasingly throughout the nineteenth century, they were viewed through a paternalistic lens, seen as an unfortunate and helpless people caught up in the exorable march of progress. They were also soon to be viewed through the lens of social Darwinism: they were an inferior race and as part of the "white man's burden," deserving of sympathy and care. But ultimately, all signs indicated that they were a dying race. The population numbers had been declining for decades, due to poverty, disease, and changes in lifestyle. While the government hoped they would assimilate into white society, it was widely agreed that by the middle of the twentieth century, there would be no more "Indians" in Canada.

By 1867, 123 treaties had been signed between the Crown and the First Nations in the area that became Canada. These treaties resulted in the various bands surrendering control of their lands in return for reserves, annuities, clothes, and tools. The agreements were signed when the colonial governments desired particular lands. The Indians were pushed onto reserves, farther and farther away from white settlements. Not surprisingly, they did not participate in shaping the new political community of Canada. "For the Europeans who fashioned the Canadian Confederation, the Aboriginal peoples were subjects on whom sovereignty could be imposed, not people with whom one formed a political community."[2]

People of French descent made up roughly a third of the total population. More than 85 percent resided in Quebec and had roots in North America extending back two centuries.

First Nations lacrosse players from the Kahnawake community near Montreal. This image depicts the national champions in the 1860s. The First Nations soon adopted the non-Aboriginals' tradition of team photographs, posed, with two players resting on their elbows on the ground at the front, others seated behind, and two standing at the back.

Source: Lee Pritzker Collection/Library and Archives Canada/C-1959.

The Acadians in the Maritimes constituted nearly 10 percent of the French-speaking population. Only 3 percent of Canada's francophones lived in Ontario, mainly in the area adjacent to Quebec.

People of British descent accounted for 60 percent of Canada's population in 1867. Some were descendants of Loyalists who had settled on British territory after the American Revolution. Most, however, were British immigrants and their descendants who had arrived in British North America during the immigration boom between 1815 and 1860, some 1.3 million in total. In 1867, the Irish made up 25 percent of the total Canadian population, the Scots 16 percent, the English 15 percent, and the Welsh 5 percent.

English and French Canadians generally lived in separate worlds. P.-J.-O. Chauveau, the first premier of Quebec after Confederation, compared Canada to the famous staircase of the Château de Chambord in France, built to allow two persons to ascend it without meeting, and even without seeing each other except at intervals. "English and French, we climb by a double flight of stairs toward the destinies reserved for us on this continent, without knowing each other, without meeting each other, except on the landing of politics."

The remaining 8 percent of the dominion's population consisted of immigrants and their descendants from Europe and the United States. The majority came from German-speaking states and were welcomed because of the close links between the British monarchy and German principalities. There were, as well, about 65,000 African Canadians. While some were of American Loyalist descent, many arrived in the mid-1800s, either as freed slaves, now facing increased discrimination in the United States, or as fugitive slaves on the eve of the American Civil War via the Underground Railroad. Although slavery had been illegal in British North America since the early nineteenth century, racial prejudice was rampant. Blacks faced discrimination in land grants, schooling, employment, and voting rights. Whereas Canadians would take pride in their nation's role in helping slaves escape, the reality in their new homes offered little justification for this pride.

Ontario and Quebec had nearly four-fifths of the new dominion's population, with more than 1.5 million in Ontario and about 1 million in Quebec. The other fifth of Canada's population resided in the Maritime provinces: roughly 400,000 in Nova Scotia and 300,000 in New Brunswick.

Social Life

In 1867, most Canadians lived and worked on their own farms, as close to neighbours, kin, and their own ethnic group as possible. In Quebec the seigneurial system had been abolished only thirteen years earlier, which meant individual farmers acquired title to their lands. Limited financial means and rudimentary transportation links made consumer goods a luxury. The village elite generally consisted of the curé, the doctor, the notary, and the local merchants. In Quebec City and Montreal, French Canadians lived amid a substantial and often better-off English population. Even though Canadians were already moving from rural areas into the growing urban centres, the Catholic Church in Quebec continued to expound the merits of rural life. On farms or in small communities, the parish priest could continue to exert influence in guiding people toward a moral life. The city, on the other hand, was perceived as

An evening with friends in Quebec. Family and friends provided social cohesion in rural Canada in the nineteenth century. Note the cross on the wall at the back, indicating the influence of the Roman Catholic Church in late-nineteenth-century Quebec.

Source: Library and Archives Canada/C-1125.

marked by vice and corruption; it was also the domain of "les anglais" who controlled the commercial levers of society. The church was concerned with the migration of French Canadians out of Quebec and to New England. It sought to stop the bleeding by directing French Catholics to take up farms in the northern areas of the province. The attempts, however, largely failed.

Next door in Ontario, most of the population consisted of recent British immigrants or children of immigrants. The majority were freehold farmers who had acquired their land within the last generation. In general, Ontario farmers were better off economically than their Quebec counterparts. They owned larger farms that were newly cultivated and subsequently more productive. People lived farther apart, however, and were divided by their different Christian denominational ties.

A HISTORICAL PORTRAIT

Josiah Henson

Josiah Henson was born into slavery on a Maryland plantation in 1789. His earliest recollection at the age of three or four was the day he saw his father return from a terrible beating. As Henson later recalled, "His right ear had been cut off close to his head and he had received a hundred lashes on his back." His father's crime? He struck a white man, the farm overseer, for brutally assaulting Josiah's mother.

Soon afterward, the Henson family was pulled apart. Josiah's father was sold to a plantation in Alabama and his mother was auctioned off, along with his brothers and sisters. Josiah's mother was successful in pleading with her new owner, Isaac Riley, to have her youngest son remain with her. Josiah worked in the fields and eventually became supervisor of the Montgomery County farm. In 1828, Henson attempted to buy his freedom, but was cheated by his owner and lost his money. Now married and with a family, Henson escaped with his wife, Nancy, and four children to Upper Canada.

In 1793, Lieutenant Governor John Graves Simcoe had passed "An Act to prevent further introduction of Slaves, and to

Reverend Josiah Henson, 1789–1883.

Source: Josiah Henson, *Truth Stranger Than Fiction: Father Henson's Story of His Own Life.* (Boston: John P. Jewett and Company, 1858).

limit the Term of Contracts for Servitude within this Province." In the decades that followed, black Loyalists from the American Revolution and refugees from the War of 1812 made their way to the colony.

The Henson family spent six weeks following the Underground Railway to Kent County, Upper Canada. On October 28, 1830, they crossed the Niagara River. Immediately, Henson fell on his knees and gave thanks. In their new home, the Hensons founded an African community named Dawn, near present-day Dresden, Ontario. With the financial assistance of a group of Boston Unitarians, they began the British American Institute for Fugitive Slaves, a school to educate ex-slaves and to teach them a trade.

In the following years, Henson expanded the settlement. Dawn's population grew to 500. Henson became a Methodist minister and spoke publically on abolition. He served as an officer in charge of a black militia unit during the Rebellion of 1837.

In the late 1840s, Henson dictated his life story. It was published in Boston in 1849 as *The Life of Josiah Henson Formerly a Slave Now an Inhabitant of Canada.* Three years later Harriet Beecher Stowe's novel *Uncle Tom's Cabin* appeared. It became the most popular anti-slavery book published before the outbreak of the American Civil War. The fact that many people identified Josiah Henson as the prototype for the fictional "Uncle Tom" made him famous. Henson made several lecture tours of Britain to raise money for the Dawn settlement.

When the American Civil War ended, many African Americans in Upper Canada returned to the United States, and the community of Dawn diminished. In his late eighties, Henson made his final visit to Britain to meet Queen Victoria at Windsor Castle. He died in Dresden at the age of ninety-three in 1883.

Already by the 1860s, Ontarians were on the move and seeking to expand. A study of several townships along Lake Ontario near Port Hope revealed that, within a five-year span, more than half the people were recent occupants or had moved from one place to another within the region. An increasing number were leaving rural areas for the cities and towns. Physical mobility, however, did not necessarily mean social mobility, even though the incentive for moving was often to better one's life. Increasingly, Ontarians looked westward as a potential area for agrarian expansion.

In the Maritimes, people lived predominantly in rural areas or in small towns. Given the sparse populations, the poor roads, and a topography that encouraged settlement along the coast, communities were often isolated. In 1867, no major railways yet existed to link communities. In addition, the region's diversified economy of fishing, lumbering, mining, and farming segregated people according to interests and livelihood.

Gender Relations

Women lacked basic rights in 1867: the right to vote, the right to higher education or professional training, and legal rights. They were not defined as individuals but by their role in the "domestic sphere," as wives and mothers at the service of husbands and children.

Women relinquished their personal property and any wages earned upon marriage. Under British common law, in effect everywhere except Quebec, husband and wife were legally one. A wife could not sign a contract, be sued in her own name, take her husband to court, or initiate divorce proceedings. Despite such restrictions, over 95 percent of women married, because not to marry was to be left to their own devices in a patriarchal society in which spinsterhood was tantamount to failure. They also had large families: 7.8 children on average by mid-century. By the end of the 1800s, that number would decline to an average of 4 children.

Marriage was more a communal than private affair. Courting generally occurred in chaperoned settings, and marriage was a public event. But diaries written by women during this period speak little of love and romance in marriage, and instead emphasize economic security. Sexuality was strictly regulated according to Victorian notions of respectability. In order to keep women in line, sex was to be enjoyed only by men, often through affairs with a mistress. Only "loose" or "fallen" women, or prostitutes, supposedly enjoyed sex. Sex within marriage was sanctioned by church and society, but it was for procreation rather than enjoyment. Such oppressive views of sexuality created rigid lines between what was accepted as "normal" and "perverse."

Women's duties consisted of the arduous work of keeping a "good" home. Their daily tasks usually consisted of cleaning house, cooking, sewing, weaving, and caring for children, elderly, and sick family members. The rhythm of daily life was often broken only by church services on Sundays, which provided a social outing. The change of seasons varied the pattern only slightly, and usually added garden and field work.

Children were the forgotten group in society, without any legal rights at all. Those from poorer families who had the opportunity to attend school usually had to leave early to help support their families. Most working-class children had little hope or opportunity of rising above their parents' social status. Social mobility remained an elusive goal. Childhood, as a result, was a brief stage of life, lasting generally until the age of ten or so, when the youth was expected to begin working or take on an apprenticeship. There was no stage between childhood and adulthood.

LE TRAVAIL.

" Tu te plains, mon pauvre mari, de tes dix heures d'ouvrage : voici quatorze heures que je travaille, moi, et je n'ai pas encore fini ma journée."

"Work," a drawing that appeared in the journal L'Opinion publique, November 2, 1871. In the late nineteenth century, gender inequality was as common as class inequality. The woman states; "You complain my dear husband, of your ten hours of labour, I have already worked fourteen hours, and my day is still not finished yet."

Source: Library and Archives Canada/C-108134.

Trade Unions

The federal government legally recognized unions in 1872. In the 1860s, the unions that did exist represented skilled workers in a particular locale or a special trade, such as typesetting, shoemaking, and moulding. The first unions for nonskilled workers appeared in shops that introduced new technologies, a development that often undermined skilled jobs. Increasingly, employers saw workers as employees rather than as apprentices. They brought workers under one roof and paid them according to the quantity, rather than quality, of their work.

As the process of industrialization transformed Canada, some workers responded to the stresses of these changed conditions in the workplace by rioting. By 1867, however, strikes and parades were replacing riots as more acceptable forms of protest, and as a means to demand better wages and working conditions. On June 10, 1867, for example, 10,000 workers paraded in the streets of Montreal as a show of worker solidarity and as an appeal for improved wages and working conditions.

Religion and Education

Religious Denominations

In 1867, most Canadians belonged to one of the major Christian denominations. The Roman Catholic Church, the largest in Canada, claimed as members 40 percent of the country's population and 85 percent in Quebec. In English Canada it was widely accepted that church and state were separate. The education system that developed was "public" and state-funded through taxation. But this separation, in essence, meant that while nominally public, the education system was unofficially controlled by Protestant denominations. The general opinion in English Canada was that the Catholic Church should not be allowed to control its own education system unless it was funded separately. The Catholic Church in Quebec controlled the Catholic education system, supplying both its teachers and its curriculum. Quebec was unique in that it had two separate school systems, created through Confederation. The English minority was accommodated through the provision of a "public" school system.

Most of the teachers came from the female religious orders. These female orders also administered the hospitals and cared for the sick, the abandoned, and the poor. They often provided their members with the opportunity to obtain an education, to occupy responsible administrative positions, and to serve as teachers, nurses, and social-assistance workers.

In Protestant Canada, Anglicans slightly outnumbered Presbyterians, who outnumbered Methodists. These denominations favoured voluntarism regarding the legal separation of church and state. They believed that religious instruction should be provided by the church only—in Sunday schools. The Catholic Church, in contrast, maintained that the school system should provide religious, as well as regular, instruction. It therefore opposed the abolition of denominational schools.

Schooling

Schooling had little priority in Canada in the 1860s, although most provinces moved to a form of taxation on property holders to finance state-operated schools. The upper classes often viewed educating the poor as a waste of time. These children were unlikely to make "proper" use of an education when they were destined to toil their lives away as labourers. In addition, educating the poor was seen as dangerous because it would possibly enlighten the downtrodden as to their miserable plight and unfair conditions. Children fortunate enough to receive formal education might have their classes in the corners of warehouses, blacksmith shops, stores, tanneries, or private homes. Their schooling rarely went beyond the basic "3 Rs"— "reading, 'riting, and 'rithmetic."

Teachers often had little more education than their students. The most important requisites for teaching were simply a willingness to work for low pay and to enforce discipline. Attitudes toward education, however, underwent significant change throughout the first half of the nineteenth century as a result of the immigration boom that brought in significant numbers of Scots and Irish of Presbyterian, Methodist, and Baptist persuasion. Some of these were educational reformers whose experiences in their homelands had given them increased expectations when it came to educating children and they put pressure on the Canadian system dominated by the Anglican Church. The process of industrialization (and the response to this process) also advanced the cause of universal education. Increasingly reformers argued that education could help cure the ills of society.

In Ontario, the middle and upper classes paid fees for their children to attend grammar schools (renamed "high schools" in 1871 by the superintendent of education, Egerton Ryerson) and collegiate institutes. In high school, the students learned English, commercial subjects, and natural science, especially agriculture. In collegiate institutes, they studied the classics in preparation for university. In Quebec, the Catholic Church operated classical colleges, which trained the province's future lawyers, doctors, and priests.

Most of the seventeen universities in existence in 1867 were affiliated with a religious denomination, but four nondenominational universities already existed: the University of Toronto, McGill in Montreal, Dalhousie College in Halifax, and the University of New Brunswick in Fredericton. Universities served an elite of only 1500 students in total, mostly sons of the well-to-do (women were not admitted) or a few aspiring members of the upper middle class. Within the university curriculum, the faculties of arts and theology dominated, as teaching and the clergy were the favoured career options after graduation. The arts course was traditional, with an emphasis on classical languages, mathematics, and philosophy. Natural science was assuming greater importance. Engineering courses had not yet been introduced, but law and medicine were taught at some of the larger universities.

COMMUNITY PORTRAIT

The Congregation of Notre Dame of Montreal

Founded in 1658 by Marguerite Bourgeoys as a religious community of uncloistered women to live and work among the common people and "less fortunate," and as a teaching order to provide schooling for the young women of New France, the Congregation of Notre Dame became, by the late nineteenth and early twentieth centuries, the largest and most prestigious religious community of women teachers in Quebec. By 1920, it had over 1600 members and over 150 Roman Catholic schools throughout Quebec, Nova Scotia, New Brunswick, and Ontario.

Bourgeoys claimed to have a vision that the Congregation would not be another typical women's religious community cloistered behind walls. Based on the example of Mary, mother of Jesus, it was to provide the opportunity for

The teachers of Mont Ste-Marie Convent School, 1889.

Source: Congregation de Notre-Dame, 2330 ouest, rue Sherbrooke, PQ, H3E 1G8, (514) 931-5891.

women to be active agents of change. It was the temporary home for some of the King's Daughters (Filles du Roi) when they arrived from France.

The Congregation forged a role in educating children in Quebec City and Montreal, as well as the surrounding areas. It received civil recognition from King Louis XIV in 1671. Bourgeoys established schools throughout New France to educate young girls and children, including First Nations children. When Bourgeoys retired in 1693, after forty years of work, the Bishop of Quebec imposed restrictions upon the Congregation. Marguerite Bourgeoys died in 1700.

As the Congregation grew, it also became more affluent. Its members enjoyed improved diets of fresh fruits, vegetables, butter, and pastries. The sisters had lighter manual workloads, and thus more time for leisure activities together and for communal prayers. But prosperity also caused strains in the Congregation's communal life. In the 1880s, *les soeurs converses*, or domestic servants, were brought into the community to do the manual work previously done by the sisters themselves. Thus a two-tiered

social order emerged, evident in the separation of recreation, clothing habits, and assigned work of the two groups. Furthermore, the Congregation's growth resulted in a more bureaucratic structure that mitigated its earlier sense of a community of equals. Now a General Superior ruled and administered affairs at the centre, while local and provincial superiors in the Congregation's six "provinces," each corresponding to the regional district of the schools owned by the community, carried out the rulings of the central council and regulated the everyday activities of the sisters. A constitution dictated the rights and responsibilities of each office and outlined the procedure for the appointment of superiors. Nominally, sisters who had been with the community for at least ten years could cast a vote for their leaders, but in reality each chapter selected delegates who made the final decision. And within the community, nuns from upper- and middle-class households wielded greater power than those nuns from working-class or farming backgrounds.

Still, the community of the Congregation of Notre Dame provided its members with a communal and supportive setting in which women lived a religious life while also acquiring a profession. In 1908, the Congregation supported the establishment of the first French-language women's college in Quebec: the École d'enseignement supérieur (renamed the Collège Marguerite Bourgeoys in 1926). In this way, the Congregation of Notre Dame assisted French-Canadian females to obtain an education equal to that of their male counterparts.

The Congregation of Notre Dame still exists today in Canada and around the world. In 1982, Marguerite Bourgeoys was canonized by the Roman Catholic Church and became Canada's first female saint.

FURTHER READING

Patricia Simpson, *Marguerite Bourgeoys and the Congregation of Notre Dame*, 1665–1700 (Montreal/Kingston: McGill-Queen's University Press, 2005).

Marta Danylewycz, *Taking the Veil: An Alternative to Marriage, Motherhood and Spinsterhood in Quebec, 1840–1920* (Toronto: McClelland and Stewart, 1987).

Danielle Juteau and Nicole Laurin, *Un métier et une vocation: Le travail des religieuses au Québec de 1901 à 1971* (Montreal: Les Presses de l'Université de Montréal, 1997).

Nadia Famy-Eid and Micheline Dumont, *Les couventines: L'éducation des filles au Québec dans les congrégations religieuses enseignantes*, 1840–1960 (Montreal: Boréal, 1986).

SUMMARY

The Dominion of Canada was formed in 1867 but, in size at least, the nation was only a shadow of what it soon was to become. When Canada was created, even its architects were well aware that its growth was only beginning. The experiment in nation building was about to take on a new phase of expansion that would result in serious growing pains. Politically, the new nation was setting out on a new two-party system and with a new constitution that left relationships between the new federal government and the provincial governments to be resolved.

But in reality, Confederation had little immediate effect on the life of the average person. Canada in 1867 was a rural, predominantly farming society. Social distinctions divided the rural population, and great physical distances isolated communities. One result was that the dominion lacked a sense of nationalism; few saw "Canadian" as their primary sense of identity. According to Prime Minister John A. Macdonald, Confederation "now in the gristle" needed to "harden into bone."

NOTES

1. John McCallum, *Unequal Beginnings: Agriculture and Economic Development in Quebec and Ontario Until 1870* (Toronto: University of Toronto Press, 1980), p. 5.

2. Peter H. Russell, *Constitutional Odyssey: Can Canadians Become a Sovereign People?*, 2nd ed. (Toronto: University of Toronto Press, 1993), p. 4.

BIBLIOGRAPHY

The best work that deals with the interpretation of Confederation is Paul Romney, *Getting It Wrong: How Canadians Forgot Their Past and Imperilled Confederation* (Toronto: University of Toronto Press, 1999). The three best general texts on Confederation, all written in the 1960s and now dated, are Donald Creighton, *The Road to Confederation: The Emergence of Canada, 1863–1867* (Toronto: Macmillan, 1964); W.L. Morton, *The Critical Years: The Union of British North America, 1857–1873* (Toronto: McClelland & Stewart, 1964); and P.B. Waite, *The Life and Times of Confederation, 1864–1867: Politics, Newspapers, and the Union of British North America* (Toronto: University of Toronto Press, 1962). Christopher Moore takes a more recent look at the topic in *1867: How the Fathers Made a Deal* (Toronto: McClelland & Stewart, 1997). Primary sources include P.B. Waite, ed., *The Confederation Debates in the Province of Canada, 1865* (Toronto: McClelland & Stewart, 1963); Janet Ajzenstat et al., eds, *Canada's Founding Debates* (Toronto: Stoddart, 1999); G.P. Browne, ed., *Documents on the Confederation of British North America* (Montreal and Kingston: McGill-Queen's University Press, 2009).

On the Maritimes and Confederation, see Phillip A. Buckner, "The 1860s: An End and a Beginning," in Phillip A. Buckner and John G. Reid, eds., *The Atlantic Region to Confederation: A History* (Toronto: University of Toronto Press, 1994), pp. 360–86; and J. Murray Beck, *Joseph Howe* (Montreal: McGill-Queen's University Press, 1984). One of the best sources on Quebec and Confederation in English remains A.I. Silver, *The French-Canadian Idea of Confederation, 1864–1900* (Toronto: University of Toronto Press, 1982). Parts Three and Four of Yvan Lamonde, trans., Phyllis Aronoff and Howard Scott, *The Social History of Ideas in Quebec, 1760–1896* (Montreal: McGill-Queen's University Press, 2013) help contextualize the French-Canadian response to Confederation.

On the American influence on Confederation, consult Robin Winks, *Canada and the United States: The Civil War Years* (Montreal: Harvest House, 1971 [1960]); Greg Marquis, *In Armageddon's Shadow: The Civil War and Canada's Maritime Provinces* (Montreal/Kingston: McGill-Queen's University Press, 1998); Adam Mayers, *Dixie and the Dominion: Canada, the Confederacy and the War for the Union* (Toronto: Dundurn Press, 2003); and Claire Hoy, *Canadians in the Civil War* (Toronto: McClelland and Stewart, 2004). More recent studies include Richard M. Reid, *African Canadians in Union Blue: Enlisting for the*

Cause in the Civil War (Vancouver: UBC Press, 2014), and John Boyko, *Blood and Daring: How Canada Fought the American Civil War and Forged a Nation* (Toronto: Knopf Canada, 2013). Studies of Britain's influence include C.P. Stacey, *Canada and the British Army, 1841–1871*, rev. ed. (Toronto: University of Toronto Press, 1963 [1936]), and Ged Martin, *Britain and the Origins of Canadian Federation, 1837–67* (Vancouver: University of British Columbia Press, 1995).

For a study of Canada's Irish community at the time of the Fenian Raids, see William Jenkins, *Between Raid and Rebellion: The Irish in Buffalo and Toronto, 1867–1916* (Montreal-Kingston: McGill-Queen's University Press, 2013). For the impact of the Fenian Raids on the Canadian state, see Reg Whitaker, Gregory S. Kealey, and Andrew Parnaby, *Secret Service: Political Policing in Canada from the Fenians to Fortress America* (Toronto: University of Toronto Press, 2012).

Portraits of Canada's first prime minister are available in Donald G. Creighton, *John A. Macdonald: The Old Chieftain* (Toronto: Macmillan, 1955) and P.B. Waite, *Macdonald: His Life and World* (Toronto: McGraw-Hill Ryerson, 1975). More recent studies include Ged Martin, *Favourite Son? John A. Macdonald and the Voters of Kingston, 1841–91* (Kingston: Kingston Historical Society, 2010); Richard Gwyn, *John A., The Man Who Made Us: The Life and Times of John A. Macdonald, Volume One: 1815–1867* (Toronto: Random House, 2007) and *Nation Maker: Sir John A. Macdonald: His Life, Our Times, Volume Two: 1867–1891* (Toronto: Random House, 2011); and Patrice Dutil and Roger Hall, eds., *Macdonald at 200: New Reflections and Legacies* (Toronto: Dundurn, 2014).

There are good biographies on a number of the Fathers of Confederation. On Cartier, see Brian Young, *George-Étienne Cartier: Montreal Bourgeois* (Montreal/Kingston: McGill-Queen's University Press, 1981). On George Brown, see J.M.S. Careless, *Brown of* The Globe (Toronto: Dundurn, 1989). On D'Arcy McGee, see David Wilson, *Thomas D'Arcy McGee, Volume 1: Passion, Reason, and Politics, 1825–1857* (Montreal/Kingston: McGill-Queen's University Press, 2008) and *Thomas D'Arcy McGee: The Extreme Moderate, 1857–1868* (Montreal-Kingston: McGill-Queen's University Press, 2013). Gordon T. Stewart discusses the formation of political parties in *The Origins of Canadian Politics: A Comparative Approach* (Vancouver: University of British Columbia Press, 1986).

For a review of the Canadian economy at the time of Confederation, consult Michael Bliss, *Northern Enterprise: Five Centuries of Canadian Business* (Toronto: McClelland & Stewart, 1987); Kenneth Norrie and Douglas Owram, *A History of the Canadian Economy*, 4th ed. (Toronto: Nelson, 2008); and, in the case of Quebec, P.-A. Linteau, R. Durocher, and J.-C. Robert, *Quebec: A History, 1867–1929* (Toronto: James Lorimer, 1983). Andrew Smith's *British Businessmen and Canadian Confederation: Constitution Making in an Era of Anglo-Globalization* (Montreal/Kingston: McGill-Queen's University Press, 2008) reflects new work in the field.

For a study of social life in Confederation-era Montreal, see Bettina Bradbury, *Wife to Widow: Lives, Laws, and Politics in Nineteenth Century Montreal* (Vancouver: UBC Press, 2011). Sandra Gwyn provides a glimpse of governing society in Ottawa from 1867 to 1914 in *The Private Capital: Ambition and Love in the Age of Macdonald and Laurier* (Toronto: McClelland & Stewart, 1984). The best overview of African Canadians remains Robin Winks, *The Blacks in Canada: A History*, 2nd ed. (Montreal/Kingston: McGill-Queen's University Press, 1997).

On women at the time of Confederation, see the relevant sections of Alison Prentice et al., *Canadian Women: A History*, 2nd ed. (Toronto: Harcourt Brace, 1996). For Quebec, see Marta Danylewycz, *Taking the Veil: An Alternative to Marriage, Motherhood, and Spinsterhood in Quebec, 1840–1920* (Toronto: McClelland & Stewart, 1987); for the Maritimes, see Janet Guildford and Suzanne Morton, *Separate Spheres: Women's Worlds in the 19th-Century Maritimes* (Fredericton: Acadiensis Press, 1994).

Craig Heron's *The Canadian Labour Movement: A Short History*, 2nd ed. (Toronto: Lorimer, 1996) surveys Canadian labour history. See as well Bryan D. Palmer, *Working-Class Experience: Rethinking the History of Canadian Labour, 1800–1991* (Toronto: McClelland & Stewart, 1992).

For further discussion of religion, see John W. Grant, *A Profusion of Spires: Religion in Nineteenth-Century Ontario* (Toronto: University of Toronto Press, 1988). For a discussion of religion and religious practice in English-speaking Quebec, see J.I. Little, *The Other Quebec: Microhistorical Essays on Nineteenth Century Religion and Society* (Toronto: University of Toronto Press, 2006).

On education, consult Susan E. Houston and Alison Prentice, *Schooling and Scholars in Nineteenth-Century Ontario* (Toronto: University of Toronto Press, 1988); Bruce Curtis, *Building the Educational State: Canada West, 1836–1871* (London: Althouse Press, 1988); and J. Donald Wilson, Robert M. Stamp, and Louis-Philippe Audet, eds., *Canadian Education: A History* (Toronto: Prentice-Hall, 1970).

The best work that deals with the interpretation of Confederation is Paul Romney, *Getting It Wrong: How Canadians Forgot Their Past and Imperilled Confederation* (Toronto: University of Toronto Press, 1999).

Part 1

EXPANDING THE NEW DOMINION, 1867–1914

INTRODUCTION

The mid-to-late-nineteenth century was an era of nationalism throughout the Western world. The creation of Canada did not occur in a vacuum. The process was set against an international backdrop that included the formation of Germany in 1866 and Italy in 1871, and a war to hold the nation together in the United States in the early 1860s. But Canada's exercise in nation building did not end in 1867 and the decades to follow produced what can best be called a "second Confederation."

The "Fathers" were well aware that Confederation was the first step to building a nation "from sea to sea." What they did not realize, however, was how rapidly expansion was going to occur and how the process was going to strain the bonds of the new nation. Within ten years, the country expanded to include all of the existing British North American colonies with the exception of Newfoundland. The new nation also expanded to the Pacific and the Arctic Oceans. In order to expand and eventually settle the vast Northwest, Canada negotiated seven treaties with the First Nations that, according to the government, effectively extinguished Aboriginal title to the territory. But in the process, the new dominion drove the First Nations to the point of starvation and sickness carrying out a policy of "cultural genocide." Canada engaged in two serious conflicts with the mixed-blood population of the Northwest, and pursued an overly ambitious transportation policy that nearly bankrupted the treasury and resulted in a scandal that toppled the government.

Creating the physical boundaries of a new nation state proved easier than fostering a sense of nationalism. The Canadian nation was not forged in blood or revolution. Instead, Canada was founded on compromise and manipulation. Because the traditional components of cultural nationalism—a common language, a common cultural tradition, and a common religion—were absent, nationalists looked to empire, geography, and government policies of railway building, protective tariffs, and large-scale immigration to generate, instill, and promote a sense of nation.

Canada, from the outset, was hampered by fundamental disagreements over the structure of the new dominion. The decision to create a federal union with political power divided between Ottawa and the provinces created a quagmire of intergovernmental squabbles that became a mainstay of Canadian politics. Dominion–provincial conflict was exacerbated by cultural and religious tensions between French and English, Catholic and Protestant. A century of bitterness and suspicion between these two dominant groups preceded 1867. Confederation temporarily buried the division by halting the designs of assimilation and providing the French Canadians with their own provincial government with control over their own local affairs. But the divisions remained, simmering beneath the surface of the new nation. Within a decade, they resurfaced.

Canada needed to reforge relations with Britain and the United States. The Dominion took pride in its role as the "eldest daughter" of the Empire and Confederation was viewed in both nationalistic and imperialistic terms. At the same time, Canada needed to rebuild its relationship with the United States after decades of annexationist fears.

Chapter Two

THREE OCEANS, ONE COUNTRY: 1867–80

TIME LINE

1867	Nova Scotia, New Brunswick, Quebec, and Ontario join Confederation
1868	Nova Scotia attempts to secede from Confederation
1869	Canada purchases Rupert's Land from the Hudson's Bay Company Act passed for the Temporary Government of Rupert's Land and the North-Western Territory Outbreak of Red River Resistance under Louis Riel Newfoundland rejects union with Canada
1870	Manitoba becomes fifth province Wolseley expedition sent to the Red River colony
1871	British Columbia joins Confederation The first of seven numbered treaties signed between First Nations and Canadian government to extinguish Aboriginal title to Prairie West
1873	Prince Edward Island joins Confederation Macdonald Conservatives win federal election
1876	Treaty Six signed with Canadian government covering the territory of present-day central and northern Saskatchewan and Alberta Indian Act passed
1877	Treaty Seven signed with the Canadian government covering the territory of present-day southern Alberta
1880	Britain transfers jurisdiction over Arctic Islands to Canada

As the nation's first prime minister, John A. Macdonald worked to keep the fragile creation called Canada together, despite the attempts of such provinces as Nova Scotia to secede. He also greatly expanded the country by having Britain purchase for Canada the vast northwestern territory known as Rupert's Land from the Hudson's Bay Company (HBC). In the next six years, three new provinces joined Confederation: Manitoba in 1870, British Columbia in 1871, and Prince Edward Island in 1873. The majority of the Northwest became a colony under Canadian control. Negotiations were carried out with Newfoundland, but the colony was unhappy with the terms offered and refused to join. By 1880, Canada had acquired the Arctic archipelago from Britain.

But expansion came at a heavy price and with its share of challenges. Macdonald wanted to wait for settlement and the development of the West before carving out new provinces. The Red River Resistance led by the Métis forced his hand and resulted in the creation of Manitoba. The signing of the numbered treaties in the Prairie West and then the passage of the Indian Act in 1876 highlighted the tragic plight and treatment of the First Nations despite the government's paternalistic belief that it was ultimately aiding these "doomed" people. Still fearing American annexation, and in particular excursions into the undefended western territory, the Canadian expansion was done with remarkable haste and even reckless abandon. Expectations were unrealistic and promises were made that could not be kept.

The Nova Scotia Repeal Movement

Nova Scotia opposed union with the Canadas from the beginning. Charles Tupper, the province's pro-Confederation premier since 1863 and the leader responsible for bringing the colony into Confederation, refused to hold a referendum or even to debate the question in the legislative assembly. He knew his government would lose on the issue. A report in the anti-Confederation newspaper, the *Novascotian*, made no secret of Tupper's unpopularity for supporting union: "Dr. Tupper was burned in effigy here on Monday night last. We are only sorry it was not in person." The Halifax *Morning Chronicle* included an obituary notice for the province in its issue of July 1, 1867.

When Nova Scotians were finally provided an opportunity to vote in the federal election of September 1867, they demonstrated their discontent and anger by electing anti-confederates to 18 of the 19 seats. Tupper was the only confederate to win his seat, and then by less than a hundred votes. In a provincial election the same year, Nova Scotians elected 36 anti-confederates and only 2 pro-confederates. In the first meeting of the provincial legislature, the anti-confederates presented repeal resolutions to end the "bondage" of Confederation.

The Anti-Confederation League, later renamed the Nova Scotia Party, was formed in 1866 and led by Joseph Howe. This popular and seasoned politician, the "Father of Responsible Government in Nova Scotia" and premier from 1860 to 1863, represented a generation of Nova Scotians who remembered the colony's once-flourishing triangular trade with Britain and the West Indies. Howe wanted to strengthen the colony's ties with Britain, not weaken them through British North American union. After the Repealers' stunning victories over the Unionists in the elections of 1867, Howe headed a committee to London in early 1868 to obtain the Colonial Office's sanction for Nova Scotia's release from Confederation. The colonial secretary, however, refused to meet with Howe. Britain wanted to lessen, not increase, its obligations to its British North American colonies through greater colonial autonomy. There was no going back.

Other anti-confederates, particularly the business interests in the province, favoured annexation to the United States. After Britain adopted free trade in the 1840s, Nova Scotians developed a lucrative trade with the United States through the Reciprocity Treaty of 1854, until a protectionist American Senate rescinded it in 1866. In 1867, many Nova Scotians preferred a renewal of reciprocity—even annexation to the United States—rather than union with Canada.

Prime Minister Macdonald saw Canada's opportunity. He knew Howe opposed union with the United States. Hoping that Howe realized that Confederation was a fait accompli and fearing pro-American sentiments, the prime minister promised Howe a cabinet position as well as control over political patronage in the province. In addition, Macdonald offered better financial terms for Nova Scotia—an increased debt allowance and a 25 percent increase in the federal subsidy to the province. Although Howe's opponents accused him of betraying Nova Scotia, he accepted the offer and ran for federal office in a by-election. Assisted by a very generous campaign donation, supplied jointly by the federal Conservative government and central Canadian business interests, Howe won and subsequently joined the federal cabinet.

Howe's "conversion" to Canadian federalism destroyed the repeal movement. Only the annexationists remained. In June 1869, the Anti-Confederation League formally changed its name to the Annexation League. The timing could not have been worse: the group's manifesto, advocating closer relations with the United States, coincided with a brief period of prosperity that undermined its economic grievances. Furthermore, the United States did not appear interested in annexing Nova Scotia.

The offer of better terms for Nova Scotia won over the moderate anti-confederates, but Confederation remained the central issue facing the province for generations to come. In order to weaken opposition to Confederation, Tupper, Howe, and New Brunswick's Charles Tilley successfully pressured Macdonald to give priority to the construction of the Intercolonial Railway. The 800-kilometre publicly funded railway line was completed in 1876 and ran from Rivière-du-Loup in Quebec along New Brunswick's north shore to link up with existing lines to Halifax and Saint John. Regardless, on July 1 in the years that followed, flags were flown at half-mast in Nova Scotia to mourn Confederation.

The Acquisition of Rupert's Land (1869 - 70)

Macdonald's Conservative government faced serious trouble in the Northwest that would require more than a lucrative cabinet position to satisfy opposition. Once again, the fear of American annexation loomed in the background. In this case, however, the threat was more tangible. American senators and congressmen talked openly of annexing the territory. In 1864, the United States Congress granted a charter for the construction of the Northern Pacific Railway from St. Paul, Minnesota, to Seattle, Washington. It was to be built close to the international border with the intention of capturing the trade of the British territory through the building of spur lines.

For decades, there had been discussion in British and colonial government circles as to what do with the vast northwestern territory known as Rupert's Land. Government officials generally viewed the southern part of the territory as a valuable agricultural frontier. It was seen as open and empty, because it was inhabited by the First Nations and the mixed-blood populations emerging from the fur trade who did not make "effective" use of the land. The Hudson's Bay Company charter came up for regular renewal, and it was generally accepted as early as the 1850s that the time was near at hand to transfer control to British North America. The Confederation negotiations were carried out with the expectation that the transfer would soon follow and the new nation would be handed Rupert's Land as its own colony.

In 1868, the Canadian government began negotiations in London with the British government and representatives of the HBC to acquire Rupert's Land, roughly defined as all territory whose rivers flowed into Hudson Bay. Thus, unlike the American West, which was won by military conquest, the Canadian West was purchased by a government. The agreement reached in 1869–70 constituted one of the largest real estate deals in history. For an area ten times the size of what was then Canada, the British government agreed to pay the HBC a cash sum of £300,000 (approximately $1.5 million) and to allow the company to retain one-twentieth (roughly 2.8 million hectares) of the land of the "fertile belt" (the area along the North Saskatchewan River), as well as the land immediately surrounding its trading posts. (Over time, the company would receive over $120 million from the sale of this land.) The company agreed to transfer the land to the British government, which then turned the territory over to Canada. Historian Chester Martin maintained that the land deal "transformed the original Dominion from a federation of equal provinces … into a veritable empire in its own right."[1] The Canadian government would rule the region as a colonial possession, suppressing any challenge to its authority, demanding conformity, and refusing to consult with the territory's inhabitants.

Administering the Northwest

While the negotiations were under way, the Canadian government made preparations to administer the new territory. In June 1869, Parliament passed the "Act for the Temporary Government of Rupert's Land and the North-Western Territory." It provided for a colonial system of government with an appointed governor and council—a political structure similar to those that existed in the BNA colonies prior to the granting of elected assemblies. Representative and responsible government, and provincehood, would await substantial white settlement and accompanying infrastructure.

The Canadian government made immediate plans to build a road from the Lake of the Woods to Fort Garry in the Red River colony, and dispatched a survey crew to the Red River to prepare for an eventual railway to link the Northwest to the rest of Canada. As well, it appointed William McDougall from Ontario as the first lieutenant governor. McDougall—a "Father of Confederation"—set off by way of St. Paul, Minnesota, to take up his administrative duties in the Red River colony. But he never reached his destination. A group of in the colony, led by Louis Riel, a Montreal-educated 25-year-old from a well-established Red River family, forbade McDougall and his entourage to enter the colony. The Métis also drove out the survey crew. Because the HBC had not yet officially transferred Rupert's Land to Canada, Ottawa had no legal authority to deal with the resistance.

The Red River colony of the time consisted of over 10,000 people. About half were French Métis, offspring of French fur traders and First Nations women. Another third were the "country born," descendants of Scottish and First Nations parents. The rest were descendants of Selkirk's original Scottish settlers and newly arrived immigrants from the Canadas, who together numbered about 1000 people.

The Red River Resistance of 1869–70

Most residents of Red River were angry that they had not been consulted over the sale of what they considered their homeland. They also disliked the aggressive action and haughty attitude of the small group of Canadian "expansionists" working to bring the colony into Confederation. These Canadians' local newspaper, *The Nor'Wester*, ridiculed the Métis and proclaimed Canada's right to take control of the Northwest. The Métis reacted by occupying Upper Fort Garry, the local seat of government, on November 2, establishing their own provisional government, and thus gaining effective control of the Red River colony.

Without waiting for the announcement of the official transfer of the Red River colony to Canada on December 1, William McDougall forged his own royal proclamation, to which

A family of Métis traders in camp, early 1870s. The Red River cart, built without any metal, allowed the Métis to harvest the buffalo herds, which at this point had been greatly depleted on the Canadian side of the border.

Source: Archives of Manitoba: Boundary Commission (1872–1874) 167 (N14100).

he attached Queen Victoria's name. On the night of November 30, he crossed the border to proclaim Canada's sovereignty over the Red River colony. He did so without knowing that the Canadian government had decided to delay taking over the territory until the dispute was resolved.

Fearing that the United States (which only two years earlier had purchased Alaska from the Russians and had expressed interest in taking over the Northwest) might annex the area, Prime Minister Macdonald acted. He had little choice but to negotiate with the Métis. Railway construction was gradually making travel across Canada possible, but there was no quick and easy way to get troops to Red River. In particular, the areas north of Lake Superior had to be crossed by foot. In winter, the possibility of moving troops was even more daunting, if not impossible. Macdonald dismissed William McDougall and asked the influential Catholic Bishop of the Red River colony, Alexandre Taché, to return from Rome where he had been attending the Vatican Council and assist in reaching a settlement. He also appointed Donald A. Smith of the Hudson's Bay Company to negotiate with the Métis on behalf of the Canadian government. Once again, fears of American annexation forced the government's hand, resulting in hurried negotiations. But even while Ottawa was negotiating, a military force was organized to be dispatched with all due haste.

Louis Riel's provisional government drew up a bill of rights in November 1869, outlining its grievances and demands. The bill became the basis for negotiations with Ottawa. At two well-attended public meetings in the Red River colony held in mid-January, Smith discussed entry into Canada, promising a satisfactory deal to be decided by a committee of Métis and the Canadian government.

Meanwhile, the Canadian expansionist party in the Red River colony took matters into its own hands, and prepared to oppose Riel's provisional government. The group saw financial and political potential in having the territories transferred to Canada. The expansionists shared the desire to see the Northwest, in becoming a colony of Canada, also become an extension of Ontario. They were furious that the Catholic "half-breeds" would dare resist the expansion of Canada and the British Empire. The general store owned by John Schultz, editor of *The Nor'wester* and the leader of the Canada Party, became its headquarters. The Métis raided the store and imprisoned the Canadians. The Métis agreed to release those prisoners who promised either to leave the colony or to obey the provisional government. A few, like Schultz, refused to comply. Schultz managed to escape by using a knife, hidden in a pudding by his wife, to cut the ropes on the windows and lower himself out. He then gathered his supporters for an ill-fated attack on Upper Fort Garry. The Métis again captured members of the raiding party, including Thomas Scott, a 28-year-old Protestant Irishman, government surveyor, and member of the Orange Lodge.

According to the Métis, Scott was a difficult prisoner. He insulted and provoked his guards and made threats against Riel's life. Riel decided to make an example of Scott, at the same time demonstrating to the expansionists and Canadian government that the Métis were serious in their demands. He put the Irish Ontarian on trial for contempt against the provisional government. The court ruled to execute him. Riel agreed, claiming it would "make Canada respect us." Some historians have since argued that Riel complied with the court order to prevent internal dissension among the Métis. On March 4, 1870, a firing squad executed Thomas Scott in Upper Fort Garry. Some contemporary accounts indicate that Scott was not yet dead when he was placed in his coffin.

Louis Riel (seated directly in the centre) with his council, 1870. The Red River Resistance led to the Manitoba Act of 1870, which brought Manitoba into Confederation as the fifth province.

Source: Library and Archives Canada/PA-12854; Manitoba Museum of Man and Nature/3661.

Thomas Scott, executed March 4, 1870. The Scott Memorial Hall in Winnipeg was erected in his memory between 1900 and 1902 by the provincial Grand Lodge of the Orange Order. See "Great Day for the Orangemen," Manitoba Free Press, July 13, 1900.

Source: Archives of Manitoba/Archives du Manitoba, Thomas Scott 1, N16492.

The execution proved to be a fatal error for Louis Riel. It turned the Métis resistance in Canada from a distant western struggle into a national crisis. Protestant Ontario now had its martyr. When a group of Scott's Red River associates, led by Schultz, arrived in Toronto to enlist support for their cause, a huge crowd assembled to hear their version of the uprising in the west:

> It would be a gross injustice to the loyal inhabitants of Red River, humiliating to our national honour, and contrary to all British traditions for our Government to receive, negotiate or meet with the emissaries of those who have robbed, imprisoned and murdered loyal Canadians, whose only fault was zeal for British institutions, whose only crime was devotion to the old flag.

A different perception prevailed in Quebec. French Canadians viewed Riel as the protector of the French Catholic Métis against an aggressive group of expansionists from Ontario backed by the Orange Order. Lost amid the religious and ethnic rivalry between Ontario and Quebec were the Métis and the legitimate grievances of the Red River colony. As newspapers in the two provinces ramped up the rhetoric and took shots at one another for their own purposes, the colonists were left to negotiate amid the divisive atmosphere.

John A. Macdonald had little choice but to compromise. To appease the Métis (and now the French Canadians of Quebec), his government passed the Manitoba Act in May 1870, based on negotiations between the three-person delegation from Red River and the Canadian government. Despite Macdonald's desire to have the entire Northwest as a colony under Canadian control, the Red River colony entered Confederation as a province. To satisfy Ontarians, the prime minister agreed to send an armed force to the Red River colony to secure the Northwest and ensure it did not fall into American hands.

The Manitoba Act

The Manitoba Act created the new province of Manitoba, which included only the 35,000 square kilometres around the Red River settlement and Portage la Prairie to the west. The rest of the area became the North-West Territories. Manitoba (dubbed the "postage stamp province" due to its small size and shape) received its own legislative assembly, four federal members of Parliament, and two senators. But, unlike the other provinces in Confederation, Manitoba was denied control over its public lands and natural resources. The same was true of the North-West Territories. The land and resources remained under the federal government's control, to be used "for the purposes of the Dominion." In particular, Macdonald wanted Ottawa to maintain control of land in order to control the settlement of the West.

Ontario had long pushed for westward expansion as a means of increasing its own influence and overwhelming the French Catholic population in Quebec once and for all. To this end, if any new provinces were to be created, it was expected they would follow the Ontario model. In many ways, however, Manitoba was created as a "little Quebec." The Manitoba Act addressed the issue of linguistic and educational rights of the Métis, who made up 80 percent of the population. The Fathers of Confederation had not determined the rights of French Canadians outside the province of Quebec; they preferred to address the issue on an ad hoc basis when new provinces joined Confederation. Manitoba became the first new province to join, forcing Macdonald's Conservative government to address the thorny issues of language rights and separate schools. Should French be recognized as an official language? Should denominational schools be permitted in provinces with a sizable Catholic population at the time of union with Canada? The Manitoba Act recognized both French and English as official languages. It also established a confessional school system on the Quebec model, with separate Protestant and Catholic divisions that would receive government funding. Most importantly, the Act promised a 1.4-million-acre land grant for the Métis and their descendants. While this provision was not in the early drafts of the bill, it was added later in response to Macdonald's refusal to allow provincial control over Manitoba's natural resources.

The debate and ensuing controversy over the Manitoba Act highlighted an important issue. As Canada expanded, what would be the essential characteristics of new provinces? Some historians have argued that the Fathers of Confederation intended to create a bilingual and bicultural country in which French Canadians would have the same linguistic and educational rights as English Canadians. Other historians have disagreed. Donald Creighton, for example, argues that no evidence exists that the Fathers of Confederation, particularly Macdonald, intended to create a bilingual and bicultural nation. According to Creighton, Macdonald agreed to French-language rights and separate schools only because he was being pressured to act quickly by a "dictatorial Riel"[2]—otherwise Canada might lose the Northwest to American expansionists. Ralph Heintzman disagrees and argues that the Manitoba Act reflected an ongoing "spirit of Confederation" evident between English and French Canadians at the time of Confederation.[3]

The Wolseley Expedition

Amnesty – an official pardon

Tension continued in the region even after Manitoba's entry into Confederation. Riel wanted an amnesty but the prime minister refused. In May of 1870, Macdonald sent out a military force of over 1000 men under Colonel Garnet Wolseley. It consisted of a British imperial unit, the 60th Rifles, and Ontario militia units. Without a rail link, the journey was arduous. For three months, the Expedition travelled from Toronto, through the Great Lakes and the Lake of the Woods, to Red River. As the troops approached the settlement in late August, most of Riel's men had left for the annual buffalo hunt. Riel received word of the force's arrival and fled south to the United States. The troops reported finding his breakfast still warm on the table. Upon finding Fort Garry abandoned, Wolseley reported in his diary: "Personally, I was glad that Riel did not come out and surrender, as he at one time said he would, for I could not then have hanged him as I might have done had I taken him prisoner when in arms against his sovereign." It soon became apparent that the military force was dispatched for more than symbolic reasons. When the troops failed to capture Riel, they proceeded to invoke a reign of terror upon the Métis population that included intimidation, destruction of property, and violence. Riel fled, however, convinced that he had won a great victory for the Métis people.

Riel's victory proved transitory, however. Once secure, and despite the promises inherent in the Manitoba Act, the demographics of the new province changed quickly. Settlers from Ontario moved into Manitoba and took over land once occupied by the Métis. One group seized Métis land on the Rivière aux Ilets de Bois and, in a symbolic gesture of defiance, renamed the river "the Boyne," after William of Orange's decisive victory over the Catholics in Ireland in 1690. Ontarians soon dominated the political, economic, and social life of the new province. They worked to undermine the rights of the Métis population by introducing amendments to the Manitoba Act that made it difficult for the Métis to prove they owned the land. Discouraged, many Métis left the province and went farther west into either the North-West Territories or the Dakotas and Montana to pursue their traditional livelihoods of fur trading, hunting buffalo, and small-scale agriculture along the riverbanks. Louis Riel, Manitoba's "Father of Confederation," remained in exile.

Treaties with the First Nations

Having acquired the Northwest, the federal government took control of Indian affairs in the territory. The Crown was replaced by the federal government in having responsibility for this population, but the paternalistic handling of the First Nations as "wards of the state" was maintained. The purchase and transfer of Rupert's Land was intended to open the West to Canadian settlement. While the Red River Resistance put a kink in Macdonald's plan, the federal government proceeded with its design. The next step necessitated convincing and manipulating the First Nations across the Northwest to surrender title to their lands through treaty. The government adhered to the Royal Proclamation of 1763, which prohibited settlers from occupying territory that the First Nations had not first surrendered to the Crown. The Canadian government also made treaties to avoid the bloody and costly "Indian wars" that were occurring in the United States. By the time of Confederation, 123 treaties had been signed in the area that became Canada. Most of these agreements were small in scale, and usually involved a First Nation surrendering its land in return for an annuity, some clothes, and some tools.

The treaties in the Northwest would be much more substantial, both in the amount of land and number of people involved. They would also be negotiated over a much shorter period of time. Between 1871 and 1875, the government negotiated numbered Treaties One through Five, affecting the Ojibwa and Cree peoples in what is now northwestern Ontario, Manitoba, and southern Saskatchewan. In 1876, Treaty Six was signed with the Cree of present-day central Saskatchewan and Alberta. The last of the treaties on the Plains, Treaty Seven, followed in 1877 with the Blackfoot-speaking nations, and the Sarcee (Tsuu Tina) and Stoneys.

According to the government's interpretation of the treaties, the First Nations agreed to "cede, release, surrender, and yield up to the Government . . . all their rights, titles, and privileges whatsoever" to the lands in question forever in return for certain reserve lands, amenities, and the right to fish and hunt on Crown lands. In the case of Treaty Six, the federal government also promised a "medicine chest"—assistance in the event of "any pestilence" or "general famine." The Cree insisted on these additional clauses because of the devastating effects of disease and starvation as a result of declining buffalo herds. The Blackfoot in the Treaty Seven area envisioned the treaty as a pact of friendship, peace, and mutual support between the two parties. They did not intend to surrender their sovereignty. Some of the Cree in Treaty Six believed the agreements allowed the newcomers only the use, not the ownership, of their land. First Nations people in general viewed the treaties as their only hope of survival against the rapid encroachment and takeover by white settlers. Canadian officials, on the other hand, viewed the treaties and the establishment of Indian reserves as the first step toward the assimilation of the First Nations people.

Historians disagree over the interpretation of the treaty process. The focus has shifted away from viewing the First Nations as victims and toward native "agency." Just as with the fur trade, historians argue that the First Nations were not a simple and uncivilized people duped by the superior whites. First Nations understood the plight of their people and their probable fate at the hands of

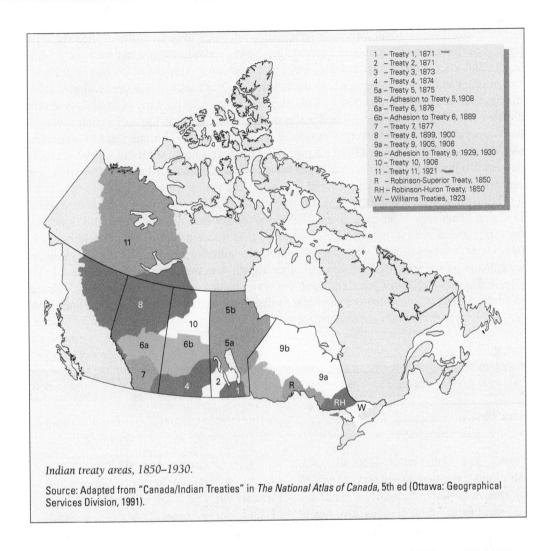

1 – Treaty 1, 1871
2 – Treaty 2, 1871
3 – Treaty 3, 1873
4 – Treaty 4, 1874
5a – Treaty 5, 1875
5b – Adhesion to Treaty 5, 1908
6a – Treaty 6, 1876
6b – Adhesion to Treaty 6, 1889
7 – Treaty 7, 1877
8 – Treaty 8, 1899, 1900
9a – Treaty 9, 1905, 1906
9b – Adhesion to Treaty 9, 1929, 1930
10 – Treaty 10, 1906
11 – Treaty 11, 1921
R – Robinson-Superior Treaty, 1850
RH – Robinson-Huron Treaty, 1850
W – Williams Treaties, 1923

Indian treaty areas, 1850–1930.

Source: Adapted from "Canada/Indian Treaties" in *The National Atlas of Canada*, 5th ed (Ottawa: Geographical Services Division, 1991).

the newcomers. The Indian Wars in the United States was evidence enough of what would befall the First Nations if they took the path of resistance. The Plains tribes were in a deplorable state by the 1870s. Disease and sickness (in the form of smallpox, measles, and tuberculosis)—the seemingly inevitable effects of contact with the Europeans—were ravaging the Native population. The devastation was made worse by the slaughter of the bison herds, which eliminated the main foodstuff and cultural symbol of the Plains people. Yet, while miscommunication and misunderstanding marred the treaty process and led to anger and frustration, and while the First Nations were negotiating from a position of weakness, the gains made in the treaties were impressive. As each deal was negotiated, additional gains were added retroactively. The First Nations leaders sought agreements whereby they could protect their people from the immediate threats while allowing the least traumatic transition from the old world to the new. But notwithstanding the degree of agency that First Nations exercised in treaty negotiations, the results were still traumatic.

The Canadian government was not interested in negotiating a treaty for the entire Northwest. Instead, Ottawa wanted only the lands required for settlement. This included the Prairie West. Future treaties would be signed for the northern regions (Treaties 8 through 12), but only when the government believed there was some form of wealth to be gained. Once Indian title was extinguished through treaty, the government next established the Indian Act in 1876, amended in 1880, which regulated all aspects of First Nations peoples' lives. It legally defined the First Nations people as minors or special wards of the Crown, without citizenship privileges. It went further and even defined what it was to be "Indian" (although this definition was in constant flux in order to fit the shifting needs of the government) and set out one universal governing structure for all First Nations across Canada, despite the fact that the various "tribes" were very different in culture and tradition. The Act effectively became Ottawa's tool in handling, controlling, manipulating, and ultimately assimilating the First Nations. This one piece of legislation would be amended more than a hundred times over the next century. Whenever the government decided that it needed to alter its handling of this population, it amended the Act. Over time, the Indian Act became the most racist piece of legislation in Canadian history.

From the government's perspective, the treaty process and the ensuing reserve system it created were temporary. As far back as the 1840s, government statistics and reports indicated that the First Nations were a dying people. It assumed that within a century they would be gone. Government officials believed they were alleviating the suffering of this dying race by easing its assimilation into white society. The process, they argued, was inevitable as well as desirable. As John A. Macdonald pointed out, "The great aim of our legislature has been to do away with the tribal system and assimilate the Indian people in all aspects with the inhabitants of the dominion, as speedily as they are fit for the change."

WHERE HISTORIANS DISAGREE

The Treaties

Before the Constitution Act of 1982, Aboriginal treaties could be amended or altered by federal statute, without the approval of the First Nations. The Act of 1982 entrenched treaty rights and the Supreme Court has since made clear that Aboriginal rights exist under Canadian law.

Duncan Campbell Scott, deputy superintendent of Indian affairs from 1913 to 1932, wrote the first history of federal Indian administration in 1914. The federal civil servant stressed the honourable and just nature of Indian policy: "As may be surmised from the record of past Indian administration, the government was always anxious to fulfill the obligations which were laid upon it by these treaties. In every point, and adhering closely to the letter of the compact, the government has discharged to the present every promise which was made to the Indians."[1]

George Stanley became the first professional historian to study the western treaties. In *The Birth of Western Canada* (1936) Stanley presents a more sophisticated analysis of the treaties, yet he reached a similar conclusion: "On the whole, Canada has followed the tradition of the Imperial Government in its relations with native tribes, and has endeavoured to deal fairly with her aboriginal wards."[2] For the next thirty-five years, historians essentially accepted the "honourable and just" interpretation of the treaties—or ignored the agreements altogether. Historical debate did not emerge until the 1970s.

Much of the new attention came from First Nations people frustrated that their side of the story had not received attention. The civil rights movement and the focus on racial issues led to the challenging of old interpretations. In 1969, Harold Cardinal, a young Cree politician and author, published

The Unjust Society, an indictment of Canadian Indian policy: "The truth of the matter is that Canadian Indians simply got swindled. Our forefathers got taken by slick-talking, fork-tongued cheats."[3] First Nations oral traditions of the treaties also appeared, such as the interviews in a book edited by Richard Price, *The Spirit of the Alberta Indian Treaties,* and the Treaty Seven Elders and Tribal Council's accounts of Treaty Seven.[4]

Other historians joined the debate by focusing on "agency."[5] They argued that the First Nations were active agents in the treaty process who helped shape the process. The First Nations recognized that it was in their interest to secure the best terms possible and they negotiated to this end. Problems arose, however, when the federal government did not fulfill the First Nations' oral understandings of the treaties.

In 1983 George Stanley re-entered the debate. He still dismissed the idea that there were deliberate attempts to deceive the First Nations during the treaty negotiations. Instead he saw the problems as arising from the misunderstandings of treaty terms. "The probability that promises were made to the Indians, which they remember and the Whites have forgotten, seems strong."[6] Changing social attitudes and changes in the historical profession with the rise of social history, combined with the availability and use of Aboriginal oral testimony and a new postcolonial context for discussion, contributed to the debate.

According to Gerald Friesen, the First Nations did possess agency in the treaty process, although their autonomy had declined over the twenty-five years leading up to Treaty One in 1871. The Canadian government, for its part, had both limited finances and a minimal military presence in the Northwest. Prime Minister John A. Macdonald feared an "Indian Uprising." As a result, both sides took the negotiations very seriously. Where they differed, however, was in their interpretations of their meaning. According to Friesen, the Crown viewed the treaty "as a single transaction" that extinguished Aboriginal land title. The First Nations, on the other hand, viewed the process as forging an alliance that was subject to annual renewal. These diverging interpretations set the tone for Canadian–First Nations relations for the next century.[7]

In 1986, Jean Friesen argued that the treaties must be understood in their historical context. They were agreements developed over two centuries of contact through the fur trade. The picture that emerged revealed the striking differences that existed between First Nations and government agents over the nature of treaty-making. The Europeans "did not understand the significance of the social contract the Indians were making" which was one of "mutual obligation" and a belief that peace had to be renewed annually. The First Nations were forced to negotiate but their position was not based upon ignorance and deception.[8]

J.R. Miller agreed that fur-trade practices remained an integral part of treaty-making but he emphasized the fundamental misunderstandings between the two groups. Aboriginal rituals including gift-giving, equestrian demonstrations, and pipe ceremonies, along with references to the Great White Mother, demonstrated that "First Nations were making kin of the Canadians with ceremonies." Because they were "surrendering the use of the territory that had given them life and a living, they expected that the Crown reciprocate by guaranteeing them protection and assistance to maintain their livelihood in a dramatically changed world." The Crown, however, was not interested in making long-term commitments.[9]

Olive Dickason agreed that the process was based on misunderstanding but argued that, it was only the First Nations who were being misled. She interpreted the treaties as a tool used by the Crown to extinguish Aboriginal land rights so western settlement and development could proceed as quickly as possible. The First Nations did not immediately recognize this intention, because "by their custom, agreements were not considered permanent, subject as they were to changing conditions that would necessitate renegotiation and renewal." The Crown, on the other hand, viewed the treaties as granting Aboriginals privileges at its pleasure. While the Aboriginals involved in the negotiations were very skilled, the language barrier remained an obstacle that worked to the advantage of the government.[10]

Interpretations of the treaties and the government's handling of the First Nations have become increasingly critical in recent years. In 2001, Maureen Lux argued that racism infused government policies that led to the precipitous decline in the health of First Nations on the Prairies. In 2013, Jim Daschuk moved away from an emphasis on the racist ideology of the Canadian state and instead focused on the material conditions that resulted for First Nations. He highlighted the devastating role of infectious diseases and environmental change that led to widespread starvation. It was in the context of these shocking conditions that the treaties were signed. According to Daschuk, the Canadian government failed to meet its treaty obligations of providing food and medicine to the suffering First Nations. Instead, food was used to control the population. In this way, the government of John A. Macdonald committed genocide against the First Nations of Canada.[11]

1   Duncan Campbell Scott, "Indian Affairs, 1867–1912," in Adam Short and Arthur G. Doughty, eds., *Canada and Its Provinces* (Toronto: Glasgow, Brook and Co., 1914), p. 600.

2   George F.G. Stanley, *The Birth of Western Canada* (London: Longmans, Green, 1936; Toronto: University of Toronto Press, 1960), p. 214.

3   Harold Cardinal, *The Unjust Society* (Edmonton: Hurtig, 1969), p. 39.

4   Richard Price, ed. *The Spirit of the Alberta Indian Treaties* (Montreal: Institute for Research on Public Policy, 1979; 3rd ed., Edmonton: University of Alberta Press, 1999); Treaty Seven Elders and Tribal Council, *The True Spirit and Original Intent of Treaty 7* (Montreal/Kingston: McGill-Queen's University Press, 1996).

5   To list several of them: John Leonard Taylor, in his essays "Canada's Northwest Indian Policy in the 1870s: Traditional Premises and Necessary Interventions" and "Two Views of Treaties Six and Seven," in Price, ed., *Spirit*, pp. 3–46; John L. Tobias, "Canada's Subjugation of the Plains Cree, 1879–1885," *Canadian Historical Review*, 64(4) (1983): 519–48; David Hall, "'A Serene Atmosphere'? Treaty 1 Revisited," *Canadian Journal of Native Studies*, 4(2) (1984): 321–58; Jean Friesen, "Grant Me Wherewith to Make My Living," in Kerry Avel and Jean Friesen, eds., *Aboriginal Resource Use in Canada: Historical and Legal Aspects* (Winnipeg: University of Manitoba Press, 1991), pp. 141–56.

6   George F.G. Stanley, "As Long as the Sun Shines and Water Flows: An Historical Comment," in Ian A.L. Getty and Antoine S. Lussier, eds., *As Long as the Sun Shines and Water Flows* (Vancouver: University of British Columbia Press, 1983), p. 16.

7   Gerald Friesen, *The Canadian Prairies: A History* (Toronto: University of Toronto Press, 1984), pp. 137, 148–9.

8   Jean Friesen, "Magnificent Gifts: The Treaties of Canada with the Indians of the Northwest 1869–76," *Transactions of the Royal Society of Canada*, series 5, vol. 1(1986), pp. 42–3, 48–9.

9   J.R. Miller, *Compact, Contract, Covenant: Aboriginal Treaty-Making in Canada* (Toronto: University of Toronto Press, 2009), pp. 184–5; J.R. Miller, *Lethal Legacy: Current Native Controversies in Canada* (Toronto: McClelland & Stewart, 2004), pp. 144–5.

10   Olive Dickason, *Canada's First Nations: A History of Founding Peoples from Earliest Times* (Toronto: McClelland & Stewart, 1992), pp. 275–6.

11   Maureen Lux, *Medicine That Walks: Disease, Medicine, and Canadian Plains Native People, 1880–1940* (Toronto: University of Toronto Press, 2001), pp. 5–19; James Daschuk, *Clearing the Plains: Disease, Politics of Starvation, and the Loss of Aboriginal Life* (Regina: University of Regina Press, 2013).

Future Prime Minister W.L. Mackenzie King with two Plains First Nations people, taken on his western trip of 1905. King later served as leader of the federal Liberal Party for thirty years and as prime minister for twenty-one. While he was Liberal leader and prime minister, Aboriginal issues were rarely on the national agenda.

Source: Library and Archives Canada/C14157.

The design of the Canadian government was based on a paternalistic desire to assimilate the First Nations through the reserve system. The First Nations would surrender their culture (spirituality, language, dress, etc.), take up agriculture on a reserve, convert to Christianity, accept white education within a residential school system, and pursue enfranchisement by relinquishing Indian status and receiving the full "privileges" of citizenship. Adult males deemed of good character, free of debt, and fluent in English or French were eligible. They could, after a probationary period of three years, apply to relinquish their treaty and statutory rights under the Indian Act, as well as their right to live in the reserve community. In return, they gained British citizenship with all legal privileges including the right to vote, as well as private ownership of their share of band reserve lands and funds. Initially, the First Nations peoples of western Canada were excluded from this procedure, because the government considered them still too "uncivilized."

Regardless, the policy of enfranchisement was a failure. Few of Canada's First Nations people agreed to enfranchisement because it meant complete assimilation and absorption into white society; it meant surrendering any benefits and protection offered by the treaties; it meant entering a society that was already racially charged against them. Only 102 First Nations people applied and were enfranchised between Confederation and the end of World War I. Status Indian women who married non-Indians (whites, Métis, or Native people not governed by the Indian Act) had no choice in the matter. Under the Indian Act, they lost their Indian status automatically when they married.

Under pressure from missionaries, the federal government attempted to assimilate the Native people by outlawing their cultural and spiritual practices. Particularly offensive from the government's perspective was the West Coast ritual of the potlatch—a gift-giving ceremony to distribute wealth. The government used various tactics to dispense with potlatch, including making it an offence in the amended Indian Act of 1884. Indian agents were instructed to collect evidence to use in court cases (playing off Christian Native converts who opposed the potlatch against traditionalists). They used extortion to pry ceremonial regalia from West Coast Native people. Despite these efforts

Before and after: Propaganda photos used to promote the benefits of Native residential schools. From Thompson Ferrier, Indian Education in the North West (Toronto: Department of Missionary Literature of the Methodist Church, 1906), pp. 4–5.

Source: Library and Archives Canada/C-104585 and C-104586.

to end the potlatch, it survived and, in some areas, continued to flourish. The same held true for the Sun (Thirst) dances on the Plains. While some bands altered certain practices to prevent a total ban on the dances, they ensured the customs continued to be practised—albeit subversively.

Residential schools were the most draconian of the assimilation schemes. The federal government quickly realized just how expensive some of its treaty promises were, the most obvious being education. The leaders who negotiated the treaties recognized that white education was essential to allow the next generation an opportunity to compete in the changing world. They wanted schools placed on reserves. In order to offload costs and responsibility, the government gave Christian missionaries control of residential schools. Included were industrial schools that taught skills in agriculture and trades for boys and household skills for girls between the ages of 14 and 18. The first three were established in western Canada in 1883–84, at Qu'Appelle, Dunbow (just east of High River), and Battleford. By the turn of the century, twenty such schools operated in the West.

The residential school experience was brutal. Approximately 150,000 Native children were forcefully removed from their homes and families, and sent away to one of what was eventually ninety schools across the country. The object was to "take the Indian out of the child." Students were prohibited from speaking their language, wearing cultural dress, and pursuing their traditional spirituality. "I want to get rid of the Indian problem," Duncan Campbell Scott announced in 1920. ". . . Our objective is to continue until there is not a single Indian in Canada that has not been absorbed into the body politic."

Retribution to those who broke the rules was harsh. The result was decades of physical, emotional, and sexual abuse. First Nations families were torn asunder and seven generations were traumatized. To make matters worse, the schools were poorly maintained and administered. A low estimate has 6000 of the children dying of sickness or malnutrition. They were often buried without their families being notified.

The residential schools lasted until the 1960s. In 2008, the Canadian government offered an official apology to the First Nations and in 2015, the Truth and Reconciliation Commission issued its report formally labelling the system as "cultural genocide."

British Columbia Joins Confederation

With the Northwest secured, the Canadian government began negotiating with the colony of British Columbia to join Confederation, fulfilling Macdonald's vision of a nation "from sea to sea." Although First Nations constituted the majority of the population along the Pacific coast, they were not consulted about Confederation. Over the years, two separate colonies had evolved, one on Vancouver Island and the other on the mainland. In 1866, the two united into the single colony of British Columbia. The united colony now had three options as to its future: remain a separate British colony, join the United States, or unite with Canada.

Economically, British Columbia was tied closely to the United States. Many of the colony's businesses were American branches. Much of its trade in raw materials went south. The colony communicated with the outside world via the United States. American vessels, for example, provided the only regular steamship service. Mail required both local and American stamps on letters abroad, because it went via San Francisco. When railways made transcontinental travel feasible, it was an American line, the Union Pacific, completed in 1869, that provided British Columbia with connections to the Atlantic seaboard. The strong American presence caused the old ghost of annexation to rise up once again.

British loyalties, however, remained firm. The non-Native population saw British Columbia as "a British outpost on the edge of an American frontier."[4] The Royal Navy provided protection and the colonial government followed British parliamentary tradition. The colony also had a predominance of British politicians, from the governor to the majority of representatives in the legislative council. By contrast, the Americans, although large in numbers, had relatively few supporters in government.

While British Columbia had strong economic ties with the United States and even stronger political and cultural ones with Britain, it had little contact with Canada. Few Canadians resided in the colony. Nor did any overland route exist to link the West Coast colony to the rest of British North America. Nevertheless, the small Canadian community that did reside in the colony constituted an influential and vocal minority, including Amor de Cosmos ("Lover of the Universe," alias William Smith) and John Robson, who headed the Confederation movement in the colonial

British Columbia's settler population was very small in the 1870s. This photo, taken outside the legislative buildings in Victoria, shows the entire British Columbia civil service in 1878.

Source: British Columbia Archives/HP-17826.

assembly. Prime Minister Macdonald corresponded with these pro-Confederation politicians. As well, Macdonald asked the British government to appoint Anthony Musgrave, the governor of Newfoundland and a known supporter of Canadian Confederation, as the new governor of British Columbia when Governor Seymour, who had opposed union, died in 1869. The Colonial Office agreed, since the British government wanted to lessen its commitment to its West Coast colony without losing it to the United States.

Britain valued British Columbia as an important link in its "all red route to the Orient"—an imperial trading network tying Britain to India and China through British territory. By convincing British Columbia to join Confederation, Britain could achieve both objectives. British Prime Minister William Gladstone argued that Victoria, as "the San Francisco of British North America," could achieve greater commercial and political power as part of Canada than as "the capital of the isolated colony of British Columbia."

The Canadian Government Negotiates

Soon after taking office, Governor Musgrave appointed a three-member delegation to open up negotiations with the Canadian government. The committee drew up its list of demands. British Columbia would consider joining Confederation if the Canadian government agreed to: assume the colony's $1 million debt; grant responsible government to the province; undertake a public works program; and complete a road to link British Columbia with the rest of the country.

The British Columbia delegation found a receptive audience in Ottawa. A committee headed by George-Étienne Cartier agreed to all the demands. As with so much of its nation-building endeavours, the federal government felt pressured to get a deal done quickly to avoid the threat of American annexation. Ottawa would assume the provincial debt and request Britain to implement responsible government. It would undertake a public works program to include underwriting a loan to build a dry dock and maintain a naval station at Esquimalt. In addition, the Canadian government promised not merely a road but a railway to join west with east, to be begun within two years of British Columbia's entry into Confederation and completed within ten years—a most ambitious (and unrealistic) promise. The United States, with ten times Canada's population, had only recently, and with great difficulty, built its first transcontinental railway.

On July 20, 1871, British Columbia joined Confederation. Canada now stretched from the Atlantic to the Pacific Ocean. In the same year, by the Treaty of Washington, Britain and the United States confirmed the borders between Canada and the United States, thereby ending the threat of an American seizure of lands above the 49th parallel. The treaty, however, was intended to heal the breach between Britain (and by extension, Canada) and the United States. In particular it was to deal with the American demands for compensation resulting from incidents during the Civil War, including damage and losses inflicted by the *Alabama*. Even though foreign affairs remained in the hands of Britain, Macdonald participated in the negotiations on behalf of Canada. The resulting treaty succeeded in improving relations among the nations. The Americans gained access to Canada's inshore Atlantic fisheries. But the British offset this Canadian offering by providing Canada loan guarantees for railway construction.

The agreement with British Columbia left one important issue unresolved—Aboriginal lands. At the time of British Columbia's entry into Confederation, fourteen land treaties had been concluded for only a tiny portion of Vancouver Island. In 1873, the federal government requested that British Columbia acknowledge Aboriginal land title and increase the allotment of reserve land for a family of five from 10 to 80 acres (4 to 32 hectares). Premier George Walkem objected, claiming that the Native peoples already had enough land. His government reflected the prevailing attitude of the time that the First Nations never owned the land and that land ownership was a right reserved for non-Native settlers only. British Columbia was placed in the unique situation of not having undergone a full treaty process.

The Federal Election of 1872

In 1872, the first federal election in which the new provinces of Manitoba and British Columbia participated was held. Politicians could no longer sit in both provincial and federal legislatures, so Edward Blake resigned as premier of Ontario and became de facto leader of the federal Liberals. His party won 95 seats, but the Conservative government of John A. Macdonald was re-elected with 99.

An Unwilling Newfoundland and a Reluctant Prince Edward Island

Canada had expanded massively in a very brief period of time. Only the British colonies of Newfoundland and Prince Edward Island remained as potential new provinces. Of the two, Newfoundland seemed more likely to join. Although the colony had not sent representatives to the Charlottetown Conference in September 1864, it did send two representatives—Frederick B.T. Carter, leader of the opposition, and Ambrose Shea, Speaker of the House of Assembly—to the Quebec Conference a month later. Both men became converts to Confederation, especially after hearing the generous financial terms that Macdonald and the other representatives from the Canadas promised. But neither they nor the governor of Newfoundland, H.W. Hoyes, could convince a dubious public, especially the merchants in St. John's and the Roman Catholic population, about the benefits of Confederation.

Opposition to Confederation in Newfoundland

In the 1860s, Newfoundland had little association with the other British North American colonies. Many Newfoundlanders believed that their island's destiny lay to the east—the Atlantic Ocean and Britain—rather than to the west in a transcontinental nation. Their economy was based on cod fishing and sealing. Eighty percent of the island's working population earned its living from the sea. Newfoundlanders traded with Britain and the West Indies, not with British North America.

Newfoundland Catholics opposed joining Confederation because they feared that a wider union would offset their favourable position in the colony. They had their own government-funded schools, which many believed a union with "Protestant Ontario" might threaten. Also, Irish Catholics saw Confederation as comparable to the reviled union of Ireland and England.

Union with Canada became the chief campaign issue in the local elections of 1869. Charles Fox Bennett, a St. John's merchant, headed the anti-Confederation faction. He pointed out that Confederation would result in the imposition of Canadian taxes on boats and fishing gear, and in exploitive competition from the mainland. He reminded Newfoundlanders of Nova Scotia's opposition to Confederation, while injecting his own strong dose of local Newfoundland nationalism. A contemporary folk song summed up the sentiment:

> *Would you barter the rights that your fathers have won?*
> *No! Let them descend from father to son,*
> *For a few thousand dollars Canadian gold,*
> *Don't let it be said that our birthright was sold.*
> *Newfoundland's face turns to Britain*
> *Her back to the Gulf.*
> *Come near at your peril*
> *Canadian wolf!*

Pro-Confederationists were on the defensive. They presented union with Canada as an uncertain alternative to the current depressed economy of Newfoundland rather than as a bold

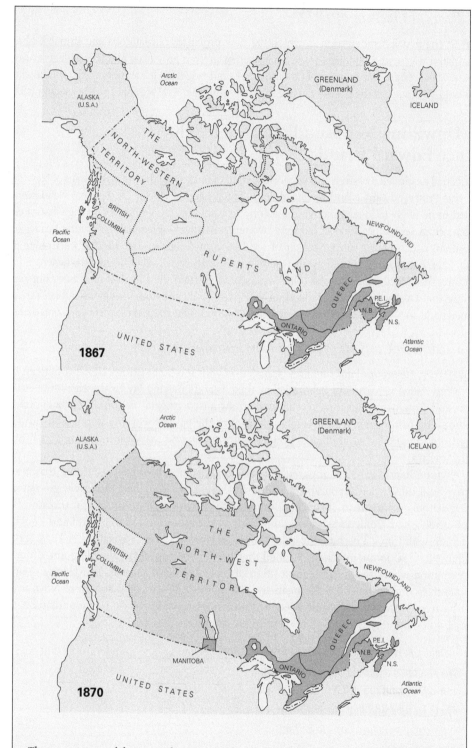

These two maps and the two on the next page show Canada's territorial evolution, 1867 to 1905.

Source: These maps are based on information taken from National Topographic System map sheet no. MCR 2306. © 1969, Her Majesty the Queen in right of Canada with permission of Energy, Mines and Resources Canada.

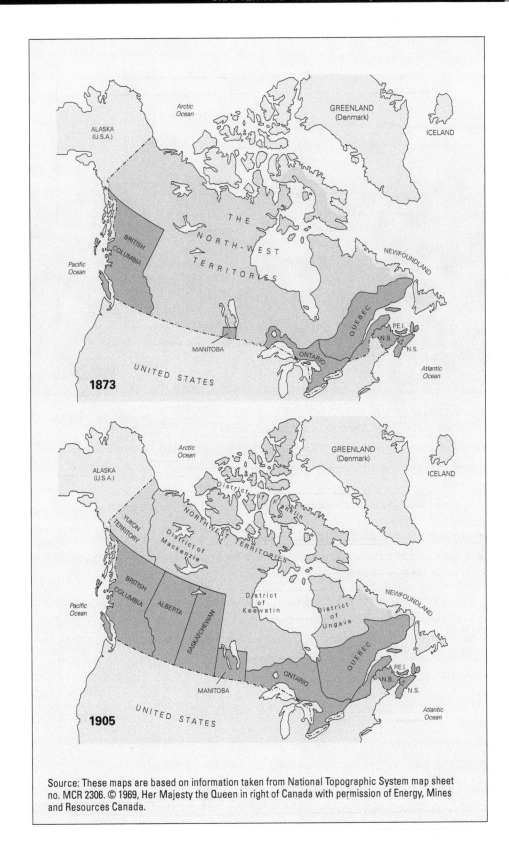

Source: These maps are based on information taken from National Topographic System map sheet no. MCR 2306. © 1969, Her Majesty the Queen in right of Canada with permission of Energy, Mines and Resources Canada.

St. John's, around 1890. Its harbour and the heavily settled part of the island faced the Atlantic Ocean and Britain, not the North American continent and Canada.

Source: Archives and Special Collections/Queen Elizabeth II Library/Memorial University of Newfoundland.

positive move. Furthermore, an improved sealing and fishing season in 1869 worked against their cause.

In the end, Newfoundlanders rejected Confederation, with 19 seats in the colonial assembly going to anti-confederates and only 8 to confederates. According to one account, as soon as the election results became known,

> *the fishermen and mechanics of St. John's . . . put together a large coffin labeled "Confederation," which was placed on a vehicle draped in black, and this was drawn by scores of willing hands through the town, headed by a band playing the Dead March, and escorted by an immense crowd, to the head of the harbour, where a grave was dug below highwater mark and the coffin solemnly interred.*

The defeat effectively ended the Confederation debate in Newfoundland for the next twenty-five years.

Opposition to Confederation in Prince Edward Island

Initially, Prince Edward Island opposed Confederation more strongly than Newfoundland. Its representatives at the Charlottetown and Quebec conferences pressed the Canadian delegates the furthest on the possible negative effects of Confederation for the Maritime region. Furthermore, only recently had some islanders succeeded in freeing themselves from British absentee landlords who had extracted onerous rents from them. They had no desire to substitute a new set of Canadian landlords. Even pressure through the Colonial Office in Britain failed to persuade the islanders to join Confederation. If anything, economic union with the United States had more appeal to many islanders, who saw it as a possible return to the prosperity the island had enjoyed during the period of the Reciprocity Treaty (1854–66). In 1868, American congressman Benjamin Butler visited Charlottetown to negotiate a reciprocal trade agreement.

Fear of American annexation led Prime Minister Macdonald to reopen negotiations with Prince Edward Island. Late in 1869, he extended another invitation to the islanders to join Confederation. Macdonald agreed to more generous financial terms than in 1864, guaranteed communication and transportation links with the mainland, and promised islanders assistance in buying off the remaining British absentee landlords who still owned large tracts. At the same time, the Canadian prime minister convinced Britain to block a reciprocal trade agreement between Prince Edward Island and the United States. Still the islanders resisted.

By the early 1870s, however, financial problems on Prince Edward Island made Confederation more appealing. A coalition government headed by J.C. Pope embarked in 1871 on an ambitious railway-building scheme that threatened to push the island into bankruptcy. In 1872, work on the railway ceased due to a lack of funds. The Union Bank of Prince Edward Island, which held large numbers of the railway debentures, feared a financial collapse and appealed to Britain for assistance. London financiers replied that the island would be in a better negotiating position if it joined Canada.

This time Charlottetown approached Ottawa. In early 1873, the Canadian government renewed its earlier offer: to assume the island's debt, to pay the annual interest on an $800,000 imperial loan, to provide a special subsidy of $45,000 to buy out the absentee landowners and thus bring all land under provincial control, and to take over the railway guarantee. As well, it promised to establish and maintain an efficient all-year steamer service between the island and the mainland.

In the election of April 1873, the choice became Confederation or the imposition of increased taxes to pay off the debt. In the end, provincial debt and railways were the real "Fathers of Confederation" in Prince Edward Island. On July 1, 1873, Prince Edward Island joined the Dominion of Canada as its seventh province. The Charlottetown newspaper the *Patriot* recorded the public's response:

> On Tuesday, July 1st, whether for weal or woe, Prince Edward Island became a province of the Dominion of Canada. At 12 o'clock noon, the Dominion flag was run up on the flag staffs at Government House and the Colonial Building, and a salute of 21 guns was fired from St. George's battery and from HMS Spartan now in port. The church and city bells rang out a lively peal, and the volunteers under review at the city park fired a feu de joie. So far as powder and metal could do it, there was for a short time a terrible din. But among the people who thronged the streets there was no enthusiasm.

The North

With the exception of Newfoundland and the Arctic Archipelago, Macdonald's Conservative government had now completed the consolidation of British North America. Initially, Canada had no interest in the far north and the Arctic Archipelago, seeing it only as a frozen wasteland. Britain had secured a prior claim to the region as a result of the sixteenth- and seventeenth-century journeys of Martin Frobisher, John Davis, and William Baffin, as well as the mid-nineteenth-century

The Alert, a ship in the British expedition led by Captain George Nares, by an ice floe, Dobbin Bay, 1875–1876. It was the first vessel to land on the shores of northern Ellesmere Island.

Source: Library and Archives Canada/C52521.

British naval expeditions in search of Sir John Franklin, whose party of more than 100 had disappeared in the mid-1840s in an attempt to find the Northwest Passage. In July 1880, the British government transferred title of its Arctic "possessions" to Canada, once again without bothering to consult the Aboriginal peoples in the region.

SUMMARY

Three oceans, one country—in little more than a decade after Confederation, Canada had acquired three new provinces and an enormous geographic area, becoming one of the largest nations on earth. Fear of American encroachment was a major factor in its rapid expansion, but internal economic pressures such as the need for more land for agricultural development, the necessity of east–west trade, and a growing railway-building program also contributed. Nationalism served as the fuel for the nation-building engine. By 1880, Canada had become a transcontinental nation but at a considerable cost that included land promises to the Métis, a promise of a transcontinental railroad to British Columbia, the assumption of colonial debts, and First Nation treaty obligations. Now came the challenge of working out new dominion–provincial relations, reconciling regional differences, and creating a dominion-wide economic policy.

NOTES

1. Chester Martin, *Dominion Lands Policy* (Toronto: McClelland & Stewart, 1973), p. 9.

2. Donald G. Creighton, "Macdonald, Confederation, and the West," in *Towards the Discovery of Canada: Selected Essays* (Toronto: Macmillan, 1972), p. 234.

3. Ralph Heintzman, "The Spirit of Confederation: Professor Creighton, Biculturalism, and the Use of History," *Canadian Historical Review*, 52 (1971): 267–68.

4. Hugh Johnston, "Native People, Settlers and Sojourners, 1871–1916," in H.J.M. Johnston, ed., *The Pacific Province: A History of British Columbia* (Vancouver: Douglas & McIntyre, 1996), p. 177.

BIBLIOGRAPHY

Students interested in the Atlantic region's resistance to Confederation should consult Ged Martin, *Britain and the Origins of Canadian Confederation, 1837–67* (London: Macmillan, 1995) and his edited collection *The Causes of Canadian Confederation* (Fredericton: Acadiensis, 1990). A summary of historical developments in the Atlantic region since 1867 is E.R. Forbes and D.A. Muise, eds., *The Atlantic Provinces in Confederation* (Toronto: University of Toronto Press, 1993).

For Nova Scotia, see George Rawlyk, ed., *The Atlantic Provinces and the Problems of Confederation* (St. John's: Breakwater, 1979); and Colin D. Howell, "Nova Scotia's Protest Tradition and the Search for a Meaningful Federalism," in David J. Bercuson, ed., *Canada and the Burden of Unity* (Toronto: Macmillan, 1977), pp. 169–91. Joseph Howe's views are presented in J. Murray Beck, *Joseph Howe*, vol. 2, *The Briton Becomes Canadian, 1848–1873* (Montreal/Kingston: McGill-Queen's University Press, 1983).

On Newfoundland's resistance to Confederation, see James Hiller, "Confederation Defeated: The Newfoundland Election of 1869," in *Newfoundland in the Nineteenth and Twentieth Centuries: Essays in Interpretation* (Toronto: University of Toronto Press, 1980), pp. 67–94; and the relevant section in Frederick W. Rowe, *A History of Newfoundland and Labrador* (Toronto: McGraw-Hill Ryerson, 1980).

Francis Bolger reviews Prince Edward Island's decision to join Canada in *Prince Edward Island and Confederation* (Charlottetown: St. Dunstan's University Press, 1964). See also Catherine Hennessey, *The Landscapes of Confederation: Charlottetown, 1864* (Charlottetown, PE: PEI Museum and Heritage Foundation, 2010), and Rusty Bittermann and Margaret McCallum, "Upholding the Land Legislation of a 'Communistic and Socialist Assembly': The Benefits of Confederation for Prince Edward Island," *Canadian Historical Review*, 87(1) (2006): 1–28. Popular studies include Donald Weale and Harry Baglole, *The Island and Confederation: The End of an Era* (Charlottetown: Williams & Crue, 1973) and the chapter "Confederation" in D.O. Baldwin, *Land of the Red Soil: A Popular History of Prince Edward Island*, rev. ed. (Charlottetown: Ragweed Press, 1998). Ronald Tallman, "Annexation in the Maritimes? The

Butler Mission to Charlottetown," *Dalhousie Review*, 53 (1973): 97–112 shows the American influence, which almost caused Prince Edward Island to reject Confederation.

Alvin C. Gluek, *Minnesota and the Manifest Destiny of the Canadian Northwest: A Study in Canadian–American Relations* (Toronto: University of Toronto Press, 1965) examines American annexationist sentiments toward the Canadian Northwest. Doug Owram, *Promise of Eden: The Canadian Expansionist Movement and the Idea of the West, 1856–1900* (Toronto: University of Toronto Press, 1980) looks at the geography from a Canadian perspective.

On the Riel Resistance, see George F.G. Stanley, *The Birth of Western Canada* (London: Longmans, Green, 1936; rep. Toronto: University of Toronto Press, 1960) and J.M. Bumsted, *The Red River Rebellion* (Winnipeg: Watson & Dwyer, 1996). On the military expedition, see George F.G. Stanley, *Toil and Trouble: Military Expeditions to Red River* (Toronto: Dundurn Press, 1989). For a postcolonial examination of Louis Riel, see Jennifer Reid's *Louis Riel and the Creation of Modern Canada: Mythic Discourse and the Postcolonial State* (Albuquerque: University of New Mexico Press, 2008).

On Manitoba's entry into Confederation, see W.L. Morton, *Manitoba: A History* (Toronto: University of Toronto Press, 1957); Donald G. Creighton, "John A. Macdonald, Confederation and the Canadian West," *Historical and Scientific Society of Manitoba*, 3rd series, no. 23 (1966–67), reprinted in Donald G. Creighton, *Towards the Discovery of Canada: Selected Essays* (Toronto: Macmillan, 1972), pp. 229–37; and Ralph Heintzman, "The Spirit of Confederation: Professor Creighton, Biculturalism, and the Use of History," *Canadian Historical Review*, 52 (1971): 245–75. There are several studies on the Métis in the Red River and Manitoba in the late nineteenth century. For general overviews, see Thomas Flanagan, *Métis Lands in Manitoba* (Calgary: University of Calgary Press, 1991); Irene Gordon *A People on the Move: The Métis of the Western Plains* (Surrey: Heritage House, 2009); Nicole St-Onge, Carolyn Podruchny, Brenda Macdougall, eds., *Contours of a People: Métis Family, Mobility, and History* (Norman: University of Oklahoma Press, 2012); and Gerhard J. Ens and Joe Sawchuk, *From New Peoples to New Nations: Aspects of Métis History and Identity from the Eighteenth to the Twenty-first Centuries* (Toronto: University of Toronto Press, 2015). For histories with a particular emphasis on Red River, see Frits Pannekoek, *A Snug Little Flock: The Social Origins of the Riel Resistance 1869–70* (Winnipeg: Watson & Dwyer, 1991) and Dale Gibson, *Law, Life, and Government at Red River: Settlement and Governance 1812–1972* (Montreal/Kingston: McGill-Queen's University Press, 2015). Gerhard Ens, *Homeland to Hinterland: The Changing Worlds of the Red River Métis in the Nineteenth Century* (Toronto: University of Toronto Press, 1996) and Michael Hogue, *Métis and the Medicine Line: Creating a Border and Dividing a People* (Regina: University of Regina Press, 2015) both highlight the Métis ability to adapt to various political and economic situations on the Prairies, while Chris Andersen's *"Métis": Race, Recognition, and the Struggle for Indigenous Peoplehood* (Vancouver: UBC Press, 2015) reveals how the very definition of Métis has evolved over time. Sarah Carter's *Aboriginal People and Colonizers of Western Canada to 1800* (Toronto: University of Toronto Press, 1999) also provides useful summary of developments in the Red River and on the Prairies.

Useful surveys of First Nations relations with Canada that cover the 1870s include J.R. Miller, *Skyscrapers Hide the Heavens: A History of Indian–White Relations in Canada*, 3rd ed. (Toronto: University of Toronto Press, 2000); Olive P. Dickason, *Canada's First Nations: A History of Founding Peoples from Earliest Times* (Don Mills, ON: Oxford, 2002); A.J. Ray's *I Have Lived Here Since the World Began* (Toronto: Key Porter, 1996); and his *The Canadian Fur Trade in the Industrial Age* (Toronto: University of Toronto Press, 1990). See also J.R. Miller, *Compact, Contract, Covenant: Aboriginal Treaty-Making in Canada* (Toronto: University of Toronto Press, 2009). Shelley A.M. Gavigan, *Hunger, Horses, and Government Men: Criminal Law on the Aboriginal Plains, 1870–1905* (Vancouver: UBC Press, 2012) looks at Aboriginal participation and resistance in the courtroom after the implementation of the 1876 Indian Act.

On the numbered treaties on the Plains, see Richard Price, ed., *The Spirit of the Alberta Indian Treaties*, 3rd ed. (Edmonton: University of Alberta Press, 1999), which contains valuable essays and transcripts of interviews made in the mid-1970s with Native elders. D.J. Hall's *From Treaties to Reserves: The Federal Government and Native Peoples in Territorial Alberta, 1870–1905* (Montreal/Kingston, McGill-Queen's University Press, 2015) also explores the Albertan treaties. Jean Friesen's "Magnificent Gifts: The Treaties of the Indians of the Northwest, 1869–70," *Transactions of the Royal Society of Canada*, series 5, vol. 1 (1986), pp. 41–51 and Arthur J. Ray, Jim Miller, and Frank Tough's *Bounty and Benevolence: A History of Saskatchewan Treaties* (Montreal/Kingston: McGill-Queen's University Press, 2000) study the other numbered treaties. In *Indian Treaty-Making Policy in the United States and Canada, 1867–1877* (Toronto: University of Toronto Press, 2001), Jill St. Germain reviews American and Canadian experiences. An examination of the white settlers' perspective on land settlement through the use of law can be found in Sherene H. Razack, *Race, Space and the Law: Unmapping a White Settler Society* (Toronto: Between the Lines, 2002). James Daschuk's *Clearing the Plains: Disease, Politics of Starvation, and the Loss of Aboriginal Life* (Regina: University of Regina Press, 2013) provides important context for the treaty-making process by examining the environmental, medical, and racial politics that drove Aboriginal communities to sign the numbered treaties.

Several good biographies of Prairie chiefs have been published by Hugh A. Dempsey: *Crowfoot* (Edmonton: Hurtig, 1972), *Red Crow* (Saskatoon: Western Producer Prairie Books, 1980), and *Big Bear* (Vancouver: Douglas & McIntyre, 1984). Dempsey established the troubled context of the early 1870s on the northern Plains in *Firewater: The Impact of the Whisky Trade on the Blackfoot Nation* (Calgary: Fifth House, 2002). For Big Bear, see as well J.R. Miller, *Big Bear (Mistahimusqua)* (Toronto: ECW Press, 1996). Edward Ahenakew's *Voice of the Plains Cree* (Toronto: McClelland & Stewart, 1973) provides a valuable Native assessment of conditions for the First Nations of the Canadian Prairies in the early twentieth century. Shorter treatments of these and other First Nations leaders appear in the *Dictionary of Canadian Biography*, vols. 11, *1881 to 1890* (1982), 12, *1891 to 1900* (1990), 13, *1901 to 1910* (1994), and 14, *1911 to 1920* (1998) (Toronto: University of Toronto Press). For a visual look at Aboriginal people in this era, see Edward Cavell, *Classic Images of First Nations (1880–1920)* (Surrey: Heritage House, 2009).

Indian policy is reviewed by Brian Titley in the early chapters of his *A Narrow Vision: Duncan Campbell Scott and the Administration of Indian Affairs in Canada* (Vancouver: University of British Columbia Press, 1987). Titley provides portraits of all the Indian Commissioners in *The Indian Commissioners: Agents of the State and Indian Policy in Canada's Prairie West, 1873–1932* (Edmonton: University of Alberta Press, 2009). The government's farming policy for the Native peoples is outlined in Sarah Carter, *Lost Harvests: Prairie Indian Reserve Farmers and Government Policy* (Montreal/Kingston: McGill-Queen's University Press, 1990). A good case study of an eastern-Canadian Indian reserve in the late nineteenth century is Hélène Bédard's *Les Montagnais et la réserve de Betsiamites: 1850–1900* (Quebec: Institut québécois de recherche sur la culture, 1988). Daniel Rueck's "Commons, Enclosure, and Resistance in Kahnawá:ke Mohawk Territory, 1850–1900," *Canadian Historical Review* 95, no. 3 (September 2014): 352–381 shows how the federal government generally tried to undermine Aboriginal land ownership. Two important historical studies of Indian residential schools are: J.R. Miller, *Shingwauk's Vision: A History of Native Residential Schools* (Toronto: University of Toronto Press, 1996); and John S. Milloy, *A National Crime: The Canadian Government and the Residential School System 1879–1986* (Winnipeg: University of Manitoba Press, 1999). More recently, Andrew Woolford's *This Benevolent Experiment: Indigenous Boarding Schools, Genocide, and Redress in Canada and the United States* (Winnipeg: University of Manitoba Press, 2015) provides a transnational comparison of Indigenous boarding schools in Manitoba and New Mexico.

On British Columbia and Confederation, see Margaret Ormsby, *British Columbia: A History* (Toronto: Macmillan, 1958), and Ormsby's "Canada and the New British Columbia," *Canadian Historical Association Report* (1948), pp. 74–85. W. George Shelton's *British Columbia and Confederation* (Victoria: Morriss Printing [for the University of Victoria], 1967) is a worthwhile collection of essays. See also Jean Barman, *The West Beyond the West: A History of British Columbia*, rev. ed. (Toronto: University of Toronto Press, 1996), and Hugh J.M. Johnston, ed., *The Pacific Province: A History of British Columbia* (Vancouver: Douglas & McIntyre, 1996).

For maps and charts, see L.R. Gentilcore et al., eds., *Historical Atlas of Canada*, vol. 2, *The Land Transformed, 1800–1891* (Toronto: University of Toronto Press, 1993).

Source: Library and Archives Canada/NMC 11868.

Chapter Three

A "NATIONAL POLICY"?

TIME LINE	
1868	Founding of Canada First Movement
1869	Joseph Guibord dies
1872	Dominion Lands Act passed
1873	North-West Mounted Police (NWMP) established Pacific Scandal topples Macdonald government
1874	Liberal Party wins federal election under Alexander Mackenzie
1875	Supreme Court of Canada established
1876	Alexander Graham Bell makes the first long-distance call, from Brantford, Ontario
1878	Conservatives re-elected under John A. Macdonald
1879	National Policy established
1880	Canadian Pacific Railway Company formed
1882	Conservatives re-elected under John A. Macdonald
1885	Completion of Canadian Pacific Railway
1887	"Head tax" imposed on Chinese immigrants Conservatives re-elected under John A. Macdonald
1891	Conservatives re-elected under John A. Macdonald
1896	Liberal Party wins federal election under Wilfrid Laurier Western immigration boom begins
1897	British preferential tariff established as part of Liberals' national policy
1901	First transatlantic wireless signal received by Marconi at Signal Hill, St. John's, Newfoundland

In 1874, Edward Blake, the premier of Ontario and future leader of the Liberal Party, identified what he perceived as the major challenge facing the nation: "The future of Canada depends very much upon the cultivation of a national spirit."

In the late nineteenth century there were numerous definitions of what it meant to be a "Canadian." When Quebeckers referred to "les Canadiens," they spoke of themselves alone. They called English Canadians *les Anglais*. English Canadians, in turn, considered Quebeckers "French Canadians." The Native peoples did not use the term "Canadians" to describe themselves, because they had their own designations for their own nations, such as Dene, Haida, Mi'kmaq, Anishinaabeg (Ojibwa), Innu (Montagnais), and Haudenosaunee (Iroquois). The assumed basis of national unity—common language, religion, and ethnic origin—did not apply to Canada. Nor did geography or history, both of which tended to divide rather than unite the population. As the Confederation experience demonstrated, even the process of forging the nation did not produce a powerful national spirit in Canada.

Could economic goals and interests unite Canadians? John A. Macdonald's Conservative government believed it would at least aid in the process. In 1879, his party proposed a dominion-wide economic policy of nation building based on a "National Policy" or national tariff to protect Canada's developing manufacturing industries. Once in place, the Conservatives believed, the tariff would provide the capital to pay the expenses of building the transcontinental railway. The railway, in turn, would link an industrialized East with the soon-to-be-developed agricultural West, providing transportation for goods as well as people to settle the new region. The growth of central Canadian industry, the settlement of the West, and the building of the transcontinental railway would continue the process of creating the nation.

After 1896 and the defeat of the federal Tories, the Liberals under Wilfrid Laurier implemented their own version of the national policy. But the shaping of this policy for the benefit of central Canadian manufacturing and business interests created regional discontent in western and eastern Canada. As well, the conformist attitude of the dominant British Canadian population created resentment among new "ethnic" Canadians. These trends brought into question whether the national policy was indeed "national" and actually served to unite the country.

Emerging Expressions of Nationalism

In the spring of 1868, five members of the Ontario elite met in Ottawa to launch the Canada First Movement: George Denison, Henry Morgan, Charles Mair, William Foster, and Robert Haliburton. Concerned about the lack of myths, symbols, and national spirit surrounding Confederation, these men sought to identify and promote a nationalism for the new Dominion of Canada. They believed that Canada's greatness lay in its northern climate and rugged landscape, which combined to create a superior Anglo-Saxon and Aryan race. They saw English Canadians as the "Northmen of the New World."

The national vision of the Canada First Movement represented a distinctly Anglo-Protestant and Ontarian brand of nationalism. "Canada First" meant "English Canada First." The group supported John Schultz' and Charles Mair's Canadian expansionists in Red River. The Canada Firsters cast aspersions on the French Canadians (including the Métis) as a "bar to progress, and to the extension of a great Anglo-Saxon Dominion across the Continent." The execution of Thomas Scott was a major catalyst for the movement and the group organized a protest in Toronto when Schultz and Mair returned from Red River in 1870. Its members were disappointed with the Treaty of Washington in 1871 and advocated imperial federation as providing a voice for the young dominion with the Empire. Canada first flirted with the idea of becoming a political party in the early 1870s but speculation ended when Edward Blake became Liberal leader.

While Canada First sought a British and Protestant Canada, many French Canadians were themselves caught up in a renewed Catholic nationalism. The late nineteenth century witnessed a resurgence of French Catholic sentiment in Quebec. This sentiment was attached to ultramontanism, a Catholic philosophy that gave precedence and authority to the Pope and Vatican in Rome, even over secular political leaders. The Quebec government cultivated closer ties with France under Napoleon III, especially after the French helped to protect the papal lands in central Italy against Giuseppe Garibaldi's army and then fought for the unification of Italy. Five hundred volunteer soldiers, the Papal *Zouaves*, or "mercenaries of the Lord," left Quebec between 1868 and 1870 to serve in the papal army.

Ignace Bourget, the influential bishop of Montreal, and his disciple, Louis-François Laflèche, later named bishop of Trois-Rivières, led the ultramontane movement within the Quebec Catholic Church. Laflèche lay down the basic principles of ultramontane nationalism in 1866:

> A nation is constituted by unity of speech, unity of faith, uniformity of morals, customs, and institutions. The French Canadians possess all these, and constitute a true nation. Each nation has received from Providence a mission to fulfill. The mission of the French Canadian people is to constitute a centre of Catholicism in the New World.

Church above state

Ultramontanes believed in the subordination of the state to the church. In their view, the Pope constituted the supreme authority over religious and civil matters. Bourget reminded his followers in a circular in 1876: "Let us each say in his heart, 'I hear my *curé*, my *curé* hears the bishop, and the bishop hears the Pope, and the Pope hears our Lord Jesus Christ.'"

While the ultramontanes gained influence in Quebec as early as the 1840s, their political influence increased in the 1870s with the Vatican's declaration of the dogma of papal infallibility. In Quebec the ultramontanes issued a *Programme catholique*, which proclaimed the church's right to advise Roman Catholics on how to vote. Catholics were expected to vote for the *bleus* (Conservatives), blessed with the colour of heaven, and not for the *rouges* (Liberals), damned by the colour of the fires of hell (and associated with the secular liberalism of Garibaldi's movement threatening the Vatican in Italy). The ultramontanes favoured candidates who endorsed the church's views on marriage, education, and social order. A number of French-Canadian politicians, including such Conservatives as George-Étienne Cartier and Joseph-Adolphe Chapleau, opposed this mixing of religion and politics. In general, the movement brought up the old debate over the divisions of church and state. For English Canadians, this debate had been ended with the English Civil War in the seventeenth century. As a result, they viewed the ultramontanes as backward and Quebec as a "priest-ridden society." Philosophies aside, the ultramontane movement rekindled the religious bigotry between Catholics and Protestants, French and English that had seemingly been put aside with Confederation.

The ultramontanes also encountered resistance among liberals in Quebec. A particularly vocal group, the *Institut canadien*, formed in Montreal in 1844. The group consisted of about 200 young Quebec liberals and professionals who established a public library and debating room. (There was no French-language university or even a public library in Montreal.) Later, other centres founded

Recruits for the Zouaves needed a letter of recommendation from their parish priest. They had to be unmarried, or widowers without young children, and between the ages of 15 and 40. The photo shows nine Quebec papal Zouaves in Italy in 1868. A former Zouave, Ephrem Brisebois, Inspector of the NWMP, founded what later became known as Calgary in 1875. Initially, Fort Calgary was known as Fort Brisebois.

Source: Archives de la chancellerie de l'Archevêché de Montréal/ACAM-FP-Zouaves pontificaux.

branches of the Institut throughout Lower Canada. Initially organized as literary societies and debating clubs, branches of the Institut encouraged free thought and sponsored their own libraries free of church censorship. Many of the Institut's members were influenced by the writings of such French liberal thinkers as Voltaire, Rousseau, and Montesquieu, as well as by British liberal writers such as Bentham and Mill. They believed in the separation of church and state. Many members of the Institut supported the Parti rouge in the 1850s and later the Liberals.

The Guibord Affair (1869)   Consecrated - declared sacred.

Bishop Bourget viewed the Institut canadien as a direct challenge to the authority of the church in Quebec and the Vatican in Rome. He condemned the organization, even going so far as to deny the sacraments to its members, including the right of burial in consecrated soil. The battle between the ultramontanes and the Institut became a celebrated case in Quebec when Joseph Guibord, a former vice-president of Montreal's Institut, died in November 1869 and the Catholic Church refused to give him a Christian burial. Since the case addressed the larger issue of civil versus ecclesiastical supremacy, the Institut supported Henriette Brown, his widow, when she took her local curé to court. As the case moved through the various appeal courts, Guibord's coffin rested for six years in a vault in Montreal's Mount Royal cemetery. Finally the Judicial Committee of the Privy Council, the supreme law court in the British Empire, ruled in 1874 that burial was a civil right.

Henriette Brown died shortly before this judgment. She was peacefully buried in the family plot in the Catholic cemetery. Friends of her late husband now demanded that he join her in their final resting place. The decision aroused passions and it took two attempts to carry the coffin to the cemetery. An angry mob prevented the first attempt. Only with an escort of more than 1200 militiamen and regular soldiers did the authorities succeed. They placed Guibord's coffin on top of his wife's grave in poured cement to prevent vandalism. Immediately, Bishop Bourget deconsecrated Guibord's plot, although he left the wife's, only centimetres beneath the husband's body, in a state of grace. Guibord's body still lies in unconsecrated soil in Montreal's Côte des Neiges cemetery.

The rise of ultramontanism in Quebec and the reaction to the movement in English Canada made clear the religious, ethnic, and even sectarian tensions simmering below the surface of Confederation. These tensions worked counter to the creation of one Canadian nationalism and posed a threat to national unity. While extremists came to vocalize these movements, they demonstrated that nationalisms in Canada continued to be defined in cultural rather than political terms. In Quebec the nationalist debate took shape between ultramontanes and gallicans (those who believed in the restriction of papal authority and the autonomy of national churches); in English Canada it took the form of a debate between imperialists and autonomists. Thus, by 1870, conflicting nationalisms surfaced in both English and French Canada. They reinforced the realization that in Canada, nationalism had to be based on an identity other than a common ethnicity, religion, or language.

Liberal Rule

The Pacific Scandal (1873-1878)

The Conservatives won the federal election of 1872 but just one year later a political scandal broke. It was revealed that Macdonald and Cartier had accepted more than $300,000 in campaign funds from Sir Hugh Allan, president of a large shipping concern, whose newly created Canada Pacific Company was a major contender for the government charter to build the transcontinental railway promised to British Columbia. The major financial backing for Allan's group came from financial interests in the United States, raising the old spectre of American influence and control. Prime Minister Macdonald moved quickly to eliminate the American connection by forcing the consortium to cut its ties with the financial interests and form an all-Canadian bid. But it was too late; the damage was done.

An American railway tycoon, angry at his exclusion from the consortium, supplied the Liberal opposition with incriminating evidence of a financial kickback to the Conservatives from Allan and his American backers. While donations and patronage were part of the political customs of the day and generally tolerated, the scandal with its American connection went too far and threatened the government of John A. Macdonald. Until this time, the Liberals remained a fractured and divided group. They lacked leadership, a coherent and united platform, and an efficient and wealthy party organization. In Quebec, where the party was staunchly opposed by the Catholic Church, the party could make no inroads. The Liberals accused the Conservatives of immorality and corruption, and the charges began to have an effect. Macdonald denied involvement. "These hands are clean," he assured the House of Commons. But fearing a want-of-confidence vote, he announced his cabinet's resignation on November 5, 1873. The governor general asked the Liberals to form a government, which they did without an election being held. Two months later, in January 1874, the new prime minister, Alexander Mackenzie, dissolved Parliament and called an election, with the Pacific Scandal as the major issue. The Liberals won office with 138 of 206 seats and 53.8 percent of the popular vote.

Liberal Leadership

Alexander Mackenzie, a poor farmer's son, was born not far from Macdonald's birthplace in Glasgow. He came to Canada from Scotland at the age of twenty and worked as a stonemason. The acerbic political critic Goldwin Smith once remarked that if Mackenzie's strong point as prime minister consisted in his having been a stonemason, his weak point consisted in his remaining one: cold, hard, and colourless.

Mackenzie inherited numerous political problems. For one thing, the Liberal Party was divided. Whereas the Conservatives were able to unite in the mid-nineteenth-century and overcome their ethnic cleavages, largely as a result of their shared commercial interests, the Liberal Party remained fractured. It was a coalition of factions—rouges, Clear Grits, and Reformers—that had come together less out of a sense of common philosophy or a unified party platform than out of a common dislike for the Conservatives and their program. Canadian Liberals did share the general tenets of British and European liberalism based around liberty, equal rights, democracy, the market economy, and a secular society. In the Canadian context, they distrusted big business interests, idealized rural life, endorsed a lower tariff, criticized imperialism, and championed minority and provincial rights. But they were divided by factionalism.

The Liberal Party needed a strong leader (which Alexander Mackenzie was not) to pull its divergent groups together and to provide direction. George Brown had been such a leader—at least for English-Canadian Liberals—but he resigned after his defeat in the 1867 election. The fact that a number of influential party members challenged Mackenzie's leadership compounded the problem. Brown lurked in the background; Richard Cartwright, a Conservative defector who left after Macdonald denied him the post of minister of finance, wanted a senior post; and Antoine-Aimé Dorion led the party's rouge faction and sought the role of Mackenzie's Quebec lieutenant. Finally, Mackenzie faced the enigmatic Edward Blake, who was a former premier of Ontario (1871–72) and a brilliant parliamentary debater but indecisive about whether to stay in the party. In essence, the Liberal party was catapulted into office due to the Pacific Scandal, whether it was ready to lead the nation or not.

The Mackenzie Government

Prime Minister Alexander Mackenzie took office just as Canada entered an economic recession. Two months earlier, the North American and European financial boom of the 1860s and early 1870s ended. As trade declined, the federal debt increased sharply. The Liberals had opposed Macdonald's unrealistic promise of a transcontinental railway to British Columbia. Now facing a recession, Mackenzie responded by slowing down the inherited railway-building scheme, despite British Columbia's threat to leave Confederation over Ottawa's broken promises. The completion date of the promised railway was extended to 1890, while the province was given a line from Esquimalt to Nanaimo as compensation in the meantime. While the Liberals delayed the building of the transcontinental, they did see to the completion of the Intercolonial Railway linking Central Canada to the Maritimes.

Yet despite the challenges, the Mackenzie government ushered in an impressive spate of reform measures. The Liberals concentrated on constitutional and political questions to divert attention away from the faltering economy. In 1875, they established the Supreme Court of Canada as a national appeal court as part of their mandate to increase Canadian autonomy within the Empire. While final appeal still rested with the Judicial Committee of the Privy Council in Britain and continued to do so on civil matters until 1949, the Supreme Court became the first Canadian court to review Canadian laws. The Liberals also restricted the powers of the governor general, Britain's representative in Canada, by withdrawing his right to disallow legislation without consulting the Canadian Parliament.

The Liberals introduced the secret ballot and the practice of holding the entire general election on the same day in each constituency across the country. They also closed taverns on election day to reduce the possibility of buying votes for drinks. Contested elections were transferred out of the hands of parliamentarians and into the courts. Prime Minister Mackenzie and his cabinet extended the federal franchise effectively to all non-Native males, whether they held property or not. The Liberals also ended the system of dual representation that allowed an individual to hold a federal and a provincial seat simultaneously.

The Mackenzie government also reformed Canada's department of militia and defence by establishing a national military college to train officers. One of the major expenditures the Liberals incurred came from the establishment of the Royal Military College in Kingston in 1876.

A MECHANIC'S HOME

UNDER THE NATIONAL POLICY.
NO WORK, NO MONEY.

UNDER A FREE TRADE OR REVENUE TARIFF.

According to the Conservatives, the National Policy's supporters, a high tariff meant prosperity (top); free trade meant unemployment and poverty. To the Liberals a high tariff and free trade meant the exact opposite.

Source: Library and Archives Canada, Acc. no. 1983-33-1117.

The National Policy of John A. Macdonald

But as is often the case, the economic recession destroyed the government unfortunate enough to be in office at the time. The Liberals' cautious approach to railway construction may have been financially prudent, but it lacked the nationalistic lustre of the Conservatives' dream of a transcontinental railway to link the nation from sea to sea. The Mackenzie government also lacked an economic agenda. It attempted to negotiate a reciprocity treaty with the United States similar to the one signed in 1854, and in 1874 a draft treaty was drawn up. But the American Senate defeated the bill, leaving the Liberals without a viable commercial policy.

The Conservatives intensified their nationalist rhetoric and transformed it into a campaign platform. On the eve of the 1878 election, a lobbying group of the Canadian Manufacturers' Association convinced Macdonald and the Conservative Party to endorse a protective system of higher tariffs. Increased import duties, they argued, would promote manufacturing in Canada, thus diversifying the economy, but more importantly fostering a national manufacturing sector and protecting it from American competition. Macdonald pointed out that import duties in Britain and the United States enabled these countries to advance industrially and that the same could happen in Canada. He argued that the creation of an east–west economy by means of a transcontinental railway provided the answer to the recession. Such a railway link would allow for settlement of the West. Farmers from this new region could help their Ontario counterparts to feed the growing number of industrial workers in central Canada, who in turn could supply the farmers throughout Canada with agricultural equipment and other manufactured goods. While the Macdonald Conservatives had themselves been proponents of reciprocity with the United States, and indeed had attempted on several occasions to negotiate a trade deal, they embraced protectionism and made it a major plank in their political platform. In the federal election of 1878, the Conservatives returned to power with 142 seats to the Liberals 64.

This policy of nation building—the "national policy," as Macdonald called it—rested on three essentials: the system of protective tariffs; the completion of a transcontinental railway; and the settlement of the West through immigration. While historians in hindsight interpret the National Policy as an integrated entity, it was not viewed as such at the time. In 1879, the immediate focus was on the tariff. The Conservatives raised the tariff on textiles, iron and steel products, coal, and petroleum products by 10 to 30 percent, thus achieving their first objective. In the budget speech, the Conservatives referred to the tariff as the National Policy, an integral part of the larger "national policy" of nation building.

Debate over the National Policy

The Conservatives argued that a protective tariff would shift trade from a north–south to an east–west axis. If trade was allowed to follow the natural contours of geography, it would flow north–south. Dangerous examples of such a result had already been seen in Red River and British Columbia. If Canada was to be a nation from sea to sea, trade needed to flow in the same direction. The provinces needed to trade with each other. The tariff would also provide Canadians with their own national market, reducing their dependency on the United States. Furthermore, manufacturers—both Canadians and foreigners building plants in Canada—would ensure more jobs for Canadian workers, technicians, and managers. If Canada was to be a competitive industrial nation, it required its own viable and vibrant manufacturing sector.

In contrast, the Liberals argued that the tariff would erect an artificial and obstructive fiscal barrier around the country. Philosophically, they were opposed to trade restrictions imposed by the heavy hand of government. Furthermore, they claimed, while the tariff or National Policy was "National" in name, it was regional in interest. It mainly served the needs of central Canadians, and more specifically, the needs of the manufacturers and industrialists of the urban centres of Ontario and Quebec. The tariff would serve to heighten divisions among the various regions, pitting the

Maritimes and the West against Ontario and Quebec. Furthermore, it would put the burden of national unity on the hinterland regions, which would become the suppliers of raw materials for the more prosperous metropolitan centres. In social terms, a corresponding inequality would develop, since workers, farmers, and fishers would have to pay a higher price for consumer goods, whether imported (as a result of the higher tariff) or produced in Canada (as a result of higher production costs). The tariff protected domestic manufacturing. It did nothing, however, to protect domestic agriculture, because grain prices were determined on the world market. As a result, the tariff forced farmers to pay more for their manufactured goods (tools and implements), while offering no such protection for the goods they produced. The Liberals drove home the point in a pamphlet published in 1882:

> The farmer starting to his work has a shoe put on his horse with nails taxed 41 percent; with a hammer taxed 40 percent; cuts a stick with a knife taxed 27-½ percent; hitches his horse to a plough taxed 30 percent; with chains taxed 27-½ percent. He returns to his home at night and lays his wearied limbs on a sheet taxed 30 percent, and covers himself with a blanket on which he has paid 70 percent tax. He rises in the morning, puts on his humble flannel shirt taxed 60 percent, shoes taxed 30 percent, hat taxed 30 percent, reads a chapter from his Bible taxed 7 percent, and kneels to his God on a cheap carpet taxed 30 percent . . . and then he is expected to thank John A. that he lives under the freest Government under heaven.

Not surprisingly, most farmers across Canada became critics of the National Policy, and of high tariffs in general. As the West was settled as the nation's breadbasket, the tariff became increasingly viewed as a national injustice and the major issue of western alienation.

Building the Canadian Pacific Railway

Although not originally tied to the National Policy, the dream of a transcontinental railroad remained an essential plank of Macdonald's nation-building enterprise. Settlers wishing to go from Toronto to Manitoba via British territory in the 1870s, for example, had to travel by steamboat across the Great Lakes and over eastern Manitoba's lakes and rivers, with wagon journeys at the portages, then by wagon on the newly completed Dawson Road to Winnipeg, and finally by wagon on rough roads to their destination. The alternative was to go through the United States, where American immigration agents often succeeded in persuading Canadian travellers to settle in the American West. Furthermore, British Columbia's entry into Confederation depended on the "trail of iron" as the only means to link the isolated colony to central Canada. Finally, a transcontinental railway, it was felt, would allow Canada to compete with the United States as a great North American nation.

Government Involvement in Railway Building

Prior to the construction of the Canadian Pacific Railway the Canadian government had a history of involvement in railway building. Whether it was building railways or canals, these massive transportation endeavours were expensive. Their commercial and nationalistic appeal was strong, but their profit potential was questionable and usually years away. As a result, they failed to draw adequate private capital investment. The problem was compounded by the fact that the young colonies and later dominion did not possess enough investors. In the 1840s and 1850s, the government of the Canadas went into heavy debt to help finance the Grand

Trunk Railway and other colonial lines. As part of the Confederation agreement, the Canadian government itself financed the extension of the Grand Trunk line, known as the Intercolonial Railway, from Rivière-du-Loup, the eastern terminus, to Halifax, adding substantially to the dominion's debt. But this debt load had limits. Macdonald's government received a reprieve in the form of further loan guarantees from Britain, compensation for the Treaty of Washington in 1871.

Yet, despite the expense of the Intercolonial Railway, the Conservative government embarked on the even more ambitious and riskier railway to the Pacific Ocean. This line, when completed, would be two-thirds longer than any other single railway line then existing in the world. It would run across 5000 kilometres of forest, prairies, mountains, and shield to link 3.5 million people scattered over vast distances. Alexander Mackenzie in 1872 called it "an act of insane recklessness," although his administration was pressured into continuing the project, albeit only through piecemeal construction. The building of the CPR took on the dimensions of a national dream—and, at times, the qualities of a political nightmare. The Pacific Scandal was only the first act.

WHERE HISTORIANS DISAGREE

The National Policy

The National Policy of high tariffs, railway building, and immigration, first established by the Conservative government in the late nineteenth century, once generated considerable debate among historians and economists. As social history rose to prominence and political and economic history declined, however, the topic received less attention.

In the 1950s, Donald Creighton represented the central Canadian nationalist tradition in arguing that the National Policy, especially the protective tariff of 1879, was an essential component of Canada's growth as an independent nation: "In international affairs, the tariff asserted the principle of independence as against both Britain and the United States. In domestic matters, it expressed the hope for a new varied and self sufficient national life."[1] Canada needed its own manufacturing sector, east–west trade was essential, and regional interests had to be sacrificed for the dream of nation. Craig Brown agreed, and noted the success of the National Policy in instilling a feeling of nationalism in Canada when traditional national symbols were absent.[2]

In 1986, Ben Forster pointed to other factors important in shaping Canada's National Policy. He highlighted a wide range of political and economic factors and interests, including business, industry, agriculture, and government, as all having made a contribution from 1825 to 1879 in shaping the policy.[3]

John Dales questioned the success of the National Policy, concluding that it was a "dismal failure." Railway building became an expensive undertaking for the Canadian taxpayer through heavy government subsidies to the Canadian Pacific Railway Company, established in 1880 to build the transcontinental line. Immigration and the settlement of the West did not occur until well after the National

Policy was in place and then for reasons independent of the policy. Lastly, the high tariff pitted region against region. It created an artificial climate for industrial growth that ironically made Canada more, not less, dependent on the United States through a branch-plant economy. Dales questioned to what extent international economic trends dictated Canadian economic policy.[4]

Historians in the West and the Maritimes not surprisingly focused on the negative impact of the National Policy on their region. The tariff was the most important political issue in the West from the 1880s until the 1930s. W.L. Morton went so far as to claim that it began the agrarian revolt in 1911. David Bercuson pointed out that the tariff was the major issue in advancing western alienation.[5] In fact, all three planks of the National Policy became issues of regional discontent in the Prairie West.[6]

Kenneth Norrie countered this viewpoint in reference to the West: "The claims of prairie economic discrimination currently so casually thrown about are not supported by the evidence."[7] The economic development of the Prairies occurred after the tariff was already in place. Norrie argues that the lack of industrial development in the West had nothing to do with the National Policy and everything to do with the region's location—away from the heart of North American development— and its lack of a sufficient population base to make industrialization viable. According to Norrie, there were few feasible alternatives to the National Policy.

Gerald Friesen notes that while Norrie may be generally correct, "his arguments are based on 'counterfactual' propositions." Regardless of what would have happened if other policy alternatives had been put into place, "the National Policy was designed to integrate the west into the nation, it eventually became a subject of bitter debate because it set the price for western participation in the nation." For Friesen, the National Policy must be understood in broad terms. It encompassed not only tariffs, railways, and settlement but also freight-rate agreements, First Nations Treaties, and the creation of the North West Mounted Police. As a grand design, some scholars even argue "that Confederation itself was a plank in the entrepreneurs' National Policy."[8]

1   Donald Creighton, *Dominion of the North* (Toronto: Macmillan, 1957), p. 346.

2   Craig Brown, *Canada's National Policy, 1883–1900: A Study in Canadian–American Relations* (Princeton: Princeton University Press, 1964).

3   Ben Forster, *A Conjunction of Interests: Business, Politics, and Tariffs, 1825–1879* (Toronto: University of Toronto Press, 1986).

4   J.H. Dales, *The Protective Tariff in Canada's Development* (Toronto: University of Toronto Press, 1966).

5   W.L. Morton, *The Progressives* (University of Toronto Press, 1950); David Bercuson, ed., *Canada and the Burden of Unity* (Toronto: Macmillan, 1977).

6   Robert Wardhaugh, *Mackenzie King and the Prairie West* (Toronto: University of Toronto Press, 2000).

7   Kenneth Norrie, "The National Policy and Prairie Economic Discrimination, 1870–1930," in Donald Akenson, ed., *Canadian Papers in Rural History*, vol. 1 (Gananoque, ON: Langdale, 1978).

8   Gerald Friesen, *The Canadian Prairies: A History* (Toronto: University of Toronto Press, 1987), pp. 163, 186, 194.

The Conservative government agreed to undertake the Canadian Pacific Railway for several reasons. First, the United States in the past had threatened to annex the Northwest and was in a position to do so, especially after the completion of its first transcontinental—the Union Pacific Railway—in 1869. Only with a Canadian railway could the dominion secure effective control over the region of the North-West Territories that it had acquired in 1869–70. Second, the railway would serve as a link in the British Empire's "all red route to the Orient," a route to Asia entirely through British territory. Third, Canadian politicians believed in the resource potential of the Northwest. Two scientific expeditions into the region, the British Palliser and the Canadian Hind expeditions in the late 1850s, while disagreeing on the extent of the fertility of the soil in the area, reported that the Northwest contained millions of hectares of fertile land. Fourth, while nationalism remained nascent in Canada, the building of the transcontinental was seen as an essential component of uniting the new nation. Finally, the promise to British Columbia of a transcontinental railway within ten years of the province's entry into Confederation obliged even the Liberal government to build it, albeit belatedly.

The Search for a Private Company

Macdonald's Conservative government initially favoured a private company to undertake the ambitious project. Before the recession of the mid-1870s, two companies competed for the contract: the Interoceanic Company of Toronto, headed by Senator David Macpherson and backed by British financiers, and the Canada Pacific Company, a Montreal consortium under Sir Hugh Allan, president of the Merchants' Bank, with American financial backing. For nationalist reasons, Macdonald favoured a merger of the two companies, but neither Macpherson nor Allan would agree. The government awarded the contract to the Canada Pacific Company in return for generous financial contributions on Allan's part to the Conservative campaign fund in the election of 1872. The resulting Pacific Scandal forced the Macdonald Conservative government to resign and ended the short-lived Canada Pacific Company.

The Mackenzie Liberal government continued the railway, but only on those sections where settlement warranted construction and only as public money became available, relying on waterways and even American lines, meanwhile, to fill the gaps. To build piecemeal, as demand necessitated, however, meant reneging on the Conservatives' promise of completing the railway to British Columbia in ten years. Edgar Dewdney, a surveyor and MP for British Columbia, insisted on "The Terms, the Whole Terms and Nothing But the Terms."

When the Conservatives returned to office in 1878, an economic upturn enabled them to find a new private company, the Canadian Pacific Railway Company (CPR), made up of a group associated with the Bank of Montreal, headed by George Stephen, R.B. Angus, and Donald Smith. The syndicate agreed to build the railway across northern Ontario from Callander (near North Bay) to Port Arthur and from Winnipeg to Kamloops by May 1, 1891. In return, the government offered $25 million in financing and 25 million acres (10 million hectares) of land consisting of alternate sections not already sold in a belt nearly 40 kilometres wide on both sides of the track across the Prairies. Land not "fit for settlement" could be exchanged for better land elsewhere. The company also obtained free of charge the 1200 kilometres of track already completed or under construction, which had an estimated worth of $31 million. The government promised exemption of construction materials from duty. As well, CPR property and its capital stock would be free from taxation. Its grant of 10 million hectares of land remained tax-exempt for twenty years or until sold. The "monopoly clause," however, would become the most controversial aspect of the deal: the government agreed that no competing line could be built south of the main CPR line until 1900.

In Parliament, Liberals, and even some Conservative backbenchers, questioned the need for such generous terms. The two-month debate that followed proved one of the longest and most bitter in the history of Parliament. As Pierre Berton pointed out, more than a million words were spoken, more than in the Bible's Old and New Testaments combined.[1] Yet Macdonald held his party together, and the Conservatives voted down the 25 amendments proposed by the Liberal opposition.

The CPR Route

The new CPR company decided to alter the route of the railway. Rather than follow the northerly route proposed by Sandford Fleming's survey team in the early 1870s—along the North Saskatchewan River and through the Yellowhead Pass—it would take a southerly route through Pile O' Bones Creek (Regina), Swift Current, Fort Calgary, and the Kicking Horse Pass. A number of reasons accounted for this sudden shift. First, the CPR feared that farmers in the southern Prairies would use the American Northern Pacific Railway rather than the Canadian line. If the CPR was built closer to the American border, western Canadian settlers would be more likely to use it. Second, coal deposits discovered near Lethbridge could be exploited as a source of fuel for the locomotives on the southern route. Third, John Macoun, a botanist and leader of a scientific expedition in the West who had visited the area during the wettest decade in more than a century, reported that the southern Prairies were not the desert that John Palliser had earlier described. (Palliser had seen that area in the 1850s, one of the driest periods.) The CPR also hoped that the sudden switch would bypass speculators who had already bought up land along the proposed northern route. When speculators attempted to do the same along the southern route—guessing where divisional points and stations might be—the company arbitrarily changed its plans and placed stations and divisional points at spots not originally intended. In this way, the CPR retained control over

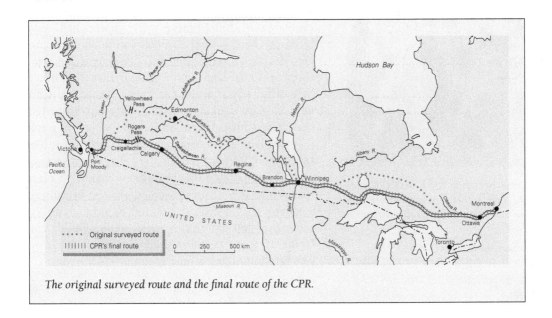

The original surveyed route and the final route of the CPR.

A Canadian Pacific Railway work crew laying track in British Columbia. The CPR's construction project was a massive undertaking. Building the rail line through the mountain ranges proved one of the most challenging tasks facing the Canadian Pacific Railway Company and cost the lives of hundreds of Chinese workers.

Source: Royal BC Museum, BC Archives/A-07021.

Although Chinese labourers built the British Columbia section of the CPR, there are few contemporary photos of them. This is one, a shot of a Chinese railway camp at Kamloops, B.C., 1886.

Source: Royal BC Museum, BC Archives/D-04712.

the land profits to be made in building the railway from Brandon to Revelstoke. But the change in route angered many who had already moved into the West in anticipation of the coming of the CPR.

Once the government confirmed the route, construction began. In 1881 the syndicate hired William Cornelius Van Horne, an experienced American engineer, to oversee construction. Van Horne drove his men hard. He boasted that his construction gang, which at one time had 5000 workers and 1700 teams of horses, could lay 800 kilometres of prairie track in a year. The line reached Calgary in August 1883.

But building across the Prairies was the easy part. Still ahead lay the difficult mountain terrain. In addition, sections across the rugged shield north of Lake Ontario still had to be completed. Surveyors had already chosen the Kicking Horse Pass through the Bow River valley, despite its steep incline, as the best route through the Rocky Mountains. Only late in the summer of 1882, however, did Major A.B. Rogers, an experienced railway surveyor, locate a pass that allowed the CPR to cross the more westerly Selkirk Mountains. He insisted that the pass bear his name. Difficulties abounded, including laying track along the sides of mountains, blasting tunnels through rock, and bridging swift mountain rivers.

The construction of the British Columbia section, particularly that built by Andrew Onderdonk from Port Moody on the coast nearly 400 kilometres into the interior, cost enormous amounts of time and money and took the lives of hundreds of the estimated 17,000 Chinese workers who had been hired as cheap labour to do the difficult and dangerous tasks of tunnelling and handling explosives. Chinese Canadians had a saying that "for every foot of railway through the Fraser Canyon, a Chinese worker died." Onderdonk himself estimated that three Chinese died for every kilometre of track that was laid. It is estimated that Chinese labourers saved the CPR $3.5 million. The Canadian government demonstrated its gratitude by making it clear that while the Chinese were desirable as railway workers, they were not wanted as immigrants in the region and nation they were helping build. The Chinese faced the most draconian restrictions on immigration of any ethnic group.

Financial Troubles

Construction costs increased, yet the arduous task of building along the north shore of Lake Superior still lay ahead. This meant blasting through hundreds of kilometres of what Van Horne called "engineering impossibilities"—Precambrian rock. In addition, the company had to buy up eastern lines to connect the Pacific railway with Toronto and Montreal. When the CPR's construction boss was asked about the prospect of not having sufficient funds to complete the project, he replied, "If we haven't got enough, we'll get more." The money did come—from investors, from the sale of stock, and from bank loans. When these sources proved inadequate, however, the company turned to the only remaining source—the government.

By the summer of 1883, the CPR was in trouble. The company needed an estimated $22.5 million—an enormous sum, almost an entire year's revenue for the federal government. Meanwhile, the Conservatives were re-elected in the general election of 1882. Pressed by opposition within his own party against further concessions, Macdonald replied that the CPR might as well ask for the planet Jupiter. But J.H. Pope, Macdonald's secretary, reminded his leader: "The day the Canadian Pacific bursts, the Conservative Party bursts the day after." The prime minister convinced his party to agree to another loan, but only after the CPR agreed to mortgage the entire main line, all the rolling stock, and everything else connected with the railway. The CPR also promised to make the railway even more political. It would provide more political appointees to jobs; secretly it would back several Conservative newspapers; and it would construct a terminus at Quebec City to please French-Canadian voters. The money kept construction going through 1884, but by the end of that year, the company once again teetered on the edge of bankruptcy. The transcontinental, while symbolic of the dream of nation, was in reality a financial disaster.

On the evening of March 26, 1885, George Stephen met with Macdonald to appeal for more government money. The prime minister turned him down. Macdonald knew his party would never agree to another loan. Stephen returned home convinced the railway would, after all, go under. Then, in the morning, came extraordinary news: the Métis of the Saskatchewan region had rebelled under Louis Riel, defeating the North-West Mounted Police in a battle near Duck Lake in the North-West Territories (see Chapter 4). Macdonald's luck saved him once again. The federal government was forced to negotiate with Riel and the Métis in 1870, in part because there was no railway to get troops into the region. The same would not happen again. The North-West Rebellion justified the railway. That day in Parliament, the federal government voted to send troops out on the railway to fight Riel and the Métis. It also introduced a bill to finance the remaining mountain section of the line.

The Last Spike (Nov 7, 1885)

On November 7, 1885, Donald Smith drove in the last spike at Craigellachie, named for a rocky crag in Scotland where he grew up. Despite all the headaches, it was a proud nationalist moment. The American-born Van Horne remarked that "to have built that road would have made a Canadian out of the German Emperor!" He boasted that a train could now make the trip from Montreal to Vancouver in a mere 85 hours, with a first-class ticket costing $123.35 (a railway labourer then earned $2 a day). In 1886, daily mail service was inaugurated across the nation.

The driving of the last spike, November 7, 1885, 9:30 a.m., at Craigellachie, British Columbia. The important CPR financial backer Donald Smith (later Lord Strathcona) holds the heavy spike hammer. Behind Smith stands white-bearded Sandford Fleming, former engineer-in-chief, and to the left is the burly figure of W.C. Van Horne, CPR general manager.

Source: Glenbow Archives, Calgary, Canada/NA-218-3.

Prime Minister Laurier with his secretary, M. Boudrias, in the library of his home in Ottawa, now a national historic site, 1897.

Source: Library and Archives Canada/C-61705.

But the cost of such national pride was high. The Pacific railway cost the Canadian government 10.4 million hectares of the best prairie land, an estimated $63.5 million in public funds, and government loans of $35 million. Yet as a private company it did very well, and by 1905 it had capital worth $228 million. Questions as to whether the project was worth the effort and expense had been answered, in Macdonald's mind, by the beginning of Riel's North-West Rebellion. The CPR allowed for the immediate dispatch of over 3000 troops westward.

Two New Transcontinental Railways

During the economic boom of the Laurier era (1896–1911), Canada added two new transcontinental railways. The first was the Canadian Northern Railway (CNR). Begun by two Ontario-born entrepreneurs, Donald Mann and William Mackenzie, the company built sufficient rail lines in the West and sufficient financial strength by 1901 (through the building of branch lines and the incorporation of rival companies' near-defunct charters, which often included substantial land grants—a policy discontinued during the Laurier era) to expand transcontinentally. The CNR applied for financial assistance from the federal government to build from Port Arthur (now Thunder Bay) to Montreal. The second new transcontinental—the eastern-based Grand Trunk Railway—wanted to build a line westward to profit from prairie grain traffic. The logical solution was for the two companies to cooperate, but each feared that the other would dominate in any joint venture. At the same time, Prime Minister Laurier believed the country could support three transcontinental railways. He assured Parliament: "This is a time for action. The flood tide is upon us that leads on to fortune; if we let it pass it may never recur again."

The Liberals backed the Grand Trunk. They even offered to build the difficult 2880-kilometre-long eastern section of the railway, at government expense, through Ontario and Quebec to Moncton, New Brunswick. This section, known as the National Transcontinental, was leased to the Grand Trunk for fifty years at a modest annual rate of 3 percent on construction costs. The first seven years of operation were rent-free. A new company—the Grand Trunk Pacific (GTP), a subsidiary of the Grand Trunk—built the western section from Winnipeg to the Pacific. The federal government agreed to guarantee 75 percent of the bond money for its construction. Despite such financial support, the line was a failure.

Meanwhile, Mann and Mackenzie went ahead with their transcontinental line, convinced that Ottawa would assist. As a result, in many areas of the West, these competing lines ran parallel to each other and sometimes within sight of one another. As T.D. Regehr notes, "a short distance west of Portage la Prairie, a traveller going north could cross eight parallel east–west lines within the space of 55 km."[2] The Conservative opposition denounced the Liberals' railway-building scheme as a "$200 million vote catcher, designed to carry elections rather than passengers." Ultimately, both lines ended in bankruptcy.

But the two companies added 18,000 kilometres of prairie railway—six times more line than the CPR had when completed in 1885. By 1914, it gave Canada the dubious distinction of having more kilometres of rail line per capita than any other country in the world. The new lines also opened up lucrative mining areas in northern Ontario and Quebec, and provided employment for thousands during the construction and operational phases.

The first Canadian Pacific Railway through-train from the Atlantic to the Pacific arriving in Port Arthur.

Source: Library and Archives Canada/C-014464.

New Inventions and the Onset of Modernity

As industrialization reshaped society in late-nineteenth-century Canada and ushered in an age of "modernity," it also helped unite the country through technological innovations. Due to transportation and communication revolutions, standard notions of space and time were reformulated. In 1884, the first electric telegraph line was built in the United States. Soon other countries, such as Canada, realized the benefits of this new rapid means of communication for business and pleasure. Then in 1876, inventor of the telephone Alexander Graham Bell, at the time a Canadian resident, placed the first "long-distance" call—15 kilometres—between Brantford and Paris, Ontario. Before long, every business and household coveted a telephone.

In the late nineteenth century, the energetic Sandford Fleming, dubbed "the Father of Canadian Communications," turned his attention to building first a transatlantic and then a transpacific underwater cable to link Canada to Britain and to the other British possessions in the Pacific. Then in 1901, Guglielmo Marconi picked up the first wireless signal sent across the Atlantic Ocean by erecting an antenna on Signal Hill in St. John's, Newfoundland. Marconi's Wireless Telegraph Company of Canada, created in 1902, operated a transatlantic radio link between Glace Bay, Nova Scotia, and London, England.

Such rapid means of communication, transportation, and trade heightened the inadequacy and inconsistency of timekeeping methods in each locality. It proved difficult, for example, to create a train schedule in which the time varied from place to place. So railway companies demanded a standardized approach. It was Sanford Fleming who "invented" standard time, by dividing the world into 24 time zones and persuading governments throughout the world to standardize time within their own time zones to ensure conformity and uniformity.

Canada and the Northwest

Immigration into the West constituted the third plank of Macdonald's National Policy. Without a populated West, no justification existed for a transcontinental railway. Without a railway, east–west trade could not occur. And without internal trade, the National Policy of tariff protection was meaningless.

Settlement

In preparation for settlement, the Canadian government surveyed the land into townships similar in size to those in the American West. Each township was 36 square miles (92 square kilometres) and consisted of 36 sections. Each section was 1 square mile (2.6 square kilometres) and contained 640 acres (259 hectares) each. Sections were subdivided into more manageable quarter-sections of 160 acres (65 hectares).

Not all land was available for settlement. The Hudson's Bay Company (HBC) received "one twentieth of the land of the fertile belt" as part of the sale of Rupert's Land to the Canadian government in 1869. In Manitoba, as part of the Manitoba Act of 1870, the Canadian government appropriated 1.5 million acres (600,000 hectares), or one-seventh of the new province, for the benefit of the Métis. The CPR received 25 million acres (10 million hectares), and other railway companies also received land as part of their contracts until the practice ended in 1894. Additional land was set aside for schools. The remaining land belonged to the federal government to sell or to turn over to private land companies to sell. This latter scheme proved disastrous. Most of the 26 colonization companies in existence in 1883 were owned by friends of Macdonald's government and held up to 3 million acres (1.2 million hectares) of land, most of which remained idle either as a result of failed immigration or speculation on the part of the companies that land prices would rise.

To encourage settlement, the government passed the Dominion Lands Act in 1872. Following the American example in settling its West, the Act provided a quarter-section of free land to each head of family or 21-year-old male if he fulfilled certain conditions. He had to pay a $10 registration fee, reside on the land for three years, cultivate 30 acres (12 hectares), and build a permanent dwelling. At the time, conventional wisdom held that a farm of this size could support a family.

While men were offered free land, women's property rights in the West were seriously curtailed. Married women did not qualify for free land under the Dominion Lands Act, and only a few widowed women succeeded in receiving the 160-acre (65-hectare) land grant. In 1886, the government of the North-West Territories abolished a woman's right to the dower—a one-third interest in her husband's property upon widowhood. Western Canadian women protested the dower legislation for over thirty years before it was rescinded in 1917.

A survey of a standard prairie township.

Source: D.G. Kerr, ed., *Historical Atlas of Canada* (Don Mills, ON: Nelson, 1981), p. 62.

Law and Order in the Northwest

To ensure "peaceful" settlement, the federal government established territorial courts and organized the North-West Mounted Police (NWMP) in 1873, establishing what some historians have called the fourth plank of the National Policy. The settlement of the West was proceeding at a disappointingly slow pace, so the NWMP was created and sent into the region as a symbol of Canadian–British law and order. The Canadian government feared an Indian uprising and the wars that were plaguing American settlement. Ottawa also wanted the NWMP to monitor the American border. Whisky traders and wolf hunters were crossing the international boundary at their leisure. The Cypress Hills Massacre— a tragic event that saw a camp of Assiniboines attacked by a group of American wolf hunters allegedly looking for stolen horses in a traditional native sanctuary in what would become southern Saskatchewan—was the last straw in the creation of the NWMP. But the police force was also intended to provide security during the negotiations of the numbered treaties in the Prairie West.

The 300 "Mounties" began their work in the Northwest in 1874 after a long, arduous march across the southern Prairies. They established important posts throughout the region: Fort Walsh in the Cypress Hills, Fort Macleod on the Old Man River, and Fort Calgary at the junction of the Bow and Elbow Rivers. The NWMP administered Canadian law to the Native peoples, curtailed the whisky traders, and assisted the early settlers. By most accounts, the NWMP were remarkably successful. They were generally respected and trusted by the First Nations and the settlers. Perhaps their success can best be measured by their transition into an enduring symbol, albeit mythologized, of the law and order of the Canadian frontier, particularly when juxtaposed against the American "wild west." Their red tunics and white helmets symbolized British over American "blue-coat" law and tradition, a collective as opposed to an individual authority. As the novelist Wallace Stegner pointed out, "One of the most visible aspects of the international border was that it was a colour line: blue below, red above, blue for treachery and unkept promises, red for protection and straight tongue."[3]

NWMP Commissioner James Macleod, standing second from right, with his men at Fort Walsh in the Cypress Hills, in what is now southwestern Saskatchewan, in the late 1870s. Macleod reportedly treated the Native peoples with dignity and respect. The Blackfoot called him "Stamixotokan," or "Bull's Head."

Source: Glenbow Archives, Calgary, Canada/NA-52-1.

Ranching

Ranching became one of the first major occupations in the newly surrendered western lands, with beef the major export. The foothills region and the southern grasslands, with their short grass, numerous coulees and streams to provide water for livestock, and winter winds known as *chinooks* that regularly melted the snow and exposed the grass for winter pasture, proved suitable for cattle ranching.

Initially, ranching existed as a small-scale operation. A few Mounties bought small ranches after their three-year enlistment terms expired. They knew the terrain and lifestyle, and had already established relations with the First Nations. At times, they supplied beef for the NWMP and for Indians' rations in the early 1880s, once the prairie bison herds had been decimated.

By the 1880s, ranching became big business. Wealthy "gentlemen" ranchers from Ontario, Quebec, France, and Britain established large operations—the most famous being the Cochrane Ranch, the North West Cattle Company, the Walrond Ranch, and the Oxley Ranch Company— which monopolized the business. The large ranchers benefited from the coming of the CPR to the southern Prairies in 1883, together with the federal government's embargo on live cattle imports from the United States, and a generous land-lease system that allowed ranchers to lease up to 100,000 acres (40,000 hectares) for twenty-one years at the modest rate of two cents a hectare.

Western Immigration and Settlement

Until the turn of the century, the settlement plank of the National Policy was a failure. As long as free land remained available in the American West, European settlers went south to the warmer climate and the more established frontier. Most new settlers in the West were migrants from Ontario, English-speaking Quebec, and the Maritimes. Being the first to arrive, they became the established commercial and political elite, ensuring that the region became integrated with the rest of the country. While the American West welcomed "desirable" settlers from Europe, those they categorized as "undesirables"—often fleeing persecution and seeking a new home—were willing to take up homesteading in Canada.

Of the limited number of foreign immigrants, the first to arrive were the Mennonites, descendants of the radical Anabaptists of the Reformation era and followers of Menno Simons (1496–1561), a religious leader in the Netherlands. They left their homes in southern Russia (now Ukraine) as a result of the intense Russification policy of the Tsarist government and its introduction of universal military conscription. These policies went against the sect's religious beliefs in pacifism, noninvolvement with government, and a strict interpretation of the Bible. The Canadian government provided travel assistance and a promise that the Mennonites could settle in communal villages, or *strassendorffs*, and enjoy religious freedom as well as exemption from military service. The 7000 Mennonites who arrived in the 1870s settled on two reserves, one southeast and the other southwest of Winnipeg.

In the mid-1870s, 2000 Icelanders left their homeland, with its limited supply of fertile land and declining fishing industry, to settle on the shores of Lake Winnipeg. They named their new western settlement Gimli, meaning "paradise." Floods in 1879 and 1880 forced many to resettle elsewhere in Manitoba or move into the Dakotas. Despite these setbacks, the original settlement prevailed and even began to prosper by the turn of the century.

Selected groups of Jewish immigrants came to western Canada in the 1880s. Sir Alexander Galt, Canada's high commissioner in London, joined the archbishop of Canterbury and several titled English gentlemen in aiding victims of Russia's pogroms (massacres of Jews) and offered the Canadian Prairies as a refuge. The Canadian government encouraged the new settlers to farm, and they established rural farming communities such as New Jerusalem near Moosomin, and Wapella and Hirsh, in Saskatchewan, but few remained in these rural communities. Most chose instead to become small shop owners, merchants, or labourers in urban centres, particularly Winnipeg, Canada's major western city at the turn of the century.

The Mormons were the single largest American group to arrive in western Canada before 1896. Charles Ora Card, a religious leader, entrepreneur, and colonizer from Utah, first led them northward in 1887 to establish farms at Lee's Creek (later renamed Cardston in honour of their leader), Sterling, and Magrath in present-day southern Alberta. The Canadian government encouraged them to settle in the Palliser Triangle area because they had practised dryland farming in Utah. By 1912, some 7000 Mormons lived in Alberta. They built a temple at Cardston, which when completed in 1923 was the only Mormon temple outside of the United States at the time.

The Immigration Boom

Between 1896 and 1914, more than 1 million people immigrated to western Canada in what would be the last great continental land rush, ensuring the success of the third plank of the National Policy. What had changed by 1896 to account for this tremendous influx of immigrants? Both "push" and "pull" factors played a role.

Share of Population by Province, Census Years 1871–1911 (percentage of total)

	1871	1881	1891	1901	1911
Maritimes	20.7	20.1	18.2	16.7	13.0
Prince Edward Island	2.5	2.5	2.3	1.9	1.3
Nova Scotia	10.5	10.2	9.3	8.6	6.8
New Brunswick	7.7	7.4	6.6	6.2	4.9
Quebec	32.3	31.4	30.8	30.7	27.8
Ontario	43.9	44.6	43.7	40.6	35.1
Prairie Provinces	0.7	1.4	3.2	7.9	18.4
Manitoba	0.7	1.4	3.2	4.8	6.4
Saskatchewan	—	—	*	1.7	6.8
Alberta	—	—	*	1.4	5.2
British Columbia	1.0	1.1	2.0	3.3	5.4
Yukon	—	—	—	0.5	0.1
North-West Territories	1.3	1.3	2.0	0.4	0.1

*Included with North-West Territories.

Source: Calculated from M.C. Urquhart and K.A.H. Buckley, eds., *Historical Statistics of Canada* (Toronto: Macmillan, 1965), Series A2-14. Reproduced in Kenneth Norrie and Douglas Owram, *A History of the Canadian Economy*, 2nd ed. (Toronto: Harcourt Brace, 1996), Chapter 16.

The "push" factors varied as widely as the migrants themselves. Many left because of limited prospects in their homeland. The industrial revolution in Europe raised the number of births and lowered the death rate, thus overpopulating the continent. In the countryside, particularly in eastern Europe, farmers divided their relatively poor agricultural land into smaller parcels to provide for their offspring. In Galicia, the northeastern province of the Austro-Hungarian Empire, each peasant family needed about 7 hectares for subsistence, yet most farms were only half that size and some families had to get by on less than a hectare. A new class of landless peasants emerged.

In the European cities, working-class people lived in cramped slum quarters. The Canadian government's promise of 160 acres (65 hectares) of good farmland offered an escape. For the Americans who moved north and the prosperous British immigrants who came on the advice of friends or relatives already in Canada, the move promised adventure and a chance to strike out on their own to become self-sufficient. Many American settlers had already received free homesteads in the United States. They were now able to sell these and move north into Canada where they received more free land.

Others, like the Mennonites, Hutterites, and Doukhobors, sought religious freedom from the oppressive regime of the Russian Tsar. Both Galician Slavs and Jews faced ethnic persecution in the Austro-Hungarian Empire. A large number of Asians came to work on the railroads in British Columbia as contract labourers or simply in search of a better life. Many immigrants were single men ("sojourners") who hoped to make enough money either to return home prosperous or, if they were married, to bring their families to Canada.

The "pull" factors were equally varied, and related to world conditions in general and the Canadian West's attractions in particular. The rapid growth of international trade after 1896 meant jobs. Prosperity increased demand for raw materials, especially food for the growing urban population. Farmers in the West could benefit from a ready market and a high price for Canadian wheat. Increased prosperity also meant declining interest rates and lower freight rates, which in turn resulted in higher profits for exports of Canada's bulky natural resources. Most importantly, Canada benefited from the closing of the American frontier after 1890. After the best land—especially well-watered land—in the American West ceased to be available, the Canadian Prairies became the "last best West."

Improved farming conditions also made the Canadian West attractive. Better strains of wheat such as Marquis—discovered by the Canadian plant breeder Charles Saunders in 1909—matured earlier than Red Fife, thus enabling it to be grown in northern areas of Alberta and Saskatchewan without risk of frost damage. The price of wheat quadrupled between 1901 and 1921. Better machinery such as the chilled-steel plough (introduced from the United States), improved harrows and seed drills, and tractors and threshers also aided western farmers. A steam-thresher could process more in a day than a farmer could by physical labour for an entire season.

Clifford Sifton

Clifford Sifton, an energetic Manitoba politician with a business background and Prime Minister Laurier's minister of the interior, also played a significant role in the western immigration boom. He reorganized the department of the interior and used it as the headquarters for western settlement. Sifton pressured the HBC and the CPR to sell their reserved lands at reasonable rates to prospective settlers. He discontinued the practice of using land grants as incentives to railway promoters. Sifton also simplified the procedure for obtaining a homestead and encouraged settlers to buy up an adjacent section, if available, by allowing them the right to preempt such land (to make an interim claim on it and to purchase it at a reduced rate from the government later on).

Sifton's department produced numerous pamphlets—such as *The Wondrous West*; *Canada: Land of Opportunity*; *Prosperity Follows Settlement*; and *The Last Best West*—that contained glorified descriptions of conditions in the Canadian West. In 1896 alone, the Department of the Interior printed 65,000 pamphlets; four years later, the figure reached 1 million. Brochures were sent out to prospective immigrants in the United States and Europe, in over a dozen languages. As well, the department advertised in thousands of newspapers, arranged for lecture tours and promotional trips for potential settlers (particularly Americans), and offered bonuses to steamship agents based on the number of immigrants they brought to Canada. Sifton's agents targeted mainly young, white, British and American males. When insufficient numbers came, they targeted western and eastern Europeans.

Immigrant Groups

Sifton's promotional campaign reflected the government's desire and intention to shape the new society being created in the West. There was no mistaking this design: the new society was to be white, Anglo-Saxon, and Protestant. Anglo-conformity was to be the model used in assimilating any and all who did not fit the design. In order to achieve this end, Sifton had his own immigration hierarchy with the desirable immigrants on the top and the undesirables on the bottom.

British immigrants came mostly on their own and at their own expense. There were exceptions. The Barr colonists, a group of Londoners who came together under the aegis of Reverend Isaac Barr at the turn of the century, settled in the Lloydminster area on the border between Saskatchewan and Alberta. Also, some 80,000 "Home Children" came to Canada between

1867 and 1924 to work as agricultural and domestic servants. They were organized and sent by child-care organizations in England, the largest being the Barnardo Home. Despite some known incidents of gross neglect and child abuse, the government supported the movement and deemed it successful.

Most British immigrants adjusted relatively easily to Canadian life. They were the "host society" and held hegemonic sway. They did not have to learn a new language or radically different customs, and many were relatively well off. Those who lacked farming experience, however, had a more difficult time adjusting. Some drifted into the booming Prairie towns in search of work; others first learned how to farm as hired hands. But not all British received a warm welcome;

"NOW THEN, ALL TOGETHER"

"Now Then, All Together!" A cartoon in the 1904 Liberal election pamphlet Laurier Does Things *suggests that immigrants—male at least; no women appear—could live together in harmony in western Canada. It was unlikely, however, that a "Frenchman" would want to sing "The Maple Leaf Forever," English Canada's unofficial anthem. The song praises James Wolfe, the English victor at Quebec in 1759.*

Source: Saskatchewan Archives Board R-A 12, 402.

some employment ads read "No English Need Apply." Canadians resented the haughty attitude of upper-class Englishmen in particular, many of whom refused to fit into Canadian society. In addition, the British were often highly urbanized and were deemed lazy and "soft" workers.

American immigrants were high on Sifton's list of desirable settlers, often being preferable even to the British. The majority were of Anglo-Saxon extraction. Because they already spoke English and were usually Protestant, they mixed easily with their Canadian neighbours and participated fully in their new communities. In addition to being culturally desirable, many were experienced farmers. Some sold their farms at home at a high price and bought new ones in Canada at a low price. One Iowa farmer, for example, sold his old homestead for $250 per hectare and bought good land in Manitoba for $18 per hectare. About a third of those coming from the United States were newcomers from Europe, such as Germans and Scandinavians who had initially settled in the American West. As part of the Aryan race, they were also deemed culturally desirable.

But not all Americans were welcome. Canada's immigration policy was shaped by racism and was by no means an "open door." Sifton put considerable importance on the immigrants assimilating into Canadian society; visible minorities were deemed inassimilable. African Americans were at the bottom of the immigration hierarchy. While Canadian agents assured white Americans that the climate of the West was mild and healthy, they warned black Americans of the region's rigorous and severe climate. When a group of well-to-do African Americans from Oklahoma crossed into Canada in 1910 en route to Edmonton, local newspapers warned of an "invasion of Negroes." In the end, the effort to restrict black immigrants succeeded. Between 1901 and 1911, fewer than 1500 African Americans came to Canada, as against hundreds of thousands of other Americans. The nation that congratulated itself for the success of the Underground Railway and aiding slaves during the Civil War closed its doors on further black immigration.

A HISTORICAL PORTRAIT

Robert, a Barnardo Boy

Robert Francis was a "Home Child," one of some 80,000 British boys and girls sent to Canada between 1868 and 1925 to work as agricultural and domestic servants. He belonged to the Barnardo Homes, the largest of the child-care organizations in England, begun by Dr. Thomas Barnardo in 1870 in London's East End to assist waifs, strays, orphans, and street urchins by providing them with a "home." The original Barnardo Home had a sign out front that read: "No destitute child ever refused admission." While in operation, the Barnardo Homes took in over 30,000 destitute children.

Robert was admitted into the home on November 23, 1921, at the age of nine, along with an older brother, Alfred, and a younger brother, Harold. Another brother, Sidney, was old enough to be on his own. Their mother, Emily, had died from pregnancy complications in 1920, and their father, Edward, a brewer's labourer, died a year later from pneumonia. A maiden aunt, Annie, took them in for a brief time, but when she was unable to care for them any longer, they were admitted to the home. They were given the familiar Barnardo uniform of a tunic, a pair of red-striped trousers, and a hat like that of a Salvation Army officer.

From the beginning, Dr. Barnardo had arranged to send his "children" overseas to "the colonies," where he believed they had a better chance at a new life than in the slums of London. Robert had a choice of going to either Canada or Australia, and chose Canada. He and his brother Harold left England on the SS *Melita* on September 18, 1924, with the customary "Barnardo trunk" that contained all of

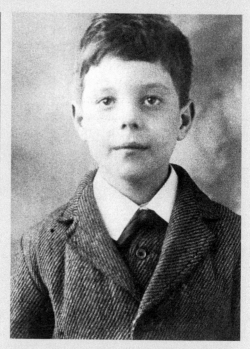

Robert Francis, as a young boy.
Source: R. Douglas Francis.

their earthly possessions; Alfred stayed in England with Sidney. It was the last time the four brothers would see each other.

Upon arrival in Canada, Robert and Harold were sent to the Barnardo's Canadian Office and Distributing Home for Boys in Toronto. From here, they were sent north to Bracebridge to a bush farm in Muskoka, where a widow had requested two boys as farm workers. Like so many Home Children, the boys did not have a good initial experience in Canada. The widow saw them as indentured labourers. They ate separately from the family and slept in an unheated section of the house. They were underfed, and Robert recalled drinking the cow's milk from the bucket before taking it into the house. They attended school but missed many days when needed around the farm. Robert wrote to the officials in Toronto to complain about the harsh conditions, and an inspector came out, but only after informing the widow of his impending visit. Robert recalled that day as the only time they ate with the family and had a scrumptious meal. When the official left, conditions became even more intolerable.

It was customary for employers of Home Children to pay them a wage when they reached the age of fifteen. When Robert turned that age, the widow sent the boys away. They went to the Niagara Peninsula, where a large number of Barnardo boys were located, to assist on the fruit and vegetable farms. Robert's new "home" was a wonderful contrast to his first; the farm owner, Sidney Wright, had been a Barnardo boy himself. Robert was treated as part of the family. When the Depression struck, the family could no longer afford to keep him. He moved to another farm in the area, where once again he was treated as "just a Barnardo boy." He stuck it out until he married a local girl and took over the family farm. The couple had three children and lived in the community for the remainder of their lives.

European Immigrants

The Canadian government had little success in attracting large numbers of western European immigrants. France, for example, had a low birth rate and a well-balanced economy that provided ample work for its population. It also had its own colonies to populate, such as Algeria. Moreover, the French government openly discouraged Canadian immigration agents because it feared a future war with Germany, whose population was almost double that of France.

The Scandinavian countries also restricted emigration, especially of skilled workers. Germany prohibited immigration agents within its borders and fined steamship lines for carrying emigrants. Still, between 1901 and 1911 the German population in the three Prairie provinces increased from 46,844 to 147,638. Many of these immigrants came from German-speaking settlements in eastern Europe rather than directly from Germany. They were sponsored by German Catholic organizations, the most successful being the German-American Land Company, a joint religious–lay venture that established the Saskatchewan colonies of St. Peter and St. Joseph.

To get around these emigration restrictions, Clifford Sifton allowed W.T.R. Preston, Canada's immigration inspector in London, to set up a clandestine organization, the North Atlantic Trading Company, in 1899 to work with European shipping agents to bring western Europeans to Canada. Each agent received a $5 bonus for every healthy man, woman, or child over 12 who was a bona fide farmer, farm worker, domestic servant, or accompanying family member. This illegal scheme ended in 1905 after public outcry against undue profiteering, but not before the company had succeeded in bringing in 50,000 emigrants from western Europe.

Immigrants in "Sheepskin Coats"

Eastern Europeans, or what Sifton called "peasants in sheepskin coats," filled the middle ranks of the immigration hierarchy. While they were not culturally desirable (they did not speak English and were not Protestant), they were at least white. In addition, they fit Sifton's second criterion of being experienced farmers, having settled in the harsh Russian Steppes. Upon coming to the Canadian West, they generally wished to settle together in blocs, and Sifton realized they were unlikely to quit farming for the urban areas. As a result, he encouraged immigrants from eastern Europe, particularly Ukrainians, seeing them as ideal farmers. By World War I, 170,000 Ukrainians had come to Canada from the Austro-Hungarian Empire. They left Ukraine for a variety of reasons, but were attracted to Canada for one main reason—*vilni zemli*, or free land. The first group of 4000 Ukrainians—or Galicians, as the immigration agents called them because they came from the province of Galicia—settled at Star and Josefberg, 65 kilometres east of Edmonton. This forested area assured them an abundant supply of wood, a scarce commodity back home. Soon the tightly knit farming communities grew into villages of timber and whitewashed-clay houses with thatched roofs, and distinctive churches with onion-shaped domes.

Some 7000 Doukhobors (meaning "spirit wrestlers") came from Russia in the late 1890s to escape persecution for their pacifist and anti-tsarist beliefs. Leo Tolstoy, the great Russian novelist, and Peter Kropotkin, a leading Russian anarchist, admired their simple, communal lifestyle and assisted them to emigrate from Russia. James Mavor, a professor of political economy at the University of Toronto and a friend of Kropotkin, helped settle them in Canada. They founded three Saskatchewan colonies—two near Yorkton and another near Saskatoon. They held land collectively, in a special arrangement agreed upon by the Canadian government, and lived in communal villages.

All was peaceful until a radical wing calling itself the Sons of Freedom marched toward Winnipeg in search of Christ and a new earthly paradise, and in expectation of the arrival of their leader, Peter Veregin, recently released from captivity in Russia. The group walked naked through the Doukhobor villages in a quest for a state of purity akin to that of Adam and Eve before the Fall. Public outcry provided an excuse for Frank Oliver, Clifford Sifton's successor as minister of the interior (1905–11), to confiscate half of their Saskatchewan land. He did so on the grounds that the Doukhobors refused to cultivate quarter-sections, to swear allegiance to the Crown, or to register births and deaths. (The federal government had exempted them from these conditions originally.) In protest, 5000 Doukhobors trekked to the Kootenay district near Grand Forks, British Columbia, where Peter Veregin had purchased private land.

Doukhobor women pulling a plough. During their first spring in Canada the Doukhobors had no farm animals. With most of their men away working on railway construction to earn money for the community, the women hitched themselves to the ploughs.

Source: Saskatchewan Archives Board #SPA R-B 1964 (1).

Although Sifton tolerated eastern European immigrants as potentially good farmers, he disdained southern Europeans. He believed them to be migratory labourers who would settle only in urban centres. "I don't want anything done to facilitate Italian immigration," the minister of the interior warned his assistants. As a result, Italian immigrants who did arrive mostly came illegally through the help of *padros*, or employment agents, who worked with the railway companies and business interests to find them work.

Asian Immigrants

Joining black people at the bottom of the list were immigrants from Asia. For reasons of geography, Asian immigration occurred mainly on

The tax certificate for Lau Shong (or Shing), 1912, for $500, the amount required to bring in Chinese immigrants.

Source: Library and Archives Canada/C-96443.

Canada's Pacific Coast. In the 1850s, at the time of the Fraser River gold rush, the first Chinese immigrants, Chang Tsoo and Ah Hong, arrived. They were followed about twenty years later by a small number of Japanese. By 1911, nearly 10 percent of British Columbia's population was Asian. But like black people, "Orientals" were seen as inassimilable, their presence an obstacle to creating the desired Anglo-Saxon society.

The Canadian government went to extreme measures to restrict further Chinese immigration. While free land and transportation was being offered as an incentive to desirable immigrants, Ottawa imposed a head tax on all Chinese immigrants—first of $50 in 1885, which increased to $100 in 1900 and then to $500 by 1903. Still, many paid the tax, enabling Ottawa to collect $4,381,550 in head taxes between 1885 and 1908. The Chinese were welcome to come, work, and die building Canada's railways but they were not welcome to make Canada home. The government was prevented from imposing a similar tax on the Japanese, because Japan was then a military ally of Britain and a major trading partner of the Empire. Instead, the Canadian and Japanese governments agreed to restrict Japanese immigrants to Canada to 400 people a year.

The head tax succeeded in reducing overall Chinese immigration, particularly female immigrants, since many married men could not afford to bring their wives and few single men could pay the tax for single women who might become their wives. Some companies, such as the railways, paid the head tax, or simply brought in Chinese males illegally because they worked hard and for low wages. Asians also worked in mining, land clearing, public works, lumbering, salmon canning, and market gardening.

A few immigrants came from India. As British subjects, they had a special claim for entry into another country within the British Empire. Dr. Sundar Singh spoke for his Sikh community when

Sikh mineworkers at CPR station, Frank, Crow's Nest Pass, Alberta, 1903.
Source: Library and Archives Canada/PA 125112.

he reminded the Empire Club in 1912: "We are subjects of the same Empire." But West Coast citizens generally opposed their entry. In May 1914, the ship the *Komagata Maru* brought nearly 400 Punjabis, mostly Sikhs, to Vancouver. But for two months, port authorities refused them entry. In the end, the Punjabis were forced back to India, amid cries of "White Canada forever" and the refrain of "Rule Britannia."

Nativist Attitudes

Despite government attempts to keep them out, the "foreign" element increased in Canada. With their arrival, concern arose as to their place in society. The dominant model was Anglo-conformity, a hegemonic ideal that pushed the foreign "other" to surrender his or her culture and assimilate into that of the host society. The British elite feared the degradation of its culture should the "foreigners" not be forced to adopt its perceived superior ways.

Such attitudes led to "nativism"—the idea that positive and negative traits are "native" to particular racial groups, so some groups should be given favoured status for immigration over others. At the time, most English Canadians held to the theories of social Darwinism. As Howard Palmer notes, it was based on each group's "physical and cultural distance from London (England) and the degree to which [its] skin pigmentation conformed to Anglo-Saxon white."[4]

Visible minorities faced the most overt discrimination. While many Chinese immigrants were kept out by the head tax and Japanese immigrants by a quota system, those Asians who did enter the country remained marginalized. They were denied the vote in the western provinces, barred from the professions, and subjected to discrimination in housing and in access to public places. They also faced physical persecution. In 1907, for example, the Asiatic Exclusion League of Vancouver led a march of 10,000 people through Chinatown, brandishing sticks, stones, bricks, and bottles, and damaging buildings and assaulting residents. They also entered the Japanese quarter but were pushed out. It took the police four hours to control the crowd. The government responded to the violence by further restricting Asian immigration.

The federal government meanwhile put pressure on First Nations communities to surrender land recently reserved by treaty to make way for immigration and settlement. A number of illegal losses of reserve lands occurred, particularly in the last years of Wilfrid Laurier's Liberal government. Frank Oliver, as Laurier's minister of Indian affairs and minister of the interior, passed a law in 1908 that allowed the government to remove Native people from reserves near towns of more than 8000 residents. Then, in 1911, he amended the Indian Act to allow companies and municipalities to expropriate reserve land for roads, railroads, or other public purposes.

Underlying these attitudes was the desire to create the "ideal" Canadian society. White Anglo-Saxon Canadians believed they were at the pinnacle of human civilization. They sought to create a homogeneous culture based on British-Canadian customs and the English language. They looked to the churches and especially the schools to inculcate these values and one language. Most English Canadians believed that "foreign" immigrants could become Canadians only by abandoning their own customs and language and assimilating.

In September 1907, a mob of 10,000, incited by the Asiatic Exclusion League, invaded Vancouver's Chinatown and then moved into the Japanese quarter of the city. The photo shows the damage to a Japanese Canadian grocery store. The Japanese men pushed back the mob that rushed into their neighbourhood.

Source: William Lyon Mackenzie King Collection/Library and Archives Canada/C-014118.

SUMMARY

By 1914, the era of nation building was complete. It was accomplished with a national economic policy (the National Policy); the completion of the transcontinental Canadian Pacific Railway; and settlement of the West through large-scale immigration. But the remarkably rapid expansion came with its share of growing pains. And while the Fathers of Confederation attempted to paint the national enterprise in suitable and celebratory nationalist colours, within a few years the old divisions and bigotries that had long plagued colonial Canada emerged again, threatening the new nation's fragile unity. Even the national dream of building the transcontinental railway was marred by scandal, racism, and financial problems. In addition, certain groups, classes, and regions of the country felt alienated or neglected. Their discontent contributed to a new era of protest.

NOTES

1. Pierre Berton, *The National Dream* (Toronto: McClelland & Stewart, 1970), p. 363.

2. T.D. Regehr, "Triple Tracking," *Horizon Canada* 7 (1986), p. 1878.

3. Wallace Stegner, *Wolf Willow: A History, a Story, and a Memory of the Lost Plains Frontier* (New York: Viking, 1966), p. 101.

4. Howard Palmer, "Reluctant Hosts: Anglo-Canadian Views of Multiculturalism in the Twentieth Century," in R. Douglas Francis and Donald B. Smith, eds., *Readings in Canadian History: Post-Confederation*, 7th ed. (Toronto: Thomson Nelson, 2006), p. 176.

BIBLIOGRAPHY

The nationalism of the Canada First Movement is discussed in a chapter in F.H. Underhill, *The Image of Confederation* (Toronto: Canadian Broadcasting Corporation, 1964) and in David Gagan, "The Relevance of 'Canada First,'" *Journal of Canadian Studies*, 5 (November 1970): 36–44. See too Carl Berger, *The Sense of Power: Studies in the Ideas of Canadian Imperialism* (Toronto: University of Toronto Press, 1970).

On French-Canadian nationalism in the 1870s, see Jean-Paul Bernard, *Les rouges: Libéralisme, nationalisme et anti-cléricalisme au milieu du XIXe siècle* (Montreal: Presses de l'Université du Québec, 1971); Nive Voisine and Jean Hamelin, eds., *Les ultramontains canadiens-français* (Montreal: Boréal Express, 1985); Arthur Silver, *The French-Canadian Idea of Confederation, 1864–1900*, 2nd ed. (Toronto: University of Toronto Press, 1997); and "The Clerical Offensive" in Susan Mann, *The Dream of Nation: A Social and Intellectual History of Quebec*, 2nd ed. (Montreal/Kingston: McGill-Queen's University Press, 2002), pp. 115–31.

Dale Thomson's *Alexander Mackenzie: Clear Grit* (Toronto: Macmillan, 1960) provides a decent if dated portrait of Canada's second prime minister. On Edward Blake, see Joseph Schull's two-volume biography *Edward Blake: The Man of the Other Way* (Toronto: Macmillan, 1975), and *Edward Blake: Leader in Exile* (Toronto: Macmillan, 1976).

The ideas underlying Canadian liberalism in the 1870s are examined by F.H. Underhill in "The Political Ideas of the Upper Canadian Reformers, 1867–1878," in his *In Search of Canadian Liberalism* (Toronto: Macmillan, 1960), pp. 68–84. On the politics of the Laurier era, see R.C. Brown and R. Cook, *Canada, 1896–1921: A Nation Transformed* (Toronto: McClelland & Stewart, 1974) and three now-dated biographies of Laurier: Joseph Schull, *Laurier: The First Canadian* (Toronto: Macmillan, 1965); Richard Clippendale, *Laurier: His Life and World* (Toronto: McGraw-Hill Ryerson, 1979); and Réal Bélanger, *Wilfrid Laurier: Quand la politique devient passion* (Quebec City: Presses de l'Université Laval, 1986).

On the national policy, see Ben Forster, *A Conjunction of Interests: Business, Politics, and Tariffs, 1825–1879* (Toronto: University of Toronto Press, 1986); R.C. Brown, *Canada's National Policy, 1883–1900: A*

Study in Canadian–American Relations (Princeton, NJ: Princeton University Press, 1964); and John Dales, *The Protective Tariff in Canada's Development* (Toronto: University of Toronto Press, 1966). The *Journal of Canadian Studies*, 14 (Autumn 1979) is devoted to "The National Policy, 1879–1979."

Pierre Berton's two-volume popular study *The National Dream: The Great Railway, 1871–1881* (Toronto: McClelland & Stewart, 1970) and *The Last Spike: The Great Railway, 1881–1885* (Toronto: McClelland & Stewart, 1974) describes the building of the Canadian Pacific Railway. For a less nationalistic view of the railway, see A.A. den Otter, *The Philosophy of Railways: The Transcontinental Railway Idea in British North America* (Toronto: University of Toronto Press, 1997). On the Chinese contribution to the building of the CPR, see Paul Yee, *Building the Railway: The Chinese and the CPR* (Toronto: Umbrella Press, 1999).

On railway building during the Laurier era, consult T.D. Regehr, *The Canadian Northern Railway: Pioneer Road of the Northern Prairies, 1895–1918* (Toronto: Macmillan, 1976) and G.R. Stevens, *Canadian National Railways*, 2 vols. (Toronto: Clarke Irwin, 1960). On the Grand Trunk Pacific, see Frank Leonard, *A Thousand Blunders: The Grand Trunk Pacific Railway and Northern British Columbia* (Vancouver: University of British Columbia Press, 1996). In *The Canadian Pacific Railway and the Development of Western Canada* (Montreal/Kingston: McGill-Queen's University Press, 1989), John A. Eagle examines the CPR's contributions to western Canadian economic growth between 1896 and 1914. On the relationship of railways and government, see Ken Cruikshank, *Close Ties: Railway, Government, and the Board of Railway Commissioners, 1851–1933* (Montreal/Kingston: McGill-Queen's University Press, 1991). Suzanne Zeller's *Inventing Canada: Early Victorian Science and the Idea of a Transcontinental Nation* (Toronto: University of Toronto Press, 1987) examines the role of scientists in shaping the idea of a transcontinental nation.

On the development of the Canadian West in the 1870s and 1880s, see Gerald Friesen, *The Canadian Prairies: A History* (Toronto: University of Toronto Press, 1984). On settlement patterns in the West, see Chester Martin, *"Dominion Lands" Policy*, published in an abridged form (Toronto: Macmillan, 1973). For an account of homesteading, see the essays in David C. Jones and Ian Macpherson, eds., *Building Beyond the Homestead: Rural History on the Prairies* (Calgary: University of Calgary Press, 1985). A detailed study of settlement in one Prairie town is Paul Voisey, *Vulcan: The Making of a Prairie Community* (Toronto: University of Toronto Press, 1988). For a discussion of the North-West Mounted Police see R.C. Macleod, *The North-West Mounted Police and Law Enforcement, 1873–1905* (Toronto: University of Toronto Press, 1976). William Baker has edited a collection of articles on the early NWMP in *The Mounted Police and Prairie Society, 1873–1919* (Regina: Canadian Plains Research Center, 1998). On ranching, see David Breen, *The Canadian Prairie West and the Ranching Frontier, 1874–1924* (Toronto: University of Toronto Press, 1983); Warren Elofson, *Cowboys, Gentlemen and Cattle Thieves* (Montreal/Kingston: McGill-Queen's University Press, 2000); Elofson's *Frontier Cattle Ranching in the Land and Times of Charlie Russell* (Montreal/Kingston: McGill-Queen's University Press, 2004); and Simon Evans, Sarah Carter, and Bill Yeo, eds., *Cowboys, Ranchers and the Cattle Business: Cross-Border Perspectives on Ranching History* (Calgary: University of Calgary Press, 2000).

Overviews of immigration to western Canada are available in R.C. Brown and R. Cook's chapter "Opening Up the Land of Opportunity," in *Canada, 1896–1921: A Nation Transformed* (Toronto: McClelland & Stewart, 1974); Gerald Friesen's *The Canadian Prairies: A History* (cited above); and the relevant chapters in Ninette Kelley and Michael Trebilcock, *The Making of the Mosaic: A History of Canadian Immigration Policy* (Toronto: University of Toronto Press, 1998).

On immigration to western Canada in the pre-1896 era, see Frances Swyripa, *Storied Landscapes: Ethno-Religious Identity and the Canadian Prairies* (Winnipeg: University of Manioba Press, 2010) and Norman Macdonald, *Canada: Immigration and Colonization, 1841–1903* (Toronto: Macmillan, 1966). For social histories of specific immigrant groups during the western immigration boom, see Robert Painchaud *Un rêve français dans le peuplement de la Prairie* (Saint-Boniface, MB: Éditions des Plaines, 1987); Royden K. Loewen, *Family, Church, and Market: A Mennonite Community in the Old and the New Worlds, 1850–1930* (Toronto: University of Toronto Press, 1993); John C. Lehr, *Community and Frontier: A Ukrainian Settlement in the Canadian Parkland* (Winnipeg: University of Manitoba Press, 2011); and Ryan Eyford, *White Settler Reserve: New Iceland and the Colonization of the Canadian West* (Vancouver:

UBC Press, 2016). Clifford Sifton's role in promoting immigration to the West is examined in D.J. Hall's two-volume biography *Clifford Sifton*, vol. 1, *The Young Napoleon, 1861–1900* (Vancouver: University of British Columbia Press, 1981) and vol. 2, *The Lonely Eminence, 1901–1929* (Vancouver: University of British Columbia Press, 1985). To explore the role that immigrant agents played, consult Angelika Sauer "A Weak Woman Standing Alone: Home, Nation and Gender in the Work of German-Canadian Immigration Agent Elise von Koerber, 1872–1884," in *Beyond the Nation? Immigrants' Local Lives in Transnational Cultures*, ed. Alexander Freund (Toronto: University of Toronto Press, 2011), 137–162.

The immigration of British Home Children is the subject of Joy Parr's *Labouring Children: British Immigrant Apprentices to Canada, 1869–1924* (Montreal/Kingston: McGill-Queen's University Press, 1980) and Kenneth Bagnell's *The Little Immigrants: The Orphans Who Came to Canada*, rev. ed. (Toronto: Dundurn Press, 2002). On American farmers' immigration to western Canada, see Carl Bicha, *The American Farmer and the Canadian West, 1896–1914* (Lawrence, KS: Coronado Press, 1968) and Harold Troper, *Only Farmers Need Apply* (Toronto: Griffin House, 1972). European immigration more generally is discussed in Donald Avery, *"Dangerous Foreigners": European Immigrant Workers and Labour Radicalism in Canada, 1896–1932* (Toronto: McClelland & Stewart, 1979).

Black immigration to western Canada is covered in Robin Winks, *The Blacks in Canada: A History*, 2nd ed. (Montreal/Kingston: McGill-Queen's University Press, 1997) and Sharon Hepburn, *Crossing the Border: A Free Black Community in* Canada (Urbana: University of Illinois Press, 2007). On Asian immigration to British Columbia in the pre–World War I era, see Peter Ward, *White Canada Forever: Popular Attitudes and Public Policy Toward Orientals in British Columbia*, 3rd ed. (Montreal/Kingston: McGill-Queen's University Press, 2002); Patricia Roy, *A White Man's Province: British Columbia Politicians and Chinese and Japanese Immigrants, 1885–1914* (Vancouver: University of British Columbia Press, 1989); and Hugh Johnston, *The Voyage of the Komagata Maru: The Sikh Challenge to Canada's Colour Bar* (Delhi: Oxford University Press, 1979).

Historians have recently moved away from focusing exclusively on the racism Asian immigrants encountered. Instead, they explore how Asian immigrants challenged Canadian racism through transnational ties to the pacific world, political activism, and religion. See Lisa Rose Mar, *Brokering Belonging: Chinese in Canada's Exclusion Era, 1885–1945* (Toronto: University of Toronto Press, 2011); Timothy J. Stanley, *Contesting White Supremacy: School Segregation, Anti-Racism, and the Making of Chinese Canadians* (Vancouver: UBC Press, 2011); Kornel Chang, *Pacific Connections: The Making of the U.S.–Canadian Borderlands* (Berkeley: University of California Press, 2012); Alison R. Marshall, *The Way of the Bachelor: Early Chinese Settlement in Manitoba* (Vancouver: UBC Press, 2011); and *Cultivating Connections: The Making of Chinese Prairie Canada* (Vancouver: UBC Press, 2014). On nativist attitudes and the creation of racial hierarchies, see Howard Palmer, *Patterns of Prejudice: A History of Nativism in Alberta* (Toronto: McClelland & Stewart, 1982) and Renisa Mawani, *Colonial Proximities: Crossracial Encounters and Juridical Truths in British Columbia, 1871–1921* (Vancouver: UBC Press, 2010).

Chapter Four

THE FRAGILE UNION

TIME LINE

1872	Oliver Mowat elected Liberal premier of Ontario
1885	North-West Rebellion occurs; Louis Riel is executed
1886	Parti national wins office in Quebec under Honoré Mercier
1887	First interprovincial premiers' conference held Conservatives re-elected under John A. Macdonald
1888	Jesuits' Estates Act passed in Quebec
1889	Manitoba Schools Question begins
1891	Conservatives re-elected under John A. Macdonald John A. Macdonald dies
1896	Liberals win federal election under Wilfrid Laurier
1897	Laurier–Greenway compromise ends Manitoba Schools Question
1900	Liberals re-elected under Wilfrid Laurier
1904	Liberals re-elected under Wilfrid Laurier
1905	Autonomy Bills passed; Saskatchewan and Alberta become provinces

"We have come to a period in the history of this country," Liberal leader Wilfrid Laurier wrote in the early 1890s, "when premature dissolution seems to be at hand." The outcome of the experiment in nation building was still very much in doubt. Bickering between Ottawa and the dominion's seven provinces was endemic. A provincial-rights movement emerged to challenge the centralist domination of the federal government; secessionist sentiments resurfaced in Nova Scotia; and the Northwest was the site of a second and much more serious resistance, this time in the form of the Riel Rebellion of 1885. In Quebec, French–English and Catholic–Protestant antagonism resurfaced, both in reaction to the execution of Louis Riel and in the course of the debate concerning the Jesuits' Estates Act and Manitoba's denominational schools. To make matters worse, these divisions threatening the fragile unity of the new nation were set against the backdrop of a deep economic recession, resulting in 1 million people leaving for the United States in the 1880s.

The Provincial-Rights Movement

During the negotiations leading to Confederation, John A. Macdonald sought a union with a strong central government. While his desire for a legislative union was resisted, after 1867 Macdonald proceeded to act as prime minister of a centralist federation regardless. The quest to consolidate and expand the nation explains, perhaps even justifies, the powerful centralist federation that emerged, but Macdonald also advanced his cause through such extraordinary powers as disallowance, the right granted to the federal government in the BNA Act to disallow any provincial law considered to conflict with federal law. (Disallowance was used 96 times between 1867 and 1920.) It is debatable whether the form of federalism that came to govern Canada reflected the original designs of Confederation. It fell to the most affluent provinces to resist Ottawa's temptations to centralize power.

Oliver Mowat, one of the Fathers of Confederation and Liberal premier of Ontario from 1872 to 1896, led the provincial-rights movement. He endorsed the provincial-compact theory—a belief that Confederation constituted a compact among the provinces and one that could be altered only with their consent. The British North America Act set out the jurisdictions of the two levels of government but there were many grey areas. Dominion–provincial relations became a quagmire that frustrated many a politician in Canada for decades to come.

The Ontario Boundary Dispute

One such issue was the location of the boundary line between Ontario and Manitoba. The origins of the boundary dispute dated back to pre-Confederation days. The British had never established a precise boundary line between Rupert's Land and the colony of Upper Canada. As premier, Mowat argued that Ontario's western boundary should run due north from the source of the Mississippi River, which was slightly west of Lake of the Woods at a place called Rat Portage (present-day Kenora). He referred to western explorations during the French regime to justify his claim. In contrast, Manitoba governments believed that the boundary should be drawn near Port Arthur on Lake Superior. Macdonald's federal Conservative government (which had "created" Manitoba in 1870) waded into the provincial controversy by opposing Mowat's position. It was no coincidence that Mowat led a Liberal government and that the two men were political foes. Macdonald wanted to restrict Ontario's size to lessen its influence in Confederation.

The issue remained unresolved when the federal Liberals under Alexander Mackenzie came to power in 1874. The following year, the two Liberal governments agreed to establish an arbitration board, which ruled in favour of Ontario. But before the board's decision became law, the federal Liberals were defeated in 1878 and the newly elected Conservatives refused to ratify the

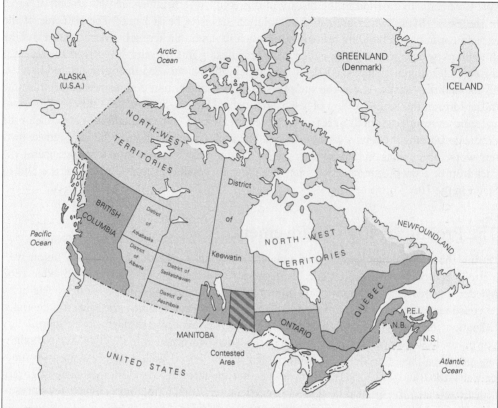

For years, the Canadian, Ontario, and Manitoba governments fought over the boundary line between Ontario and Manitoba. This map of Canada in 1882 shows the contested area.

Source: Based on information taken from National Topographic System map sheet no. MCR 2306. © 1969, Her Majesty the Queen in Right of Canada with permission of Energy, Mines and Resources Canada.

arbitrators' award. Instead, in 1881 Macdonald unilaterally awarded the disputed territory—from Lake of the Woods eastward to Thunder Bay—to Manitoba. Since the federal government maintained control of Manitoba's natural resources, it was in a position to control the land and the mineral rights. The prime minister granted timber rights to logging companies in the disputed area.

After two years of legal chaos, both governments agreed to submit the issue to the Judicial Committee of the Privy Council in London, the supreme legal authority in the British Empire. Mowat himself pleaded Ontario's case, and won. In 1884 the Judicial Committee fixed the western limits of Ontario at the northwest angle of Lake of the Woods (the present boundary). Still Prime Minister Macdonald delayed. Not until 1889 did the federal government confirm Ontario's boundaries and its right to the natural resources within the disputed territory.

Powers of the Lieutenant Governor and Federal Disallowance

Premier Mowat also won a series of victories in other disputes with the federal government, notably over the powers of the lieutenant governor (the Crown's representative in the province) and the federal power of disallowance. According to the BNA Act, the federal government appointed lieutenant governors, paid their salaries, and had the right to dismiss them at any time. The lieutenant governors had the power to reserve provincial legislation so the Crown could test its validity. At the time of Confederation, Macdonald hoped this influence would keep provincial policies in harmony with national objectives.

Mowat argued that the lieutenant governor had the same position in the province as the governor general had in the federal government. In his view, the provinces coordinated sovereignties on a par with the federal government on constitutional matters. He viewed Macdonald's ploy as an attempt by Ottawa to dominate the provinces. Once again the Judicial Committee of the Privy Council upheld Mowat's position. In its ruling of 1892, it declared that a lieutenant governor "is as much the representative of Her Majesty, for all purposes of provincial government, as the Governor General himself for all purposes of the Dominion Government."

The Ontario premier advanced provincial interests on yet another front. While perhaps seeming minor, this issue went to the very heart of federalism—jurisdictional control. Mowat argued that the provinces had certain legal powers before Confederation that they retained after 1867; one was the right to issue liquor licences. In 1884 the Ontario government passed the Act Respecting Licensing Duties, which the federal government immediately disallowed. Ontario took the dispute to court in the case of *Hodge v. the Queen*. The Judicial Committee sustained Ontario's position, deciding that the provinces had full authority in their own realm of legal jurisdiction. Thus, by 1896 and the end of Conservative rule, Mowat had succeeded in strengthening provincial powers and Ontario's rights, at the expense of the federal government. But Mowat's victories rang hollow. In the era of rapid nation building, Macdonald succeeded in strengthening Ottawa's powers in other ways. The strength of the provincial-rights movement ebbed and flowed during the first half of the twentieth century, but federal power increased steadily.

Protest in Atlantic Canada

Mowat was not alone in his struggle for provincial rights. The Ontario premier found ready allies in Atlantic Canada. The anti-confederate sentiments of the mid-1860s re-emerged in the 1880s as Maritimers protested their perceived inferior position in the new dominion. The custom, for example, of flying flags at half-mast on July 1, which first began in 1867, continued in many Atlantic communities. The dream of nation stirred powerful emotions but expansion westward also further diminished the national influence of the Atlantic provinces. It was difficult to argue that the National Policy was designed to aid the Maritimes.

The Maritimes faced difficult economic times in the 1880s. The Conservatives' high protective tariff of 1879 contributed to regional dissatisfaction. Fish and lobster exports dropped a staggering 75 percent in the early 1880s when the United States raised import duties on Maritime fish in response to the high Canadian tariff. Shipbuilding declined, as iron steamers replaced wooden sailing ships. Yarmouth, for example, once a thriving centre of Nova Scotia's shipbuilding industry, built only six vessels in 1880, four in 1884, and none in 1887. Many Maritimers left in search of jobs elsewhere.

Secession Threats in Nova Scotia

From 1878 to 1884, Nova Scotia's Conservative government asked Ottawa for financial assistance. But Prime Minister Macdonald's top priority remained the CPR and the development of the West. The unwillingness of Ottawa to help contributed to the Liberals' provincial victory in 1884 on a wave of anti-confederate sentiment. W.S. Fielding, the new Liberal premier, also attempted to extract larger subsidies from Ottawa. When he proved no more successful than his Conservative predecessor, he introduced a secessionist resolution in the Nova Scotia legislature in 1886. The premier appealed to the other Maritime provinces to secede as well and to create an independent Maritime nation.

The other two provinces declined. New Brunswick saw Nova Scotia's offer of Maritime union as a ploy to benefit Halifax. Also, New Brunswick had just received federal financial support for a rail line to Saint John. Prince Edward Island feared the loss of its autonomy in a Maritime union. Fielding himself retreated because, despite winning 29 of the 39 seats in the provincial election of 1886, he sensed insufficient support for separation within the province. At the same time, his pressure tactics worked: the federal Conservative government lowered freight rates and offered generous financial assistance for railway building in the province.

Newfoundland Considers Joining Confederation

In Newfoundland, major economic changes in the late nineteenth century led to renewed interest in union with Canada. The fishing industry, which by 1885 employed nine out of ten of the island's workforce and accounted for nearly all of its exports, experienced a serious slump. Between the early 1880s and the late 1890s, industry earnings fell by a third as a result of decreased exports to the United States and increased competition from other fishing nations such as Norway, Denmark, and France.

The Newfoundland government successfully negotiated a reciprocity agreement with the United States in 1890, only to have the Colonial Office in Britain veto it. The Colonial Office acted on advice from the Canadian government claiming that, if ratified, the agreement would hurt the fishing industry within the Maritimes.

Newfoundland was experiencing other financial troubles as well. In 1894, the colony suffered a bank crash. A year later the Newfoundland government defaulted on interest payments on its loans. Premier Whiteway approached the Canadian government about discussing terms of union. But this time, the Canadians rejected the offer. Even though Ottawa had offered terms to Newfoundland only a few years earlier, by 1895 the political climate had changed. John A. Macdonald had died in 1891 and the current prime minister, Mackenzie Bowell, feared that better terms for Newfoundland would lead to appeals from other provinces for better terms. Nevertheless, there was little enthusiasm on the island for union. Canada had just scuttled Newfoundland's reciprocity negotiations with the United States. Discussions broke down and Newfoundland would wait another half-century before joining Confederation.

Discontent in the Northwest

By the mid-1880s the federal government was again facing problems in the West. Settlers in Manitoba who came prior to 1870 compiled a list of grievances, including demands for a land grant similar to the one received by the Métis in the Manitoba Act. They complained of problems with federal homesteading policies, as well as high transportation costs to get their goods to market. In particular, settlers complained that the lack of transportation competition in the West kept freight rates artificially high. They paid more to ship their goods than did central or eastern Canadians because the monopoly clause that prohibited competitive lines for twenty years after the completion of the CPR gave the railway free rein to charge exorbitant rates.

The Manitoba government responded by chartering competitive rail lines to the American border. The Macdonald government disallowed these provincial charters on the grounds that they were not in the "national interest." The new Liberal premier, Thomas Greenway, then began building a railway from Winnipeg south to Emerson to connect with American lines. He warned Ottawa that if federal politicians opposed it, he would solicit American financial—and, if need be, military—support. The Macdonald government gave in and bought out the CPR monopoly. Two planks of the National Policy—tariffs and railways—were major causes of discontent in Manitoba.

But a much more serious threat was emerging further northwest. The First Nations, particularly the Cree in the Treaty Six area (which is now central Alberta and Saskatchewan), felt betrayed by the federal government's failure to keep its treaty promises of providing food rations in times of scarcity. The bison had disappeared and the government had inserted the "famine clause" in Treaty Six in 1876. Despite its promise, however, the debt-ridden federal government did little, aside from supplying insufficient amounts of poor-quality food. The Cree also resented the government's refusal to allow them to choose their own reserve lands, as promised in the treaty. Fearing an Indian uprising, the government prevented the establishment of large concentrations of reserves in the Cypress Hills area (a traditional sanctuary) and then around Battleford (the capital of the Northwest). With the decline of the bison, the move onto reserves, and the spread of disease, the First Nations were sick and starving. Not surprisingly, they were reaching the point of desperation and the warrior societies were stirring for action.

The Métis in the region were also frustrated and angry. They resented Ottawa's failure to act on their land claims. After the Red River Resistance of 1869–70, many of the Manitoba Métis moved farther into the Northwest to the South Saskatchewan River Valley, in the area of St. Laurent and Batoche. Here, they established their traditional lifestyles based around the river lot and the buffalo hunt. Other Métis moved onto the southern Prairies, to the area of the Qu'Appelle Valley. Inevitably, however, their livelihoods were threatened as white settlers moved in.

The Métis in the Saskatchewan River Valley appealed to the federal government to provide them a land grant as their brethren in Manitoba had received, recognize their land claims, and allow them to keep their river-lot system instead of making them conform to the rectangular township plan imposed elsewhere in the territories. Macdonald had been forced to negotiate with Louis Riel and the Métis in 1869–70. The prime minister had been pressured into accepting Riel's demands and providing the Métis a land grant and Red River provincial status. With the Northwest firmly in Canadian control, the transcontinental railway nearing completion, and the Treaties signed, the federal government's position was now very different. By the end of 1884, Ottawa had still not responded to the petitions of the Métis.

Many of the white settlers in Prince Albert, northeast of Batoche, were also discontented. The CPR's decision to reroute the railway through the southern region was a devastating blow that left them hundreds of kilometres away from a rail link to eastern markets. As well, the settlers demanded an elected assembly for the Northwest Territories and representation in the federal Parliament.

The Return of Louis Riel

In June 1884, a group of Métis (led by Gabriel Dumont) from the St. Laurent area rode south to Montana on horseback to ask Louis Riel to return and again lead his people against the Canadian government. To Dumont and the Métis, the issues to be addressed were generally the same as in 1870 in Manitoba. They hoped for a similarly successful result. But much had changed in the intervening fifteen years.

The Métis (both French and English mixed-bloods) welcomed back Louis Riel to lead their protest. But Riel had undergone significant changes since 1870. He had been forced to flee the Manitoba he helped create, and despite being elected as a Member of Parliament for the new province in 1873 and 1874, he was banished from Canada for five years for his part in the execution of Thomas Scott. He became an American citizen and a school teacher in Montana, married, and had a family.

Gabriel Dumont was among the Métis who travelled northwest following the Red River Resistance. He was a skilled marksman, rider, and leader of the buffalo hunt in the South Saskatchewan River Valley, and he petitioned Ottawa to take action on Métis land claims. Dumont was among the group that rode down to Montana to ask Riel to return and lead his people. During the 1885 Rebellion, he became the military leader of the Métis. When Riel surrendered, Dumont escaped to the United States. He is seen here in a portrait by Orlando Scott Goff.

Source: Glenbow Archives, Calgary, Canada/NA-1177-1.

Riel remained active in politics during this fifteen-year period but he suffered psychologically. He suffered a nervous breakdown in the late 1870s and was hospitalized (against his wishes) in two mental asylums in Beauport, Quebec. Riel's religious thinking also changed during these years, or at least became more extreme. He had always been a devout Catholic but his religion increasingly became entwined with his political mission to lead the Métis. Riel came to believe that God appointed him "prophet of the New World," responsible for creating a reformed Roman Catholic state on the Prairies. Indeed, he believed that western Canada was the ideal location to establish a new Vatican. When Dumont arrived in Montana, Riel was convinced that it was part of God's plan.

The North-West Rebellion of 1885

Upon returning to the Northwest in 1884, Riel attempted to follow the same strategy as when he successfully led the resistance in 1869–70. The Métis petitioned Ottawa on December 16, 1884, to ask for more generous treatment for the First Nations, a land grant for the mixed-bloods, responsible government for the North-West Territories, western representation in Ottawa, a reduction of the tariff, and the construction of a railway to Hudson Bay as an alternative to the CPR. The federal government acknowledged receipt of the petition and promised to appoint a commission to investigate problems in the Northwest. Early in 1885, the Macdonald government finally took action on the growing discontent by setting up the Half-Breed Commission to settle the land claims (in the area not covered by the Manitoba Act) put forward by the Métis. But it was too late.

Subsequently in mid-March, Riel continued to follow the Red River precedent. He established a provisional government with himself as president and Gabriel Dumont as adjutant general. But the Métis leader underestimated just how much the situation had changed in fifteen years. In 1885, a federal police force—the NWMP—existed in the North-West Territories; hundreds of settlers had

The University of Toronto's "K" Company, Queen's Own Rifles, shown immediately after their return from the Northwest, by the doorway of University College. A grateful university honoured its undergraduate soldiers by exempting them from their annual examination and automatically giving them their academic year.

Source: University of Toronto Archives/A73-0093-002 (39).

moved in; a newly completed railway linked the region to central Canada; and there was no fear of American annexation. Prime Minister Macdonald was not under the same pressure to negotiate. Moreover, the Métis were quickly becoming isolated. The white settlers in Prince Albert soon broke their informal alliance with Riel. The Cree leaders, despite the suffering of their people, realized the inevitable results of joining the Métis: they would be blamed and ultimately punished. The recent and tragic example of Sitting Bull and the Sioux in the United States loomed large. Influential Cree chiefs such as Poundmaker and Big Bear attempted to pacify their young warriors and avoid taking active part in the resistance. To make matters worse, Riel's unorthodox religious views lost him the support of the Catholic Church and the sympathy of Quebec. He was denounced as a heretic.

WHERE HISTORIANS DISAGREE

Louis Riel and the Métis

Few topics in Canadian history have led to as much disagreement among historians as Louis Riel and the Métis. The issues go to the very core of Canadian identity. Early English-Canadian historians blamed the North-West Rebellion of 1885 on one man: the traitor Louis Riel. The rebel leader incited violence and rebellion against the new Dominion of Canada and the British Empire; his actions and his religious delusions were condemned as those of a lunatic. In 1905, R.G. MacBeth wrote that "rebellion was rampant with a madman at its head."[1] In contrast, French-Canadian writers portrayed Riel as a French Catholic martyr who suffered at the hands of Anglo-Saxon bigotry.[2] Both groups portrayed Riel and the Rebellion in the context of the antagonism between English and French, Protestant and Catholic. The Aboriginal perspective was ignored.

Canadian historiography took a new turn in the 1930s and 1940s. Influenced in part by the "frontier thesis" (already well established in American historiography by Frederick Jackson Turner), some historians perceived the Métis as frontier hunters and nomads who opposed the advancing frontier of a different cultural group. George F.G. Stanley portrayed the

rebellion of 1885 as a clash between "primitive and civilized peoples."[3] French ethnologist Marcel Giraud[4] also subscribed to this cultural-conflict thesis, while Lionel Groulx maintained the French-Canadian position that Riel's treatment reflected bigotry against Catholics.[5]

In the 1950s, historian W.L. Morton rejected "frontierism" and presented the Métis as the founders of the pluralistic tradition in the West.[6] They embodied French and English, Catholic and Protestant, Aboriginal and white. The Riel Resistance and 1885 Rebellion were also chapters in the story of western alienation. By 1885, the Métis formed part of a larger western Canadian society that felt aggrieved by the indifference of Ottawa to regional concerns. The Rebellion was therefore more than a Métis uprising incited by one man; it was a resistance by the people of the Northwest, including, at least initially, the First Nations, Roman Catholic clergy, and white settlers in addition to the Métis. It was the first of a series of western protest movements against central Canada in general, and the federal government in particular, for their failure to address western complaints. By the 1960s, writing was increasingly critical of nineteenth-century Anglo-Canadian expansionist policy and those orchestrating it, such as John A. Macdonald.

By the 1970s and 1980s, Stanley's "civilization–savagery" theory was challenged and replaced by more sophisticated interpretations. According to Emma Laroque, the issue for the Métis "was not some great, psychosocietal, static conflict between a supposed savagery versus civilization, but rather colonization and eventual powerlessness."[7] For writers such as George Woodcock, Dumont and Riel were heroes fighting against the odds to defend their people against a greedy, racist, and distant government.[8]

In 1985, while preparing a work on the centennial of the Rebellion, political scientist Thomas Flanagan questioned whether the Métis were forced into rebellion. Flanagan reversed his earlier, more positive interpretation of Riel as a messianic leader. The result was a controversial work that was critical of Riel and supportive of Macdonald's government. Flanagan claimed that "the Métis grievances were at least partly of their own making; that the government was on the verge of resolving them when the Rebellion broke out; that Riel's resort to arms could not be explained by the failure of constitutional agitation." Flanagan did not exonerate Ottawa completely but claimed that the government's mistakes were "in judgment, not part of a calculated campaign to destroy the Métis or deprive them of their rights."[9] Riel acted as much out of self-interest as for his people. As a result, the Rebellion was not justified and Riel got what he deserved.

D.N. Sprague challenged Flanagan's assertion that the government acted fairly. He argued that Métis grievances over land claims in Manitoba during and after the resistance of 1869–70 continued to poison Métis–Ottawa relations in Saskatchewan, where so many Métis had fled when the situation in Manitoba became intolerable. According to Sprague, the federal government deliberately provoked Riel into forming a second provisional government so that he could be accused of treason.[10] By the 1990s both Flanagan and Sprague were working as expert witnesses in court cases over land claims in Manitoba between the federal government and the Métis.

The debate gradually shifted away from Riel and to the Métis. This shift in perspective led to the study of Métis society in an effort to explain what conditions prevailed within the community that caused its members to follow Riel into rebellion. Historians followed the lead of First Nations historians by arguing that the Métis exercised agency. They were not helpless victims caught up in the inexorable march of "civilization." Gerhard Ens argues that the economy and society of the Red River Métis underwent dramatic change between 1840 and 1890—from being pre-capitalist and "subsistence" to a dynamic capitalist market economy, based on the buffalo-robe trade, in the North-West Territories. The Métis proved remarkably resilient at adapting to new economic conditions. The result was out-migration from the Red River colony well before 1870. In other words, the Métis were not simply forced out by the incoming Ontario settlers. Ens maintains that migration after 1870 was part of this earlier trend as economic opportunities for the Métis in Manitoba continued to decline, along with the added economic difficulties experienced as a result of the incoming settlers.[11] But it did not occur because of actions taken by the Canadian government that stripped the Métis of their lands.

Since the 1990s, the tenor of this heated debate has cooled. Some historians have criticized Riel for seeking to manipulate the First Nations in order to gain their support during the Rebellion.[12] Historians are also seeking to shift the focus away from Riel and the events in both Red River and the Northwest (what they term "Red River myopia") and to shed light on Métis communities across Canada. Historians such as Jennifer Brown, Karl Hele, David McNab, Nicole St-Onge, Heather Devine, and Brenda Macdougall use gender, ethnicity, race, and family as tools to highlight the fact that there is more to Métis history than resistance and rebellion.[13]

Yet, as J.M. Bumsted points out, despite the fact that more biographical work has been written on Louis Riel than on any other Canadian figure, he remains the most enigmatic historical figure in Canada. According to Jennifer Reid, "from the earliest works about Riel, there has been a tendency among writers to see in him some reflection of their own cultural values and agendas."[14]

---

1   R.G. MacBeth, *The Making of the Canadian West* (Toronto: W. Biggs, 1905), p. 144.

2   Jennifer Reid, *Louis Riel and the Creation of Modern Canada: Mythic Discourse and the Post-Colonial State* (Winnipeg: University of Manitoba Press, 2012), pp. 33–56.

3   George F.G. Stanley, *The Birth of Western Canada* (London: Longmans, Green, 1936), p. vii.

4   Marcel Giraud, *The Métis in the Canadian West.* 2 Volumes. (1945) Translated by George Woodcock. (Edmonton: University of Alberta Press, 1986).

5   Lionel Groulx, *Louis Riel et les événements de la Rivière-Rouge en 1869–1870,* (Montréal: les Éditions de l'Action nationale, 1944).

6   W.L. Morton, *Manitoba: A History* (Toronto: University of Toronto Press, 1957).

7   Emma Laroque, "The Métis in English Canadian Literature," *The Canadian Journal of Native Studies,* 3(1) (1983): 88.

8   George Woodcock, *Gabriel Dumont: The Métis Chief and His Lost World* (Edmonton: Hurtig, 1975).

9   Thomas Flanagan, *Riel and the Rebellion: 1885 Reconsidered* (Saskatoon: Western Producer Prairie Books, 1983), pp. 146, 147.

10   D.N. Sprague, *Canada and the Métis, 1869–1885* (Waterloo, ON: Wilfrid Laurier University Press, 1988).

11   Gerhard Ens, *Homeland to Hinterland: The Changing Worlds of the Red River Métis in the Nineteenth Century* (Toronto: University of Toronto Press, 1996), p. 170.

12   Blair Stonechild and Bill Waiser, *Loyal Till Death: Indians and the North-West Rebellion* (Calgary: Fifth House Ltd., 1997).

13   Jacqueline Peterson and Jennifer S.H. Brown, *The New Peoples: Being and Becoming Métis in North America* (Winnipeg: University of Manitoba Press, 1985); Karl Hele, "Manipulating Identity: The Sault Borderlands Métis and Colonial Invervention," in Ute Lischke and David T. McNab, eds., *The Long Journey of a Forgotten People: Métis Identities & Family Histories* (Waterloo, ON: Wilfrid Laurier University Press, 2007); Nicole St-Onge, *Saint-Laurent, Manitoba: Evolving Métis Identities, 1850–1914* (Regina: Canadian Plains Research Center, 2004); Heather Devine, *The People Who Own Themselves: Aboriginal Ethnogenesis in a Canadian Family, 1660–1900* (Calgary: University of Calgary Press, 2004); Brenda Macdougall, *One of the Family: Metis Culture in Nineteenth-Century Northwestern Saskatchewan* (Vancouver: UBC Press, 2010).

14   Reid, p. 47.

The Military Campaign

Riel and his provisional government continued to follow the path set in Red River fifteen years earlier. This entailed securing the local fort as the military, administrative, and supply centre. The problem, however, was that Fort Carleton was also the base of the local North-West Mounted Police detachment. Riel demanded that Leif Crozier, NWMP commander, surrender the fort. Crozier refused and dispatched fifteen Mounties and seven settler-volunteers to get supplies from the local store at Duck

Lake. They were turned back by an entrenched force of over thirty Métis, led by Gabriel Dumont. Crozier sent out a larger force of almost a hundred as well as a cannon. On March 26, 1885, Riel—armed only with a cruxifix—led his men in the Battle of Duck Lake. He and twenty-five Métis successfully routed the NWMP. When victory was apparent, Riel refused to allow his men to pursue and finish off the government troops. The NWMP suffered 10 dead and 13 wounded; the Métis suffered 5 dead and 3 wounded. The Battle of Duck Lake had immediate consequences. Blood had now been spilled. For the federal government and Canadian society in general, this uprising now crossed the line into rebellion.

Word of the victory also provided impetus to the Cree, particularly their younger warriors. Riel urged the Cree to join the cause. Chief Poundmaker refused and instead led his band to the settlement of Battleford in an attempt to secure rations (which were being withheld by the government) for his starving people. The citizens of the town, however, assumed the Cree had come to attack and they took refuge in the fort. These fears seemed to be validated when some looting occurred. Fears that the rebellion was turning into an "Indian uprising" increased when Cree from Big Bear's band killed nine people on April 2 at the HBC store at Frog Lake, northwest of Battleford.

Backed by popular support in both English and French Canada to crush the rebellion, the federal government dispatched troops to the Northwest on its almost-completed railway. Within a month, more than 3000 troops under the command of Major General Frederick Middleton

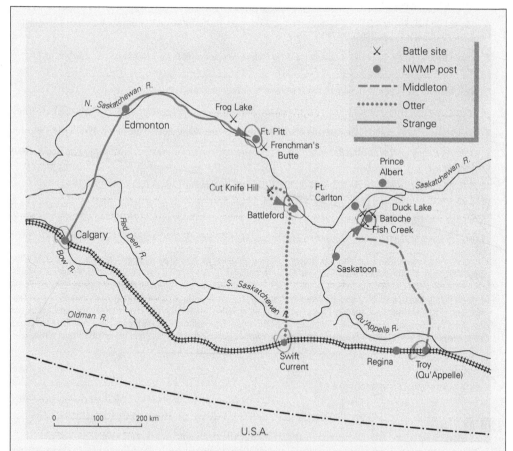

Military operations in the North-West Rebellion, 1885. This map shows the routes of the three military columns: to Batoche, under Major General Middleton; to Battleford, under Lieutenant Colonel Otter; and to the Ft. Pitt area, under Major General Strange. After the fighting was over, the three military units gathered at Battleford and were then dispersed.

Big Bear (front row, second from the left) and Poundmaker (front row, far right), shown at their trials, 1885. Father André (back row, second from the right) spent the night before Riel's execution in prayer with him. He walked with him to the scaffold.

Source: Glenbow Archives, Calgary, Canada/NA-3205-11.

arrived, joining the 2000 volunteers and Mounties already in the Northwest. Middleton organized the troops in three columns, at Qu'Appelle, Swift Current, and Calgary. They moved against Riel's forces and the Cree.

The Métis ambushed Middleton and his field force of 800 men at Fish Creek, south of Batoche, on April 24. Again led by Dumont the 150 Métis and Aboriginal warriors used the terrain to their advantage and refused to fight the Canadian troops in an open, pitched battle. Middleton's forces had superior numbers and the Métis were poorly equipped. The clash ended in a stalemate but it provided a moral victory to the Métis. Middleton's forces suffered 10 dead and over 40 wounded; the Métis suffered 4 dead and 1 wounded.

From Swift Current, Lieutenant Colonel William Otter and 762 troops marched to Battleford. The Canadian force relieved the settlement on April 24 and Otter decided to "punish" Poundmaker. Despite orders from Middleton to stay put, Otter led 325 troops (equipped with a Gatling gun) to attack Poundmaker's camp at Cut Knife Hill. On the morning of May 2, fewer than 100 Cree and Assiniboine warriors forced Otter's forces to withdraw. The defeat would have turned into a slaughter had Poundmaker not prevented his warriors from routing the fleeing troops. The Canadians suffered 8 killed and 14 wounded; Poundmaker's people suffered 6 dead and 3 wounded.

Major General Thomas Bland Strange led the Alberta Field Force of 1000 troops from Calgary, by way of Edmonton and the North Saskatchewan River. Troops were left to protect isolated white settlements while 300 continued east to Fort Pitt in an attempt to trap Big Bear's Cree. The Cree, led by war chief Wandering Spirit and numbering 250 warriors, burned Fort Pitt and retreated to the nearby hills. After several days of skirmishes, the two sides met at Frenchman's Butte on May 28. The encounter was a draw, with both sides retreating and no fatalities.

While Dumont urged Riel to continue using Aboriginal hit-and-run tactics, Riel claimed that God wanted the Métis to stand and fight. Unsettled by the defeats and near disasters, Middleton's force of 800 troops approached Riel's capital at Batoche with caution. The 300 Métis and First Nations warriors meanwhile dug rifle pits along their defensive line. Middleton's forces approached the church at Batoche on the morning of May 9 and began the attack. The Métis were dug in but Middleton was able to determine that they were fewer in number than he previously believed. Dumont's forces were also poorly equipped. By the third day, they had to resort to searching for bullets fired by enemy troops so that they could fire them back. The Métis defences collapsed when the Canadians charged.

Dumont prepared to flee to the United States and he urged Riel to follow. The Métis leader, however, again followed divine providence. Claiming that God wished him to articulate the case of his people, Riel surrendered on May 15. Middleton recorded Métis casualties at 51 dead and 173 wounded (but other reports indicate that only 16 were killed and 30 wounded). His own forces suffered 8 dead and 46 wounded.

Poundmaker also surrendered. Big Bear held out for a brief period of time but then turned himself in to a startled policeman at Fort Carleton on July 2. In the end, only about 4 percent of the First Nations in the region joined Riel, yet, despite the attempts to stay out of the conflict, the Cree were perceived as having openly participated in the Rebellion.

Fears that their people would be made the scapegoats proved justified. In the trials that followed, the Canadian government prosecuted more than 125 First Nations people—44 were convicted and 8 hanged at Battleford, including Wandering Spirit for the killings at Frog Lake. This mass hanging, the largest in Canadian history, demonstrated Ottawa's determination to punish any challenge to its authority and to send a message to the First Nations against further resistance. Big Bear and Poundmaker each received prison sentences of three years. "Everything I could do was done to stop bloodshed," Poundmaker protested in court. "Had I wanted war, I would not be here now. I should be on the prairie. You did not catch me. I gave myself up. You have got me because I wanted justice." Big Bear suffered the additional humiliation of having his hair cut. Poundmaker and Big Bear were released before their terms ended because of poor health, but they were broken men. Both died within a year of their release.

Riel's Trial

If Louis Riel expected justice when he surrendered to Canadian authorities, he was to be disappointed. The five-day trial in late July of 1885 became one of the most sensational in the nation's history. A jury of six men, all of British Protestant background, tried the Métis leader for six counts of treason in a courtroom in Regina, the new capital of the Northwest. The proceedings took place in English, Riel's third language. The trial judge, Hugh Richardson, owned property in the looted town of Battleford, raising questions as to his impartiality.

Riel pleaded not guilty. His lawyers wanted to fight for acquittal on the grounds of insanity but the Métis leader refused to comply. An admission of insanity would have undermined his cause and ensuing actions. Riel maintained that it was the federal government that was insane. "The federal government," he claimed, "besides doing nothing to satisfy the people of this great land, has even hardly been able to answer once or give a single response. That fact indicates an absolute lack of responsibility, and therefore insanity complicated by paralysis." Two doctors— James Wallace of Hamilton and Daniel Clark of Toronto—examined Riel during the trial. Both concluded he was sane, which according to the standards at the time meant he could distinguish right from wrong. Dr. François Roy, who had treated Riel at the Beauport asylum in Quebec, testified that Riel was insane and in no condition "to be master of his acts."

Riel addressed the jury on two occasions, defending his actions and the cause of his people. Both speeches were in English, and they were both eloquent and impressive. He explained his reasons for involvement in the Rebellion:

> No one can say that the Northwest was not suffering last year ... but what I have done, and risked, and to which I have exposed myself, rested certainly on the conviction I ... was

Louis Riel's address to the jury during his trial in Regina, late July 1885.

Source: Glenbow Archives, Calgary, Canada/NA-1081-3.

called upon to do something for my country.... I know that through the grace of God I am the founder of Manitoba.... Even if I was going to be sentenced by you, gentlemen of the jury, I have the satisfaction if I die—that if I die I will not be reputed by all men as insane, as a lunatic.... Gentlemen of the jury, my reputation, my liberty, my life are at your discretion.

The jury deliberated for an hour before reaching its verdict: Riel was found guilty of treason. But Riel had made a powerful impression. The sentence for high treason in the British Empire was death, but the jury recommended mercy. This recommendation was the last thing Prime Minister Macdonald wanted to hear because it handed the issue back to the government.

The Execution of Riel

When the Rebellion broke out, Canada was united against it. Quebec no longer felt affinity with Riel and the Métis. The events did not represent the resistance of a French Catholic community against an uncaring and distant government, as was perceived to have occurred in Manitoba in 1869–70; this was a "half-breed" and Aboriginal uprising led by a mad and dangerous heretic. "The revolt has made an evil cause of a just one," one Quebec newspaper noted.

But during the course of the trial, as Ontario clamoured in the press for Riel's head in revenge for the earlier killing of Thomas Scott and as the issue increasingly became one of Catholic versus Protestant and English versus French, Quebec became defensive and demanded that Riel be exonerated. "Riel did not really have a trial," *L'Electeur* reported. "It was a sort of inquisition set up by the government, not for the purpose of enquiring into the guilt or innocence of the prisoner, but only in order to deliver up his head to the fanatics under the cover of a sham trial." Macdonald watched nervously as the issue threatened national unity and the Conservative Party's hold on both influential provinces. Only the federal cabinet could commute the court's decision. Appeals for clemency came from Canada, the United States, Britain, and France.

Macdonald was now in a no-win situation. Twice, he postponed the execution. The second time, he appointed a medical commission to re-examine the question of Riel's sanity. If he was found insane, the prime minister would have no choice but to grant clemency. The commissioners concluded that Riel was sane. November 16, 1885, became the new execution date. Riel must hang, Macdonald was quoted as saying, "though every dog in Quebec bark in his favour." And the "dogs" were indeed "barking." As far as Quebec was concerned, the people who were demanding that Riel hang were "those people who hate everything which is French-Canadian and Catholic. Riel is only a name. It's the whole French-Canadian and Catholic population that they'd like to see dancing at the end of a rope!" On that clear and chilly morning, Louis Riel mounted the gibbet at Regina. The executioner, who had been imprisoned by Riel in Fort Garry in 1869, placed the rope around Riel's neck, the priest performed the last rites, and the trap door was sprung.

Macdonald had decided that "Riel must swing" to keep Ontario loyal to the Conservative Party. The prime minister gambled that Quebec would continue to give its support to the Conservatives, because there seemed little chance the province would move to the anti-clerical Liberals. Aside from the political factors, Macdonald believed that Riel was guilty of treason and that the courts would hold him accountable for his actions. Regardless, the prime minister's French-Canadian ministers—Hector Langevin, Adolphe Caron, and Joseph-Adolphe Chapleau—were denounced as traitors for standing by their leader. Macdonald was burnt in effigy in the streets of Montreal. The Liberals saw an opportunity to finally make their breakthrough in Quebec. Wilfrid Laurier, a young French-Canadian Liberal politician, declared at a huge Montreal rally: "If I had been on the banks of the Saskatchewan, I too, would have shouldered a musket." Riel's execution contributed to the demise of the Conservatives in Quebec. The party would not recover for a century.

The furor in central Canada, however, obscured the issues that led to the crisis. The North-West Rebellion of 1885 marked a transition on the Prairies; henceforth the white settler society would dominate. Many events symbolized the transition: the execution of Riel and the imprisonment of Big Bear and Poundmaker; the use of the newly completed CPR to transport troops west to suppress the insurgents; and the establishment of an elected territorial assembly a year later, in 1886, in which no Métis were present. The grievances of the Métis and the Cree were not only ignored and forgotten in the aftermath; these two groups were blamed and punished for the Rebellion. The Métis, once considered the "new nation," now found that they had no place in Canada. Neither First Nations nor white, they became the "forgotten people." They were not included in the Treaties, nor were they accepted by white society. Meanwhile, the federal government used the Indian Act to tightly monitor, control, and punish the First Nations. The Rebellion became a convenient justification for draconian assimilative measures, including the imposition of a pass system on First Nations people to control their movements and prevent them leaving their reserves, the creation of the residential schools system, and the banning of First Nations culture, such as language, dress, and rituals.

A HISTORICAL PORTRAIT

William Jackson (Honoré Jaxon)

William Jackson, secretary to Louis Riel in 1884–85, was one of the most interesting individuals to emerge from the North-West Rebellion. The former University of Toronto student, labour activist, and English Canadian-turned-Métis spent a lifetime helping others, but died in poverty at the age of 90 in New York City in 1952.

Jackson was born into a Methodist family in Toronto on May 3, 1861. Several years later the family moved to Wingham, about 150 kilometres northwest of Toronto, where his father opened a store. A good student, William completed high school and then studied classics for three years at the University of Toronto. His father's sudden bankruptcy, however, prevented William from completing his final year. In 1882, he followed his family to Prince Albert in the North-West Territories, where his father began a farm implement business.

The young Jackson was elected secretary of the local farmers' union. The short man with a loud, booming voice soon became a familiar sight, riding on horseback to meetings throughout the Prince Albert district. He criticized the federal government's harsh land regulations and its misadministration of the Northwest. He advocated a settlers' alliance with the Métis at neighbouring Batoche, when Louis Riel returned from the United States. After becoming Riel's secretary, Jackson was baptized a Catholic, with the Métis leader serving as his godfather and giving him the name "Honoré Joseph Jaxon."

After the Battle of Batoche, on May 12, 1885, Canadian troops took Jackson into custody and sent him to Regina to be tried. The Regina court committed the prisoner, who was long-haired with a full beard and wore a Métis headband, to the lunatic asylum at Lower Fort Garry in Winnipeg. There he wrote his assessment of Riel: "The oppression of the aboriginal has been the crying sin of the white race in America and they have at last found a voice."

On November 2, 1885, Jackson escaped and crossed the border into the United States. He now identified as Métis and went only by the name Honoré Jaxon. In Chicago, he became a

Honoré Jaxon, sitting by his library, much of which was about to be transported to the New York City dump, December 13, 1951.

Source: *New York Daily News* Archive/Getty Images.

labour organizer and helped the carpenters fight for an eight-hour working day. In 1894 he joined Coxey's Army of unemployed as they marched on Washington, D.C. Three years later he converted to Bahá'í, the new world religion from Persia, which stressed the simplicity of living and service to suffering human beings.

Jaxon returned to Canada for two years, from 1907 to 1909, but was disillusioned by the old injustices that remained. He went back to the United States and ended up in New York City in the 1920s. He loved the city, with its museums and libraries. His life mission became the establishment of a library for the Aboriginal people of Saskatchewan. Throughout the 1930s and 1940s he collected old books, pamphlets, and newspapers.

His dream died on December 12, 1951, when he was evicted. His library went first to the street, then to the New York City dump. In poor health and broken in spirit, Honoré Jaxon died in New York one month later, on January 10, 1952.

Immediately after Riel's execution on November 16, 1885, French Canadians rose in protest against the federal government. In Montreal, demonstrators burned Sir John A. Macdonald in effigy at the base of the statue of Queen Victoria in Victoria Square.

Source: *Frank Leslie's Illustrated Newspaper,* November 28, 1885. Saskatchewan Archives Board/R-D1776.

French-Canadian Nationalism

The aftermath of 1885 contributed to the growing rift between French and English Canada. The Riel controversy stirred French-Canadian nationalism. Honoré Mercier, leader of the Liberal Party in Quebec after 1883, expressed this nationalist position in the mid-1880s. At the same rally in Montreal at which Laurier declared his support for the Métis, Mercier denounced the federal Conservative politicians who had been responsible for Riel's execution: "Riel, our brother, is dead, victim of fanaticism and treason—of the fanaticism of Sir John and some of his friends, of the treason of three of our people who sold their brother to keep their portfolios." Mercier appealed to his fellow Quebeckers to form the Parti national, an exclusive French-Canadian party, one that would put their interests first: "We felt that the murder of Riel was a declaration of war against Quebec; and that, therefore, French Canadians had a duty to cease their fratricidal quarrels and unite in a crusade to preserve the nation in Quebec from encroaching federal power." Mercier and the Parti national won the provincial election of 1886. As premier, Mercier found an ally in Oliver Mowat in advancing provincial rights but more particularly in resisting the encroachments of Macdonald's federal government.

In 1887, Wilfrid Laurier became the federal Liberal leader. Edward Blake had just led the party to another federal election defeat at the hands of the "Old Chief." Laurier articulated an alternative brand of French-Canadian nationalism to Mercier, one that included French Canadians across the country. Laurier's views had changed over time. Initially, in the 1860s, he opposed Confederation. But he became reconciled to union in the early 1870s when elected to the House of Commons. While he blamed the federal government for neglecting the Métis grievances, he appealed for moderation on both sides. Laurier presented a message of toleration reminiscent of Georges-Étienne Cartier at the time of Confederation:

> We form here, or wish to form, a nation composed of the most heterogeneous elements, Protestants and Catholics, English and French, German, Irish, Scottish, each, let us not forget, with its own traditions and prejudices. In each one of these opposing elements, however, there is a common point of patriotism, and the only veritable politics is that which dominates this common patriotism, and brings these elements toward a unified goal and common aspirations.

While Laurier stood for compromise and conciliation between French and English Canada, he was an ardent liberal. He believed strongly in the separation of church and state, free trade, and the autonomy of Canada within the British Empire. The question, however, was whether Quebec would support the Liberals, even with one of its own as party leader.

The First Interprovincial Conference

Honoré Mercier called a conference of all the provincial premiers in 1887, the first of its kind. Two provinces declined the invitation—British Columbia and Prince Edward Island, both of which had Conservative governments—while the other four provincial Liberal governments

A photo of the first interprovincial conference, called by Honoré Mercier in 1887, to challenge the authority of the federal government. The Quebec premier appears seated second from the left. Ontario's Oliver Mowat, the "Father of Provincial Rights," is seated in the centre. W.S. Fielding, who tried during his premiership to take Nova Scotia out of Confederation, is beside Mowat on the right.

Source: Library and Archives Canada/C-11583.

accepted. Macdonald's federal Conservative government ignored the conference, dismissing it as a partisan gathering of provincial Liberals. Increasingly, the Liberals were associated as the defenders of provincial rights.

The premiers summed up the provincial-rights position. They argued that Confederation was a contract among the British North American colonies that had agreed to establish a new country. Therefore, the provinces should have increased powers and more influence within a Canadian federal system that gave too much power to Ottawa. Among the demands were appeals for larger federal subsidies, abolition of the federal power of disallowance, and Senate reform to strengthen provincial power.

Cultural and Religious Division

Laurier's appeal for unity between English Protestants and French Catholics went unheeded in the ethnically and religiously charged atmosphere of the late nineteenth century. Two issues— the Jesuits' Estates Act and the Manitoba Schools Question—revealed the extent of the bitterness.

The Jesuits' Estates Controversy

The dispute over the Jesuits' Estates began in 1888. During the *ancien régime* of New France, the Jesuit order obtained large grants of land. After the conquest of 1763 and the disbanding of the order by the Pope in 1773, ownership of these Jesuit properties passed first to the British government and then to the colony of Lower Canada. The Jesuit order was restored in 1814. In 1842, as part of the ultramontane resurgence, the order was reformed and Bishop Ignace Bourget brought it back to Quebec. The Jesuit order appealed to the provincial government to have its property returned or to receive financial compensation for its losses. Premier Mercier appealed to Pope Leo XIII to act as arbiter. On the basis of the Pope's recommendation, Mercier agreed to distribute $400,000 (a sum well below the actual value of the land) among the Jesuits, the Université Laval in Quebec City, and the Catholic dioceses of the province. He awarded a further $60,000 to Protestant postsecondary educational institutions in Quebec. This became the basis of the Jesuits' Estates Act in 1888.

Many in English Canada reacted vehemently to the idea of papal intervention, particularly over an overtly political issue. Britain had long ago divorced church and state, yet to English Canadians, Quebec seemed backward and caught up in its past, one that gave far too much influence to the Catholic Church. The issue seemed to belie much of what distinguished Quebec from the rest of Canada. It also went to the very heart of Protestant bigotry. D'Alton McCarthy, a Conservative MP from Ontario, insisted that the Pope had no right to meddle in Canadian political affairs. He moved a resolution in the House of Commons to have the federal government disallow the Jesuits' Estates Act. He and his twelve supporters became known as "the noble thirteen" or "the devil's dozen." McCarthy insisted on one common Canadian nationality based on the English language and a British Protestant culture. Prime Minister Macdonald wanted nothing to do with the issue and refused to intervene. McCarthy lost this battle but the war was far from over. Sectarian tensions soon emerged again in what became known as the "Schools Question."

The New Brunswick Schools Question

Schools have long served as a battleground between church and state and therefore were a contentious topic for politicians in British North America and, later, Canada. In 1867, the Fathers of Confederation were well aware of their potential for dispute and division. While education was placed under local and therefore provincial jurisdiction, the federal government was responsible for protecting minority rights. In Quebec a separate school system was created, with a Catholic system for the majority and a Protestant (state) system for the influential English minority. But Quebec was an exception. The French Catholic minorities in the other provinces were not awarded such status. The BNA Act recognized only separate schools that existed by law before the union in the four original provinces.

The first dispute over denominational schools since Confederation occurred in New Brunswick. The problem was that Catholic schools existed by custom, not law, in New Brunswick before the union. In 1871 the New Brunswick government proposed legislation to amend the province's Schools Act to introduce a nonsectarian school system, which would deny public support to "separate" parish schools teaching French and providing religious instruction. The quality of education at these schools was suspect and the provincial government wanted to provide more children with mandatory, nondenominational schooling. To New Brunswick Catholics, both Acadian and Irish, this legislation would deprive them of a right that they had enjoyed in fact, if not in law, at the time of Confederation. They requested that the federal government disallow the act under section 93 of the BNA Act, which included the right to intervene to protect the educational rights of a minority.

The federal government refused to intervene due to the controversial nature of the issue. Macdonald argued that the legislation lay within the province's jurisdiction. Roman Catholics did not lose any rights that they had had by law at the union or that they had acquired since. The prime minister refused disallowance or federal remedial action under section 93. Furthermore, he was reluctant to interfere in education—an area under provincial jurisdiction in the BNA Act. The federal government did appeal to the New Brunswick legislature to consider minority rights, but its willingness to become involved ended there.

New Brunswick's Schools Question provided the only precedent for the courts and the politicians when Manitoba's Schools Question arose in the late 1880s and early 1890s. But because the New Brunswick situation dealt with Catholic schools in a founding province of Confederation whose rights had been written into the original BNA Act, it was not applicable. Furthermore, the Manitoba Act of 1870 guaranteed rights and privileges to Catholic and Protestant schools not only in practice but also in law, unlike the case in New Brunswick.

The Manitoba Schools Question

When Manitoba became a province in 1870, Louis Riel made sure to include cultural protections for French Catholics. The Manitoba Act granted language as well as denominational school rights. By 1890, however, the demographic situation had changed dramatically in the province. The English Protestant population increased tenfold, significantly outnumbering French Catholics. Many Métis left the province and moved farther northwest. Moreover, French Canadians from Quebec did not join their English compatriots to the same extent in moving west in the late nineteenth century, despite a concerted effort by the Catholic clergy in the region. For French Canadians contemplating leaving Quebec, New England was closer and more convenient, and most had relatives or friends living there. Quebeckers could also be assured jobs as factory workers or labourers in New England. Should they want to farm, opportunities existed in the American West, with much easier access than in the Canadian West before the completion of the CPR in 1885. Thus the Northwest held little appeal for Quebec. Ontario, going back to the days of George Brown, had looked upon the Northwest as its own frontier. These designs for expansion were problematized by Riel's Red River Resistance, but it merely delayed the inevitable.

Main Street and City Hall Square in Winnipeg, about 1897. View looking southward toward Portage and Main. The Winnipeg monument to the Canadians who fought in 1885 appears on the extreme left.

Source: Provincial Archives of Manitoba/Simons Marguerite 5 (N10911).

The Manitoba Act of 1870 made the province a "little Quebec"; by the 1890s a flood of Ontarian immigration created a "little Ontario."

In August 1889, D'Alton McCarthy (fresh from the front lines in the battle over the Jesuits' Estates Act) delivered an emotional speech at Portage la Prairie, Manitoba, in which he railed against French-Canadian nationalism. A few months earlier, he had supported the formation of the Equal Rights Association, which claimed in its platform to stand for "equal rights of all religious denominations before the law, special privileges for none." The platform was a rationale for a single language—English—and a single system of public school under government control. According to McCarthy and his followers, "as long as Frenchmen learned their laws and their history in French, they would remain French in sentiment. . . . Now is the time, when the ballot box will decide this great question before the people, and if that does not supply the remedy in this generation, bayonets will supply it in the next."

On the same platform as McCarthy at Portage la Prairie sat Joseph Martin, attorney general for Manitoba's Liberal government. He pledged his government's support in abolishing the dual school system, as well as French as an official language, in Manitoba. The provincial government was already contemplating such action.

In 1890, the Manitoba government passed a Schools Act that established a provincial department of education and a system of nonsectarian public schools that alone would receive the provincial grant for education. Denominational schools could still exist but without government funding. Those wishing to contribute to such schools had to do so in addition to their public-school taxes. The same session of the legislature abolished French as an official language, contrary to section 23 of the Manitoba Act of 1870. In one fell swoop, the provincial government broke the promises made to Riel and the Métis. The government claimed that Manitoba was now a very different province.

Manitoba Catholics Fight Back

Discontented Catholics in Manitoba had three options: appeal to the federal government to use disallowance of the provincial legislation; take the issue to the courts to have the legislation declared *ultra vires* (unconstitutional); or appeal to Ottawa to intervene on behalf of the minority through remedial legislation as set out in section 93 of the BNA Act. Eventually, they pursued all three possibilities.

Macdonald and the Conservatives again won office in the federal election of 1891. The prime minister resisted using the federal government's power of disallowance, fearing that a public outcry would only strengthen the provincial government. He favoured court action to decide such a contentious issue and agreed that the federal government would pay the legal costs. The provincial court in the case of *Barrett v. the City of Winnipeg* upheld the Manitoba government's position. It then went to the Supreme Court of Canada, which reversed the decision and upheld the right of the Catholic minority to have state-supported separate schools. Finally, the Judicial Committee of the Privy Council in London reversed this decision in favour of the Manitoba government. During the same period, the territorial assembly of the North-West Territories in 1892 followed Manitoba's lead in denying the French language official status in the legislature, the courts, and the schools—all rights granted in the North-West Territories Act of 1875, as amended in 1877.

One final option remained. The Manitoba Catholics appealed to the federal government for remedial action under section 93 of the BNA Act. The Judicial Committee of the Privy Council eventually ruled that the federal government had the constitutional right to intervene on behalf of the minority even though the Manitoba law had been judged valid. Despite John A. Macdonald's attempts to avoid the issue, it was thrown back into Ottawa's lap.

But Macdonald had died only months after winning office in 1891. The Conservative government introduced the remedial legislation bill in Parliament in January 1896. The government established a nine-member board to run the separate-school system, to be supported by Catholic tax revenue; the schools in this system would share a portion of the provincial educational grant; and, to ensure proper standards, the separate schools would be inspected regularly and funds would be withheld if they were judged inefficient. But Parliament was dissolved on April 23, with the bill still not passed into law. Four days later, Mackenzie Bowell resigned as Conservative leader under pressure from the Orange wing of his party, who were angered over his handling of the Schools Question.

The Laurier Era

The Election of 1896

The Conservatives entered the federal election of 1896 with another new leader, Charles Tupper. By the time of Macdonald's death in 1891, the party was old and in need of revitalization. The candidates for the leadership (and because an election had just take place, the position of prime minister) reflected this fact. Four men took on the mantle of prime minister between 1891 and 1896: John Abbott, John Thompson, Mackenzie Bowell, and Charles Tupper.

The Manitoba Schools Question proved to be only one of several contentious issues in the election, although an important one. In Quebec, the Conservatives stressed that they had introduced remedial legislation on behalf of the Manitoba Catholics. In English Canada, Conservative candidates emphasized that the bill was not, and might never become, law. Outside Quebec, the Conservatives also remained on the defensive over their high-tariff policy and were blamed for an economic recession.

The Liberals were finally in an advantageous position. The winds of change were blowing. Other than the brief interlude with Alexander Mackenzie as a result of the Pacific Scandal, the Conservatives had dominated federal government since Confederation. The death of the "Old Chieftain" gave the Liberals hope. As the opposition, they could denounce the Tories without offering concrete alternative policies. On the controversial Schools Question, for example, Wilfrid Laurier did not take a strong stand during the stormy parliamentary session of 1896. During the election campaign, the Liberal leader simply promised that his Liberal government, if elected, would end the dispute through compromise with the Manitoba Liberal government in a way that would respect provincial rights. "If it was in my power," he said in 1895, "and if I had the responsibility, I would try the sunny way" (a reference to Aesop's fable involving a contest between the wind and the sun). To voters weary of the wrangling between the federal government and the provinces, the "sunny way" seemed appealing. The Liberals won fewer votes in the election of 1896 but they won more seats. In English Canada they tied the Conservatives in the number of seats, but in Quebec they obtained two-thirds of the province's share and, after nearly two decades in opposition, returned to power.

The Laurier–Greenway Compromise

Prime Minister Laurier opened negotiations with the Manitoba government and reached a compromise with the Liberal premier, Thomas Greenway. Religious instruction would be allowed in the public schools for half an hour at the end of each day. Catholic teachers could be employed in urban schools with at least 40 Roman Catholic pupils or in rural districts with at least 25 Catholic pupils. On the language question, it was agreed that, when at least 10 of the pupils in any school system spoke French (or any language other than English as their native language), the teaching of such pupils would be conducted in English and French (or the other language) "upon the bilingual system."

It might have been labelled a "compromise" by the Liberals, but it was another defeat to the Catholic minority, who would have obtained more under the Conservatives' remedial legislation. The compromise allowed religious instruction for a brief period of time at the end of each day but led to the abolition of the state-supported separate-school system. French would be retained only when sufficient population warranted it; hence, it lost the status of equality with English that it had had under the Manitoba Act of 1870. Moreover, it became a language like any other in Manitoba, all of which were unofficial except English. In 1916, at the height of World War I, even the bilingual clause of the Laurier–Greenway compromise was abolished, making English the only language of instruction in the province's schools.

The Roman Catholic hierarchy in Canada accused Laurier of capitulating to the English-Canadian Protestants. Laurier argued that the agreement was the best that could be hoped for, given the Catholics' minority position. Some Canadian bishops appealed to the Pope to intervene on behalf of the Manitoba Catholics. The Pope sent Monsignor Merry del Val to investigate the issue. The papal adviser reported that while the compromise was unsatisfactory, these terms were the best that the Catholics could, under the circumstances, obtain.

The Autonomy Bills

The Laurier Liberals were returned to power in the federal elections of 1900 and 1904, increasing their seat totals each time. The Schools Question arose again in 1905, however, with the creation of the two new provinces of Saskatchewan and Alberta. The original ordinances of the North-West

Interior of a school near Vulcan, Alberta, at the turn of the century. Teachers insisted that children from non-English-speaking countries speak English in the classroom. Legally in Alberta, even French-Canadian students were obliged to do so after their first two years of elementary school as a result of ordinances passed by the territorial government in the early 1890s.

Source: Glenbow Archives, Calgary, Canada/NA-748-41.

Territories Act of 1875, as amended in 1877, provided for both Protestant and Roman Catholic schools to receive public funding. As well, both French and English could be used as languages of instruction. In the sectarian atmosphere of the early 1890s, however, the territor-ial govern-ment made English the official language of instruction in the Catholic school system, restricting French to only French-speaking children in the primary grades. Then, in 1901, the territorial government restricted religious instruction to the last half hour of the school day, as was the case in Manitoba.

When the time came to draw up the Autonomy Bills to create Saskatchewan and Alberta, Charles Fitzpatrick (the federal minister of justice and a Quebec Catholic), in Alberta along with Henri Bourassa, drafted the educational clause to restore the original system of 1877. The clause permitted the free establishment of Catholic and Protestant schools as well as the use of French in the school system. Clifford Sifton, minister of the interior and the most influential politician in all of western Canada, who had once been a cabinet minister under Manitoba Premier Greenway, opposed the educational clause, claiming it went against the wishes of the government of the North-West Territories. Sifton was appalled at the results of the ensuing situation in Manitoba, which he argued was allowing other ethnic and religious groups to take advantage of the Laurier–Greenway compromise. Immigrant groups were avoiding the government's assimilative designs, and as a result "a babel of languages" was being spoken on the streets of Winnipeg. He believed the same would happen in the two new provinces. Sifton resigned from the cabinet in protest.

Laurier intervened and allowed Sifton to redraft the educational clause, although he did not invite him back into the cabinet. Sifton's revised clause restricted the rights of the French-Canadian Catholic minorities to the limited concessions granted in the ordinance of 1901. Laurier accepted the "honourable compromise," as he described the Sifton amendment. But Bourassa denounced it as a sellout. It infringed on the rights of French Canadians as set out in the original North-West Territories Act. He maintained that French-Canadian Catholics in the West should enjoy the same rights that English-Canadian Protestants enjoyed in Quebec. In the end, however, the Sifton amendment became law.

SUMMARY

The period from 1880 to 1914 witnessed a resurgence of French–English, Catholic–Protestant antagonism in Canada. It also highlighted regional and provincial divisions within the federation. Provincial rightists successfully challenged the power of the central government on a number of constitutional issues. Regional protests arose in the Maritimes with the attempt by Nova Scotia once again to secede from Confederation and in the West over the North-West Rebellion of 1885. As well, English- and French-speaking Canadians feuded over Riel's execution, over the Jesuits' Estates Act in Quebec, and over linguistic and religious rights in schools, first in New Brunswick, then in Manitoba, and then in Saskatchewan and Alberta. These disputes contributed to the defeat of the Conservatives in the 1896 election and the coming to power of the Liberals under Wilfrid Laurier.

BIBLIOGRAPHY

For an overview of dominion–provincial relations in the late nineteenth century, see P.B. Waite, *Canada, 1874–1896: Arduous Destiny* (Toronto: McClelland & Stewart, 1971). The provincial-rights movement in Ontario is discussed in Christopher Armstrong, *The Politics of Federalism: Ontario's Relations with the Federal Government, 1867–1942* (Toronto: University of Toronto Press, 1981). Paul Romney's *Getting It Wrong: How Canadians Forgot Their Past and Imperilled Confederation* (Toronto: University of Toronto Press, 1999) challenges the dominant interpretation of Confederation and provides a critique of the emphasis on centralization and a strong federal government by Canadian historians. See, as well, Margaret Evans's biography *Sir Oliver Mowat* (Toronto: University of Toronto Press, 1992).

On political protest in Atlantic Canada in the 1880s, see Judith Fingard, "The 1880s: Paradoxes of Progress," in E.R. Forbes and D.A. Muise, eds., *The Atlantic Provinces in Confederation* (Toronto: University of Toronto Press, 1993); T.W. Acheson, "The Maritimes and 'Empire Canada,'" in D.J. Bercuson, ed., *Canada and the Burden of Unity* (Toronto: Macmillan, 1977), pp. 87–114; E.R. Forbes, *Aspects of Maritime Regionalism, 1867–1927* (Ottawa: Canadian Historical Association, 1983); and George Rawlyk, ed., *The Atlantic Provinces and the Problem of Confederation* (St. John's: Breakwater Books, 1979). Rawlyk also deals with developments in Newfoundland in the 1880s and 1890s, as does Frederick W. Rowe in *A History of Newfoundland and Labrador* (Toronto: McGraw-Hill Ryerson, 1980). On western Canada, see T.D. Regehr, "Western Canada and the Burden of National Transportation Policies," in D.J. Bercuson, ed., *Canada and the Burden of Unity* (Toronto: Macmillan, 1977), pp. 115–41. David Cruise and Alison Griffiths discuss the impact of the CPR rates in *Lords of the Line* (Toronto: Viking, 1988).

On the North-West Rebellion, see Bob Beal and Rob Macleod, *Prairie Fire: The 1885 North-West Rebellion* (Edmonton: Hurtig, 1984). For the First Nations perspective on the 1885 Rebellion, see Blair Stonechild and Bill Waiser, *Loyal Till Death: Indians and the North-West Rebellion* (Calgary: Fifth House, 1997). See Walter Hildebrandt, *Views from Fort Battleford: Constructed Visions of an Anglo-Canadian West* (Regina: Canadian Plains Research Center, University of Regina, 1994) and Jennifer Reid, *Louis Riel and the Creation of Modern Canada* (Albuquerque: University of New Mexico Press, 2008). On the aftermath of 1885 for the First Nations, see Edward Ahenakew's *Voices of the Plains Cree* (Toronto: McClelland and Stewart, 1973; Regina: Canadian Plains Research Center, 1995). For the impact of disease, consult Maureen K. Lux, *Medicine That Walks: Disease, Medicine, and Canadian Plains Native People, 1880–1940* (Toronto: University of Toronto Press, 2001) and James Daschuk, *Clearing the Plains: Disease, Politics of Starvation, and the Loss of Aboriginal Life* (Regina: University of Regina Press, 2013). For a gendered perspective, see Sarah Carter, *Capturing Women: The Manipulation of Cultural Imagery in Canada's Prairie West* (Montreal/Kingston: McGill-Queen's University Press, 1997). For biographical works, see Hugh A. Dempsey, *Big Bear* (Vancouver: Douglas & McIntyre, 1984); J.R. Miller, *Big Bear (Mistahimusqua)* (Toronto: ECW Press, 1996); and George Woodcock, *Gabriel Dumont* (Edmonton: Hurtig, 1975).

On Louis Riel, see the sources cited in the Bibliography in Chapter 2 of this book, as well as the titles listed in "Where Historians Disagree" in this chapter. All of Riel's writings have been edited by

George F.G. Stanley et al., *The Collected Writings of Louis Riel*, 5 vols. (Edmonton: University of Alberta Press, 1985). For a discussion of the military engagement at Batoche, see Walter Hildebrandt, *The Battle of Batoche: British Small Warfare and the Entrenched Métis* (Ottawa: National Historic Parks and Sites, Parks Canada, 1985). George F.G. Stanley reviews the various interpretations of Riel in "The Last Word on Louis Riel—The Man of Several Faces," in F. Laurie Barron and James B. Waldram, eds., *1885 and After: Native Society in Transition* (Regina: Canadian Plains Research Center, University of Regina, 1986), as does Doug Owram in "The Myth of Louis Riel," *Canadian Historical Review*, 63(3) (September 1982): 315–36. George Melnyk's *Radical Regionalism* (Edmonton: NeWest, 1982) and his edited collection *Riel to Reform: A History of Protest in Western Canada* (Saskatoon: Fifth House, 1992) examine the roots of western protest and its relationship to regional identity. For an examination of Louis Riel in Canadian culture, see Albert Braz, *The False Traitor: Louis Riel in Canadian Culture* (Toronto: University of Toronto Press, 2003). The life of Will Jackson (1861–1952), Riel's secretary in 1884/85, later known in the United States as Honoré Jaxon, is told by Donald B. Smith in *Honoré Jaxon: Prairie Visionary* (Regina: Coteau Books, 2007).

Quebec's views on federal–provincial relations are analyzed in R. Cook, *Provincial Autonomy: Minority Rights and the Compact Theory, 1867–1921* (Ottawa: Queen's Printer, 1969) and Arthur Silver, *The French-Canadian Idea of Confederation, 1864–1900* (Toronto: University of Toronto Press, 1982). See also Mason Wade, *The French Canadians: 1760–1945* (Toronto: Macmillan, 1955), pp. 331–446; and Susan Mann, *The Dream of Nation: A Social and Intellectual History of Quebec*, 2nd ed. (Montreal/Kingston; McGill-Queen's University Press, 2002), pp. 150–66. Honoré Mercier's views are presented in Gilles Gallichan, *Honoré Mercier: La politique et la culture* (Sillery, PQ: Septentrion, 1994). J.R. Miller's *Equal Rights: The Jesuits' Estates Act Controversy* (Montreal: McGill-Queen's University Press, 1979) deals with that subject in depth.

On the Manitoba Schools Question and its impact on the election of 1896, consult Paul Crunican, *Priests and Politicians: Manitoba Schools and the Election of 1896* (Toronto: University of Toronto Press, 1974). On Rome's position in the controversy, see Roberto Perin, *Rome in Canada: The Vatican and Canadian Affairs in the Late Victorian Age* (Toronto: University of Toronto Press, 1990). Lovell Clark has compiled a collection of sources in *The Manitoba School Question: Majority Rule or Minority Rights* (Toronto: Copp Clark, 1968). On D'Alton McCarthy's role, see J.R. Miller, "D'Alton McCarthy, Equal Rights, and the Origins of the Manitoba Schools Question," *Canadian Historical Review*, 54 (December 1973): 369–92. Gilbert L. Comeault, "La question desécoles du Manitoba—un nouvel éclairage," *Revue d'histoire de l'Amérique française*, 33(1) (June 1979): 3–23, stresses the local origins of the Manitoba Schools Question. Treatment of the schools question in Alberta and Saskatchewan can be found in Manoly R. Lupul, *The Roman Catholic Church and the North-West School Question: A Study in Church–State Relations in Western Canada* (Toronto: University of Toronto Press, 1974). On Sifton's contribution, see D.J. Hall, *Clifford Sifton*, vol. 2, *The Lonely Eminence, 1901–1929* (Vancouver: University of British Columbia Press, 1985). For subsequent school questions that occurred in central Canada, see David Fraser, *Honorary Protestants: The Jewish School Question in Montreal, 1867–1997* (Toronto: University of Toronto Press, 2015), and Jack D. Cecillon, *Prayers, Petitions, and Protests: The Catholic Church and the Ontario Schools Crisis in the Windsor Border Region, 1910–1928* (Montreal: McGill-Queen's University Press, 2013).

Birdseye View of Dawson, Yukon Ter., 1903.

Source: Library and Archives Canada/NMC 21044.

Chapter Five

IMPERIALISM, CONTINENTALISM, AND NATIONALISM

TIME LINE	
1871	Treaty of Washington signed
1884	Imperial Federation League formed
1891	Conservatives win federal election under John A. Macdonald
1896	Liberals win federal election under Wilfrid Laurier
1897	Queen Victoria's Diamond Jubilee
1899	Outbreak of the South African (Boer) War
1900	Liberals win federal election under Wilfrid Laurier
1903	Founding of the Ligue nationaliste Alaska Boundary Dispute settled
1904	Laurier Liberals win federal election
1908	Laurier Liberals win federal election
1909	Department of External Affairs established
1910	Naval Service Bill introduced
1911	Reciprocity Treaty negotiated with the United States but rejected in federal election Conservatives win federal election under Robert Borden
1912	Conservatives impose closure to pass Naval Aid Bill

[handwritten: Imperialists - Engl CAN/ON/ Conservative Party]

Confederation indicated a change in status for Canada—a maturing process from colony to nation—but it was not meant to sever the imperial tie to Britain. Canada remained the "eldest daughter of Empire" and most Canadians perceived no conflict between their nationalist and imperialist sentiments. Indeed, as historian Carl Berger demonstrates, nationalism and imperialism were flip sides of the same coin. But when Canadians debated the future of the country, the "imperial question" dominated the discussion.

While the majority of Canadians maintained an emotional tie to the British Empire, there was disagreement over the role the Empire would play in Canada and the role Canada would play in the Empire. Canadians were grateful for the protection the imperial navy had long provided British North America. Other than from the United States, there had been no fear of external attack since the end of the colonial wars with France in 1763. By the 1840s, the British Empire reached the peak of its power and was unrivalled on the global stage. But by the 1880s the geopolitical situation was changing. Germany posed a new challenge. This threatened Canada's passive role within the Empire and demanded a change to the relationship. For the first time, Canada was called on to aid the Empire, even in distant and remote places. This request posed yet another threat to the nation's fragile unity.

George Ross, Ontario's minister of education (and later premier, 1899–1905) reflected the view of the imperialists. "As Canadians," he stated in 1896, "we should teach more of Canada and in teaching Canada we should teach it as only one colony of the vast British Empire on whose dominion the sun never sets." This view was strong in English Canada (particularly Ontario) and increasingly associated with the Conservative Party. It did not propose colonial subservience to Britain but rather that Canada had an active and formal role to play in the Empire.

The autonomists, on the other hand, reflected not only the dominant opinion in Quebec but also that of the Liberal Party and those on the left throughout English Canada. This group agreed that Canada was evolving from colony to nation but opposed such notions as imperial federation or centralization. They advanced autonomy through Canada becoming involved only in imperial matters that directly impacted Canadians.

A fringe group of English Canadians favoured closer economic or even political association with the United States—continentalism. Goldwin Smith, a historian-cum-journalist and long-time critic, advanced this position in his controversial book *Canada and the Canadian Question* (1891). There were others less extreme in their position who argued that as Europe declined in significance and the old world gave way to the new, Canada's destiny inevitably lay in a North American identity. *[handwritten: Autonomists - QC / Liberal Party]*

All three options were bound up in what became known in Canada as "the imperial question" and were heatedly debated in the context of events such as the Boer War, the naval crisis, and the failed reciprocity agreement with the United States. The issues divided French and English Canadians, Liberals and Conservatives, farmers and manufacturers.

The North Atlantic Triangle and the Treaty of Washington

The triangular relationship among Canada, Britain, and the United States broke down in the 1860s. After the North won the American Civil War in 1865, it immediately demanded compensation from Britain for supporting the South. The British government had allowed Confederate agents to purchase ships and ammunition in Britain. One British-built warship, the *Alabama*, inflicted heavy losses on American merchant shipping. Other British vessels, such as the *Trent*, carried Confederate envoys to England to raise money for the Southern cause. As a final irritant, Confederate sympathizers, on at least one occasion, used British North America as a sanctuary from which to attack the North.

The Americans also contributed to the tensions. The American Congress cancelled the Reciprocity Treaty in 1866, and some members of Congress assumed that economic collapse north of the border would follow, causing the British North American colonies to seek union with the United States. In addition, the American government did nothing to prevent the Fenian Brotherhood—a radical group of Irish Americans who hoped to capture Canada for use as a bargaining tool for the independence of Ireland—from making raids across the border. The Fenians continued their attacks until 1871. Prominent American leaders also talked openly of annexing Canada as part of their "manifest destiny" to control the North American continent. Canadians viewed Britain as their military protector and welcomed the 15,000 British troops garrisoned in the new dominion in 1867. It was the British government, seeking to reduce expenses, who insisted on their withdrawal by 1871.

In order to alleviate tension and repair damaged relations, British and American leaders agreed to hold a conference in Washington to settle outstanding disputes between the two countries, in particular the *Alabama* claims. The United States also wanted to bargain for the right to fish in the territorial waters of the Maritimes and to use those provinces' ports—privileges denied since 1818, except during the term of the Reciprocity Treaty from 1854 to 1866. Canada hoped to use the fisheries as leverage to convince the Americans to renew reciprocity. In addition, Canada wanted compensation for damages caused by Fenian raids. On the Pacific Ocean, a clear boundary line between Vancouver Island and the American mainland needed to be drawn. But while Confederation made Canada a nation, its sovereignty was limited. Control of external policy remained in British hands and Canada did not have the authority to negotiate foreign treaties.

For the first time, in 1871, a Canadian prime minister attended an international conference as a participant. Although he spoke for Canada, John A. Macdonald belonged officially to the five-member British delegation to Washington. This dual role, however, placed Macdonald in an awkward position: "If things go well my share of the kudos will be but small, and if anything goes wrong I will be made the scapegoat at all events so far as Canada is concerned." From Macdonald's perspective, the British proved once again too willing to bargain away Canadian interests for a lasting Anglo–American peace. It was not the last time Canadian interests were sacrificed on the altar of American friendship.

The Americans did well by the Treaty of Washington of 1871. They succeeded in keeping the question of compensation to Canadians for the Fenian raids off the conference agenda, yet obtained $15.5 million as a settlement for their *Alabama* claims. They won the right to fish in British North American territorial waters in return for a cash payment, subsequently agreed upon by an arbitration committee to be $5.5 million. The United States also obtained free navigation in perpetuity on the St. Lawrence River. The treaty also provided for the arbitration of the San Juan boundary dispute.

Canada gained only the right to free navigation on three remote Alaskan rivers and the removal of duties on Canadian fish exported into American markets. Most notably, Canada did not obtain its desired reciprocity deal. The United States did at least recognize Canada as a separate nation in North America and promised to respect its borders. The threat of American annexation, so long a spectre in Canada, apparently vanished.

Prime Minister Macdonald was irritated by the treaty results yet, as a junior member of the delegation, he felt he had no choice but to sign. He returned to face vociferous opposition from the Canadian press and the Liberal opposition in Parliament. But the wily politician looked to turn the embarrassment to his advantage. He informed the House that through secret negotiations with Britain and the United States, Canada would receive a cash payment for use of the fisheries in lieu of compensation for the Fenian Raids. Britain had also agreed to guarantee loans for construction of the Canadian Pacific Railway. Regardless, Macdonald returned from Washington determined to

The Treaty of Washington commissioners in 1871. Prime Minister John A. Macdonald is third from the left. This was the first international conference in which a Canadian leader participated. The settlement was advantageous to the United States and was generally regarded as having sacrificed Canadian interests on the altar of American friendship.

Source: M.B. Brady/Library and Archives Canada/C-2422.

obtain a greater voice in British imperial policy affecting Canada. The prime minister later appointed Alexander Tilloch Galt, who briefly served as the dominion's first finance minister in 1867, as high commissioner for Canada in London. Only reluctantly did the British government approve the new quasi-diplomatic post, and then only on the condition that Canada would not use the term "minister." Galt's tasks included the promotion of Canada's exports to Britain and of British investment in Canada, as well as the encouragement of British emigration to the Canadian Northwest.

Continentalism

Whereas the Conservatives became the party increasingly associated with closer ties to the British Empire, the Liberals favoured stronger continental ties as a means of advancing Canadian autonomy. These ties took the form of free trade or reciprocity with the United States, a principle and platform of both British and Canadian liberalism. Partisanship aside, free trade appealed particularly to the exporters of fish, agricultural products, and timber, and as a result, took on regional dimensions. The Liberal Party supported a return to the Reciprocity Treaty of 1854 or a restricted reciprocity agreement, which would apply to natural products only. Some favoured unrestricted reciprocity in some manufactured goods in addition to natural resources. A select few proposed commercial union—an integrated economic union with the United States with a free interchange of all products, a sharing of internal revenue taxes, and a common tariff policy against other countries.

Free trade could occur, however, only if the Americans were open to such an agreement. The signing of the Treaty of Washington in 1871 did not lead to such a deal but it did at least improve relations. Protectionists dominated the American Senate and the Republican administrations turned down Canadian offers to renegotiate a reciprocity treaty. Even the Conservatives in Canada recognized the value of the Reciprocity Agreement and the benefits it had brought. Macdonald actively sought a renewal of the agreement after Confederation. It was only in the face of the American refusal that the Conservatives moved toward the National Policy, the tariff, and protectionism.

The Trade Question and the 1891 Election

The trade issue was front and centre in the election of 1891. The Liberals worked for closer Canadian–American ties, although they differed on what form these ties should take. The most extreme position was put forward by Goldwin Smith, who advocated political union with the United States. Smith was a British historian and a Liberal, but he vocally supported the North during the American Civil War and opposed many of the imperial policies of British Liberal Prime Minister William Gladstone. He moved first to the United States and then to Canada in 1871, where he worked as a journalist. Smith regarded Canada as an "unnatural" country economically, geographically, and culturally. Political expediency alone held it together and Canada's natural destiny lay in a larger North American nation. Smith looked toward continental union as the means to assimilate the French Canadians, whom he regarded as a backward people.

Richard Cartwright, former minister of finance in the Liberal government of Alexander Mackenzie, was one of the most vocal advocates for unrestricted reciprocity with the United States. He decried the Conservative National Policy, claiming that only "parasites" gained from high tariffs. By contrast, Edward Blake, former leader of the federal Liberal Party (1881–87), opposed unrestricted reciprocity, seeing it as a threat to national interests. Wilfrid Laurier, as party leader, stood in the middle. He pressured Blake into silence on his opposition until after the election, at which time Blake publicly denounced the policy in an open letter to his constituency. Laurier committed the Liberal party to unrestricted reciprocity.

Canadian manufacturers opposed any form of reciprocity. In 1887, they published a manifesto warning that reciprocity would adversely affect the infant industries of Canada that were still struggling under the National Policy to survive a recession. Prime Minister Macdonald now claimed that unrestricted reciprocity threatened Canada's independence, because it would ultimately lead to political union with the United States. The Liberal position was "veiled treason." He maintained that protectionism was the means to prevent American assimilation and uphold the British connection. He declared his loyalty to Britain in his popular campaign slogan—"A British subject I was born, and a British subject I will die"—and proceeded to drape himself in the British flag. The spectre of American assimilation had clearly not disappeared; it had rather changed form. The threat was now not military; it was economic. In time, it would also become cultural.

The 1891 Election Results

The Conservatives won the election of 1891, but only by a narrow majority of 27 seats. They lost seats to the Liberals in close votes in the rural areas, which tended to support free trade, but won most of the urban vote in Ontario and Quebec, where protectionism was strong. They made their real gains, however, in the outlying provinces—"the shreds and patches

Rife with visual symbolism, including Uncle Sam, Miss Canada, and the British Lion, this electoral poster from 1891 depicts John A. Macdonald as "Miss Canada's Rescuer."

Source: Library and Archives Canada, Acc. no. 1983-33-1096.

of Confederation," as the disgruntled Richard Cartwright called them. The Conservatives won in all three Maritime provinces and returned fourteen out of a possible fifteen members in the West. With the open backing of the CPR, they won every seat but one (in Manitoba) along the railway's main line from Vancouver to Montreal. When asked about that one loss, Cornelius Van Horne, president of the CPR, replied that it must have been a case of oversight on the CPR's part. The election of 1891 temporarily shelved unrestricted reciprocity as a Liberal policy. Two decades would pass before the Liberals would champion it once again in the election of 1911.

Imperialism

Many English Canadians favoured stronger British ties. After 1875, British attitudes to empire changed. Prime Minister Benjamin Disraeli's statement in the 1850s that colonies were "mill-stones around the neck of the British" gave way to what was considered a "new imperialism" in the late nineteenth century. Indeed, Disraeli himself, as Conservative prime minister, became one of its most ardent supporters, having come to appreciate the importance of colonies in maintaining Britain's military and economic supremacy. In particular, overseas colonies proved important for British hegemony, as Germany and Italy became major European powers and as the United States threatened to supplant Britain as the leading English-speaking country in the world. As British power was challenged, policy shifted from informal (economic) to formal (military) empire. Informal empire was most evident in Britain's move to an imperial policy of free trade in the 1840s and the saying that "trade follows the flag." Formal empire was much more costly and entailed putting troops on the ground in the distant corners of the world. The new imperialism also took the form of an aggressive outpouring of emotional attachment to the Empire. People assumed it represented a strengthening of imperial sentiment. While this may have been the case, it was a direct response to threats now challenging British supremacy. In hindsight, it signalled the long decline of the Empire.

Imperialism, however, represented more than trade, tariffs, and guns. It was an intellectual and spiritual ideology. Most British subjects believed implicitly in the superiority of the Anglo-Saxon race. Applying Charles Darwin's theory of evolution in the animal kingdom to human society, theorists argued that some races were born superior and were better fit to survive and adapt than others. A quick glance at race relations around the globe seemed to provide evidence as to which races were inferior. Imperialists argued that the white race's superior position made it imperative for Anglo-Saxons to spread their "virtues"—their British values and Christian beliefs—to the lesser races of Asia, Africa, and the Pacific. In the words of the unofficial poet laureate of Empire, Rudyard Kipling, it was the "white man's burden."

Imperialism crossed gender and class lines. Its cultural sway led many in the working classes to offer their support. While labourites used the writings of Karl Marx and Vladimir Lenin to argue that imperialism was simply the highest stage of capitalism and to the detriment of the working classes, the emotional appeal of imperialism and the racial superiority it offered appealed to the masses.

Women also played an important role in the imperialist movement. Organizations such as the Imperial Order Daughters of the Empire (IODE), founded by Scottish Canadian Margaret Polson Murray during the South African War, became strong advocates of imperial sentiment. The organization's motto—"One Flag, One Throne, One Country"—summarized its aspirations. Through its first chapters in Fredericton and Montreal, the IODE sought to promote the British Empire and its institutions in schools. By World War I, it was one of the largest women's voluntary associations in English Canada.

These women, however, were much more than advocates of imperialism; they were symbols of it and represented the moral, religious, and spiritual components of its ideology. They were the bearers of British civilization and thus the true "Empire builders." Their children were the offspring of the dominant race and thus the means to ensure its survival. English-Canadian imperial literature extolled the virtues of the fairer sex of the Empire builders, by contrasting the noble attributes of British women with the "degenerate qualities" of "coloured women" in the subservient colonial society. As well, protecting this "fairer sex" became a pretext for suppressing and controlling the Indigenous population. Once again, racism and imperialism were fused to accentuate the superiority of the conqueror by emphasizing the inferiority of the conquered, the "other," in the imperial–colonial relationship.

Imperialism as Nationalism

In her novel *The Imperialist* (1904), novelist Sara Jeanette Duncan presented an Ontarian community that was deeply loyal and affectionately attached to Britain. Imperialists believed that Canada could offer much to the Empire. The new dominion represented a rejuvenation of British values. In return, the Empire could protect and advance Canada's national interests. In this sense, as historian Carl Berger has written, "imperialism was one form of Canadian nationalism."[1] They believed that Canada was destined to become the heart of the British Empire. Throughout history, they argued, all great races had come out of northern climates. English Canadians were the last group of Anglo-Saxons to struggle in a cold, rugged, northern climate, and this struggle "in the true north, strong and free" strengthened their will to survive. It prepared them to assume the mantle of imperial grandeur as it inevitably passed from British hands. At the same time, imperialists argued that in aiding the Empire, Canadians would also be helping themselves. They envisioned an "imperial federation" as a means to free Canada from economic depression, ethnic tension, provincialism, and threatened American annexation, thus enabling it to reach greater heights. Imperial federation was a proposal advanced across the Empire to replace colonial imperialism. The general idea was to create a federal state with a common Parliament made up of all British colonies. The colonies would be provided more of a voice in imperial policy, while the British government would be able to share the costs of imperial defence. In 1887 a Canadian branch of the Imperial Federation League was formed, an organization begun in Britain three years earlier.

A HISTORICAL PORTRAIT

Sara Jeannette Duncan

Sara Jeannette Duncan symbolized the "new woman" of the late nineteenth century. She was the first Canadian woman to become a journalist and counted among her friends Pauline Johnson, the Mohawk poet, and Augusta Stowe, the daughter of Emily Stowe, the first woman to graduate from a Canadian medical school.

Duncan was born in Brantford, Ontario, in 1861. She became a teacher but decided instead to pursue a career in journalism. She published poetry, and obtained a job as a travel writer and then a columnist for the Toronto *Globe*, writing under the pseudonym "Garth". Duncan moved to Washington, D.C., in 1885 to work for The *Washington Post*. She was put in charge of the literature department but also took over the "Woman's World" section. She also began publishing under her own name. Two years later, Duncan became parliamentary correspondent for the *Montreal Star* and moved to Ottawa.

In 1888, she and a female friend embarked on a world tour—unchaperoned—by going "the wrong way" via Asia rather than Europe. They visited Japan, Ceylon, and India before arriving in England. Duncan participated in what were considered "unladylike activities" for the time: riding a locomotive cowcatcher through the Rockies; travelling by donkey, camel, and elephant in India; and taking a catamaran to Ceylon. Her account of her tour came out in serial form in a popular

British magazine as "A Social Departure," and then appeared in book form under the same title. Upon marriage to an English official she met in India, she settled there but she split her time between England and India.

Duncan wrote poetry, short stories, plays, and novels. Most of her novels were set in India but she is best known for *The Imperialist*, published in 1904. Modelled on Brantford, Ontario, it combined her intimate knowledge of Canada with her wider knowledge of the British Empire, acquired through her world travels.

Duncan viewed imperialism along the lines of the Canadian imperialists of her day. She too admired Britain as the mother country, but was repulsed by its materialism and militarism. What imperialism needed was a new seat of power and Duncan saw Canada as the logical new location: "In the scrolls of the future it is already written that the centre of the Empire must shift—and where, if not to Canada?" The imperial tie boosted Canadian nationalism and warded off the danger of absorption into the United States. *The Imperialist*, however, was not particularly well received at the time and only gained attention in the 1960s as one of the first modern Canadian novels. Sara Jeannette Duncan died of chronic lung disease on July 22, 1922, in England.

Sara Jeannette Duncan, poet, novelist, travel writer, and journalist, was a keen observer of Canadian society and the British connection.

Source: Library and Archives Canada/C-46447.

The Imperial Federation League

An influential and well-connected group of white Ontario men advanced the cause of the Imperial Federation League in Canada. Colonel George Taylor Denison came from a wealthy family in Toronto and played a role in organizing Canada's military forces. He saw active service in the Fenian raids in 1866 and the North-West Rebellion in 1885, and wrote a book in 1892 entitled *The Struggle for Imperial Unity*. George Monro Grant was a Presbyterian minister from Nova Scotia who became principal of Queen's College in Kingston. He advanced spiritual unity to overcome Canada's linguistic, cultural, and racial divisions. A teacher from New Brunswick, George Parkin also worked for the League, travelling across New Zealand and Australia speaking on the issue of imperial unity. He argued that the British Empire had to remain at the top of the communications (telegraph) and transportation (sea and rail) revolutions in order to stave off threats to its imperial power. As the senior dominion and an integral part in the all-red route, Canada was positioned as the keystone of the Empire. The Anglo-Saxon race had to resist the temptations of materialism and the trappings of power, in order to use the Empire as a moral means of spiritual regeneration. He saw himself as "a wandering Evangelist of Empire." In 1896 Parkin was appointed principal of Upper Canada College in Toronto, a position he held until 1902, at which time he became the organizing secretary for the Rhodes Scholarship Trust, an educational fund honouring Cecil Rhodes, the British South African arch-imperialist and mining magnate. The scholarships enabled students from the British Empire to attend Oxford University.

WHERE HISTORIANS DISAGREE

Canada's British Connection

Historians have long debated the evolution of Canada's relationship with Great Britain. Responding to early historians who emphasized the historical ties, shared values, and mutual interests, Oscar Skelton, later Undersecretary of State for External Affairs (1925–41), was wary of ties to the Empire, because he viewed them to as inimical to the development of a Canadian nationalism acceptable to both French and English Canadians. In his historical works on Wilfrid Laurier in the 1920s, Skelton defended the value of Canada's British cultural heritage but advanced the dominion's unique interests that required greater autonomy within the Empire.[1]

Writing in the 1930s, Frank H. Underhill echoed Skelton's liberal-autonomist position, insisting that Canada's British connection was at odds with its own interests. His stance changed, however, as Canada reached its zenith of international influence as a middle power by the end of World War II. Underhill employed the colony-to-nation framework to describe the loosening of the British connections as a positive and inevitable process resulting in Canada's maturation into an autonomous nation. The British connection while lessening, however, was not to be completely severed. Canada remained a member of the British family.[2]

In the aftermath of World War II, it was clear that Britain was being surpassed by the United States as the new imperial power. Donald Creighton and other conservative-nationalist historians such as Arthur Lower and W.L. Morton, looked to the British connection as the counterforce to the pull of continentalism, and thus Canada's means of maintaining its distinct identity in North America.[3] As Adele Perry points out, "in the heady years following the Second World War, historians of Canada writing in English traded in the rubric of the empire for that of the nation."[4] Creighton mourned the loss of the British connection and was irked by the new English-Canadian cultural nationalism. In *The Forked Road: Canada 1939–1957*, he argued that the Liberal governments of prime ministers Mackenzie King and Louis St. Laurent abandoned Britain in its blind rush for autonomy and were responsible for thrusting Canada into the arms of the United States, thereby betraying Canada's past while sabotaging its future.[5]

In the 1960s, the writings of philosopher George Grant (grandson of George Monro Grant) highlighted Canada's search for an identity, caught between hegemonic British and American forces. In *Lament for a Nation*, Grant claimed that the idea of a British nation surviving in North America was a romanticized dream.[6]

A new generation of historians in the 1970s and 1980s downplayed the British connection and reimagined Canada as a multicultural, peacekeeping, and tolerant nation. In this reconstructed history Empire and imperialism "slipped from view."[7] Carl Berger, in his influential 1970 work *The Sense of Power*, argued that despite the political split between conservative imperialists and liberal autonomists, and the longstanding division over the imperial question, "imperialism was one form of Canadian nationalism."[8]

Berger's work remained unchallenged in part because the attention of Canadian historians drifted even further from the ideas of empire. The rise of multiculturalism in the 1970s focused the gaze of historians on Canada's "limited identities." Works appeared on the nation's numerous "ethnic" groups. The British, however, as the hegemonic group, were not deemed ethnic.

With the turn of the millennium, some Canadian historians began returning to empire, arguing that this connection remained significant much longer than previously claimed. Phillip Buckner criticized Berger's focus on the elite men who supported the Imperial Federation League, such as Denison, Grant, and Parkin. By drawing attention to the imperialism of other social groups, such as the Orange Order, the Imperial Order Daughters of the Empire (IODE), and the Canadian Legion, Buckner asserted that Canada continued to be part of a "British world" that was less monolithic and more widespread, flexible, and enduring. "Support for the British connection in Canada survived well into the twentieth century because the imperial relationship had real meaning to a majority of English-speaking Canadians and fed into their sense of national identity."[9]

Diplomatic historians are also pointing to the longevity of the British connection. Francine McKenzie argued that while Canada was less willing after 1945 to contribute to British and Commonwealth strength, significant independent (rather than centralized) collaboration between Canada and Great Britain continued to be "in the national interest."[10] Robert Bothwell emphasized both the patriotic and the economic importance of Canada's British connections. Ultimately, however, he concluded that Britain's inability to rebound from the war made these efforts a "dead end" by 1947 and forced Canada to increasingly depend on the United States.[11]

Adele Perry argued that Canadian historians must finally break free from their nationalist confines and move toward more "transnational" and "postcolonial" approaches: "The rediscovery of imperial frames of reference also is providing another route by which Canadian history is finding more global frames of reference," one that will "prompt us to question the meaning, impact, and limits of the nation as an experience and a tool of analysis."[12]

1   O.D. Skelton, *The Life and Letters of Sir Wilfrid Laurier, vols. 1 and 2* (Toronto: Oxford University Press, 1921).

2   Frank H. Underhill, *The British Commonwealth: An Experiment in Co-operation Among Nations* (Durham: Duke University Commonwealth-Studies Center, Duke University Press, 1956).

3   Carl Berger, *The Writing of Canadian History: Aspects of English-Canadian Historical Writing Since 1900*, 2nd ed. (Toronto: University of Toronto Press, 1986), pp. 128–36, 251–6.

4   Adele Perry, "Nation, Empire and the Writing of History in Canada in English," in Christopher Dummit and Michael Dawson (eds.), *Contesting Clio's Craft: New Directions and Debates in Canadian History* (London: Institute for the

Study of the Americas, 2009), p. 129; J.E. Igartua, *The Other Quiet Revolution: National Identities in English Canada, 1945–1971* (Vancouver, UBC Press, 2005).

5   Donald G. Creighton, *The Forked Road: Canada 1939–1957* (Toronto: McClelland and Stewart, 1976).

6   George Grant, *Lament for a Nation: The Defeat of Canadian Nationalism*. (Toronto: McClelland and Stewart, 1965).

7   Perry, p. 131.

8   Carl Berger, *The Sense of Power: Studies in the Ideas of Canadian Imperialism, 1867–1914* (Toronto: University of Toronto Press, 1970), p. 259.

9   Phillip A. Buckner, "The Long Goodbye," in Phillip A. Buckner, ed., *Rediscovering the British World* (Calgary: University of Calgary Press, 2005), p. 203.

10 Francine McKenzie, "In the National Interest: Dominions' Support for Britain and the Commonwealth after the Second World War," *Journal of Imperial and Commonwealth History*, 34(4): 553–76.

11 Robert Bothwell, *Alliance and Illusion: Canada and the World, 1945–1984* (Vancouver: UBC Press, 2007), p. 39.

12 Perry, p. 140.

Stephen Leacock was a younger member of the Imperial Federation League, and later of the British Empire League, as the organization came to be known after 1896. Leacock, best remembered as one of Canada's finest humorists, expressed his serious side in his writings on imperialism. He saw imperial unity as a means by which Canadians could transcend their parochial and narrow provincial concerns to achieve a "Greater Canada," to use the title of one of his writings.

These men—Denison, Grant, Parkin, and Leacock—became the intellectual leaders of the imperial movement in Canada in the pre–World War I era. But the imperial question was divisive. While large numbers of English Canadians identified with their message, French Canadians, Catholic Irish Canadians, First Nations peoples, and the growing number of non-Anglo-Saxon immigrants often did not.

Queen Victoria's Diamond Jubilee

The strength of imperial sentiment peaked in the 1890s. Joseph Chamberlain, appointed to the Colonial Office in 1895, personified the imperial spirit and spearheaded the movement. Two years later, Queen Victoria celebrated her Diamond Jubilee—sixty years as the ruling monarch—in a spectacular celebration to show the world the splendour and the might of the British Empire. Representatives from all the colonies, including Canada's new prime minister, Wilfrid Laurier, travelled to London, England, to join in the festivities. Back in Canada, communities across the nation joined in the military parades and reviews, assemblies of school children, patriotic speeches, unveiling of monuments, and numerous banquets. The occasion was used to remind new immigrants of their membership in the greatest Empire the world had seen. Schools—the primary agents of assimilation—celebrated the jubilee in grand fashion. Special commemorative stamps were issued, among them a Canadian stamp showing a map of the world splashed with red for all the British possessions. The inscription read: "We hold a vaster empire than has been." A year after Queen Victoria's Diamond Jubilee, several provinces established Empire Day on May 23—the day before the Queen's birthday. Ontario, Nova Scotia, and the Protestant schools of Quebec celebrated the occasion in 1898, and other provinces followed suit. The day was designed to use the public schools for promoting patriotic sentiments.

But beneath the celebrations, all was not well. While in London for the jubilee, the dominion leaders were taken on a tour of the British shipyards. They were shown the latest weapon in the naval arsenal—the dreadnought. But at the same time, they were given a sombre message: British supremacy of the seas was being challenged by Germany. Steel manufacturing was fuelling the German economy and used to build a formidable navy. For the first time, Canada and the other dominions were informed that they might be asked to contribute to imperial defence. This message was particularly sobering for Prime Minister Laurier (now "Sir" Wilfrid after the festivities). Laurier was well aware that the imperial question would threaten national unity back home.

The Boer War

In 1899, the British Empire extended over a quarter of the earth's land surface and contained nearly a quarter of its people. The Royal Navy, the largest in the world, made Britain the greatest maritime power. When British imperial expansion in southern Africa led to conflict with the Boers—the descendants of European settlers, mainly Protestants from the Netherlands—the result seemed a foregone conclusion. The British coveted diamonds discovered in the region and conflict erupted between Cecil Rhodes, prime minister of the Cape Colony, and Paul Kruger, leader of the Boer republics. Kruger threatened war if the British did not withdraw their troops. The British assumed an easy victory over the two small Boer republics: the Transvaal and the Orange Free State. Yet the war turned out quite differently. Initially, the Afrikaners inflicted a series of defeats on the British. They knew the country and effectively practised guerrilla warfare techniques. Britain turned to its dominions, including Canada, for help.

The response demonstrated the strength of imperial sentiment in Canada. Most newspapers, especially those in Montreal and Toronto, demanded Canadian participation. After all, Britain had long defended Canada. Should Canada shy away from its duty and responsibility when called upon? Lord Minto, the governor general, and Major General Edward Hutton, commander of the Canadian militia, worked out plans for a Canadian contingent without even informing Prime Minister Laurier. A cable from Joseph Chamberlain, the British colonial secretary, thanked the self-governing dominions for their "offer to serve in South Africa." His thanks were premature, however, since the Canadian government had not yet made an official statement of support. The cable was leaked to the press.

Prime Minister Laurier tried to temper this enthusiasm. While he admired the British Empire as the world's leading protector of liberty and justice, he opposed imperial federation. It was one thing to fight to defend Canada or even Britain; it was another to die fighting to maintain imperial control over conquered peoples in the distant corners of the world. Laurier believed that the Canadian Parliament, not the British colonial secretary, should decide Canada's participation.

The Boer War aroused strong anti-imperialistic sentiments in Quebec. If French Canadians sympathized with anyone in the struggle, it was with the Boers, whom they regarded as a kindred oppressed minority. Henri Bourassa, a young Liberal politician and impressive orator like his grandfather, the legendary Louis-Joseph Papineau, leader of the Rebellion of 1837 in Lower Canada, opposed Canadian involvement in this distant imperialist war. Bourassa equated imperialism with militarism and commercialism. He condemned the British Empire "not because it is British, but because it is Imperial. All empires are hateful. They stand in the way of human liberty, and true progress, intellectual and moral. They serve nothing but brutal instincts and material objects." He was not, however, prepared to advocate Canadian independence, believing that internal divisions between English and French Canadians within an independent Canada might lead to annexation to the United States, which he opposed.

He favoured an autonomous Canada within the British Empire, a country in which the two linguistic groups respected each other.

Compromise

Laurier feared the imperial question because it caused the traditional divisions within Canada to resurface. And as with the Riel question, it created a no-win situation. For two days, Laurier's cabinet met to find a solution. On October 13, 1899, the prime minister devised a compromise. He proposed that "in view of the well-known desire of a great many Canadians who are ready to take service under such conditions," the Canadian government would equip and transport a volunteer force of 1000 men for service alongside the British. Once in South Africa, however, the troops would become the British government's responsibility and would fight as British soldiers. The British would train and equip them. Laurier informed English and French Canadians alike that this decision to send troops should not be "construed as a precedent for future action."

Canada assembled volunteers as the 2nd Battalion of the Royal Canadian Regiment, and they sailed to South Africa. After two months of training amid the extreme heat and suffering from typhoid fever, the Canadians marched into action in the interior. They won a strategic victory at

Canadian soldiers in Ottawa departing for the Boer War. In total, some 7300 Canadian volunteers fought in the South African war (1899–1902). The enthusiasm of the volunteer effort surprised Prime Minister Laurier.

Source: Library and Archives Canada/C-003950.

Paardeburg but were then subject to the Boer guerrilla tactics. As the war dragged on, Canada sent 7300 volunteers to fight in South Africa. When the war ended in 1902, 245 had died overseas, more than half from disease. The British emerged victorious and the two republics (the Transvaal and the Orange Free State) were annexed to the Empire, eventually becoming part of the Dominion of South Africa in 1910.

Laurier's compromise policy pleased no one. The Toronto *Globe* demanded that Canada assume full responsibility for Canadian troops in South Africa. Many English Canadians were appalled and embarrassed by what they considered the weak response offered by their country. In Montreal, a group of McGill students attacked the offices of the French-language newspapers in the city and fought street battles with French-Canadian university students. Henri Bourassa, on the other hand, denounced Laurier as *un vendu*, a sellout to the English-Canadian imperialists. He warned that the sending of troops established a dangerous precedent, since Britain would now expect support every time the Empire became entangled in future wars. Bourassa resigned his parliamentary seat in protest on October 18, 1899, only to be re-elected as an independent by acclamation six months later. Laurier was losing critical support in Quebec and his compromising policy on the imperial question was unlikely to gain back that support in English Canada.

In 1902, Joseph Chamberlain, hoping to capitalize on the imperial sentiment generated by the Boer War, called a colonial conference to promote imperial federation. But Prime Minister

Thousands of Torontonians crowded city streets on June 5, 1901, to celebrate the announced end of the Boer War (which actually continued until 1902) and the final submission of the Afrikaner troops.

Source: Archives of Ontario, F 1143-1, S 1244, York Pioneer and Historical Society Fonds.

Laurier resisted closer imperial unity. On the eve of the colonial conference, he assured Parliament that he would not "bring Canada into the vortex of militarism which is the curse and blight of Europe." At the conference, he opposed Canada becoming part of a consolidated imperial defence force. Laurier would only agree that Canadians contribute to their own defence. The issue was not about loyalty or even attachment to Britain; it was a debate over the role that Canada would play within the Empire. If Canada maintained control over its imperial commitments, it would control the potential for division.

To this end, Canada assumed responsibility for the British-controlled ports of Halifax, Nova Scotia and Esquimalt, British Columbia, in 1904. In 1909 Joseph Pope, former private secretary to Sir John A. Macdonald and secretary of state after 1896, established the department of external affairs to deal with aspects of the dominion's foreign affairs. Laurier believed the department would allow Canada to become more autonomous in its external relations without offending British or English-Canadian imperialists.

Quebec and French-Canadian Nationalism

Imperialist sentiments in English Canada contributed to a parallel French-Canadian nationalism in Quebec. Inspired by Henri Bourassa, a group of nationalists founded the *Ligue nationaliste in 1903* and their own newspaper, *Le nationaliste*, a year later. The organization had a three-point program: Canadian autonomy within the British Empire; provincial autonomy within the federal state; and the development of Canada's resources. Other nationalists founded the *Association catholique de la jeunesse canadienne-française* (ACJC), or "Catholic Association of French-Canadian Youth," in 1904. This group, under the leadership of Lionel Groulx, a Catholic priest and historian, recruited new members from the classical colleges.

Jules-Paul Tardivel, a Franco-American born in Kentucky who came to Quebec in 1868 to study French and then took up the causes of ultramontanism and French-Canadian nationalism, took a more extreme position. In his newspaper, *La vérité*, and in his futuristic novel *Pour la patrie* (1895), Tardivel proposed Quebec's separation from Canada to create a Catholic state on the banks of the St. Lawrence River. In an exchange published in 1904, Tardivel and Bourassa outlined their different conceptions of French Canada. "Our own nationalism is French-Canadian nationalism. . . . For us our fatherland is—we do not say precisely the Province of Quebec—but French Canada; the nation we wish to see founded at the hour marked by Divine Providence is the French-Canadian nation." Bourassa replied:

> For us the fatherland is all Canada, that is, a federation of distinct races and autonomous provinces. The nation that we wish to see develop is the Canadian nation, composed of French Canadians and English Canadians, that is of two elements separated by language and religion, and by the legal dispositions necessary to the preservation of their respective traditions, but united in a feeling of brotherhood, in a common attachment to the common fatherland.

In this interchange lay the essence of two currents of twentieth-century French-Canadian nationalism: one leading to separatism, the other to a bilingual and bicultural nation.

The Alaska Boundary Dispute

At the turn of the century, a new dispute arose between Canada and the United States, this time over the boundary between Alaska and the Yukon Territory. The dispute had its origins in the Anglo–Russian Treaty of 1825, which established an ambiguous boundary line, "to follow

Miners packing their equipment and supplies up the Chilkoot Pass, 1897–98, on their way to the Klondike gold fields. On reaching the summit, they had to return to get another load. It took many ascents, because the North-West Mounted Police required each miner to have a year's supply (about 500 kilograms) of provisions upon entering Canada.

Source: E.A. Hegg/Library and Archives Canada/C-5142.

the summit of the mountains situated parallel to the coast," between British and Russian territory running north from Portland Channel. The territory, however, encompassed many mountain chains and an uneven coast.

The Americans adopted the Russian stance on the border after they purchased Alaska in 1867. They sought a continuous border along the Pacific coast, and after British Columbia joined Confederation in 1871, they denied Canada's claim to several fiords with access to the Yukon. As would become consistent with Canada's policy toward the North, the issue emerged only when the remote region offered up resource riches. The news that gold had been discovered in the Yukon in 1897 suddenly made the boundary question of utmost importance and access to the area became hotly contested. Following the precedent set by the California gold rush of the 1840s, prospectors crossed the mountain passes into the Yukon, and by the summer of 1898, Dawson City had a population of more than 20,000 people, making it temporarily the largest Canadian city west of Winnipeg. The North-West Mounted Police were sent to the new frontier to impose law and order. In June 1898, the Canadian government made the Yukon a separate territory with its own commissioner to help prevent the area from becoming a de facto part of Alaska. The government also responded to First Nations' requests for treaty, in order to have the local groups surrender title to the land.

The Americans and Canadians (and British, since Canada still had no formal place in matters of external affairs) tried to settle the issue with a joint commission. Britain asked the Laurier government to appoint four Canadians as representatives to the British "side" of the commission.

The number of Canadians appointed (particularly in relation to the precedent of the Washington Treaty of 1871) was testament to the developments within the dominion's autonomy over the previous two decades. It appeared at first as though a quick settlement could be reached, but negotiations broke down as each side refused to compromise.

To break the deadlock, the three countries agreed in 1902 to appoint a six-member tribunal, three from each side, to review the disputed border. Britain appointed a British judge and two Canadian lawyers for its side. The United States appointed three members who came to the bargaining table determined to secure the full acceptance of the American claim. Furthermore, President Theodore Roosevelt informed the British that if the Americans failed to win the case, he would "run the line" on their claim.

In the end, Lord Alverstone, the lone British member of the tribunal, sided with the Americans. He agreed that the boundary line should run around the heads of the inlets, giving the United States territorial control. He also agreed to the equal division of the four islands at the mouth of Portland Channel. In a vote of four to two, the commission favoured this settlement. But the two Canadian commissioners were opposed and refused to affix their signatures to the agreement.

Canadian historians have debated the justifications for Alverstone's decision. The instinctive nationalistic response was that once again Canadian interests were sacrificed to maintain American friendship. Alverstone, however, was under pressure from the British government not to allow a deadlocked decision. More recently, historians argue that the Canadian position was in fact the weaker of the two. Regardless, Canadians at the time, including the prime minister, considered Alverstone's decision to side with the Americans to be "one of those concessions which

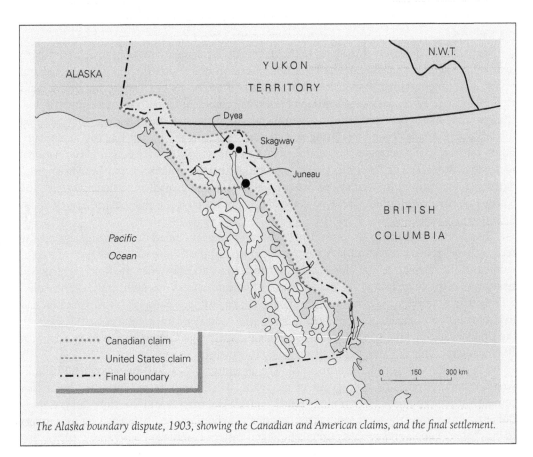

The Alaska boundary dispute, 1903, showing the Canadian and American claims, and the final settlement.

have made British diplomacy odious to Canadian people." The issue did demonstrate the need for Canada to control its own foreign policy.

Relations with Britain and the United States damaged Laurier's government, but the Liberals remained in office. The West was booming and the economy remained prosperous. Nova Scotian lawyer Robert Borden became leader of the Conservatives in 1901, but he lost the elections of 1904 (137 Liberals; 70 Conservatives) and 1908 (133 Liberals; 85 Conservatives).

Revisiting Reciprocity

After the contentious Alaska boundary dispute, Canadian–American relations did improve. By 1910, closer trade relations seemed possible. This time the Americans took the initiative to open up negotiations. President William Howard Taft, who came to office in 1909, favoured lower tariffs, arguing that expanding American industries needed Canadian raw materials. On January 26, the Liberals made a surprise announcement in Parliament: a reciprocal trade agreement had been reached with the United States that, in essence, renewed the popular Reciprocity Treaty of 1854. The proposal would allow Canadian natural products free entry into American markets in exchange for American manufactured goods entering Canada at a lower tariff rate. Contrary to the previous deal, however, this agreement was to come into effect through concurrent legislation passed by the two governments rather than by treaty, enabling Canada to avoid seeking British approval. The American Congress passed the legislation in July 1911. It remained only for the Canadian Parliament to give its approval. After decades of seeking another reciprocity deal, and in the face of a deteriorating political situation as a result of the imperial question, it seemed the Laurier Liberals had pulled a rabbit out of the hat.

Very quickly, however, opposition to the reciprocity agreement arose in the manufacturing heartland of central Canada. But the basis for opposition was couched mainly in national and imperial sentiment, rather than economics. Clifford Sifton, no longer a westerner but rather a well-established Torontonian, led a group of eighteen prominent Ontario manufacturers, industrialists, and financiers to petition the government against the agreement because they believed it threatened Canada's economic future and its close ties with the British Empire. Reciprocity, Sifton warned, spells "retrogression, commercial subordination, the destruction of our national ideals and displacement from our proud position as the rising hope of the British empire." Sifton's group went on to become the core of a newly created Canadian National League. The league published a pamphlet, *The Road to Washington*, in which it warned that the United States intended to annex Canada.

Inopportune statements by imprudent American politicians aided the campaign against the reciprocity agreement. Champ Clark, speaker-designate of the House of Representatives, commented on the agreement: "I am for it, because I hope to see the day when the American flag will float over every square foot of the British North American possessions clear to the North Pole." President Taft himself noted that "Canada stands at the parting of the ways." The dominion had to choose between remaining an isolated protectionist country or integrating economically with the United States. But the statement was interpreted to mean that Canada had to choose between Britain and the United States, imperialism and continentalism.

The debate, however, was also regional. The agricultural West and the farm belt of southwestern Ontario were firmly in favour of reciprocity. High tariffs meant little to regions that primarily produced grains to be traded on the international market and therefore did not enjoy domestic protection. The tariff symbolized "economic subordination" because it forced farmers to purchase materials and supplies from central and eastern Canada at higher costs, rather than purchasing them more cheaply from the United States. Laurier had gone so far as to connote the tariff with bondage. After years of pressure and lobbying, the "free-trading" Liberals were finally acting on their promise to take action on the tariff.

The Naval Crisis

By 1911, the Laurier Liberals had been in power for fifteen years. Although their reign coincided with a "golden era" of prosperity, the imperial question had taken its toll. The successful negotiation of the reciprocity deal, it was assumed, spelled sure re-election. The Conservatives meanwhile were stunned by the news. But controversy over the agreement emerged and it soon joined with the imperial question to threaten the Liberals.

Tension between Germany and Britain increased at the turn of the century, and was demonstrated through the Boer War. In 1908, the British press openly warned of Germany's growing naval strength, which threatened Britain's control of the high seas. Critics demanded that the British government immediately build eight super-battleships, or dreadnoughts. Many in Canada insisted that the dominion contribute to the cause. French-Canadian nationalists such as Henri Bourassa opposed such a move, claiming it would lead to greater Canadian involvement in imperial wars.

Both the Liberals and the Conservatives agreed that in the long term Canada should establish a Canadian navy, rather than contribute funds regularly and directly to the British admiralty. But the two parties differed on the best short-term policy. The Conservatives supported an emergency direct cash contribution to Britain in the present crisis, while the Liberals favoured the immediate establishment of a Canadian navy under Canadian command, to be used by Britain in the event of war if the Canadian Parliament approved. Again, the debate centred on how Canada should contribute to imperial policy.

In January 1910, the Laurier government introduced the Naval Service Bill. It proposed that Canada construct five cruisers and six destroyers and establish a naval college to train Canadian officers. The government could, "in case of war," place the force under imperial command with the approval of Parliament.

Opposition to the Naval Service Bill

The government's decision once again divided imperialist and autonomist, Conservative and Liberal. On the one hand, the Conservatives denounced what they derisively labelled a "tin-pot navy" as a disgrace to Canada's role in the Empire. Laurier's compromise position would produce an ineffective force that would effectively aid neither Canada nor the Empire. On the other hand, Bourassa and the nationalistes in Quebec opposed the Naval Service Bill because it went too far. They asserted that the navy would be used to fight imperial wars. "It is the most complete backward step Canada has made in half a century," Bourassa declared. He could support a navy for home defence, but not one that might involve Canada in the "whirlpool of militarism." He questioned whether Canada needed a navy at all, since the only threat to the country could come from the United States, with whom Canadians had enjoyed a century of peace.

Bourassa's attacks against Laurier had become increasingly strident. By 1907, he abandoned the federal Liberals for provincial politics, where he attacked the Quebec government's close links with foreign entrepreneurs who wanted to exploit the province's natural resources. In 1910, he established a daily newspaper, *Le devoir*, in which he championed his vision of Canada as an independent member of the British Empire, one that placed Canadian interests first. In that year, the nationalistes in Quebec ran a candidate against the Liberals in a federal by-election in the "safe" seat of Drummond–Arthabaska. Laurier, who had represented the district in the Quebec legislature, campaigned personally on behalf of the Liberal candidate, only to see the nationalistes win. If the Liberals were losing their base of support in Quebec, the party was in trouble. It was hoped that the reciprocity deal would save the day—and the government.

The 1911 Election

During the 1911 federal election campaign, Laurier faced vigorous attacks from both imperialists in Ontario (who branded him a continentalist on the reciprocity issue) and nationalists in Quebec (who called him an imperialist on the naval issue). "I am neither," an exasperated Laurier protested during an election rally in St. Jean, Quebec, in August. "I am a *Canadian*." His policy, he claimed, was one of "true Canadianism, of moderation, of conciliation." The Liberals, however, tarnished by corruption and inefficient government after fifteen years in office, lost the election. The results were a reversal of the 1908 contest: the Conservatives won 132 seats to the Liberals' 85. Westerners were stunned. Their long-sought reciprocity deal vanished before their eyes. It seemed that neither the Liberals nor the Conservatives could satisfactorily represent western interests. The "agrarian revolt" was under way.

Borden's Conservative Government

Robert Borden became the new Conservative prime minister. He ran an efficient government but limited French-Canadian representation weakened his administration significantly.

One of the government's first decisions concerned the naval issue. The Liberal Naval Service Bill was now dead. Despite strong Quebec opposition, Prime Minister Borden, as his own secretary of state for external affairs, introduced the Naval Aid Bill in December 1912. It provided a direct cash contribution of $35 million to Britain to build three dreadnoughts. One of Borden's few Quebec cabinet ministers resigned in protest, but the prime minister persevered. The Liberals attacked the Naval Aid Bill as an inadequate alternative to Laurier's naval program. Eventually, the Conservatives imposed closure—for the first time in Canadian legislative history—to end the debate. The Liberals countered by using their strong majority in the Senate (after being in power for fifteen years) to defeat the bill. By this time, however, the point was largely moot: military experts questioned the efficiency of dreadnoughts against the new technological innovation—submarines. Thus, on the eve of World War I, after fifteen years of discussion and debate, the dominion had neither made a contribution to the British navy nor built a navy of its own. Canada entered the most devastating conflict the world had ever witnessed completely unprepared.

SUMMARY

For half a century after Confederation, Canadians debated the nation's destiny. There was no question that Canada should maintain a connection to Britain and its Empire, but there was strong disagreement over the nature and extent of those ties. The imperial debate divided Liberals and Conservatives, French and English Canadians. But there was another facet to the debate, one that had long dominated and even shaped the nation: Canada's relationship with the United States. While the debate posed serious divisions, it was far from over.

NOTE

[handwritten annotation: Imperialists - Engl CAN / ON / Conservatives / involvement / matters that directly impact CAN / Autonomists = QC / Liberals : only imperial period]

1. Carl Berger, *The Sense of Power: Studies in the Ideas of Canadian Imperialism, 1867–1914* (Toronto: University of Toronto Press, 1970), p. 259.

BIBLIOGRAPHY

Canada's relations with Britain and the United States are covered in C.P. Stacey, *Canada and the Age of Conflict: A History of Canadian External Relations*, vol. 1, *1867–1921* (Toronto: Macmillan, 1977), and W.L. Morton, *The Critical Years: The Union of British North America, 1857–1873* (Toronto: McClelland & Stewart, 1964). For a more recent overview of Canada's Empire relations see Phillip Buckner, *Canada and the British Empire* (Oxford: Oxford University Press, 2008).

Canadian–American relations in the late nineteenth century are dealt with in John Herd Thompson and Stephen J. Randall, *Canada and the United States: Ambivalent Allies*, 4th ed. (Montreal/Kingston: McGill-Queen's University Press, 2008) and Norman Hillmer and J.L. Granatstein, *For Better or for Worse: Canada and the United States into the Twenty-First Century* (Toronto: Thomson Nelson, 2007). See also Damien-Claude Belanger's *Prejudice and Pride: Canadian Intellectuals Confront the United States, 1891–1945* (Toronto: University of Toronto Press, 2010), and "L'Antiaméricanism et l'antimodernisme dans le discours de la droite intellectuelle du Canada, 1891–1945," *Revue d'histoire de l'Amerique francaise*, 61(3–4) (2008): 501–530; and Edward P. Kohn, *This Kindred People: Canadian–American Relations and the Anglo-Saxon Idea, 1895–1903* (Montreal/Kingston: McGill-Queen's University Press, 2004). Goldwin Smith's *Canada and the Canadian Question* (Toronto: Hunter, Rose, 1891; rep. University of Toronto Press, 1971) is an interesting contemporary statement. P.B. Waite's biography *The Man from Halifax: Sir John Thompson, Prime Minister* (Toronto: University of Toronto Press, 1985), provides an approach to the politics of the period. Allan Smith provides a collection of interpretative essays in *Canada—An American Nation? Essays on Continentalism, Identity, and the Canadian Frame of Mind* (Montreal/Kingston: McGill-Queen's University Press, 1994).

Norman Penlington's *The Alaska Boundary Dispute: A Critical Appraisal* (Toronto: McGraw-Hill Ryerson, 1972) and John Munro's *The Alaska Boundary Dispute* (Toronto: Copp Clark, 1970) cover this issue in Canadian–American relations. A third study that touches on the question of Canada's sovereignty in the Yukon dispute is W.R. Morrison's *Showing the Flag: The Mounted Police and Canadian Sovereignty in the North, 1894–1925* (Vancouver: University of British Columbia Press, 1985). In *Land of the Midnight Sun: A History of the Yukon* (Edmonton: Hurtig, 1988), Ken S. Coates and William R. Morrison provide an overview. See also David G. Haglund and Tudor Onea, "Victory Without Triumph: Theodore Roosevelt, Honour, and the Alaska Panhandle Boundary Dispute," *Diplomacy & Statecraft*, 19(1) (2008): 20–41. For the impact of the Gold Rush, see Charlene Porsild, *Gamblers and Dreamers: Women, Men, and Community in the Klondike* (Vancouver: University of British Columbia Press, 1998).

Carl Berger's *The Sense of Power: Studies in the Ideas of Canadian Imperialism, 1867–1914* (Toronto: University of Toronto Press, 1970) remains the dominant work on the imperial connection. For women and imperialism, see Lisa Chilton, *Agents of Empire: British Female Migration to Canada and Australia 1860s–1930* (Toronto: University of Toronto Press, 2007). Norman Penlington's *Canada and Imperialism, 1896–1899* (Toronto: University of Toronto Press, 1965) discusses Canadian imperialism in the context of the South African War. More recent studies are Carman Miller, *Painting the Map Red: Canada and the South African War 1899–1902* (Montreal/Kingston: Canadian War Museum, McGill-Queen's University Press, 1992) and Miller, "Framing Canada's Great War: A Case for Including the Boer War." *Journal of Transatlantic Studies* 6, no. 1 (2008): 3–21. See also Robert Page, *The Boer War and Canadian Imperialism* (Ottawa: Canadian Historical Association, 1987), and his book on the subject, *Imperialism and Canada, 1895–1903* (Toronto: Holt, Rinehart and Winston, 1972). Social histories of the Boer War include Gordon Heath, *A War with a Silver Lining: Canadian Protestant Churches and the South African War, 1899–1902* (Montreal/Kingston: McGill-Queen's University Press, 2009), and Amy Shaw's chapter on masculinity in Patrizia Gentile and Jane Nicholas, eds., *Contesting Bodies and Nation in Canadian History* (Toronto: University of Toronto Press, 2013). A useful collection of essays is Colin M. Coates, ed., *Imperial Canada 1867–1917* (Edinburgh: Centre of Canadian Studies, University of Edinburgh, 1997).

On the Boy Scout movement and imperialism, see Robert H. MacDonald, *Sons of the Empire: The Frontier and the Boy Scout Movement, 1890–1918* (Toronto: University of Toronto Press, 1993). On literature and the Empire see Barrie Davies, "'We Hold a Vaster Empire Than Has Been': Canadian Literature and the Canadian Empire," *Studies in Canadian Literature* 14(1) (1989): 18–29; and Sara Jeannette Duncan, *The Imperialist* (1904; rep. Toronto: McClelland & Stewart, 1990). On Duncan's life, see Marian Fowler, *Redney: A Life of Sara Jeannette Duncan* (Toronto: Anansi, 1983) and Thomas E. Tausky, *Sara Jeannette Duncan: Novelist of the Empire* (Port Credit, ON: P.D. Meaney, 1980). For a discussion of Duncan's ideas, see Misao Dean, *A Different Point of View: Sara Jeannette Duncan* (Montreal/Kingston: McGill-Queen's University Press, 1991). On the IODE, see Katie Pickles, *Female Imperialism and National Identity: Imperial Order Daughters of the Empire* (Manchester: Manchester University Press, 2002). Margaret MacMillan's biography of Stephen Leacock is useful for understanding the life of one of Canada's most prominent imperialists: *Stephen Leacock* (Toronto: Penguin Books Canada, 2009).

French-Canadian views on imperialism and nationalism during this era can be found in M. Wade, *The French Canadians, 1760–1945* (Toronto: Macmillan, 1955), pp. 447–535, and in Susan Mann, *The Dream of Nation: A Social and Intellectual History of Quebec*, 2nd ed. (Montreal/Kingston: McGill-Queen's University Press, 2002), pp. 167–83. Joseph Levitt's *Henri Bourassa on Imperialism and Bi-culturalism* (Toronto: Copp Clark, 1970) and his pamphlet *Henri Bourassa, Catholic Critic* (Toronto: Canadian Historical Association, 1976) summarize the ideas of this French-Canadian thinker.

For a popular account of the 1891 election, see Chris Pennington, *The Destiny of Canada: Macdonald, Laurier, and the Election of 1891* (Toronto: Allen Lane Canada, 2011). The 1911 federal election is discussed in Patrice A. Dutil and David Mackenzie, *Canada 1911: The Decisive Election That Shaped the Country* (Toronto: Dundurn Press, 2011). The issue of reciprocity in the 1911 election is analyzed in Paul Stevens, ed., *The 1911 General Election: A Study in Canadian Politics* (Toronto: Copp Clark, 1970). On the formation of the Department of External Affairs, see John Hilliker, *Canada's Department of External Affairs*, vol. 1, *The Early Years, 1909–1946* (Montreal/Kingston: McGill-Queen's University Press, 1990).

The fortunes of the Conservative Party are discussed in R.C. Brown, *Robert Laird Borden: A Biography*, vol. 1, *1854–1914* (Toronto: Macmillan, 1975); and in John English, *The Decline of Politics: The Conservatives and the Party System, 1901–20* (Toronto: University of Toronto Press, 1977).

For maps and charts on the period, see the *Historical Atlas of Canada*, vol. 2, *The Land Transformed, 1800–1891*, edited by L.R. Gentilcore et al. (Toronto: University of Toronto Press, 1993) and vol. 3, *Addressing the Twentieth Century, 1891–1961*, edited by Donald Kerr and Deryk W. Holdsworth (Toronto: University of Toronto Press, 1990).

Part 2

INDUSTRIAL CANADA, 1867–1914

INTRODUCTION

At the turn of the twentieth century, Canada underwent rapid industrial and urban change. But the new nation lagged behind developments in Britain and the United States. Canada lacked the financial and economic infrastructures to keep pace with these more populated countries. Canada did, however, possess an abundance of natural resources now in demand for industrialization. Canadians remained "hewers of wood and drawers of water." The exploitation of natural resources, along with manufacturing, allowed economic expansion from 1867 to 1914.

Canada's transformation was evident by comparing the dominion in 1867 and 1914. In 1867 80 percent of the population lived on farms or in villages, and worked in primary industries such as farming, fishing, and lumbering. By 1914, nearly 50 percent lived in towns or cities and worked in secondary or service industries. Such development fostered optimism in Canada's future.

While all Canadians were affected by the changes from industrialization, not all benefited to the same extent. Central Canada became the industrial heartland. The West prospered through immigration and agricultural development. The Maritimes industrialized but had difficulties competing with Ontario and Quebec.

Race, ethnic, class, and gender lines also determined who benefited from industrialization. British Canadians maintained hegemony, and were relatively more prosperous and influential than other ethnic groups. Industrial capitalism ensured that the upper and middle classes enjoyed greater advantages over the working class. As the demographic shift continued from rural to urban, the poor were worse off in the cities. Patriarchy shaped gender relations. Males worked in jobs with higher wages than women and dominated both the public and private realms.

Industrialization ushered in such rapid and significant change, however, that even the elite feared that the system was teetering under its own weight. Only reform would save society from itself. In the past, the churches played the role of taking care of the poor, sick, and downtrodden through charity. They would continue to play this role; but change was occurring so quickly that they could not keep up. The rising middle class took up the challenge. If the reform movement could not cure social ills, the state would be called in to help.

Source: James Salmon Collection, City of Toronto Archives fonds 1231, item 432.

Chapter Six

BOOMTIME: INDUSTRIALIZATION AT THE TURN OF THE CENTURY

TIME LINE	
1869	Timothy Eaton opens his first dry-goods store in Toronto
1873	Economic recession begins
1877	Establishment of the Laurentide Company, Canada's first major newsprint company
1883	Discovery of nickel in Sudbury, Ontario
1891	Ontario government establishes Bureau of Mines
1895	First smelter at Rossland, British Columbia
1902	International Nickel Company of Canada (Inco) incorporated
1904	Over 1800 freight cars pass through Winnipeg every day
1906	Creation of Ontario Hydro
1908	Henry Ford introduces Model T
1910	Combines Investigation Act passed Federal government establishes the Royal Commission on Industrial Training and Technical Education Steel Company of Canada created
1914	Completion of Panama Canal

Industrialization/Urbanization

"To visit Canada just now is a bracing experience," J.A. Hobson, the English economist and journalist, wrote in 1906. "For Canada is conscious, vocally, uproariously conscious, that her day has come. . . . A single decade has swept away her diffidence, and has replaced it by a spirit of boundless confidence and booming enterprise." A number of factors came together to enable Canada to undergo its own industrial revolution, including financial investment, industrial development, and rising prices for raw materials. And with industrialization came urbanization.

Not all regions, however, experienced uniform and sustained growth. The Maritimes lan- *uneven* guished, while the West developed as an impressive agricultural area, and central Canada became *growth* the heartland of industrial growth. Yet even there growth was uneven. Ontario outperformed Quebec, and the minority Anglophone population in Quebec maintained its hold on the economic levers of power. Still, Canada entered an age of general prosperity through industrialization and resource extraction that led Prime Minister Wilfrid Laurier to predict that the twentieth century "belongs to Canada."

Canada's Economic Expansion

At the turn of the century, the National Policy was producing results. Growth in the primary industries—farming, fishing, lumbering, and mining—increased the demand for secondary industries, such as road construction, rail transportation, and shipbuilding. Through the tariff and the railway, the National Policy was successful at creating an east–west trade nexus. The CPR and the two new transcontinental railways—the Canadian Northern and Grand Trunk Pacific/National Transcontinental—brought hundreds of thousands of immigrants westward and transported that region's natural resources to eastern ports and markets. Railways were also major employers. By 1914, Canada prided itself on having 55,000 kilometres of track, spanning the country from coast to coast.

A growing farm population in the Prairie West required manufactured goods, from agricultural implements to common household items. Stimulated by additional foreign investment, industry and manufacturing expanded to meet the increased demand for consumer goods. Employers needed workers in iron and steel foundries, agricultural-implements works, machine shops, textile and shoe factories, and a host of other manufacturing plants that supplied consumer goods. Service industries, as well as governments (national, provincial, and municipal), became major employers. Indeed, by 1921 as many people worked in service industries as in the primary sector.

Canada's Population (in thousands), 1861–1921

	NATURAL INCREASE*	IMMIGRATION	EMIGRATION	NET MIGRATION	POPULATION
1861					3230
1861–71	610	260	410	−150	3689
1871–81	690	350	404	−54	4325
1881–91	654	680	826	−146	4833
1891–01	668	250	380	−130	5371
1901–11	1025	1550	740	810	7207
1911–21	1270	1400	1089	311	8788

*Natural increase is the number of births minus the number of deaths.

Source: From Fielding/Evans. *Canada: Our Century, Our Story*, 1E. © 2001 Nelson Education Ltd. Reproduced by permission: www.cengage.com/permissions.

Financial Investment

Canada's abundant natural resources and increasing population made it an attractive country for investment. This attraction was important because in the past, major initiatives (such as canals and railways) faltered when investors hesitated or shied away. The federal government provided direct, as well as indirect, financial assistance to private companies. The governments of Ontario and Quebec invested heavily in development. They offered bonuses, subsidies, and guarantees to industrialists to locate new plants within their borders. Banks provided another source of internal revenue. Like business corporations, they too consolidated, declining in number from 48 to 18 between 1880 and 1920 (although the number of branches increased from 300 to nearly 5000). The three largest—the Bank of Montreal, the Royal Bank (also with its headquarters in Montreal), and the Toronto-based Bank of Commerce—centralized their operations, invested in new industries, and provided capital for entrepreneurs.

Foreign investment increased as well, especially from Britain, since Canada was the preferred country for capital investment in the Empire. British financiers invested in railways, construction, and industry, chiefly in the form of indirect portfolio investments (loans in the form of bonds). In contrast, American investors preferred ownership to indirect investment. They built branch plants in Canada to avoid tariff restrictions. By 1913, 450 American-owned branch plants existed in Canada, with assets of over $400 million. Many Americans invested heavily in mining and in the growing pulp and paper industry. Canadians generally looked favourably on American investment as an assurance of more jobs in Canadian industries, and as a means to stem the emigration of Canadians to the United States.

Large-scale industrial production required substantial capital, and large corporations predominated. In 1902, only a handful of consolidated companies existed in Canada; by 1912, there were nearly 60. Approximately 250 smaller companies consolidated through mergers. Massey and Harris, for example, merged in 1890, followed by the amalgamation of smaller companies (including some American firms) in the following two decades, to make the Massey-Harris Company Canada's largest producer and exporter of agricultural implements. Another involved Dominion Canner Limited, which in 1910 amalgamated 34 smaller canning factories. Canada Cement, a consolidation of 11 cement companies in 1909, and Stelco (the Steel Company of Canada), formed in 1910 out of several small Ontario and Quebec iron and steel mills, are other examples. The young New Brunswick financier Max Aitken—a Presbyterian minister's son who eventually became Lord Beaverbrook and who created Canada Cement and Stelco—became the "merger king" by buying and combining companies to form trusts and larger companies. After Aitken's death, a friend said he could now "set about merging heaven and hell."

The State and the Economy

As the popular saying went, "The best government is that which governs least." The federal government did not attempt to regulate the monopolies, apart from passing the Combines Investigation Act of 1910. This act allowed the state to investigate monopoly price-fixing. But during its nine-year lifespan, the investigation board dealt with only one case. Corporations took advantage of the division of powers among the federal, provincial, and municipal governments over regulations and often played one government off against the other. This frequently led to infighting between governments, and to regional divisions and animosity. Business enjoyed a free hand in the boom years before World War I, and if the state interfered, it did so on the side of business.

But limited government involvement in the economy did occur, and the role of the state was changing in the early decades of the twentieth century. In the case of Ontario Hydro, public ownership came about because of the need for cheap energy on the part of businesses in Toronto and other southern Ontario towns and cities. When it seemed likely that a small privileged business group alone might harness the tremendous energy power of Niagara Falls, business interests urged the Ontario government to create a Crown corporation of the hydroelectric power industry.[1]

Educating and Training the Workforce

The new economy necessitated a new managerial class and a skilled industrial labour force. In many ways, primary schools became training grounds for the workplace. In what were factory-like institutions, teachers taught children the values of punctuality, hard work, obedience, thrift, and self-discipline— values seen as essential for an industrial society. "Children learned to obey clocks."[2] Girls studied domestic science, while boys learned mechanical skills or how to prepare for business. In 1903, Ontario granted money to schools for shop and domestic-science courses. Under the Industrial Education Act, Ontario established trade schools. The Quebec government also built secondary technical-education schools in Montreal and Quebec City but in general the provincial government resisted the moves toward progressive education that were taking shape in the rest of Canada. Nova Scotia opened the Technical University of Nova Scotia in 1907, a postsecondary trades college.

A statue of Sir Adam Beck, erected in 1934 in Toronto, Ontario. Beck was a Canadian politician and early promoter of hydroelectricity. He founded the Hydro-Electric Power Commission of Ontario.

Source: Bert Hoferichter/Alamy.

Since education was outside federal jurisdiction, Ottawa could not intervene directly in the provincial area of technical education. It did, however, establish the Royal Commission on Industrial Training and Technical Education in 1910, which investigated the current state of Canadian education. Four years of war intervened before the federal government could act on the report. In 1919, the federal Technical Education Act established a fund of $10 million for technical education over the next decade.

Canadians had numerous role models for success emerging from the world of big business. Herbert Holt was a billion-dollar recluse who founded the Montreal Light, Heat and Power Company in 1902 and became president of the Royal Bank. Henry Pellatt was active in the formation of Canadian General Electric and owner of Toronto's Casa Loma, one of the most palatial residences in North America. Joseph W. Flavelle was president of the William Davies Meat Packaging Plant in Toronto and chair of the Bank of Commerce and the National Trust Company. Francis H. Clergue was founder of the Algoma Steel Company of Sault Ste. Marie, Ontario. Patrick Burns was owner of the Burns Meat Packing Company of Calgary. Max Aitken was a millionaire by the age of 30 and used his Royal Securities Corporation as an investment bank to fund his own mergers.

Few Canadian businessmen eclipsed the success of Timothy Eaton, who opened his Toronto dry-goods store at Yonge and Queen Streets in 1869. Eaton introduced two new revolutionary practices to Canadian merchandising. First, he accepted cash only. Second, he promised "money refunded if goods not satisfactory." Even more importantly, however, Eaton realized the emerging value of advertising and took out full-page ads in the Toronto newspapers. By 1882, his business grew to such an extent that he transformed his operation into a department store with three floors, 35 departments, electric lights (the first in a Canadian store), the first elevator, and the first store restaurant–café. In the late 1880s, he introduced evening closings at 6 p.m., and in the summer months, a Saturday afternoon holiday. He started the famous Eaton's mail-order catalogue, a volume soon to be termed "the Prairie Bible" in western Canada. By the time of his death in 1907 at age 72, Timothy Eaton employed over 9000 people. His "empire" extended across the country and the world, often undermining local retailers who found it difficult to compete.

Stenographer pool, land department, CPR Department of National Resources, Calgary, 1915. Women did clerical work at the turn of the century, but became ghettoized at the lowest levels of office work.

Source: Glenbow Archives, Calgary, Canada/NA-5055-1.

Rise of a Managerial Class

Canadian entrepreneurs and other corporate leaders relied on a new, skilled managerial class to run the complex, day-to-day operations of their expanded business: increased production data, costs, personnel, and internal communications. These managers were often trained in "scientific management," a term coined by American Frederick W. Taylor. "Scientific managers" used workers to complete simple and routine jobs at a proficient speed for a minimum wage. Indeed, a process of "deskilling" occurred. Employers used new technology to break down skills into more narrowly specialized tasks that could be performed by less skilled, lower-paid workers—in some industries by women and children. Concerned only with growth and profit, they gave little thought to the aesthetics of the workplace, the needs of workers, or the possibility of profit sharing. Work was judged only in terms of efficiency. Offices, as they became automated with the introduction of such devices as typewriters,

COMMUNITY PORTRAIT

The T. Eaton Company

Timothy Eaton created Canada's most successful department store by the early twentieth century. Eaton's modest upbringing on a farm outside Ballymena in Northern Ireland, and his own harsh

beginning in retail as a young man, made him sympathetic to his employees, albeit in a paternalistic way. "The Governor," as he became known, tried to cultivate a personal relationship with his staff,

Photo of a woman touching the boot of the statue of Timothy Eaton in the Winnipeg downtown Eaton's store. People rubbed the boot for good luck.

Source: *Winnipeg Free Press*, October 23, 2002, p. A5.

his "loyal subjects," that engendered respect, cooperation, and enthusiasm on their part. Stories became legendary of his kindness and generosity to loyal workers who experienced financial difficulties. Employees absent from work for extended periods of time due to illness continued to receive their pay, often along with an order of coal to keep them warm if the illness occurred in the winter months. During one particularly severe winter, Eaton set aside $3000 to assist workers who were in need of help. "When it's gone, let me know," he informed his accountant, as he was prepared to provide more money.

When his Toronto store at the corner of Queen and Yonge (opened in 1883) became too large to allow him to supervise his staff by himself, and when other stores opened across the country, Eaton hired managers. He handpicked and trained them to ensure that they felt an identity with the company. "When you discover a young person doing anything which he or she should be corrected for," he informed managers, "speak to them alone and never before customers." Employees dismissed for errors in judgment often gained reinstatement when they apologized. "The Governor" personally held meetings in his store at which employees could air grievances and suggest ways to improve good relations (and thus increase sales). As he reminded his managers: "None of us are too wise to learn, even from our juniors." To cultivate the sense of community, Eaton provided his associates with additional benefits such as a 10 percent discount on merchandise, low-interest loans to those wishing to buy a home, a welfare department, a pension and life insurance plan, and deposit accounts with generous interest rates.

Timothy Eaton attempted to cultivate the same strong sense of community among his customers. As one store brochure stated: "The Eaton Spirit is the combined faith and enthusiastic loyalty we have for the store and for our fellow employees . . . [T]he spirit of the store too, demands the customer's satisfaction at any cost." Store windows offered artistic displays to teach the shopping public how modern goods might be used and showcased in the home. With the introduction of its iconic catalogue in 1884, the Eaton's community stretched across the country. In rural communities, the Eaton's catalogue allowed access to modern merchandise ordered through the mail (often from the mail-order warehouse in Winnipeg) that would otherwise be impossible to obtain. One enthusiastic westerner proclaimed that "the Eaton catalogue is as much a Western institution as the wheat itself." During World War I, the catalogue even cultivated a sense of community among Canadian soldiers on the front. Some soldiers found half-charred copies of the catalogue in training camps, in hastily abandoned buildings, or even in trenches at the front. Among soldiers, the catalogue became known as "The Wish Book," since soldiers ordered items (such as a wristwatch) that they wished to own—and that Eaton's often provided at no cost—or dreamed of having when they returned home.

When Eaton died on January 31, 1907, several thousand of his employees followed the funeral entourage from Timothy Eaton Methodist Church to the Mount Pleasant Cemetery. In 1919, twelve years after his death, and on the occasion of the fiftieth anniversary of the founding of the T. Eaton store, company employees presented a life-sized bronze statue of Timothy Eaton for the main store as a gift to the Eaton family. A copy of the statue was also given to the main western Canadian store in Winnipeg. From that day on, passersby would rub the toe of the left shoe to the point of making it shiny, hoping that Eaton's good fortune might rub off on them. The T. Eaton Company remained in operation until 1999, when it filed for bankruptcy.

FURTHER READING

Joy L. Santink, *Timothy Eaton and the Rise of His Department Store* (Toronto: University of Toronto Press, 1990).

Rod McQueen, *The Eatons: The Rise and Fall of Canada's Royal Family*, rev. ed. (Toronto: Stoddart, 1999).

Patricia Phenix, *Eatonians: The Story of the Family Behind the Family* (Toronto: McClelland and Stewart, 2002).

the Hollerith punchcard machine, and the Burroughs adding machine, resembled factories in terms of routine production. Technology, efficiency, and productivity became the new watchwords of success and progress.

Beneath this managerial class, and closely supervised by it, were the clerical workers who carried out the daily routine office jobs. Increasingly, women performed the mechanized and highly specialized jobs. Female clerks did not replace male clerks, but rather ended up doing inferior clerical work under them. This "feminization of clerical work" occurred at a rapid rate in the decade from 1910 to 1920, when clerical positions in general more than doubled. Women acquired most of the new typewriting jobs. During the war years (1914–1918), in particular, females replaced male clerks who went off to war. By 1920, male managers and female secretaries had become the norm in most offices.

Urbanization

With industrialization came cities. Industrial growth required factories, large banks, commercial institutions, and transportation services in large urban centres. These institutions in turn required workers and employees. During the period from 1890 to 1920, Montreal and Toronto—the two largest and most advanced industrial cities in Canada—almost tripled their populations, each surpassing the half-million mark. But the most rapid urban growth in this time period occurred in the West, due mainly to large-scale immigration. Winnipeg's population increased sevenfold; Vancouver's increased twelvefold (growing at a rate of 1000 new residents per month in the peak year of 1910); and Calgary's increased sixteenfold. Of all the major western cities, Saskatoon eclipsed the rest in rate of growth, rising from several hundred to nearly 10,000 people in the first decade of the new century. From 1901 to 1911, the Canadian urban population increased 63 percent. In 1901, Canada had 58 urban centres with a population greater than 5000; by 1911, that number had grown to 90.

Canadian urban centres became heartlands that controlled their surrounding hinterlands, providing the rural inhabitants with manufactured goods and services. But these centres in turn became hinterlands dependent on larger cities beyond Canadian borders. Montreal and Toronto, for example, the only two Canadian metropolises that were not hinterlands of other Canadian cities, were dependent on metropolitan centres outside Canada such as London, New York, and Chicago. The dominance of Montreal and Toronto dated back to the mid-nineteenth century and the railway boom. After 1885 and the completion of the CPR, Montreal's and Toronto's influence reached to the Pacific. Their real growth, however, occurred in the 1890s and early 1900s, due to rapid industrialization.

Regional Economic Development

The nature and extent of industrial and urban growth varied across the country. In Newfoundland, the economy remained highly dependent on the cod and seal fisheries as the major industries, employing 85 percent of the island's population in the late nineteenth century. A serious decline in both industries prompted Sir William Whiteway's government in the early 1890s to implement a Newfoundland version of Canada's National Policy, the "Policy of Progress." Its centrepiece consisted of a railroad across the island that, like the CPR, would link east and west coasts and stimulate industrial growth. A moderate tariff would in turn protect small manufacturers in St. John's. But with a bank failure in 1894, financing of the railroad came under Canadian control when the Reid Newfoundland Company, actually based in Montreal, underwrote the costs. As well, the iron ore deposits on the island were shipped out to Cape Breton rather than processed at home.

In the Maritimes, the resource-based economy lost much of its momentum. The West Indies sugar trade fell dramatically in the 1870s, when a world glut of sugar caused prices to collapse, resulting in a decline in trade between Nova Scotia and the West Indies. In the same decade, Britain's demand for Maritime lumber and wooden ships fell, seriously weakening the economies of Nova Scotia and New Brunswick. An industrial economy developed to supplement the region's resource economy. Businesspeople in Nova Scotia, for instance, invested in steel products, such as steel rails and locomotives, to take advantage of the Cape Breton coal fields. At one point in the early 1880s, due in large part to the Intercolonial Railway, high tariffs, and a vigorous iron and steel industry, Nova Scotia's industrial growth on a per capita basis actually outstripped that of Ontario and Quebec.

In the long run, however, the industrial expansion of the Maritimes faltered. Some historians have pointed to the region's lack of extensive and diverse resources. Although Cape Breton had coal, timber, iron ore, and fish, its agriculture could not compete. Distance from the large markets of central Canada and the small regional population in Atlantic Canada combined to create significant obstacles to expansion for factories. Furthermore, Maritime investors, like their Canadian counterparts elsewhere, saw western and central Canadian development as potentially more lucrative. Local banks, for example (themselves swallowed up by central-Canadian-owned banks) invested outside the region. As well, the "Boston States" acted as a magnet to draw population from the Atlantic provinces, causing one Maritime historian to conclude that the pull to the south "may have resulted in the decapitation of Maritime society."[3]

As industrialization proceeded slowly, Maritime cities grew at a slower rate than those elsewhere. Halifax's population increased by only 16,000 people between 1871 and 1911 to a total

A market slip in Saint John, New Brunswick, from the early 1900s. Several examples of the harbour's ill-fated wooden ships are visible in the background.

Source: John Woodruff/Library and Archives Canada/PA-021517.

of 46,619, while that of Saint John, New Brunswick, actually declined, then regained a modest number of inhabitants, to bring its population to 42,500 by 1911. These cities remained small, with modest hinterlands of their own. They became dependants of Montreal and, to a lesser extent, Toronto.

Growth in the West

British Columbia's economy shifted from its Pacific orientation (southward to California) toward central Canada, thanks to the completion of the CPR. The provincial economy remained predominantly resource-based: mining, forestry, fisheries, and agriculture. Mining speculation ran at a fever pitch by the turn of the century—so much so, a local journalist noted, that British Columbia was cursed with a "class of crooks who prefer to mine the public instead of the ground." Extraction of lode gold and silver began in the Slocan and Boundary districts in the 1890s, but copper, lead, and zinc superseded precious metals after 1900. The smelting (or refining) of these base metals required large-scale smelters. The first successful smelter opened near the Rossland mines at Trail Creek in 1895, and a second, Cominco, in the Kootenays. Coal mining, especially in and around Nanaimo on Vancouver Island, also contributed to the province's economy.

But forestry surpassed mining in terms of both wealth and employment. Logging increased by 400 percent between 1900 and 1910, and wood-product manufacturing provided numerous jobs. Until 1912 and the passage of the Forestry Act, trees were cut without concern for reforestation or the preservation of Crown land.

Fisheries, especially the salmon fisheries, expanded and consolidated in a highly competitive business that pitted First Nations, Euro-Canadians, and Japanese Canadians against each other. Denied treaties, the First Nations were excluded by the newcomers from their ancestral fisheries used for consumption and trade. British Columbia Packers Association emerged as the most powerful salmon packing company after 1902 and used the most modern technology, including the "Iron Chink"—a racist term applied to the butchering machine for processed fish that replaced work previously done by Chinese-Canadian and Japanese-Canadian workers. The small port of Steveston became known as the sockeye capital of the world.

Agriculture was slow to get established in British Columbia but by World War I, it ranked second to forestry in terms of output. Fruit farming was the most commercially viable, especially after the introduction of refrigerated rail cars at the turn of the century, since much of the fruit was exported. Even manufacturing grew in the late nineteenth century, surpassing that of the Prairie provinces and almost reaching Ontario standards. In 1880, British Columbians contributed over 1 percent of the net value of Canadian manufactures; by 1890, the figure was close to 5 percent, more than equal to the growth of its share of the national population. Still, the province's distance from the centre of the industrial development in central Canada, combined with the high freight rates and the small regional market, prevented the province from becoming a substantial and ongoing secondary-manufacturing base. Rather, British Columbia, like the Maritimes, became another hinterland region.

In the Prairie West, wheat was king. The world demand for wheat after 1896 opened up areas on the northern fringe and in the arid Palliser Triangle to production, thus increasing substantially both the wheat lands and yields. In 1901, 55,000 Prairie farms occupied 15.4 million acres (6.2 million hectares), of which 70 percent grew wheat; by 1911, 200,000 farms occupied over 58 million acres (23.5 million hectares), of which 59 percent grew wheat. In terms of yields, a record crop of 208 million bushels was harvested in 1911. Such growth justified and necessitated new rail lines, especially to service the new areas of settlement. Rail lines in the region doubled from 1885 to 1900, to 6000 kilometres, and then tripled again to 18,000 kilometres by 1913. But the Prairie region faced the same problem as British Columbia and the Maritimes: the regional market was too small to foster substantial secondary manufacturing. Thus, as the National Policy made inevitable, the region became subservient to central Canada in terms of economic growth and dominance.

Cities in the West

Victoria and Vancouver vied for dominance in West Coast trade. Vancouver won out by 1914 because of the impressive dock and terminal facilities on Burrard Inlet, as well as its role as the western terminus of the CPR. This new status fostered the growth of transportation, wholesaling, and resource companies in the city. By 1914, its population reached 155,000, while that of Victoria, the provincial capital, stood at only 35,000. Again, such growth necessitated a variety of retail, manufacturing, and professional services.

The completion of the Panama Canal in 1914 enabled Vancouver to surpass Winnipeg as Canada's major western city; Prairie farmers could now ship wheat to European markets through Vancouver. On the eve of World War I, Vancouver stood between two worlds. As historian Robert McDonald notes:

> At one level Vancouver functioned as a metropolitan city, managing resource industries, directing transportation and commerce, and providing a growing range of business and professional services for the region. At another it continued to be a city on the frontier, a

Vancouver, British Columbia, in the early 1900s. In the foreground is the growing business section of the city. The R.M.S. Aorangi is entering Burrard Inlet in the background.

Source: Albertype Company/Library and Archives Canada/PA-031695.

new society different from Burrard Inlet's nineteenth-century lumber communities yet still subject to the vicissitudes of a regional economy narrowly based on resource extraction and promotion.[4]

Such urban developments proceeded without regard to First Nations' land claims. The situation in British Columbia differed from that in the rest of Canada. The process of contact occurred so much later than in the East, and the consequences came much later. But the lack of an agricultural frontier and the process of land settlement meant that no treaties were negotiated. Land was taken for resource extraction without surrendering First Nations claims.

Urbanization occurred at a rapid rate on the Prairies. In 1870, at the time of the region's incorporation into Confederation, no urban centres existed in the region; by 1911, there were 17 incorporated cities and 150 incorporated towns. Five dominant cities emerged by 1914: Winnipeg, Saskatoon, Regina, Edmonton, and Calgary. Each serviced a surrounding agricultural hinterland.

Winnipeg's location as the "gateway to the West" with rail links to central Canada made the entire Prairie region its hinterland. Due to this strategic location, it became the third-largest manufacturing city in pre-World War I Canada. Nicknamed the "Hub City" and the "Chicago of the North," it stood at the junction of three transcontinental railways. It processed rural agricultural products and, in return, sold construction materials to settlers—lumber, bricks, finished steel, and cement, as well as some manufactured goods. The city employed thousands in its rail yards, the largest in the world by 1904, with as many as 1800 freight cars passing through in a single day. But the central cities in turn dominated even Winnipeg. Ultimately, all western rail lines led to Toronto and Montreal.

An immigrant woman and her children waiting on a curb in front of the CPR Station in Winnipeg, around 1909. Almost everyone who came west passed through this station, built in 1904.

Source: Used with Permission from The United Church of Canada, 93.049/3111N, Immigrants in front of Winnipeg Station.

Industrialization and Urbanization in Central Canada

At the turn of the century, industrialization occurred largely in Ontario and Quebec. In 1900, the provinces together produced over four-fifths (82 percent) of the total value of Canadian manufacturing. Ontario's growth initially was based on small-scale consumer goods industries in a series of towns and cities throughout southern Ontario that fed the demands of a booming agricultural hinterland economy. These industries depended mainly on coal as a source of energy and on iron production. In both cases, Ontario had an advantage over Quebec because of the province's proximity to the Pennsylvania coal fields and the Minnesota iron ranges.

But Canada created its own iron and steel companies that increased production sixfold between 1877 and 1910 and another tenfold by 1913, producing over 900,000 tonnes of iron at peak production. Already by 1911, iron and steel industries surpassed the traditional dominant industry of textiles in terms of both production and employment. A network of rail lines crisscrossed Ontario, linking the numerous towns and cities to the rural countryside and to other urban centres. By the turn of the century, Ontario already had numerous manufacturing centres scattered from Windsor to Cornwall—London, Berlin (later called Kitchener), Guelph, and Peterborough, with the largest concentration at the western end of Lake Ontario, including Toronto, Hamilton, Brantford, St. Catharines, and Niagara Falls. These centres produced tariff-protected goods such as engines, farm implements, stoves, furniture, and canned goods. Hamilton, a steel-producing town, became the home of large railcar shops. But most of Ontario's largest head offices, financial institutions, factories, and warehouses were located in Toronto. Historian Peter A. Baskerville notes that in the first decade of the twentieth century alone "manufacturing output in Ontario's major cities almost doubled—the greatest increase of any time before World War II."[5]

In Quebec, much of the new industry was small-scale and labour-intensive. Quebec had only two major manufacturing and industrial cities: Montreal and Quebec City. A few small textile towns grew up in the Eastern Townships, but most did not develop into manufacturing centres comparable to the smaller towns and cities of Ontario. The province instead concentrated on the small-scale manufacturing of shoes, textiles, lumber, and foodstuffs (flour, sugar, dairy products)—light industries utilizing cheap and abundant labour for a limited domestic market. These industries were concentrated near the rail facilities of the two main cities of Montreal and Quebec City. Montreal had the advantage over Quebec City, the latter becoming more isolated from the major canals and rail networks without a bridge over the St. Lawrence. Montreal also had the majority of financial institutions to provide capital for businesses in the city. Quebec City's shipbuilding had declined by the late nineteenth century.

A new phase of industrialization began in Quebec by 1911, when hydroelectric power replaced steam as the main source of industrial energy. Pulp and paper, and later minerals, became the new resource products. Even during this "second industrial revolution," Ontario continued to outperform Quebec, due to mineral production, the pulp and paper mills in northern Ontario, and hydroelectric power, especially in and around Niagara Falls.

In the Laurentian Shield, Quebec had vast spruce forests for the pulp and paper industry, and an abundance of water power for electricity. Between 1900 and 1910, power production in the province tripled. The pulp and paper industry experienced similar phenomenal growth in the same period due to American demand for newsprint. Unencumbered by a perceived need to make treaties with the First Nations, Quebec simply allowed pulp and paper operations to push northward. The federal government did conclude Treaty Nine with the First Nations of northern Ontario in 1905–06 (and 1930), but northern Quebec remained unsurrendered land until the last quarter of the twentieth century. Regardless of any desire for treaty by First Nations, Ottawa recognized that they were expensive and produced increased responsibility. As a result, treaties were negotiated only when white society desired the land for resource extraction.

Initially, the pulp produced by Canadian-based companies went for processing in the United States. But at the turn of the century the Quebec government, at the urging of nationalists, put an embargo on exports of pulp from Crown lands. Subsequently, Quebec pulp mills began producing their own newsprint for export. The Laurentide Company, established in 1877, became Canada's first and largest newsprint maker at the time. By 1914, Quebec had become a leading industrial province. More than two-thirds of its population worked in non-agricultural activities, and roughly one-half of its population lived in urban centres.

Quebec's Industrial Development

For French Canadians, Quebec's industrialization had a unique and disturbing aspect: they had little control over it. In 1910, only 2.5 percent of Canada's entrepreneurs was French-speaking. French Canadians were the labourers, and only rarely the owners of industry. Part of the reason for the dominance of Anglophones in Quebec's halls of industry was the limited pool of French-Canadian capital, but Quebeckers faced other obstacles. The language of business was English, young Quebeckers were discouraged from entering business by their own elites, and the business community in the province was already securely in the hands of "les anglais." Historian Michel Brunet has argued that in the early twentieth century "the Quebec English-speaking business community constituted a select private club into which only a few assimilated former French Canadians were admitted."[6]

Education was also a factor. The Catholic Church emphasized a humanistic education, particularly at the classical college level, over science and commerce. And despite the increasing role of the state, education remained in church control. The Quebec government tried to correct this imbalance by offering financial support for the establishment of technical schools. In 1907 it created the *École des hautes études commerciales* (HEC), a university-level business school. Yet, many graduates still faced the need to work in English, at least at the managerial level.

The French-Canadian Response to Industrialism

French-Canadian intellectuals debated their involvement in industrialization. According to Jules-Paul Tardivel, the ultramontane nationalist and editor of the newspaper *La vérité*, the world of industry and commerce was not conducive to the goals of French-Canadian nationalists. On the contrary, to participate in this world would only open the assimilative floodgates: "It is not necessary for us to possess industry and money. . . . We would no longer be French Canadians but Americans like the others. . . . To cling to the soil, to raise large families, to maintain the hearths of spiritual and intellectual life, that must be our role in America." Others, like Errol Bouchette, a French-Canadian economist, urged Quebeckers to accept industrialism as the best means to survive in North America. Not even agriculture could survive, he argued, if outsiders controlled the rest of Quebec's economy. "Emparons-nous de l'industrie" (Let us take over industry) was his rallying cry.

Traditional French-Canadian nationalism was rooted in notions of an agricultural utopia. With the church as the bastion of this nationalism through the teachings of such influential priests as the historian Lionel Groulx, French Canadians were urged to avoid the sinful industrial cities and instead stay on the land where they would farm and raise large families. The problem, however, was twofold. First, this defensive type of nationalism was already anachronistic by the turn of the century. The reality was that Quebec was industrial and urban, regardless of the desires of the church. Second, the church's message only further engrained the dominance of the Anglo minority that already controlled Quebec's economy.

"New Ontario"

The pace of industrialization was most impressive in southern Ontario, especially in the period from 1890 to 1914, which historian Ian Drummond calls the province's "heroic age."[7] The high protective tariff helped, as did the extensive railway system that tied the industrial core at the western end of Lake Ontario to the rest of the province and to all of Canada. But another decisive factor was the wealth of timber and minerals in northern Ontario. Suddenly this area—"New Ontario"—ceased to be perceived as an unproductive wasteland of rocks, lakes, and muskeg, and was seen instead in terms of its resource potential. Several northern Ontario towns became synonymous with minerals: Sudbury—nickel; Cobalt—silver; Timmins—gold. By 1914, the mineral-resource base of northern Ontario became accessible through rail transport to major urban centres outside the region.

Mining required sophisticated and expensive equipment and large consolidated companies. In nickel production, for example, the ore had to be mined from the rock and then burned in the open air to concentrate the metal and reduce the sulphur content. The environmental cost of development was high. The miners cleared the land of trees to fuel the roasting process, while sulphur and arsenic fumes escaped from the smokestacks into the atmosphere and poisoned the surrounding vegetation. A Bureau of Forestry was created in 1898, but it had limited influence in regulating the cutting of forest reserves in the region.

WHERE HISTORIANS DISAGREE

Industrial Growth in Quebec

During the Quiet Revolution of the 1960s, Quebec historians began to question why their province lagged behind Ontario in terms of industrial growth, and why French Canadians lagged behind the minority English Canadians as the owners of industry. These questions led historians to look back at the beginning of industrialization in Quebec for answers.

In the early 1950s, two Quebec economists, Albert Faucher and Maurice Lamontagne, argued that Canadian industrialization occurred in two stages, or two "industrial revolutions"—one from 1866 to 1911, the other after 1911. In the first, industrial growth depended chiefly on the ability to produce iron and steel, resources that Quebec had in short supply and that were unavailable nearby. Ontario, by contrast, benefited from its proximity to the Pennsylvania coal fields and the Minnesota iron ranges. In the second stage, growth depended on the availability of hydroelectric power, which by 1911 had become the new source of industrial energy. Here Quebec was well blessed, but by this time Ontario had already developed an industrial infrastructure, and Quebec could not catch up.

Other economic historians questioned Faucher and Lamontagne's identification of the "industrial takeoff" period in Quebec. John Dales contended that hydroelectricity experienced its greatest growth—310 percent—in the first decade of the twentieth century.[1] André Raynauld argued that in some decades, such as the period 1910–20, Ontario accelerated faster than Quebec, but that over the extended period 1870–1957, the two provincial economies grew at almost parallel rates, each one taking its turn as the leader in industrial growth. Thus, overall, Quebec did not lag behind.[2]

H.V. Nelles and C. Armstrong agreed. They claimed that by 1920, both Ontario and Quebec produced the same quantity of hydroelectric power. But the two provinces differed in the nature of control of this key energy source. In Ontario it was publicly owned through Ontario Hydro, making it available to a larger industrial base, whereas in Quebec two very large privately owned companies controlled profits and alone benefited.[3]

John Isbister examined the differing agricultural economies of the two provinces. Quebec produced insufficient surplus food to serve its urban centres. Agriculture in the province was "a subsistence sector, economically isolated, not integrated into the wider market system," unlike in Ontario. Cultural explanations, according to Isbister, explain the difference; Quebec had "a different attitude toward the farming life. The Quebec habitant was a peasant, poor and self-sufficient, not a man of business."[4] Only in the twentieth century would this attitude change, and by then Ontario farmers had surged ahead.

Quebec historians Paul-André Linteau, René Durocher, and Jean-Claude Robert questioned whether Quebec industrialized at a slower pace than Ontario even at the turn of the century. They argued that by dwelling on the resource-oriented industries, historians and economists overlooked the sustained growth in manufacturing in Quebec at the turn of the century, which showed the period to be one of industrial takeoff.[5]

The second question—why French Canadians failed to become the leaders of industry in their own province—has also proven contentious. Maurice Séguin and Michel Brunet blamed the Conquest of 1759–60 for the disadvantage. They contended that New France had a dynamic business class, but that its members were forced to return to France after the conquest because of poor business opportunities under the British conquerors. With the departure of the French bourgeoisie, British interests stepped in, causing French Canadians to lose their economic role from that point onward.[6] Fernand Ouellet challenged this interpretation.[7] He denied the existence of a viable business class in New France. Rather, the French Canadians' conservative business mentality led to British commercial superiority. In any event, the two sides agreed that Anglophone business interests already controlled the economy of Quebec by the nineteenth century.

Another debate revolves around the question of how this small Anglo minority was able to maintain its favoured position. Some historians blamed the church-dominated educational system, with its emphasis on a classical education rather than on training in science and commerce, for the failure of French Canadians to succeed in business. But more recent research does not entirely bear this out. Some science and commerce courses were in fact part of the school curriculum in Quebec.[8] Craig Brown and Ramsay Cook argued that where the church and the schools erred was in putting nationalism ahead of practical economic considerations: "Education . . . had a moral and patriotic function, to which practical training for economic life was secondary."[9] Linteau, Durocher, and Robert explained the gap in industrial leadership of French-Canadian businesspeople in terms of limited technological knowledge. Unlike English-speaking immigrants in Quebec, whose contact with their place of origin provided them with important business links and an international perspective, French Canadians lacked an "information network."[10] Their contacts and know-how never extended beyond the confines of Quebec.

1   John Dales, *Hydroelectricity and Industrial Development in Quebec, 1898–1940* (Cambridge, MA: Harvard University Press, 1957).

2   André Raynauld, *Croissance et structure économique de la province de Québec* (Quebec: Ministère de l'industrie et du commerce, 1961).

3   H.V. Nelles and C. Armstrong, "Contrasting Development of the Hydro-Electric Industry in the Montreal and Toronto Regions, 1900–1930," in Douglas McCalla, ed., *The Development of Canadian Capitalism: Essays in Business History* (Toronto: Copp Clark Pitman, 1990), pp. 167–190.

4   John Isbister, "Agriculture, Balanced Growth, and Social Change in Central Canada Since 1850: An Interpretation," in Douglas McCalla, ed., *Perspectives on Canadian Economic History* (Toronto: Copp Clark Pitman, 1987), p. 67.

5   Paul-André Linteau, René Durocher, and Jean-Claude Robert, *Quebec: A History 1867–1929* (Toronto: James Lorimer, 1983).

6   Maurice Séguin, "The Conquest and French-Canadian Economic Life," translated from "La Conquête et la vie économique des Canadiens," *Action nationale*, 28 (1947): 308–26, in Dale Miquelon, ed., *Society and Conquest: The Debate on the Bourgeoisie and Social Change in French Canada, 1700–1850* (Toronto: Copp Clark Publishing, 1977), pp. 67–80; and Michel Brunet, "The British Conquest and the Decline of the French-Canadian Bourgeoisie," translated

from "La Conquête anglaise et la déchéance de la bourgeoisie canadienne," in *La présence anglaise et les canadiens* (Montreal: Beauchemin, 1958), pp. 49–109; also in Miquelon, *Society and Conquest*, pp. 143–61.

7   See the conclusion of Fernand Ouellet's *Histoire économique et sociale du Québec 1760–1850* (Montreal: Fides, 1966), pp. 539–596. This work is available in translation: *Economic and Social History of Quebec 1760–1850* (Toronto: Gage, 1980), pp. 547–609.

8   W.J. Ryan, *The Clergy and Economic Growth in Quebec, 1896–1914* (Quebec: Presses de l'Université Laval, 1966).

9   R.C. Brown and R. Cook, *Canada, 1896–1921: A Nation Transformed* (Toronto: McClelland and Stewart, 1974), p. 132.

10 Linteau, Durocher, and Robert, *Quebec: A History, 1867–1929*, p. 404.

The building of two new transcontinental railways across northern Ontario in the early twentieth century opened up vast areas of First Nations hunting and trapping grounds to settlement and resource development. It also eliminated Aboriginal peoples' jobs as freighters. The photo shows HBC Aboriginal voyageurs on their way to Flying Post with supplies from Biscotasing on the CPR, northwest of Sudbury, around 1900.

Source: Archives of Ontario/Acc. no. 10144.

The investment capital and technical skill required for large-scale production led to consolidated companies. In 1902, the Canadian Copper Company in Sudbury amalgamated with several smaller American companies to form the International Nickel Company of Canada (Inco). In the Porcupine district, three large companies—Hollinger (Canadian-owned), Dome (American-owned), and McIntyre (Canadian-owned after 1915)—soon controlled 90 percent of the gold production. In Sault Ste. Marie, F.H. Clergue, an American-born entrepreneur, built an industrial empire, the Consolidated Lake Superior Company, by using largely American capital.

The Ontario government assisted promoters. During Oliver Mowat's time as premier (1872–96), the Ontario government invested heavily in the north for a handsome return of some $17 million, enabling the Ontario government to be debt-free at a time when most other provincial governments had large deficits. In 1891, in response to the recommendations of a royal commission on Ontario's mineral resources, the government established the Bureau of Mines "to collect and publish information and statistics on the mineral resources and mining industry." It also established the School of Mining at Queen's University in the early 1890s (later merged into the university's Faculty of Applied Sciences). As well, the provincial government handed out loans, railway land grants, timber leases, and mineral rights. Only when production began did the province demand royalty payments. By 1904, one-quarter of the province's revenue came from mining and another quarter from forestry.

Mining Towns in Northern Ontario

A host of mining towns appeared. Some, such as Golden City, Elk Lake, and South Porcupine, were little more than camps made up of shacks and log cabins; others became company towns, built and owned by the town's only employer. Only a few, such as Sudbury and Timmins, became main service or distribution centres for the entire region. All of these northern Ontario mining communities depended on the capricious rise and fall of world metal prices. In time they came under the dominance of Toronto—the provincial capital, their main supply base, the focus of their rail transport, and the source of money for many of the mining and forestry companies.

SUMMARY

From 1880 to 1914, Canada underwent its industrial revolution as a result of the success of the National Policy, large-scale financial investment from within the country and abroad, exploitation of a seeming unlimited supply of natural resources, and government cooperation. Manufacturing and large-scale industrial production, and accompanying urban growth, transformed the dominion. But not all regions of the country, nor all social classes, benefited equally from the economic expansion. The social costs of rapid change were high.

NOTES

1. H.V. Nelles, *The Politics of Development: Forests, Mines and Hydro-Electric Power in Ontario, 1849–1941* (Toronto: Macmillan, 1974), pp. 248–49.

2. Michael Cross, "The Canadian Worker in the Early Industrial Age," in Gregory S. Kealey and W.J.C. Cherwinski, eds., *Lectures in Canadian Labour and Working-Class History* (St. John's: Canadian Committee on Labour History and New Hogtown Press, 1985), p. 49.

3. Judith Fingard, "The 1880s: Paradoxes of Progress," in E.R. Forbes and D.A. Muise, eds., *The Atlantic Provinces in Confederation* (Toronto: University of Toronto Press, 1993), p. 97.

4. Robert A.J. McDonald, *Making Vancouver: Class, Status, and Social Boundaries, 1863–1913* (Vancouver: University of British Columbia Press, 1996), p. 148.

5. Peter A. Baskerville, *Ontario: Image, Identity and Power* (Toronto: Oxford University Press, 2002), p. 157.

6. Michel Brunet, "The French Canadians' Search for a Fatherland," in Peter Russell, ed., *Nationalism in Canada* (Toronto: McGraw-Hill, 1966), p. 55.

7. Ian Drummond, *Progress Without Planning: The Economic History of Ontario from Confederation to the Second World War* (Toronto: University of Toronto Press, 1987), p. 104.

BIBLIOGRAPHY

Michael Bliss's *Northern Enterprise: Five Centuries of Canadian Business* (Toronto: McClelland & Stewart, 1987) provides a comprehensive history of Canadian business. See, as well, Graham Taylor and Peter Baskerville, *A Concise History of Business in Canada* (Toronto: Oxford University Press, 1994). On economic developments, consult Kenneth Norrie and Douglas Owram, *A History of the Canadian Economy*, 4th ed. (Toronto: Nelson, 2008). Two chapters—"The Triumph of Enterprise" and "French Canada and the New Industrial Order"—in R.C. Brown and R. Cook, *Canada, 1896–1921: A Nation Transformed* (Toronto: McClelland & Stewart, 1974) deal with industrialization and urbanization in English and French Canada, respectively. For women and wealth, see Peter Baskerville, *A Silent Revolution? Gender and Wealth in English Canada, 1860–1930* (Montreal/Kingston: McGill-Queen's University Press, 2008). On Quebec, consult also Paul-André Linteau, René Durocher, and Jean-Claude Robert, *Quebec: A History, 1867–1929* (Toronto: James Lorimer, 1983), and Susan Mann, *The Dream of Nation: A Social and Intellectual History of Quebec*, 2nd ed. (Montreal/Kingston: McGill-Queen's University Press, 2002), pp. 132–49 and 167–83. On the links between industrialization and immigration policy, see Ninette Kelley and Michael Trebilecock, *The Making of the Mosaic: A History of Canadian Immigration Policy* (Toronto: University of Toronto Press, 1998). See too Joy Parr, *The Gender of Breadwinners: Women, Men, and Change in Two Industrial Towns, 1880–1950* (Toronto: University of Toronto Press, 1990).

Michael Bliss deals with Canadian business's attitudes in *A Living Profit: Studies in the Social History of Canadian Businessmen, 1883–1914* (Toronto: McClelland & Stewart, 1974). Fernande Roy studied the economic outlook of francophones in Montreal in *Progrès, harmonie, liberté: Le libéralisme des milieux d'affaires francophones à Montréal au tournant du siècle* (Montreal: Boréal Express, 1988). Joy L. Santink's *Timothy Eaton and the Rise of His Department Store* (Toronto: University of Toronto Press, 1990) is an important study of this prominent Canadian merchant. Lord Beaverbrook's dealings are discussed in Gregory P. Marchildon, *Profits and Politics: Beaverbrook and the Gilded Age of Canadian Finances* (Toronto: University of Toronto Press, 1996). For a general debate on industrialism in Ontario, consult Ian Drummond, Louis P. Cain, and Majorie Cohen, "CHR Dialogue: Ontario's Industrial Revolution," *Canadian Historical Review*, 69(3) (September 1988): 283–314. Russell Johnston, *Selling Themselves: The Emergence of Canadian Advertising* (Toronto: University of Toronto Press, 2001) examines advertising during the period while Donica Belisle looks at the growth of Canadian department stores in *Retail Nation: Department Stores and the Making of Modern Canada* (Vancouver: UBC Press, 2011).

On industrialization in the Maritimes, see T.W. Acheson, D. Frank, and J. Frost, *Industrialization and Underdevelopment in the Maritimes, 1880–1930* (Toronto: Garamond Press, 1985); Kris Inwood, *Farm, Factory and Fortune: New Studies in the Economic History of the Maritime Provinces* (Fredericton: Acadiensis Press, 1993); the relevant chapters in E.R. Forbes and D.A. Muise, eds., *The Atlantic Provinces in Confederation* (Toronto: University of Toronto Press, 1993); and W. Acheson, "The National Policy and the Industrialization of the Maritimes, 1880–1910," in G. Stelter and A.F.J. Artibise, eds., *The Canadian City: Essays in Urban and Social History* (Toronto: McClelland & Stewart, 1977; rev. ed., Ottawa: Carleton University Press, 1984), pp. 93–124.

On industrialization and rural society, see Daniel Samson, ed., *Contested Countryside: Rural Workers and Modern Society in Atlantic Canada, 1800–1950* (Fredericton: Acadiensis Press, 1994). For Newfoundland, see David Alexander, "Economic Growth in the Atlantic Region, 1880–1940," in E. Seager, L. Fisher, and S. Pierson, comp., *Atlantic Canada and Confederation: Essays in Canadian Political Economy* (Toronto: University of Toronto Press, 1983), pp. 51–78; and the relevant sections of Margaret R. Conrad and James K. Hiller, *Atlantic Canada: A Region in the Making* (Toronto: University of Toronto Press, 2001). On the impact of out-migration on industrialization, see Patricia Thornton, "The Problem of Out-Migration from Atlantic Canada, 1871–1921: A New Outlook," *Acadiensis*, 15(1) (Autumn 1985): 3–34.

On British Columbia, see Allen Seager, "The Resource Economy, 1871–1921," in Hugh J.M. Johnston, ed., *The Pacific Province: A History of British Columbia* (Vancouver: Douglas & McIntyre, 1996), pp. 205–52; Frank Leonard, *A Thousand Blunders* (Vancouver: University of British Columbia Press, 1996); Jeremy Mouat, *Roaring Days: Rossland's Mines and the History of British Columbia* (Vancouver: University of British Columbia Press, 1995); and Martin Robin, *The Rush for Spoils: The Company Province, 1871–1913* (Toronto: McClelland & Stewart, 1972).

Studies in English of industrialization in Quebec include A. Faucher and M. Lamontagne, "History of Industrial Development," in M. Rioux and Y. Martin, eds., *French-Canadian Society* (Toronto: McClelland & Stewart, 1964), pp. 257–71; J.H. Dales, *Hydroelectricity and Industrial Development in Quebec, 1898–1940* (Cambridge, MA: Harvard University Press, 1957); and W.J. Ryan, *The Clergy and Economic Growth in Quebec, 1896–1914* (Quebec: Presses de l'Université Laval, 1966). See, as well, John Dickinson and Brian Young, *A Short History of Quebec*, 3rd ed. (Montreal/Kingston: McGill-Queen's University Press, 2003). For information on Quebec's banks, consult Ronald Rudin, *Banking en français* (Toronto: University of Toronto Press, 1985); and, for background on its credit unions, Ronald Rudin, *In Whose Interest? Quebec's Caisses Populaires*, 1900–1945 (Montreal/Kingston: McGill-Queen's University Press, 1990).

For Ontario's resource development, see H.V. Nelles, *The Politics of Development: Forests, Mines and Hydro-Electric Power in Ontario, 1849–1941* (Toronto: Macmillan, 1974); Duncan McDowall, *Steel at the Sault: Francis H. Clergue, Sir James Dunn, and Algoma Steel Corporation, 1901–1956* (Toronto: University of Toronto Press, 1984); Keith Fleming, *Power at Cost: Ontario Hydro and Rural Electrification, 1911–1958* (Montreal: McGill-Queen's, 1992); and Jean L. Manore, *Cross-Currents: Hydroelectricity and the Engineering of Northern Ontario* (Waterloo, ON: Wilfrid Laurier University Press, 1999).

For the impact of industrialization and urbanization and resource developments on the Aboriginal peoples in Ontario, consult Edward S. Rogers and Donald B. Smith, eds., *Aboriginal Ontario* (Toronto:

Dundurn Press, 1994); and for British Columbia, Rolf Knight, *Indians at Work: An Informal History of Native Labour in British Columbia, 1848–1930* (Vancouver: New Star Books, 1996). For Western Canada more generally, see Keith D. Smith, *Liberalism, Surveillance, and Resistance: Indigenous Communities in Western Canada, 1877–1927* (Edmonton: Athabaska University Press, 2009).

Also of importance for Canada as a whole is Christopher Armstrong and H.V. Nelles, *Monopoly's Moment: The Organization and Regulation of Canadian Utilities, 1830–1930* (Philadelphia: Temple University Press, 1986). On Canadian investment abroad, the following studies are important: C. Armstrong and H.V. Nelles, *Southern Exposure: Canadian Promoters in Latin America and the Caribbean, 1896–1930* (Toronto: University of Toronto Press, 1988); and Duncan McDowall, *The Light: Brazilian Traction, Light and Power Company Limited, 1899–1945* (Toronto: University of Toronto Press, 1988).

On urbanization, see J.M.S. Careless, *Frontier and Metropolis: Regions, Cities and Identities in Canada Before 1914* (Toronto: University of Toronto Press, 1989). Consult as well Richard Preston, "The Evolution of Urban Canada: The Post-1867 Period," in R.M. Irving, ed., *Readings in Canadian Geography*, 3rd ed. (Toronto: Holt, Rinehart and Winston, 1978), pp. 19–46; and the collection of articles in Stelter and Artibise, eds., *The Canadian City* (cited earlier). The Canadian Museum of Civilization has sponsored eight volumes in its series of histories of major Canadian cities: *Regina* (1989) by J. William Brennan, *Ottawa* (1986) by John H. Taylor, *Winnipeg* (1977) by Alan Artibise, *Calgary* (1978) by Max Foran, *Vancouver* (1980) by Patricia Roy, *Hamilton* (1982) by John C. Weaver, *Toronto to 1918* (1983) by J.M.S. Careless, and *Toronto Since 1918* (1985) by James Lemon. On Montreal, see Sherry Olson and Patricia Thornton, *Peopling the North American City, 1840–1900* (Montreal/Kingston: McGill-Queen's University Press, 2011), and Nicolas Kenny, *The Feel of the City: Experiences of Urban Transformation* (Toronto: University of Toronto Press, 2014).

For a detailed study of urbanization in the Maritimes, see J.M.S. Careless, "Aspects of Metropolitanism in Atlantic Canada," in M. Wade, ed., *Regionalism in the Canadian Community, 1867–1967* (Toronto: University of Toronto Press, 1969), pp. 117–29. On British Columbia, see Robert A.J. McDonald, *Making Vancouver: Class, Status, and Social Boundaries, 1863–1913* (Vancouver: University of British Columbia Press, 1996); and Norbert McDonald, *Distant Neighbors: A Comparative History of Seattle and Vancouver* (Lincoln: University of Nebraska Press, 1987). On the Prairies, consult Paul Voisey, "The Urbanization of the Canadian Prairies, 1871–1916," *Histoire sociale/Social History*, 8 (1975): 77–101; A.F.J. Artibise, "The Urban West: The Evolution of Prairie Towns and Cities in 1930," *Prairie Forum*, 4 (1979): 237–62; A.F.J. Artibise, ed., *Town and City: Aspects of Western Canadian Urban Development* (Regina: Canadian Plains Research Center, University of Regina, 1981); Jonathan Hildebrand, "Class, Community, and Urban Consciousness: The Winnipeg Street Railway, 1902–1910," *Manitoba History*, 60 (2009): 2–13; and Kurt Korneski, "Reform and Empire: The Case of Winnipeg, Manitoba, 1870s–1910s," *Urban History Review*, 37(1) (2008): 48–62.

Source: City of Toronto Archives, Series 372, Subseries 32, Item 259.

Chapter Seven

THE IMPACT
OF URBAN AND
INDUSTRIAL GROWTH

TIME LINE

1872	Trade Union Act passed
1879	Provincial Workmen's Association for coal miners in Nova Scotia founded
1883	Founding of the Trades and Labor Congress of Canada (TLC)
1889	Royal Commission on the Relations of Labour and Capital issues report
1892	Criminal Code outlaws contraceptives
1894	Labour Day established as national holiday
1897	Herbert Ames publishes *City Below the Hill*, a sociological study of Montreal
1900	Department of Labour established
1905	Founding of the Industrial Workers of the World (IWW) or "Wobblies"
1907	The Industrial Disputes Investigation Act passed
1908	The Fishermen's Protective Union founded in Newfoundland by William Ford Coaker
1913	Publication of John MacDougall's *Rural Life in Canada: Its Trends and Tasks* Ontario Housing Act passed
1914	Workmen's Compensation Act passed in Ontario
1917	The Order of Sleeping Car Porters formed, the first African-Canadian railway union in North America

Industrialization and urbanization transformed the lives of Canadians. Rural areas experienced the migration of younger members of farm families into the towns and cities in search of work. Farming increasingly changed from a subsistence, family-organized vocation to a form of business. Machinery replaced people and tasks became more routine.

Industrialization also transformed the northern areas of Canada, even where agriculture was not practised. First Nations people in all regions of the country, but especially in the north, had to adjust to increased competition from other interest groups. The fur trade (and subsistence trapping) steadily declined. New industries moved into the shield regions, including lumbering, mining, pulp and paper, and hydroelectric power. But it was the cities that witnessed the most rapid and dramatic change. Urban infrastructure had to adapt quickly to both rural migration and immigration from abroad. This led to urban problems such as poverty, overcrowding, disease, and poor health and hygiene. Industrialization reinforced the class system in Canada.

Industrialization and urbanization also reshaped the meaning of time and space for the average Canadian. No longer was the workday framed around daylight and the season; it was now controlled by the clock. Spaces were separated by gender and divided into the public and the private (although these lines were often blurred). Above all, industrial capitalism was driven by profit. Increasingly, urban workers worked outside the home in factories or offices that were often substandard in terms of cleanliness and safety. They worked long hours for meagre pay. Women and many working-class children worked for lower wages even when doing the same job as men.

Industrial capitalism reshaped the class system but then blamed the masses for their inevitable and miserable plight. The downtrodden, as in the past, looked to the churches for aid. Workers looked to charitable institutions for assistance, fraternal organizations and clubs for camaraderie and identity, and unions for better wages and working conditions. The working classes began to organize, and this response alarmed the elites as the fear of class war cast an ominous shadow over the cityscapes. While, overall, Canadians enjoyed a higher standard of living in 1914 than in 1867, social and gender inequality and poor living and working conditions persisted, causing social reformers to target these concerns. Society was being transformed, but critics wondered whether the result was ultimately for the better.

The Impact on Rural Society

On the eve of Canada's urban and industrial revolution, farming remained a fairly stable occupation, with the family farm a relatively self-sufficient unit. Farm families produced food that they consumed and sold the surplus. Farmers looked to pass their farms down from generation to generation, usually to the eldest son. Many younger sons worked to save money to purchase their own farms in order to expand the operation. Daughters helped on the farm in preparation for marriage, often to a young farmer in the district.

Industrialization, however, transformed rural life. The introduction of labour-saving machines — hay mowers, reapers, threshers, and tractors—enabled a farmer to bring more land under cultivation. A mechanical hay mower, for example, allowed a farmer to cut 10 acres (4 hectares) a day, or 40 times as much as had been the case previously. By 1900, farmers, who used labour-saving machinery, produced a bushel of wheat in one-hundredth of the time required only thirty years earlier. Now a farmer required greater revenue from the farm to pay for the expensive equipment. Large-scale farms became common. Dairy and fruit farming also became agribusiness. As well, improved and increased rail and steamship service that included cold-storage facilities and lower freight rates made it possible for Canadian farmers to sell their produce abroad.

The nature of work also changed. It became more routine and specialized. Farmers began to take over what had previously been considered women's work. As economist Marjorie Cohen notes, "As large dairy herds developed, dairying ceased to be a part-time occupation for farm women and more and more became the major work of males on the farms."[1] Large-scale dairy farms produced the milk to supply cheese factories that, by 1901, produced 40 percent of Canadian cheese. As was the case with cheese, the production of butter and the canning of fruit, traditionally women's work, now occurred in factories instead of on farms. The result transformed the economy of the family household. It transformed gender relations but also changed the relationship between young and old.

Mechanization reduced the number of older children needed to work the farm. This encouraged some youth to seek jobs or to work at least seasonally in the cities. Better-paying jobs also lured the younger generation from the land. Rural depopulation became a concern. Many social commentators, such as John MacDougall, a minister from Spencerville, Ontario, whose lectures on rural life were incorporated in *Rural Life in Canada: Its Trends and Tasks* (1913), warned of the dire consequences of a declining rural population. Like MacDougall, society at large continued to associate rural living with good moral values and clean living.

The Impact on First Nations People

The First Nations and the Métis were once again caught up in the rapid and tumultuous change. The Canadian government continued in the late nineteenth century to view the "Indians" as a dying race. But as part of a "civilized" and philanthropic empire, it was the "white man's burden" to alleviate the suffering of an inferior people struggling to adapt to modernity. The government negotiated the treaties to create reserves—temporary spaces upon which the Aboriginal peoples would have the time needed to make the transition to white society. The old ways were gone and change was inevitable. The only option was assimilation and white society lost patience with the process. The idea of the "noble savage" was long gone. Racist attitudes prevailed and the image of the "drunk and lazy Indian" dominated. Ottawa's tools of assimilation included religion, education, and agriculture. When First Nations individuals were ready to make the leap into the dominant society, they were expected to become white citizens and leave the reserves. Absorption into a racist and hostile society, however, was hardly inviting. Not surprisingly, most First Nations people preferred to remain on the "temporary" reserves.

On the West Coast, salmon processing came under the control of the British Columbia Packers Association after 1902. The company replaced Aboriginal people with Japanese immigrants as fishers, boat builders, and processors, since the latter would work for lower wages, could be relied on for year-round fishing, and were less prone to strike. Asians also replaced First Nations people in the canneries, although both groups were subordinate to Euro-Canadians as managers. The introduction of modern assembly line and processing equipment eliminated jobs in fish-processing plants.

First Nations peoples were adversely affected by commercialization in the northern fur trade. Initially, at the turn of the century, this was not the case. Rising prices and increased demand for furs in Europe created a lucrative market. New companies, such as the Revillon Frères of Paris and the Northern Trading Company, undermined the Hudson's Bay Company's monopoly, resulting in increased demand, higher prices, and cash fur buying. Prosperity had its downside, however. The influx of non-Aboriginal hunters and trappers led to increased competition and a rapid decline in furs. The federal and provincial governments introduced conservation methods and laws to provide protection for wildlife, but they failed to appreciate the Aboriginal peoples' commercial, ceremonial, and subsistence needs as well as their treaty rights.

This shot of the interior of a salmon cannery, on the Skeena River in northwestern British Columbia, shows four Native women doing butchering work.

Source: Library and Archives Canada/PA-118162.

The loss of trading and employment opportunities within the fur industry would not have been so dramatic if the northern First Nations people and Métis had possessed viable alternative means of livelihood, but they did not. Even such traditional alternatives as working on the railroads, supplying the railway ties, or working in mining areas as above-ground workers erecting buildings, clearing sites, and constructing roads were increasingly given to new immigrants. "By mid-century," historian Arthur Ray notes, "many northern Native groups were probably more dependent on hunting and trapping than they had been at anytime since the late eighteenth century."[2]

Life in the Industrial City

As a result of industrialization, cities became more socially stratified, with working-class districts physically separated from middle- and upper-class areas. In the past, the rich and poor lived side by side, and no exclusive neighbourhoods existed. In a western city such as Calgary or Edmonton, for example, people in mansions looked out on plank or dusty sidewalks, and occasionally on a stray cow. The urban "elite" in the late nineteenth century wanted their homes close to their businesses or places of work. But with the arrival of the electric streetcar and later the automobile, the middle and upper classes had an option. They could leave the inner city for neighbourhoods away from downtown congestion and pollution.

The city centres became both business and industrial districts in which the majority of the working class lived. A number of long-established cultural institutions, such as churches and social clubs, were removed from the city centre and relocated in more luxurious and pleasant areas. Many city centres became ghettoized and undesirable places to live. The Commission of Conservation, established by the federal government in 1909, noted in its *Annual Report* of 1914:

> *Industrial smoke disfigures buildings, impairs the health of the population, renders the city filthy, destroys any beauty with which it may naturally be endowed and tends, therefore, to make it a squalid and undesirable place of residence, and this at a time when economic influences are forcing into cities an ever increasing proportion of our population.*

In Montreal and Toronto, the two largest and most industrialized Canadian cities, most working-class people rented rooms in either boarding or tenement houses—old wooden cottages or two-storey buildings with little or no yard area. Rent could be as high as $10 or $12 a month for basement rooms, roughly 25 percent of an unskilled worker's wages. Some philanthropists, such as Toronto's Sir Joseph Flavelle and Hart Massey, subsidized workers' houses near their factories. In 1913, the Ontario government passed the Ontario Housing Act to provide municipal support for upgraded working-class districts. But before World War I, most working-class families had to face intractable landlords on their own. Few families owned their own houses, since house prices remained well beyond the means of the ordinary worker.

An average working-class family of five typically lived in a one- or two-room flat: damp, unventilated, inadequately lit, and poorly heated. Overcrowding was a constant problem. In Toronto, for example, rapid growth led to a housing shortage. Some families lived in hastily constructed shacks, in backyard tents, or even on the street. With only rudimentary sewage and sanitation, in summer a stench rose from the cesspools and outdoor privies. The first sense to be experienced when walking into a nineteenth-century city was undoubtedly the smell.

New social conditions led to changes in gender relations. No longer did males and females of the same family work alongside each other. Formal work became the domain of men. They were the "breadwinners" and they controlled the finances. The public realm was that of the male; the private or domestic realm was that of the female. But while this spatial distinction was pronounced, in reality the lines were blurred. Most working-class households could not survive with only one income. As a result, women and children had to work the peripheries of the formal economy in the public realm. Aside from maintaining the household, women worked as domestic servants or in factories.

The breadwinner model reinforced patriarchy within the household. Domestic violence and sexual abuse occurred among all social classes. Often such violence in working-class districts was associated with drinking, unemployment, and destitution. Wives had little legal recourse, because male-dominated courts rarely challenged the husband's proprietary right over his wife's person and her sexuality. Judges questioned the woman's character and the courts remained distinctly male spaces. Because of high legal costs, divorce also remained out of the question for most women.

There were fewer age categories in the nineteenth century. Childhood was a brief stage that abruptly ended around the age of ten and was replaced by adulthood. The concept of a "teenager" did not begin to emerge until around World War II. Children, particularly those of the working class, enjoyed even fewer rights and privileges than did women at the turn of the

A slum courtyard in Toronto. Several dwellings opened out onto this common space used for hanging laundry, for storage, and as a play area for children. Note the buildings are constructed of wood with tar paper roofs. Photo taken November 26, 1913.

Source: City of Toronto Archives, Series 372, Subseries 32, Item 259.

century. They had to assume family responsibilities at an early age, and to grow up and mature quickly. In Montreal, a maximum third-grade education was common for working-class children. In Ontario in 1871, John Sandfield Macdonald's Liberal government passed legislation that made school attendance compulsory to the age of 16, but the law was not rigorously enforced. Critics (usually the upper classes) of universal education argued that schooling was a privilege not to be wasted on the poor, who were destined to work in factories or on farms. Children had to enter the workforce as soon as possible (age 11 or 12 being the norm) to supplement the family income. The census of 1871 reveals that 25 percent of boys and 10 percent of girls between the ages of 11 and 15 held jobs outside the home; these statistics did not include boys hired to do odd jobs or girls working as domestics. In the 1880s, Ontario and Quebec passed Factory Acts prohibiting the hiring of boys under 12 and girls under 14, but they had little impact due to poor enforcement and the difficulty of taking recalcitrant factory owners to court. Those children unfortunate enough to end up in court were more likely to be penalized than protected, and sent to harsh probationary institutions, such as the Toronto Mercer Reformatory or the Vancouver Boys' Industrial School.

In Montreal, Canada's most industrialized city, daughters were less likely than sons to be employed outside the home, since girls, by the age of 15 or 16, made only one-half to two-thirds of the wages paid to boys of the same age for doing a similar job. Patriarchal attitudes militated against girls working in factories. As well, girls up to the age of 16 were required at home to help run the household and care for younger family members. Still, poorer working-class families had to send their daughters out to work because of economic necessity.

Untreated waste from Toronto, and virtually every other Canadian and American municipality in the Great Lakes basin, polluted the region's water systems.

Source: City of Toronto Archives Fonds 1244, Item 1122A.

WHERE HISTORIANS DISAGREE

New Historical Paradigms: Age and Generation

The "youth" challenged the established order so frequently in the twentieth century that historians have described it as a "century of adolescence."[1] The "flower children" of the 1960s and 1970s are obvious examples of such challenge and protest, but the youth problem has concerned parents, as well as the state, since the 1860s. Throughout the twentieth century, a number of groups emerged that defined themselves in generational terms. These include the "lost" generation of World War I, the Baby Boomers, and the Gen-Xers.

Yet, despite the rise of social history and the obvious importance of age and generation, these categories have received relatively little attention. Instead historians more commonly employ such paradigms as race, ethnicity, gender,

class, religion, and sexuality. Each is essential to the formation of identity but as historian Cynthia Comacchio argued, "the status changes that take place over the life course and that are directly related to age are critical formative factors."[2] Moreover, "each generation has a story to tell."[3] In Canada, the study of age/generation is in its infancy. Some historians are focusing on the emergence of adolescence and the teenager years as a distinct life stage; others are turning to the history of childhood and the elderly.

As with gender and sexuality, the historical study of age and generation relies on theoretical concepts used in other disciplines such as sociology and anthropology. Perhaps the most influential are the sociologists Karl Mannheim and Maurice

Halbwachs. Mannheim's research pioneered the idea of generations and their influence on social change, while Halbwachs focused on how generations formed, including the importance of shared rituals and the creation of collective memory. Contemporaries of Mannheim, V.F. Calverton and Samuel D. Schmalhausen, also explored the concept of age, describing generational conflict between parents and children in the family and household as a "war of the generations."[4]

Canadian historians are also taking their lead from those working on age/generation in other countries. One of the earliest to focus on the impact of family and household conditions was the French medieval historian Philippe Ariès, who offered some of the first child-centred histories.[5] The American historian Paula Fass has studied age and its relation to specific eras (in her case the 1920s). She argued that youth is more than a biological or physical fact. It is "a cultural expression of social relationships and a product of a specific set of historical conditions."[6] American historians William Strauss and Neil Howe have also observed that generations repeat themselves by means of recurring "personality patterns," which they identify as the "generational cycle."[7] Moreover, Robert Wohl has tested the idea that generations are formed by social responses to a collective trauma, such as World War I. His work highlights how single events can produce multiple generations.[8]

Doug Owram was one of the first Canadian historians to examine generation. His work seeks to explain the social conditions, the shared culture, and common experiences that allowed the emergence of a distinct generation—the "Baby Boomers." The economic prosperity at the end of World War II, but also the sense of relief after the difficult years of war and depression that plagued the first half of the century, shaped this generation's sense of "special-ness." The Boomers saw themselves, and were recognized by society, as a distinct generation, making them a highly influential group who dictated social, cultural, and governmental trends and policies as they matured. While the Boomers were certainly youthful, it was their identification as a generation, rather than their age, that interests Owram.

Neil Sutherland pioneered the study of early childhood in Canada. His work seeks to describe growing up "from the perspective of children themselves."[9] Cynthia Comacchio has built on Sutherland's work. She explores the emergence of a distinct stage of adolescence. Prior to the twentieth century, life stages included childhood (until the age of around ten years) and adulthood. Youth were expected suddenly to stop being children and enter the harsh world of grownups, complete with expectations of working and earning money. These expectations began to change gradually in the decades from the 1920s to the 1950s with the emergence of leisure and popular culture. Comacchio also noted that generational "self-awareness" and "consciousness" were "most acute during the adolescent years." Her research demonstrates how adolescents increasingly viewed themselves as a group and how their parents, teachers, and the government tried to ensure they lived up to social ideals.

According to Comacchio, "historic events affect people of all ages, but age shapes the experience of them." By exploring the development of Canadians' ideas about adolescence, she is able to show how they were "refashioned into a distinct socio-cultural space between childhood's end and full adult citizenship." Rather than focusing on one generation's experience, Comacchio argues that it is the experience at a specific age that explains the creation of a new life stage. Both Sutherland and Comacchio show how generations are socially constructed, arguing that childhood and adolescence vary from society to society and that the experiences are "a matter of human decision rather than a biological necessity."[10]

Michael Gauvreau provides a similar cultural explanation for generational conflict. His research, however, highlights an explicit link between modernity and generation by outlining how the clergy in Quebec helped foster the idea of a generation gap in the 1930s. The "youth" constituted a "different class."[11] Gauvreau portrays adolescents in Quebec as a distinct generation, whose sense of self was recast to embody modern ideals. Ultimately, he argues that the youth's power to reject the past was unsettling to many in Quebec, including the church. The desire to harness the power of the generation gap was, therefore, important.

Although specific to Quebec, Gauvreau's research fits within a larger trend of studying how society, with the aid of the state, has attempted to regulate youth and the problem of delinquency. Historians Franca Iacovetta, Joan Sangster, and Tamara Myers examine how the state has tried to regulate young girls and women.[12] Although these works place young women at the centre, the primary focus is the state's responses to them. The concept of age, therefore, is utilized differently.

The distinction between Comacchio's and Owram's work illustrate how historians can use age and generation to reach conclusions about groups who perceive themselves, and are perceived, in generational terms. They can also use these categories to study specific life stages and the social responses to them. As a prism, age/generation provides historians a distinct way of viewing society.

1   Philippe Ariès, *Centuries of Childhood: A Social History of Family Life* (New York: Knopf, 1962), p. 27.

2   Cynthia Comacchio, *The Dominion of Youth: Adolescence and the Making of Modern Canada, 1920 to 1950* (Waterloo, ON: Wilfrid Laurier University Press, 2006), p. 6.

3   Doug Owram, *Born at the Right: A History of the Baby Boom Generation* (Toronto: University of Toronto Press, 1996), p. ix.

4   V.F. Calverton and Samuel D. Schmalhausen, eds., *The New Generation: The Intimate Problems of Modern Parents and Children* (London: George Allen & Unwin, 1930), p. 7.

5   Comacchio, "Foreword," in Neil Sutherland, *Children in English-Canadian Society: Framing the Twentieth-Century Consensus* (Waterloo, ON: Wilfrid Laurier University Press, 2000), p. v.

6   Paula S. Fass, *The Damned and the Beautiful: American Youth in the 1920s* (New York: Oxford University Press, 1977), p. 6.

7   William Strauss and Neil Howe, *Generations: The History of America's Future, 1584 to 2069* (New York: William Morrow & Co., 1991), p. 8.

8   Robert Wohl, *The Generation of 1914* (Cambridge: Harvard University Press, 1979), p. 36.

9   Neil Sutherland, *Growing Up: Childhood in English Canada from the Great War to the Age of Television* (Toronto: University of Toronto Press, 2002), p. ix.

10 Comacchio, pp. 8, 3; Sutherland, *Growing Up*, p. xi.

11 Michael Gauvreau, *The Catholic Origins of Quebec's Quiet Revolution, 1931–1970* (Montreal/Kingston: McGill-Queen's University Press, 2006), p. 15.

12 Franca Iacovetta, *Gatekeepers: Reshaping Immigrant Lives in Cold War Canada* (Toronto: Between the Lines, 2006); Joan Sangster, *Regulating Girls and Women: Sexuality, Family, and the Law in Ontario, 1920–1960* (Oxford: Oxford University Press, 2001); and Tamara Myers, *Caught: Montreal's Modern Girls and the Law, 1869–1945* (Toronto: University of Toronto Press, 2006).

Working Conditions in Canada's Cities

Industrialization created harsh working conditions. Because there was no regulation, it was up to factory owners to set the rules and create the labour conditions. Not surprisingly, profit was the driving force and the workers suffered. In times of demand, the average labourer spent at least ten to twelve hours a day, six days a week, at work. Factories were poorly ventilated, noisy, and dirty. Factory foremen ran the factory to ensure maximum efficiency. They often fined workers for tardiness or for talking to fellow workers on the job. Industrial accidents and deaths occurred frequently.

Job security did not exist. Victims of industrial accidents had no workers' compensation. Layoffs, especially during the slower winter months, occurred regularly. Even in good times, unemployment was common, a by-product of the capitalist system. Before the federal government introduced unemployment insurance in 1940, layoffs could mean months of subsistence without wages.

But the city was the centre of modern life and this in itself was attractive. Cities offered the attractions of the bright lights, the hustle and bustle of a burgeoning population, and a new array of leisure activities. They may have seemed strange, dangerous, and full of vice, but these traits were also alluring. Young people, both men and women, left the farm in increasing numbers to find work in the congested, noisy cities. While the working hours were long, they were still shorter than those on the farm, with at least Sunday off and, sometimes, Saturday afternoon. Factory wages also tended to be higher than farm wages. As well, cities had taverns, sports events, music halls, and, soon, the cinema for entertainment.

Photo of advertisement from the Montreal Star, April 4, 1903. At the time, the average labourer made less than $11 a week.

Source: Library and Archives Canada/18635.

The Standard of Living

The cost of living in urban centres increased continually and outpaced urban wages. The federal Department of Labour issued "typical weekly expenditure" budgets listing those items necessary for a family of five to enjoy a minimum standard of living. Although it allowed for only 0.6 kilograms of fresh meat per week per person, less than a litre of milk a day for a family of five, and no fresh vegetables or fruit, this minimum was more than the average working-class family could afford. In 1901, the estimated cost of living was $13.38 a week. But the average male worker (without layoffs) made $425 a year in 1901, or an average of $8.25 a week. The modern definition of poverty is any individual or family having to spend more than 70 percent of total income on basic needs such as food, fuel, and shelter. Thus, many working-class families needed at least two incomes to stay above the poverty line.

Women in the Workplace

At the turn of the century, women made up about one-seventh of the paid workforce. Even though the views of the day dictated that "respectable" women remain in the private sphere, reality necessitated that they cross into the public. Usually they worked outside the home between the ages of 14 (the youngest age permissible for girls to work after 1885) and 24 (the average marrying age). Once married, they returned to paid work only as a result of economic necessity, widowhood, desertion, or illness in the family. The routine of housework—rearing children, cleaning, cooking, washing, mending, and shopping—meant full and exhausting days. Marriage, motherhood, and domesticity remained intertwined in the minds of most women, no matter to which class they belonged. This was considered the women's "proper sphere." Men dominated the "public sphere." Nevertheless, many women supplemented the family income by taking in boarders, doing part-time sewing, or taking in laundry.

Economic realities often necessitated work outside the home in female-related jobs in textile factories, as waitresses, or as domestics. Women without familial support had to find work. In these cases, they had to rely on friends, neighbours, relatives, or working-class associations to assist with children. Sometimes immigrant women could count on the support of their own ethnic community to provide mutual aid and, occasionally, employment agencies. Increasingly, however, there arose a segment of unmarried working, non-immigrant girls, popularly known as "working girls," who performed non-domestic waged work outside the home. Single, young, independent, and alone, they became the concern of moral reformers who saw the "girl problem" as a threat to the ideal of a Canadian society made up of morally upright, married, and motherly women.

Middle-class women depended on domestic help at the turn of the century. Families were larger, homes harder to keep clean, and food preparation much more time-consuming. Domestics tended to be young girls from rural areas or immigrant women. Indeed, the demand for domestic servants was so great that they were considered "preferred" immigrants. In 1891, 40 percent of all women working outside the home were employed as domestics.

Domestic servants, if working away from the protection of family or friends, were vulnerable to sexual exploitation. Their gender, age, class, and often ethnic affiliation made them second-class citizens, and upper-class men often took full advantage. If these women were brave enough to face the social stigma and attempt to use the legal system for protection, they rarely received justice. The courts were gendered, hierarchal spaces, and usually more concerned with castigating women for their apparent "loose" morals and protecting the reputations of the men. The most typical response of those victimized was simply to leave the community. There were exceptions, however. Carrie Davies, an 18-year-old servant of Charles Albert Massey, a member of the farm machinery family founded by Hart Massey, opposed his sexual advances and finally shot and killed him. About a thousand sympathetic supporters in Ontario contributed to Davies' trial-defence fund in 1915. The jury acquitted her of murder.

Women preferred factory work to domestic service because of higher wages and shorter hours. Still, in 1900, most women worked up to 60 hours a week. Sexism meant textile and shoe factories hired women because they could pay them lower wages (approximately half of what men earned) and because they were better workers for the type of work to be done. Women made up about two-thirds of the workforce in the textile industry in 1880 and almost half by 1900. Historian Jacques Rouillard describes the exhausting working conditions in a textile factory:

> It was not so much the physical effort required by the machines, as the tremendous speeds at which they functioned and the attention they demanded, which taxed the nervous system of the worker. The noise caused by the hundreds of weaving machines as well as the high degree of humidity in the spinning and weaving rooms were especially irritating. This damp atmosphere, maintained to keep the thread from breaking, resulted in fatigue among the workers and often led to loss of appetite and anemia. Many of the young women had to quit their jobs, unable to overcome the tension they suffered in this atmosphere.[3]

This store at the turn of the century shows the diversity of items available to those who had money to purchase them, including Jell-O, which had just come on the market in 1897. Note the method of displaying goods at the time, from floor to ceiling.

Source: Provincial Archives of New Brunswick/P18-163.

A HISTORICAL PORTRAIT

Emily Jennings Stowe

Emily Jennings Stowe became the first female public-school principal in Upper Canada, and, immediately after Confederation, the first Canadian woman to practise medicine openly. She was also one of the country's first suffragists.

Stowe was born near Norwich, Upper Canada on May 1, 1831, and came from a Quaker background. Since the Society of Friends (Quakers) gave women the same status as men, she grew up in an atmosphere of relative gender equality. Her struggle to achieve equality for women began in 1852 when she applied for admission to Victoria College in Cobourg. Refused on the grounds that she was female, she then applied successfully to the Toronto Normal School.

She graduated with first-class honours in 1854. She taught until her marriage in 1856 to John Stowe, owner of a carriage business in neighbouring Mount Pleasant.

Shortly after the birth of their third child in 1863, John Stowe contracted tuberculosis and had to leave the family for treatment. With the financial help of the Jennings family and the support of her sister, Cornelia, who agreed to care for Emily's children, Emily Stowe prepared for a medical career.

Barred from medical school in Canada because she was female, Emily enrolled at the New York Medical College for Women, a homeopathic (natural medicine) institution in New York City. She graduated in 1867. But when she

Emily Howard Jennings Stowe, 1831–1903, was an early Canadian activist and promoter of women's rights. She was also the first female to openly practise medicine in Canada.

Source: Wilfrid Laurier University Archives & Special Collections U57_1191.

returned to Canada, the College of Physicians and Surgeons refused to certify her. For over a decade Stowe practised medicine in Toronto without a licence. She was not prosecuted but she was charged in 1879 with having performed an abortion. In the lengthy trial that followed, Stowe successfully defended her qualifications, skill, and professional conduct. After her acquittal, the College of Physicians and Surgeons granted her a medical licence.

Dr. Stowe helped to organize the Women's Medical College in Toronto (the forerunner of Women's College Hospital) in 1883. That same year, her daughter Augusta achieved her mother's own goal of twenty years earlier—she obtained a medical degree from the University of Toronto. Augusta Stowe became the first woman to receive a Canadian medical degree.

When John Stowe regained his health, Emily supported him while he retrained as a dentist. After his graduation, the Stowes practised side by side at 111 Church Street in Toronto until Emily retired in 1893.

While in New York City as a medical student, Emily Stowe became interested in feminist causes. Upon her return to Canada she launched the Toronto Women's Literary Club, a pseudonym for a suffrage group, the first in Canada. The organization issued a magazine, *The Citizen*, which championed women's education and enfranchisement. In 1883, the group reconstituted itself as the Canadian Women's Suffrage Association. Six years later, the group helped to form the Dominion Women's Enfranchisement Association. Dr. Stowe became its first president, a position she held until her death in 1903.

In a note she wrote in 1896, Emily Stowe provided her own best epitaph: "My career has been one of much struggle characterised by the usual persecution which attends everyone who pioneers a new movement or steps out of line with established custom."

Women sought office jobs away from the noise and pressure of the factory. By the turn of the century, women were employed in most clerical jobs. Conventional wisdom held that their "natural" feminine characteristics—sympathy, adaptability, courtesy, and even nimble fingers—made them particularly suitable for clerical work. Male clerks, however, retained the senior managerial positions. Women also worked as department-store clerks or telephone operators, two of the most "feminized" occupations at the turn of the century.

Amherst, Nova Scotia, telephone exchange, around 1909. Telephone operators belonged to the elite of female clerical workers.

Source: Cumberland County Museum, 184-78-2.

After domestic, factory, and office work, teaching was the most common female occupation. Public schools had expanded across Canada in the late nineteenth century. At the turn of the century, women constituted three-quarters of the teaching profession. Teaching was considered an acceptable occupation for women, one that allowed for upward social mobility, although it provided little financial security. Women received low salaries and had little chance of advancing to become department heads or principals. Generally, female teachers were expected to give up their teaching positions when they married so they could return to their "natural" calling as wives, mothers, and keepers of the home.

A small number of women worked as nurses. Thanks to Florence Nightingale's popular example during the Crimean War, nursing, although not yet recognized as a profession, had become a respectable occupation at the turn of the century. Again, this choice of profession was shaped by conventional views regarding femininity and masculinity. Although women were viewed as natural healers and had played this role for centuries, the rise of science and the patriarchal nature of society discouraged most women from aspiring to be doctors. But they could aid doctors: many women gravitated to the Victorian Order of Nurses (VON), formed in 1897 as a model public-health nursing service.

Only a handful of women entered Canadian medical schools. For one thing, few hospitals would provide them with hospital privileges after graduation. Unable to attract enough patients, a number of Canada's early female doctors became medical missionaries overseas instead.

In all the professions that women entered at the turn of the century, they experienced lower pay than men, lack of control over their work, and pressure to quit once they married.

Health

Health issues became one of the central concerns of social reformers. Frequent illness complicated the normal daily problems of living and working. These concerns were increasing rapidly with the expansion of cities. Montreal in particular remained a most unhealthy city in which to live, especially for children. At the turn of the century, approximately one out of every four infants died before the age of one. Urban reformers claimed that only one other city in the world exceeded this death rate—Calcutta, India. City inhabitants suffered from impure water and unpasteurized milk. Families had neither sick benefits nor hospital or life insurance to protect them. Women were expected to provide essential health care at home. Nevertheless, Ontario established a Board of Health in 1882, modelled on Britain's Public Health Act of 1875, to carry out preventive measures. The other provinces followed suit by 1909.

Despite overpopulation and crowding, society generally denounced attempts to limit family size. Church and state merged to stifle fertility control. A nation seeking to increase its population had a stake in encouraging women to have large families. Limitation of family size, in both English and French Canada, was considered "race suicide." According to section 179 of the Criminal Code of Canada, prepared in 1892:

> Everyone is guilty of an indictable offence and liable to two years' imprisonment who knowingly, without lawful excuse or justification, offers to sell, advertise, publish an advertisement of or has for sale or disposal any medicine, drug or article intended or represented as a means of preventing conception or causing abortion.

Despite such threats, many married women, anxious to limit their family size, sought birth-control information. Attempts to control women's fertility, whether by church or state, forced the practices underground. Many women lacked even the basic information on sexuality, fertility, and reproduction. According to historian Angus McLaren: "Doctors would not discuss the merits of the most reliable forms of contraception—the condom, douche, and pessary—because they associated them with the libertine, the prostitute, and the midwife."[4] A few doctors performed abortions, but since they were illegal it is difficult to know how many occurred. As well, many women underwent self-induced abortions. Statistics of women who died from botched abortions are available for a later period and speak to the magnitude of the problem: between 1926 and 1946, an estimated 4000 women died.

Charitable and Social Institutions

At the turn of the century, churches and private philanthropic organizations administered limited charitable help to those in need. Early in the century, Toronto had more than 50 charitable organizations and 20 churches providing relief to the poor. Montreal had nearly 30 shelters and out-door-relief agencies, as well as about a dozen old-age homes and a dozen orphanages. Between 1900 and 1911, these institutions provided relief for 2000–3000 families in their respective cities every year—usually a meal of soup, bread, and tea, and a bath and a bed. According to societal views, with the exception of the handicapped and the aged, individuals alone remained responsible for their plight. As a result, charities provided only temporary relief.

Skilled workers looked to fraternal organizations and clubs for financial and emotional support. Associations and lodges such as the Orange Lodge, the Masons, the Oddfellows, and the Independent Order of Foresters gave their male members a sense of importance and self-worth, and a feeling of camaraderie. Females could not belong to the fraternal or sporting clubs, but in some instances, such as the Oddfellows, women could belong to a parallel gendered organization, such as the Rebekahs. Some associations had mutual-aid plans to care for sick members and to assist widows and orphans in the event of a member's death. They also gave workers a means to express publicly and collectively their discontent with industrial capitalism by supporting parades through the streets of towns and cities to show both solidarity and defiance. Association life was, as historian Bryan Palmer notes, "a realm apart from the troubled conflicts of the workplace"[5] and an important phase on the road to a working-class consciousness. These clubs were, however, quite exclusive and their membership was based around such commonalities as gender, profession, religion, and ethnicity.

In a study of the mining communities on Vancouver Island in the mid- to late nineteenth century, historian John Belshaw noted their transition from a "British" to a "Canadian" identity. He argued that as these communities matured through industrialization and urbanization, they took on more North American qualities. Drinking became a favourite pastime, but it came up against the opposition of employers, social reformers, and even union leaders who wanted to eliminate "demon rum." Miners identified more with fraternal associations than with unions, because the former provided a source of identity and support beyond the workplace. In other words, class meant more than the job one did at the workplace: it shaped culture. Belshaw argued that British Columbia miners were not more radical than miners elsewhere in Canada: "Skills, custom, and security were the principal 'British' watchwords, not rebellion, racism, revolution, or socialism."[6]

Unions

Between 1850 and 1890, labour unions took root in Canada in direct response to industrialization. At first, most unions were local, dispersed across the country, and specialized. Initially, the government refused to grant them legal recognition or to accept workers' right to collective bargaining. The state was not seen to have a role in industrial relations. But as industrial discord and even class war became acknowledged threats, the role of government increased. The state prided itself on being an "impartial umpire" between industry and labour, but in a capitalist system there was little doubt where its support lay.

Knights of Labor procession, King Street, Hamilton, 1885. Parades were an expression of workers' solidarity and a means to achieve public recognition.

Source: W. Farmer/Library and Archives Canada/PA-103086.

Young Cape Breton miners at the pit head, 1903. Allie, on the far left, was a boy of only nine, who worked as a trapperboy. He opened and closed the door for horses bringing coal carts out of the mine. He regularly worked a thirteen-hour shift, six days a week, for 55 cents a day. Canada's industrial revolution depended on coal, and Cape Breton Island contained the richest coal deposits in eastern Canada. By 1901, it produced half of Canada's coal.

Source: Beaton Institute, University College of Cape Breton.

Regardless, labour fought for its rights. The first victory came in 1872, after more than 100 Toronto printers stayed off the job for almost two months. They went on strike for a nine-hour day, protesting that "nine hours a day, six days a week is enough for any man to work." George Brown, one of the Fathers of Confederation and editor of the Toronto *Globe*, opposed the strikers. But his arch-rival, Prime Minister John A. Macdonald, enacted the Trade Union Act, which recognized the right of unions to exist and to organize without fear of prosecution as illegal associations, as long as they registered with the government. Aided by the act, the Toronto printers eventually won better wages and a 54-hour work week. The implementation, at the same time, of the Criminal Law Amendment Act, however, constituted a step backward. This act imposed severe penalties, including a prison sentence, for most forms of picketing and union pressure. Picketing remained illegal in Canada until 1934.

In the late nineteenth century, only a minority of Canadian workers belonged to unions. Three unions dominated the labour movement: the Knights of Labor, the Provincial Workmen's Association, and the American Federation of Labor.

The Knights of Labor, an American organization founded in 1869, enjoyed its greatest success among workers in Ontario and Quebec, although it had branches across the country. Its secret rituals enjoyed great popularity among its followers and its name demonstrated the desire for a code of honour and respectability. At the moment of greatest expansion, the Knights had more than 450 assemblies and over 20,000 members across Canada. The group believed in developing a working-class consciousness through the organization of workers by industry rather than by craft. As industrialization spread, this distinction gained importance. It reflected a move away from skill or craft-based organizations and toward the industry-based factory floors. The organization used its newspapers, the *Pallidium of Labour* and the *Labour Advocate*, to educate the working class to its ideals. The Knights' platform urged, wherever possible, arbitration instead of strikes, an eight-hour workday, an end to child labour, the passage of health and safety legislation, and equal pay for equal work. As an industrial union, rather than a craft union, the Knights took in semiskilled and unskilled workers as well as women and blacks, although not Asians.

Most unions refused to support women, arguing that by improving female wages they encouraged them to remain at work, where they took jobs away from men. Despite such attitudes, some unions, such as the Knights of Labor and others, attempted to organize female telephone operators, retail clerks, laundry workers, waitresses, and even domestics. In some industries, women formed their own unions. In the garment industry, for example, a number of women joined locals of the International Ladies' Garment Workers Union. Their success in this particular industry came in part from the support of male trade unionists, who needed their female counterparts to mount effective strikes. Still, unionized women workers remained more the exception than the rule. Even within this class struggle for equality and justice, the male breadwinner model worked against gender equality.

Most unions also refused to support visible minorities such as blacks and Asians, seeing them as cheap labour that would undermine unionization. Since these minorities ended up working only part-time or seasonal jobs, it was difficult to form their own unions. One exception was the occupation of railroad employee. In 1917, porters formed the Order of Sleeping Car Porters—the first African-Canadian railway union in North America. Many of its members came from Africville, an African-Canadian neighbourhood in Halifax, while others were more recent immigrants from the American South and the Caribbean. Although the Canadian Brotherhood of Railway Employees initially refused to accept the union, it did so in 1919, making it the first craft union to lift racial restrictions on memberships. Regardless, the labour movement demonstrated the same bigoted views toward gender, race, and ethnicity as seen throughout Canadian society.

The Provincial Workmen's Association, founded in 1879 by the coal miners of Springfield, Nova Scotia, became the Maritime equivalent of the Knights of Labor, and Canada's first industrial union. After a slow beginning, it became recognized as the voice of the coal miners, and later represented other Maritime workers in seeking protection and compensation. In 1909, however, the Scottish immigrant J.B. McLachlan helped introduce to Cape Breton a more militant union, a branch of the American-based United Mine Workers of America. Ten years later, miners at last won the eight-hour day and made important gains in their standard of living. Resource communities, based around mining and timber, were the most fertile ground for union organization. The vast majority of people in the community relied on that one industry and formed a community based around their class identity. It was here where the most radical unions formed and also where class-consciousness was strongest.

In Newfoundland, William Ford Coaker founded the Fishermen's Protective Union (FPU) in 1908 to protect fishers from the vagaries of curing weather, fish migration, and volatile markets. Its motto, "To each his own," signified that fishers did not enjoy the benefits of their own labour nor the right to a decent living. The objective of the union was to promote the commercial welfare of the fishermen by securing the highest price for their fish and lowest price for their supplies. In addition, Coaker advocated a "national plan" that consisted of free and compulsory education, a night-school system, nondenominational education in small outposts, outpost hospitals, and universal old-age pensions. The FPU turned to politics to attempt to achieve its objectives and won eight seats in the Newfoundland Legislature in the 1913 election.

The Knights of Labor controlled the Trades and Labor Congress of Canada (TLC), the central labour organization founded in 1883 by the Toronto Trades and Labor Council as a successor to the Canadian Labor Union (1873–77). Originally it brought together trade unionists from Ontario only. By 1900, however, it became a dominion-wide organization. Union leaders realized quickly that in order to organize effectively, they had to cross not only craft and trade lines, but also political boundaries, both provincial and national. They heeded theorist Karl Marx's call: "Workers of the world unite." International unionism spread into Canada even though it raised the ire of the government.

The TLC moved away from the Knights' approach to reform and organization by industry when it established strong ties with the American Federation of Labor (AFL), a strictly craft-union organization. The conservative leadership of the AFL believed that the primary purpose of unions should be to improve the material benefits of its workers—better wages and hours and safer working conditions—rather than to radically reform the capitalist system. It expelled industrial unions such as the Knights from its membership.

With the decline of the Knights of Labor in the early twentieth century, unskilled workers looked increasingly to politics or radical unions to achieve their objectives. Some called for political involvement and worked to create an independent socialist party, while others, who had given up hope that the AFL would become more militant, supported radical unions, such as the Industrial Workers of the World (IWW), founded in 1905. The "Wobblies," as they became known, attempted to organize all workers, regardless of their trade, skill, or gender, into one large union for the purpose of calling a general strike to bring down the capitalist system. The first sentence of their constitution revealed their view of North American society: "The working class and the employing class have nothing in common." The IWW had little impact in eastern Canada but had greater success in western Canada, particularly in the resource camps.

The West was becoming more radical than the rest of Canada. While the philosophy of individualism and a sense of "frontierism" existed, it ran up against a developing philosophy of collective action. Much of western radicalism came from the expectation that it was a "new" society, apart from the "old" society of central and eastern Canada. Immigration of workers and farmers from Britain and central Europe brought in new ideas and increased the expectation that the new society would somehow be an improvement over the old. As an assumed "land of opportunity," the region became infused with the spirit of reform. Yet generally conditions remained poor for western workers. Wages were exceptionally low, inflation high, employment sporadic, especially in the primary industries, and working conditions, especially in the mines and railway camps, atrocious. Large-scale immigration into the region proved to be both the strength and the weakness of unions. On the one hand, many European, and especially British, immigrants were well versed in socialist ideas and experienced in union organizations, and contributed to labour protest and union building in Canada. On the other hand, immigration provided a large pool of unskilled workers who hindered the growth of unions by their willingness to work as "scabs" for low wages.

Quebec sat in contrast to the rest of Canada. The Roman Catholic Church assisted in providing church-affiliated unions as an alternative to what it considered to be socialist and anti-clerical international unions that undermined the church's position among the working class. The clergy first intervened directly in a labour dispute in the Quebec shoe-workers' strike of 1906. One year later, the church founded a union. Its successor would be the *Confédération des travailleurs catholiques du Canada* (CTCC), an exclusively Catholic organization founded in 1921, with a priest, as chaplain, effectively in charge of each local.

The Limitations of Unions

In general, unions had limited success prior to World War I. As late as 1911, less than one-tenth of the national workforce belonged to unions. Most unskilled workers and virtually all women remained non-unionized. Unions were also divided, and their leaders suspicious of one another. Divisions existed over skilled and unskilled, over whether to become affiliated with American and international organizations, and over objectives, tactics, and philosophies. Furthermore, unions had few rights. Employers could still fire union workers at will, or demand that workers sign contracts in which they promised not to join a union. As well, employers brought in immigrant labourers on the condition that they work as strike-breakers or for extremely low wages.

Workers fought back by pressuring the Laurier government to pass the Alien Labour Act in 1908, which prohibited "any person, company, partnership, or corporation, in any manner to pre-pay the transportation of, or in any other way to assist or solicit the importation of immigration of any alien or foreigner into Canada under control or agreement." But the act was rarely enforced and had no impact on controlling companies wanting cheap labour. Unions also faced a hostile and indifferent managerial class. The views of one Montreal mill manager, as reported in *La presse* in 1908, characterized the general attitude of managers to workers: "It was not at all his concern whether his employees could live on the wages he paid them. If they don't like it, they can go work somewhere else."

Nevertheless, unions did organize strikes—1000 disputes were recorded between 1900 and 1911, mainly in the manufacturing, construction, transportation, and mining industries. Workers protested against low wages, inadequate working conditions, and managerial tyranny. But most strikes ended without workers gaining any significant concessions. Many of them erupted into physical violence, with the government calling out the militia to end them. This happened on more than 30 occasions before 1914.

Governments clearly favoured business interests over workers. The same government that supported employers by means of tariffs or other economic incentives argued against intervention on behalf of workers on the basis of a laissez-faire philosophy. The federal Conservative government did, however, establish the Royal Commission on the Relations of Labour and Capital, which in its report in 1889 documented the negative impact of the Industrial Revolution. Few reforms resulted from the report, although in 1894 the Conservatives officially established Labour Day, the first Monday of September, as a national holiday for working people.

The Liberal government of Wilfrid Laurier created the Department of Labour in 1900 to settle strikes as well as to enforce a fair wage policy. In 1907 it also passed the Industrial Disputes Investigation Act, which prohibited strikes and lockouts in mines or public utilities until a three-member board had investigated the dispute. The Ontario government under James Whitney introduced the Workmen's Compensation Act in 1914, but only after the act met with the approval of employers, who realized that they would also benefit from government compensation to injured workers.

Increasingly, skilled workers tried to gain influence through politics. They set out their own agenda, such as the sixteen-point program of the Trades and Labor Congress that passed at its meeting in 1898, in which they demanded free compulsory education, an eight-hour day, a minimum wage, tax reform, public ownership of railways and telegraphs, extension of the franchise, abolition of the Senate, prohibition of prison and contract labour, legislative elimination of child labour, and opposition to Chinese immigration (since the Chinese were perceived as a threat to labour's employment opportunities and wages). Then they tried to pressure the two traditional parties to adopt some or all of their recommendations. When this approach failed, they fielded their own labour candidates in federal, provincial, and municipal elections. While a few were elected, most labour politicians had limited success and impact, particularly at the federal and provincial levels. Greater success occurred at the municipal level. By 1920, fully 271 working-class candidates ran for political office in 44 municipalities; 111 were elected, including labour mayors in Fort William, Port Arthur, Sault Ste. Marie, and Moncton. Overall, however, workers had a weak political voice.

Cities – socially/physically stratified inequalities [handwritten annotation]

SUMMARY

At the turn of the century, Canadians lived well by world standards but social injustice and inequalities persisted. Farming underwent significant change. The family farm had to adjust to mechanization, higher costs, fewer workers, and routine and specialized jobs. Many left the land for the growing urban centres. This was a trend that would continue for decades. Cities became socially and physically stratified, with working-class districts in the city centre and middle-class areas in the surrounding neighbourhoods. Both male and female workers lived in cramped quarters and worked long hours, under poor conditions, in factories and offices. In times of need, they looked to charitable and social institutions, and ultimately to unions, for assistance. By the early twentieth century, the injustices had become so noticeable that they gained public attention, especially among a rising group of middle-class social reformers.

NOTES

1. Marjorie Griffin Cohen, *Women's Work, Markets, and Economic Development in Nineteenth-Century Ontario* (Toronto: University of Toronto Press, 1988), p. 106.

2. Arthur J. Ray, *I Have Lived Here Since the World Began* (Toronto: Key Porter, 1996), p. 291.

3. Jacques Rouillard, "A Life So Threadbare," *Horizon Canada*, 25 (1985): 594.

4. Angus McLaren, "A Motherhood Issue," *Horizon Canada*, 87 (1986): 2074.

5. Bryan Palmer, *Working-Class Experience: The Rise and Reconstitution of Canadian Labour, 1800–1980* (Toronto: Butterworths, 1983), p. 80.

6. John Douglas Belshaw, *Colonization and Community: The Vancouver Island Coalfield and the Making of the British Columbian Working Class* (Montreal/Kingston: McGill-Queen's University Press, 2002), p. 214.

BIBLIOGRAPHY

Histories that examine the dynamics between rural life and urban and industrial growth are Daniel Samson, ed., *Contested Countryside: Rural Workers and Modern Society in Atlantic Canada, 1800–1950* (Fredericton: Acadiensis Press, 1994); R.W. Sandwell, ed., *Beyond the City Limits: Rural History in British Columbia* (Vancouver: UBC Press, 1999); and Kenneth Michael Sylvester, *The Limits of Rural Capitalism: Family, Culture and Markets in Montcalm, Manitoba, 1870–1940* (Toronto: University of Toronto Press, 2001). Rod Bantjes, *Improved Earth: Prairie Space as Modern Artefact, 1869–1944* (Toronto: University of Toronto Press, 2005) provides an exploration of space in the Prairie West. Royden Loewen and Gerald Friesen, *Immigrants in Prairie Cities: Ethnic Diversity in Twentieth-Century Canada* (Toronto: University of Toronto Press, 2009) examines the immigrant experience to urban centres in the Prairie West.

On the impact of industrialization and commercialization on the First Nations, see Arthur Ray, *I Have Lived Here Since the World Began* (Toronto: Key Porter, 1996); Diane Newell, *Tangled Webs of History: Indians and the Law in Canada's Pacific Coast Fisheries* (Toronto: University of Toronto Press, 1993); Bruce Hodgins and Jamie Benidickson, *The Temagami Experience: Recreation, Resources, and Aboriginal Rights in the Northern Ontario Wilderness* (Toronto: University of Toronto Press, 1989); and Kerry Abel, *Drum Songs: Glimpses of Dene History* (Montreal/Kingston: McGill-Queen's University Press, 1993).

Working-class life in the major industrial city of Montreal at the turn of the century is discussed in T.J. Copp, *The Anatomy of Poverty: The Condition of the Working Class in Montreal, 1897–1929* (Toronto: McClelland & Stewart, 1974), and in J. Rouillard, *Les syndicats nationaux au Québec de 1900 à 1930* (Quebec: Presses de l'Université Laval, 1979), as well as in his *Histoire du syndicalisme québécois* (Montreal:

Boréal Express, 1989). For family life in Montreal, see Bettina Bradbury, *Working Families: Age, Gender and Daily Survival in Industrializing Montreal* (Toronto: McClelland & Stewart, 1993). For Toronto, see Gregory Kealey, *Toronto Workers Respond to Industrial Capitalism, 1867–1892* (Toronto: University of Toronto Press, 1980), and Michael Piva, *The Conditions of the Working Class in Toronto, 1900–1921* (Ottawa: University of Ottawa Press, 1979); also Christina Burr, *Spreading the Light: Work and Labour Reform in Late-Nineteenth-Century Toronto* (Toronto: University of Toronto Press, 1999). For a look at Calgary, see David Bright, *The Limits of Labour: Class Formation and the Labour Movement in Calgary, 1883–1929* (Vancouver: UBC Press, 1998). See also Craig Heron and Steve Penfold, *The Workers' Festival: A History of Labour Day in Canada* (Toronto: University of Toronto Press, 2005). A comparative study of one industry is Craig Heron's *Working in Steel: The Early Years in Canada, 1883–1935* (Toronto: University of Toronto Press, 1988).

On epidemics, see Michael Bliss, *Plague: A Story of Smallpox in Montreal* (Toronto: HarperCollins, 1991). For the unemployed, see Peter Baskerville and Eric W. Sager, *Unwilling Idlers: The Urban Unemployed and Their Families in Late Victorian Canada* (Toronto: University of Toronto Press, 1998). On the experience of ethnic minorities, see Franca Iacovetta et al., eds., *A Nation of Immigrants: Women, Workers, and Communities in Canadian History, 1840s–1960s* (Toronto: University of Toronto Press, 1998). For how Canadians dealt with sickness, see Mona Gleason, *Small Matters: Canadian Children in Sickness and Health, 1900–1940* (Montreal/Kingston: McGill-Queen's University Press, 2013).

On women workers, see the relevant sections in Alison Prentice et al., *Canadian Women: A History*, 2nd ed. (Toronto: Harcourt Brace, 1996); the relevant essays in Veronica Strong-Boag, Mona Gleason, and Adele Perry, eds., *Rethinking Canada: The Promise of Women's History*, 4th ed. (Toronto: Oxford University Press, 2002); Marjorie Griffin Cohen, *Women's Work: Markets and Economic Development in Nineteenth-Century Ontario* (Toronto: University of Toronto Press, 1988); and Graham S. Lowe, *Women in the Administrative Revolution: The Feminization of Clerical Work* (Toronto: University of Toronto Press, 1987). Mary Kinnear, ed., *First Days, Fighting Days: Women in Manitoba History* (Regina: Canadian Plains Research Center, University of Regina, 1987) contains several essays on women workers. See also J. Acton et al., eds., *Women at Work: Ontario, 1850–1930* (Toronto: Canadian Women's Educational Press, 1974); and Wayne Roberts, *Honest Womanhood: Feminism, Femininity and Class Consciousness Among Toronto Working Women, 1893 to 1914* (Toronto: New Hogtown Press, 1976).

A comparative study of men and women workers in the two Ontario towns of Paris and Hanover is provided in Joy Parr, *The Gender of Breadwinners: Women, Men, and Change in Two Industrial Towns, 1880–1950* (Toronto: University of Toronto Press, 1990). For the Maritimes, see Janet Guildford and Suzanne Morton, *Separate Spheres: Women's Worlds in the 19th-Century Maritimes* (Fredericton: Acadiensis Press, 1994). For women in the professions, see Mary Kinnear, *In Subordination: Professional Women, 1870–1970* (Montreal/Kingston: McGill-Queen's University Press, 1995). Gender conflict is reviewed in Franca Iacovetta and Mariana Valverde, eds., *Gender Conflicts: New Essays in Women's History* (Toronto: University of Toronto Press, 1992). On women in the medical profession, see Kathryn McPherson, *Bedside Matters: The Transformation of Canadian Nursing, 1900–1990* (Toronto: Oxford University Press, 1996) and Denyse Baillargeon, translated by W. Donald Wilson, *Babies for the Nation: The Medicalization of Motherhood in Quebec, 1910–1970* (Waterloo, ON: Wilfrid Laurier University Press, 2009).

On working families see Bettina Bradbury, ed., *Canadian Family History: Selected Readings* (Toronto: Copp Clark Pitman, 1992); and R. Marvin McInnis, "Women, Work and Childbearing: Ontario in the Second Half of the Nineteenth Century," *Histoire sociale/Social History*, 24(48) (November 1991): 237–62. Women and the law are the subject of Constance Backhouse's *Petticoats and Prejudice: Women and Law in Nineteenth Century Canada* (Toronto: The Osgoode Society, 1991); and Amanda Glasbeek, *Feminized Justice: The Toronto Women's Court, 1913–1934* (Vancouver: UBC Press, 2009). On the "girl problem," see Carolyn Strange, *Toronto's Girl Problem: The Perils and Pleasures of the City, 1880–1930* (Toronto: University of Toronto Press, 1995), and Tamara Myers, *Caught: Montreal's Modern Girls and the Law, 1869–1945* (Toronto: University of Toronto Press, 2006).

On changing notions of sexuality, see Gary Kinsman, *The Regulation of Desire: Homo and Hetero Sexualities in Canada*, 2nd ed. (Montreal: Black Rose Books, 1996); Sharon Dale, *Lesbians in Canada*

(Toronto: Between the Lines, 1990); and Angus McLaren and Arlene Tigar McLaren, *The Bedroom and the State: The Changing Practices and Politics of Contraception and Abortion in Canada, 1880–1980* (Toronto: McClelland & Stewart, 1986). McLaren has also written a short popular article, "A Motherhood Issue," *Horizon Canada*, 87 (1986): 2072–77, on birth control in Canada in the late nineteenth and early twentieth centuries. For the development of the social work profession, see Therese Jennissen and Colleen Lundy, *One Hundred Years of Social Work: A History of the Profession in English Canada* (Waterloo, ON: Wilfrid Laurier Press, 2009).

The labour movement is discussed in Craig Heron, *The Canadian Labour Movement: A Short History*, rev. ed. (Toronto: James Lorimer, 1996); Bryan Palmer, *Working-Class Experience: Rethinking the History of Canadian Labour, 1800–1991* (Toronto: McClelland & Stewart, 1992); Desmond Morton with Terry Copp, *Working People: An Illustrated History of the Canadian Labour Movement* (Toronto: Summerhill Press, 1990); Desmond Morton, *Working People: An Illustrated History of the Canadian Labour Movement*, 5th ed. (Montreal/Kingston: McGill-Queen's University Press, 2007); Ian McKay, *Reasoning Otherwise: Leftists and the People's Enlightenment in Canada, 1890–1920* (Toronto: Between the Lines, 2008). Also useful are Laurel Sefton MacDowell and Ian Radforth, eds., *Canadian Working Class History: Selected Readings*, 3rd ed. (Toronto: Canadian Scholars' Press, 2006); G. Kealey and P. Warrian, eds., *Essays in Canadian Working-Class History* (Toronto: McClelland & Stewart, 1976); and Craig Heron and Steve Penfold, *The Workers' Festival: A History of Labour Day in Canada* (Toronto: University of Toronto Press, 2005). On the Provincial Workmen's Association, see Ian McKay, "'By Wisdom, Wile or War': The Provincial Workmen's Association and the Struggle for Working-Class Independence in Nova Scotia, 1879–97," *Labour/Le travail*, 18 (Fall 1986): 13–62, and for the Fishermen's Protective Union, see Ian D.H. McDonald, *"To Each His Own": William Croaker and the Fishermen's Protective Union in Newfoundland Politics, 1908–1945* (St. John's: ISER, Memorial University, 1987). David Frank has written *J.B. McLachlan: A Biography—The Story of a Legendary Labour Leader and the Cape Breton Miners* (Toronto: James Lorimer, 1999).

On the making of a working-class community in the coalfields of Vancouver Island, see John Douglas Belshaw, *Colonization and Community: The Vancouver Island Coalfield and the Making of the British Columbian Working Class* (Montreal/Kingston: McGill-Queen's University Press, 2002). Women and unions are discussed in Julie White, *Sisters and Solidarity: Women and Unions in Canada* (Toronto: Thompson Educational, 1993). D. Owen Carrigan, *Crime and Punishment in Canada: A History* (Toronto: McClelland & Stewart, 1991) deals with this important subject. On the Order of Sleeping Car Porters union, see Sarah-Jane (Saje) Mathieu, "North of the Colour Line: Sleeping Car Porters and the Battle Against Jim Crow on Canadian Rails, 1880–1920," *Labour/Le travail*, 47 (Spring, 2001): 9–41. For race relations, see Constance Backhouse, *Colour-Coded: A Legal History of Racism in Canada, 1900–1950* (Toronto: University of Toronto Press, 1999).

Source: City of Toronto Archives/SCI-3.

Chapter Eight

AN ERA OF SOCIAL REFORM: 1890–1914

TIME LINE	
1874	Founding of the Woman's Christian Temperance Union (WCTU)
1875	Mount Allison University becomes first university in the British Empire to grant a degree to a woman, Grace Annie Lockhart
1877	The Toronto Women's Literary Club becomes the first Canadian women's suffrage organization
1878	Canadian Temperance Act (Scott Act) passed
1885	Banff National Park established
1887	Establishment of the first bird sanctuary in North America at Last Mountain Lake, North-West Territories
1893	Wilfred Grenfell begins mission in Newfoundland and Labrador Algonquin Provincial Park established in Ontario
1894	Fred Victor Mission founded in Toronto
1895	Reading Camp Association, forerunner of Frontier College, created by Alfred Fitzpatrick
1897	The first Women's Institute founded near Stoney Creek, Ontario
1898	National Referendum on prohibition held
1900	Alphonse Desjardins establishes *caisses populaires* (credit unions) in Quebec
1903	Founding of *Ligue nationaliste* in Quebec
1904	Founding of the *Association catholique de la jeunesse canadienne-française* (ACJC)
1909	Jack Miner establishes a bird sanctuary in Kingsville, Ontario
1911	Founding of the *École sociale populaire* (ESP)

Social reform movements emerged across Canada around the turn of the century to deal with disruptions brought about by large-scale industrialization and rapid urbanization. Traditionally, the churches played the leading role in social reform, but more effort was needed to deal with the serious challenges posed by industrialization. As part of a much broader reinterpretation of the role of the individual in society, social reformers believed that the churches had to be concerned not only with individual salvation in the afterlife but also with improving social conditions in this life. In the face of social problems brought on by industrialization, they believed that the state should join the churches in dealing with these issues.

Education was seen as an essential means of improving society. It was viewed as a panacea for social ills and a means of creating productive workers, obedient citizens, and "good Canadians." Reformers pushed for universal, progressive education that provided a nurturing, healthy environment and practical training that prepared children with good work habits and strong morals for the new industrial age. Urban reformers sought to improve the cityscape by focusing on pleasing architecture, natural spaces, the elimination of ghettos, and adequate social services. Conservationists emerged to campaign for the preservation of wildlife and the wilderness. Women reformers fought for political equality and suffrage based on the belief that their gender would use the power of the ballot to bring about social reform. They also spearheaded the prohibition movement to eliminate the "demon drink," which they saw as one of the root causes of social decay. Together, these reformers made positive changes in society but their goal of an ideal, reformed Canada still eluded them on the eve of World War I.

Social Evangelism and Reform in English Canada

Many social reformers emerged from the ranks of the Protestant churches. Protestant clergymen called for a "revitalization of evangelicalism" to deal with the "increasing social distress and conflict."[1] Social evangelism was part of a larger movement of religious revival in Britain and the United States with roots in the Great Awakenings of the nineteenth century. This revivalism emphasized conversion (being "born again"), the authority of the Bible as God's revelation to humanity, and a commitment to evangelism. The movement looked to apply Christianity to correct society's ills, both public and private. It sought the "New Jerusalem" and to create the "Kingdom of God on Earth."

Social reformers regarded people as inherently good. If individuals erred, they did so not simply because of human weakness or maliciousness of character, but because of their environment. If reformers could improve social conditions, then people's character would change for the better, which would result in an ideal Christian society—the creation of the New Jerusalem. They argued that Jesus was a social reformer in that he preached against the injustices of society, and sought active change and reform.

Social evangelicals were concerned with the problems leading to an apparent collapse in morality: prostitution, alcoholism, gambling, violence, poverty, and a lack of hygiene. The Reverend S.D. Chown of the Methodist church in Kingston, Ontario, summed up the attitude in a lecture in 1905: "The first duty of a Christian is to be a citizen, or a man amongst men. We are under no obligation to get into heaven, that is a matter entirely of our own option; but we are under obligation to quit sin and to bring heaven down to this earth." Social evangelicals strove to create in this world a humane society based on the Christian principles of love, charity, humanity, and brotherhood.

Social reformers worked to give immediate assistance to the destitute through the establishment of missions and settlement houses. In 1890, the Reverend D.J. Macdonnell founded St. Andrews Institute in Toronto to bring the Presbyterian Church closer to the working people. In Newfoundland, Dr. Wilfred Grenfell, who trained as a doctor in London's notoriously poor

A Salvation Army meeting in Calgary, late August 1887. Meetings featured testimony, prayer, music, and song. The Salvation Army, begun by General William Booth in England, came to Canada in 1882.

Source: Library and Archives Canada/C-14426.

East End, established his Grenfell Mission in 1893 to help improve the appalling social conditions he found in northern Newfoundland outposts and along the Labrador coast. He challenged church leaders to provide better schooling; merchant capitalists to provide greater financial support to fishers and their families; and politicians to provide more hospitals. His efforts led to the establishment of a Newfoundland public health movement that addressed in particular the serious tuberculosis epidemic in the British colony.

Settlement houses were set up by middle-class reformers in poor urban neighbourhoods to help the unfortunate; Toynbee Hall in London, England, and Hull House in Chicago were noted examples. Sara Libby Carson started the first Canadian settlement house in 1902, and helped found others in Toronto and McGill universities. Originally established to help the poor, they increasingly focused on helping immigrants and women. By 1920, at least thirteen settlement houses existed in Canada, offering the basic necessities of food, shelter, and medical care, as well as programs such as night schools and nurseries.

The Salvation Army, started by William Booth in England, also established centres in Canada at the turn of the century to help the poor. The organization modelled itself after the regular army, and the members wore military-style uniforms and insignia. The ministers were called "officers" and the converts were "soldiers." At their peak, their "field force" enlisted nearly 150,000 in Canada to fight sin and poverty. Among their field force were a number of women—"Hallelujah lasses"—who preached on street corners and worked in shelters and homes to alleviate the misery of their "sisters."

Morality, Social Control, and the State

Some reformers, labelled social purity activists, concerned themselves with issues associated with morality and vice, such as gambling, alcoholism, promiscuity, and prostitution (often referred to as "the social evil"), along with homosexuality, venereal disease, "feeblemindedness," and abortion. They sought to regulate and legislate sexual relations as a means to ensure social control and even racial purity. English-Canadian social purists feared that the influx of large numbers of "foreigners" into Canada would lead to "inter-breeding" and dilute the dominant and superior Anglo-Saxon race. Reverend S.D. Chown linked the two: "The immigration question is the most vital one in Canada today, as it has to do with the purity of our national life-blood."

The churches sat at the vanguard of this social panic and called for social control. From the pulpit, ministers addressed moral concerns such as extramarital sex, masturbation, homosexuality, prostitution, and abortion. Reverend W.J. Hunter lectured to as many as 1500 men a night at St. James Methodist Church in Montreal on such topics. Reverend C. Sharp told his Toronto congregation in 1908: "God abhors the spirit as prevalent nowadays which condemns motherhood," in reference to the feminist and women's suffrage movement. "How it must grieve Him when He sees what we call race suicide; when He sees the problems of married life approached lightly and wantonly, based on nothing higher and nobler than mere luxury, and gratification of passion."

The Methodist and Presbyterian churches established social reform agencies under the umbrella of the Moral and Social Reform Council of Canada, established in 1907, which later changed its name to the Social Service Council of Canada. The Methodist Church also recommended and distributed sex manuals, especially the popular eight-volume "Self and Sex" series.

The Woman's Christian Temperance Union (WCTU) hired purity reformers such as William Lund Clark, Arthur Beall, and Beatrice Brigden to tour schools to warn young people against "self-abuse" and promiscuity. Clark recommended that "they drink neither tea nor coffee and refrain from dancing and that they seek improved ventilation and take frequent baths." The WCTU also built homes for "fallen women."

Increasingly, however, regulation of sexuality shifted from the family, community, and church to the state. The early decades of the twentieth century witnessed the rise of the middle class, the state, and the scientific expert. This development had significant impact on the social ideas of the time. Cities hired social workers, experts on prisons, and psychiatrists to present the latest "scientific" theories, to educate the public on proper moral standards, and to work with the "sexual deviants" in the jails and mental institutions. Some social theorists, known as eugenicists, argued for selective breeding by preventing people deemed to have undesirable mental and physical traits from reproducing. Not coincidentally, all too often the "unfit" and "inferior" were also foreigners, thus adding a racial and ethnic component to the eugenics movement. Some cities, such as Toronto, established morality departments to arrest and prosecute anyone involved in prostitution or in same-sex relationships. The department targeted in particular young single women—"working girls"—who frequented amusement parks and dancehalls, where, it was assumed, they became easy prey for lusty young men or pimps.

The courts became the arm of the state in regulating morality. In 1892, the Criminal Code included a comprehensive system of offences to "protect" young girls and women by imposing stiff penalties of up to fourteen years on brothel operators and those who enticed women into prostitution. It also legislated against "gross indecency," which referred to homosexual acts. Punishment was set at a minimum of five years, with provisions for whipping. In 1907, the federal government passed the Juvenile Delinquents Act, which created separate courts and different

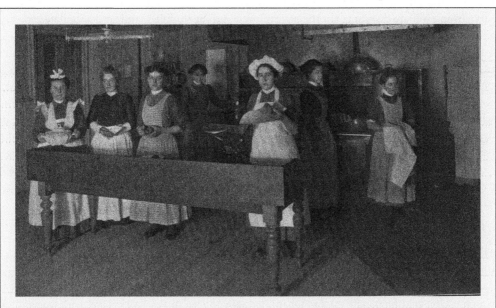

The Andrew Mercer Ontario Reformatory for Females taught virtues of domesticity to "fallen women." In prison, strict time-management was instituted to encourage regular work habits.

Source: Ontario Prisons, *Annual Report of the Inspector of Prisons and Public Charities*, [Sessional Papers] 35 (1903): 87. This appears as an illustration in Carolyn Strange, *Toronto's Girl Problem: The Perils and Pleasures of the City, 1880–1930*, p. 87.

punishments for young offenders than for adults. These courts, like the morality squad and the sexual purists, aimed to regulate sex for the "good of society" and the "purity of the race." Juvenile courts, however, worked to the detriment of children, contrary to the intentions of their founders, since accused children lost many of the rights of due process and faced more indiscriminate sentencing than the accused in adult courts. Often the courts committed them to industrial or training schools, like Toronto's Mercer Reformatory, where they were lectured on morality while receiving agricultural, manual, or domestic training.

Social reformers also worked to shape social attitudes through education. The argument for the link between education and morality was added to the arsenal of those advocating universal education. It helped convince the upper classes that there *was* a purpose to educating the masses. Reformers believed that attitudes of greed, competition, and materialism caused society's problems. Through education, people could learn of the benefits of living in a society governed by Christian principles. In 1918, William Lyon Mackenzie King, then a Canadian labour conciliator but one year away from becoming the leader of the federal Liberal Party, published *Industry and Humanity*. He called for moral regeneration through the application of Christian principles. Social salvation, he argued, would come to a society that practised the ethical laws of Christianity.

Reformers gradually advocated an increased role for the state in reforming society. The problems of a modern society were simply too much for the churches and voluntary groups to handle. They argued that the concept of laissez-faire—the belief that governments should not upset the natural laws of the marketplace—had been used by the wealthy in society to exploit the poor. But such an argument would not be enough for the elites unless it was appended with the assertion that the state could help alleviate social problems, thereby providing an improved atmosphere for the marketplace. It made sense for the middle classes to call on state intervention. An activist government operating on Christian principles would ensure that all people—not just the elite—benefited from the well-being of society. Government involvement could provide essential social services and welfare assistance for the unemployed and the disabled, and could regulate industry and nationalize key industries to ensure that they served the public good.

For a few social evangelicals, such as J.S. Woodsworth—then a Methodist minister but later the founder of the Co-operative Commonwealth Federation (CCF)—these reforms served as a prelude to a more fundamental restructuring of society. Woodsworth believed that the "ideal Kingdom of Jesus" was a socialist paradise where everyone worked for the well-being of the whole rather than for its individual parts. True social reform meant replacing the profit motive of capitalism with Christian charity through socialism. But even Woodsworth was caught up in the dominant thinking of his day. After working as a missionary and social reformer with the "foreign element" in Winnipeg's "shantytown," he openly advocated their assimilation and even certain aspects of eugenics to control their reproduction.

The Impact of Social Reform

The reform movement raised public awareness of social injustices. It spurred such causes as prohibition and women's suffrage, as well as the urban, labour, and farm movements. Reformers' combined efforts contributed to the passing of Ontario's Workmen's Compensation Act in 1914, which established financial benefits for individuals injured in the workplace. Later expanded, the legislation served as a model for similar measures in Nova Scotia (1915), British Columbia (1916), Alberta (1918), and New Brunswick (1918). Social reformers also played a role in the passage in 1916 of the Manitoba Pensions Act, which provided a basic allowance to widowed, divorced, or deserted wives with children. Ultimately, the movement contributed to the rise of such political parties as the Progressives in the 1920s and the CCF and Social Credit in the early 1930s, and prepared the way for the establishment of the social welfare system after World War II.

Historians have debated whether the social evangelical and reform movements led to a more secular society. They agree that the movements led to a religious re-evaluation but differ in measuring the results. The secularists argue that the rise of industrial capitalism and modernity ultimately led to a decline in the role and influence of religion in the everyday lives of Canadians. Declining church attendance and the increasing role of the state are cited as obvious examples. Social gospellers, in attempting to make religion more relevant to everyday concerns and thus to move it away from abstract, theological issues, ironically denied religion its distinctive spiritual function and traditional role. Religious leaders became indistinguishable from social scientists, the clergy became lay sociologists, the sacred became secular.

The revivalists, on the other hand, argue that the social evangelical movement was a time of renewal and rebirth for the churches. The churches were dynamic organizations, able to adapt to new social conditions. Religion continued to play a formative role in the lives of most Canadians. The churches accommodated their faith to the new modern age, even to the rise of the social sciences, thus enabling them to remain active agents of social change well into the twentieth century. Historians, the revivalists argue, have miscast this linear path toward a secular society, and in doing so have miscast the central role of religion.

By World War I, the forces of social reform were in full swing. Scientific and secular approaches were becoming more prominent, but the impetus of reform continued mainly under the guidance of the Protestant churches. Reformers were often professionally trained in the social sciences; social activists were replaced by social workers and sociologists; moral purists were replaced by doctors and psychiatrists in the medical profession and by lawyers and judges in the legal profession. These new professionals relied on surveys as a "scientific" way of documenting problems. They also allied themselves with the state to bring about social change, thus contributing to increased government control over the regulation of individuals, even in their private lives. But, as Nancy Christie and Michael Gauvreau argue, social reform was not a purely secular process: "Until the late 1930s almost every facet of social investigation and social policymaking fell under the aegis of Christian leadership."[2]

Social Reform in Quebec

When English-Canadian reformers looked at Quebec, they saw what they perceived as a backward and priest-ridden society. They believed that Protestantism was progressive while Catholicism was conservative. In many ways, however, Quebec's path to reform paralleled that in English Canada. The forces of modernization, and their cultural and social impact, were similar. As in English Canada, the social significance of religion did not diminish. In Quebec, the Catholic Church responded to these forces and led the reform impetus.

The origins of social reform in Quebec lay in the Roman Catholic Church's emphasis on personal humanity, and on its principles of social justice and Christian charity. In his encyclical *Rerum Novarum* (1891), Pope Leo XIII urged that "some opportune remedy be found quickly for the misery and wretchedness pressing so unjustly on the majority of the working class." Social reformers in Quebec believed that the Catholic faith constituted the "remedy." They believed that the family and the church, rather than the state, were the best institutions to deal with social problems. The ideal Christian social order, church leaders argued, rested on the household and the French-Canadian nation. It was also viewed as essential for the survival of French-Canadian culture. Thus, in Quebec, Catholic values and French-Canadian nationalism became intertwined with social reform.

The Role of the Church

Recognizing the social problems caused by industrialization and urbanization, most particularly in Montreal, the Catholic Church initiated and supported various social reform movements. In this sense, the church was continuing its traditional role. In 1911, for example, the Jesuits founded the Montreal-based *École sociale populaire* (ESP) to develop a Catholic social doctrine. The ESP published pamphlets, organized study groups and retreats, and worked to sensitize the clergy to the social needs of their parishioners. In 1902, priests at Université Laval established the *Société du parler français* to increase French Canadians' awareness of French vocabulary in a largely English-language oriented urban and industrial society, and to eliminate anglicisms in business and industry.

In the classical colleges, religious instructors created the *Association catholique de la jeunesse canadienne-française* (ACJC) in 1904. It sought to encourage among Quebec's youth a unique French-Canadian and Catholic response to the province's social problems. The popular Abbé Lionel Groulx of Valleyfield became the chief leader of the ACJC. In 1907, the Quebec diocese started a newspaper in Quebec City, *L'Action sociale*, later renamed *L'Action catholique*, that addressed social problems. It campaigned for the prohibition of alcohol or at least strict government control of the manufacturing and sale of alcoholic beverages. It also called for the abolition of movie theatres to protect Catholics from corruption.

Many priests supported the *caisses populaires*, the credit unions founded in 1900 by Alphonse Desjardins, as another way of reforming Quebec society. Desjardins believed that a lack of capital handicapped French Canadians in business. He established his savings and lending cooperatives to assist French-Canadian enterprises to get started, hoping to improve the living standards of the working class and to bring economic liberation to the Quebec people. By 1907, the caisses had sufficient assets to establish new cooperative ventures. By the time of Desjardins' death in 1920, more than 200 caisses populaires existed, mainly in Quebec but also among French Canadians in Ontario, Manitoba, and Saskatchewan, and among Franco-Americans in New England.

French-Canadian priests also promoted Catholic unions for Quebec workers (see Chapter 7). Church leaders feared that workers in secular unions, especially American-controlled ones, would become too materialistic and too socialistic in their outlook. The church rejected the idea of organizing workers along class lines, favouring instead Catholic unions based on a spirit of Christian charity and employer–employee cooperation. But the church's control over unions was also self-serving. It was a means to avoid class conflict, which could ultimately undermine the importance of religion and the position of the Catholic Church by giving impetus to the "godless" socialists. Any reform coming to Quebec would first have to go through the powerful and influential Roman Catholic Church.

The church did lend its moral support to the *Ligue nationaliste*, a middle-class group of reformers founded in 1903. Besides concerning themselves with Canada's position in the British Empire and Quebec's status within Canada, they formulated a French-Canadian and largely Catholic response to problems arising out of Quebec's urbanization and industrialization on the assumption that French Canadians needed to retain their identity in an increasingly secularized society. They believed in the family and the household as the fundamental social unit of society and in Christian values as the bulwark of society. They viewed individual or family businesses as compatible with Catholic teachings, while opposing large-scale capitalism, which, they felt, was guided by foreign and mercenary concerns. The state, they argued, should curtail the excessive monopolization of big business by preventing private control of utilities. Ultimately, they favoured a society based on Christian values of cooperation and a concern for the public good.

Educational Reformers

Education and social reform went hand in hand. Early educators concerned themselves with preparing children for the workplace by teaching good work habits. They viewed children as miniature adults, to be placed into adult society. By the turn of the century, however, a new generation of educators emerged who were influenced by such intellectuals as Friedrich Froebel, a European philosopher who advocated child-oriented education by providing students with love and protection from the harsh realities of adult life.

To some educational reformers, "kindergartens" provided one answer. James L. Hughes, a Toronto school inspector, and his future wife, Ada Marean, established the first Canadian public-school kindergarten in 1883 to provide, in Hughes' words, "reverent love for the child, profound respect for his individuality … and freedom and self-activity as the condition of most perfect growth physically, intellectually, and spiritually." Four years later, in 1887, Ontario formally incorporated kindergartens into the public-school system. The Free Kindergarten Association in Winnipeg advocated the same for Manitoba, arguing that "the proper education of children during the first seven years of their lives" did much to "reduce poverty and crime in any community."

In Quebec, the Catholic Church maintained control over education, at least for the French-Canadian majority. In Montreal and Quebec City, nuns ran *salles d'asile* or day-care centres for children of working parents. Between 1898 and 1902, more than 10,000 children attended. In addition to these centres, which offered care on a daily basis, there were orphanages, provincial asylums, and homes for the poor to provide care for children of destitute families.

Other educational reformers worked for different objectives. Some called for temperance education to warn children of the evils of alcohol, while others asked for social programs in public health and in physical and mental hygiene. Reformers also advocated practical or "manual training" in farming and industrial work to prepare children for future jobs. They were successful in getting a number of provinces to introduce technical courses in domestic science, gardening, and shop or industrial arts. Increasingly, educational curricula were breaking free from the constraints of the traditional humanities-based system and becoming more practical.

Educational reformers appreciated the importance of extended and free (universal) schooling. They succeeded by 1905 in getting all provinces except Quebec to legislate free schooling and compulsory attendance for youngsters up to the age of twelve. School attendance soared, especially in elementary school and increasingly in secondary schools as well, doubling from 1891 to 1921.

Two notable educational reformers in Canada were John Kelso and Alfred Fitzpatrick. Kelso, a young police reporter for the Toronto *World*, was concerned about the street urchins who could not be reached through the regular educational system. He quit journalism to begin the Humane Society. When its members

Norman Bethune (third from the left), a labourer/teacher with Frontier College, near Whitefish on the north shore of Georgian Bay, 1911. Bethune would become famous for his medical assistance during the 1930s, first to Spanish civilians during the Spanish Civil War and then to Chinese fighting against Japanese invaders.

Source: Frontier College Collection/Library and Archives Canada/C-56826.

seemed only marginally interested in the plight of children, he began yet another organization, the Children's Aid Society. In 1899, Reverend Alfred Fitzpatrick, a Presbyterian minister from Nova Scotia, created the Reading Camp Association, later called Frontier College, to bring education to immigrant workers in the lumber shanties and railway bunkhouses across northern Canada. Fitzgerald recruited university-student volunteers to give night classes in the "three Rs" and in basic civics. One of the young men whose social conscience was aroused by his work in the camps was Norman Bethune, later renowned for his medical work in Spain and China in the 1930s.

The Urban Reform Movement

The push to clean up the cities was an essential aspect of the social reform movement. Inspired by the "City Beautiful" movement in the United States and Europe, reformers in Canada believed that change must focus on the urban environment—the physical structure of the city, its aesthetic nature, and the quality of its municipal government—in order to deal directly with industrial problems. According to historian Paul Rutherford, what united urban reformers was "less a single creed and more a common approach to a wide variety of urban problems."[3] They worked to transform the existing urban environment, marred by the ugliness and filth of the industrial landscape, into a humane and beautiful one.

The earliest urban reformers included newspaper editors who concentrated on the sordid side of urban life. Through their sensational and inexpensive newspapers (the penny press)— among them Montreal's *Daily Star* and *La presse* and Toronto's *Telegram* and *World*—the editors appealed to readers' emotions both to sell newspapers and to raise public concern over child abuse, slums, prostitution, and political corruption. While they were able to highlight the problems, seldom did they offer solutions.

Reform-minded businesspeople and concerned citizens also helped raise public consciousness. Herbert Ames financed a sociological study of a working-class ward in Montreal, entitled *The City Below the Hill* (1897). G.A. Nantel wrote *La métropole de demain*, a grandiose scheme for the better governance of Montreal. Samuel Wickett spoke and wrote in Toronto regularly on the importance of efficient and expert municipal governments as the first step to urban reform. In Winnipeg, J.S. Woodsworth wrote the highly acclaimed *My Neighbour* (1911), about the problems of living in the modern city.

A host of professionals and experts—engineers, architects, surveyors, medical people, and urban planners—offered advice on how to create the perfect city. Architects emphasized the need for stately buildings, while urban planners stressed parks, treed boulevards, and adequate housing. Medical professionals argued for clean water and air, and campaigned for pasteurized milk.

These urban reformers had limited success in the era prior to World War I because vested interests generally opposed their proposals. Developers, for example, saw little profit in expensive urban renewal. Established businesses saw only expenses when faced with suggested modifications. Nor were badly funded municipal governments prepared to act, because the reforms suggested often came at a high price, resulting in increased taxes.

The Children's Aid Society, founded by John Kelso, opened its first shelter in Toronto in 1892. This photo of the shelter was taken in the mid-1890s.

Source: City of Toronto Archives/SCI-3.

Wilderness and Wildlife Conservation

The idea of conservation emerged slowly in Canada. With such a vast geography and a small population, the need to conserve held little immediacy. The popular Canadian naturalist Farley Mowat recalls in his book *Sea of Slaughter* a story about his grandfather:

> One autumn weekend in 1884, he and three companions left on a weekend duck hunting trip. They left armed with double-barrelled 10-gauge shotguns. They returned with 140 canvasbacks, 227 redheads, about 20 scaups, 84 blacks, about five dozen teal, and enough additional assorted kinds to quite literally fill the four-wheeled farm wagon that brought them and their trophies home.[4]

But some Canadians started to question such excessiveness. The conservation movement that began in the late nineteenth century called for the planned and efficient use of natural resources to ensure their permanence. Foresters in the 1880s were the first Canadians to organize for conservation, because they saw overcutting and forest fires as wasting the nation's forest wealth. Conservationism spread to watershed and wildlife protection, and eventually to urban planning and even public health.

In 1885, the federal government reserved to the Crown more than 26 square kilometres of land around the mineral springs near the railway station of Banff in present-day Alberta. It would protect the hot springs and the scenery from private exploitation. Ottawa had taken the first step in the creation of Canada's national parks. Two years later, it extended the area to 675 square kilometres. Banff began largely as a recreation park, a playground for people to enjoy their leisure time rather than a conservation area, although the latter would become its chief function.

In 1887, the first bird sanctuary in North America opened at Last Mountain Lake, in present-day Saskatchewan. In 1893, the Ontario government established Algonquin Park, south of North Bay, as the province's first wilderness area. Other provinces followed Ontario's example in establishing their own provincial parks.

The overexploitation of the country's wildlife was a growing concern. The problem was not new as evident by the over-trapping of animals during the fur trade, but major improvements in firearm technology, combined with the increasing commercial value of certain types of wildlife, had led to the extermination of certain species. The Plains bison herds disappeared on the Canadian side of the border as early as 1879. By 1900, the great Prairie herds of pronghorn antelope declined to a tiny fraction of their original number. Hunted thoroughly, the passenger pigeon vanished from Nova Scotia by 1857, from Manitoba by 1898, and from Ontario by 1902. The last surviving member of this once-abundant species died in an Ohio zoo in 1914. By 1900, trumpeter swans disappeared from eastern Canada, as had wild turkeys before them.

Conservationism was cultivated by many Canadians' growing interest in nature. The upper classes got back to nature by building cottages in the Georgian Bay and Muskoka areas of Ontario, the Lake of the Woods region near the Manitoba–Ontario border, the Laurentians and Murray Bay in Quebec, and the Bras d'Or Lakes on Nova Scotia's Cape Breton Island (and in doing so put pressure on wilderness areas). Field naturalists' clubs, the Alpine Club of Canada, Woodcraft Clubs, and the Boy Scouts and Girl Guides troops all flourished, promoting the importance of experiences in nature for good health, spiritual rejuvenation, and as a refuge from hectic city life. Schools in British Columbia, Nova Scotia, Ontario, and Alberta developed nature study classes in the first decade of the twentieth century through the initiative of naturalists' societies, farm organizations, and experimental farms.

Coinciding with this shift in mentality was an increase in leisure time. Industrialization created a working population that lived within the confines of the cityscape and whose time was dictated by the clock. As labour reform freed up time for leisure pursuits (such as the weekend), workers sought new places to play. A revolution in transportation, leading to rail travel and later to automobile travel, provided the necessary mobility. No longer were these sublime nature locales restricted to the wealthy who could afford cottages. These developments also led to tourism and the government was quick to realize the profits to be accrued by exploiting one of Canada's seemingly infinite resources—nature.

The federal government also responded to the need for conservation. It established the Commission of Conservation (1909–21), which helped to secure the passage in 1917 of the Canada–United States Migratory Birds Convention Treaty, an agreement that was supposed to ensure international protection for migratory bird populations throughout their ranges. The government created the Dominion Parks Branch in 1911, the first agency in the world devoted to national parks, under the leadership of J.B. Harkin. In 1919, the Canadian government convened the first national wildlife conference to discuss with the provinces how best to conserve the country's wildlife.

Where Historians Disagree

Conservation and the Environment

Interest in the field of environmental history in Canada arose in part as a response to suggestions from American environmental historian Roderick Nash that Canada had no environmental consciousness. In a 1968 speech to the National and Provincial Parks Association of Canada, Nash argued that "the Canadian public's sensitivity to and enthusiasm for wilderness values lags at least two generations behind opinion in the United States." Canadian parks, according to Nash, were established for the economic purposes of natural resource and tourism development.[1]

Nash's controversial comments caused a reaction among Canadian historians. Janet Foster was one of the first to take up the gauntlet. Her 1978 book, *Working for Wildlife: The Beginning of Preservation in Canada*, argued that early twentieth-century Canada saw a number of important conservation efforts, initiated "through the determination, understanding, and foresight of a small group of remarkably dedicated civil servants who were able to turn their own goals of wildlife preservation into a declared government policy."[2]

Focusing on a few individuals, in particular J.B. Harkin, Canada's first commissioner for national parks, Foster asserted that a national conservation consciousness and standard were successfully established through their efforts. Foster's "great man" biographical approach paralleled work being done in other fields and became the standard work on Canadian conservation for two decades.

By 2000, the field of environmental history was finally making inroads in Canada, and its practitioners were exploring the complexities underlying historical relationships between people and nature. Alan MacEachern's *Natural Selections: National Parks in Atlantic Canada, 1935–1970* questioned the degree to which the conservation movement was a simple story of a few progressive civil servants. He claimed that Foster's study downplayed the broader societal interest in conservation on the one hand and the often utilitarian and pragmatic concerns that drove conservationists on the other. MacEachern argued that a primary motivation underlying the establishment of national parks in eastern Canada was economic, to attract tourism to an underdeveloped part of the country, rather than conservationist, to protect these pieces of Canadian nature: "Historians' eagerness to see Harkin's drive for dollars as a strategy rather than a philosophy tells us more about them than about him."[3]

Painting yet a different picture, Tina Loo's *States of Nature: Conserving Canada's Wildlife in the Twentieth Century* analyzes the development of the Canadian conservation movement in terms of the expansion of state power over both humans and the natural world. Game laws and the "scientific management" of natural resources were, according to Loo, "instruments of colonization, imposing an urban and bourgeois sensibility about wildlife on rural Canada." Despite the increased role of the state, private wildlife organizations (such as Ducks Unlimited) and environmentally minded individuals (such as author Farley Mowat) continued to play an active role in shaping the nature of Canadian conservation. Presenting conservation as a broad and far-reaching cultural phenomenon, Loo further adds to the historiographical debate by asserting that "wildlife conservation was about the values that should govern humans' relationships with nature."[4] She notes the significance of an urban, bourgeois, male elite in the formation of these values. Her study emphasizes intellectual, social, and cultural factors that contributed to the creation and maintenance of the conservation movement from the bottom up, alongside the government's initiative to regulate wildlife from the top.

The issue of conservation and the development of environmental thinking remains a central facet of Canadian environmental history. As the field continues to expand, current trends are taking greater account of the dominant role of science and scientific discourses of nature in shaping popular understandings of the natural world and how we should properly interact with it. In his book *Nature's Experts: Science, Politics, and the Environment*, Stephen Bocking presents the role of formal science in defining and assessing recourse management policy goals under the context of ecosystem and biodiversity. Bocking argues that while "other people may be included in the process," they are only incorporated as "objects to be studied, managed, and occasionally consulted." This body of scholarship reminds us that environmental thinking in Canada derived from many sources.[5] It serves as a framework for thinking about how diverse visions of Canada's "nature" have converged to form present understanding of the environment and human interaction with it.

1   Roderick Nash, "Wilderness and Man in North America," in R.C. Scace and J.G. Nelson, eds., *Canadian National Parks: Today and Tomorrow* (Calgary: University of Calgary, 1969), pp. 73, 75.

2   Janet Foster, *Working for Wildlife: The Beginning of Preservation in Canada* (Toronto: University of Toronto Press, 1978), p. 3.

3   Alan MacEachern, *Natural Selections: National Parks in Atlantic Canada, 1935–1970* (Montreal: McGill-Queen's Press, 2001), p. 26.

4   Tina Loo, *States of Nature: Conserving Canada's Wildlife in the Twentieth Century* (Vancouver: UBC Press, 2006), pp. 6, 40.

5   Stephen Bocking, *Nature's Experts: Science, Politics, and the Environment* (New Jersey: Rutgers University Press, 2004), p. 98.

Later, in the 1930s, the international popularity of Grey Owl (born Archie Belaney in England) assisted the conservation movement. Through his books, films, and lectures, he advocated the protection of Canada's wilderness and wildlife. When the young white man arrived at Lake Temagami in northeastern Ontario from England in 1907, he came to appreciate the Ojibwa culture and its approach to nature. Eventually, he assumed an Aboriginal identity. Much of what he wrote as Grey Owl in the 1930s attacked the notion that humans should "have dominion over" all creatures. It was not until after his death that the public discovered Grey Owl's true identity. Regardless, his work was important in highlighting the need for conservation.

Women and Social Reform

The late nineteenth century became the era of the "New Woman." With the family and household seemingly under siege by the forces of change, women took up the fight to protect social institutions and relations. But they were not simply defending the status quo; they were often leading the vanguard of change. Middle-class women used the social reform movement to push for an active role in society. Local, provincial, and national women's organizations such as the Woman's Christian Temperance Union (WCTU), the National Council of Women, the Young Women's Christian Association (YWCA), and the Dominion Women's Enfranchisement Association assisted women in reaching out to society. By 1912 an estimated one out of every eight adult women—the majority of them middle-aged, middle-class, English-speaking Protestants—belonged to a women's group, thus making these organizations influential agents of social change.

The spirit of reform could be seen at all levels of society, both at work and play. The bicycle, for example, aided the liberation of the new woman. This popular new vehicle enabled women to abandon restrictive, ankle-length, tight skirts in favour of comfortable, loose-fitting clothes such as bloomers (loose trousers gathered at the knees). Some clergy voiced their concerns about the impact of the bicycle on morals, since women could now go out without chaperones.

A HISTORICAL PORTRAIT

Grey Owl

Archie Belaney was born in Hastings, Sussex, England, on September 18, 1888. Abandoned by his parents, he was raised by two maiden aunts. As with many boys in Britain, he was fascinated by North American Indians and dreamed of living among them. His aunts wanted him to take up a profession after leaving grammar school, but finally they gave their consent for him to emigrate to Canada. He left in 1906.

In 1910, Belaney married Angele Egwuna, an Ojibwa woman from Lake Temagami, Ontario. She taught him how to canoe, trap, and speak some Ojibwa. But the marriage did not last. Following in his father's footsteps, he abandoned his wife and their young daughter in 1912.

Belaney served in the Canadian Expeditionary Force during World War I and served as a sniper while fighting in France. He was wounded and, while recovering in England, he married Constance (Ivy) Holmes (even though he was still married to Egwuna). The marriage failed and Belaney returned to Canada in

1917. In 1925 the 37-year-old Belaney married a young Iroquois woman, 19-year-old Gertrude Bernard—whom he called Anahareo—in a traditional Aboriginal ceremony in northern Quebec. She convinced him to abandon trapping and to work and write for the conservation of Canada's wildlife and forests. It was at this point that Belaney took on a Native identity, claiming a mixed-race identity. He also took the name "Grey Owl" (*Wa-sha-quon-asin*).

Grey Owl was a highly skilled and prolific nature writer and his "Indian" perspective drew notice. The Canadian *Who's Who* of 1936–37 summarized his romantic stories about his origins: "Born encampment, State of Sonora, Mexico; son of George, a native of Scotland, and Kathrine (Cochise) Belaney; a half-breed Apache Indian ... adopted as blood brother by Ojibway tribe, 1920 ... speaks Ojibway but has forgotten Apache." Impressed by his first articles, the Canadian government invited Grey Owl to join the Canadian Parks Branch as a "caretaker of park animals." His first book, *Men of the Last Frontier*, a collection of his published stories and others, appeared in 1931. Three years later came *Pilgrims of the Wild*, a moving account of his life with Anahareo and their struggle to preserve wildlife and the wilderness. Two other books followed: a children's book *The Adventures of Sajo and Her Beaver People* (1935) and *Tales of an Empty Cabin* (1936).

Grey Owl's books became bestsellers. Films were made with him at his new home in Prince Albert National Park in Saskatchewan. The public loved the fact that the beaver built their lodge outside—and partially inside—his cabin. He made two lecture tours of Britain, each of several months' duration. During his last visit, in

Grey Owl and a beaver, June 1931.

Source: Glenbow Archives, Calgary, Canada/ NA-4868-213.

December 1937, the tall, hawk-faced man in buckskin performed at Buckingham Palace for the royal family. No one discovered his true identity, not even in Hastings, which he visited twice. His aunts knew, but, intensely proud of him, they kept his secret.

The tours were demanding, and the constant threat of having his secret revealed was very real. Shortly after Grey Owl's return to Beaver Lodge in early April 1938, he was rushed to hospital in Prince Albert, where he died on April 13. Swift detective work in Canada and England in the weeks after his death revealed his true identity. His contributions as a writer and spokesperson for conservation received new recognition in the 1970s, when the preservation of the natural environment became a recognized concern.

Two women cyclists, Flo and Jessie McLennan, Owen Sound, Ontario. Bicycles liberated women from restrictive clothing—and from chaperones.

Source: Glenbow Archives, Calgary, Canada/ NA-2685-61.

But despite the new spirit, most women accepted the prevailing "scientific" (not to mention religious) stereotyping of them as womanly and motherly. Consequently, they accepted the belief that their primary task was to maintain the home. A plethora of books on proper mothering reinforced this belief. But a few women believed that their maternal instincts should be used to reform society. "Rocking the cradle for the world" was how Nellie McClung, an influential reformer, expressed the new role of women. Men had controlled society for ages; now, with society under constant challenge, it was women's turn:

> Women must be made to feel their responsibilities. All this protective love, their instinctive mother love, must be organized in some way, and made effective. There is enough of it in the world to do away with all the evils which war upon childhood: undernourishment, slum conditions, child labour, drunkenness. Women could abolish all these if they wanted to.

The women's movement fought for better education. It was in the Maritimes that the first woman was admitted to a university. In 1875, Mount Allison University in Sackville, New Brunswick, conferred a bachelor's degree in science and literature to Grace Annie Lockhart. She became the first woman in the British Empire to receive a university degree. The University of Toronto followed, first opening its doors to women in 1884. Many male professors opposed the decision. Daniel Wilson, a professor of history and English literature, considered that a mixed class posed serious problems in the teaching of Shakespeare due to the sexual allusions in several of the playwright's works. Such allusions were not deemed appropriate for the "fairer sex." His objection was overruled.

Adelaide (Hunter) Hoodless helped to further the women's cause in another way. Born in 1857, the twelfth child in the family, she received little education beyond elementary school. She married John Hoodless, a wealthy furniture manufacturer. Their fourth child, a son, died in 1889 at the age of fourteen months, presumably from the unpasteurized milk that farmers delivered in open cans, which exposed it to bacterial contamination. Seeing an urgent need to teach women nutrition and proper health measures, she offered domestic science or home-economics classes through the YWCA. Later the dedicated reformer assisted in having the subject introduced in schools and, eventually, at the Ontario Agricultural College in Guelph and at Montreal's McGill University. In 1897, she started the first Women's Institute near Stoney Creek, south of Hamilton, Ontario—an equivalent, for women, of the Farmers' Institutes. The new organization helped women to increase their knowledge of farm and household management.

Mount Allison University graduates, 1875. Grace Annie Lockhart, the lone woman in this photo, was the first woman in the British Empire to receive a degree from a recognized university.

Source: Mount Allison University Archives/005 540.

Thanks to her unflagging efforts, the University of Toronto eventually created the School of Household Economics. Hoodless also helped found the Victorian Order of Nurses to offer nursing and housekeeping services to impoverished invalids. Although she worked to improve women's role in society, Adelaide Hoodless parted company with the suffragists on the "vote question." She believed that a woman's primary role was to be a wife and mother and that the vote would not aid them in this task. She feared that the right to vote might actually lead to the breakdown of home and family.

The Women's Suffrage Movement

Many women reformers viewed the vote as the most effective means to reform society. The Canadian women's suffrage movement began in Ontario with leaders such as Dr. Emily (Jennings) Stowe. But if Ontario launched the first suffrage movement, momentum came from the Prairie provinces. In the newer settler society of the West, women found a greater degree of equality and such "progressive" ideas were more generally embraced. In establishing a homestead and building a farm, women worked alongside their husbands, although Prairie wives had to fight their husbands for an equal right to the family farm. Early on, they won the support of western farm organizations that also struggled for national recognition, and therefore empathized with women's efforts for equality. The Prairie farmers' newspaper, the *Grain Growers' Guide*, founded in 1908, added a women's column to its paper in 1911, while the Grain Growers' Association of Manitoba, Saskatchewan, and Alberta endorsed women's suffrage as early as 1912.

The presence of a large immigrant population on the Prairies helped the suffrage cause in an ironic way. The women's movement was led by white, middle-class women who possessed nativist views toward "foreigners." Women suffragists protested against giving recent male immigrants the vote while denying it to long-standing female citizens. As one suffragist bluntly put it: "What an outrage to deny to the highest-minded, most cultured native-born lady of Canada what is cheerfully granted to the lowest-browed most imbruted foreign hobo that chooses to visit our shores."

The West was home to many women actively involved in the struggle for female suffrage, such as Henrietta Edwards, Emily Murphy, Louise McKinney, Nellie McClung, and Irene Parlby. McClung, with her intelligence, gift for oratory, energy, and sense of humour, best epitomized the suffrage movement. Her leadership rallied many others to the cause.

Nellie (Mooney) McClung was born in Ontario in 1873 but educated in Manitoba, where her family began homesteading in 1880. After attending Winnipeg Normal School and teaching for several years, she married Wes McClung, a pharmacist and later an insurance company manager, in 1896. Her fiancé promised her before marriage that he would not stand in the way of her writing career, a promise he kept. Between 1897 and 1911, she had four sons and a daughter, but still found time to write—first poems, sketches, and editorials for Sunday school publications, and later adult stories in leading North American magazines. Early on, her interest in reform led her to write her best-selling novel, *Sowing Seeds in Danny*. In 1912, she joined the Winnipeg Political Equality League, whose president was Lillian Beynon Thomas, another reformer. McClung wrote her witty but powerful social commentary on suffrage, *In Times Like These*, for the 1916 election in Manitoba, in which suffrage was a major issue. The suffragists made their first breakthrough in that election when the Liberals came to power. The new government introduced a suffrage bill, making Manitoba the first province in Canada to grant women the vote.

[handwritten margin note: — I like this person!]

Presentation of a petition by the Winnipeg Political Equality League for the Enfranchisement of Women, December 23, 1915. Mrs. Amelia Burritt, then ninety-three years old, gave the document to the provincial government. In 1916, Manitoba became Canada's first province to grant women the franchise.

Source: Provincial Archives of Manitoba/Events 173/3 (N9905).

Women Reformers in Quebec

Women in Quebec had a more difficult battle due to the more conservative nature of French-Canadian society and the resistance of the Catholic Church. Archbishop Bruchési of Montreal defined *féminisme* as "the zealous pursuit by woman of all the noble causes in the sphere that Providence has assigned to her." He added: "There will be no talk in your meetings of the emancipation of woman, of the neglect of her rights, of her having been relegated to the shadows, of the responsibilities, public offices and professions to which she should be admitted on an equal basis with man."

Despite such stern warnings, some French-Canadian women spoke out for the feminist cause, often through membership in the local council of the National Council of Women of Canada. In 1907, Marie Lacoste Gérin-Lajoie, Caroline Béique, and Josephine Dandurand founded the *Fédération nationale Saint-Jean-Baptiste* to consolidate Quebec women's activities in charitable associations, in education, and in the workforce. Marie Lacoste Gérin-Lajoie directed the federation's activities for the first twenty years. The Fédération offered a forum for Quebec women to fight for a variety of causes, including the pasteurizing of milk to reduce infant mortality, better working conditions for women, and the elimination of alcoholism and prostitution. It also contributed to better women teachers' pensions, improved working conditions for women in factories and stores, increased home-economics courses, and established pure milk depots.

The Fédération, along with the Sisters of the Congregation of Notre Dame, petitioned Archbishop Bruchési to obtain approval for a classical college for women. He agreed only when the newspaper *La patrie* announced the opening of a French *lycée*, a lay-administered classical college for women. In 1908, Bruchési granted permission to the Congregation of Notre Dame to open the *École d'enseignement supérieur pour les filles*. But the École had to wait until 1926 before gaining the right to call itself a *collège*; it then became the *Collège Marguerite-Bourgeoys*, named after the founder of the Sisters of the Congregation of Notre Dame. In 1910, Marie Gérin-Lajoie, the daughter of Marie Lacoste Gérin-Lajoie, became the École's first graduate. She had the further distinction of coming first in the provincial university-entrance examinations for the province, much to the consternation of the all-male examiners. But she did not obtain the award. Because women could not attend university, first prize was given to the male who placed second.

Marie Lacoste Gérin-Lajoie led the fight for women's suffrage in Quebec. She obtained her legal education by studying her father's law books and under his supervision. Shocked to learn that the legal status of a woman was that of an adjunct of her husband, with no personal financial or civil independence, she initially considered refusing her future husband's marriage proposal. Only after her suitor pledged his support for the equality of the sexes did she accept. She spent her early married life writing a legal handbook for women while raising her children.

With an English-speaking colleague, Marie Lacoste Gérin-Lajoie created the Provincial Franchise Committee in 1921 to put pressure on Quebec politicians to grant women the franchise. The committee had no success, and ironically the strongest opposition often came from other women who saw suffrage as a threat to their identity as wives and mothers. The fatal blow came when in 1922 the Archbishop of Montreal expressed his disapproval of women voters. In protest, Marie Lacoste Gérin-Lajoie resigned her post as head of the francophone section of the Provincial Franchise Committee, although she continued to promote women's rights. Women in Quebec did not obtain the provincial franchise until 1940, a generation later than women in other provinces.

The Prohibition Movement

The first women reformers were, for the most part, "maternal feminists." They sought gender reform rather than full equality. They worked to gain the vote in the hope that by bringing the voice of women to the many problems threatening society, they would bring a feminine and motherly concern. While suffrage was the main political issue in the women's movement, prohibition was the main social issue. Throughout Canada, most women reformers worked to ban booze. Alcohol was viewed as a vice of men, because "respectable" women did not drink. "Demon drink," they argued, wrecked home life. Much-needed wages were spent in taverns rather than on family sustenance. Drinking often led to domestic violence and abuse. It was assumed that it was the less educated and less controlled working classes who were becoming servants to the demon.

With the rise of the state, prohibitionists argued that the only way to eradicate drinking was to prohibit it through government legislation. They reminded governments that they had a right and an obligation to pass laws for the good of society. If society needed to be cleaned up, prohibition was the first step. The division of jurisdiction over alcohol between the federal and provincial governments complicated the question, however. The federal government had the power to restrict the manufacture of, and interprovincial trade in, alcoholic beverages. Provincial governments, however, controlled retail sales. Thus, prohibitionists had to apply pressure on both levels of government.

They achieved an initial victory in 1878 with the passage of the Canadian Temperance Act, popularly known as the Scott Act, which allowed the residents of each municipality or county to decide by a simple majority vote whether their constituency would be "wet" or "dry." But to prohibitionists, this measure did not go far enough because it still left open the possibility of wet constituencies. They demanded that governments outlaw the liquor trade completely. The federal Conservative government delayed acting on this contentious issue until the mid-1890s, when it established the Royal Commission on the Liquor Traffic. Before the commission set out its recommendations, a federal election ensued. During the election campaign of 1896, Laurier and the Liberals promised a plebiscite on the question of prohibition if they gained office. When they won, the prohibitionists held them to their promise.

The results of Canada's first plebiscite were split. Every province except Quebec voted on the dry side. But voter turnout throughout Canada was low—only 44 percent. Furthermore, of those who did vote, only a small majority of about 13,000 favoured prohibition. Laurier used these "indecisive" results to avoid enacting legislation that he feared would divide the nation. The Liberals' refusal to follow through on their promise angered the prohibitionists and gave them even greater resolve to banish booze.

Prohibition became one of the main planks in the social reform movement and Protestant churches provided many of the leaders. They urged drinkers to sign "the pledge" card, by which they promised, "by the help of God, to abstain from the use of all intoxicating drinks as a beverage."

The Woman's Christian Temperance Union (WCTU), formed in Ontario in 1874, but quickly becoming a national organization with some 16,000 members by 1914, focused on the importance of the home and the sanctity of the family. It identified alcoholism as the greatest single cause of domestic violence and divorce, leading to a breakdown in the family unit. Initially, the WCTU campaigned for prohibition by issuing petitions, circulating literature, and giving speeches. But WCTU members soon developed a new strategy. If women had the right to vote, they argued, alcohol abuse would end. As the first superintendent of the Ontario WCTU's Franchise Department noted, "The liquor sellers are not afraid of our conventions but they are afraid of our ballots." Prohibition and women's suffrage became mutually supportive causes.

The vision of a purified Anglo-Saxon society inspired many prohibitionists. Drunkenness became associated with "foreigners." Controlling alcohol offered a means of regulating immigrants and of ensuring their conformity in an otherwise heterogeneous society. The greatest support for prohibition came, therefore, from the majority of British descent, who believed themselves superior to other groups that succumbed to alcohol.

Despite their efforts, however, prohibitionists remained in the minority before World War I. On the eve of the Great War, only Prince Edward Island had implemented provincial prohibition, while on the national level the federal government had resisted pressure to restrict the production and interprovincial distribution of "demon rum" and all liquor in general.

SUMMARY

Between 1880 and 1914, social reform movements arose to correct the injustices brought about by large-scale industrialization, rapid urbanization, and immigration. Without vigilant reform, society seemed on the edge of collapse. This collapse threatened such fundamental institutions as the family. Not surprisingly, reform was led by another fundamental institution—the church. On the eve of World War I, the reformers had accomplished much, but they still fell short of their ultimate goal of social regeneration. The war would spur many of these reforms forward, particularly women's suffrage and prohibition.

NOTES

1. Nancy Christie and Michael Gauvreau, *A Full-Orbed Christianity: The Protestant Churches and Social Welfare in Canada, 1900–1940* (Montreal: McGill-Queen's University Press, 1996), p. 245.

2. Christie and Gauvreau, p. xi.

3. Paul Rutherford, "Tomorrow's Metropolis: The Urban Reform Movement in Canada, 1880–1920," in G.A. Stelter and A.F.J. Artibise, eds., *The Canadian City: Essays in Urban History* (Toronto: McClelland & Stewart, 1977), p. 370.

4. Farley Mowat, *Sea of Slaughter* (Toronto: McClelland & Stewart, 1984), p. 69.

BIBLIOGRAPHY

Chapters 15 and 16 in R.C. Brown and R. Cook, *Canada, 1896–1921: A Nation Transformed* (Toronto: McClelland & Stewart, 1974) provide an overview of the social reform movements. The best books on religion and social reform are Nancy Christie and Michael Gauvreau, *A Full-Orbed Christianity: The Protestant Churches and Social Welfare in Canada, 1900–1940* (Montreal/Kingston: McGill-Queen's University Press, 1996); Nancy Christie and Michael Gauvreau, *Christian Churches and Their Peoples, 1840–1965* (Toronto: University of Toronto Press, 2010); and Michael Gauvreau and Ollivier Hubert, eds., *The Churches and Social Order in Nineteenth- and Twentieth-Century Canada* (Montreal: McGill-Queen's University Press, 2006).

The social gospel is studied by Richard Allen, *The Social Passion: Religion and Social Reform in Canada, 1914–28* (Toronto: University of Toronto Press, 1971), and Ramsay Cook, *The Regenerators: Social Criticism in Late Victorian English Canada* (Toronto: University of Toronto Press, 1985). On the social gospeller J.J. Kelso, see Andrew Jones and Leonard Rutman, *In the Children's Aid: J.J. Kelso and Child Welfare in Ontario* (Toronto: University of Toronto Press, 1981). On Wilfred Grenfell, consult Ronald Rompkey, *Grenfell of Labrador: A Biography* (Toronto: University of Toronto Press, 1991). Kenneth McNaught's study of J.S. Woodsworth, *A Prophet in Politics* (Toronto: University of Toronto Press, 1959), reviews the life of this important social gospel figure. See also Allen Mills, *Fool for Christ: The Political Thought of J.S. Woodsworth* (Toronto: University of Toronto Press, 1991). For background to religious life in Ontario at the turn of the century, see John Webster Grant, *A Profusion of Spires: Religion in Nineteenth-Century Ontario* (Toronto: University of Toronto Press, 1988); William Westfall, *Two Worlds: The Protestant Culture of Nineteenth-Century Ontario* (Montreal/Kingston: McGill-Queen's University Press, 1989); and Lynne Marks, *Revivals and Roller Rings: Religion, Leisure, and Identity in Late-Nineteenth-Century Small-Town Ontario* (Toronto: University of Toronto Press, 1996). For a history of social policy and practice, see Alvin Finkel, *Social Policy and Practice in Canada: A History* (Waterloo: Wilfrid Laurier University Press, 2006).

On religion and moral reform, consult Mariana Valverde, *The Age of Light, Soap, and Water: Moral Reform in English Canada, 1885–1925* (Toronto: McClelland & Stewart, 1991), and Carolyn Strange, *Toronto's Girl Problem: The Perils and Pleasures of the City, 1880–1930* (Toronto: University of Toronto Press, 1995).

On the question of secularism versus religious renewal, see Phyllis D. Airhart, *Serving the Present Age: Revivalism, Progressivism and the Methodist Tradition in Canada* (Montreal/Kingston: McGill-Queen's University Press, 1992); David B. Marshall, *Secularizing the Faith: Canadian Protestant Clergy and the Crisis of Belief, 1850–1940* (Toronto: University of Toronto Press, 1992); and John G. Stackhouse, Jr., *Canadian Evangelicalism in the Twentieth Century* (Toronto: University of Toronto Press, 1993). James Opp, *The Lord for the Body: Religion, Medicine, & Protestant Faith Healing in Canada, 1880–1930* (Montreal/Kingston: McGill-Queen's University Press, 2005) examines the relationship between religion and medicine.

On Canadian women in foreign missions, see Rosemary R. Gagan, *A Sensitive Independence: Canadian Methodist Women Missionaries in Canada and the Orient, 1881–1925* (Montreal/Kingston: McGill-Queen's University Press, 1992); Ruth Compton Brower, *New Women for God: Canadian Presbyterian Women and India Missions, 1876–1914* (Toronto: University of Toronto Press, 1990); and Hamish Ion, *The Cross and the Rising Sun: The Canadian Protestant Missionary Movement in the Japanese Empire, 1872–1931* (Waterloo, ON: Wilfrid Laurier University Press, 1989). The evolution of the social work profession has been profiled in Therese Jennissen and Collen Lundy, *One Hundred Years of Social Work: A History of the Profession in English Canada* (Waterloo, ON: Wilfrid Laurier University Press, 2009).

Educational reform in the context of social reform is the subject of Neil Sutherland's *Children in English-Canadian Society* (Toronto: University of Toronto Press, 1976). The public-library movement is discussed in Lorne Bruce, *Free Books for All: The Public Library Movement in Ontario, 1850–1930* (Toronto: Dundurn Press, 1994). On higher education, see Paul Axelrod and John Reid, eds., *Youth, University and Canadian Society: Essays in the Social History of Higher Education* (Montreal/Kingston: McGill-Queen's University Press, 1989) and Catherine Gidney, *Tending the Student Body: Youth, Health, and the Modern University* (Toronto: University of Toronto Press, 2015; and for Ontario, A.B. McKillop, *Matters of Mind: The University in Ontario, 1791–1951* (Toronto: University of Toronto Press, 1994). Paul Rutherford's "Tomorrow's Metropolis: The Urban Reform Movement in Canada, 1880–1920," *Canadian Historical Association Report* (1971): 203–24, and his edited anthology, *Saving the Canadian City, 1880–1920* (Toronto: University of Toronto Press, 1974), deal with urban reform. See, as well, G. Stelter and A. Artibise, eds., *The Canadian City: Essays in Urban History* (Toronto: McClelland & Stewart, 1977), pp. 337–418.

On the conservation movement, see Janet Foster, *Working for Wildlife: The Beginning of Preservation in Canada* (Toronto: University of Toronto Press, 1978); Michel F. Girard, *L'Écologisme retrouvé: Essor et déclin de la Commission de la conservation du Canada* (Ottawa: Les Presses de l'Université d'Ottawa, 1994); Darcy Ingram, *Wildlife, Conservation, and Conflict in Quebec, 1840–1914* (Vancouver: UBC Press, 2013); and Tina Loo, *States of Nature: Conserving Canada's Wildlife in the Twentieth Century* (Vancouver: UBC Press, 2006). On the conservation movement in the Canadian west, see George Colpitts, *Game in the Garden: A Human History of Wildlife in Western Canada to 1940* (Vancouver: UBC Press, 2002), and in the north, see John Sandlos, *Hunters at the Margin: Native People and Wildlife Conservation in the Northwest Territories* (Vancouver: UBC Press, 2007). Donald Smith's *From the Land of Shadows: The Making of Grey Owl* (Saskatoon: Western Producer Prairie Books, 1990) tells the story of the transformation of trapper Archie Belaney to conservationist Grey Owl.

E.J. Hart has written a biography of Canada's first commissioner of the Dominion Parks Branch: *J.B. Harkin: Father of Canada's National Parks* (Edmonton: University of Alberta Press, 2010). Other useful works on parks include Claire Campbell, ed., *A Century of Parks Canada, 1911–2011* (Calgary: University of Calgary Press, 2011); Alan MacEachern, *Natural Selections: National Parks in Atlantic Canada, 1935–1970* (Montreal: McGill-Queen's University Press, 2001); and Paul Kopas, *Taking the Air: Ideas and Change in Canada's National Parks* (Vancouver: UBC Press, 2007). For environmental history generally, see Laurel Sefton MacDowell, *An Environmental History of Canada* (Vancouver: UBC Press, 2012); Graeme Wynn, *Canada and Arctic North America: An Environmental History* (Santa Barbara: ABC-CLIO, 2007); Neil Forkey, *Canadians and Their Environment to the Twenty-First Century* (Toronto: University of Toronto Press, 2012); Alan MacEachern and William J. Turkel, *Method and Meaning in Canadian Environmental History* (Toronto: Nelson, 2009); and Chad and Pam Gaffield, eds., *Consuming Canada: Readings in Environmental History* (Toronto: Copp Clark, 1995).

For women and social reform see Chapter 7, "The 'Woman Movement,'" in Alison Prentice et al., *Canadian Women: A History*, 2nd ed. (Toronto: Harcourt Brace, 1996); Linda Kealey, ed., *A Not Unreasonable Claim: Women and Reform in Canada, 1880–1920* (Toronto: Canadian Women's Educational Press, 1979); Micheline Dumont et al., *Quebec Women: A History* (Toronto: Women's Press, 1987); and Carole Gerson, *Canadian Women in Print, 1750–1918* (Waterloo, ON: Wilfrid Laurier University Press, 2010). Biographical sketches of Emily Jennings Stowe and Adelaide Hunter Hoodless appear in volume 13 of the *Dictionary of Canadian Biography* (Toronto: University of Toronto Press, 1994). On Nellie McClung, see Mary E. Hallett and Marilyn Davis, *Firing the Heather: The Life and Times of Nellie McClung* (Saskatoon: Fifth House, 1993), and Charlotte Gray, *Nellie McClung* (Toronto: Penguin Canada, 2008). On farm women and social reform, see Monda Halpern, *And on That Farm He Had a Wife: Ontario Farm Women and Feminism, 1900–1970* (Montreal/Kingston: McGill-Queen's University Press, 2001). The story of Marie Gérin-Lajoie and her daughter is told in Hélène Pelletier-Baillargeon, *Marie Gérin-Lajoie* (Montreal: Boréal Express, 1985).

On the suffrage movement consult Carol Bacchi, *Liberation Deferred? The Ideas of the English-Canadian Suffragists, 1877–1918* (Toronto: University of Toronto Press, 1983); and Catharine L. Cleverdon, *The Woman Suffrage Movement in Canada: The Start of Liberation, 1900–20* (Toronto: University of Toronto Press, 1974 [1950]). On women socialist reformers, see Janice Newton, *The Feminist Challenge to the Canadian Left, 1900–1918* (Montreal/Kingston: McGill-Queen's University Press, 1995); and Linda Kealey, *Enlisting Women for the Cause: Women, Labour, and the Left in Canada, 1890–1920* (Toronto: University of Toronto Press, 1998). On the impact of the medical profession on women and reform, see Wendy Mitchinson, *The Nature of Their Bodies* (Toronto: University of Toronto Press, 1991), and her *Giving Birth in Canada, 1900–1950* (Toronto: University of Toronto Press, 2002).

Prohibition in the Maritimes is examined in E. Forbes, "Prohibition and the Social Gospel in Nova Scotia," *Acadiensis*, 1 (1971): 11–36; in Ontario, in Gerald Hallowell, *Prohibition in Ontario, 1919–1923* (Toronto: Ontario Historical Society, 1972); and on the Prairies, in James Gray, *Booze: The Impact of Whiskey on the Prairie West* (Toronto: Macmillan, 1972). On the Woman's Christian Temperance Union, see Wendy Mitchinson, "The WCTU" in *A Not Unreasonable Claim* (cited earlier); and Sharon Anne Cooke, *"Through Sunshine and Shadow": The Woman's Christian Temperance Union, Evangelicalism, and Reform in Ontario 1874–1930* (Montreal/Kingston: McGill-Queen's University Press, 1995).

Paul-André Linteau, René Durocher, and Jean-Claude Robert, *Quebec: A History, 1867–1929* (Toronto: James Lorimer, 1983); and Susan Mann, *The Dream of Nation: A Social and Intellectual History of Quebec*, 2nd ed. (Montreal/Kingston: McGill-Queen's University Press, 2002) discuss social reform in Quebec. Jean Hamelin and Nicole Gagnon, *Histoire du catholicisme québécois; le XXe siècle*, vol. 1, *1898–1940* (Montreal: Boréal Express, 1984), discuss the role of the Quebec church in social reform. Joseph Levitt's *Henri Bourassa and the Golden Calf* (Ottawa: University of Ottawa Press, 1969) analyzes the views of the Ligue nationaliste on social questions. On the caisses populaires, see Ronald Rudin, *In Whose Interest? Quebec's Caisses Populaires, 1900–1945* (Montreal/Kingston: McGill-Queen's University Press, 1990).

Source: National Gallery of Canada, Ottawa. Royal Canadian Academy of Arts diploma work, deposited by the artist, Toronto, 1880.

Chapter Nine

CULTURE: 1867–1914

TIME LINE

1867	Founding of the Society of Canadian Artists Founding of National Lacrosse Association
1875	First regulated Canadian hockey game played in Montreal
1880	Calixa Lavallée composes "O Canada" Creation of Canadian Academy of the Arts Ned Hanlan wins world rowing championship
1882	Royal Society of Canada established
1886	Founding of Amateur Hockey Association of Canada, first national hockey association
1890	Women's Art Association formed
1891	James Naismith invents basketball
1893	Lord Stanley donates Stanley Cup
1894	Founding of Toronto Mendelssohn Choir
1895	Founding of *École littéraire de Montréal*
1899	Ralph Connor's popular novel, *The Sky Pilot*, published
1902	The Edison Electric Theatre, Canada's first permanent movie house, opens in Vancouver
1903	*Hiawatha, the Messiah of the Ojibway*, the first single-reel film produced in Canada
1908	Celebration of the tercentenary of Champlain's founding of Quebec Lucy Maud Montgomery publishes first novel, *Anne of Green Gables*
1909	Governor General Earl Grey donates Grey Cup

Canada's status as a colony and then a dominion of the British Empire shaped its cultural identity. Immigrants were expected to conform to the dominant British culture by checking their own cultures at the door when they arrived. First Nations were expected to assimilate to white culture in order to make the transition to "civilization." But what was this dominant culture? Was there anything distinctly Canadian about it? What role did continentalism and proximity to the United States play?

Culture generally refers to a set of shared beliefs and values, and activities associated with education and leisure. In the late nineteenth and early twentieth centuries, high culture was expressed in the fine arts—music, drama, and the visual arts—along with literature. But already a form of popular culture was emerging—culture that appealed to the rising middle and growing working classes. The middle class found enjoyment in such leisure activities as attending movie theatres and fairs. The working class also increasingly enjoyed the same activities, but, due to financial restrictions, was more inclined to find enjoyment and camaraderie in taverns, picnics, and festivities. All three social classes—upper, middle, and lower—enjoyed sport, although the kinds of sport they participated in and supported varied.

By 1914, the forces of modernity shaped a popular culture that was more influential than high culture in constructing a Canadian identity. This cultural expression, however, was also becoming more Americanized. Increasingly in the twentieth century, it was within the realm of culture that American influence became so pervasive and often threatening. The nationalistic desire to create a distinctly Canadian culture amid the struggle between British and American influences ensured that other influences were marginalized. First Nations people did not share in mainstream Canadian culture, except as contributors to fairs and on display in exhibitions. The same was true of "ethnic" Canadians. As part of the process of assimilation, these groups were expected to participate in the dominant cultural activities of the host society.

High Culture

High culture in the pre-World War I era referred to the interests and activities of the social elite. Wealth and privilege ensured that this elite had more time for leisure activities than the middle and lower classes. In Canada, the values and beliefs as maintained and expressed by the upper classes were expected to trickle down and shape those of the masses through such hegemonic institutions as churches, schools, and social organizations. This process was particularly important in a new nation, where cultural identity was besieged on all sides by the forces of immigration and continentalism. Cultural activities were a means of transferring the values, beliefs, and ideals of British society to Canada and then maintaining them. For the elite, these activities, if controlled, were one way to ensure a continuity with the mother country and Empire, thus offsetting the limitations of living in an isolated part of the world where harsh conditions and a small population militated against cultural sophistication and living next door to the United States posed a constant threat.

Music

While music was the most widespread of cultural activities in the late nineteenth century in both English and French Canada, only a few choral

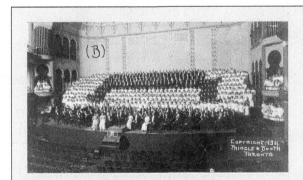

Toronto's famed Mendelssohn Choir, circa 1911.

Source: Canada Patent and Copyright Office/Library and Archives Canada/PA-029791.

groups or orchestras achieved national fame or performed at the level of comparable groups in European society. The James Street Baptist Church Choir in Toronto, consisting of 250 voices and led by choirmaster Augustus Stephen Vogt, had a national reputation. Out of Vogt's choir came the nucleus of the famous Toronto Mendelssohn Choir, which Vogt himself conducted from its founding in 1894 until 1917. In Quebec, the Montreal Oratorio Society, formed in 1864, acquired both a national and an international reputation by the turn of the century, as did the *Société musicale des montagnards canadiens* and *Les orphéonistes de Montréal*. These choirs and their audiences favoured oratorios, cantatas, and masses—especially works by baroque and classical masters such as Bach, Handel, Haydn, and Beethoven.

Notable Canadian composers included Guillaume Couture, organist and conductor of the Montreal Philharmonic Society, known for his religious compositions, and William Reed, who composed the organ recital *Grand Choeur in D Major*, still considered one of the finest organ works written by a Canadian. By far the most popular was Calixa Lavallée. His fame came from his music for "O Canada" in 1880, first performed at the request of the Société Saint-Jean-Baptiste in Quebec City. It was an immediate hit. Only after Lavallée's death did his other compositions come to light and begin to be performed. The English-Canadian equivalent of "O Canada" was "The Maple Leaf Forever," written by Alexander Muir, a Toronto school principal, in 1867. Before setting it to music, Muir entered it in a Montreal poetry contest; it won second prize.

Local church choruses, bands, and orchestras proliferated in the late nineteenth century. Almost every city in Canada had singing groups such as the Orpheus Club in Halifax, Nova Scotia, or the Oratorio Society in Saint John, New Brunswick. Many of the brass bands formed around militia camps as a form of local entertainment for the troops, but some of the most impressive were started in First Nations residential schools as a means to impose discipline and order. The Septuor Haydn chamber ensemble, consisting of a string quintet, flute, and piano, and conducted by Arthur Lavigne of Quebec City, was founded in 1871. By 1903, it had grown into the city's Société symphonique.

It was assumed that only the sophisticated, educated, and "respectable" could appreciate opera. If social constraints did not prevent the non-elite from attending, the price of admission certainly did. Tour companies performed a variety of operas from grand to ballad and comic. Most of these tours originated in Europe and then came to North America. Cities in the Maritimes and central Canada were part of the North American circuit, along with such American cities as Boston, New York, Chicago, and Philadelphia. By the turn of the twentieth century, the major cities of Montreal, Quebec City, and Toronto each had its own local opera company.

Music historians refer to the nineteenth century as "the age of the virtuoso"—a time when gifted soloists astounded

Canada's opera superstar, Marie Lajeunesse, better known by her stage name, Emma Albani.

Source: William Hicock Low, *Marie-Emma Lajeunesse, Dite Madame Albani*, 1877, oil on canvas, 226.4 x 126.2 cm. Collection Musée national des beaux-arts du Québec, 1949.83, Photo: MNBAQ, Patrick Altman, photographer.

the public with superb performances. Canada's most internationally known virtuoso was Emma Albani. Born Marie-Louise-Emma-Cécile Lajeunesse in Chambly, near Montreal, in 1847, she adopted her stage name while on a European tour in the early 1870s. The French-Canadian diva performed at the best opera houses in Europe and the United States, and was renowned in Canada as the "queen of song."

A HISTORICAL PORTRAIT

Calixa Lavallée

Calixa Lavallée, the composer of "O Canada," was born on December 28, 1842, in Verchères, Canada East. His father, a blacksmith by trade, taught Calixa to play the piano, organ, violin, and cornet. Calixa's own musical talent advanced when the family moved to St. Hyacinthe, where he took piano lessons with Paul Letonal and Charles Sabater, two distinguished French pianists who for some time resided in Canada.

Calixa Lavallée, the composer of "O Canada." Canada's national anthem since 1980 was originally composed in 1880 for Saint-Jean-Baptiste Day, which Quebec now recognizes as its *Fête nationale*.

Source: Library and Archives Canada/C-070448.

At age 15, Lavallée left Canada to seek his fortune in the United States. A piano competition in New Orleans, in which he won first prize, resulted in a tour of South America, Mexico, and the West Indies as an accompanist for a Spanish violinist. In 1861, he became a musician in the Union army, a position that lasted only one year when he was discharged after being wounded in the battle of Antietam, in Maryland. In 1867, he married Josephine Gently, an American, and settled in Boston where he became a composer, teacher, and virtuoso performer.

The talented musician returned to Montreal in 1872. The following year, with financial support from a wealthy friend, he went to Paris to advance his study of piano and to take classes in harmony and composition. Two years later, Lavallée returned to his native Quebec where he became a well-known composer and choirmaster.

Lavallée was asked to compose a national song for the convention of the French-Canadian patriotic organization, the Société Saint-Jean-Baptiste, in 1880 in Quebec City. He took the words of a patriotic poem written by Judge Adolphe-Basile Routhier and set them to music; the result was "O Canada." The song soon became popular throughout Quebec, and, decades later, in several versions in English Canada as well.

On July 1, 1980, a century after the song's creation, Parliament made both the French and English versions of "O Canada" the national anthem. It was a great honour, but a century earlier Lavallée's financial position had become so precarious that he had felt he could no longer support himself and his family comfortably in Canada. He returned to the United States, settling permanently. Ironically, the composer of "O Canada" publicly declared himself in favour of Canada joining the United States.

Lavallée died in Boston in 1891. Forty-two years later, in 1933, a group of Lavallée's admirers brought his body back to Montreal and had it interred in the Côte-des-Neiges Cemetery after a funeral service at the majestic Notre-Dame Basilica.

The Visual Arts

In 1860, on the occasion of the official opening of the Victoria Bridge—a magnificent structure that spanned the St. Lawrence River from Montreal to Longueuil—the government of the Canadas held a "Great Exhibition" of Canadian art in Montreal. The exhibition contained paintings by Quebec's famed Cornelius Krieghoff, known for his quaint depictions of habitant life, and by Charles Jones Way, a younger artist from England who painted majestic scenes of Canadian landscapes. Also on exhibit were photographs by William Notman, a Scot who by 1860 had established a thriving photograph studio in downtown Montreal. In the 1860s and 1870s, the Notmans opened over a dozen branches in Ottawa, Saint John, Halifax, and even several eastern American cities. Many of Canada's aspiring artists of the day began their careers in Notman's Studio.

After the Great Exhibition, English-speaking artists in the city formed the Art Association of Montreal. It became the nucleus for the Society of Canadian Artists, founded in 1867. Many of its members were recent immigrants. John Bell-Smith, an English artist who had arrived in Montreal a year earlier, became its first president. The society held its first exhibition in 1868. The society set an ambitious goal: to foster a pan-Canadian artistic tradition to make its artists known both within Canada and abroad. Shortly after the formation of the Montreal society, the Ontario Society of Artists formed in 1872. These artists also promoted Canadian art, including holding annual exhibitions of their works and working toward the building of a permanent public art gallery in Toronto.

Out of these two societies grew the Canadian Academy of the Arts in 1880 (which Queen Victoria prefixed "Royal" the same year). Lucius O'Brien became its first president, a position he held for ten years. Women countered with their own organization, the Women's Art Association. Established in 1890, it soon spawned branches throughout the country to support women artists.

O'Brien and the Royal Canadian Academy of the Arts embodied the new spirit of the age. Born at Shanty Bay near Barrie, Ontario, and educated at Upper Canada College in Toronto, O'Brien first painted scenes of his home region of Lake Simcoe. But he clearly "felt a calling to reflect the majestic beauty of his native land,"[1] and sought opportunities to paint the diverse Canadian landscape. He was among the first Toronto artists to travel on the Intercolonial Railway in 1877 to paint the areas of southern Quebec and the Baie des Chaleurs region of New Brunswick through which it passed. One of O'Brien's most famous paintings, *Sunrise on the Saguenay, Cape Trinity* (1880), came out of these trips. It dominated the opening exhibition of the Royal Canadian Academy of the Arts in 1880.

Lucius O'Brien was also the chief Canadian contributor (with almost one-quarter of the 500 illustrations) to the two-volume *Picturesque Canada*, the most ambitious Canadian publishing

Lucius R. O'Brien, Sunrise on the Saguenay, Cape Trinity, *1880. This painting, first exhibited at the opening of the Royal Canadian Academy of the Arts in 1880, won O'Brien much praise and recognition. Sunrise is traditionally considered to have been the first work entered into the collection of the National Gallery of Canada.*

Source: National Gallery of Canada, Ottawa. Royal Canadian Academy of Arts diploma work, deposited by the artist, Toronto, 1880.

project of the day when launched in 1876. The book of landscape prints and essays was based on the highly successful *Picturesque America*. Two Americans, the Belden brothers of Chicago, launched the project. The investors employed Americans who had worked on the previous book on the United States to complete three-quarters of the Canadian illustrations. O'Brien was the token Canadian—the Belden brothers claimed that Canadian artists were not experienced enough in preparing work for the volumes, a viewpoint that caused an uproar in the Canadian art community. The response did, however, highlight the struggle for recognition that Canadian artists of all genres faced, and would continue to face for decades.

George Monro Grant, principal of Queen's University and a Canadian art enthusiast, edited the *Picturesque Canada* text. He overlooked the American visual contributions and instead underscored the importance of the volumes for the growth of a pan-Canadian nationalism. "I believe that a work that would represent its characteristic scenery and the history and life of its people," he wrote, "would not only make us better known to ourselves and to strangers, but would also stimulate national sentiment and contribute to the rightful development of the nation."

Grant's text and O'Brien's paintings together reflected the growing national spirit of Canadians who looked to the landscape for the essence and the soul of the nation. It was, however, a landscape void of its original inhabitants. Grant did not look to the First Nations as a source of future strength for Canada. In *Picturesque Canada*, the principal of Queen's University

Many art galleries in the late nineteenth century had to rely on a coal stove for "climate control."

Source: William James Topley/Library and Archives Canada/PA-136767.

contributed the article on "The North-West Manitoba," in which he wrote: "The Indians of Manitoba are gradually disappearing before the stronger races."

While some artists looked for Canada's identity in its landscape, others found it in its "country folk." Many of these artists, who emerged in the 1880s and 1890s, were trained in Europe, especially in Paris, its art centre. They returned to Canada prepared to apply European art styles and subject matter to Canadian scenes. Some were influenced by the French Barbizon school that looked for the essence of a country in its inhabitants. Wyatt Eaton of Quebec, influenced by Millet's paintings of French peasants in rural settings, took the Quebec habitant as his subject, in paintings such as *Harvesters at Rest*. Homer Watson did the same for Ontario rural folk. Paul Peel was an Ontario artist who also studied in Paris. He became one of Canada's best-known painters in Europe in the late nineteenth century.

Canadian artists received an opportunity for international fame when the British government invited Canada to contribute paintings to the Colonial and Indian Exhibition in London, England, in 1886, the year preceding Queen Victoria's Golden Jubilee. The Canadian display included works by established painters but it was the paintings of the younger, Paris-trained group that caught the attention of British art critics. The Canadian artists, however, had to struggle to emerge from their colonial vestiges in order to gain international recognition.

At the turn of the twentieth century, English-Canadian art came of age. James Wilson Morrice and Maurice Cullen, both from Quebec, became the leading Canadian practitioners of European Impressionism and Post-Impressionism. Morrice was born into a wealthy, established Montreal family. In 1890 he sailed for Europe on the advice of Sir William Van Horne, the manager of the Canadian Pacific Railway and an art connoisseur. Morrice won instant international acclaim. His works were purchased by a number of the great European galleries, as well as by the French government and Parisian art connoisseurs. Ironically, he was hardly known in Canada. Recognition in Europe would change that.

Morrice's contemporary, the Newfoundland-born Maurice Cullen, influenced a whole generation of Canadian painters with Impressionism. After an unsuccessful initial career in business in Montreal, he left for Paris in 1888 to practise sculpture. There he met the great French Impressionists, most notably Monet. Five Cullen canvases were exhibited in the 1894 Salon. The Salon was the official art exhibition of the French Academy of Fine Arts. The following year he was elected to the distinguished Société Nationale des Beaux-Arts. Yet, despite such recognition in Europe, he returned to Canada in 1895 where his acceptance was slow and difficult. His work later inspired A.Y. Jackson, a young Montreal avant-garde artist of the time and a future member of the Group of Seven.

Literature

English-Canadian poetry became established in the 1880s. The "Confederation Poets"—the name literary critics have given to Charles G.D. Roberts, Bliss Carman, Archibald Lampman, and Duncan Campbell Scott—provided a nationalist dimension to the era. The first volume of poetry by Roberts, *Orion and Other Poems*, inspired Lampman, who later wrote: "It seemed to me a wonderful thing that such a work could be done by a Canadian, by a young man, one of ourselves." As with the painters, the Confederation Poets sought the essence of Canada in the sublime, in nature—in the physical world of rocks, streams, and woods, and in the country lifestyle

Philippe Hébert, one of Canada's best-known monumental sculptors, loved the history of New France. He appears here in his Montreal studio with a plaster model (at left) of his famous Sans merci, *a depiction of the struggle of an early French settler with a reaping hook in his hand against a First Nations warrior.*

Source: Louis-Philippe Hébert à l'atelier avec le groupe *Sans Merci* au premier plan, 1910-11, Musée national des beaux-arts du Québec, Fonds Hébert (H-21/H-17).

of the farmer and lumberjack. They depicted nature in the highly romantic terms of the British Romantic poets who inspired them, such as Wordsworth, Keats, and Shelley. The Confederation Poets were the literary equivalent of the Canada First Movement and of the Royal Canadian Academy of the Arts, seeking to discover "the soul of the new nation."

Isabella Valancy Crawford was another poet who drew inspiration from the Canadian landscape. She depicted nature as half-human, as possessing a soul that was very much in tune with the human soul. Both "souls" struggled with love and death—common themes in her nature poetry. But Pauline Johnson became the most famous female poet in the late nineteenth century. Born the daughter of a Mohawk chief and his English wife, Johnson (or Tekahionwake, her Mohawk name) celebrated her Iroquois heritage while at the same time expressing a Canadian and imperial identity. In her poem "Canadian Born" she expressed her imperialistic fervour:

> *The Dutch may have their Holland, the Spaniard have his Spain,*
> *The Yankee to the south of us must south of us remain;*
> *For not a man dare lift a hand against the men who brag*
> *That they were born in Canada beneath the British flag.*

In Quebec, a generation of poets used François-Xavier Garneau's magisterial *Histoire du Canada*, published between 1845 and 1848, along with folklore, patriotic feeling, and religion, as themes for their poetry. Not surprisingly, survival (*la survivance*) was a dominant motif. Octave Crémazie, for example, expressed a patriotic sentiment for the French-Canadian homeland and

Cousins Bliss Carman (left) and Charles G.D. Roberts (right), two of the "Confederation Poets."
Source: Provincial Archives of New Brunswick, Miscellaneous Photograph Collection: P37-402.

looked to Quebec's past during the French *ancien régime* for the nation's moments of greatness. In the same way, Louis Fréchette, considered the unofficial poet laureate of nineteenth-century French Canada, wrote a series of patriotic poems, *La légende d'un peuple* (1887), inspired by dramatic moments of Canada's past from the arrival of Jacques Cartier to the hanging of Louis Riel.

Quebec's poetry came into its own with the École littéraire de Montréal. Founded in 1895, it received acclaim for its poetry, which broke free of the dominant patriotic–romantic verse. The school's famous member was Émile Nelligan, who produced 170 poems when he was between the ages of seventeen and twenty. Perhaps his best known was "Le vaisseau d'or" (Ship of Gold). Unlike other members, Nelligan found his inspiration for poetry less in romantic nature, historical subjects, or patriotic fervour, and more in what Wordsworth called "the still, sad music of humanity," the poetry of the spirit. Sadly, Nelligan spent the last forty-one years of his life in mental institutions.

English-Canadian novelists and short-story writers also emerged in the late nineteenth century. Again, the Canadian identity being constructed through art was usually based on nature and the wilderness. Both Charles G.D. Roberts and Ernest Thompson Seton had popular reputations for their realistic animal stories. Seton was born in England, raised in Ontario, and lived in Manitoba in the early 1880s before leaving permanently for the United States in 1896. He published his first collection of animal stories, *Wild Animals I Have Known*, in 1898. Eight years later his classic of children's literature, *Two Little Savages*, based on his boyhood experiences of "playing Indian" in Ontario, was published.

Despite the nationalistic overtones, many of the best Canadian novels had regional settings. Norman Duncan's *The Way of the Sea* (1903) and Theodore Goodridge Roberts's *The Harbour Master* (1913) were set in Newfoundland. Lucy Maud Montgomery's first novel, *Anne of Green*

Gables (1908), captured the spirit of her native province of Prince Edward Island through her beloved orphan character, Anne Shirley. An instant success, the novel made her, and the island, world-famous. Gilbert Parker's *The Seats of the Mighty* (1898), a historical novel about New France, became an international bestseller. One of the most popular French-Canadian novels of the Quebec rural countryside was Ernest Choquette's *Claude Paysan* (1899). But excommunicated priest Charles Chiniquy outdistanced all of his Quebec contemporaries in terms of the number of editions and translations of his works. His *The Priest, the Woman and the Confessional* (1875), *Fifty Years in the Church of Rome* (1885), and *Forty Years in the Church of Christ* (1899) were popular among Protestant extremists throughout the world because of their vitriolic attacks on the Roman Catholic Church.

Stephen Leacock acquired international recognition as one of the great humorists writing in the English language. *Sunshine Sketches of a Little Town* (1912), an affectionate satire of small-town Ontario life in the fictitious town of Mariposa, and *Arcadian Adventures with the Idle Rich* (1914), a parody of city life, were the best known of about sixty books that earned Leacock a reputation as the "Mark Twain of the British Empire." But there was more to Leacock's novels than humour. He questioned the values and virtues of liberal capitalism and advocated a more humane and spiritual society.

In the West, the settlement of the Prairies provided a rich subject and inspiration for a generation of novelists. Authors such as Ralph Connor (Charles Gordon), Robert Stead, Nellie McClung, and Janey Canuck (Emily Murphy) wrote of the pioneer experience with highly utopian depictions of the region. The successful novels of Ralph Connor sold in the millions and, as was often the case, had a larger audience outside the country than within it. He made his reputation with his first novel, *The Sky Pilot* (1899), the story of a North-West Mounted Police officer. All of his western novels capitalized on the romance, adventure, and physical beauty of the early West. His novels also dealt with the familiar theme of good Christians challenged by scoffers and nonbelievers who, in the end, were won over to the purer life. In British Columbia, Martin Allen Grainger's *Woodsmen of the West* (1908) captured life in the logging industry on the West Coast. Robert Service's verse, published in his *Songs of a Sourdough* (1907), *The Spell of the Yukon* (1907), and *Ballads of a Cheechako* (1909), established his reputation as a writer of humorous ballads.

Theatre

Canadian theatre grew slowly in the period from 1867 to 1914, and was restricted to the major urban centres. In Montreal, the New Dominion Theatre opened in 1873 to cater to professional drama touring groups. It succumbed, however, to vaudeville or music hall troupes by 1876, a reflection of the type of culture in demand at the time. In Toronto, a new Grand Opera House opened in 1880, which, along with the Princess Theatre and the Academy of Music,

Pauline Johnson was one of Canada's greatest poets in the late nineteenth and early twentieth centuries. She travelled across the dominion many times on tour. When one old dowager asked the Mohawk poet if her father really was an Indian, she replied, "Was your father really a white man?"

Source: Durnford, H./Library and Archives Canada/PA-127297.

Émile Nelligan (1879–1941), the legendary Quebec poet and member of the École littéraire de Montréal. The intense young man already was confined to a mental asylum at the time this photo was taken in 1904. His poetry is still widely read in Quebec, where the tragic figure has legendary status.

Source: Library and Archives Canada/C-88566.

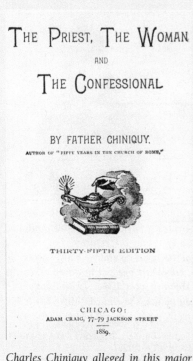

THE PRIEST, THE WOMAN

AND

THE CONFESSIONAL

BY FATHER CHINIQUY.

AUTHOR OF "FIFTY YEARS IN THE CHURCH OF ROME,"

THIRTY-FIFTH EDITION

CHICAGO:

ADAM CRAIG, 77–79 JACKSON STREET

1889.

Charles Chiniquy alleged in this major work that the confessions of female parishioners caused some Roman Catholic priests to end their vows of celibacy. This certainly had been his own experience and led to his excommunication. The Protestants embraced him when he began his furious campaign against the "Church of Rome."

Source: Copyright 1880, by Rev. Charles Chiniquy.

housed most of the important cultural events that came to Toronto between 1880 and 1914. These theatre houses welcomed American and British touring companies.

The prevailing mood in late nineteenth-century Canada, according to the theatre historian Murray Edwards, was "essentially anti-theatre."[2] Few Canadians attended productions, fewer still supported their actors, and theatre productions were seldom reported in the local newspapers. One reason for such a low opinion of acting was its association with "immorality and debauchery" in the mind of church leaders. The stage was regarded "as the gate of Hell." Regardless, Sarah Bernhardt, the flamboyant French actress, succeeded in "packing the house" no matter where she performed in the country.

By the turn of the century, theatre was well established, thanks to large-scale urbanization. It remained a largely foreign phenomenon. American money built most of the new theatres, and American touring companies provided nearly all the shows.

Some patrons of the arts became concerned about this "Americanization." But instead of supporting Canadian actors, they brought in British touring groups. For a while, in the period from 1910 to 1914, a battle existed between these two external groups for the domination of Canadian theatre. With the outbreak of war, however, the British "theatrical invasion" of Canada ended. The Great War also curtailed American productions in Canada. Only in the interwar years did a respectable Canadian theatre develop, in competition with the new moving-picture industry.

Quebec theatre often had a political theme. In May 1880, Louis Fréchette's *Papineau* appeared at Montreal's Académie de musique, and his *Retour de l'exilé* (The Return of the Exile) played in June of the same year. Both plays concerned the heroes and events of 1837–38, and advocated a reconciliation of French and English, while holding out hope of the *canadiens* one day freeing themselves from British rule. Another play, *Un bonheur en attire un autre* (One Piece of Luck Attracts Another), written by Félix-Gabriel Marchand, premier of Quebec between 1897 and 1900, was performed in 1883 at "a benefit for the families of those killed during the 1837/38 Rebellion."

The Promotion of Canadian Culture

The governors general in Canada, as British aristocrats, played an important role in promoting Canadian high culture. As the symbolic representatives of the Crown and the Empire, they viewed the promotion of a distinctly British form of Canadian culture as an integral part of their mandate. As their roles became increasingly ceremonial, the governors general became more involved in cultural rather than political issues.

Often the governors general bought and displayed Canadian art in their official residences. When serving the Empire on the periphery, it seemed only reasonable that these British aristocrats would use their wealth, influence, and station to serve as patrons of the arts in general, and promote local, "colonial" artists in particular. Lord Dufferin, Canada's third governor general (1872–78), went further. He laid the groundwork for the establishment of the Royal Canadian Academy of the Arts, modelled after the British Royal Academy. Dufferin's successor, the Marquis

The Sherman Grand Theatre opened in Calgary in February 1912, at the height of the city's pre–World War I economic boom. From 1901 to 1911, the city's population grew from 4000 to 44,000. The Grand, with a "stage one foot larger than that of the Royal Alexandra in Toronto," served as Calgary's centre for the performing arts for over a generation.

Source: Illustration from *The Western Standard*, June 12, 1913. Glenbow Library.

of Lorne, brought the Academy, along with the National Gallery of Canada, its successor, into existence in the early 1880s.

For the first thirty years, the National Gallery housed only government purchases, donations, bequests, and commissions. Then, in 1907, the federal government established the three-person Advisory Arts Council to promote "the growth of a true taste and general interest in public arts amongst the people of Canada." Three years later, the gallery's first full-time curator, Eric Brown, arrived from England. In the 1910s, Brown encouraged Canadian artists to develop works "along national lines." He helped begin the Canadian War Memorial Fund, which sponsored Canadian artists to go abroad to paint the carnage of World War I.

The prosperity and expansion of Canada at the turn of the twentieth century led to new initiatives. Earl Grey (Canada's ninth governor general, 1904–1911) sponsored the Earl Grey Musical and Dramatic Trophy Competition, which held national competitions in different Canadian cities yearly in an effort to promote and elevate the quality of Canadian talent. Grey, a fervent imperialist, also sponsored lecture tours to promote the British Empire both within Canada and abroad. Stephen Leacock, who toured Canada, Great Britain, Australia, New Zealand, and South Africa in 1907, became one of the beneficiaries. Grey purchased an entire printing of Robert Stead's book *The Empire Builders* (1908) because he liked its imperial

An appreciative audience watching a movie at the Innisfail Opera House, Innisfail, Alberta, 1910.
Source: Glenbow Archives/NA-1709-23.

message. To promote the study of Canadian and British history, Grey founded the Historical Landmark Association of Canada, the precursor of the Historical Sites and Monuments Board of Canada, in 1907. It had as its mandate the establishment of national historic sites such as the Plains of Abraham, a difficult site to interpret due to strong and conflicting feelings on the part of English and French Canadians over the conquest.

By the turn of the century, the growing business community in Canada was beginning to serve as patrons of the arts. As entrepreneurs, their interests were not only those of the elite wishing to foster a respectable arts scene and a nationalism for the fledgling nation; they also saw the arts as a means of promoting their financial interests. The Canadian Pacific Railway Company, for example, hired artists in the 1880s to create works for their hotels, chateaus, railcars, and offices and to design their promotional posters. Portraits of the rugged Canadian landscape served as ideal promotional material for the CPR that linked the young dominion from sea to sea. Later the CPR gave Dominion Drama Festival finalists a round-trip ticket to Ottawa for the price of a one-way fare to make it possible for the finalists to participate in the annual competitions. For writers and dramatists it often provided free passes to enable authors to read their works across the country and dramatists to stage their plays.

Wealthy families and their businesses also supported the arts. They generally viewed such patronage as part of their duty to society as elites. As early as the 1870s, the Massey Manufacturing Company, owned by the wealthy Massey family of Toronto, established a company band (the Massey Concert Band), a glee club, an employees' orchestra, and even a literary magazine, *Massey's Illustrated*, published between 1882 and 1895. As well, the Massey family purchased a number of church organs for Methodist churches in Toronto. In 1894, Hart Massey built the magnificent Massey Hall, with a seating capacity of 4000, and underwrote the costs of the Toronto Symphony Orchestra and the Toronto Mendelssohn Choir. The family business would continue its patronage under Hart's grandson, Vincent, in the interwar years. While elites were expected to have a natural appreciation for the arts through their lineage, education, and upbringing, it also allowed them to feel as if they were giving something back to society.

Popular Culture

"Popular culture" generally refers to beliefs and pursuits practised by the masses of society. Historians have debated what constitutes popular culture and who defines it. Lawrence W. Levine, one of the leading authorities on American popular culture, describes it as "culture that is widely accessible and widely accessed; widely disseminated, and widely viewed or heard or read."[3] He notes that such diffusion generally occurred in the late nineteenth and early twentieth centuries by such media of communication as national magazines and syndicated newspapers, and then, by the 1920s, through radio and film. These media allowed for mass production and widespread dissemination and thus led to the rise of mass culture. Industrialization led to mass consumption and the beginning of the "modern" age.

Several factors worked against the formation of a recognizable and national popular culture in Canada. The size and diverse geography of the new nation posed obstacles to communication, and therefore to the dissemination of popular culture through media. Regional barriers thwarted cultural dissemination and worked against the formation of a national culture. In addition, leisure time was in short supply for the majority of Canadians.

"Leisure" has been defined in two ways: as synonymous with cultural enrichment and learning, and as "free time." This second concept of leisure emerged out of the Industrial Revolution, when work occurred for defined periods of time, leaving demarcated periods of time for non-work-related activities. But the upper and middle classes became increasingly worried about how the masses were "spending" their "free" time. Leisurely pursuits seemed to be slipping into the realm of vice, and they would continue to do so, it was believed, unless productive, healthy, and moral alternatives were offered.

Newspapers

In the late nineteenth century, most newspapers were local rather than national, each the product of a particular city or town and serving its urban audience and surrounding rural hinterland. By the turn of the century, however, new technology enabled newspapers to widen their coverage to national and international events, and to reach a wider and larger audience. By the early twentieth century "steam-powered production machinery, cheap newsprint, telegraph communications, a comprehensive rail network, and efficient postal delivery combined to create the penny-a-copy urban daily that made information gleaned worldwide available to more and more Canadians."[4] Some of the more popular mass-produced newspapers were the Montreal *Star* and *La presse* in Montreal, and the *Telegraph*, the *World*, the *News*, and the *Star* in Toronto. These inexpensive and independent newspapers, whose product was known as "yellow journalism," or "the people's press," altered the nature of news. It became less informational and more sensational, focusing on subjects of popular interest such as war and crime. They also began to include advertisements from large department stores that catered to the consuming "masses," such as Eaton's, as a means of defraying production costs. According to historian Paul Rutherford, these publications also promoted Canadian nationalism; the three key ideas that all the popular newspapers emphasized—nationalism, progress, and democracy—were interrelated.

Magazines

Few Canadian magazines existed in the late nineteenth century, but there was a host of American options. As with other emerging forms of cultural media, Canadian enterprises found it difficult to compete with those from the United States. In 1907 one of the popular American magazines, *Saturday Evening Post*, had a Canadian circulation of 60,000—more than all the major Canadian

Mary Pickford (1893–1979). The Canadian-born golden-haired girl, nicknamed "America's Sweetheart," became the most popular movie actress of her time. Alfred Cheney Johnston, the official photographer of the Ziegfeld Follies, took this photo in 1920.

Source: Alfred Cheney Johnston, Library and Archives Canada, Acc. no. 1991-334, PA-185967.

magazines combined. These American magazines contained an abundance of advertising to absorb the cost of production and to keep prices low. They also targeted the rising and increasingly consuming middle class. It was feared that these American imports hindered the growth of a Canadian popular culture. Only in the interwar years would popular Canadian magazines appear to rival the American ones, but they still often depended on the American magazines for feature articles.

Cinema

Movie theatres made their debut in Canada at the turn of the century. The first permanent movie house, the Edison Electric Theatre, opened on Cordova Street in Vancouver in 1902. Winnipeg's Unique and Dreamland followed in 1903, Montreal's Ouimetoscope (an impressive 1000-seat cinema named after Ernest Ouimet, its owner) in 1904, and the York Theatre in Saint John, New Brunswick, in 1906. They charged their customers a nickel, hence the name "nickelodeon" for these early movie theatres.

Developing a Canadian movie industry was a constant struggle. Quebec cinematographers looked to Europe, especially France, for inspiration, content, and support, while cinematographers in the rest of Canada looked to the United States. The challenge was to carve out a Canadian perspective in films unique from that of Hollywood.

James Freer, a farmer from the Brandon area of Manitoba, became Canada's first cinematographer. He filmed agricultural subjects in 1897, with the blessing of the Canadian government and the Canadian Pacific Railway Company, as promotion literature to attract settlers, especially from Britain, to the Canadian West. At the turn of the century, Freer toured Britain with his moving pictures that showed the potential of the Canadian West. At the same time, a number of "scenic" films depicted popular and exotic Canadian sites, paralleling illustrations in many of the weekly or monthly "illustrated news" magazines. Since these films resembled photographs or pictures, they were called "moving pictures."

Hiawatha, the Messiah of the Ojibway (1903) became the first single-reel film produced in Canada. It was filmed on a First Nations reserve in Ontario, using Aboriginal performers. But the inspiration for the film was American, based on Henry Wadsworth Longfellow's poem, *The Song of Hiawatha*. The film's appeal, according to George Melnyk, was its ability to "fit the colonizing culture's late nineteenth- and early twentieth-century fascination with Native Americans and their supposed doomed way of life."[5] Such productions, however, made no attempt to discern the diverse cultures of the First Nations. Instead, a romanticized version of the "Indian" was produced for mass consumption. This version was usually based on the stereotypical depiction of the Plains Indian, complete with such cultural icons as the tepee and the mounted warrior with feathered war bonnet. Longfellow mistakenly portrayed Hiawatha as an Ojibway (Anishinaabeg) when in fact the figure emerged from Iroquois legend. The popular image of the Indian was one frozen in time, taken from a constructed and romanticized version of the past. It had no connection to the harsh realities being faced by the marginalized First Nations at the time.

Film companies between 1912 and 1914 produced films on Canadian subjects in an effort to create a Canadian-based fictional narrative, quickly becoming the popular style of film of the day. The British American Film Company produced *The Battle of the Long Sault*, about the Iroquois attack on Montreal in 1660. A Montreal production company made *Madelaine de Verchères*, about the Quebec heroine who defended a fort against the Iroquois. The All-Red Feather Company did *The War Pigeon*, an account of the War of 1812, while the Canadian Bioscope Company made *Evangeline*, based on another of Longfellow's popular poems set in the Acadian deportation of 1755. Each company had its moment of glory, but quickly died out in the competition with more sophisticated and well-funded Hollywood feature films. Many Canadian filmmakers headed south, and along with them went Canadian actors. The most famous of these was Gladys Mary Smith—or to use her stage name, Mary Pickford. She became "America's Sweetheart," coming to symbolize youthful female beauty. In the end, Canadian silent cinema suffered the fate of other forms of popular culture in Canada. The attempts to construct a national popular culture were defeated by the same forces that allowed popular culture to be created, disseminated, and consumed. Increasingly, national boundaries meant little to communication media.

Sport

Sport developed in Canada during the half-century after Confederation, from an activity for the elite to a popular form of leisure for the middle and lower classes. Increasingly it was viewed not only as a means of leisure and creating a healthier society but also as a form of social control. It also went from being amateur to professional and, along with this transition (as with other forms of culture), from being Canadian to American-dominated.

Amateur Sport

Amateur sport clubs existed in major urban centres at the time of Confederation for hunting, curling, golf, lawn tennis, and, in port cities, yachting. They provided social meeting places for Canada's political, economic, and commercial elites who possessed the leisure time and money to afford such pursuits. Membership was usually restricted to people with certain ethnic, religious, and educational backgrounds and denied to racial minorities. But wealth and social position also became criteria, allowing entry to a new professional and business class, such as lawyers, doctors, entrepreneurs, and bank managers. Women were active in these clubs, although in a clearly defined and subservient role. Racial minorities were forced to create their own teams and clubs. In Nova Scotia, African Canadians in the community of Africville, on the outskirts of Halifax, formed their own baseball and hockey teams. On the West Coast, Japanese Canadians formed a baseball team, called the Asahi. Out of these organizations came a number of key figures in the development of amateur sport.

Organized team sport, such as football, baseball, lacrosse, and hockey, increased in popularity. As people settled in urban centres and worked clearly

Isobel Stanley, dressed in white, playing outdoor hockey near Rideau Hall, circa 1890. Stanley was the daughter of Canada's Governor General Lord Stanley of Preston, and she played a key role in convincing her father to create the Stanley Cup.

Source: Brian McFarlane - Toronto: Stoddart, 1994 - xvii, p. : ill., ports.; 20 x 27 cm - ISBN 0773728368 - P. 6. © Public Domain nlc-5953.

defined hours in factories or offices, their regimented schedules produced some free time for sport. Better transportation facilities and communication links also enabled intercity competition. The standardization of rules in sport, in turn, led to the creation of local, provincial, and national associations. The Amateur Athletic Union of Canada became the first truly national association when it was formed in 1909. By 1912, it already included 1300 clubs and over 100,000 individual members, and regulated all aspects of amateur sport.

A few women athletes formed their own clubs and teams in the 1890s in sports such as basketball, hockey, and baseball. The Young Women's Christian Association, which first emerged in the 1890s in the large urban centres, assisted by providing athletic facilities and clubhouses for young, urbanized working girls. Most girls and young women, however, pursued athletic interests and team sport in the sanctum of schools, colleges, and universities until a more receptive audience for women athletes and more public facilities were available.

Social reformers reacted to women's involvement in sport. Concerned about the decline of the birth rate among the British-Canadian population and the influx of large numbers of foreign immigrants, some reformers urged women to improve their health through physical activity in expectation of having healthy, robust children. Others equated sport with qualities of manliness and masculinity, and viewed athletic women as challenging dominant notions of femininity. The advocates of "muscular Christianity" argued that, through athleticism and rugged team sport, young males would become vigorous fighters for their faith, their country, and the British Empire.

In general, however, despite concerns about females participating, sport was viewed as a means to control and shape society. If the lower classes were to have free or leisure time, it had to be regulated, lest it be wasted on unproductive pursuits or turned to vice, such as drinking, smoking, gambling, and other even less reputable activities. Sport provided a suitable alternative. It was a healthy activity at a time when the urban and industrial population was becoming increasingly less active and working indoors. It emphasized such traits as discipline, hierarchy, competition, perseverance, cooperation, and teamwork.

Team Sports

Although football made its debut in Canada in the late nineteenth century, it became a recognized national sport in 1909 when Governor General Earl Grey donated the cup that bears his name. At first the sport remained largely the preserve of an anglophone Canadian elite associated with universities in the larger cities of central Canada. Only in the first decade of the twentieth century did football spread to the smaller towns of Ontario and the Prairies. It also became more of a spectator sport. In so doing, it became more "Americanized," except that it retained the oval ball and the rules of rugby—both Canadian contributions to the game.

Soccer was also played, particularly by British immigrants, but it failed to catch on despite its appeal to the lower classes. By the time soccer was becoming popular in Britain during World War I, Canada was turning to other team sports such as baseball, hockey, and football. Still, in 1904, the Galt Football Club of Galt, Ontario, represented Canada at the Olympic Games in St. Louis, Missouri, and won the soccer gold medal.

Baseball, despite its reputation as "America's past-time," was highly popular in Canada, particularly prior to World War I. The game gained both fans and players in English Canada because it required minimal facilities. During the 1870s, baseball clubs emerged, and intra-town leagues became popular by the 1880s. In rural areas, baseball was often played during a picnic or other gathering associated with celebrations, such as May 24 (later Victoria Day), Dominion Day, and Labour Day.

To those seeking a distinctly Canadian team sport, lacrosse—a game of First Nations origins—seemed the perfect choice. The National Lacrosse Association, founded in 1867, and its slogan—"*Our* Country and *Our* Game"—certainly claimed that status. George Beers, a Montreal dentist, promoted it as such when he wrote in 1867: "We may find that lacrosse will do as much for our young Dominion as the Olympian games did for Greece or cricket for our Motherland." Lacrosse was closely associated with the game of baggataway, which was played by several First

Smirle Lawson of the Varsity Blues hurdles the McGill defence in October 1909. The University of Toronto went on to defeat Toronto Parkdale that fall, to win the first Grey Cup.

Source: Canadian Football Hall of Fame and Museum.

Choosing sides, boys before a hockey game, Sarnia, Ontario, December 29, 1908.

Source: Photo by John Boyd/Library and Archives Canada/PA-60732.

Nations. On the very day of Canada's creation, Kahnawake took the Dominion lacrosse title—at the time, the equivalent of world championship—by defeating the Montreal Lacrosse Club 3 to 2. The First Nations in eastern North America originated the sport, but Euro-Canadians altered the game by drawing up new "rules." Even so, the Kahnawake team defeated the Montreal team even while playing under the new rules.

Lacrosse had a sporadic history before 1914. After an enthusiastic beginning in the 1860s, it ebbed in the early 1870s as a result of the presence of "rowdy" or undesirable elements at many of the matches. The roughness of the game was an attraction—a masculine trait that set Canadians apart from their "softer" British counterparts—but was also a distraction, particularly to social reformers who wanted sport to inculcate respectable values. The game revived in the 1880s, but also changed from amateur to professional. This change was evident in the shift from exhibition games arranged occasionally, to systematized leagues that met and competed on a regular basis for spectators. The game also became a "national" sport, with teams located in urban centres across the country, although the sport lacked a national association until 1912.

Hockey, a sport that contained the masculine physicality of lacrosse but set it in the nationalistic realm of a northern icy climate, was *the* Canadian sport by World War I. The first regulated game dates back to 1875 in Montreal, when two nine-man teams from the Montreal Football Club looking for some winter training, confronted each other. Soon, companies that sponsored the local "amateur" teams hired men both to work and to play hockey—the first professional players. Already players earned more money from hockey than from their regular work.

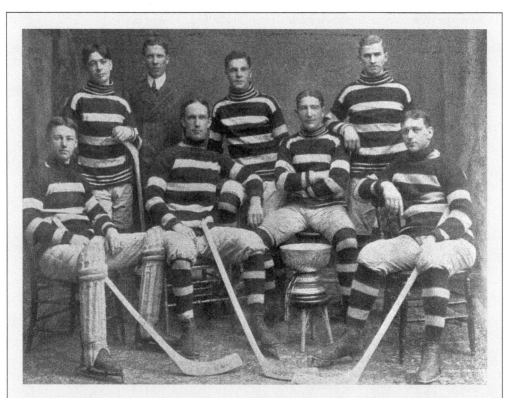

Ottawa's *"Silver Seven,"* winners of the 1905 Stanley Cup, shown in the centre of the photo. The team was later renamed the Senators.

Source: Library and Archives Canada/Credit: Thomas Patrick Gorman/Thomas Patrick Gorman Fonds/PA-091046.

Many of the early teams began in Canada's mining, lumbering, and farming towns, resulting in tough games and ferocious intercommunity rivalry. The sport caught on quickly. By 1880, the number of players per side was reduced from nine to seven, and a standardized set of rules was in place. Montreal held the "world championship" in 1883, in which the McGill University team was victorious.

Three years later, in 1886, the Amateur Hockey Association of Canada was formed. Initially the association was made up of clubs from Montreal, Quebec City, and Ottawa only. Teams from these three cities dominated hockey between 1883 and 1893, the year Lord Stanley, governor general of Canada, donated the Stanley Cup to go to the league's winning team. (Remarkably, the first recipient, the Montreal Hockey Club, refused the Cup because of a feud with its parent organization, the Montreal Amateur Athletic Association, which accepted it on their behalf.)

A group of colleges, universities, and military and athletic clubs founded the Ontario Hockey Association in 1890. Similar associations sprang up in the Maritimes and the West. Montreal had more than 100 hockey clubs in 1895, and by 1905, hockey teams existed across Canada. The cities of Saint John, Montreal, Ottawa, Toronto, and Edmonton even had a few women's teams.

In 1904, the International Hockey League (IHL) was formed, consisting of five communities in the United States and Ontario. It lasted only three years, however, due to the difficulty of getting professional players, because local elite Canadian leagues professionalized players to prevent them from migrating to the IHL. In 1909, this organization was replaced by the National Hockey Association, the forerunner of today's National Hockey

Residents of Nelson, British Columbia, celebrated Dominion Day in 1898 with a horse race down the town's main street.

Source: British Columbia Archives/HP-6225.

League, which launched its inaugural season with seven teams: three from Montreal, one of which was the Canadiens, the new French-Canadian team, with other teams from Ottawa, Renfrew, Haileybury, and Cobalt. They employed professional players. By 1912, the three small-town teams folded, victims of rising costs. The league now consisted of two teams from Montreal, two new ones from Toronto, and a team from both Ottawa and Quebec City. Also by 1912, the first artificial-ice rinks appeared, making playing conditions more stable and allowing ice hockey to become a West Coast sport. A Pacific Coast Hockey Association formed, which, in 1917, affiliated with the National Hockey Association to create the National Hockey League (NHL).

In four major sports in Canada—football, baseball, lacrosse, and hockey—professionalization took over by World War I. Good players could make a living from sports alone, because there now existed a group of consumers, mostly middle class, willing and able to support spectator sports. From this point onward, money and victory overrode gentlemanly conduct and pleasure as the main objectives. Sports became a business. Even the

WHERE HISTORIANS DISAGREE

Sport and Culture

Sport has been a vibrant aspect of Canadian culture for the past two centuries. Yet, despite its cultural importance, prior to the 1960s sport was not a serious subject of historical inquiry. It was viewed as a pedestrian and "low culture" activity, with no significant impact on society. Books on sport were left to journalists who were more interested in writing about their heroes and favourite teams.

Max Howell was an Australian rugby player and educator who became a pioneer of sport history in Canada. His historical survey of sports and games, written with his wife Nancy Howell in 1969, went a long way in filling a void. The work was built upon by such historians as Alan Metcalfe, and then by Don Morrow and Kevin Wamsley. These efforts focused on the distinct development of Canadian sports, separate from what was happening in the United States.[1]

As sport history developed, its methodology became more complex. Most of the practitioners of early sport history were trained as physical educators,

not historians. Narrative descriptions that chronicled the achievements of individuals and teams in the 1970s and early 1980s gave way to systematic analysis and social theory to interpret data.

The rise of social history led to the introduction of such analytical tools as class, race, and gender. Metcalfe, for example, demonstrated the link between class structure and leisure activities, by arguing that for most of the nineteenth century, sport was used by the middle and elite classes to control the masses. The lower classes were expected to be "productive" during their meagre leisure time, and sport was perceived as a healthy activity that could be used to control workers while teaching them valuable lessons about citizenship, morality, and discipline. Sport historians in Canada turned their attention to race, particularly the role of First Nations. Victoria Paraschak has explored how those marginalized have been treated by the Eurocentric system of domestic athletics. Ann Hall provided the first complete history of women's sport in Canada, arguing that women were active in opening sport to both genders in Canada. Hall claims that women were not victims of an oppressive sport structure, but rather were committed agents in creating sport for their children, particularly their daughters.[2]

Because sport has been so male-dominated, the role of masculinity is receiving considerable attention from historians. In the mid-1980s, Patricia Vertinsky examined Canadian athletics as gendered events. Philip White and Kevin Young focused on a wide array of gender and sexuality issues, including homophobia and masculinity.[3] According to Varda Burstyn, "masculinism, through sport, encourages and promotes other ideologies and other forms of inequality—notably economic, racial, and biotic hierarchies."[4] For Burstyn, it was a matter of social priorities. Sport and the "cultural matrix" it sustains, promote competition, a winner-take-all philosophy, and a "hypermasculinity"—an embellished ideal of manhood linked mythically and practically to the role of the warrior. Kevin Wamsley is one of the most prolific

in the field. His work explores the relationship between violence and athletics.

Not surprisingly, historians have focused on the relationship among hockey, culture, and national identity in Canada. Richard Gruneau and David Whitson have explored the "myths" surrounding Canadians and their love for hockey. They argue that the centrality of hockey in Canadian cultural life is not as deep-rooted as we usually assume. David Brown argues that hockey's cultural impact is linked to Canada's identity as a northern nation. Carly Adams's work represents the growing female interest in hockey.[5]

While hockey is explored as a national passion, emphasis is being put on the role of regionalism and localism. Bruce Kidd puts Ontario at the centre of Canada's sporting movement. The province's status as the national heartland came with the obligations of national leadership. Nancy Bouchier examines sport in the small-town milieu. Sandy Young and Colin Howell analyze sport in the Maritimes. Donald Guay's work remains an important book about Quebec's sporting past.[6]

---

1   Maxwell and Nancy Howell, *Sports and Games in Canadian Life: 1700 to the Present* (Toronto: Macmillan Company of Canada, 1969); Alan Metcalfe, *Canada Learns to Play: The Emergence of Organized Sport, 1807–1914* (Toronto: McClelland and Stewart, 1987); Don Morrow and Kevin Wamsley, *Sport in Canada: A History* (Don Mills, ON: Oxford University Press, 2005).

2   Victoria Paraschak, "Doing Race, Doing Gender: First Nations, 'Sport,' and Gender Relations," in Kevin Young and Philip White, eds., *Sport and Gender in Canada*, 2nd ed. (Don Mills: Oxford University Press, 2007), pp. 137–54; M. Ann Hall, *The Girl and the Game: A History of Women's Sport in Canada* (Peterborough, ON: Broadview Press, 2002).

3   Patricia Vertinsky, "God, Science and the Marketplace, the Bases for Exercise Prescriptions for Females in Nineteenth Century North America," *CJHS*, 17(1) (May 1986): 38–45; Philip White and Kevin Young, eds., *Sport and Gender in Canada* (Don Mills, ON: Oxford University Press, 1999).

4   Varda Burstyn, *Rites of Men: Manhood, Politics, and the Culture of Sport* (Toronto: University of Toronto Press, 1999), p. 5.

5   Richard Gruneau and David Whitson, *Hockey Night in Canada: Sport, Identities and Cultural Politics* (Toronto: Garamond Press, 1993); David Brown, "The Northern Character Theme and Sport in Nineteenth Century Canada," *Canadian Journal of History of Sport*, 20(1) (1989): 47–56; Carly Adams, *Queens of the Ice: They Were Fast, They Were Fierce, They Were Teenage Girls* (Toronto: James Lorimar and Company, 2011).

6   Bruce Kidd, "Ontario and the Ambition of Sports." *Ontario History* 90(2) (Autumn 1998): 157–72; Nancy Bouchier, *For the Love of the Game: Amateur Sport in Small-Town Ontario, 1838–1895* (Montreal: McGill-Queen's University Press, 2003); A.J. Young, *Beyond Heroes: A History of Sport in Nova Scotia*, 2 vols. (Hantsport, NS: Lancelot Press, 1988); Colin Howell, *Northern Sandlots: A Social History of Maritime Baseball* (Toronto: University of Toronto Press, 1995); Donald Guay, *Introduction a l'histoire des sports au Québec* (Montreal: VLB Editeur, 1987).

The cover of an awards list depicting the 1885 Industrial Exhibition. The fair played an important role in shaping Canadian ideas about modern life.

Source: Courtesy of Exhibition Place (Direct Energy Centre/ Allstream Centre).

newest sport, basketball—invented only in 1891 by James Naismith, a Canadian physical education instructor at the School of Christian Workers in Springfield, Massachusetts—later became professionalized. These team sports also reflected the dominant cultural values of a competitive urban and industrial society.

Middle-Class Culture

By the turn of the century, the rising middle class emerged as the primary shapers and consumers of culture in Canada. Middle-class male leisure activity often crossed class lines to incorporate working-class men as well. What united them was gender—male bonding (a shared sense of masculinity)—more than class affiliation. Such willingness to cross class lines occurred less frequently among women. Middle-class women had their own separate and acceptable social organizations, including the church, which was deemed "respectable." They would have little to do with working-class associations, including the Salvation Army (which they regarded as a working-class religion) and dance halls.

In the cities, leisure centres arose, such as dance halls, amusement parks and theatres, and fairs. The most popular in the Victorian era was Toronto's Industrial Exhibition, the forerunner of the Canadian National Exhibition. Founded in 1879, it entertained a broad segment of the populace of Toronto and its surrounding hinterland in the last few weeks of summer. Historian Keith Walden points out that, while it entertained, the exhibition also helped to "shape understanding in a society being altered profoundly by industrial capitalist production, technological developments, and new ideas and values, including consumerism."[6] Industrial fairs expressed the perspective of the dominant or hegemonic groups in society, usually the industrial and mercantile members of the rising middle class. These fairs and exhibitions in the larger urban centres provided "respectable" leisure to the rising middle class. They reflected the new spirit of "modernity" by putting on show the latest technologies, consumer goods, and cultural pursuits. At the same time, however, they became "liminal" spaces in which the borderlands among classes, ethnicities, genders, and identities were displayed and negotiated.

Working-Class Culture

A working-class culture emerged in both English and French Canada in the late nineteenth century. It took shape through a proliferation of associations, societies, clubs, and lodges that formed earlier but took on a new importance as they replaced institutions of self-help (mechanics' institutes) and community protection (finance companies). They provided a place where male workers (female workers could not belong) of common background and interests could meet and enjoy each other's company. Taverns served the same purpose. Joe Beef's Canteen, established in Montreal in the 1860s by Charles McKiernan, an Irish Protestant ex-soldier, became one such place. Because of its rowdy atmosphere, the establishment was the target of reform zealots. But for casual labourers, the unemployed, and transients, it provided a haven from the harsh realities of daily life in the slums and factories. The Canteen offered its working-class clientele food, drink, and accommodation—a blanket and access to a tub, a barber, "medical" advice, and "cures"—all for ten cents.

By the 1880s, larger working-class associations such as the Knights of Labor assumed the role that Joe Beef's Canteen and other, similar establishments (such as Dan Black's Tavern in Hamilton) had played. Through the American-based organization's ritualistic procedure of secret pledges, obedience, and committed charity, working men and women bonded and shared a sense of pride. Festivals, dinners, picnics, and workers' balls provided social gatherings to "cement the bonds of unity." Until the Knights' decline in the 1890s, workers held labour parades and demonstrations, often drawing thousands to such events from both towns and cities, thus providing visual reminders of labour's strength and solidarity.

The many working-class societies, clubs, lodges, and associations of the pre–World War I era helped to build a working-class culture. As historian Julia Roberts has demonstrated, however, taverns, being public sites, allowed a diverse range of races, ethnicities, and classes to intermingle and negotiate identities.

Aboriginal Culture

Although most Canadians in the late nineteenth century had a romanticized regard for the First Nations peoples, it did not extend to a belief that they had a right to maintain their cultures. When John A. Macdonald proposed the creation of a separate Department of Indian Affairs in 1880, he noted:

> We must remember that they are the original owners of the soil, of which they have been dispossessed by the covetousness or ambition of our ancestors. Perhaps, if Columbus had not discovered this continent—had left them alone—they would have worked out a tolerable civilization of their own.

Yet, in the same speech, Macdonald went on to justify the need for a Department of Indian Affairs "to advance the interests of the Indians, civilizing them and putting them in the condition of white men." The First Nations were caught up in the exorable march of "progress and civilization." It was the "white man's burden" to help alleviate the resulting suffering, and part of that burden included helping the "Indians" make the transition to white society. Assimilation was seen as inevitable.

These views were in keeping with the age. Canadians, like the majority of the Western world, believed that Aboriginal peoples were inferior and therefore had to be assimilated into the "superior" white culture. Edward Blake, former premier of Ontario and federal leader of the Liberal Party prior to Wilfrid Laurier, described the First Nations peoples in 1888 as "an inferior race, and in an inferior state of civilization." This negative perspective justified suppressing any aspect of Aboriginal culture that might get in the way of achieving assimilation. It would only postpone the inevitable. It was one thing to romanticize the First Nations through the adoption of practices such as lacrosse or by putting them on show in parades, official visits, fairs, and exhibitions; it was another to allow their languages, religion, and rituals to survive. Thus, while Canadians at the turn of the century concerned themselves with cultivating their own cultural traditions, they failed to have the same regard and concern for the culture of the First Nations.

Canadians believed that the First Nations were disappearing. As a result, they became increasingly fascinated with a people they saw as quaint and dying. This tragedy led to a romanticization of their role in the nation's history. Canadian society wanted to include First Nations ceremonies and customs in their country fairs and stampedes as an example of the dominion's distinct history. This display worked against the federal government's policy of assimilation, and, not surprisingly, the government undermined such popularizing of First Nations customs and ceremonies. Thus, when organizers of the Dominion Exhibition, the forerunner of the Calgary Stampede, invited a number of First Nations people to participate, Frank Pedley, the deputy superintendent-general of Indian affairs, appealed to the minister of agriculture not to give any financial support to the exhibition unless the organizers cancelled the "Indian performance."

The Six Nations Council, around 1910. After Sir John A. Macdonald gave his speech to the Council a quarter of a century earlier on the value of becoming citizens, it was translated into Mohawk. A council speaker then replied that they need not become Canadian citizens, because they already constituted a sovereign nation with their own political institutions.

Source: Department of Indian Affairs and Northern Development Collection/Library and Archives Canada/ C-33643.

COMMUNITY PORTRAIT

The Wendat (Huron) Community of Wendake

When the French first visited the Wendat people in the early seventeenth century, they lived on a small peninsula between Georgian Bay and Lake Simcoe in southern Ontario. The French called them "Huron." By the early 1650s, the Iroquois from present-day New York State drove the Wendat from their territory. A small group of them retreated to the region around Quebec City. In 1697, they moved to their new home of Lorette, or Wendake, near the St. Charles River, 15 kilometres north of Quebec.

Two hundred years later, Léon Gérin, a French-Canadian federal civil servant and pioneer sociologist, visited Wendake. He found a community of about 400 people who, in terms of their housing, dress, and religion, appeared to be almost identical to their French-Canadian neighbours. The village consisted of 50 houses or so, low-roofed wooden buildings, small whitewashed structures in double rows. Some homes had very small gardens beside them, while others were placed so closely together that no room existed for a garden. Encroachments by non-Aboriginal settlers had reduced the village site itself to a very small tract. The Wendat also had a reserve for hunting as well as a timber tract, but neither was adjacent to the village site. In terms of dress, only one old Wendat woman, in her nineties, dressed in her traditional costume of the last century. The men dressed like the French Canadians around them, but, for special occasions, the chiefs and leading men wore their traditional native costumes. Apart from a handful of Protestants, all the Wendat were Catholics.

Prosper Vincent had become a priest. While he could not speak Wendat, he was one of the last members of the community to know a number of Wendat dances and songs.

The Wendat at Wendake spoke the same French as the white community around them. The use of Wendat as a daily language had effectively died out half a century earlier. Other changes had also occurred. No longer were the clans as important as they had once been. In the past a member obtained a clan identification from his or her mother; now many Wendat men had married French-Canadian women, ending the traditional importance of female lineage.

Their immediate locality was not well adapted to agriculture and, as a result, the Wendat gradually abandoned their farming activities. Some members still practised hunting, trapping, and guiding, but the vast majority worked in the village itself, especially in the manufacturing of moccasins and snowshoes. On average, 10,000 to 15,000 hides were cut annually at Wendake. In 1898, the Wendat made 140,000 pairs of moccasins and about 7000 pairs of snowshoes. The improved transportation system of the late nineteenth century allowed for the expansion of the market for the sale of these items throughout Canada and the United States.

In 1869, the federal "Act for the graduate enfranchisement of Indians," later incorporated into the federal Indian Act of 1876, made rules that further eroded the community's Native traditions. The Act ruled that when an Indian woman married a non-Indian, or someone not subject to the Indian Act, she automatically lost her Indian status. The same would be true for their children. It did stipulate that when a non-Indian woman married an Indian under the Indian Act, she gained Indian status, as did any future children they might have. But the Indian Department worked to achieve the complete assimilation of the Wendat into the surrounding French-Canadian population by encouraging the "enfranchisement" or voluntary giving up of Indian status by adult Wendat males. (Under Bill C-31 in 1985, Canada gave up enfranchisement, and amended the Indian Act to permit those who had given up or lost their status to regain it.)

Despite such changes, Léon Gérin also found evidence that the Wendake Wendat were determined to resist assimilation and to maintain their unique Native traditions and customs. For example, they still held all their land communally. They also fought to maintain their traditional hunting rights, and resisted the leasing of reserve lands in their hunting grounds to sport clubs. Gérin found that the people of Wendake saw themselves as a culturally separate community, different and distinct from the larger French-speaking community because of their Wendat roots and traditions. They refused to abandon their First Nations status, and Wendake.

FURTHER READING

Léon Gérin, "The Hurons of Lorette," offprint from the *Transactions of the Ottawa Literary and Scientific Society*, June 26, 1900: 69–92.

Denys Delâge, sous la direction de, "Les Hurons de Wendake," special issue of *Recherche amérindiennes au Québec*, 30(3) (2000): 3–97.

Denis Vaugeois, sous la direction de, *Les Hurons de Lorette. Léon Gérin. Jean-Charles Falardeau. Christian Morissonneau. Denys Delâge. Marcel Trudel. Cornelius Jaenen. Alain Beaulieu* (Sillery, QC: Les éditions du Septentrion, 1996).

"Our people are at peace." The Wendat chief Ovide Sioui, at left, accepts the pipe from Six Nations chief Andrew Staats, in centre. In early August 1921, the Wendat and the Iroquois made peace at the tercentenary commemoration of Champlain's landing at Penetanguishene, on Georgian Bay in Ontario.

Source: Toronto Reference Library/T 33409.

Immigrant Culture

By 1900, the cultural traditions of other ethnic groups emerged, as immigrants came in large numbers and brought with them their customs, ceremonies, and festivities. According to the dominant assumptions of Anglo-conformity, the newcomers were expected to assimilate and adopt the British-Canadian culture. The fact that many of these customs were frowned upon by the host society did not prevent newly arrived ethnic groups from enjoying their own customs within their own communities.

In the Prairie West, the cultural clash was most evident. As historian Gerald Friesen pointed out,

> the population of the western interior had been overwhelmingly Canadian by birth and
> British by national origin in the late nineteenth century, but within one generation the

cultural composition changed dramatically. Almost half of all prairie residents at the start of the First World War had been born in another country.[7]

These "origins" included Ukrainian, Austro-Hungarian, Polish, Russian, German, Dutch, and French. Adjustment for most of these "foreigners" in a "strange land" was very difficult. It included both economic survival and cultural accommodation. While the host society looked to absorb the ethnic groups, discrimination often left them marginalized. Instead, they formed kinship networks and ethnic "webs" that provided a sense of welcome within their own enclaves. Here, they were able to practise and maintain their own cultural traditions.

SUMMARY

In the years 1867 to 1914, Canadian culture was in its infancy. While a strong desire to create a distinctly national spirit was certainly at work, such a process was proving difficult in the face of British and American influences. Also, the vastness of the country led to regional barriers. Most cultural endeavours began as amateur and local, and only slowly evolved into being professional and national. As well, elite culture increasingly gave way to popular culture. Just as Canada was slow to cultivate a national political culture, so too the country only gradually developed a national popular culture.

NOTES

1. Dennis Reid, "Lucius Richard O'Brien," *Dictionary of Canadian Biography*, vol. 12, *1891–1900* (Toronto: University of Toronto Press, 1990), p. 793.

2. Murray D. Edwards, *A Stage in Our Past: English-Language Theatre in Eastern Canada from the 1790s to 1914* (Toronto: University of Toronto Press, 1968), p. 28.

3. Lawrence W. Levine, "The Folklore of Industrial Society: Popular Culture and Its Audiences," *AHR Forum, American Historical Review*, 97(5) (December 1992): 1373.

4. R. Louis Gentilcore et al., eds., *Historical Atlas of Canada*, vol. 2 (Toronto: University of Toronto Press, 1993), p. 133.

5. George Melnyk, *One Hundred Years of Canadian Cinema* (Toronto: University of Toronto Press, 2004), p. 21.

6. Keith Walden, *Becoming Modern in Toronto: The Industrial Exhibition and the Shaping of a Late Victorian Culture* (Toronto: University of Toronto Press, 1997), p. xi.

7. Gerald Friesen, *The Canadian Prairies: A History* (Toronto: University of Toronto Press, 1987), p. 244.

BIBLIOGRAPHY

For an overview of the arts in Canada, consult Maria Tippett's *Making Culture: English-Canadian Institutions and the Arts Before the Massey Commission* (Toronto: University of Toronto Press, 1990). For the Laurier era, see as well Robert J. Lamb, *The Arts in Canada During the Age of Laurier: Papers from a Conference Held at the Edmonton Art Gallery* (Edmonton: University of Alberta Press, 1988). The *Dictionary of Canadian Biography*, vols. 9–14, has good biographical sketches of some of the major cultural figures of this period. For a contemporary commentary on the cultural divisions of French and English Canadians at the turn of the century, see André Siegfried, *The Race Question in Canada* (Toronto: McClelland & Stewart, 1966 [1907]). On the role of the Canadian Clubs in promoting culture, consult Russell R. Merifield, *Speaking of Canada: The Centennial History of the Canadian Clubs* (Toronto: McClelland & Stewart, 1993). An analysis of the tercentenary celebration of the founding of Quebec can be found in H.V. Nelles, *The Art of Nation-Building: Pageantry and Spectacle at Quebec's Tercentenary* (Toronto: University of Toronto Press, 1999).

Music is discussed in Helmut Kallmann's *A History of Music in Canada, 1534–1914* (Toronto: University of Toronto Press, 1960), and his edited *Encyclopedia of Music in Canada*, 2nd ed. (Toronto: University of Toronto Press, 1992); Timothy J. McGee's *The Music of Canada* (New York: W.W. Norton, 1985); and, for the early twentieth century, George A. Proctor, *Canadian Music of the Twentieth Century: An Introduction* (Toronto: University of Toronto Press, 1980). For a discussion of Canadian opera, see Rosemary Cunningham, *Bravo! The History of Opera in British Columbia* (Madeira Park, BC: Harbour Publishing, 2009). For Quebec, see as well Annette Lasalle-Leduc's *Music in French Canada* (Quebec: Ministry of Cultural Affairs, 1967).

On the history of painting, consult J. Russell Harper, *Painting in Canada: A History*, 2nd ed. (Toronto: University of Toronto Press, 1966); Dennis Reid, *A Concise History of Canadian Painting*, 2nd ed. (Toronto: Oxford University Press, 1988); Dennis Reid, *"Our Own Country Canada": Being an Account of the National Aspirations of the Principal Landscape Artists in Montreal and Toronto, 1860–1890* (Ottawa: National Gallery of Canada, 1980); Marylin McKay, *Picturing the Land: Narrating Territories in Canadian Landscape Art, 1500–1950* (Montreal: McGill-Queen's University Press, 2011); and Karen Stanworth, *Visibly Canadian: Imaging Canadian Collective Identities in the Canadas, 1820–1910* (Montreal/Kingston: McGill-Queen's University Press, 2015). For Quebec, see also Guy Viau, *Modern Painting in French Canada* (Quebec: Department of Cultural Affairs, 1967). David Karel's *Horatio Walker* (Quebec: Musée du Québec, 1987) looks at the life and paintings of this artist. For a review of the renowned sculptor Philippe Hébert, see Bruno Hébert, *Philippe Hébert* (Montreal: Fides, 1973); and Yves Lacasse, "Philippe Hébert," in the *Dictionary of Canadian Biography*, vol. 14, *1911–1920* (Toronto: University of Toronto Press, 1998), pp. 467–70. For a review of photography, see Roger Hall, Gordon Dobbs, and Stanley Triggs, *The World of William Notman: The Nineteenth Century Through a Master Lens* (Toronto: McClelland & Stewart, 1993). For architecture, consult Harold Kalman, *A Concise History of Canadian Architecture* (Toronto: Oxford University Press, 2000).

Literary history is documented in Carl F. Klinck, ed., *Literary History of Canada*, 2nd ed. (Toronto: University of Toronto Press, 1976); and Eugene Benson and William Toye, eds., *The Oxford Companion to Canadian Literature*, 2nd ed. (Toronto: Oxford University Press, 1997). For Quebec, see Guy Sylvestre, *Literature in French Canada* (Quebec: Department of Cultural Affairs, 1967). Interest in First Nations literature has led to several studies of Pauline Johnson: Sheila M.F. Johnson, *Buckskin and Broadcloth: A Celebration of E. Pauline Johnson—Tekahionwake 1861–1913* (Toronto: National Heritage Books, 1997); Veronica Strong-Boag and Carol Gerson, *Paddling Her Own Canoe: The Times and Texts of E. Pauline Johnson* (Toronto: University of Toronto Press, 2000); and Charlotte Gray, *Flint and Feather: The Life and Times of E. Pauline Johnson, Tekahionwake* (Toronto: Harper Flamingo, 2002). The life of Charles Chiniquy is discussed by Marcel Trudel in *Chiniquy* (Trois-Rivières: Éditions du bien public, 1955). On John William Dawson, see Susan Sheets-Pyenson, *John William Dawson: Faith, Hope, and Science* (Montreal/Kingston: McGill-Queen's University Press, 1996).

For the history of Canadian theatre in English-speaking Canada, see Murray D. Edwards, *A Stage in Our Past: English-Language Theatre in Eastern Canada from the 1790s to 1914* (Toronto: University of Toronto Press, 1968). For western Canada, consult E. Ross Stuart, *The History of Prairie Theatre: The Development of Theatre in Alberta, Manitoba and Saskatchewan 1833–1982* (Toronto: Simon and Pierre, 1984); and Eugene Benson and L.W. Conolly, eds., *The Oxford Companion to Canadian Theatre* (Toronto: Oxford University Press, 1989). For Quebec, see Elaine F. Nardocchio, *Theatre and Politics in Modern Québec* (Edmonton: University of Alberta Press, 1986); and Jean Hamelin, *The Theatre in French Canada* (Quebec: Department of Cultural Affairs, 1967). On the colourful performances of Sarah Bernhardt, see Ramon Hathorn's lecture to Canada House in London, *Sarah Bernhardt's Canadian Visits* (Leeds: University of Leeds for Canada House, 1992).

Canadian folklore is discussed in Edith Fowke's *Folklore of Canada* (Toronto: McClelland & Stewart, 1990) and *Canadian Folklore* (Toronto: Oxford University Press, 1988); and in Paul Rutherford's *A Victorian Authority: The Daily Press in Late Nineteenth-Century Canada* (Toronto: University of Toronto Press, 1982).

On popular culture, see Mary Vipond, *The Mass Media in Canada* (Toronto: James Lorimer & Co, 1989); and for cinema, George Melnyk, *One Hundred Years of Canada Cinema* (Toronto: University of Toronto Press, 2004). See also Clarence Karr, *Authors and Audience: Popular Canadian Fiction in the Early Twentieth Century* (Montreal/Kingston: McGill-Queen's University Press, 2000); and for the West, Frances W. Kaye, *Hiding the Audience: Viewing Arts and Arts Institutions on the Prairies* (Edmonton: University of Alberta Press, 2003). For women and print culture, see Carole Gerson, *Canadian Women in Print, 1750–1918* (Waterloo, ON: Wilfrid Laurier University Press, 2010).

For sport in Canada, see Alan Metcalfe, *Canada Learns to Play: The Emergence of Organized Sports, 1807–1914* (Toronto: McClelland & Stewart, 1987); and Colin Howell, *Blood, Sweat, and Cheers: Sport in the Making of Modern Canada* (Toronto: University of Toronto Press, 2001). See, as well, the relevant essays in Morris Mott, ed., *Sports in Canada: Historical Readings* (Mississauga, ON: Copp Clark Pitman, 1989). On hockey, see Daniel Mason, "The International Hockey League and the Professionalization of Ice Hockey, 1904–1907," *Journal of Sport History* 25(1) (Spring 1978): 1–17; William Houston, *Pride and Glory: 100 Years of the Stanley Cup* (Toronto: McGraw-Hill Ryerson, 1992); and Dan Diamond, ed., *The Official National Hockey League 75th Anniversary Commemorative Book* (Toronto: Firefly Books, 1991); John Chi-Kit Wong, ed. *Coast to Coast: Hockey in Canada to the Second World War* (Toronto: University of Toronto Press, 2009). On lacrosse, see Donald Fisher, *Lacrosse: A History of the Game* (Baltimore, MD: Johns Hopkins University Press, 2002). For women and sport, see M. Ann Hall, *The Girl and the Game: A History of Women's Sport in Canada* (Peterborough: Broadview Press, 2002); and Nancy Bouchier, *For the Love of the Game: Amateur Sport in Small-Town Ontario, 1838–1895* (Montreal: McGill-Queen's University Press, 2003). For a more general discussion of sport, popular culture, and immigration, see Gillian Poulter, *Becoming Native in a Foreign Land: Sport, Visual Culture, and Identity in Montreal, 1840–1885* (Vancouver: UBC Press, 2009).

For a discussion of an emerging middle-class culture in English-speaking Canada, see Lynne Marks, *Revivals and Roller Rinks: Religion, Leisure, and Identity in Late Nineteenth Century Small-Town Ontario* (Toronto: University of Toronto Press, 1996); and Keith Walden, *Becoming Modern in Toronto: The Industrial Exhibition and the Shaping of a Late Victorian Culture* (Toronto: University of Toronto Press, 1997). One of the best discussions of culture can be found in Ian McKay, *The Quest of the Folk: Antimodernism and Cultural Selection in Twentieth-Century Nova Scotia* (Montreal: McGill-Queen's University Press, 1994).

On working-class culture, the best source is Bryan Palmer, *Working-Class Experience: The Rise and Reconstitution of Canadian Labour 1880–1991*, 2nd ed. (Toronto: Butterworths, 1993). An insightful and now-classic article on taverns and working-class culture is Peter de Lottinville, "Joe Beef of Montreal: Working-Class Culture and the Tavern, 1869–1889," reprinted in R. Douglas Francis and Donald B. Smith, eds., *Readings in Canadian History: Post-Confederation*, 7th ed. (Toronto: Nelson Thomson, 2006), pp. 226–46. On the role of taverns, see Julia Roberts, *In Mixed Company: Taverns and Public Life in Upper Canada* (Vancouver: UBC Press, 2008).

Among the best studies of the impact of the dominant society on the First Nations are Katherine Pettipas, *Severing the Ties That Bind: Government Repression of Indigenous Religious Ceremonies on the Prairies* (Winnipeg: University of Manitoba Press, 1994); Brian E. Titley, *A Narrow Vision: Duncan Campbell Scott and the Administration of Indian Affairs in Canada* (Vancouver: University of British Columbia Press, 1986); and Edward Ahenakew, *Voices of the Plains Cree* (Toronto: McClelland & Stewart, 1973). For an overview, see Olive P. Dickason, *Canada's First Nations: A History of Founding Peoples from Earliest Times*, 3rd ed. (Don Mills, ON: Oxford University Press, 2002); J. R. Miller, *Skyscrapers Hide the Heavens: A History of Indian–White Relations in Canada*, 3rd ed. (Toronto: University of Toronto Press, 2000); and Arthur J. Ray, *I Have Lived Here Since the World Began* (Toronto: Key Porter, 1996).

WAR AND DEPRESSION, 1914–45

INTRODUCTION

The first half of the twentieth century was tumultuous and Canada did not escape the era's wrath. Until World War I, Canada was protected by the British Empire and had a limited military tradition. In contrast, the nation sent over 600,000 men into battle in the "Great War," of which 60,000 died. In World War II, the country sent 1 million, with 40,000 deaths. An even greater number returned home maimed in body and mind from both wars. Canadian soldiers, sailors, and pilots distinguished themselves in battle, contributing greatly to the Allied cause. Canada's national recognition was advanced considerably abroad.

World War I transformed Canada. Governments struggled to deal economically with a war of this magnitude and the disastrous implications plagued the Western world for decades, leading to the Great Depression. The war also altered the role of the state in society. The government intervened in the lives of Canadians to a greater extent than ever before.

With such large numbers of men fighting in Europe, women were called on to work outside the home. Women obtained the vote in these years but it was assumed that changes in gender roles were temporary. In a nation of recent immigrants, nativist sentiments seemed justified and the war was deeply divisive for Canadian society. The war also had a major impact on Canada's political system. A coalition government implemented military conscription, bitterly dividing English and French Canadians for decades to come.

When the war ended, Canada slid back into recession. It was not until the mid-1920s that prosperity seemed to be finally returning. The prosperity that led the decade to be dubbed "the Roaring Twenties" was short-lived. A new third party, the Progressives, appeared to challenge the two traditional parties and the political system. Internationally, meanwhile, Canada took control over its foreign relations and achieved constitutional autonomy from Great Britain.

The Great Depression of the 1930s represented a crisis in capitalism and demonstrated the need for change in the relationship between individuals and the state. New political parties emerged, desperate to find a solution to the economic turmoil. The economic crisis took the Canadian federal system to the breaking point.

The world was plunged into another war in 1939. Although the federal government attempted to avoid the threats to national unity by fighting a war of limited liability, for a time Canada became Britain's ranking ally. Once again, the nation was transformed. Women were again called on to work outside the home for the war effort. This time, however, the results were more long-lasting. The role of the state again increased, but the federal government demonstrated that it had learned valuable lessons from the experience of the Great War and the Depression. Internationally, Canada had to confront changing relations with Britain (the declining empire) and the United States (the rising empire). Canada moved into the position of a middle power in a world that was rapidly embracing multilateral relations but also a new "Cold War."

Chapter Ten

CANADA IN THE GREAT WAR

TIME LINE

1914	World War I begins
	Parliament passes War Measures Act
	First Division of the Canadian Expeditionary Force leaves for England
1915	Battle at Ypres Salient
	John McCrae writes "In Flanders Fields"
1916	Battle of the Somme
	Battle of Beaumont-Hamel
	"Bilingual" schools abolished in Manitoba
	Women in the four western provinces are the first to gain the vote
1917	Battle of Vimy Ridge
	Canadian Defence Force established
	Military Service Act (the conscription bill) becomes law
	Wartime Elections Act passed
	Election of Union government under Robert Borden
	Halifax explosion
	Creation of Canadian National Railways (CNR)
	"Temporary" income tax introduced
1918	Establishment of Department of Soldiers' Civil Re-establishment, the Women's Bureau, and the Food Board
	Union government imposes national prohibition
	Canadian soldiers enter Mons
	Armistice signed ending World War I
	Women over the age of 21 (except female status Indians and female Asians) get the right to vote
	Outbreak of Spanish flu epidemic

World War I was a watershed in Canadian history. No other event had such a profound impact on the nation. Between 1914 and 1918, in a conflict that was assumed to last only a few months, Canada sent an astonishing 625,000 men to the battlefields of Europe. It was an enormous contribution for a nation of only 8 million people. Despite having such a weak military tradition, the Canadian Expeditionary Force (CEF) fought impressively in a number of key battles, but at great human cost. Caught up in the technological transitions in warfare, the world witnessed human carnage on an unprecedented scale. Twentieth-century technological innovations may have drastically increased the killing power of the weaponry, but the war was led by a generation of officers trained in nineteenth-century warfare. One in ten of those who fought on the battlefields of Europe died in the service of their country; an even greater number were wounded in the deadly trench warfare. The numbers were even higher proportionately for Newfoundlanders: an estimated one out of four died. But war always represents failure. Despite a search for silver linings, the war was a tragedy.

During the war, the federal government in Canada intervened in the affairs of its citizens to an unprecedented degree. It regulated the production, distribution, sale, and consumption of such essential resources as coal, wood, and gas fuels; it nationalized such institutions and industries as the Canadian railways and the Canadian Wheat Board; it financed the war through a federal income tax and the sale of Victory Bonds; it enacted military conscription and the War Measures Act to intern "enemy aliens" in camps. But despite the government's attempts to deal with the unprecedented changes, the war was an economic disaster, not only to Canada but to the entire Western world. The ramifications were felt long after the guns went silent in 1918.

The war initially united Canadians but ultimately divided them. Prime Minister Borden established a Union government for a united war effort, but then immediately implemented conscription, thereby breaking his promises to Quebec and deeply dividing French and English Canadians for generations. In a nation of immigrants, nativism reared its ugly head, pitting

Crowds swarmed into downtown Calgary the night war was declared, August 4, 1914.
Source: *Calgary Herald.*

Colony → Nation

neighbour against neighbour. Women assisted the war effort through volunteer work, and by filling vacancies in factories and offices left by men who went overseas. When the war ended, however, women were expected to return to their traditional roles. The struggle to give women the vote and enforce prohibition were won during the war, but the impetus of the reform movement lost momentum. The Russian Revolution occurred in 1917 and brought the forces of class conflict to the forefront.

Despite Canada's impressive contributions to the war effort, the dominion continued to be treated as a colony of Britain. Canadian leaders gradually succeeded in bringing their troops under Canadian command, and insisted on a more active role in deciding imperial war policy. At the end of the conflict, they fought for Canadian independent participation in the peace conference and for membership in the newly formed League of Nations. Canada's path from colony to nation advanced as a result of the Great War but the cost was higher than any could have imagined.

Canada Goes to War

The Great War began as a struggle among the old empires of Europe. Tensions had been building for years, and the assassination of Archduke Ferdinand, heir to the Austro-Hungarian throne, by a young Serbian nationalist in June 1914, served as the spark that ignited the powder keg. The intricate network of alliances and agreements among the European powers pushed them into war. Austria attacked Serbia, an ally of Russia. Germany backed Austria, while France came to the defence of Russia. Britain, the ally of France—which in turn was allied to Russia—had promised to defend Belgium's neutrality. When Germany invaded Belgium, Britain declared war. As a member of the British Empire, Canada was automatically at war.

As former subjects of the Austro-Hungarian Empire, many "enemy aliens," most of them ethnic Ukrainians, faced internment. These men were interned at Castle Mountain, Banff National Park. In addition to losing their freedom during the war, they were put to work on public projects, such as the Banff golf course.

Source: Glenbow Archives/NA-1870-6.

Initially, caught up in a frenzy of patriotism and loyalty to the British Empire and fuelled by propaganda, Canadians united behind the war effort. When Prime Minister Robert Borden summoned Parliament for a special war session on August 18, he told a cheering House of Commons: "As to our duty, we are all agreed, we stand shoulder to shoulder with Britain and the other British Dominions in this quarrel." Throughout the country, loyal demonstrations occurred, involving impromptu parades, flag-waving, and, in the streets of Montreal, the singing of "La Marseillaise" and "Rule Britannia." Even the anti-imperialist Henri Bourassa was caught up in the emotional appeal and initially supported Canadian participation. Most believed that the Allies would achieve a quick victory by Christmas.

The war was presented to the populace in black-and-white terms: good versus evil; democracy versus tyranny; the Anglo-Saxon versus the "Hun." Canadians had to believe this was a just war; they had to believe they were sacrificing, fighting, and dying for a just cause. And to make the ultimate sacrifice, it had to be made clear who the enemy was and why he was so dangerous. Newspapers, magazines, and films reported on the war in a way that brought it home to the average Canadian citizen, and in such a way as to distance "us" from "them." But in a young, immigrant nation like Canada, the "enemy" was already "within the gates." The propaganda efforts led to ethnic divisions on the home front. Nativist sentiments already plaguing Canadian society increased; persecution of immigrant groups (termed "foreigners" and "enemy aliens") intensified. The war justified these bigoted views and the state turned them into policy.

When war was declared in 1914, Canada was completely unprepared. For years, Canadians debated their role in imperial and national defence. Since 1897, imperialists and autonomists, Conservatives and Liberals argued over whether Canada should build its own navy or whether it should provide funds directly to Britain. The imperial question dominated Canada's role in the Boer War at the turn of the century and led to the debate over the Naval Service Bill a decade later. But partisan squabbles in the federal government mired the issue in politics, and there it remained. By the eve of war, Canada had done nothing other than debate the issue.

When Britain declared war, the Canadian Parliament unanimously passed the War Measures Act. The act suspended civil liberties and provided the government with extraordinary powers, such as regulating areas of society deemed essential for the conduct of the war. The federal government required all those classified as "enemy aliens"—people who held citizenship in enemy countries, mostly German and Austro-Hungarian immigrants—to carry identity cards and report once a month to the local police or Royal North-West Mounted Police. Those considered dangerous were interned, as well as anyone who refused to register.

The Borden government established 24 internment camps, from Halifax to Nanaimo. In very basic camps, such as the one at Castle Mountain in Banff National Park, the internees worked for 25 cents a day for 6 days a week. The imprisoned labourers, mainly Ukrainians, helped to build roads, paths, and tourist sites such as the Banff golf course. Despite notification from the British Foreign Office in January 1915 that Ukrainians from Galicia and Bukovyna (the areas of the Ukraine under Austro-Hungarian rule) should be given preferential treatment as "friendly aliens," the internment of Ukrainians and some other eastern Europeans continued.

Among those interned was a Russian revolutionary who was taken off a Norwegian ship in Halifax Harbour while travelling from New York. After his release, Leon Trotsky joined Vladimir Lenin in Petrograd, Russia, to lead the Bolshevik Revolution. During his one-month detainment at Amherst, Nova Scotia, in April 1917, he preached revolution to the 800 internees. During the war, the Canadian government imprisoned about 8000 individuals. In 1918, a further order in council forbade the printing, publishing, or possession of any publication in an enemy language without a licence from the secretary of state.

The Canadian Expeditionary Force

Canada's permanent army in July 1914 numbered only 3000, with an additional 70,000 men in the militia. Their military training consisted of one or two nights at the local armoury, supplemented by an annual seven- or ten-day training period at summer camp. Canada's navy consisted of one seaworthy but antiquated British cruiser, the *Rainbow*, and two submarines purchased by British Columbia from the United States. As a result of Canadian participation in the Boer War over a decade earlier, the country still had a few trained officers with experience on the battlefield. The energetic but eccentric Sam Hughes, who had fought in South Africa, served as the minister of militia in Borden's Conservative government. He had worked to build up the volunteer sector of the Canadian militia between 1911 and 1913, and had seen to the construction of new armouries and drill halls.

When war was declared, tens of thousands of young men answered the call for volunteers. Some came forward convinced of the righteousness of the Allied cause while others responded on the basis of patriotism and duty; some looked for adventure while others were desperate for a job during a time of economic recession. Within two months, 30,000 Canadian volunteers were trained at Valcartier, a military camp 25 kilometres northwest of Quebec City. Hughes placed them into numbered battalions of about 1000 men, then into brigades, and finally into divisions to be sent overseas. Pleased by the enlistment results and anticipating a short war, Prime Minister Borden promised that he would not implement conscription.

The First Division of the Canadian Expeditionary Force, numbering approximately 36,000, sailed for England on October 3, 1914—at the time the largest convoy ever to cross the Atlantic. More than 70 percent of the troops, known as "Hughes's Boys," were recent British immigrants. Native-born Canadians of British stock made up 25 percent of the soldiers. Among the Force were 101 volunteer nurses.

A group of soldiers, many of them from Ontario First Nations, before going overseas in World War I. The photo was taken in the North Bay area.

Source: Archives of Ontario/Acc. no. 9164 S15159.

Canadian Patriotic Fund poster.

Source: Toronto Reference Library.

A "White Man's War"

From the beginning, the conflict was considered a "white man's war." As in other allied armies, the Canadian army discouraged visible minorities from enlisting. Their presence was seen as damaging and divisive to the *esprit de corps* necessary for a fighting force. When 50 African Canadians from Sydney, Nova Scotia, attempted to enlist, the recruiting officers told them, "This is not for you fellows, this is a white man's war." The men pressed for an African-Canadian battalion. Major-General Willoughby Gwatkin, Canada's chief of the General Staff, agreed, but only if the battalion was officered by white men and it was a manual labour, construction unit. Daniel Sutherland, a contractor from Nova Scotia experienced in railway construction, commanded the No. 2 Construction Battalion (Coloured), the only African-Canadian battalion in Canadian military history. The unit recruited from across the country, but the majority of its 700 members came from Nova Scotia. Nearly 600 of them went overseas to southern France, but on a separate transport ship to avoid "offending the susceptibility of other troops." They joined the Canadian Forestry Corps where they worked in the lumber camps.

Japanese Canadians also faced discrimination in their effort to enlist. When Canadian military authorities denied them the right to join regular units, the Canadian Japanese Association of Vancouver raised an exclusively Japanese unit. The 227 enlistees drilled at their own expense, but under British veteran and militia captain R.S. Colquhoun. Eventually 185 of them served overseas in different battalions.

First Nations men faced similar obstacles. The Canadian Militia Council forbade the enlistment of status Indians on the justification that "Germans might refuse to extend to them the privileges of civilized warfare." Still, they persisted. Sam Hughes permitted them to establish their own units as long as they were under the watchful eye of white officers who could cultivate their "natural" talents as fighters and marksmen. The 114th became an all-Aboriginal unit, but it was broken up upon arrival in England, its members dispersed to various battalions, where many ended up doing labour duty. A few joined the front lines. Corporal Henry (Ducky) Norwest, a Cree Métis from Alberta, became one of the most celebrated Canadian snipers of World War I. Francis Pegahmagabow, an Ojibwa from Parry Island in Georgian Bay, was awarded the Military Medal plus two bars for bravery in Belgium and France.

By 1917, the Canadian authorities, now desperate for all possible human power, lifted restrictions on the enlistment of visible minorities. In the end, a significant number enlisted: some 3500 First Nations (registered Indians under the Indian Act), several thousand Métis, over 1000 African Canadians, and several hundred Japanese Canadians. Unfortunately, they received little in return for their service. At war's end, they returned to Canada and the same racist society they had left.

Canadian troops trained on Salisbury Plain in southern England. That first winter of the war proved the wettest in years—over a 75-day period, only 5 days were dry. Heavy mists and occasional snow curtailed training. Inadequate army clothing contributed to illness and poor morale. Then, in February 1915, the 1st Canadian Division, as it became known, joined the British army under the command of Lieutenant General E.A.H. Alderson for action in northwestern Belgium (at Flanders) and adjacent France.

The Horrors of the Great War

The troops were woefully unprepared for what they faced on the battlefields of Europe. In many ways, the Great War was the first modern war. Technological changes transformed warfare. A vast array of new weapons were tested for the first time with devastating results. While repeating rifles and Gatling guns had been used in the Crimean and American Civil Wars, never had so many new technologies emerged in one conflict, including tanks, airplanes, mortars, grenades, machine guns, barbed wire, and poison gas. But the leadership had been trained in nineteenth-century tactics and weaponry. They were just as woefully unprepared to lead the troops into this twentieth-century war.

As early as October 1914, deadlock developed on the Western Front. Neither side could make a meaningful breakthrough. As a result of the stalemate and the rapidly mounting casualties caused by the new technologies, the armies had to dig down and create trenches to avoid enemy fire. The two opposing sides faced each other, across a narrow "No Man's Land," in deep trenches stretching from Switzerland to the North Sea. Time and time again, the two sides attempted to break the other's position; wave after wave of troops went "over the top" and charged the enemy lines. Casualties mounted, reaching numbers never before seen.

On the Western Front, all soldiers faced the same intolerable conditions: mud, vermin, rotten food, and the stench of rotting flesh. The soldiers spent hours digging trenches, tunnels, dugouts, and underground shelters, only to have them washed away by the rain and mud, or abandoned in haste. Then there was the noise:

> *It has been likened to an infernal orchestra made up of ear-splitting crashes from heavy artillery, the deeper roar of mined charges, the flailing crack of field pieces, the higher-pitched note of rifles, the ghastly staccato rattle of machine-guns, the shriek and wail of shells, and the insect zip and whine of bullets, but no words can ever describe it adequately.*[1]

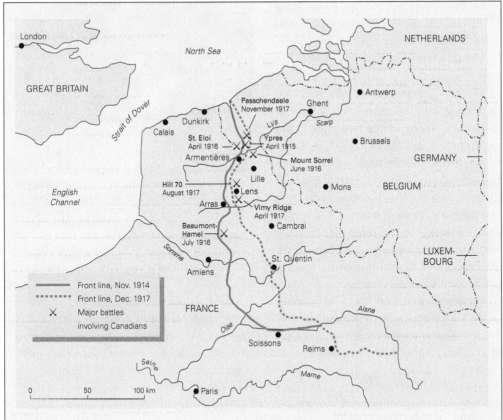

Canada at war, 1914–17. Minimal advances were made between 1914 and 1917, despite seven major battles involving Canadians.

Source: Based on Elizabeth Abbott, ed., *Chronicle of Canada* (Montreal: Chronicle Publications, 1990), p. 579.

A HISTORICAL PORTRAIT

Private Fraser

"I do make Oath that I will be faithful and bear true Allegiance to His Majesty George the Fifth, His Heirs and Successors, and that I will as in duty bound honestly and faithfully defend His Majesty, His Heirs and Successors, in Person, Crown and Dignity, against all enemies, and will observe and obey all orders of His Majesty, His Heirs and Successors, and of all the Generals and officers set over me. So help me God." With those words—repeated in every recruiting station by hundreds of thousands of Canadian volunteers—Donald Fraser, on November 14, 1914, enlisted in the 31st (Alberta) Battalion, Canadian Expeditionary Force. Aged 32, Private Fraser was older than most men in his battalion, but as a British immigrant, he shared a common background with the majority.

Fraser never explained why he decided to enlist. Although well educated in Scotland, he had drifted from job to job since coming to Canada in 1906, first as a farm labourer in Manitoba, then as a bank clerk in Calgary, and finally, on the eve of the war, as a clerk with a Vancouver trust company. He chose to return to Calgary to enlist, possibly because his friends were also enlisting and persuaded him to do so. Fraser was typical in that he had no previous military experience.

Fraser's battalion was equipped, trained in elementary military drill and discipline, and sent overseas to England in mid-May 1915. After four months of "drills and manoeuvres, trench digging ... courses of special instruction in bayonet fighting, grenade throwing, machine-gunnery, musketry, signalling and map reading," the battalion left on September 16 for France. By the end of the month the troops huddled in the trenches, "small,

A studio portrait of Private Donald Fraser, Canadian Expeditionary Force. Fraser enlisted with the 31st (Alberta) Battalion in November 1914 and served continuously until severely wounded at Passchendaele. His journal, first published in 1985, has proved an invaluable primary source for historians.

Source: Library and Archives Canada, Fraser, Donald, *The Diary of Private Fraser, 1914–1918, Canadian Expeditionary Force*, Victoria, Sono Nis Press, 1985, 334 p.

damp and cold and overrun with rats." The mud dominated many descriptions of conditions: "For want of sunshine and wind, it is impossible for the ground to dry up and after a while we learn that it is useless trying to keep the trenches passable. The rain loosens the earth and the sides cave in. With additional rain the bottom of the trenches become liquid mud which defies all efforts at drainage."

Fraser recalled one particular close scrape with death. He and four comrades were talking during an enemy shelling when

a report that sounded like a premature or a short made us bolt out of the way.... I rounded the end of the wall and threw myself flat behind it on the side nearest the line. At that moment the shell burst with a tremendous explosion on the other side of the sandbag wall where I was standing a second ago and not more than a yard away from where I lay. The report of the explosion dazed me and I was hit with all sorts of debris as they fell on me in their downward course. The concussion or whatever it is called created a terrific strain on the tissues. I felt as if I was being pulled apart, as if some unseen thing was tearing me asunder, particularly the top part of my body, and especially the head. I know I could not have stood a fraction more without bursting, the outward pull on the tissue was so immense.

Although wounded again at Passchendaele in late 1917, Fraser was one of the lucky ones: he survived, recovered, and received his honourable discharge. Of the 4500 officers and men from Private Fraser's battalion who served in World War I, nearly 1000 were killed.

In Calgary in 1919, Fraser married Caroline Mackintosh, a young woman he had known in Scotland, and they had a family. But Donald Fraser was never the same. According to his wife, "He [Donald] lost quite a bit of his strength and vigour, and thus led a quieter life than he ordinarily would have. Also, he was unable to travel any great distance without feeling unwell."

Private Donald Fraser died in 1946. His war diary was published and has been described as "one of the most vivid personal descriptions of trench life by a Canadian soldier."[1]

1   Reginald Roy, ed., *The Journal of Private Fraser, 1914–1918* (Victoria: Sono Nis Press, 1985).

A new horror was about to be added to the mix—chemical warfare. The Germans first used chlorine gas in an attempt to break the stalemate on April 22, 1915, at the Battle of Ypres in Belgium. Chlorine attacks the bronchial tubes, causing the membranes to swell, congesting the lungs, and preventing the intake of oxygen. The victims suffocated as they drowned in their own fluids. "A great wall of green gas about 15 or 20 feet high was on top of us," one officer described. "Captain McLaren gave an order to get handkerchiefs, soak them" —in urine, in hopes its ammonia would neutralize the chlorine— "and tie them around our mouths and noses." A British soldier later recalled what he saw when he and his contingent arrived to relieve the Canadians: "We stopped at a ditch at a first-aid clearing station. There were about 200 to 300 men lying in that ditch. Some were clawing their throats. Their brass buttons were green. Their bodies were swelled. Some of them were still alive. Some were still writhing on the ground, their tongues hanging out." Half of the men in surgeon John McCrae's brigade were killed or wounded. While waiting on the rear step of an ambulance for the wounded to arrive, he wrote a poem. "In Flanders Fields" became the most popular poem of the Great War and made the poppy flower the enduring symbol of those who died. But the use of chlorine, and even the more lethal mustard gas, was more of a psychological weapon. Its capacity to kill was limited, and countermeasures were quickly developed. Despite being outraged at the use of this horrific weapon, the British were using it by September 1915. The Geneva Protocol was signed in 1925 outlawing the use of poison gas in warfare.

At Ypres, the Canadians made their reputation by preventing a German breakthrough in the Allied lines that would have seen the Germans pushing toward the English Channel. But nearly 2000 Canadians lay dead, with another 3410 wounded and 775 taken prisoner, out of a total divisional fighting strength of 10,000. After Ypres, "there was no more bravado about an early victory over the Hun, no more fears of missing out on 'the fun.'"[2]

In 1915 and 1916, three more Canadian divisions joined the 1st Canadian Division in France. Lieutenant General Sir Julian Byng, a British regular officer, replaced Alderson as commander of the Canadian Corps. There was also a change in equipment. The Canadian-built Ross rifle, insisted upon by Sam Hughes, tended to jam in the difficult trench conditions. "The least thing would jam it," one soldier wrote, "—a speck of dust, a shower of rain, even a burst of rapid fire. Very often there was difficulty in loading. The Ross Rifle was a standing joke amongst the Imperial troops." In the spring of 1916, the Canadian Cabinet overruled Hughes and officially replaced the Ross rifle with the better-built British Lee-Enfield.

The Ross rifle affair highlighted the incompetence of Sam Hughes as minister of militia and defence. The governor general, the Duke of Connaught, once privately described the controversial and eccentric cabinet minister as a "conceited lunatic." Accused of corruption, of failure to attend to his departmental duties, and of incompetence in handling the administration of the war, Hughes had his responsibilities reduced by Prime Minister Borden. J.W. Flavelle, general manager of the William Davies Packing Company, took over the Imperial Munitions Board, which was responsible for producing munitions in Canada for Britain. By 1917, the board oversaw 60 factories and a quarter of a million workers who produced $2 million a day worth of shells, ships, fuses, and even airplanes. R.B. Bennett, a Calgary lawyer and Conservative member of Parliament, chaired the National Service Board, established in the fall of 1916 to increase recruiting. Sir George Perley, the high commissioner to Britain, took charge of the newly created Ministry of Overseas Military Forces to deal with the troops in Britain and at the war front. Finally, in November 1916, Sam Hughes was fired for openly criticizing the prime minister.

The State

As a result of the war, the federal government intervened in Canada's economic, social, and military affairs to an unprecedented degree. The role of the state increased throughout the early years of the twentieth century, but the war escalated the pace and justified the process. The nation had never been involved in such a conflict, and a "united war effort" demanded state control. Borden's reform of the civil service on the eve of the war helped make the transition easier. His government implemented regulations that raised the requirements for entry into the civil service. As well, the government in 1912 passed the Canadian Grain Act, which established the government-controlled Board of Grain Commissioners to supervise, inspect, and regulate grain sales. Thus, in 1917, when the Allied demands for Canadian wheat made it imperative for Canada to step up production and export, the government could intervene further without difficulty. Through the newly created Board of Grain Supervisors (after 1919 the Canadian Wheat Board), the government regulated all aspects of the production and distribution of wheat. Hectarage in wheat doubled, and the price per bushel increased by more than 50 percent. The move increased the reliance of the Prairie West on wheat production, made even more evident when the region was overlooked for munitions manufacturing or any form of manufacturing or industrial production. Thus, while towns and cities in other regions, especially central Canada, prospered from war contracts, western cities did not.

The government also regulated the production, distribution, sale, and consumption of coal, wood, and gas fuels. As military historian Desmond Morton notes, "Canadians learned to live with unprecedented government controls and involvement in their daily lives. Food and fuel shortages led to 'Meatless Fridays' and 'Fuelless Sundays.'"[3] The "boys" were making the ultimate sacrifice in the trenches; civilians on the home front were expected to do their share. Government regulations reminded Canadians of their need to contribute, whether on the war front or the home front. As well, the government nationalized two new transcontinental railways, the

Canadian Northern and the Grand Trunk Pacific. Both teetered on the edge of bankruptcy by 1915, when a royal commission recommended government takeover to avoid a total collapse, a possibility deemed unthinkable during wartime. Between 1917 and 1920, the Canadian government incorporated these railways into the publicly owned Canadian National Railways (CNR).

Such government intervention created resentment and accusations of regional favouritism. Western Canadians accused Flavelle's Imperial Munitions Board of favouring central Canadian firms. Maritimers complained of military ships being built in Quebec rather than in their ports. Workers resented the federal government's War Labour Policy, passed in 1918, which prohibited strikes and lockouts. They believed upper-class Canadians were not making the same sacrifices. Farmers and labourers demanded that wealth as well as manpower be conscripted for the war effort.

Financing the War

At the outbreak of war, the federal government depended on revenue from the tariff and the sale of federal bonds to finance the war effort. But as imports declined and as New York replaced London as the main underwriter of Canadian bonds, the government had to look for additional money. It sold "Victory Bonds," which proved to be immensely popular. More than 1 million Canadians purchased the bonds by war's end, generating close to $2 million in revenue. The government also introduced another important innovation: direct taxation. First it imposed a business-profits tax. Then, in 1917, it imposed the first federal income tax—3 percent for a family earning more than $3000 or an individual earning more than $1500. Ottawa promised, however, that the new tax would remain only for the duration of the war. While these new sources of revenue helped, costs continued to outdistance revenue, forcing the government to borrow vast sums at home and abroad, at high interest rates. The national debt increased fivefold, from $463 million in 1913 to $2.46 billion by 1918. Inflation spiralled out of control, and not just in Canada. The war was driving the Western nations into debt.

The increased cost of living hurt people on fixed incomes and cancelled the benefits workers received from increased wages. Workers joined trade unions in an effort to increase their bargaining power. The unions in turn staged strikes. Class conflict increased. The antagonism mounted as critics questioned the overall cause. This war was an imperial and capitalist war, rather than a war for democracy and freedom as portrayed through propaganda. As the struggle reached a stalemate in the trenches, and thousands of young men died over a few hundred yards of blasted earth, the absurdity was difficult to avoid. Critics pointed out that while it was the working classes who were paying the heaviest price, it was the elites who were profiteering through war contracts. Even if victory could be achieved, what was to be gained?

Women and the War

Women made major contributions to the war effort. Twenty-five hundred women served as nursing sisters in the Canadian Army Medical Corps, working overseas at station hospitals, on hospital ships, and on ambulance trains. Forty-three died. Margaret Macdonald, director of the army nursing sisters, received the Royal Red Cross and the Florence Nightingale Medal for her effort, while Matron Ethel Ridley was invested into the Order of the British Empire for her efforts as principal matron in France.

But women's main contribution came in the form of countless hours of unpaid labour through their work in voluntary organizations, including the Imperial Order Daughters of the Empire (IODE), Red Cross clubs, the Great War Veterans' Association, the Next-of-Kin Association, the YWCA, and the Women's Patriotic Leagues. They rolled bandages and knitted socks, mitts, sweaters, and scarves for the troops; they raised money to send cigarettes and candy overseas; and they

Canadian nursing sisters at 1st Canadian Field Hospital, Étaples, France. They are helping to clean up after a German shelling killed three nurses, June 1918.

Source: Library and Archives Canada/PA-3747.

marshalled support for the cause, not least by persuading wives and mothers to allow their men to enlist.

Amid the sacrifices of war, there was intense social pressure for those at home to do their part. Volunteering was a way to express patriotism, to mediate fear and grief, and to demonstrate worthiness. Women headed the Canadian Patriotic Fund, established in 1914 to assist families of soldiers overseas. They lobbied for mothers' pensions, day nurseries, and health inspection. By 1918, the government established federal agencies, such as the Women's Bureau and the Food Board, to assist them in the war effort. Children were encouraged to grow "victory gardens" to supplement food production.

Women entered the workforce in large numbers to ease the wartime labour shortage. On farms, in factories, and in offices, women filled positions previously occupied by men. In summertime, the YWCA recruited hundreds of female volunteers in the cities and towns to help on farms. The Women's Canadian Club organized a Women's Emergency Corps to recruit women for the munitions-production industries. In its first year of operation, more than 35,000 Ontario and Quebec women signed up.

In wartime industries, however, gender discrimination remained, including lower wages for women, lack of union support, and inadequate daycare facilities. Still, tens of thousands of women filled jobs previously closed to them, even in such male-dominated industries as railways and steel production. A number of women used their new bargaining position to raise social issues such as women's suffrage, child labour, and conditions in jails and asylums. But the war did not lead to increased gender equality in Canadian society. Although gender roles were transformed during the war, the gains made by women were temporary. Even then, the gains made were not evenly distributed but were further mitigated by ethnicity and class.

Fighting on the Battlefields of Europe

On June 1, 1916, Canadian soldiers fought in the Battle of Mont Sorrel in the Ypres Salient, a small triangular area around Ypres, Belgium. The Germans began an intense artillery barrage that enabled them to break through the Allied lines to capture Mont Sorrel. Brigadier-General Arthur Currie led the First Division troops that began the counterattack. By June 13, the Canadian Corps had recaptured all that had been lost to the Germans, a great victory but at the loss of 8000 men in just 12 days of fighting.

A month later, Canadian and Newfoundland soldiers joined British and French soldiers in the massive but ill-conceived Battle of the Somme against heavily fortified German positions. On July 1, the first day of the "Big Push" or Grand Assault at Beaumont-Hamel, France, the Newfoundland Regiment suffered 684 casualties—85 percent of the unit. It was the greatest single disaster in Newfoundland's history, and the heaviest loss by any army on any single day in the history of the Great War. Among the casualties was Owen Steele, a 29-year-old lieutenant from St. John's whose published diary is the best account of the Newfoundland experience in the first two years of the war, first at Gallipoli—the regiment's baptism of fire—and then at the Battle of the Somme. Britain recognized Newfoundland's efforts by awarding its regiment the title "Royal." At the end of the war, the people of Newfoundland purchased the land at Beaumont-Hamel, and erected a statute of a lone bull caribou, the regiment's emblem. For Newfoundlanders, the battle, commemorated annually on July 1, came to represent what Vimy Ridge later did for many Canadians.

Canadian soldiers made their greatest contribution to the Battle of the Somme in the assault on the Regina Trench, a shallow ditch on the outskirts of the French town of Courcelette. The Royal 22nd Regiment, the "Vandoos," led the attack. According to their commanding officer, Lieutenant-Colonel Thomas Tremblay: "If hell is as bad as what I have seen at Courcelette, I would not wish my worst enemies to go there." After a week of fierce fighting and heavy casualties, the Canadians captured the Regina Trench and the town of Courcelette. This battle was one of the last—and few—victories in the infamous Battle of the Somme, which lasted over two and a half months and resulted in 1 million casualties in all. Twenty-four thousand of those casualties were Canadians.

Canada's finest hour came in the Battle of Vimy Ridge. On Easter Monday, April 9, 1917, 70,000 Canadian soldiers under the command of Julian Byng, along with British units, made a major attack against the German-held ridge outside the town of Vimy, France. Earlier in the war, both the British and French armies, with heavy losses, failed to dislodge the Germans. This time, the Canadians took the ridge. A Paris newspaper described Vimy as "Canada's Easter gift to France." In an editorial headlined "Well Done Canada," the New York *Tribune* wrote that "every American will feel a thrill of admiration and a touch of honest envy at the achievement of the Canadian troops.... No praise of the Canadian achievement can be excessive." British Prime Minister David Lloyd George recalled in his memoirs: "The Canadians played a part of such distinction ... that thenceforth they were marked out as storm troops; for the remainder of the war they were brought along to head the assault in one great battle after another." The cost that day for such praise and national honour was devastating: 3598 killed and 7004 wounded. In years to come, the victory at Vimy Ridge became a symbolic badge of national pride for Canadians.

Canada's Enlistment/Casualty Rate, 1917

MONTH	ENLISTMENTS	CASUALTIES
January	9,194	4,396
February	6,809	1,250
March	6,640	6,161
April	5,530	13,477
May	6,407	13,457
June	6,348	7,931
July	3,882	7,906
August	3,177	13,232
September	3,588	10,990
October	4,884	5,929
November	4,019	30,741
December	3,921	7,476
Total	**64,339**	**122,946**

Source: From Fielding/Evans. *Canada: Our Century, Our Story,* 1E. © 2001 Nelson Education Ltd. Reproduced by permission: www.cengage.com/permissions.

Cyril Barraud, The Stretcher-Bearer Party, *about 1918. The stretcher bearers administered essential first aid before transporting the wounded. In the background soldiers carry duckboard, which they used to bridge trenches and to provide a secure footing in the mud.*

Source: Cyril Barraud, *The Stretcher-Bearer Party*, AN: 19710261-0019, Beaverbrook Collection of War Art, © Canadian War Museum (CWM).

Canadians and Newfoundlanders also served in the air and on the sea. Canada did not have an air force of its own, but 2500 pilots, trained in Canada by the Royal Flying Corps after 1917, joined the Royal Air Force (RAF). A number became high-scoring "aces," such as British Columbia's Raymond Collishaw, Manitoba's Billy Barker, Ontario's Roy Brown (credited with shooting down the notorious Baron von Richthofen—the "Red Baron"—in April 1918), and the legendary Billy Bishop, who was credited with shooting down 72 German fighters, earning him a Victoria Cross. But casualties were high. As the British never issued parachutes in World War I, there were no escapes from burning or disabled aircraft. The airplanes, too, were very flimsy; more pilots died in crash landings than in the air. Canadians wanting to serve at sea joined the Royal Canadian Navy, under the command of the British Royal Navy. Some 8800 Canadians and 200 Newfoundlanders joined. Among their duties was the patrolling of Canadian and Newfoundland waters against German U-boats (submarines), another Great War "innovation."

"Invite Us to Your Councils"

As the war progressed, Canadian politicians demanded a greater voice in Britain's war policy. At the outset of the war, the British government treated Canada and the other dominions as colonial subordinates, neglecting to consult them about war strategy or even to keep them informed of developments. When Prime Minister Borden first requested a stronger voice for Canada, Bonar Law, the colonial secretary (who by chance had been born in New Brunswick) replied curtly: "I fully recognize the right of the Canadian government to have some share of the control in a war in which Canada is playing so great a part. I am, however, not able to see any way in which this could be practically done."

When David Lloyd George became British prime minister in December 1916, he found a way. With the dominions and colonies contributing and sacrificing so much, some form of consultation in the war effort was desirable. He invited the dominion prime ministers to London to meet as an Imperial War Cabinet, a group consisting of the British War Cabinet and dominion representation. There, in March 1917, for the first time, Borden learned about the Allied position, discussed strategy, and, most important, became involved in the decision-making process.

The Imperial War Conference met simultaneously with the Imperial War Cabinet. The representatives passed a host of resolutions, one of which recognized in theory the equality of the dominions with one another and with Britain. It stated that Britain and the dominions agreed that their new constitutional status "should be based upon a full recognition of the dominions as autonomous nations of an Imperial Commonwealth." Only in the years following the war, however, did this symbolic recognition become official policy.

Borden also gradually replaced British senior officers with Canadian commanders. In June of 1917, Arthur Currie, the commander of the First Canadian Infantry Division, was appointed commander of the entire Canadian Corps.

Recruitment

With casualties mounting, the federal government was forced to step up its recruitment drive. On the basis of the impressive volunteer effort, however, the prime minister remained confident. In his 1916 New Year's Day address, Borden announced his "sacred promise" that Canada would send a total of 500,000 to the war front, double the current numbers. And initially, it appeared that the government could honour its commitment. In January alone, nearly 30,000 volunteers enlisted. By June 1916, total wartime recruitments numbered over 300,000. Then recruitment dropped off dramatically. In summer, young men were needed to work on farms across Canada. Munitions factories in wartime were also in need of more workers. The government responded by establishing the National Service Board with a mandate to "determine whether the services of any man of military age are more valuable to the state in his present occupation than in military duties and either to permit or forbid his enlistment." The government assigned registration cards to every male of military age. The NSB concluded that 475,000 potential recruits existed.

The government next established the Canadian Defence Force in the spring of 1917. This force was designed to get men who opposed fighting overseas to sign up for home defence. They would replace those already in uniform who were willing to serve on the war front. But as the war dragged on, and casualties mounted, the bogey man of conscription would not go away. This last, desperate attempt to get more troops without conscription failed. In the first month of operation, fewer than 200 signed up for home defence.

On June 10, 1916, the 102nd Battalion embarked for overseas from Comox, Vancouver Island. The whole Courtenay–Comox community came to the harbour to see them off.

Source: Courtenay and District Museum and Archives/ P215-1141.

National Disunity

Public pressure for conscription increased. As voluntary enlistment dried up, complaints arose about those groups who appeared reluctant to give their full support to the war effort. The pressures within Canadian society for every one to do their "duty" intensified. Seemingly able-bodied young men who were not serving in the military were under intense scrutiny and were often labelled "shirkers." Those whose loved ones were making the ultimate sacrifice found it unacceptable when they came across those who were not. These pressures further fractured a society already cracking under ethnic and regional divisions. Once again, the fault lines that divided French and English Canadians were clearly exposed. While Quebec was initially caught up in the emotion and propaganda when war broke out, that enthusiasm and support waned as it became clear the conflict would not end quickly. It waned further as English Canada increasingly scrutinized Quebec's contributions and enlistment numbers, and as calls for conscription grew louder. Increasingly the war was viewed as an imperial war that was alien and remote for French Canadians. They would fight to defend Canada, and even Britain, but they would not be forced to go and fight to defend the Empire.

In addition, the military was viewed as an English-Canadian organization. Few of the officers at the Royal Military College in Kingston (the training school for military officers) were French-speaking and English remained the sole language of instruction. In Quebec, an Anglophone elite headed the recruitment effort. Sam Hughes did little to encourage French-Canadian enlistment. He placed French Canadians in English-speaking units and seldom appointed or promoted Quebeckers to the rank of officer. Initially, apart from the one French-language battalion, the "Vandoos" (the Royal 22nd Regiment of Quebec), English was the language of the army.

The Ontario Schools Question

The ethnic divisions exacerbated by the war also took the form of another schools question. This time the controversy arose in Ontario. By 1910, French Canadians, who had been moving into northern and eastern Ontario since the late nineteenth century, made up nearly 10 percent of the province's population. These Franco-Ontarians appealed to the provincial government to protect their bilingual schools.

The schools came under attack from both the Orange Order and Irish Catholics on the justification that they were of poor quality, but in reality it was because they were French. The Orange Order believed that the use of French in schools undermined the unity of Canada. Irish Catholics feared that language concessions to French Catholics would give French Canadians control of the separate-school system. Irish Catholics favoured Catholic—but not bilingual—schools. In this regard, the Ontario Schools Question (unlike the previous three) was more about language than religion. Bishop Michael Fallon of London, Ontario, led the Irish Catholic opposition. He viewed the bilingual school system as one that "teaches neither English nor French, encourages incompetency, gives a prize to hypocrisy, and breeds ignorance."

James Whitney, the Ontario premier, appointed a commission to investigate the complaints about poor educational standards. The commissioners pointed out the inadequate training of many teachers in the schools but stopped short of making any recommendations to solve the problem. In 1912, the Whitney government implemented "Regulation 17," which made English the official language of instruction and restricted French to the first two years of elementary school. It also established a commission to enforce its policy. Both the government and opposition, apart from the handful of French-speaking members, agreed with the policy. In 1913, Whitney amended Regulation 17 to permit French as a subject of study for one hour a day. Franco-Ontarians took the government to court on the ruling. While waiting for the Judicial Committee of the Privy Council to deliberate, both sides dug in.

The Franco-Ontarian community received support in Quebec. At the Guigues school in Ottawa, an "army" of French-speaking mothers, brandishing long hatpins, stood ready to prevent any entry by authorities to remove the bilingual teachers. In Quebec, Henri Bourassa denounced the Ontario government as more Prussian than the Prussians. French Canadians need not go to Europe to fight the enemy; it resided next door. Bourassa carried his message into Ontario. But wartime emotions were running high. In Ottawa, for example, an army sergeant climbed up on the platform during Bourassa's speech at the Russell Theatre and insisted that he wave the Union Jack. In the momentary hush, Bourassa replied, "I am ready to wave the British flag in liberty, but I shall not do so under threats." The curtain fell as the crowd rushed the stage. Bourassa escaped through a back door and finished his speech for friends and newspaper reporters in the lobby of the neighbouring Château Laurier hotel.

The Ontario Schools Question dragged on for years, during which time Franco-Ontarians were deprived of schooling in their own language. Not until 1927 did the Ontario government find a solution: each school designated for bilingual education was considered on its merits by a departmental committee.

The wartime hysteria poisoned relations among ethnic groups. Whereas prior to the war Germans were considered ideal immigrants, now they were vilified as "blood-crazed madmen." The Canadian propaganda machine, through newspaper editorials, books, advertisements, movies, songs, and church sermons, ensured that this image of the enemy prevailed. It also presented the counter-image of the Allies, and especially the Canadian soldiers, as brave and noble warriors. Such propaganda played out in various ways. In Berlin, Ontario, the city government held a plebiscite on whether to change the name of this city. Although over two-thirds of the city's population was of German descent, it was decided, by a narrow vote, to rename the city "Kitchener," after the British military hero who drowned at sea on June 5, 1916.

The Conscription Crisis

In the spring of 1917, while attending a meeting of the Imperial War Cabinet in London, Prime Minister Borden visited Canadian soldiers at the front and in British hospitals. The desperate situation and the British pressure on Canada to increase its commitment of men convinced the prime minister to break his promise not to introduce conscription for overseas military service. He informed his cabinet of the decision. His Quebec ministers warned that conscription would "kill them and the party for 25 years" in the province, but that they would stand with him.

Borden favoured a coalition government of Conservatives and Liberals as the best means to introduce compulsory service, so he approached Wilfrid Laurier, leader of the Liberal Party, about the possibility. Laurier faced a dilemma. While he agreed with the need for a coalition government for the war's duration, he opposed a union government that would introduce conscription, which neither he nor his Quebec followers favoured. Laurier realized the consequences: Quebec would be delivered to the nationalists under Henri Bourassa. But coalition and conscription held strong appeal among English Liberals. By not forming a union government, the Liberal Party would be split. "I oppose this bill," he warned when the Conservatives introduced the Military Service Act in Parliament, "because it has in it the seeds of discord and disunion, because it is an obstacle and bar to that union of heart and soul without which it is impossible to hope that this Confederation will attain the aims and ends that were had in view when Confederation was effected."

Opposition to Conscription

The Military Service Act, the official title of the conscription bill, became law in July 1917, although recruitment did not get under way until January 1918, after the election of a coalition government. Throughout the summer of 1917, anti-conscriptionist riots broke out in Montreal. Crowds marched through the streets yelling "*À bas Borden*" (Down with Borden) and "*Vive la révolution*" (Long live the revolution). Soldiers passing through Quebec in the winter of 1917–18 were pelted with rotten vegetables, ice, and stones when they taunted French-Canadian youth for not being in uniform. More riots followed in the spring of 1918, upon the actual implementation of conscription. The most serious riot, an armed clash in Quebec City on the Easter weekend, left four French-Canadian civilians dead and ten soldiers wounded.

Opposition to conscription did not come only from Quebec. Many farmers resented their sons' forced departure from the farm, where they contributed to the war effort through food production. Many workers saw military conscription as the first step toward the hated compulsory industrial service, forcing them to remain at one job for the war's duration. Labour leaders became increasingly critical of the war and conscription as an imperialist and capitalist struggle. Both farmer and labour groups demanded the "conscription of wealth," heavier taxes on the rich, and the nationalization of banks and industries to ensure that financiers and businesspeople made the same sacrifice.

Pacifist groups, such as the Quakers, Mennonites, Hutterites, and Doukhobors, opposed war as inherently evil and immoral. Many of these "conscientious objectors" settled in the Canadian West on the promise given by Queen Victoria that they would never be forced to serve in the military. They upheld their beliefs despite the social pressures, the persecution, and being branded "slackers."

Others opposed war as a wasteful and destructive means of settling world problems. The Canadian Women's Peace Party, forerunner of the Women's International League for Peace and Freedom, championed peace under the leadership of Laura Hughes (cousin of Sam Hughes) and Alice Chown (niece of S.D. Chown, superintendent of the Methodist Church and an ardent supporter of the war). They advocated a nonviolent struggle at home rather than war abroad as a means to reform society in order to root out the inherent causes of violence and war.

Slander!

That man is a slanderer who says that
The Farmers of Ontario
will vote with
**Bourassa, Pro-Germans,
Suppressors of Free Speech and Slackers**

Never!

They Will Support Union Government
Citizens' Union Committee

An ad placed in The Farmer's Advocate *December 13, 1917, by the "Citizens' Union Committee." The federal election of December 1917 was one of the most divisive in Canadian history as a result of the implementation of the Military Service Act, or conscription bill, that past summer.*

Source: Courtesy University Archives, Killam Memorial Library, Dalhousie University.

Union Government and the Election of 1917

Despite Laurier's refusal to join a coalition government, Borden forged ahead. He realized that the majority of Liberals were in favour of the scheme. A number of prominent English-Canadians Liberals, at both the federal and provincial levels, abandoned Laurier—including Alberta premier Arthur Sifton (Clifford's brother) and Newton W. Rowell, leader of the Liberal opposition in Ontario—to join the Union government. Then Borden dissolved Parliament and called an election.

The formation of a Union Party consisting of Conservatives and the majority of Liberals was guaranteed victory. But Prime Minister Borden was taking no chances. Before dissolving Parliament, the Unionists implemented two bills to strengthen their chances at the polls. Realizing that soldiers were likely to support conscription, the Military Voters Act enfranchised all members of the armed forces, no matter how long or short a time they had lived in Canada. As further manipulation, the governing party could use the soldiers' vote in whatever constituency it wished, thereby providing victories in tightly contested ridings. Seemingly acting on the pressures for women's suffrage, the Wartime Elections Act gave the vote to Canadian women who were mothers, wives, sisters, or daughters of servicemen (this did not apply to female relatives of status Indian servicemen), but denied the vote to conscientious objectors and to naturalized Canadians from enemy countries who had settled in Canada after 1902. Arthur Meighen, the solicitor general, reasoned that these aliens had been banned from enlisting and so should not have the right to vote. He also realized that new Canadians tended to vote Liberal. In one fell swoop, the federal government gave the vote to certain women while taking it away from certain ethnic groups. It was one of the most blatant examples of electoral manipulation the country ever witnessed.

Both the Unionists and the Liberals (the "Laurier Rump") fought the election largely along cultural lines. A Unionist election poster claimed that a vote for Laurier was a vote for Bourassa, the Kaiser, and the Germans. A group of Union supporters issued a map of Canada with Quebec in black, the "foul blot" on the country. On the Sunday before the election, an estimated three-quarters of the Protestant ministers across Canada responded to a Unionist circular, appealing for support of the Union Party in their sermons.

In Quebec, political leaders painted conscriptionists as a greater danger to the country than the Germans. Bourassa and the nationalistes argued that Canada had done enough for the war. "Every Canadian who wishes to combat conscription with an effective logic," Bourassa declared, "must have the courage to say and to repeat everywhere: No Conscription! No Enrolment!"

The outcome of the election proved predictable. The Unionists won 153 seats to the Liberal's 82. The Union Party won two-thirds of the constituencies outside of Quebec but only 3 seats, all in English-speaking ridings, in the province. Ninety percent of the soldiers' vote went to the Union government. The federal government was now literally an English-Canadian government. The divisions within the nation were visible for all to see.

Shortly before the 1917 election, the citizens of Halifax experienced the impact of the war in an immediate and devastating way. Early in the morning of December 6, 1917, a massive explosion occurred in Halifax harbour when a Belgian relief ship, the *Imo*, collided with a French munitions ship, the *Mont Blanc*. In an instant, part of the city of Halifax was destroyed, over 1600 people were killed, 9000—nearly one person in five—were injured, and some 20,000 were left

The view from Halifax's waterfront after the great explosion caused by the collision of a Belgian vessel with a French munitions ship, December 6, 1917. The blast, the subsequent tidal wave, and the raging fire killed over 1600 people and injured 9000, including 200 blinded by flying glass.

Source: Library and Archives Canada/C-19951.

without adequate shelter for the winter, from the blast itself, or from the resulting fires and tidal wave. It would take months for the people of Halifax to rebuild their city. Until the explosion of the atom bomb on Hiroshima in 1945, the Halifax explosion was likely the largest non-natural explosion in history, certainly in a city.

The War and Social Reform

The war justified and advanced the cause of social reform. Reformers argued that just as the troops fought for a noble cause on the battlefront, so should those at home—against materialism, alcoholism, and corruption. It was easier to argue against these vices during wartime, at a time when every citizen was expected to sacrifice and do his or her duty. Time spent in leisurely pursuits was time wasted. Grain spent on alcohol was a poor use of resources. Social evangelicals saw the war as the final struggle for bringing God's kingdom to earth. As superintendent S.D. Chown of the Methodist Church told a conference on "The Church, the War and Patriotism," "the war is a divine challenge to build the Tabernacle of God amongst men."

Women's Suffrage and Prohibition

Women's suffrage and prohibition both gained support during the war. Women reformers argued that men's aggressive nature caused the worldwide cataclysm. If women had the right to vote, wars would cease. They also pointed out the inconsistency of fighting for democracy abroad while denying women the democratic right to vote at home. In 1916, the four western provinces granted women the right to vote in provincial elections. Ontario followed in 1917, Nova Scotia in 1918, New Brunswick in 1919, Prince Edward Island in 1922, and Quebec in 1940.

Federally, the franchise came in three stages: the Military Voters Act of 1917 awarded the vote to women serving in the armed forces or as nurses in the war; the Wartime Elections Act extended voting privileges to women, aged 21 years and over, who were close relatives of servicemen overseas; and finally, in 1918, all women, recognized as British citizens in Canada, over the age of 21, gained the right to vote federally. Still excluded from the franchise were status Indians, Asians, and conscientious objectors, including Mennonites and Hutterites.

The war also helped the cause of prohibition, at least temporarily. Prohibitionists equated their struggle with that of the men at the front. They criticized human and material resources being wasted to make liquor at this time of critical shortage. Their first victory came in 1915, when the Saskatchewan Liberal government closed all bars, saloons, and liquor stores. Immediately, this move brought liquor under the control of provincially operated outlets. Alberta went further by endorsing outright provincial prohibition later the same year. Manitoba followed in early 1916. By the end of 1917, every provincial government except Quebec had implemented prohibition legislation. In 1918, the newly elected federal Union government imposed prohibition on Quebec. Within a week of his electoral victory in December 1917, Prime Minister Borden moved to prohibit the manufacture, importation, and transportation of any beverage containing more than 2.5 percent alcohol.

WHERE HISTORIANS DISAGREE

Women and Reform

Historians have debated the primary motivations underlying the women's movement. The first historians to write on the subject in the 1960s and early 1970s argued that women reformers sought only the right to vote—women's suffrage—believing that political equality would bring about an era of social reform. This narrow focus on the ballot box seemed to explain why the movement for reform apparently died out so rapidly in the 1920s, once women's suffrage had been achieved.

Some historians viewed women's reform as part of a greater "progressive reform" movement that went well beyond a concern for enfranchisement. In his introduction to a reprint of Catharine L. Cleverdon's classic study, *The Woman Suffrage Movement in Canada*, Ramsay Cook linked women's reform to the larger social gospel movement. "The suffragists were a part of a more general, middle-class reform movement that was concerned to remove a wide range of injustices and evils that afflicted the country."[1] Other historians questioned this idealized image of women reformers motivated purely by religious zeal. Veronica Strong-Boag argued that power, fame, and influence motivated them, at least those associated with the influential National Council of Women of Canada: "The female relatives of Canada's powerful men, energized by a changing external environment and by their own recent access to higher education and the professions, had few formal ways of expressing their complementary desires for national leadership and influence."[2] These middle-class women reformers worried more about their own position of power in society than about the disadvantaged.

Carol Bacchi applied the feminist theories of the 1980s to the leaders of the suffrage movement in the 1910s, and found the suffragists wanting.[3] They were middle-class reformers more than they were feminists, and as such were more conservative than radical in outlook. They succeeded in getting the vote for women, according to Bacchi, only because men in positions of power at the time realized that giving women the right to vote would not upset the status quo.[4]

Margot Iris Dudly examined the women's suffrage movement in Newfoundland.[5] She discovered a group of women reformers who crossed class lines and even religious divisions between Catholics and Protestants, and who allied themselves with the International Alliance of Women, based in London, England. Her study brought into question the assumption that the women's suffrage movement in Canada was middle-class, Protestant, and narrowly national.

Some historians have concentrated on the 1920s to see whether the women's reform movement indeed died out after political emancipation. Linda Kealey and Joan Sangster studied a group of "radical women" in the 1920s to show that, for these women, left-wing politics became the means to achieve real change, something that was not possible in the more conservative social-reform movement.[6] Nevertheless, these women had to adopt male tactics and abandon the "private sphere" in order to succeed in the traditionally male-dominated "public sphere."

Veronica Strong-Boag re-entered the debate to argue that the real struggle for reform did not take place in politics—in the public sphere—but rather in a highly politicized private sphere. "Theirs was the feminism of the workplace, day-to-day life. It was not for the most part an organized movement as the campaign for enfranchisement had been, but it flowed from a similar awareness of women's oppression and a desire to end it."[7]

Linda Kealey appealed for a broader definition of "public" and "political" in dealing with women reformers to include "the home, the neighbourhood, and the community, as well as ... the union, the party, or the workplace."[8] She argued that some socialist women reformers were concerned with women workers as wage earners or working-class wives and mothers, while others advocated a radical transformation of the industrial capitalist system. In either case, they succeeded in bringing working-class women's issues into the public domain, despite opposition from men and even middle-class female reformers. Janice Newton demonstrated how Canadian women reformers within the socialist movement rejected the middle-class obsession of the suffragists to get the vote and instead worked for equality of working-class women through such organizations as the Canadian Socialists League, the Socialist Party of Canada, and the Social Democratic Party.[9]

Monda Halpern has examined social reform among Ontario farm women. She argues that farm women spoke the language of "social feminism," which she defines as "informed by domestic community needs and values." She identifies those values as nurturing, cooperation, love, and peace, ones that were closely allied with maternal feminism and cultivated through farm women's roles as wives and mothers. According to Halpern, farm women applied these values in the public domain to such success that they challenged the patriarchal system and values, and in the end had a greater impact on social reform than the equity feminists, such as the suffragists.[10]

Nancy Christie has rejected the notion that the spirit of social reform diminished after World War I. In arguing against the claim that religious institutions entered a period of decline, Christie demonstrated that the 1920s were not a "wasteland of reform activism."[11] She also argued against the separate spheres (public/private) model, and called into question the existence of the "private" as a category, because family and household spilled over into the community and the wider civic culture.[12]

1   Ramsay Cook, "Introduction," in Catharine L. Cleverdon, *The Woman Suffrage Movement in Canada* (Toronto: University of Toronto Press, 1950; rep. 1974), p. xvii.

2   Veronica Strong-Boag, *The Parliament of Women: The National Council of Women of Canada, 1893–1929* (Ottawa: Canadian Museum of Civilization, 1976), p. 410.

3   Carol Bacchi, *Liberation Deferred? The Ideas of the English Canadian Suffragists, 1877–1918* (Toronto: University of Toronto Press, 1983).

4   But see Ernest Forbes, "The Ideas of Carol Bacchi and the Suffragists of Halifax," *Atlantis*, 10(2) (Spring 1985): 119–26.

5   Margot Iris Dudley, "The Radius of Her Influence for Good: The Rise and Triumph of the Women's Suffrage Movement in Newfoundland, 1909–1925," in Linda Kealey, ed., *Pursuing Equality: Historical Perspectives on Women in Newfoundland and Labrador* (St. John's: Institute of Social and Economic Research, Memorial University, 1993).

6   Linda Kealey and Joan Sangster, *Beyond the Vote: Canadian Women and Politics* (Toronto: University of Toronto Press, 1989).

7   Veronica Strong-Boag, "Pulling in Double Harness or Hauling a Double Load: Women, Work and Feminism on the Canadian Prairies," *Journal of Canadian Studies*, 21 (Fall 1986): 34.

8   Linda Kealey, *Enlisting Women for the Cause: Women, Labour, and the Left in Canada, 1890–1920* (Toronto: University of Toronto Press, 1988), p. 10.

9   Janice Newton, *The Feminist Challenge to the Canadian Left, 1900–1918* (Montreal/Kingston: McGill-Queen's University Press, 1995).

10 Monda Halpern, *And on That Farm He Had a Wife: Ontario Farm Women and Feminism, 1900–1970* (Montreal/Kingston: McGill-Queen's University Press, 2001), p. 8.

11 Nancy Christie and Michael Gauvreau, *A Full-Orbed Christianity: The Protestant Churches and Social Welfare in Canada, 1900–1940* (Montreal/Kingston: McGill-Queen's University Press, 1996).

12 Nancy Christie, *Households of Faith: Family, Gender, and Community in Canada, 1760–1969* (Montreal/Kingston: McGill-Queen's University Press, 2002).

English-Canadian Reform

English-Canadian reformers regarded an Allied victory as a regeneration of a "New Canada." Some wrote books associating war with reform. In *The New Christianity* (1920), Salem Bland, a leading figure in the social gospel movement and a professor at Wesley College in Winnipeg, presented his vision of a socialist Canada operating on the Christian principles of love, equality, brotherhood, and democracy through a new labour church. Stephen Leacock, the political economist–cum–humorist, had doubts about the utopian nature of socialism. In his *Unsolved Riddle of Social Justice* (1920), he favoured instead legislation designed to make the workplace more appealing. In *Wake Up Canada* (1919), C.W. Paterson saw educational reform as the answer to society's ills. Two agrarian reformers, W.G. Good in *Production and Taxation in Canada* (1919) and William Irvine in *The Farmers in Politics* (1920), proposed rural values as the ideal of the future. William Lyon Mackenzie King welcomed the new urban-industrial society in *Industry and Humanity* (1918), provided that "regenerated men" directed it on Christian principles of cooperation and brotherhood.

French-Canadian Reform

French-Canadian clerics and laypeople pressed for social, not political, reform during the war. In 1917, Father Joseph-Papin Archambault, of the Jesuit-inspired École sociale populaire, issued a tract, *La question sociale et nos devoirs de catholiques*, in which he appealed to Roman Catholics to reach out to the working class. In 1920, he began the *Semaines sociales*, an annual week-long meeting of clerics and laypeople to discuss social questions.

In Bourassa's view, French-Canadian regeneration had to remain linked to Canadian Catholic reform in general. At the turn of the century, most French-Canadian nationalists, including Bourassa, looked to all of Canada as their homeland. After the conscription crisis of 1917, perspectives changed. A small group of nationalists, led by the Quebec historian Abbé Lionel Groulx, advanced the idea of an independent, Roman Catholic, and rural French-Canadian nation in the St. Lawrence valley: "For him the French Canadians possessed most of the essential attributes of a nation, and their attainment of political independence would be a normal part of their coming of age as a people."[4]

Final Year of the War

By 1917 the situation in Europe was desperate. In October, revolution broke out in Russia, and by November, Vladimir Lenin led the Bolsheviks to power. Viewing the war as an imperial and capitalist struggle, in March 1918 Russia signed the Treaty of Brest-Litovsk with Germany and pulled out of the conflict. Now the Germans could concentrate on the Western Front. German submarine attacks in the North Atlantic brought the United States into the war against Germany in April 1917, but American troops would not be mobilized in force in Europe until the summer of 1918. Meanwhile, Canada played a role in combating the communists in Russia in 1918. Forty officers and men were sent as military trainers to aid the anti-communist forces. Canada also contributed to the Allied intervention in Siberia by sending 4000 troops. The men arrived in Vladivostock but, with no clear objectives or Allied coordination, the force was soon sent home.

In October and November 1917, the Allies suffered hundreds of thousands of casualties in the last phase of Field-Marshal Haig's Flanders offensive, including 16,000 Canadian deaths in the battle of Passchendaele, an attempt to take an insignificant Belgian ridge in a sea of mud. Finally, in the spring of 1918, came the all-out German counteroffensive, launched before American troops entered the front lines. Once again the Allies faced defeat. Only with the Germans' "black day" at Amiens, France, on August 8, 1918, the beginning of the final "Hundred Days" campaign, did the Allies turn the tide. The Canadian Corps under Arthur Currie's command played a key role in the final assault. With victories in France at the Drocourt-Quéant line, and in Cambrai and Valenciennes, the Canadians pushed on to the Belgian city of Mons. As the site of Britain's first defeat at the hands of the Germans in 1914, the recapture of Mons on the night of November 10 held symbolic importance. The next morning at 11 a.m., the Germans surrendered and signed the Armistice. The guns fell silent; the "Great War" was over.

The war ended too late for Private George Lawrence Price. He became the last Canadian soldier killed when a sniper shot him at Mons three seconds before the ceasefire came into effect at

Construction underway at the Canal du Nord, which Canadians crossed with their supplies during their advance east of Arras, France.

Source: Canada Department of National Defence/Library and Archives Canada/PA-003287.

11 a.m. Local citizens commemorated his tragic death by displaying, at the Mons War Museum, a replica of the Canadian soldier's headstone at the neighbouring St. Symphorien Military Cemetery.

Few Canadian conscripts ever fought on the battlefield. While the implementation of conscription put 100,000 more men into the army by the war's end, only one-quarter of them reached the front before the armistice. Based on the damage to national unity in Canada, it is easy to argue that conscription was a failed policy and not worth the price. These reinforcements at the end of the war, however, played an important role in bringing infantry battalions back up to full strength. In Borden's defence, no one in late 1917 could have predicted that the long, drawn-out war would finally end one year later. Overall, over 600,000 Canadians fought in the Great War; 60,000 of them died.

COMMUNITY PORTRAIT

The Canadian Corps: A Community of Soldiers

The young men who joined the Canadian Expeditionary Force, or the Canadian Corps, in the late summer and fall of 1914 did so for a variety of reasons. Many sought adventure in what they believed would be a short war, over by Christmas. Unemployment led others to enlist. Most, however, joined for patriotic reasons. They believed they were fighting to protect the British Empire, democracy, and freedom from the dangerous, militaristic "Hun." In the initial two years of the war, recent immigrants from Britain formed the largest single group. French Canadians' ties to Europe were more distant and when they did join, they entered an "English" army. English was the language of command. Over time, this community of soldiers transitioned into a disciplined, hardened, unified fighting force.

Many of the Canadian-born recruits came from farming backgrounds or from small rural hamlets or villages. The fact that these young men trained together and, in most cases, fought and died together reinforced the feeling of camaraderie. In an open letter to his cousin Henri Bourassa, Talbot Papineau, a member of the Corps, noted how working together and facing death together forged a sense of community. Canadian soldiers, he wrote in 1916, "are being knit together into a new existence, because when men stand side by side and endure a soldier's life and face together a soldier's death, they are united in bonds almost as strong as the closest of blood ties." English-born Greg Neale, a farmer from Lloydminister, Alberta, recalled how he found a sense of community in the military. "For years, and especially for an impressionable boy, all my relations were there. Your battalion was there, your company was there, your platoon was there. You belonged to them. You were an identifiable person." The war united this generation for the remainder of their lives.

The commanders of the Canadian Corps reinforced this sense of unity and community. Julian Byng, who took command of the Corps in May 1916, although British, bonded with his men and worked alongside them to the point where they became identified as "the Byng Boys." When Canadian-born Major-General Arthur Currie, a former real estate agent from Victoria, replaced Byng in the spring of 1917, an even closer bond of unity and community as Canadian soldiers formed. Currie insisted that the Canadian Corps be kept together as a fighting force under Canadian command for the duration of the war.

At Vimy Ridge on Easter Monday, 1917, all four Divisions of the Canadian Corps fought together for the first time. Harold Innis, later an economist and historian at the University of Toronto, noted the importance of working together as a community of soldiers. All soldiers realized that "other men's lives depended to an important extent on how much work we did." Together, at Vimy, the Canadian Corps captured the Ridge from the Germans. Earlier attempts by both the British and French had failed. For many Canadian soldiers, it was the defining moment. Greg Clark, later a leading columnist for the *Toronto Daily Star*, recalled that although the losses were horrendous, the Vimy campaign and the war in general had created a spirit of purpose. He attributed his individual survival and the overall success "to the community of men closest to him."

While the Great War instilled a powerful sense of pride among those Canadians who served, ultimately, it was a calamity. Attempts would be made in the years and decades that followed to instill the conflict with an overriding sense of national purpose, yet this "community of men" fortunate enough to survive were left to suffer in relative silence.

FURTHER READING

Ted Barris, *Victory at Vimy: Canada Comes of Age, April 9–12, 1917* (Toronto: Thomas Allen Publishers, 2007).

Pierre Berton, *Vimy* (Toronto: McClelland and Stewart, 1986).

Terry Copp, "The Military Effort, 1914–1918," in David Mackenzie, ed., *Canada and the First World War: Essays in Honour of Robert Craig Brown* (Toronto: University of Toronto Press, 2005), pp. 35–61.

Jonathan Vance, *Death So Noble: Memory, Meaning, and the First World War* (Vancouver: UBC Press, 1997).

Demobilization

In 1919, the Canadian government faced insurrection among its soldiers stationed in demobilization camps in Britain and Europe, as rumours spread of favouritism and deliberate delays in arranging for returns. To alleviate the tension, army officials began educational classes. When this initiative proved ineffective, the Young Men's Christian Association (YMCA) established the Khaki University in the summer of 1918 under acting president Henry M. Tory, president of the University of Alberta. Its main campus was in Ripon, a medieval cathedral town in Yorkshire, with additional classes held at University College, London, and after the Armistice, at the University of Bonn, Germany. But soldiers simply wanted to get home as quickly as possible and get on with their lives.

To coordinate the demobilization effort, in early 1918 the Canadian government created the Department of Soldiers' Civil Re-establishment. Even its personnel, however, were unprepared for the difficulties involved in arranging for 300,000 troops to return and be reintegrated into civilian life. When they returned after four years of hell in the trenches, many expected to find a better world. Otherwise, what had all the sacrifices been for? Instead, they returned to a nation gripped by economic recession. When they could not even find jobs, veterans protested. They used their association, the Great War Veterans' Association (GWVA), the forerunner of the Canadian Legion, to press the government to give preferential treatment to veterans, to provide pensions for those who were disabled, to financially help wives and children of dead soldiers, and to provide proper medical care to veterans.

For What? *by Frederick Varley, one of the four war artists who later joined the Group of Seven. Varley's bleak painting of a burial party at work behind the front lines makes a powerful statement on the futility of war.*

Source: F.H. Varley, *For What?* AN: 19710261-0770, Beaverbrook Collection of War Art. © Canadian War Museum (CWM).

The Influenza Epidemic

The problem of treating disabled soldiers paled in comparison with an even greater domestic crisis at the end of the war: the Spanish influenza epidemic then sweeping the globe, brought to Canada almost certainly by returning soldiers. The first major outbreak occurred in September 1918 in Quebec. In some cities, people were ordered to wear gauze masks in public; in others, theatres and schools were closed, public meetings were banned, and church services were cancelled in an effort to check the deadly disease. Labrador was devastated by the influenza, with a third of the Inuit dying between November 1918 and January 1919. Since there was no known cure, people tried all kinds of home remedies, from camphorated oil on the chest to Epsom salts and even salted herring around the neck, while volunteers fought the dreaded disease in makeshift hospitals. In the fall of 1919, the federal government established the Department of Health to deal with the epidemic. Eventually an estimated 50,000 Canadians died from this "silent enemy"—almost as many as had died in the Great War itself. The influenza epidemic was a transformative event in Canadian history. Along with the need posed by debilitated veterans, it led to an increased role for the state to provide medical services.

SUMMARY

The wartime propaganda that the conflict would lead to a better Canada, a glorious nation of peace and prosperity, rang hollow in 1918. The war strained national unity to an unprecedented extent, leading for the first time to the formation of national parties along ethnic and regional rather than political and national lines. Equally, the war taxed the nation's capacity in both industrial production and human resources. While Canada made strides on the road to nationhood, it did so at great expense. The total of all Canadian casualties—killed, missing, prisoners of war, or wounded—reached a quarter of a million people.

Canada lost much of its optimism. As commentators would later note, the nation also lost its innocence. Fifteen years earlier, Prime Minister Wilfrid Laurier predicted that the twentieth century would be Canada's century, just as the nineteenth century belonged to the United States. In 1919, Laurier died. In many ways, his vision perished before he died, another casualty of the killing fields of Europe.

NOTES

1. John Swettenham, *To Seize the Victory: The Canadian Corps in World War I* (Toronto: Ryerson Press, 1965), p. 106.

2. Daniel Dancocks, *Welcome to Flanders Fields: The First Canadian Battle of the Great War, Ypres, 1915* (Toronto: McClelland & Stewart, 1988), p. 249.

3. Desmond Morton, "World War I," *The Canadian Encyclopedia*, vol. 4, 2nd ed. (Edmonton: Hurtig, 1988), p. 2343.

4. Mason Wade, *The French Canadians, 1760–1967*, 2 vols. (Toronto: Macmillan, 1968), vol. 2, p. 872.

BIBLIOGRAPHY

For overviews of Canada during World War I, see G.L. Nicholson, *Official History of the Canadian Army in the First World War: Canadian Expeditionary Force, 1914–1919* (Ottawa: Queen's Printer, 1964); Desmond Morton and J.L. Granatstein, *Marching to Armageddon: Canada and the Great War, 1914–1919* (Toronto: Lester & Orpen Dennys, 1989); Desmond Morton, *When Your Number's Up: The Canadian Soldier in the First World War* (Toronto: Random House, 1993); Tim Cook, *At The Sharp End: Canadians Fighting the Great War: Volume I, 1914–1916* (Toronto: Penguin Books, 2007), and *Shock Troops: Canadians Fighting the Great War: Volume II, 1917–1918* (Toronto: Penguin Books, 2008); Daniel Dancocks, *Spearhead to Victory: Canada and the Great War* (Edmonton: Hurtig, 1987); R.C. Brown and R. Cook, *Canada, 1896–1921: A Nation Transformed* (Toronto: McClelland & Stewart, 1974), pp. 212–94; and Bill Freeman and Richard Nielson, *Far From Home: Canadians in the First World War* (Toronto: McGraw-Hill Ryerson, 1999). A collection of essays is David Mackenzie, ed., *Canada and the First World War: Essays in Honour of Robert Craig Brown* (Toronto: University of Toronto Press, 2005); as is Marc Milner, ed., *Canadian Military History: Selected Readings* (Toronto: Copp Clark Pitman, 1993).

On Robert Borden, see R.C. Brown, *Robert Laird Borden: A Biography*, 2 vols. (Toronto: Macmillan, 1975, 1980); and John English, *Borden: His Life and World* (Toronto: McGraw-Hill Ryerson, 1977). For a study of party and politics during the Borden era, consult John English, *The Decline of Politics: The Conservatives and the Party System, 1901–1920* (Toronto: University of Toronto Press, 1977). Joseph Schull's *Laurier: The First Canadian* (Toronto: Macmillan, 1965), and O.D. Skelton's *The Life and Letters of Sir Wilfrid Laurier* (Toronto: Oxford University Press, 1921), deal with the leader of the opposition in the war years. The best short summary of Laurier is that by Quebec historian Réal Bélanger in the *Dictionary of Canadian Biography*, vol. 14, *1911–1920* (Toronto: University of Toronto Press, 1998), pp. 610–28.

John Swettenham, *To Seize the Victory* (Toronto: Ryerson Press, 1965), and Robert James Steel, *The Men Who Marched Away: Canada's Infantry in the First World War, 1914–1918* (St. Catharines: Vanwell, 1989), describe Canadian involvement at the front, as does Sandra Gwyn's *Tapestry of War: Politics and Passion: Canada's Coming of Age in the Great War* (Toronto: HarperCollins, 1992). See too Bill Rawling, *Surviving Trench Warfare: Technology and the Canadian Corps, 1914–1918* (Toronto: University of Toronto Press, 1992). More recent work includes Tim Cook, *No Place to Run: The Canadian Corps and Gas Warfare in the First World War* (Vancouver: UBC Press, 1999); and Kenneth Radley, *We Lead, Others Follow: First Canadian Division, 1914–1918* (St. Catharines: Vanwell, 2006).

On Canada's involvement in the Ypres Salient, see Daniel Dancocks, *Welcome to Flanders Fields: The First Canadian Battle of the Great War, Ypres, 1915* (Toronto: McClelland & Stewart, 1988). For the second Ypres battle, see Nathan M. Greenfield, *Baptism of Fire: The Second Battle of Ypres and the Forging of Canada, April, 1915* (Toronto: Harper Collins Publishers LTD, 2007); Andrew Iarocci, *Shoestring Soldiers: The 1st Canadian Division at War, 1914–1915* (Toronto: University of Toronto Press, 2008); and George H. Cassar, *Hell in Flanders Fields: Canadians at the Second Battle of Ypres* (Toronto: Dundurn, 2010).

Pierre Berton tells the story of Canada's greatest battle in *Vimy* (Toronto: McClelland & Stewart, 1986). Peter Barton and Jeremy Banning examine Vimy in their book *Vimy Ridge and Arras: The Spring 1917 Offensive in Panorama* (Toronto: Dundurn, 2010). A reconsideration of Vimy is available in the edited collection Geoffrey Hayes, Andrew Iarocci, and Mike Bechthold, eds., *Vimy Ridge: A Canadian Reassessment* (Waterloo: Wilfred Laurier University Press, 2007). Norman Leach covers the battle of Passchendaele in his work, *Passchendaele: Canada's Triumph and Tragedy on the Fields of Flanders* (Regina: Coteau Books, 2008).

G.W.L. Nicholson, *The Fighting Newfoundlander: A History of the Royal Newfoundland Regiment* (Ottawa: Government of Newfoundland, 1964) recounts Newfoundland's contribution to the Allied army. For a personal account, see David R. Facey-Crowther, ed., *Lieutenant Owen William Steele of the Newfoundland Regiment: Diary and Letters* (Montreal/Kingston: McGill-Queen's University Press, 2002). Jean-Pierre Gagnon's *Le 22e bataillon (canadien-français) 1914–1919: Étude sociomilitaire* (Quebec: Presses de l'Université Laval, 1987) reviews the story of the "Vandoos" in World War I.

For an overview of the Canadian regiment, see David J. Bercuson, *The Fighting Canadians: Our Regimental History from New France to Afghanistan* (Scarborough, ON: Harper Collins Canada, 2008). On Canada's first military commander, consult A.M.J. Hyatt, *General Sir Arthur Currie: A Military Biography* (Toronto: University of Toronto Press, 1987); Mark Osborne Humphries, ed., *The Selected Papers of Sir Arthur Currie: Diaries, Letters, and Report to the Ministry, 1917–1933* (Waterloo, ON: Wilfrid Laurier University Press, 2008); and Mark Osborne Humphries, ed., "Sir Arthur Currie and the Legacy of the Great War: Letters from the Archives of the Canadian War Museum," *Canadian Military History*, 17 (2) (2008): 51–60. On Sam Hughes, see Ronald G. Haycock, *Sam Hughes: The Public Career of a Controversial Canadian, 1885–1916* (Waterloo, ON: Wilfrid Laurier University Press, 1986). On the Canadian air force, see S.F. Wise, *Canadian Airmen and the First World War* (Toronto: University of Toronto Press, 1980); and for the navy, Michael L. Hadley and Roger Sarty, *Tin-Pots and Pirate Ships: Canadian Naval Forces and German Sea Raiders 1880–1918* (Montreal/Kingston: McGill-Queen's University Press, 1991). Ted Barris offers the first-person testimonials of soldiers in *Breaking the Silence: Untold Veterans Stories from the Great War to Afghanistan* (Markham, ON: Allen, 2009).

On ethnic relations during the war, see John Herd Thompson, *Ethnic Minorities During Two World Wars* (Ottawa: Canadian Historical Association, 1991). James W. St. G. Walker looks at race relations in the Canadian army in "Race and Recruitment in World War I: Enlistment of Visible Minorities in the Canadian Expeditionary Force," *Canadian Historical Review*, 70(1) (March 1989): 1–26. On the only African-Canadian battalion, see John G. Armstrong, "The Unwelcome Sacrifice: A Black Unit in the Canadian Expeditionary Force, 1917-19," in N.F. Dreisziger, ed., *Ethnic Armies: Polyethnic Armed Forces from the Time of the Hapsburgs to the Age of the Superpowers* (Waterloo, ON: Wilfrid Laurier University Press, 1990), pp. 178–97; and Calvin Ruck, *The Black Battalion, 1916–1920: Canada's Best Kept Military Secret* (Halifax: Nimbus, 1987). On First Nations soldiers, see Fred Gaffen, *Forgotten Soldiers* (Penticton, BC: Theytus Books, 1985); James Dempsey's *Warriors of the King: Prairie Indians in World War I* (Regina:

Canadian Plains Research Center, 1999); and Timothy C. Winegard, *For King and Kanata: Canadian Indians and the First World War* (Winnipeg: University of Manitoba Press, 2012).

On Canadian internment camps, see Bill Waiser, *Park Prisoners: The Untold Story of Western Canada's National Parks, 1915–1946* (Saskatoon: Fifth House Publishing, 1995). On Ukrainian internments, see Frances Swyripa and John Herd Thompson, eds., *Loyalties in Conflict: Ukrainians in Canada During the Great War* (Edmonton: Canadian Institute of Ukrainian Studies, 1983); and Lubormyr Luciuk, *A Time for Atonement: Canada's First National Internment Operations and the Ukrainian Canadians, 1914–1920* (Kingston: Limestone Press, 1988). For information about the nearly 4000 Canadians held in German prison camps in World War I, see Desmond Morton, *Silent Battle: Canadian Prisoners of War in Germany, 1914–1919* (Toronto: Lester, 1992). The role of propaganda on the war effort is examined in Jeffrey A. Keshen, *Propaganda and Censorship During Canada's Great War* (Edmonton: University of Alberta Press, 1996).

On the shaping of the war on the home front, see Robert Rutherdale, *Hometown Horizons: Local Responses to Canada's Great War* (Vancouver: UBC Press, 2006); and Ian Miller, *Our Glory and Our Grief: Torontonians and the Great War* (Toronto: University of Toronto Press, 2002). On voluntary contributions, see Desmond Morton, *Fight or Pay: Soldiers' Families in the Great War* (Vancouver: UBC Press, 2004). Brock Millman looks at the federal government's repressive policies during the war in *Polarity, Patriotism, and Dissent in Great War Canada, 1914–1919* (Toronto: University of Toronto Press, 2016).

The question of government intervention in the state during the war is discussed in R. Cuff, "Organizing for War: Canada and the United States During World War I," *Canadian Historical Association Report* (1969): 141–56. On the nationalization of the railways, see T.D. Regehr, *The Canadian Northern Railway* (Toronto: Macmillan, 1976); and R.B. Fleming, *The Railway King of Canada: Sir William Mackenzie, 1849–1923* (Vancouver: University of British Columbia Press, 1991).

Women's contributions to the war effort are discussed in the relevant sections of Alison Prentice et al., *Canadian Women: A History*, 2nd ed. (Toronto: Harcourt Brace, 1996); Marjorie Barron Norris, *Sister Heroines: The Roseate Glow of Wartime Nursing 1914–1918* (Calgary: Bunker to Bunker Publishing, 2002); and Ceta Ramkhalawonsingh, "Women During the Great War," in J. Acton et al., eds., *Women at Work: Ontario, 1850–1930* (Toronto: Canadian Women's Educational Press, 1974), pp. 261–308. Two recent accounts are Susan Mann, ed., *The War Diary of Clare Glass, 1915–1918* (Montreal/Kingston: McGill-Queen's University Press, 2000); and Susan Mann, *Margaret Macdonald: Imperial Daughter* (Montreal/Kingston: McGill-Queen's University Press, 2005). The most recent collection of essays on the subject is Sarah Glassford and Amy J. Shaw, eds., *A Sisterhood of Suffering and Service: Women and Girls of Canada and Newfoundland during the First World War* (Vancouver: UBC Press, 2011).

The Halifax explosion is well documented in Alan D. Ruffman and Colin D. Howell, eds., *Ground Zero: A Reassessment of the 1917 Explosion in Halifax Harbour* (Halifax: Nimbus, 1994). Jacob Remes places the explosion in a transnational framework in *Disaster Citizenship: Survivors, Solidarity, and Power in the Progressive Era* (Urbana: University of Illinois Press, 2016).

The conscription crisis is covered in J.L. Granatstein and J.M. Hitsman, *Broken Promises: A History of Conscription in Canada* (Toronto: Copp Clark Pitman, 1985 [1977]); and C. Berger, ed., *Conscription 1917* (Toronto: University of Toronto Press, 1969). Granatstein reverses his opinion in "Conscription in the Great War" in David Mackenzie's edited volume noted previously, pp. 62–75. Social histories of the conscription crisis and its impact on gender, class, and ethnic relations include Tarah Brookfield, "Divided by the Ballot Box: The Montreal Council of Women and the 1917 Election," *Canadian Historical Review* 89, no. 4 (2008): 473–501; Martin F. Auger, "On the Brink of Civil War: The Canadian Government and the Suppression of the 1918 Quebec Easter Riots," *Canadian Historical Review* 89, no. 4 (2008): 503–40; and David Tough, "'The rich . . . should give to such an extent that it will hurt': 'Conscription of Wealth' and Political Modernism in the Parliamentary Debate on the 1917 Income War Tax," *Canadian Historical Review* 93, no. 3 (2012): 382–407.

Mason Wade examines French-Canadian attitudes toward the war in *The French Canadians: 1760–1945* (Toronto: Macmillan, 1955). Students should also consult Elizabeth Armstrong, *The Crisis of Quebec, 1914–1918* (Toronto: McClelland & Stewart, 1974 [1937]). The Canadian peace movement is studied in Thomas Socknat, *Witness Against War: Pacifism in Canada, 1900–1945* (Toronto: University of Toronto Press, 1987). Amy J. Shaw addresses conscientious objection in her work, *Crisis of Conscience: Conscientious Objection in Canada during the First World War* (Vancouver: UBC Press, 2008). See D. Morton and G. Wright, *Winning the Second Battle: Canadian Veterans and the Return to Civilian Life, 1915–1930* (Toronto: University of Toronto Press, 1987) for a study of World War I veterans.

For the Ontario Schools Questions, see Chad Gaffield, *Language, Schooling, and Cultural Conflict: The Origins of the French-Language Controversy in Ontario* (Montreal/Kingston: McGill-Queen's University Press, 1987); and the articles by Marilyn Barber and Margaret Prang in R.C. Brown, ed., *Minorities, Schools, and Politics* (Toronto: University of Toronto Press, 1969). For the debate's aftermath, see Theodore Michael Christou, *Progressive Education: Revisioning and Reframing Ontario's Public Schools, 1919–1942* (Toronto: University of Toronto Press, 2012).

For the impact of World War I on social reform, consult John Herd Thompson, "'The Beginning of Our Regeneration': The Great War and Western Canadian Reform Movements," *Canadian Historical Association Historical Papers* (1972): 227–45, and his study *The Harvests of War: The Prairie West, 1914–1919* (Toronto: McClelland & Stewart, 1978).

On Canadian imperial and foreign relations during and immediately after the war, see R.C. Brown's biography of Borden (cited earlier), and his "Sir Robert Borden, the Great War and Anglo-Canadian Relations," in J.S. Moir, ed., *Character and Circumstance* (Toronto: Macmillan, 1970), pp. 201–24; as well as C.P. Stacey, *Canada and the Age of Conflict*, vol. 1, *1867–1921* (Toronto: Macmillan, 1977).

On the flu epidemic of 1918, see Esyllt Jones, *Influenza 1918: Death, Disease, and Struggle in Winnipeg* (Toronto: University of Toronto Press, 2007); and Eileen Pettigrew, *The Silent Enemy* (Saskatoon: Western Producer Prairie Books, 1983). The most recent accounts include Mark Osborne Humphries, *The Last Plague: Spanish Influenza and the Politics of Public Health in Canada* (Toronto: University of Toronto Press, 2013), and Magda Fahrni and Esyllt W. Jones eds., *Epidemic Encounters: Influenza, Society, and Culture in Canada, 1918–20* (Vancouver: UBC Press, 2013).

Sandra Gwyn's *Tapestry of War: Politics and Passion: Canada's Coming of Age in the Great War* (Toronto: HarperCollins, 1992) examines the significance of the war for Canada's advancement; while Jonathan F. Vance looks at the construction of a myth of the Great War in *Death So Noble: Memory, Meaning and the First World War* (Vancouver: UBC Press, 1997).

Donald Kerr and Deryck W. Holdsworth, eds., *Historical Atlas of Canada*, vol. 3, *Addressing the Twentieth Century, 1891–1961* (Toronto: Nelson, 1990), contains a wealth of detail in the form of maps and charts on Canadian society in the early twentieth century.

Source: Glenbow Archives, NA-2291-2.

Chapter Eleven

CANADA, 1919–29: A DECADE OF ADJUSTMENT

TIME LINE

1919	Canada participates in Paris Peace Conference and joins League of Nations Wilfrid Laurier dies Robert Borden retires Winnipeg General Strike occurs
1920	Formation of Maritime Rights Movement Founding of Group of Seven
1921	Liberals win federal election under William Lyon Mackenzie King Progressive Party wins 65 seats in federal Parliament, forcing the first minority government Agnes Macphail becomes first woman elected federally Founding of Communist Party of Canada
1922	Insulin made available for treatment of diabetes Chanak Crisis occurs
1923	Canada signs Halibut Treaty with United States Federal government bans Chinese immigration Mackenzie King plays pivotal role at Imperial Conference
1925	Liberals cling to power in federal election with Progressive support United Church of Canada established
1926	Customs Scandal breaks out Balfour Declaration signed at Imperial Conference signals shift from Empire to Commonwealth King–Byng controversy Mackenzie King resigns; Conservatives under Arthur Meighen take office Conservative government falls Liberals under Mackenzie King win majority government
1927	Federal government introduces old-age pension program National Museum of Canada created
1928	Percy Williams wins two gold medals at the Amsterdam Olympics
1929	The Privy Council's decision in the Persons Case recognizes women in Canada as "persons" for legal purposes

The decade known as the "Roaring Twenties" was in reality marked by economic recession and postwar anxiety. It was a period of adjustment to new postwar conditions and dramatic shifts in politics, economics, and social and cultural developments. While Canada seemed culturally progressive as the populace embraced modernity, it was generally a conservative era as the impetus for reform that had dominated the prewar and war years diminished or at least transformed.

Canada witnessed a serious labour situation when a general strike broke out in Winnipeg in 1919, paralyzing the city and alarming the nation. The evangelical roots of the social reform movement remained intact, particularly among middle-class Canadians "who shared the broad progressive impulse for a social reconstruction that would mediate the social tensions spawned by the warfare between capital and labour."[1] With reform firmly ensconced with the churches, much of the prewar radicalism was tempered by the realities of the communist revolution in Russia. Women continued their struggle for recognition and rights, but in the economic and the legal rather than in the political sphere. In the aftermath of the Winnipeg General Strike, the impetus for reform shifted from the urban-based labour movement to the rural-based farm movements.

In politics, a generational change occurred. Both political parties chose new leaders, but regional protest movements surfaced in the Maritimes and the West. The two-party system disappeared forever. In foreign affairs, Canada rode the nationalist momentum coming out of the war and took a number of steps on the road from colony to nation. Economically, the nation staggered under the weight of problems exacerbated by the Great War. Canadians looked increasingly to the United States rather than to Britain for trade. Consumer goods became major items of trade. The nature of the Canadian economy shifted from a preponderance of wheat to the newer staples of pulp and paper, and base metals, as the northern shield was opened for development.

Technological innovation led to rapid change in the realms of transportation and communications. The automobile industry grew at an astonishing rate, as did all the essentials for the industry such as roads and service stations. Aviation expanded, allowing for regular air-mail service and opening up the North. By far the most popular communication invention was the telephone, making regular communication possible and alleviating isolation for many families. Amid the communication and transportation revolutions, cultural activities flourished, but because of the language differences, few points of common contact existed between French and English Canada. Within a new generation that flouted its youthfulness, popular culture thrived with the advent of radio and the "talkies" in the film industry. Both cultural mediums, however, faced American domination during the decade. Canadian sport also became more professionalized and Americanized.

The Winnipeg General Strike

The world had just witnessed the most devastating conflict ever. Veterans returned home from four years of unfathomable hell in the trenches, expecting a new world that explained and justified their sacrifices; civilians looked around at their nation that had supposedly been transformed. But how much had really changed? The expectations, hopes, and dreams of the wartime generation were about to be dashed.

Widespread social unrest followed the armistice as economic recession and the influenza epidemic met the veterans upon their return. Buoyed by the victory of the workers in the Russian Revolution of 1917, strikes broke out from Halifax to Vancouver as workers tried to make up for the restraints applied in wartime and to protect themselves in an inflationary economy. At the annual meeting of the Trades and Labor Congress (TLC) in Quebec City in 1918, the more radical western delegates became frustrated with the direction of the movement and the pace of change. They broke ranks with the eastern members who controlled the meeting. A month later, the Western Labour Conference called for a single industrial union, the One Big Union (OBU), at its meeting in Calgary.

But before its organizers could hold the founding convention, new developments broke out in Winnipeg. On May 1, 1919, metalworkers' and builders' unions struck for better wages and improved working conditions. Other Winnipeg union workers, including police officers, firefighters, and telephone and telegraph operators, joined them on May 15, transforming the dispute into a "general" strike, swelling the numbers of strikers to some 30,000, and enabling labour to shut down the city. To provide essential services and to regulate the strike, the organizers created a central strike committee. Business and government officials saw this committee, with its power to dictate what went on in the city, as the beginnings of a "Bolshevik uprising." They countered by creating the Citizens' Committee of One Thousand, an anti-strike organization. Meanwhile, sympathy strikes broke out from Prince Rupert, British Columbia, to Sydney, Nova Scotia. The struggle between labour and capital was being fought in Winnipeg, and all of Canada watched nervously.

Fearing that the strike would spread to other centres, the federal government intervened. Although claiming to act as an arbiter between labour and capital, the state was on the side of business. Arthur Meighen, the minister of justice and minister of the interior, and Gideon Robertson, acting minister of labour, arrived in Winnipeg to assess the situation. They came already convinced that the strike was a conspiracy. Meighen described the strike leaders as "revolutionists of varying degrees and types, from crazy idealists down to ordinary thieves, with the better part, perhaps, of the latter type."

It was no coincidence that the general strike occurred in Winnipeg. As "gateway to the West" and the "Chicago of the North," the city was one of the most ethnic and class-divided cities in Canada. In the anti-immigrant atmosphere emerging from the Great War, the authorities blamed the "foreigners" for stirring up trouble. The truth, however, was that the most influential strike leaders were of British background. Perhaps most tragically, the strike divided the veterans. After fighting side by side in the trenches for four years, the veterans returned to the homeland they had sacrificed to defend, only to find themselves pitted against each other on the streets of Winnipeg. The government hired veterans to work as special constables; others joined the strike. As the weeks passed, tensions in Winnipeg mounted.

On the night of June 16, Meighen ordered the Royal North-West Mounted Police to arrest ten of the Winnipeg strike leaders, along with labour newspaper editors (including J.S. Woodsworth) and some returned soldiers. In protest, the strikers organized a silent parade on Saturday, June 21, thereby ignoring an order outlawing parades. Violence erupted, and the mayor of Winnipeg called in the Mounties to disperse the crowd. The confrontation saw one man killed, another wounded, and many others injured. "Bloody Saturday," as it became known, ended with the dispersal of the workers and the establishment of military control of the city. The strike collapsed. On June 26, the strike committee called off the strike, without the workers having gained any of their objectives. The strike did convince them, however, that they must send their own labour representatives to Parliament—individuals such as the social reformer J.S. Woodsworth, who had edited their strike paper and who would be elected to Parliament as a labour MP for Winnipeg in the federal election of 1921.

Where Historians Disagree

The Winnipeg General Strike

Early labour history in Canada focused on unions, labour leaders, and strikes. Not surprisingly, the Winnipeg General Strike received considerable attention and has generated considerable debate. Was Winnipeg part of the rise of a national—even international—labour militancy, or was the strike simply the product of local issues? Was Winnipeg's working class more militant than in other Canadian cities? Was labour in western Canada more radical than in the rest of the nation? Initially, the debate reflected the opposing ideological perspectives of the two sides at the time—the strike opponents seeing it as a revolution aimed at creating a Soviet-style regime in Canada, and its supporters seeing it as a legitimate tool by which workers could obtain collective bargaining to secure better wages and working conditions. Historians of labour and the left are now using the strike to offer new insights into the role of ideology, the state, class formation, and class-consciousness in Canadian cities in the first decades of the twentieth century.

In 1950, D.C. Masters wrote the first historical study of the Winnipeg General Strike. His book challenged the mainstream view that the strike was the product of Bolshevik radicals, an opinion based on the findings of the Robson Commission in a report released in the strike's immediate aftermath. Masters stressed that strike leaders were Anglo-Saxon (many of them were British immigrants) to emphasize the legitimate nature of both the leadership and the protest. Masters also argued that Winnipeg's labour leaders had no relationship with the One Big Union (OBU), a Calgary-founded labour organization that, critics argued, was a forerunner to workers' Soviets in Canada, following the model of the Russian Revolution. Significantly, Masters portrayed Winnipeg as the culmination of ongoing tensions between workers and employers in the city, emphasizing the incremental rather than radical nature of the protest. Thus, he concluded that "there was no seditious conspiracy and that the strike was what it purported to be, an effort to secure the principle of collective bargaining."[1]

Interestingly, the historical sociologist S.D. Clark, in the introduction to Masters' work, contradicted this interpretation. Clark argued that the strike was part of a revolutionary movement that had been gaining strength from the One Big Union and the rise of the Progressive Party in western Canada. To Clark, Winnipeg was evidence of continuing frontier radicalism, and was a concerted attempt to throw off central-Canadian domination.[2]

In 1974, David Bercuson published *Confrontation at Winnipeg*, in which, like Masters, he took the position that the general strike was the culmination of labour conflicts within the city that dated back to the decade before World War I. The rise of immigrant labour and the arrival of significant industrial change to Winnipeg made the city politically and geographically divided by class. Labour conflict in Winnipeg, Bercuson argued, was legitimate, and the strike did not indicate the presence of a national or transnational labour radical movement at work. He denied that the strikers were revolutionaries; instead they were common workers striking for their legitimate class concerns. The fact that they failed to achieve their objectives, however, set back "the cause of labour for at least another generation."[3]

In a 1977 article in the *Canadian Historical Review*, Bercuson expanded his analysis to include a regional dimension. He argued that at the time of the general strike, labour was more radical in western Canada than in the rest of the country because of the "frontier conditions" of the region. Immigrants had come west in search of better opportunities but had found that industrialists were as powerful in western Canada as in the east. Thus, workers were radicalized by their disappointment and became more class-conscious.[4]

Bercuson's analysis generated controversy among labour historians and drew a response from Gregory Kealey, who disagreed that the West was more radical than the rest of Canada. He questioned Bercuson's view that Winnipeg was an exceptional case by noting that throughout 1919, strikes and protests occurred across the country. Furthermore, Canada's labour conflicts were not uniquely Canadian but rather part of international unrest among the working class. Global capitalism, destabilized by World War I, was undergoing a period of significant transition and reorganization; labour conflict and the rise of solidarity movements was a logical and widespread response.[5]

Bercuson responded in 1990 in the revised edition of his book by dismissing Kealey's argument. Strikes and protest across Canada, he posited, were incidental and not evidence of an organized or concerted effort by labour to challenge the industrial order by a working-class revolt. Bercuson noted that few of the strikes were politically motivated, and those that were failed. Kealey, he claimed, was making Winnipeg into something that it was not, and referred to his analysis of the strike as "pamphleteering," not scholarship. Winnipeg's significance, he claimed, was that it was a unique event in Canadian history and could not be attached to subsequent political movements of the working class, such as the rise of the Co-operative Commonwealth Federation (CCF) in the 1930s or the rise of industrial unions during World War II.[6]

Bryan Palmer sided with Kealey and posited that Winnipeg must be seen in the context of an ongoing class struggle in Canada. Writing in 1983, even before the Bercuson–Kealey debate, Palmer was critical of much of the scholarship that "clarified the strike's aims, but does not offer any explanation as to how non-revolutionary demands can, in specific circumstances, form the foundation of a challenge to authority that proves radical,

even potentially revolutionary in its implications."[7] To Palmer, the strike was a portentous episode in the Canadian class struggle, because it revealed a new, more militant face of industrial unionism. The Central Strike Committee's initial success at running essential city services proved a dire threat to the *status quo ante*, and the growing relationship among returning war veterans, immigrant labourers, and strikers suggested that a new socioeconomic and political order was possible. This threat led to the organization of the Committee of One Thousand by the city's business elite and the violent reprisals that came on "Bloody Saturday."

Ian McKay has examined Winnipeg in *Reasoning Otherwise: Leftists and the People's Enlightenment in Canada, 1890–1920*. He rejects Bercuson's argument that Winnipeg was either exceptional or motivated by resistance to eastern industrial capitalism. Instead, McKay connects the strike to the founding of the One Big Union (OBU) in Calgary in June of 1919. The OBU mattered, he argues, because it was a new type of labour organization distinct from the traditional, more conservative craft unions. It represented "an experiment in living otherwise, a model of a 'war of position' wherein workers would wrest ever-increasing amounts of economic and cultural power from their rulers: a working-class revolution taking place through the logic of social evolution." By reintroducing the OBU into the general strike debate, McKay challenged Bercuson's claim to Winnipeg's exceptionalism but he also placed the city at the centre of a national struggle. Winnipeg, according to McKay, was actually less about organized labour and more about an episode in the left's quest for a new social order in Canada: "Winnipeg in 1919 was also, and for some participants primarily, about *other things*: about the construction of a new form of Christianity, or the achievement of women's equality, or the rights and privileges of Britons."[8]

David Bright responded to Bercuson's argument that western Canadian labour was more radical than the rest of the country in his book *The Limits of Labour: Class Formation and the Labour Movement in Calgary, 1883–1929*. According to Bright, western Canada's labour movement was not uniformly more radical. While One Big Union received widespread support in Manitoba and Saskatchewan, it was not popular in Alberta. Bright cautioned against studying industrial unionism at the regional level, arguing that city-level studies are more appropriate because each city "was also the location of unique social conditions." Bright's analysis challenges both Bercuson's emphasis on exceptionalism and

Kealey's argument that Winnipeg represented pan-Canadian or even international labour radicalism.[9]

Reinhold Kramer and Tom Mitchell have offered a novel interpretation by focusing on the Citizens' Committee and how it effectively "broke" the Winnipeg General Strike. They argued that the role of the state has been portrayed too simply. Indeed, it has been misinterpreted: "Historians have mistakenly characterized Meighen, Prime Minister Robert Borden's factotum, as the author of reaction, the antagonist in labour's story." They shifted the focus onto the local Citizens' Committee.[10] Whether Winnipeg was a local or regional conflict, or a battlefield in an international struggle between the working class and industrial capital, the strike remains a unique episode in Canadian history.

---

1   D.C. Masters, *The Winnipeg General Strike* (Toronto: University of Toronto Press, 1950), pp.127, 134.

2   Ibid., pp. vii–x.

3   David Bercuson, *Confrontation at Winnipeg* (Montreal/Kingston: McGill-Queen's University Press, 1974), p. 176.

4   David Bercuson, "Labour Radicalism and the Western Industrial Frontier: 1897–1919," *Canadian Historical Review*, 58(2) (June 1977): 154–75.

5   Gregory Kealey, "1919: The Canadian Labour Revolt," *Labour/Le travail*, 13 (Spring 1984): 11–44.

6   David Bercuson, *Confrontation at Winnipeg*, rev. ed. (Montreal/Kingston: McGill-Queen's University Press, 1990), esp. Chapter 13: "A Longer View," pp. 196–205.

7   Bryan D. Palmer, *Working Class Experience: The Rise and Reconstitution of Canadian Labour, 1800–1980* (Toronto: Butterworth & Co., 1983), pp. 173 and 174.

8   Ian McKay, *Reasoning Otherwise: Leftists and the People's Enlightenment in Canada, 1890–1920* (Toronto: Between the Lines, 2008), p. 463.

9   David Bright, *The Limits of Labour: Class Formation and the Labour Movement in Calgary, 1883–1929* (Vancouver: UBC Press, 1998), pp. 9–10, 30, 155.

10 Reinhold Kramer and Tom Mitchell, *When the State Trembled: How A.J. Andrews and the Citizens' Committee Broke the Winnipeg General Strike* (Toronto: University of Toronto Press, 2010), p. 4.

A New Generation of Political Leaders

Beginning in 1919, a generational shift occurred within the political leadership of Canada. William Lyon Mackenzie King succeeded Wilfrid Laurier (who died in February 1919) as Liberal leader, while Arthur Meighen became the Conservative leader and acting prime minister after Robert Borden's resignation in July 1920.

The Liberals chose King at a leadership convention, the first in the country's history, in August 1919. The convention was important, because it was intended to establish a new platform

"Bloody Saturday," June 21, 1919, a violent confrontation that occurred between peaceful marchers and the Mounties and special police during the Winnipeg General Strike. Note the burning streetcar.

Source: David Miller Collection/National Archives of Canada/C-33392.

for the Liberals while also seeking to heal the bitter divisions over conscription and the formation of the Union government. Not surprisingly, with the war over, the Union Party disintegrated as its members returned to their respective parties. Mackenzie King's loyalty to Laurier during the conscription crisis put him in favour in the party, especially in Quebec. As well, King appeared to represent change. The maternal grandson of William Lyon Mackenzie, leader of the Rebellion of 1837 in Upper Canada, saw himself as a reformer. After graduating from the universities of Toronto, Chicago, and Harvard with a Ph.D. in political economy, he first served as deputy minister of labour. Then in 1908, shortly after his election to the House of Commons, he became Laurier's minister of labour. Defeated in the election of 1911, King returned to the United States to work for the Rockefeller Foundation as a labour conciliator. On the basis of his experiences, he wrote *Industry and Humanity* (1918), a social reformist discussion of the labour question in Canada. Although convoluted and moralistic, the book addressed the pressing problem in the postwar era of the impact of industrialism on society. It established King as an authority on contemporary social and economic issues, and assisted in his winning the leadership of the Liberal Party in 1919.

The Conservatives met in caucus, rather than in convention, to choose Arthur Meighen as Borden's successor in July 1920. Meighen had attended the University of Toronto at the same time as King. Upon graduation, Meighen moved west to Portage la Prairie, Manitoba, to practise law. He entered federal politics in the election of 1908, the same year that his future rival, King, was first elected. Meighen, an outstanding parliamentary debater, became solicitor general in 1913 and minister of the interior in 1917.

By the time he gained leadership of the party, however, Meighen had become identified with the federal government's most controversial policies. He drafted the conscription bill, which cost him support in Quebec and among farmers in English Canada. Meighen also introduced the

Wartime Elections Act, which denied the vote to Canadians who emigrated from enemy countries after 1902, thus losing him much of the ethnic vote. In 1919, he intervened against the workers in the Winnipeg General Strike, angering labour groups.

These two leaders could not have been more different. Mackenzie King was a cautious compromiser who sought the path of least resistance. He viewed Canada as a nation of competing interests and regions, and he perfected the art of brokerage politics. While King was not a gifted orator, he surrounded himself with competent people, thereby creating a powerful team. Arthur Meighen, by contrast, was straightforward and unequivocal. He upheld principles over compromise. He was a charismatic personality and by all accounts one of the best orators and debaters the nation has seen. These two men were also ideologically opposed. It was an era when the labels of "Liberal" and "Conservative" held clear meaning. The Liberals represented autonomy, anti-conscription, free trade, and individual, minority, and provincial rights; the Conservatives represented imperial unity, conscription, protectionism, big business and the state. Each man despised the other. Whereas Laurier and Borden were perceived as "statesmen," King and Meighen were viewed as "politicians."

Regional Protest

In 1920, both new party leaders faced the problem of regional protest movements in eastern and western Canada. In the East, the Maritime Rights movement arose in an effort to obtain a greater Maritime voice in national politics, while in the West, farmers created their own party, the Progressives, to deal with regional complaints.

The Maritime Rights Movement

In the 1920s, Maritimers witnessed the continued decline in their region's influence within Confederation. More than half a million Maritimers left the region between the 1880s and the Great Depression. Thanks to "rep by pop," the region's number of seats in the House of Commons fell by one-quarter (to 31). Given that the size of the House increased substantially during this period as other regions grew in population, the relative percentage drop was even more significant. Economically, Maritime manufacturing companies re-established themselves in the larger markets of central Canada in order to become more competitive. For example, both the Canadian Car and Foundry of Amherst, Nova Scotia, and the Maritime Nail Company of Saint John, New Brunswick, transferred operations to Montreal in 1921.

A decline in demand for Cape Breton coal and steel also hurt the regional industry. The conversion to oil for heating and power lost markets for Cape Breton's coal. Shipbuilding declined as Canada competed with Britain and the United States for international sales. The market for steel rails collapsed when railway construction ceased in the postwar era. Unemployment became widespread in Cape Breton's heavy-steel industry. The British Empire Steel Company (BESCO), created from a merger of Nova Scotia's coal, steel, and shipbuilding industries, verged on bankruptcy. It responded by attempting to cut miners' and steelworkers' wages. This action, in 1921, touched off one of the most intense labour disputes in Maritime history. The provincial government had to call in troops to keep order in New Waterford, Cape Breton Island.

The Maritimes suffered from tariff reductions throughout the 1920s that formerly protected its industries. A rise in freight rates, of 200 percent or more, on the Intercolonial Railway damaged the region's economy. When the Canadian government nationalized the Intercolonial Railway as part of Canadian National Railways (CNR), it moved the Intercolonial's head office from Moncton, New Brunswick, to Montreal. The railway thus ceased to promote regional interests and became part of a national system.

"Wooing the West." Cartoonist Donald McRitchie echoes the Maritimers' complaints that the Mackenzie King government favoured the West's regional demands over their own. From the Halifax Herald, *October 3, 1925.*

Source: Reprinted by permission from *The Halifax Herald Ltd.*

Individually, the Maritime provinces seemed powerless to stem the economic decline, but many people believed that collectively their chances would be better. A.P. Paterson, a grocer from Saint John, New Brunswick, led a group of influential business and professional people in launching the Maritime Rights movement. He offered a rationale for the movement in a pamphlet, *The True Story of Confederation*, in which he put forward his version of the compact theory. He argued that all Canadians should bear the extra economic costs experienced by any region as a result of its disadvantageous geographical location. Convinced that a study of history would reinforce his argument, Paterson helped to fund the establishment of a department of history at the University of New Brunswick.

The Maritime Rights movement demanded increased federal subsidies for the Maritime provinces, more national and international trade through the ports of Halifax and Saint John, and improved tariff protection to strengthen the region's steel and coal industries. The movement's demand for a tariff increase put the Maritimes in opposition to the Prairies, which wanted a lower tariff. There was a well-founded sense in the Maritimes that the federal government had focused for too long on western expansion and development; for too long, the national policies had worked to the benefit of the West. By deciding to work for change within the traditional two-party system rather than through a third party, the Maritime Rights movement differed from the western Progressive movement.

In the election campaign of 1921, the movement pressed Maritime Liberal candidates to promise that if elected they would "advocate and stand by Maritime rights first, last and all the time." Although taking this pledge helped the federal Liberals to win all but six constituencies in the region, the Maritime members of Parliament could not keep their promises. Mackenzie King's Liberal minority government depended too much on Prairie support to be able to cater to Maritime needs, and especially to raise the tariff.

Disillusioned, Maritime voters switched to the Conservatives in the next federal election in 1925, giving the party all but 3 of the 31 seats. But the Liberals returned to power in 1926. King responded to concerns by establishing a royal commission to investigate the region's complaints. The Duncan Commission (headed by British jurist Sir Arthur Rae Duncan) recommended major changes for the Maritimes, such as a 20 percent reduction in all rail rates, aid to the steel and coal industries, and increased federal subsidies. The Liberal government, however, ended up making only minor changes. In the meantime, the Maritime Rights movement gradually disintegrated.

The Progressive Movement

Since Confederation, the federal government remained focused on developing the West, first as its own colony, then as the nation's breadbasket, and then as a region of consumers of manufactured goods. But the great hopes and expectations placed on the new region infiltrated the western consciousness; westerners shared the vision and, more importantly, their expected potential. The golden era of the turn of the century, however, was short-lived. The West, as a new society filled with immigrants seeking opportunity, was defined by a reformist and progressive mentality. At the turn of the century, western farmers attacked the two traditional parties for neglecting regional demands. They wanted reduced freight rates, an end to the elevator companies' monopoly of the grain trade, an increase in the Canadian Pacific Railway's boxcar allotment for grain trade, a railway to Hudson Bay to rival the CPR, and most of all, a reduction in the tariff.

During the Laurier era (1896–1911), western farmers gained some of their demands. The Liberal government passed the Crow's Nest Pass Agreement in 1897, by which the CPR reduced eastbound freight rates on grain and flour and westbound rates on a list of manufactured goods. In return, the CPR obtained a government subsidy to build a branch line from Lethbridge through the Crow's Nest Pass to Nelson, British Columbia. The new line enabled the CPR to exploit the mining fields of southern Alberta and British Columbia. Ottawa also passed the Manitoba Grain Act in 1900, which improved grain storage at loading platforms and warehouses. Then, in 1902, in the Sintaluta case (named after the town in Saskatchewan where the legal challenge arose) the Territorial Grain Growers' Association won its fight against the CPR for failure to provide adequate boxcars for grain shipment at peak periods.

These victories, however, still left the fundamental problem unresolved. The same economic structure—most notably the tariff, which for western farmers symbolized the inequity of Confederation—remained in place. Farmers resented having to buy their agricultural implements and materials in a closed, protected market and to sell their wheat in an open, competitive one. The tariff, they felt, worked directly against their interests, and they demanded that the government reduce it. Traditionally the Liberals were the purported party of freer trade, yet Laurier, despite his promises, held to high tariffs to maintain his central-Canadian political base, particularly in Quebec. The party seemed to be coming around with the negotiation of the Reciprocity deal with the United States in 1911. But the defeat of the Liberals and Reciprocity in the election of 1911 left the western farmers disillusioned. The "agrarian revolt" was under way. Neither traditional party seemed to represent western interests and many farmers spoke openly of creating a third party.

Then the war intervened. Out of loyalty and a desire for a united war effort, farmers rallied behind the traditional parties. With the election of a nonpartisan Union government in 1917, farmers hoped that it would reduce the tariff. When it failed to do so, Thomas Crerar, a Liberal Manitoba farmer, one-time president of the Grain Growers' Grain Company, and minister of agriculture in the Union government, resigned from cabinet in June 1919. Nine other western Unionist MPs followed. But rather than returning to the Liberal fold, they formed the nucleus of a new national Progressive Party.

Farmer candidates did well in the provincial elections held immediately after the war. In Ontario, where rural depopulation posed a serious problem, the dissident United Farmers of Ontario (UFO) won the election of 1919, much to their surprise. Neither the premier, E.C. Drury, a farmer from Simcoe County directly north of Toronto, nor most of his party had any previous legislative experience. In Alberta, in the provincial election of 1921, the United Farmers of Alberta (UFA) swept out the incumbent Liberal Party, which had been in office since 1905. The women's section of the UFA—the United Farm Women of Alberta (UFWA)—under their leader, Irene Parlby, helped the UFA win the election. In Manitoba, the United Farmers of Manitoba (UFM) formed the government in 1922 under John Bracken. In Saskatchewan, the incumbent Liberals only remained in power by implementing the farmers' platform and disassociating themselves from the federal Liberals.

The Progressive Party ran in the 1921 federal election. The results revealed the regional divisions within the country, as well as a new political reality. None of the three main parties—the Liberals, Conservatives, and Progressives—secured a majority and none had representation in all regions. Incumbent Prime Minister Arthur Meighen and the Conservatives suffered a humiliating defeat, winning only 50 seats, with two-thirds of them in Ontario. Mackenzie King and the Liberals won 116 seats, 2 short of a majority. They won every Quebec riding and did well in the

Arch Dales' cartoon in the Grain Growers' Guide in 1915 conveys western farmers' views of Canada's political and economic reality.

Source: Glenbow Archives, Calgary, Canada/NA 3055-24.

Maritimes, but west of the Ottawa River they held only 26 seats. The Progressives won an impressive 65 seats. They swept the West, winning 39 of the 56 ridings, and also gained a significant 24 seats in Ontario, but the new party had no seats in Quebec and just 1 in the Maritimes. Five independents were elected, of whom two agreed to work together to represent labour interests. At the opening of the parliamentary session, Alberta's William Irvine informed the House of Commons: "I wish to state that Mr. Woodsworth is the leader of the labour group ... and I am the group." For the first time in Canadian history, the public elected a House of Commons divided along regional lines. The two-party system was broken. It would never be restored.

The Progressives in Decline

The Progressives were more than a farmers' party. Heavily influenced by like-minded groups in the American Midwest such as the Patrons of Industry, the Grange, and the Non-Partisan League, they represented a widespread dissatisfaction with the traditional political system. The group advocated such ideas as grassroots democracy, group and cooperative government, and non-partisanship. Progressives argued that corruption dominated traditional politics and the system encouraged abuses of power through a partisan system that stifled the voice of elected members by making them responsible to their parties and leaders, rather than the electors. The unequal power relationship among Canada's regions further exacerbated the problems. The Progressive movement found strength in an antimodernist sentiment that lauded the rural and agrarian interests as the vanguard of reform.

But ironically, the Progressive ideology ultimately undermined the effectiveness of the movement. As critics of the traditional political system, the objective was to serve as a pressure group for reform. But how was this to be done without participating and supporting the same system they opposed? In addition, the Progressives were a populist party. Their principles and policies were nonpartisan and they attempted to transcend political ideology. The movement attracted a wide range of reformers, including farmers of various political stripes, urban labourites, left-wing intellectuals, social gospellers, and many people disgruntled with politics emerging from the Great War. But how could these disparate elements come together to form one party?

The divisions took their most obvious form in a split between a Manitoba-based group under Thomas Crerar and an Alberta-based group under Henry Wise Wood, an American populist farmer who came to Alberta in 1905 and became president of the United Farmers of Alberta (UFA) in 1916. Crerar wanted the Progressives to act as a pressure group to force the minority Liberal government to implement policies favourable to farmers. He hoped the Progressives would vote in unison—in essence, as a party. Wood, in contrast, seeing political parties as inherently corrupt, wanted to abolish them altogether in favour of "group government" based on all occupations in society. Wood argued that society naturally divided into distinct economic interest groups, of which the farmers constituted one—the largest on the Prairies. If each group obtained representation in Parliament, the laws passed would reflect the interests of all rather than those of the particular group that happened to control the party. In this way, group cooperation would replace party competition.

Unable to resolve their differences, the Progressives proved politically ineffective. They refused the role of official opposition after the election of 1921 even though, as the second-largest party in the House of Commons, they warranted it. Then, in 1922, Crerar resigned as leader, claiming he could not work with Wood. Robert Forke, Crerar's successor, had no better luck at uniting the party. One of his alleged followers commented that Forke "does not control one Progressive vote other than his own, and he is not always sure about that." In addition, Prime Minister Mackenzie King employed his skills of compromise and conciliation to woo the Progressives. King dismissed the Progressives as "Liberals in a hurry," and in cases such as Crerar, he was correct. The West, in King's eyes, was a natural Liberal region and by his party returning to its liberal philosophy, the region would return to its roots. This entailed implementing policies favourable to the West, including lower tariffs and freight rates. In the following elections, the Progressives declined and the moderates returned to their respective parties. A rump was left, however, that would later serve as the foundation of a new party that would prove more enduring.

In many respects, the Progressives attempted the impossible: to base a party solely on farmers at a time of rural depopulation. They wanted to preserve the family farm, to uphold rural values, and to ensure the political dominance of agricultural interests in an increasingly urban and industrial society. Still, the spirit of the Progressives lived on in the philosophy of populism and in the tradition of western protest. Two new western Canada-based parties in the 1930s—the Co-operative Commonwealth Federation and the Social Credit movement—succeeded them.

The Election of 1925

From 1921 until 1925, Mackenzie King's minority government ruled precariously, relying on the support of the Progressives. To win over the Progressives, King's Liberal government gradually reduced tariffs and restored the preferential freight rates contained in the Crow's Nest Pass Agreement of 1897, suspended during the war years. In terms of other legislation, however, the Liberals did little. John Thompson and Allen Seager note that "it is impossible to point to a single conspicuous legislative achievement between 1922 and 1925."[2] To be fair, King had to maintain the other pillar of the Liberal Party that had ensured his leadership—Quebec. In the years to come, he would have to choose between maintaining party support in the West or Quebec.

The early 1920s were difficult economically and a sense of pessimism pervaded the nation. The Liberals lost heavily in the election of 1925. Their numbers fell from 116 to 99 in a House of Commons with 248 members. Mackenzie King lost his seat, as did 8 other cabinet ministers. Only in Quebec did the Liberals retain their numbers. The Conservatives more than doubled their number of seats to 116, doing well in the Maritimes and Ontario. The Progressives saw their strength decline by almost two-thirds, to 24 seats.

The King–Byng Affair

The Conservatives under Arthur Meighen won the largest number of seats in 1925, but not enough to form a majority. Even though the Progressive numbers declined, they held even more influence in Parliament and again held the balance of power. Despite his party's setback (and not even holding the most seats in Parliament), Mackenzie King believed he could hold onto power with Progressive support. There was no chance the Progressives were going to support the high-tariff Tories. In the throne speech, King made further concessions to westerners by promising a farm-loan program, the immediate completion of a rail link from the Prairies to Hudson Bay, the transfer of the natural resources of the three Prairie provinces to their own control, and tariff revisions. To gain the support of J.S. Woodsworth and his labour followers, King promised an old-age pension plan.

A portrait of Viscount Byng of Vimy and Lady Byng during Byng's time as governor general (1921–26). Lord Byng led the Canadian Expeditionary Force at Vimy Ridge. As governor general he is best remembered for having to negotiate the minority government crisis commonly referred to as the King–Byng Affair.

Source: Rice Studios/Library and Archives Canada/C-033995.

The situation looked encouraging for the Liberals until a scandal broke out in the customs department. Civil servants had received payoffs for allowing liquor smuggling into the United States, where prohibition remained in force. The Progressives, champions of purity in government, could no longer support the Liberals.

Realizing that his government faced certain defeat, King decided to circumvent normal parliamentary procedure. He asked the governor general, Lord Byng, to dissolve Parliament and call an election before a confidence vote could be taken in the House. The prime minister had the constitutional right to make such a request, but the governor general had the right to refuse it—and he did. Byng felt that King was acting dishonourably by not accepting defeat and the verdict of the people in the recent election. King promptly resigned as prime minister (still avoiding defeat in the House) and announced to a surprised House of Commons on Monday, June 28, that the country was without a government. The governor general then asked Meighen, as leader of the opposition, to form a government. Meighen agreed. The new Conservative government lasted only three days, however, before being defeated by a single vote, giving Meighen the dubious honour of presiding over the shortest-lived government since Confederation. Now, the governor general had no choice but to dissolve Parliament and call the election that he had denied King a few days earlier.

In the 1926 election, King took up the traditional Liberal position of advancing Canadian autonomy in the face of imperialism and maintained that the governor general had acted unconstitutionally. By refusing to take the advice of his elected representative, Byng had tried to reduce Canada "from the status of a self-governing Dominion to the status of a Crown Colony." King's strategy worked. It enabled him to focus on the "Constitutional Question" and sidestep the customs scandal, which Meighen claimed was the real issue in the election. Faced with the possibility of a Conservative victory, most Progressives returned to the Liberal fold. Mackenzie King emerged from the election of 1926 with a majority government and 116 seats to the Conservatives' 91.

From Colony to Nation

In the decade from 1919 to 1929, Canada made important advancements toward autonomy from Great Britain. Prime Minister Robert Borden took the first steps along the road from colony to nation in the immediate postwar era. It was Mackenzie King, however, who made the most significant advancements.

Immediate Postwar Advancements

Borden was determined to ensure that Canada benefited from its impressive contribution to the Great War through enhanced national status and an increased voice in imperial affairs. First he pressed for dominion representation in the British Empire delegation at the Paris Peace Conference of 1919, which met to settle the war. The United States questioned why Canada should be involved in the settlement at all, until it was pointed out by the Canadian delegates that Canada had lost more men than the United States. The Big Five (Britain, the United States, France, Italy, and Japan) wanted to make the important decisions, with the "lesser states" involved only in decisions directly affecting them. Because Canada was a dominion of the British Empire, it was assumed that providing Canada a voice would, in essence, be providing Britain more say. Borden found this unacceptable, and he won representation for Canada as a power in its own right at the Paris Peace Conference, in addition to its collective representation as a member of the British Empire delegation.

Borden also insisted on Canada's right to membership in the League of Nations General Assembly as well as eligibility for membership in the governing council of the new international body. Once in the League of Nations, however, Canada wanted to limit its commitment. It opposed Article Ten of the League's charter, the heart of its collective security system, which bound members to come to the aid of other league members in times of attack. Borden feared that this article would commit Canadians to involvement in world disputes that were of no interest to them. (In the end, Article Ten remained in place.)

After 1921, King's Liberal government made significant advances in foreign policy. The prime minister sought to avoid commitments abroad that might force Canada into imperial wars and raise the bogeyman of conscription. To achieve this objective, King delegated himself minister of external affairs and appointed O.D. Skelton, a Queen's University political economist whose outlook on foreign affairs complemented his own, as his undersecretary of state for external affairs, a position Skelton held until his death in 1941.

King's government reduced military expenditures and the size of the Canadian armed forces in the early 1920s. Along with the other Western democracies, Canada consistently opposed any attempt to strengthen the military aspects of the League of Nations. Frequently, Canadian delegates, with King's support, reminded fellow league members of the hundred years of peaceful relations between Canada and the United States. "We think in terms of peace," Senator Dandurand told the league assembly, "while Europe, an armed camp, thinks in terms of war." Canadians, he went on to say, "live in a fire-proof house, far from inflammable material. A vast ocean separates us from Europe." The implication was that Canada could, and should, be isolationist.

The Chanak Crisis, the Halibut Treaty, and the Imperial Conferences

King reacted negatively to British attempts to establish a common imperial foreign policy—imperial centralization, or what was called "Imperial Federation." The test case became the Chanak Crisis. Under the Treaty of Sèvres, one of the treaties ending World War I, the British government agreed to maintain troops in Chanak, Turkey, to ensure the neutrality of the Dardanelles, the strategic straits linking the Black Sea to the Mediterranean. In 1922, Turkish nationalists attempted to oust British troops from the region.

British leaders appealed for a concerted imperial response. King replied that only the Canadian Parliament could decide Canadian participation. Parliament was not in session, and King was in no hurry to summon it. In contrast, opposition leader Arthur Meighen did not mince words. He demonstrated the Conservative approach to imperial relations. "Ready, aye, ready we stand by you" should have been Canada's answer, he asserted. By the time Parliament met, the crisis had passed. The Liberal government's refusal of automatic support in the Chanak Crisis ended the attempt on Britain's part to define a common imperial policy.

The Halibut Treaty of 1923, a Canadian–American agreement relating to fishing rights on the Pacific coast, became the next step on the road to greater Canadian autonomy. By tradition, only agents of the British government signed treaties affecting the dominions. King resented this "badge of colonialism" and decided to use the treaty to assert Canada's diplomatic independence. He arranged for Ernest Lapointe, minister of marine and fisheries, to be the sole signatory for Canada. The British reluctantly consented, fearing that opposition would prompt Canada to establish its own diplomatic relations with Washington, which would lead to even greater disruption. But the British also recognized that Canada was maturing as a nation; the "eldest daughter" of the Empire was growing up. It was preferable for the mother country to foster this independent spirit rather than try to stifle it.

It was at the Imperial Conferences, however, that Mackenzie King took his stand against a united imperial policy. At the Imperial Conference of 1923, Mackenzie King took the leading role in resisting and ultimately in killing any notion of imperial centralization. He was joined in this cause by the prime ministers of South Africa and the Irish Free State. Feeling vulnerable so far from the imperial centre, Australia and New Zealand supported a united imperial policy.

The Balfour Declaration

King and the leaders of the other dominions now sought a formal proclamation that would recognize their equality with Britain. That came with the Balfour Declaration, signed at the Imperial Conference of 1926. It recognized the dominions as "autonomous communities within the British Empire, equal in status, in no way subordinate to one another in any respect of their domestic or external affairs, though united by a common allegiance to the Crown, and freely associated as members of the British Commonwealth of Nations."

In keeping with its recognized equality, Canada established legations or embassies overseas. In 1927, Ottawa opened a legation in Washington, and the United States opened one in Ottawa. Canada also exchanged representatives with Paris and Tokyo in 1928. Britain posted a high commissioner in Ottawa, who henceforth replaced the governor general as the British government's representative. Canada had already had a high commissioner in London since 1884.

The Statute of Westminster

The final step to securing full Canadian autonomy occurred in 1931 with the signing of the Statute of Westminster. This act prohibited the British Parliament from declaring any law passed by the Canadian Parliament as being *ultra vires*, or unconstitutional, except for laws amending the British North America Act. Canada insisted on continued British approval for these laws, because of the failure of the federal and provincial governments to agree on an amending formula among themselves. Some constitutional authorities have viewed the Statute of Westminster as Canada's equivalent of the American Declaration of Independence, because it made Canada constitutionally independent of Britain, except in regard to any laws amending the BNA Act. The Statute of Westminster continued to recognize Canada's allegiance to Britain through a common sovereign.

The Economics of Adjustment

Despite the label "the Roaring Twenties," instability marked the Canadian economy during the decade. It took years to recover from the economic mishandling of the Great War. A transition from the old staple economy of fish, timber, and wheat to a new resource economy of pulp and paper, mining, and consumer production meant adjustment. In the first two years of the decade, Canada faced a crippling business depression. This was followed by several years of slow growth before a four-year boom, beginning in 1925.

The postwar world economy was in shambles. Weakened by war, Britain no longer continued as the financial and economic world leader; it devalued its pound sterling. In contrast, the buoyant economy in the United States increased the value of the American dollar. For Canada, the transition proved especially difficult because of its traditional dependency on British markets for trade and on British financial institutions for investment money. Within a decade, beginning in 1914, British investment fell to less than 46 percent of the total foreign investment in Canada. In contrast, American investment increased to 51 percent. "Never again," economic historians Kenneth Norrie and Douglas Owram note, "would the mother country come close to the United States in its investment in Canada."[3]

Canadians had to adjust to the differing approach of American, as opposed to British, investors. The British preferred indirect investment in the form of bonds and debentures, whereas American investors favoured equity investment (purchasing common shares) and direct control through branch plants. At the time, few Canadians questioned U.S. economic intervention, as they welcomed American investment of any kind. Canadians also increased substantially their exports to the United States. In 1923, for the first time, Canadians exported more to the United States than to Britain.

During this transition, and as a result of the postwar recession, a number of Canadian banks and companies closed or underwent restructuring to avoid collapse. The Home Bank, with its 71 branches across the country, folded in 1923. The Merchant Bank, the Bank of Ottawa, and the Bank of Hamilton sought mergers or were taken over by more stable institutions to avoid similar failures. This instability benefited the larger banks, because people looked to them for sound investment. As well, many companies, nearly 4000 in 1922, went bankrupt. Unemployment in the primary sector increased substantially.

A Brief Economic Boom

By 1925, the economy had temporarily rebounded. The booming American economy and an easing of U.S. protectionist policies increased demand for the traditional Canadian staples of wheat and lumber, as well as the newer staples of pulp and paper and base metals. As freight rates and tariffs declined, prices increased. Farmers expanded their hectarages of wheat production and, beginning in 1923, established wheat pools to market abundant crops. Annually, western farmers hired more than 50,000 harvesters from eastern Canada. The crop in 1928 proved to be the largest on record—567 million bushels. Prices also remained high during these years. Vancouver benefited from the wheat boom, as Prairie farmers increasingly shipped their wheat via Vancouver and the Panama Canal to Europe. By 1925, Vancouver had six storage elevators with a capacity of 6.9 million bushels.

The wheat boom of the mid-1920s did not lead to another era of expansion for farmers, however. Rather, it signalled the final phase of the long cycle of nation building based on the wheat economy. Canadian farmers now had to compete with other wheat-growing regions, such as Argentina, Australia, and the Soviet Union, for a shrinking world market. Canada may have harvested its largest crop in 1928 but it produced much more than the international market could absorb.

Pulp and paper became Canada's leading new export. At the beginning of the 1920s, paper mills in Canada produced 850 million tonnes of newsprint; by the end of the decade, this production increased more than threefold to some 2700 million tonnes—enough to print 40 billion newspapers a year. Much of the demand came from the United States, where mass-produced daily newspapers needed cheap newsprint. American branch-plant mills in Canada produced most of that newsprint. Several factors contributed to this decision: the availability of inexpensive pulpwood; cheap hydroelectric power; good transportation facilities; and lower American import duties. Politics also played a part. Provincial governments either placed an embargo on the export of pulpwood from Crown lands within their borders or imposed a stumpage charge on the number of trees cut, an amount that declined if the producers made the pulp in Canada.

Along with increased production came consolidation. By the end of the decade, three giant companies—International, Abitibi, and Canadian Power and Paper—controlled over half of the pulp production, while the next three largest companies controlled another quarter. Americans owned more than one-third of Canada's pulp production.

Mining followed a similar pattern. After a sluggish period in the early 1920s, the industry revived as a result of American demand for Canadian-based metals to produce such consumer goods as automobiles, radios, and electrical appliances. In Quebec, mineral production increased nearly thirtyfold from 1898 to 1929. Whole new areas, such as Noranda (a name combining the words "North" and "Canada"), Rouyn, Malartic, Val d'Or, and Bourlamaque, opened up with the discovery of new lodes of copper, zinc, lead, and precious metals. In British Columbia, Cominco developed new flotation techniques to mill base metals, which revived a dying industry. In Manitoba, a Canadian–American group, incorporated as Hudson Bay Mining and Smelting, refined the ore at Flin Flon, about 100 kilometres north of The Pas, and at Lynn Lake, still farther north. Ontario benefited greatly from the rich mineral deposits in shield country. The nickel companies in the Sudbury area doubled production during the 1920s, due in part to the decision of the Canadian government in 1922 to create nickel coinage. Inco, the International Nickel Company of Canada, controlled more than 90 percent of world production.

Hydroelectric production quadrupled in the mid-1920s, providing power for the pulp and paper industry and for the refineries. This energy source was particularly important for the production of aluminum from bauxite ore, a process that required substantial amounts of electricity. Provincial governments realized the importance of hydroelectric power for industrialization and the high cost involved in building hydroelectric plants. Ontario nationalized private companies and included them in Ontario Hydro. In Quebec, the industry remained in private hands but developed with the provincial government's financial support.

A Revolution in Transportation and Communications

Growth in the primary sector—wheat, timber, and minerals—multiplied markets in the secondary sector. The most spectacular secondary growth occurred in the automotive industry. Next to the United States, Canada became "the most motorized country on the globe." The numbers of cars, trucks, buses, and motorcycles on Canadian roads tripled from 408,000 in 1920 to 1.235 million a decade later, while the total capital investment in the industry more than doubled, from $40 million to $98 million.

Initially, Canada produced its own cars. At one time as many as 70 small companies manufactured, assembled, or sold automobiles in Canada. By the 1920s, however, this period ended as Canadian companies failed to keep pace with their automated American counterparts that mass-produced less expensive models. Eventually, the Canadian car manufacturers sold out to the American giants. In 1904, Gordon McGregor of the Walkerville Wagon Works obtained a franchise for Canada and the British Empire from the Ford Company of America to establish the Ford Company of Canada. Sam McLaughlin used American technology, expertise, and money to begin producing McLaughlin cars in Oshawa, Ontario, and then sold his company in 1918 to General Motors of America. From 1923 onward, the Canadian branch of General Motors oversaw the production of the entire line of GM models, including Chevrolets and Cadillacs, and sold them throughout Canada and the Commonwealth. Chrysler, the last of the "Big Three" manufacturers to appear in Canada, came when the American automobile tycoon Walter P. Chrysler bought out the ailing Maxwell-Chalmers company of Windsor in 1925 to establish the Chrysler Company of Canada. By the end of the decade, the American "Big Three" manufactured three-quarters of the cars purchased in Canada.

Traffic congestion on Toronto's Yonge Street in 1929. Streetcars had to contend with automobiles in ever-increasing numbers.

Source: City of Toronto Archives/TTC Fonds, Series 71, Item 7172 (Queen and Yonge, looking north, traffic, noon–1pm–April 30, 1929).

Airplanes sharply reduced travel time. In 1934, travellers from Fort McMurray in northern Alberta to Great Bear Lake in the Northwest Territories could choose between 30 days by steamboat or 8 hours by plane.

Source: *Canadian Geographical Journal* 10(5) (May 1935): 241.

Canadians had already begun to worship "the great god CAR."[4] By the end of the decade, one-quarter of all potential owners had an automobile. The car revolutionized the Canadian landscape as the railway had done seventy years earlier. Roads regained their dominance and in the cities, paved streets became commonplace. In 1925, Canada had 75,200 kilometres of surfaced roads; by 1930, this had increased to 128,000 kilometres. Tire companies and factories emerged to produce tires and spare parts, service stations sprang up, and tourism prospered. The car made it easier to get to vacation areas— where there were roads.

Aviation also expanded in the 1920s. Veteran World War I flying aces, using surplus war planes, opened up the North. They flew geologists and prospectors into remote areas of the Canadian Shield and provided service to isolated northern settlements. These pilots travelled by visual flying: lacking proper maps, they had to stay at low altitudes to spot landmarks. In 1924, Laurentide Air Services began Canada's first regular air-mail service, into the Quebec gold fields at Rouyn–Noranda. Other companies followed, and for several years the Canadian government permitted each company to print and issue its own postage stamps.

Innovations in communications technology became popular in the 1920s. The telephone became a standard household item. Radio, the great communications invention of the 1920s, helped to diminish isolation. The first scheduled broadcast in North America took place in Montreal in May 1920, when station XWA (later CFCF) relayed a musical program to a Royal Society of Canada meeting in Ottawa. Others were quick to realize the potential of this new invention. By mid-decade, there were numerous stations (most of them small and low-powered) across the country.

Service Industries

Service industries grew to meet the demand of the new consumer age. Retailing, wholesaling, insurance, and banking needs meant more offices and a vast amount of paperwork. The number of managerial and clerical positions grew to keep pace. Mass production, thanks to improved technology, contributed to lower consumer prices. Effective advertising kept consumer goods in the public mind, heightening the demand. Chain stores became popular, accounting for 90 percent of sales by the end of the decade. Their wide array of material goods appealed to every taste. The T. Eaton Company competed effectively with such American chain stores as Kresge's, Woolworth's, and Metropolitan. Large supermarkets, such as Safeway, Dominion, Overwaitea, A&P, Loblaws, and IGA, began replacing the small corner-grocery store and offering a larger variety of food items and cheaper prices. Women dominated as retail clerks in these large grocery and department stores, but not at the managerial level.

Disillusionment and the Decline of Reform

The initial euphoria and the hope for world peace following the "war to end all wars" died quickly after the armistice. Around the globe many nations, instead of emerging into freedom and liberty, slipped back into tyranny and oppression. The new millennium, embodied in

American President Woodrow Wilson's fourteen-point program to ensure world peace forever, never arrived. Canadians' awareness of the failed peace contributed to their disillusionment. On November 12, 1924, the *Varsity*, the student newspaper at the University of Toronto, summarized the Armistice Day address of history professor G.M. Smith, a distinguished soldier and the winner of the Military Cross in the Great War:

> *The idealism of youth, and its enthusiasm in fighting for what they considered a good cause, the optimistic spirit which filled the people during the war and reached its climax when the Armistice was signed, all this is shattered by the six years aftermath. The fourteen points became the fourteen disappointments and self-determination has become selfish-determination.*

The impetus for reform declined in part because certain aspects of the movement achieved success. By 1921, workers had a higher standard of living and had gained increased recognition from employers. Women had the franchise federally and in most provinces. Prohibitionists had succeeded in eliminating legalized drinking. Achievements for educational reformers included better schools, children staying in school longer, and better-qualified teachers. The spirit of reform died because minimal objectives had been reached, and for many, most notably those in power, this was enough. More reform meant more substantial change. In a panicky and paranoid era marked by supposed fear of "Bolshevism," the line between reform and revolution seemed murky. This fear was used to thwart change and instead to fall back on the status quo.

Prohibition and Women's Suffrage

In some instances, a reaction to reform set in. Prohibitionists, for example, saw the provincial temperance acts removed one by one. By the end of the 1920s, government-regulated outlets sold liquor in every province except Prince Edward Island. Ironically, returned soldiers—the very people prohibitionists had used as justification to fight *for* prohibition during the war years—played a large part in ending prohibition, as they demanded legalized drinking.

The women's suffrage movement obtained the vote, but the electorate returned few women to either federal or provincial governments. Agnes Macphail became the only woman elected in the federal election of 1921 and was Canada's first woman member of Parliament. She served until her defeat in 1940, and then sat for several years in the Ontario legislature as a CCF member. Only one other woman, Martha Black, sat in the House of Commons in the interwar years, representing her husband's Yukon constituency from 1935 to 1940, when he was incapacitated by poor health. Provincially, women did better at entering politics, although the results were a far cry from their expectations. By 1940, only nine women sat in provincial legislatures, all of them in the four western provinces. Mary Ellen Smith of British Columbia held the distinction of being the first woman cabinet minister in the British Empire when she was appointed in 1921 as minister without portfolio. However, she held the position for only nine months before resigning. Even the usually optimistic Nellie McClung expressed the disillusionment of the time: "When women were given the vote in 1916–17 … we were obsessed with the belief that we could cleanse and purify the world by law.… But when all was over, and the smoke of battle cleared away, something happened to us. Our forces, so well organized for the campaign, began to dwindle."

In Canadian society, women faced continued discrimination. Not until 1929, for example, were women considered "persons" in the act stipulating eligibility for the Canadian Senate and a variety of other privileged bodies. In the famous "Persons Case," five Alberta women reformers— Emily Murphy, the first woman police magistrate in the British Empire; Irene Parlby, who became, in 1921, the first woman cabinet minister in Alberta; Nellie McClung, a member of the Alberta legislature; and Henrietta Edwards and Louise McKinney, two suffragists and prohibitionists—succeeded in securing a favourable decision from the Judicial Committee of the Privy Council that women were indeed "persons" and thus eligible for membership in all Canadian legislative bodies. The victory, however, was symbolic and meant little to the advancement of women's equality on the ground.

Urban reform languished in the interwar years, in part because the middle-class group most involved in reform began to move out of the city centres and into the suburbs. Suburbanization occurred at an astonishing rate in the 1920s with the development of tramlines and the increasing popularity of the automobile.

Social evangelicals within the mainstream churches continued to advance the reform agenda. In many ways, they filled the gap left by urban progressivism. Increasingly they worked with experts (university-trained social scientists), business groups, and labour organizations to advance social investigation and policymaking. In 1925, reformers within the Methodist, Presbyterian, and Congregationalist churches created the United Church of Canada.

L'Action française

In the 1920s, conservative elements in Quebec's Roman Catholic community reacted to the forces of modernism. Abbé Lionel Groulx, the editor of *L'Action française* magazine, which had only 5000 subscribers at its peak but was widely read by nationalist elites, saw the onslaught of urban and industrial society as anathema to Quebec's traditional core values: church, family, and homeland. In his magazine, Groulx launched an all-out attack—"l'action française"—on those forces that he believed were contributing to the anglicization and Americanization of Quebec.

L'Action française called for greater French-Canadian control of Quebec's modern industrial economy. While contributors to the magazine deplored the economic weakness of French Canadians, most of them still believed that agriculture should be the cornerstone of the Quebec economy. They opposed the growing urban migration, especially to Montreal. To *L'Action française*, the migration threatened the very existence of the French Canadians as traditionally rural, agricultural people. The trend toward modernization also threatened the morale base of what was perceived as French Catholic society. The revolutions in transportation and communication exposed Quebeckers to material and cultural influences coming from English Canada, the United States, and Britain.

"Cities bred standardization, homogeneity, and ultimately, they suspected, assimilation."[5] To counter this urbanization, L'Action française stressed the traditional values of the land, the church, and the nation. Groulx put a special responsibility on women as guardians of the home and the family. In 1922, *L'Action française* flirted with the idea of political independence for Quebec, but it returned by the late 1920s to the position that French Canadians should have more rights within Confederation.

Elsie Hall, class of 1920, first woman graduate of the College of Law, University of Saskatchewan.

Women in the 1920s

Women made only modest gains in the 1920s. Few had the opportunity for a secondary education; in 1929, only 25 percent of secondary-school students were women. Of the few who entered professions, most became teachers or nurses, while only a handful became physicians, lawyers, or professors, and a very tiny number, engineers. Nursing took on new importance in the 1920s in the light of the contribution nurses made during the war and the Spanish influenza epidemic that followed. In 1919, the University of British Columbia offered the first university-degree program in nursing. Similar programs followed at the University of Toronto and McGill University in the 1920s.

Women who worked outside the home in industry or business—20 percent of the labour force in 1929—held traditional female jobs as secretaries, sales clerks in department stores, and domestics. Others worked on assembly lines in textile or tobacco factories, canneries, or fish plants. In these jobs, women earned considerably less than men doing the same job. Economic equality, like political equality, remained an elusive goal for women.

Unions did little to organize working women, even in female-dominated industries. Seldom did they support women on strike. Some union locals included males and females, but even when unions included women, they usually subordinated their interests to men's. Agreements with employers commonly included lower female wage scales. In some cases, unions demanded equal pay for women and men—not to combat discrimination against women but rather to ensure that employers would have no financial reason to replace male employees with females.

Although many farms were becoming more mechanized in the 1920s, the farmhouses remained basic. Farm wives were expected to help outside the house at critical times of the year, while they continued caring for the children, cooking, cleaning, laundering, and sewing. Women were not "pulling in double harness" but they were "hauling a double load."[6] Rural reform leaders advocated household-science courses, cooperation, and the use of more household appliances as ways of alleviating the burden.

Urban middle-class women enjoyed a higher standard of living than their rural counterparts. Many benefited from new modern labour-saving devices such as refrigerators, electric stoves, and vacuum cleaners, and from such luxuries as electricity and running water. Ironically, these "conveniences" increased the amount of time women spent in the home. In many cases, conveniences simply raised the standards expected of women in the domestic realm.

With the rise of psychology as a respected academic discipline, a plethora of "how to parent" books made child rearing more rigorous and scientific in the 1920s. In some of the books, children were viewed as "little machines" to be scheduled routinely for basic activities. Dr. Helen MacMurchy, chief of the newly created Child Welfare Division of the federal Department of Health, reminded women in 1919 that "being a mother is the highest of all professions and the most extensive of all undertakings." To prepare them for their new role, girls were encouraged to stay in school longer and to concentrate on domestic-science courses.

The women who dared to challenge gender norms, particularly around sexuality—the "flappers"— dressed more freely, smoked in public, danced, and drank at parties. The birth-control movement began in Vancouver in 1923 with the formation of the Canadian Birth Control League, the idea inspired by the visit of the American birth-control advocate Margaret Sanger. Women, however, had to wait until the 1930s for any birth-control clinics to open.

Friends near Prince Albert, Saskatchewan, each enjoying a smoke. In the 1920s women flaunted smoking cigarettes as a sign of liberation.

Source: Saskatchewan Archives Board/R-A1259.

A Culture of Youth

The 1920s witnessed an emphasis on youth. A generation of young men had been lost on the battlefields of Europe. The impact of this slaughter, combined with the new forces of modernity, led to a new youth culture. Realizing where the past had led, the new generation was more determined to live for the moment and enjoy life. Leisure time was increasing and leisurely pursuits were more available. Consumerism offered a new and wide range of goods to enjoy. Innovations in travel and communications conflated time and space, and exposed youth to a popular culture influenced by music and cinema from Europe and the United States.

The Role of the State

The role of the state increased as a result of the Great War. While some of the state's interventions into society (such as the creation of the Wheat Board) were temporary, others (such as the income tax) were permanent. The rise of the state, however, also curtailed the impetus for reform. But the state's innovations in the 1920s were conservative. Limited social assistance programs prevailed in the decade. The Department of Soldiers' Civil Re-establishment, the federal government agency responsible for veterans' affairs, administered military pensions along with retraining and employment programs. However, 80 percent of the applicants were rejected on the grounds that they were physically able to return to their previous employment. Veterans with mental disorders were seldom considered disabled and therefore denied assistance. Calls for unemployment insurance, old-age pensions, and mother's allowances, which were heard loudly in the immediate postwar era and found their way into the Liberal Platform of 1919, were shelved.

In 1925, Mackenzie King's minority Liberal government promised to work with the provinces in a jointly funded program of old-age pensions in return for political support from J.S. Woodsworth and his followers. The government fell before King could fulfill his promise, but he moved on the legislation when re-elected in 1926. The federal legislation, however, was restrictive. It provided pensions only for people over 70 whose annual income was no more than $125. Some provinces imposed further restrictions.

As part of the rise of the professional expert, social work began as a profession in the 1920s. In 1922, the Canadian Welfare Council under the direction of Charlotte Whitton was formed. Its main concern was the care of children. In 1926, the Canadian Association of Social Workers was formed. Its constitution set out its mission: "to promote professional standards, encourage proper and adequate training, and cultivate an informed public opinion which will recognize the professional and technical nature of social work." Increasingly, university-trained sociologists and social workers were called upon to produce reports and statistics on social trends in Canadian society.

First Nations

The experience of the First Nations peoples in the 1920s varied across Canada. The process and experience of contact occurred centuries apart, depending on region. By the 1920s, First Nations in the Maritimes and central Canada had been dealing with colonial subordination and the forces of assimilation since the seventeenth century; the Plains tribes had been encountering white incursions since the nineteenth century; but many groups on the Pacific coast and in the North had suffered the effects of contact since the early twentieth century. Treaty Eleven was signed in the Mackenzie Valley only in 1921. Regardless of region and era, however, the stages of contact were similar. They included economic dislocation, cultural transformation, loss of land and territory, and decimation from disease.

Much of the change to First Nations in the 1920s occurred as a result of the Shield country being opened to new resource industries. In the northern forested areas, the First Nations and Métis suffered when boom prices for furs led to an influx of non-Aboriginal trappers. As well, intensive trapping resulted in a serious depletion in the number of beaver. Wage labour, however, partially compensated for the loss of income from trapping, now necessary to buy trade goods and store food. Some First Nations and Métis people worked as tourist guides, commercial fishers, miners, railway workers, and loggers. In the south, farming on the reserves declined as heavy expenditures became necessary for the new farm machinery. Among the Iroquois, high steel rigging, although dangerous work, remained popular and lucrative. On the Pacific coast, First Nations people could obtain jobs in logging and commercial fishing. A number of independent First Nations operators owned and operated gas-powered gillnetters, trollers, and seine boats.

But for the most part, the First Nations were a forgotten people in the interwar period. It was still assumed that they were a dying race. Government policy rarely concerned itself with the First Nations. With the treaty process complete, they were expected to live on the reserves until being ready to enter society as Canadian citizens. In the meantime, they would be prepared for the transition through the agents and institutions of the state, including churches and residential schools. Their badge of citizenship, when ready, included loss of Indian status and culture, loss of their treaty rights, racial discrimination and persecution by the host society, and of course the right to pay taxes. Not surprisingly, the assimilation of the First Nations failed. Instead, the population slipped into Third-World living conditions and faced a state-sponsored apartheid system. The Canadian state and society was about to wake up to realize that this population was not going to die out or simply disappear.

A HISTORICAL PORTRAIT

Onondeyoh (Fred Loft)

Fred Loft, or Onondeyoh ("Beautiful Mountain"), a Mohawk in the Ontario civil service, sought improvement of the system of education offered to the First Nations. Immediately after World War I, the Mohawk veteran established the League of Indians of Canada, the country's first pan-Indian political association.

Fred Loft was born February 3, 1861, on the Six Nations Reserve near Brantford, Ontario. His parents (who spoke English as well as Mohawk) were devoted Anglicans. He attended a local school until the age of 12, when he boarded for a year at the Mohawk Institute, an Indian residential school in Brantford. Bitterly, he remembered the experience: "I recall the times when working in the fields, I was actually too hungry to be able to walk, let alone work.... In winter the rooms and beds were so cold that it took half the night before I got warm enough to fall asleep."

Anxious to get the best education possible, Loft attended high school in the neighbouring non-Native community of Caledonia. After graduation, he won a scholarship to the Ontario Business College in Belleville. After briefly working as a journalist for a Brantford paper, he obtained a job as an accountant in the bursar's office

Fred Loft with his company of First Nations soldiers in the Forestry Corps, Canadian Expeditionary Force, Windsor Park, England, July 1917.

Source: Photo courtesy of the late Affa Loft Matteson, daughter of Fred Loft.

at the Provincial Lunatic Asylum in Toronto, where he stayed for forty years.

In 1898, the Mohawk civil servant met and married Affa Northcote Geare, a lively, energetic woman of British descent, eleven years younger. In 1899, Affa gave birth to twins, one of whom died in 1902. Another daughter was born in 1904. For many years the family depended on Affa for extras. She had a sharp business sense; she bought and sold houses, rented to roomers, and owned stock.

The Lofts had an active social life, with season tickets to two Toronto theatres. Fred participated in the Masons and the United Empire Loyalist Association and was active in the militia. Every Sunday he attended church. He also returned regularly to the Six Nations Reserve to visit his family. His daughters spent many summers at the family farm.

Unsuccessfully, the Six Nations Council requested the federal government to select him in 1907, and again in 1917, as their superintendent.

As a staunch supporter of Britain, Fred Loft visited Ontario Indian reserves during World War I to encourage Aboriginal recruitment. Anxious to go overseas himself, he served as an officer in France in the Canadian Forestry Corps.

Upon his return from Europe, the Mohawk veteran founded the League of Indians of Canada. The first annual meetings were held in Ontario, then in Manitoba (1920), Saskatchewan (1921), and Alberta (1922). Problems surfaced immediately. Money was short, and correspondence itself proved difficult. As Fred Loft stated,

The sad want of better schooling is evidenced by the fact that scarcely five percent of the adult population on reserves are capable of corresponding intelligently....This is a most unfortunate admission to be made after 75 years of school work among Indians of Eastern Canada at least.

The Department of Indian Affairs' unrelenting opposition to the league, and Loft's poor health in the early 1930s, further weakened it.

At the time of Fred Loft's death in 1934, the league, apart from its western Canadian branches, had come to a complete halt. But Loft's example would be remembered in the creation of the Assembly of First Nations forty years later.

Labour in the 1920s

Labour unions faced difficult times in the 1920s, as business leaders attempted to limit trade union effectiveness. Wage cuts, industrial consolidation, improved technology, and managerial efficiency all weakened the labour movement. Workers retaliated by staging strikes, many of them ending in physical violence. For example, 22,000 coal miners, mainly in Alberta, walked out on strike in August 1922. In 1923, a confrontation occurred in the coal mines of Nova Scotia. J.B. McLachlan, the militant Scottish immigrant worker and socialist who helped found the

Amalgamated Mine Workers of Nova Scotia in 1917, led the strike against BESCO, the leading steel company in the region. "War is on us, class war," he proclaimed in one of his fiery speeches. The company's vice-president replied: "Let them stay out two months or six months, it matters not; eventually they will come crawling back." The company eventually mobilized its security force to break the strike. The workers won limited concessions but a legacy of anger remained. In most other strikes across the country, strikers failed to improve wages or working conditions. As a result, union membership plummeted by more than a third by mid-decade, reaching a low of 260,000 members.

Unions were also divided. The Trades and Labor Congress (TLC) continued to favour craft unions and to advocate advancement only through conciliation and government intervention. Thus the TLC refused to back the strikers against BESCO. When Samuel Gompers, founder of the American Federation of Labor (AFL) and the inspiration behind the TLC, died later that year, McLachlan, invited to the funeral, replied: "Sorry, duties will not permit me to attend, but I heartily approve of the event." In 1927, a new militant All-Canadian Congress of Labour (ACCL) union was established. It favoured industry-wide unions and strike action.

In Quebec, some workers and farmers joined Catholic unions sanctioned by the church. These unions attempted to isolate their members from the more secular and often socialistic "foreign"—American or English-Canadian—unions. The Confédération des travailleurs catholiques du Canada (CTCC) brought 20,000 workers from a variety of industries and occupations into its organization in 1921. The Union catholique des cultivateurs (UCC) in 1924 had a membership of 13,000 farmers. By the 1930s, the UCC had joined with the clergy to organize farmers' wives and to compete with the state-sponsored Cercles de fermières. Throughout the 1920s, the CTCC and the UCC failed to attract more than one-quarter of the total Quebec union membership.

Cultural Developments

Cultural life flourished in the 1920s. Arthur Lismer, one of the Group of Seven artists, later recalled: "After 1919, most creative people, whether in painting, writing or music, began to have a guilty feeling that Canada was as yet unwritten, unpainted, unsung…. In 1920 there was a job to be done." French-Canadian artists, writers, and performers shared the same aspiration, although in their case, Quebec tended to be their frame of reference. Popular culture also flourished, especially with the advent of radio in the 1920s.

Visual Arts

In English Canada, seven artists calling themselves the Group of Seven dominated contemporary art. The original members—Franklin Carmichael, Lawren Harris, A.Y. Jackson, Frank Johnston, Arthur Lismer, J.E.H. MacDonald, and F.H. Varley—had met before the war. Most worked for the Toronto commercial-art company Grip, and belonged to the Arts and Letters Club. Artist Tom Thomson was part of this circle of friends, but he drowned in a canoe accident in Algonquin Park in 1917 before the group formed. In the

The West Wind, *by Tom Thomson, 1917, one of his best-known paintings. Thomson died in a canoe accident in Algonquin Park in 1917, and thus was not a founding member of the Group of Seven when it formed in 1920. He did, however, serve as an inspiration for the group.*

Source: Tom Thomson, *The West Wind*, winter 1916–1917; oil on canvas; Overall: 120.7 × 137.9 cm (47 1/2 × 54 5/16 in.); ART GALLERY OF ONTARIO; Gift of the Canadian Club of Toronto, 1926; 784; Canadian, 1877–1917; © 2016 Art Gallery of Ontario.

year of his death, he produced *The Jack Pine* and *The West Wind*, two paintings that have become icons of Canadian art. Thomson became an inspiration and patron saint for the Group of Seven when it formed officially in early 1920.

The first Group of Seven exhibition was held in May 1920. The exhibition catalogue claimed that art must reflect "the spirit of a nation's growth." The Group of Seven believed that "spirit" could best be found in the land—in the trees, rocks, and lakes of the Ontario northland. They depicted the land in brilliant mosaics of bright colours. For the Group of Seven, the Ontario northland symbolized the nation the same way the West did in the American tradition—a mythical land that became a metaphor for the Canadian people. As well, the "North" represented a counterforce to the "South," especially the United States, where urbanization, industrialism, and materialism threatened to undermine the Canadian spirit.

Some art critics at the time denounced the group's paintings as belonging to the "Hot Mush School" and its members as "paint slingers." The Group of Seven thrived on the criticism. It indicated that their art challenged the establishment and broke new ground. The group found a strong supporter in Eric Brown, director of the National Gallery in Ottawa, who selected their paintings to represent Canadian art at the British Empire Exhibition at Wembley in 1924. By the time the Group of Seven disbanded in 1931, their members were "elevated to the status of Canadian cultural heroes and their work enshrined as national icons,"[7] even though their best-known paintings depicted only one region of Ontario, the Algoma district, a section south of the 49th parallel. The Group of Seven allowed their paintings of wilderness to be used by government officials and commercial companies to promote tourism.

COMMUNITY PORTRAIT

The Arts and Letters Club as a Cultural Community

Founded in 1908, Toronto's Arts and Letters Club brought together writers, architects, musicians, artists, and dramatists, with a minority membership of nonprofessionals "with artistic tastes and inclinations" to promote an appreciation of the arts. The membership, restricted to men, expanded rapidly in the 1910s to comprise a significant number of the Toronto arts community; it also included several wealthy Toronto entrepreneurs, friends of the arts. These entrepreneurs greatly assisted an emerging group of artists, who in 1920 became the Group of Seven. The friendly atmosphere of the club provided the members "with an opportunity to meet Toronto's wealthy elite, who were to become their first patrons."[1] These entrepreneurs found in the club

a haven from the purely commercial nature of modern Toronto. In the words of Augustus Bridle, a founding member, the Club's president in 1913–14, and author of *The Story of the Club* (1945), the Club provided for all its members "absolute escape from all that otherwise made Toronto."[2]

The members consciously created a sense of community through the Club's location, its decor, and activities. Members believed that poverty would help to draw them together as a community. Hence, despite the wealth of a number of members, they chose modest locations for their headquarters. Their first locale was a garret next door to the Brown Betty restaurant, which was opposite— not in—the opulent King Edward Hotel. It consisted of one room and a cubbyhole in which to make coffee. Evicted ten months later, club members moved to the old Assize Court room behind No. 1 Police Station, "the most impressive, inaccessible room in Toronto." Bridle boasted that "just before the inaugural dinner day we had neither gas in the kitchen nor electricity in the hall."[3] Yet the event was a great hit as members rallied in support.

In the 1920s, the club leased St. George's Hall at 14 Elm Street. According to Bridle, each move heightened the mythical belief in the spirit of community that prevailed in the previous locale, and made club members determined to create a similar ambience. So the first thing club members did in their St. George location was to build a "collegiate-gothic fireplace." Then they commissioned club member and artist George Reid to paint a mural panel of the club's Viking crest on the adjacent wall to the fireplace. The crest had been the work of artist J.E.H. MacDonald, who joined the club in 1911. It consisted of a "Viking ship with the sails full spread before the rising sun to remind us of the open sea and the great adventure."

Club members performed rituals along medieval lines, drawing examples in particular from "the brotherhood of medieval monks."[4] Members also purchased a farm to which they could retreat from the stresses of modern life. Camping and canoeing, and other club activities, contributed to a life of simplicity and friendship. As well, club members got involved in social reform activities in Toronto to enhance the sense of community in the city at large. Of particular importance to members, especially for University of Toronto political economist James Mavor, was the Guild of Civic Art.

FURTHER READING

Charles C.H. Hill, *The Group of Seven: Art for a Nation* (Toronto: McClelland and Stewart, 1995).

Karen Leslie Knutson, "Absolute Escape from All That Otherwise Made Toronto: Antimodernism at the Arts and Letters Club, 1908–1920," M.A. thesis, Queen's University, 1995.

1   Peter Mellen, *The Group of Seven* (Toronto: McClelland and Stewart, 1970), p. 19.

2   Augustus Bridle, *The Story of the Club* (Toronto: The Arts & Letters Club, 1945), p. 10.

3   Ibid., p. 2.

4   Ibid., p. 39.

In British Columbia, artist Emily Carr visited First Nations communities along the Pacific coast and in the interior of the province. She painted scenes of their villages, buildings, and totem poles. Unable to support herself by her painting alone, she ran a boarding house in Victoria. In 1927 she made a trip to eastern Canada where she met Lawren Harris and other members of the Group of Seven. Her contact with the group, particularly Lawren Harris, gave a fresh direction to her work. After first viewing Harris's works, she wrote: "Oh, God, what have I seen? Where have I been? Something has spoken to the very soul of me, wonderful, mighty, not of this world."

In 1932, at age 57, Carr launched into the most productive period of her artistic career. She emphasized nature themes over First Nations subjects in her paintings. When she suffered a heart attack in 1937, she turned to writing. Her first book, *Klee Wyck*, described her early painting trips to First Nations communities. It won her the Governor General's Award for general literature in 1941. "Klee Wyck," meaning "laughing one," was the name given Emily

Six members of the Group of Seven, plus a friend, at a 1920 luncheon at the Arts and Letters Club. From left to right: F.H. Varley, A.Y. Jackson, Lawren Harris, Barker Fairley (a strong supporter of the Group, but not a member), Frank Johnston, Arthur Lismer, and J.E.H. MacDonald. Only Franklin Carmichael is missing.

Source: Photo by Arthur Goss, The Arts and Letters Club, Toronto.

Carr by the Nuu-chah-nulth (formerly known as Nootka) people at Ucluelet on the west coast of Vancouver Island.

Literature

A new literary culture emerged in the 1920s. In English-speaking Canada, two new journals appeared to capture and epitomize the cultural renaissance: *Canadian Forum* and *Canadian Historical Review*. In the inaugural issue of *Canadian Forum* in 1920, the editors promised that the journal would "trace and value those developments of arts and letters which are distinctively Canadian." Equally, *Canadian Historical Review* noted in an article titled "The Growth of Canadian National Feeling" in the second issue that the "central fact in Canadian history" has been the evolution of a "national consciousness." The Canadian Authors' Association (CAA), founded in 1921 for the purpose of using literature "to articulate a national identity and to foster a sense of community within the country," aided young English-Canadian writers in publishing their works. The CAA sponsored summer schools and gave literary prizes. These nationalistic journals and organizations reflected the growing political nationalism of the period. They also, however, served to counteract the growing Americanization of Canadian culture. "By 1925," historian Mary Vipond notes, "it was estimated that for every domestic magazine sold in Canada, eight were imported from the United States—a total of around fifty million copies per year."[8]

In poetry, E.J. (Ned) Pratt of Newfoundland introduced modernism into Canadian poetry in his *Newfoundland Verse* (1923). A professor of English at Victoria College, University of Toronto, Pratt used familiar Canadian scenes or events, often from his native Newfoundland, as the subjects for his poems and elevated them to mythical proportions. Pratt inspired a younger generation of poets.

At McGill University, a group of young, rebellious poets known as the Montreal Group— F.R. Scott, A.J.M. Smith, A.M. Klein, and Leo Kennedy—endorsed the modernist movement. They wrote in free verse, discarded the norms of punctuation, and chose their subject material from the modern city. In Quebec, a group of young poets challenged the establishment in the pages of *Le Nigog*, the first arts magazine in Quebec, founded by architect Fernand Préfontaine, writer Robert de Roquebrune, and musician Léo-Paul Morin. Ironically, although this group and the Montreal Group resided in the same city, they worked in isolation from one another.

Most novels of the 1920s continued in the romantic tradition. Mazo de la Roche's *Jalna* (1927) chronicled the life of the fictional Whiteoaks family. Her romantic depiction of rural Ontario life sold close to 100,000 copies within a few months of publication, resulting in sixteen sequels. Three novels, however, stood out for their realism: Frederick Philip Grove's *Settlers of the Marsh* (1925), in which Grove explored the inner psychic tension of a Norwegian settler on the Prairies; Martha Ostenso's *Wild Geese* (1925), about the tyrannical patriarch Caleb Gare, who aims to dominate both his land and his family and in the process destroys himself; and R.J.C. Stead's *Grain* (1926), which describes the tensions that farm boy Gander Stake faces in having to choose between life on the farm and in the city.

Music

The University of Toronto's Faculty of Music opened in 1919. The university also housed the Hart House String Quartet, founded in 1924 by Vincent Massey of the influential Massey family. The Masseys also continued to support Massey Hall, the location of many musical performances, including the concerts of the Toronto Symphony Orchestra. Schools of Music also began at McGill in 1920, and at Laval in 1922.

The real innovation in music, however, occurred through radio broadcasting. Many Canadian musicians got their start on radio. Radio was used to celebrate the Diamond Jubilee of Confederation in 1927. Beginning in 1929, the Toronto Symphony Orchestra performed 25 concerts over the radio, the last of which was devoted entirely to music by Canadian composers. The concerts could be heard throughout the country.

By 1930, some 60 radio stations existed across the country. Offerings were sparse, as no station transmitted for more than a few hours a day. Programs consisted mainly of news, lectures, or recorded music, compared with the comedies, drama, and live variety of American programs. Canadians fortunate enough to be close to the international border listened to American radio stations, which carried popular programs and had stronger transmitters. Rather than compete, Canadian stations themselves bought the right to broadcast these American shows. By 1930, an estimated 80 percent of the programs Canadians listened to came from the United States.

Concerned about the negative impact on Canadian culture posed by the Americanization of radio broadcasting, the federal government established a royal commission—the Aird Commission—to review public broadcasting. The Aird report recommended that broadcasting become a public monopoly, without competitors and with limited commercial content. The Canadian Radio League, founded by English-Canadian nationalists Alan Plaunt, Graham Spry, and Brooke Claxton, concurred. They hoped, as did the members of the Aird Commission, that public broadcasting would help unite Canadians. Out of their efforts came the Canadian Broadcasting Corporation (CBC) in the 1930s.

Frederick Philip Grove in the early 1920s, rafting on Lake Winnipeg with his daughter, May. He was actually Felix Paul Greve, a German translator and writer who faked his own suicide in 1909 by appearing to throw himself off a boat. Having successfully escaped his creditors, three years later he surfaced as Frederick Philip Grove in Manitoba. In his lifetime no one in Canada knew his real identity. The true story was revealed twenty-five years after his death, when D.O. Spettigue published his biography of Grove, FPG: The European Years (1973).

Source: University of Manitoba Archives and Special Collections, The Libraries/PC 2, No. 10.

Popular Culture

Canadian popular culture became more Americanized in the 1920s. American-style service clubs such as Rotary, Lions, Kiwanis, and Gyro gained in popularity, although the uniquely Canadian organization the Kinsmen, founded in 1920 in Hamilton, Ontario, held its own. (Half a century later, the Kinsmen would become Canada's largest national service organization.)

Nell Shipman with a friend in Back to God's Country *(1919).*

Source: Library and Archives Canada/MISA-4857.

The Movie Industry

The Americanization of popular culture occurred most noticeably in the movie industry. Initially, it did not appear that this would be the case. Between 1919 and 1923, Canada had a thriving domestic feature film industry that used Canadian settings, casts, and crews. The country also had its own famous movie maker, Ernest Shipman. Born in Hull, Quebec, in 1871, he produced seven successful feature films between 1919 and 1922 based on Canadian wilderness tales by such popular authors as James Oliver Curwood (*Back to God's Country*) and Ralph Connor (*The Man from Glengarry*). By 1922 Canada even had its own chain of theatres, owned by the Allen brothers of Brantford, Ontario, with company headquarters in Calgary, Alberta.

Thereafter, the Canadian movie industry went into a precipitous decline. Shipman tried unsuccessfully to break into the Hollywood scene. He was also a victim of the transition in the 1920s from independent movie producers to corporate producers. Canadian companies succumbed to the "Big Five" studios in Hollywood—Paramount, MGM, Warner Brothers, Fox, and RKO. By 1929, the Big Five produced and distributed 90 percent of all feature films in North America. The introduction of the "talkies" in 1927 strengthened the American stranglehold on Canadian filmmaking because of the high production costs. As well, in 1923, the Famous Players Canadian Corporation bought out the Allen theatre chain. The federal government refused to intervene to save the feature film industry in Canada. Government officials were interested only in promotional propaganda films and documentaries.

Quebec filmmaking faced its own challenges. In January 1927, a tragic fire at the Laurier Palace theatre in Montreal killed 78, mostly children. The Quebec government reacted by prohibiting children under the age of 16 from attending the cinema—a law that remained in effect until 1967. The film industry also faced opposition from the Catholic Church, which saw movies as immoral and an insidious form of Americanization. The Quebec government established a strict censor board to screen all films for immoralities.

Sport

The professionalization of Canadian sport continued in the 1920s. This meant indoor stadiums, artificial ice, and large payrolls. It also meant greater Americanization. At the beginning of the 1920s, professional hockey was solely Canadian. The Pacific Coast League (formed in 1911), the Western Canadian League (begun in 1921), and the National Hockey League (NHL, inaugurated in 1917) competed for the coveted Stanley Cup. Then the NHL expanded into the lucrative urban market of the United States. By 1927, the NHL consisted of five American and five Canadian teams. The Ottawa Senators dominated the NHL in the early years of the decade, winning the Stanley Cup four times.

The NHL dominated hockey throughout the 1920s. It paid the average player $900 a year, with a few exceptional players earning upward of $10,000. Although interest in the amateur trophies—the

Allan Cup and the Memorial Cup—continued in the smaller centres, the focus remained on the NHL even after the league shrank to six teams, with only two of the teams being Canadian: the Toronto Maple Leafs and the Montreal Canadiens. Almost all the NHL players were Canadians.

New trophies were donated throughout the decade: the Hart Trophy, for most valuable team player; the Lady Byng Trophy (donated by the governor general's wife), to the player exhibiting the highest sportsmanship and gentlemanly conduct; the Vezina Trophy, to the goaltender allowing the fewest goals against his team; and the Prince of Wales Trophy, which, beginning in 1927, was awarded to the season's top American Division team.

In other sports, a number of Canadian amateurs won international recognition. Track and field athlete Percy Williams won a gold medal at the 1928 Olympics. Williams was known, for a time, as "the world's fastest human." George Young made a name for Canada in swimming by winning the 32-kilometre race from the California mainland to Catalina Island. In the Maritimes, Captain Angus Walters won the International Fisherman's Trophy three years in succession—in 1921, 1922, and 1923. His schooner, the *Bluenose* (the nickname for Nova Scotians), which never lost a race, was immortalized on the Canadian dime.

Female athletics came into its own in the 1920s, enabling women to take control of their own sports. Certainly the success of the Edmonton Grads women's basketball team—setting a world record by winning 502 games and losing only 20 between the team's inception in 1915 and when it disbanded in 1940—helped to promote women in sport. So too did the success of Canadian women in the Olympic Games. In the 1928 summer Olympics in Amsterdam, Canada's "Matchless Six" women competitors won more points than any other nation, including a gold medal for Ethel Catherwood in track and field to match that of Percy William for men's track and field in the same games.

Just as professional men's sport teams emerged in the 1920s, so did professional women's sport teams, especially in basketball, ice hockey, and softball. Working-class women formed their own athletic clubs, organizations, and leagues. Some companies that employed large numbers of young, single women, such as Eaton's and the Hudson's Bay Company, provided recreational and athletic facilities. By 1926, sufficient numbers of women's sport teams existed to form the Women's Amateur Athletic Federation of Canada with a nationwide membership of 1200. It regulated all women's sport.

The Bluenose *in full sail—Canada's most famous ship. Winner of the International Fisherman's Trophy for three successive years (1921, 1922, 1923), the schooner became immortalized in 1937 with its reproduction on the Canadian dime.*

Source: Commercial Photo Service (Halifax), National Archives of Canada/PA-41990.

SUMMARY

The Great War cast a long shadow over the decade that followed. Mackenzie King and the Liberal Party dominated politics. King succeeded in diffusing the Maritime Rights movement in the East and undermining the Progressive movement in the West, but a new regionalism had emerged. King did succeed in moving Canada along the road to autonomy within the British Commonwealth. Women and labour unions made gains, but both groups were still far from achieving gender or class equality in Canadian society. A new brand of Canadian nationalism was evident but it remained Anglo-Saxon and white. Ethnic groups and First Nations were still under intense pressure to assimilate. Yet even the hegemonic group in Canada was under pressure on all fronts from "Americanization." While the 1920s may not have been "roaring," few Canadians suspected, as the decade came to an end, that it would be followed by the worst depression in world history.

NOTES

1. Nancy Christie and Michael Gauvreau, *A Full-Orbed Christianity: The Protestant Churches and Social Welfare in Canada, 1900–1940* (Montreal: McGill-Queen's University Press, 1996), p. 245.

2. John Herd Thompson with Allen Seager, *Canada 1922–1939: Decades of Discord* (Toronto: McClelland & Stewart, 1985), p. 112.

3. Kenneth Norrie and Douglas Owram, *A History of the Canadian Economy*, 3rd ed. (Toronto: Nelson, 2002), p. 322.

4. A.R.M. Lower, *Canadians in the Making: A Social History of Canada* (Toronto: Longmans, Green, 1958), p. 424.

5. Susan Mann, *The Dream of Nation: A Social and Intellectual History of Quebec*, 2nd ed. (Montreal/Kingston: McGill-Queen's University Press, 2002), p. 223.

6. Veronica Strong-Boag, "Pulling in Double Harness or Hauling a Double Load: Women, Work and Feminism on the Canadian Prairie," *Journal of Canadian Studies*, 21 (Fall 1986): 36.

7. Douglas Cole, "Artists, Patrons and Public: An Enquiry into the Success of the Group of Seven," *Journal of Canadian Studies*, 13(2) (1978): 76.

8. Mary Vipond, *The Mass Media in Canada* (Toronto: James Lorimer & Co., 1989), p. 24.

BIBLIOGRAPHY

On the Winnipeg General Strike, see "Where Historians Disagree: The Winnipeg General Strike" in this chapter. See as well Kenneth McNaught and David Bercuson, *The Winnipeg Strike: 1919* (Toronto: Longman, 1974); and with regard to the One Big Union, David Bercuson, *Fools and Wisemen: The Rise and Fall of the One Big Union* (Toronto: McGraw-Hill Ryerson, 1978). To examine the Winnipeg General Strike in the wider perspective of strikes elsewhere in Canada, see Craig Heron, ed., *The Workers' Revolt in Canada, 1917–1925* (Toronto: University of Toronto Press, 1998); and Benjamin Isitt, "Searching for Workers' Solidarity: The One Big Union and the Victoria General Strike of 1919," *Labour/Le travail*, 60 (2007): 9–42. To study the aftermath of the strike, consult Stefan Epp-Koop, *We're Going to Run This City. Winnipeg's Political Left after the General Strike* (Winnipeg: University of Manitoba Press, 2015). Michel S. Beaulieu's study portrays labour struggles outside of Winnipeg in *Labour at the Lakehead: Ethnicity, Socialism, and Politics, 1900–35* (Vancouver: UBC Press, 2011).

For an overview of the 1920s, consult John Herd Thompson with Allen Seager, *Canada, 1922–1939: Decades of Discord* (Toronto: McClelland & Stewart, 1985). Robert Bothwell, Ian Drummond, and

John English supply considerable material on the 1920s in *Canada, 1900–1945* (Toronto: University of Toronto Press, 1987). For the Maritime provinces, see Margaret R. Conrad and James K. Hiller, *Atlantic Canada: A Region in the Making* (Don Mills, ON: Oxford University Press, 2001); and David Frank, "The 1920s: Class and Region, Resistance and Accommodation," in E.R. Forbes and D.A. Muise, eds., *The Atlantic Provinces in Confederation* (Toronto: University of Toronto Press, 1993). For an investigation of intellectual attitudes vis-à-vis the United States, see Damien-Claude Belanger, *Prejudice and Pride: Canadian Intellectuals Confront the United States, 1891–1945* (Toronto: University of Toronto Press, 2010).

On Mackenzie King's political life in the 1920s, see the latter part of R.M. Dawson, *William Lyon Mackenzie King: A Political Biography*, vol. 1, *1874–1923* (Toronto: University of Toronto Press, 1958); and H.B. Neatby, *The Lonely Heights*, vol. 2, *1924–1932* (Toronto: University of Toronto Press, 1980). A popular study is J.L. Granatstein's *Mackenzie King: His Life and World* (Toronto: McGraw-Hill Ryerson, 1977). On King's association with the West, see Robert A. Wardhaugh, *Mackenzie King and the Prairie West* (Toronto: University of Toronto Press, 2000). Roger Graham's *Arthur Meighen: A Biography*, vol. 2, *And Fortune Fled* (Toronto: Clarke Irwin, 1963) and his pamphlet *Arthur Meighen* (Ottawa: Canadian Historical Association, 1965) deal with King's political rival in the 1920s. On political scandal in the 1920s, consult T.D. Regehr, *The Beauharnois Scandal: A Story of Canadian Entrepreneurship and Politics* (Toronto: University of Toronto Press, 1989). On the liquor trade of the time, see Craig Heron, *Booze: A Distilled History* (Toronto: Between the Lines, 2003), and Dan Malleck, *Try to Control Yourself: The Regulation of Public Drinking in Post-Prohibition Ontario, 1927–44* (Vancouver: UBC, 2012) for its aftermath. On the King–Byng affair, consult the King and Meighen biographies cited earlier in this paragraph; and Roger Graham, *The King–Byng Affair, 1926* (Toronto: Copp Clark, 1967).

Maritime protest in the 1920s is discussed in E.R. Forbes, *The Maritime Rights Movement, 1919–27: A Study in Canadian Regionalism* (Montreal/Kingston: McGill-Queen's University Press, 1979); and David J. Bercuson, ed., *Canada and the Burden of Unity* (Toronto: Macmillan, 1977). David Frank, "Class Conflict in the Coal Industry: Cape Breton 1922," in G.S. Kealey and P. Warrian, eds., *Essays in Canadian Working-Class History* (Toronto: McClelland & Stewart, 1976), pp. 161–84, recounts the story of labour strife on Cape Breton Island.

On the Progressive movement, see the relevant chapters in Gerald Friesen, *The Canadian Prairies: A History* (Toronto: University of Toronto Press, 1987); John Thompson, *Forging the Prairie West: The Illustrated History of Canada* (Toronto: Oxford, 1998); Walter Young, *Democracy and Discontent* (Toronto: Ryerson Press, 1969); and W.L. Morton, *The Progressive Party in Canada* (Toronto: University of Toronto Press, 1950). On the United Farmers of Ontario, see Kerry A. Badgley, *Ringing in the Common Good: The United Farmers of Ontario, 1914–1926* (Montreal/Kingston: McGill-Queen's University Press, 2000); and for the United Farmers of Alberta, see Bradford James Rennie, *The Rise of Agrarian Democracy: The United Farmers and Farm Women of Alberta, 1909–1921* (Toronto: University of Toronto Press, 2000). J.E. Rea's *T.A. Crerar: A Political Life* (Montreal/Kingston: McGill-Queen's University Press, 1997) is a biography of this important Western farm leader. On the plight of Prairie farmers in the 1920s, see David Jones, *Empire of Dust: Settling and Abandoning the Prairie Dry Belt* (Edmonton: University of Alberta Press, 1987).

On the economics of the 1920s, see the chapter "The Stuttering Twenties," in Michael Bliss, *Northern Enterprise: Five Centuries of Canadian Business* (Toronto: McClelland & Stewart, 1987); and Kenneth Norrie and Douglas Owram, *A History of the Canadian Economy*, 4th ed. (Toronto: Harcourt Brace, 2008). Consult, as well, Tom Traves, *The State and Enterprise: Canadian Manufacturers and the Federal Government, 1917–31* (Toronto: University of Toronto Press, 1979). Other studies of the Canadian economy and business leaders include Don Nerbas, *Dominion of Capital: The Politics of Big Business and the Crisis of the Canadian Bourgeoisie, 1914–1947* (Toronto: University of Toronto Press, 2013). For Quebec, see Paul-André Linteau, René Durocher, and Jean-Claude Robert, *Quebec: A History, 1867–1929* (Toronto: James Lorimer, 1983). For a look at the working class, see Desmond Morton, *Working People: An Illustrated History of the Canadian Labour Movement*, 5th ed. (Montreal and Kingston: McGill-Queen's University Press, 2007). For an examination of social welfare policy, see James Struthers, *No Fault of Their Own: Unemployment and the Canadian Welfare State, 1914–1941* (Toronto: University of Toronto Press, 1983). For an examination of economics and its impact upon emigration, see Marjorie Harper and Nicholas

J. Evans, "Socio-economic Dislocation and Inter-war Emigration to Canada and the United States: A Scottish Snapshot," *Journal of Imperial and Commonwealth History*, 34(4) (2006): 529–52.

For an examination of religion and social reform in Canada, see Nancy Christie and Michael Gauvreau, *A Full-Orbed Christianity: The Protestant Churches and Social Welfare in Canada, 1900–1940* (Montreal: McGill-Queen's University Press, 1996); Nancy Christie and Michael Gauvreau, *Christian Churches and Their Peoples, 1840–1965* (Toronto: University of Toronto Press, 2010); and Michael Gauvreau and Ollivier Hubert, *The Churches and Social Order in Nineteenth- and Twentieth-Century Canada* (Montreal: McGill-Queen's University Press, 2006).

Church union is considered in John W. Grant, *The Canadian Experience of Church Union* (London: John Knox Press, 1967), whereas opposition to church union is the subject of N. Keith Clifford, *The Resistance to Church Union, 1904–1939* (Vancouver: University of British Columbia Press, 1985). For a case study on anti-Catholic sentiment, see James M. Pitsula, *Keeping Canada British: The Ku Klux Klan in 1920s Saskatchewan* (Vancouver: UBC Press, 2014). Other studies on Catholicism during this period include Maurice Demers, *Connected Struggles: Catholics, Nationalists, and Transnational Relations between Mexico and Quebec, 1917–1945* (McGill-Queen's University Press, 2014). Susan Mann Trofimenkoff's *Action française: French-Canadian Nationalism in the Twenties* (Toronto: University of Toronto Press, 1975) analyzes this French-Canadian group.

On women in the 1920s, consult Veronica Strong-Boag, *The New Day Recalled: Lives of Girls and Women in English Canada, 1919–1939* (Toronto: Copp Clark Pitman, 1988); Susan Mann Trofimenkoff and Alison Prentice, eds., *The Neglected Majority: Essays in Canadian Women's History*, vol. 1 (Toronto: McClelland & Stewart, 1977) and vol. 2 (1985); Suzanne Morton, *Ideal Surroundings: Domestic Life in a Working-Class Suburb in the 1920s* (Toronto: University of Toronto Press, 1995); and Penny Tinkler and Cheryl Krasnick Warsh, "Feminine Modernity in Interwar Britain and North America: Corsets, Cars, and Cigarettes," *Journal of Women's History*, 20(3) (2008): 113–43. For perceptions of women in the interwar years, see Jane Nicholas, *The Modern Girl: Feminine Modernities, the Body, and Commodities in the 1920s* (Toronto: University of Toronto, 2014), and Wendy Mitchinson, *Body Failure: Medical Views of Women, 1900–1950* (Toronto: University of Toronto Press, 2013).

Women and politics are discussed in Linda Kealey and Joan Sangster, eds., *Beyond the Vote: Canadian Women and Politics* (Toronto: University of Toronto Press, 1989); and Robert J. Sharpe and Patricia I. McMahon, *The Persons Case: The Origins and Legacy of the Fight for Legal Personhood* (Toronto: University of Toronto Press, 2007). On Canada's first woman MP, see Terry Crowley, *Agnes Macphail and the Politics of Equality* (Toronto: James Lorimer, 1990).

On Quebec women, see, as well, Micheline Dumont et al., *Quebec Women: A History* (Toronto: Women's Press, 1987); and Susan Mann, *The Dream of Nation: A Social and Intellectual History of Quebec*, 2nd ed. (Montreal/Kingston: McGill-Queen's University Press, 2002). For Ontario, see Janice Acton et al., eds., *Women at Work: Ontario, 1850–1930* (Toronto: Canadian Women's Educational Press, 1974); and, for the Prairies, Veronica Strong-Boag, "Pulling in Double Harness or Hauling a Double Load: Women, Work and Feminism on the Canadian Prairie," *Journal of Canadian Studies*, 21 (Fall 1986): 32–52. For the Maritimes, see Linda Cullum and Marilyn Porter, eds., *Creating This Place: Women, Family, and Class in St. John's, 1900–1950* (Montreal/Kingston: McGill-Queen's University Press, 2014). On the topic of eugenics, see Angus McLaren, *Our Own Master Race* (Toronto: McClelland & Stewart, 1990), and Erika Dyck, *Facing Eugenics: Reproduction, Sterilization, and the Politics of Choice* (Toronto: University of Toronto Press, 2013).

On social assistance and the rise of social work in the 1920s, see Therese Jennissen and Colleen Lundy, *One Hundred Years of Social Work: A History of the Profession in English Canada* (Waterloo, On: Wilfrid Laurier University Press, 2009); the relevant section in Alvin Finkel, *Social Policy and Practice in Canada: A History* (Waterloo: Wilfrid Laurier University Press, 2006); Ken Moffat, *A Poetics of Social Work: Personal Agency and Social Transformation in Canada, 1920–1939* (Toronto: University of Toronto Press, 2001); and selected articles in Raymond B. Blake and Jeff Keshen, eds., *Social Welfare Policy in Canada: Historical Readings* (Toronto: Copp Clark, 1995).

On the impact of suburbia in the interwar years, see Richard Harris, *Creeping Conformity: How Canada Became Suburban, 1900–1960* (Toronto: University of Toronto Press, 2004). Canadian culture is dealt with in "The Conundrum of Culture," in *Canada, 1922–1939* (as cited earlier), pp. 158–92; and Carl Klinck, ed., *Literary History of Canada: Canadian Literature in English*, 2nd ed. (Toronto: University of Toronto Press, 1976). On cultural nationalism, see Mary Vipond, *The Mass Media in Canada* (Toronto: James Lorimer, 1992). For the Maritimes, see, as well, Gwendolyn Davies, *Myth and Milieu: Atlantic Literature and Culture, 1918–1939* (Fredericton: Acadiensis Press, 1993); and Ian McKay, *The Quest of the Folk: Antimodernism and Cultural Selection in Twentieth-Century Nova Scotia* (Montreal/Kingston: McGill-Queen's University Press, 1994).

Painting in the interwar years is discussed in J. Russell Harper, *Painting in Canada: A History*, 2nd ed. (Toronto: University of Toronto Press, 1977); Dennis Reid, *A Concise History of Canadian Painting*, 2nd ed. (Toronto: Oxford University Press, 1988); and Ann Davis, *The Logic of Ecstasy: Canadian Mystical Painting, 1920–1940* (Toronto: University of Toronto Press, 1992). On the Group of Seven, consult Charles C. Hill, *The Group of Seven: Art for a Nation* (Ottawa: National Gallery of Canada, 1995), and Ross King, *Defiant Spirits: The Modernist Revolution of the Group of Seven* (Vancouver: Douglas & McIntyre, 2010).

On theatre in Quebec, see Elaine F. Nardocchio, *Theatre and Politics in Modern Quebec* (Edmonton: University of Alberta Press, 1986); and Jean Hamelin, *The Theatre in French Canada, 1936–1966* (Quebec: Department of Cultural Affairs, 1968). For music, see Timothy J. McGee, *The Music of Canada* (New York: W.W. Norton, 1985); and George A. Proctor, *Canadian Music of the Twentieth Century* (Toronto: University of Toronto Press, 1980).

On popular entertainment in the West, see Don Wetherell and Irene Kmet, *Useful Pleasures: The Shaping of Leisure in Alberta 1896–1945* (Regina: Alberta Culture and Multiculturalism/Canadian Plains Research Center, University of Regina, 1990). Radio is discussed in Mary Vipond, *Listening In: The First Decade of Canadian Broadcasting, 1922–1932* (Montreal/Kingston: McGill-Queen's University Press, 1992). For Canadian sport in general, see Colin Howell, *Blood, Sweat, and Cheers: Sport in the Making of Modern Canada* (Toronto: University of Toronto Press, 2001); and for women and sport, see M. Ann Hall, *The Girl and the Game: A History of Women's Sport in Canada* (Peterborough: Broadview Press, 2002).

Important reviews of First Nations history in the interwar years include Arthur Ray, *The Canadian Fur Trade in the Industrial Age* (Toronto: University of Toronto Press, 1990), and his *I Have Lived Here Since the World Began* (Toronto: Key Porter, 1996); Stan Cuthand, "The Native Peoples of the Prairie Provinces in the 1920s and 1930s," in Ian A.L. Getty and Donald B. Smith, eds., *One Century Later: Western Canadian Reserve Indians Since Treaty 7* (Vancouver: University of British Columbia Press, 1978), pp. 31–42; and John Leonard Taylor, *Canadian Indian Policy During the Inter-war Years, 1918–1939* (Ottawa: Indian and Northern Affairs Canada, 1984). On Indian residential schools during this period, see J.R. Miller, *Shingwauk's Vision: A History of Native Residential Schools* (Toronto: University of Toronto Press, 1996); and John S. Milloy, *A National Crime: The Canadian Government and the Residential School System, 1879 to 1986* (Winnipeg: University of Manitoba Press, 1999). For working conditions of First Nations people, see Rolf Knight, *Indians at Work: An Informal History of Native Indian Labour in British Columbia, 1853–1930* (Vancouver: New Star Books, 1978). For developments among the First Nations, see Edward Ahenakew, *Voices of the Plains Cree* (Toronto: McClelland & Stewart, 1973); and for those among the Métis in Western Canada, consult Murray Dobbin, *The One-and-a-Half Men: The Story of Jim Brady and Malcolm Norris, Métis Patriots of the 20th Century* (Vancouver: New Star Books, 1981); Emma Larocque, *When the Other Me Is Me: Native Resistance Discourse, 1850–1990* (Winnipeg: University of Manitoba Press, 2008); and Yale D. Belanger, "The Six Nations of Grand River Territory's Attempts at Renewing International Political Relationships, 1921–1924," *Canadian Foreign Policy*, 13(3) (2007): 29–44. A helpful study of northern development beginning in this period is Liza Piper, *The Industrial Transformation of Subarctic Canada* (Vancouver: UBC Press, 2009); see also René Fumoleau, *As Long as This Land Shall Last: A History of Treaty 8 and Treaty 11, 1870–1939* (Toronto: McClelland and Stewart, 1973).

Students should consult the maps and charts in Donald Kerr and Deryck W. Holdsworth, eds., *Historical Atlas of Canada*, vol. 3, *Addressing the Twentieth Century, 1891–1961* (Toronto: University of Toronto Press, 1990).

Source: Library and Archives Canada/C-029399.

Chapter Twelve

CANADA IN THE GREAT DEPRESSION

TIME LINE	
1929	"Black Tuesday" and stock-market crash signal beginning of Great Depression
1930	Conservatives win federal election under R.B. Bennett
1931	Statute of Westminster recognizes Canadian autonomy from Britain
1932	Imperial Economic Conference in Ottawa Founding of Co-operative Commonwealth Federation (CCF) Party
1934	Birth of the Dionne quintuplets, world's first surviving quintuplets
1935	Creation of Bank of Canada On-to-Ottawa Trek ends in Regina Riot Liberals win federal election under Mackenzie King Social Credit Party elected in Alberta under William Aberhart
1936	Founding of Canadian Broadcasting Corporation (CBC) Union nationale elected in Quebec under Maurice Duplessis Dorothea Palmer arrested for distributing birth-control literature
1937	General Motors strike in Oshawa Creation of the Royal Commission on Dominion–Provincial Relations Establishment of governor general's awards
1939	King George VI and Queen Elizabeth tour Canada

In the 1930s, the "Great Depression"—the worst economic crisis ever to hit the Western world—ravaged Canada. While the spectacular crash of the New York stock market on "Black Tuesday" in October 1929 signalled the beginning of the crisis, the causes lay in the financial mishandling of the Great War. It was followed by bank failures, a decline in international trade, plummeting commodities prices, spiralling government debts, and massive unemployment. The crisis was deepened by the response of foreign governments who threw up protective walls to insulate their economies. The Prairie West, a region so recently beset with high hopes, was further crippled by drought and crop failure, leading to the decade's label, "The Dirty Thirties."

Canada and the United States experienced the Western world's most severe decline in industrial production and gross national product. Unemployment soared. With no jobs available, hundreds of thousands of Canadians faced the humiliation of going on public relief. Young single men rode the rails in search of jobs, and when unable to find work, ended up in "relief camps." Increasingly, society looked to government for answers.

But the federal government was unprepared for the magnitude of the crisis. The Mackenzie King Liberals were caught unaware and knocked from power in the 1930 election. The Conservatives under R.B. Bennett attempted to deal with this unprecedented economic disaster, but when they failed, they were blamed for the Depression. The Liberals returned to office in 1935. The failure of the two traditional parties to take Canada out of depression once again led to a search for new political alternatives. Capitalism was clearly in crisis, but the Depression also demonstrated a crisis in Canadian federalism. Provincial governments were no more successful at finding solutions and many teetered on the edge of bankruptcy. The system was broken.

The 1930s was a rough decade for both labour and gender relations in Canada. Progress and advancements during the economic crisis were difficult. The labour movement traditionally suffers during times of economic downturn. Soaring levels of unemployment left many men out of work. There was little space for women to advance their positions in the workplace. The male breadwinner model was further entrenched by the state through its relief and unemployment policies.

The Depression experience shaped a generation. Some remember these years as the best of times, demonstrating the importance of community, thrift, sacrifice, and perseverance. People pulled together to help each other. Others remember them as the worst of times, pointing to the failure of political, economic, and social institutions. People struggled to eke out a living. The Great Depression was only ended by the onset of another world war.

The Beginning of the Great Depression

On October 29, 1929—"Black Tuesday"—the crash of the New York stock market precipitated similar crashes around the world. Bank failures followed throughout Europe and the United States, causing financial instability. International trade declined as nations imposed high tariffs on foreign trade in an effort to protect industries and workers in their own countries from competition. Worldwide overproduction of commodities such as wheat, newsprint, and metals—all important Canadian exports—caused prices to plummet. Unemployment rose to record highs.

But the crisis did not appear suddenly out of the blue. There were certainly portents. Since the end of the Great War, a generation of university-trained economists pointed to the disastrous financial legacy of the conflict. Led by the British economist John Maynard Keynes, they theorized on new methods of both domestic and international finance, particularly when it came to the role of the state and the market. While the late 1920s showed signs of financial recovery, the optimism led to speculation. Property and farms were purchased at exaggerated prices; a stock-market balloon was created. By the late 1920s the real estate industry showed signs of serious difficulty. Farmers expanded their operations by going into debt to take advantage of high prices, but they produced more than the market could absorb. A new phenomenon appeared—widespread unemployment. By the end of the decade, municipal and provincial governments were complaining to Ottawa about the long lines of men who were out of work with nowhere to turn for assistance.

The Great Depression affected the entire Western world. It hit Canada severely, because the national economy had expanded so rapidly and so extensively in the first three decades of the twentieth century. Having risen so high, it had farther to fall. Industrial production fell by over one-third between 1929 and 1932. During the same period, Canada's gross national product sank by two-fifths in current dollars. Imports declined in volume by about 55 percent and exports by 25 percent. The unemployment rate soared to a record high of 20 percent of the *total* civilian labour force by 1933.

Dust storm near Lethbridge, Alberta—a familiar sight in Prairie Canada during the Dirty Thirties.

Source: Glenbow Archives, Calgary, Canada/NA-1831-1.

Within Canada, the Prairie West and British Columbia suffered most because of their dependence on primary industries, especially wheat production, and their overexpansion in the previous decades. Furthermore, Canada was heavily dependent on one market—the United States—which was greatly affected by the economic downturn and imposed high tariffs in response. Compounding this economic depression, the Prairie West also suffered from a particularly harsh episode in its recurrent cycle of climatic disaster: ten years of exceptional and persistent drought, extreme summer and winter temperatures, unusual weather patterns, and grasshopper infestations. In the Dirty Thirties, the topsoil turned to dust and blew away. British Columbia contended with high numbers of transients. Due to its milder climate, Vancouver became known as "the Mecca for the unemployed."

Canada's wheat—previously the nation's staple resource—was now difficult to sell. After a bumper crop in 1928, over the next four years prices fell from $1.29 to $0.34 a bushel for No. 1 Hard, the best wheat on the market. Prices for lesser grades were considerably lower. Farmers could not afford to pay the costs of shipping grain to the Lakehead. Some found it cost less to burn their crops than to harvest them.

The wheat pools felt the repercussions. When Ottawa refused to re-establish the Wheat Board at the end of the Great War, the pools emerged in 1923 as an alternative solution to stabilizing prices. They advanced (in the fall and winter seasons) a portion of the money expected on the next year's crop. This practice was intended to assist farmers in buying seed and getting the wheat crop planted. They also helped guarantee returns in a highly uncertain industry by holding back the produce if market prices were unsatisfactory. In the fall and winter of 1928–29, the pools had advanced farmers $1 a bushel. When wheat prices fell below that price in the fall of 1929 and entered a downward spiral that lasted for five consecutive years, the wheat pools went bankrupt.

Elsewhere, similar dramatic conditions prevailed in the primary resource sector. Thousands of investors lost everything when mining share prices became worthless. Mines closed down for lack of business. The pulp and paper industry, another major resource industry, suffered a similar fate. The industry overexpanded in the 1920s as a result of an insatiable American demand. Expenses could be recouped only if the market continued at record highs. When the Depression hit, the newsprint market collapsed and, along with it, the pulp and paper industry. According to one industry analyst, by 1933 the industry was operating at only half of its capacity. Even then, the bottomed-out prices kept production costs barely above bankruptcy.

Money markets followed. Banks and other financial institutions approved loans in the 1920s, hoping to capitalize on the boom. Foreign capital entered the country to take advantage of good times. With the advent of the Depression, however, financial investors could not retrieve their money or cover their debts. Foreign investment from Canada's two traditional sources ceased. Britain and the United States recalled their loans to cover demands at home. On October 29, Black Tuesday, "The Toronto *Star's* index of sixteen key Canadian stocks fell $300,000,000—a million dollars for every minute that markets were open for trading."[1]

Average Canadian investors could not pay loans now recalled by the banks. Nor could they meet their mortgage payments or pay their property taxes. Debt levels for farmers often exceeded the value of their operations. Interest payments alone often exceeded an average farmer's annual income. People abandoned their homes and farms, leaving banks with property that no one could afford and hence had little monetary value.

Companies and factories cut back on wages and employees in an effort to survive. Clerks at Eaton's and Simpson's in Toronto, for example, earned only $10 to $13 a week, while those in Montreal earned much less. Weekly pay for male workers in the furniture industry averaged $10, but "boys" of 19 often earned as little as $3. In the textile industry, the Royal Commission on Price Spreads, appointed by the Conservative government in 1934, reported on shocking conditions. A seamstress in Quebec, for example, was paid 9.5 cents for sewing a dozen dresses.

Tens of thousands of workers lost their jobs. By 1933, over 20 percent of the entire Canadian labour force—one worker out of every five—was unemployed. In some regions of the country, the figures rose as high as 35 percent and even 50 percent. Traditionally, unemployment (known as "poor-law relief") was left to the local authorities—churches and charities—to handle. When they could not handle the increasing problem, they turned to the local municipality and then the province for aid. When the provinces became overwhelmed, they turned to the federal government.

R.B. Bennett's Conservatives and Bad Timing

At the outset of the Great Depression, the Liberals were in office. Confident of another victory based on the prosperity of the late 1920s, party organizers remained apathetic and indifferent throughout the election campaign of 1930. The Liberals believed, as did many other politicians in the Western world, that this crisis was just another temporary dip in the economy. Canada, with its reliance on natural resource staples, had proven particularly susceptible to cycles of boom and bust. As a result, neither mainline party perceived a need to propose sweeping economic reform during the election campaign.

Prime Minister Mackenzie King did not anticipate the severity of the coming storm and he clung to orthodox methods of handling economic crises: fiscal restraint and balanced budgets. But danger signs for the federal Liberals were apparent at the provincial level. By the time of the federal election in 1930 almost every province in Canada had voted in a Conservative government. While under attack in Parliament on the issue of spiralling unemployment, the usually cautious King made an uncharacteristic political blunder. He responded that his government "would not give a five-cent piece" for these "alleged unemployment purposes" to provincial governments "diametrically opposed" to his own. The comment was used to demonstrate that the Liberals had lost touch with what was happening to the economy, the nation, and its people. In contrast, Richard Bedford Bennett, the Conservative leader, promised that if elected, he could and would solve the problems of the Depression. He won the election with 134 seats and 48 percent of the vote to the Liberals' 90 seats and 46 percent.

Once in power, the new prime minister acted. Bennett followed Conservative tradition (as well as the lead of most other trading nations) and introduced a high-tariff policy on manufactured goods. But the high tariffs undermined Canada's competitive edge. As a major exporting nation, Canada depended on the export of key staples—wheat, pulp and paper, and minerals—to foreign markets, especially the United States. Bennett also followed Conservative tradition by attempting to turn the direction of Canadian trade back toward Britain and the Commonwealth. In 1930, the United States retaliated with the Smoot–Hawley tariff on foreign imports. The Western world entered an era of protectionism.

Prime Minister Bennett's policy on the issue of "relief" differed little from that of the Liberals. While the BNA Act made no mention of who was responsible for unemployment, by precedent it was assumed to be within provincial jurisdiction because it was viewed as a local issue. Provincial premiers, however, were realizing that they simply could not shoulder the burden, based on the existing division of powers and their sources of revenue. Premier John Bracken of Manitoba led the provincial charge in arguing that the federal government did have some responsibility for unemployment because the problem was tied to immigration, an issue clearly in federal jurisdiction.

Like King, Bennett wanted no responsibility for unemployment. The federal treasury was already strained. Instead, the prime minister criticized the provinces for mishandling their finances, which only exacerbated dominion–provincial discord. Regardless, within his first five

Eviction in Montreal during the Depression. By 1933 over one-third of the city's francophones were on relief, with many simply forced into the streets.

Source: Library and Archives Canada/C-30811.

weeks in office, Bennett introduced the Unemployment Relief Act, which provided $20 million of assistance—a considerable sum out of a total federal budget of $500 million. But the prime minister soon discovered that much more was needed. Despite blaming the provinces and seeking to avoid federal responsibility, Ottawa was dragged kicking and screaming into paying the costs. Between 1930 and 1938, the federal government provided nearly $350 million in relief for the jobless and for destitute farmers, while municipal and provincial governments added another $650 million. Most of the money went to work-incentive programs.

The federal government underestimated the destitution of local governments. Already heavily in debt, municipal and provincial governments had overextended themselves in the boom years of the 1920s. Furthermore, their tax base eroded as people could no longer pay local property taxes. Indeed, all levels of government faced mounting deficits on a decreased tax base. Toronto's budget for relief increased twentyfold between 1929 and 1933. By the outbreak of war, Montreal's per capita debt was twice Toronto's. When the province of Quebec, more tight-fisted toward its towns and cities than other provinces, refused to come to Montreal's rescue, the city was forced to declare bankruptcy in 1940.

Municipal, provincial, and federal governments responded by trying to balance their budgets through cutbacks on services. This austerity, in turn, increased unemployment and slowed down the recovery. Governments had few alternatives, given the magnitude of the debt and their low level of revenue. To make matters worse, opportunities to borrow abroad did not exist. All countries faced debt and dealt with it the same way—by trying to balance budgets.

As the economic crisis deepened, Bennett looked to Britain and the other Commonwealth countries for increased trade. In 1932, Canada hosted an Imperial Economic Conference to explore ways to combat the Depression. Overall, the conference failed, but Canada did gain a limited preference in the British market for its wheat, lumber, apples, and bacon. In return, Canada gave preference to British manufactured goods by simply raising the level of the general tariff on all but British goods.

Relief

For the first time, thousands of Canadians faced the personal humiliation of going on relief—"pogey," as it was called. In a society built on a philosophy of individual initiative, relief was an admission of failure. Many people lost their sense of self-worth. The jobless had no choice but to fall back on charity, both public and private. Society was based on the "breadwinner model." According to gender norms, men were expected to be the sole breadwinners for the family and household, even though in reality women often had to supplement the breadwinner's income through work on the side.

Those on relief faced the further humiliation of having to acknowledge their failure publicly. They lined up in church basements or fire halls waiting for relief. When their turn came, they had to proclaim their destitution and swear that they did not own a car, a radio, or a telephone. Recipients of relief generally had to be in arrears in rent payments and to have received notice of discontinuation of electricity and water service, as well as impending eviction. Then the authorities gave them food vouchers to purchase the minimum necessities at local stores—a further reminder of one's impoverished condition. In Ontario, these relief vouchers averaged $8.07 a person for a week in the winter months. In 1933, North York gave families on relief a maximum of $11.60 a week, although the Toronto Welfare Council estimated that a family of five needed $28.35 a week to maintain an adequate living standard. In Prince Edward Island, relief vouchers amounted to only $1.93, and in New Brunswick they averaged a meagre $1.67.

In the Prairie West—once the "breadbasket of the nation"—food, along with used clothing and fuel, often came in railcar loads from central and eastern Canada. The situation seemed absurd when grain was rotting in the bins after being withheld from the market by the wheat pools until prices increased. There seemed to be "poverty in the midst of plenty."

Societies based on the capitalist work ethic balked at the notion of their governments handing out money without work being done. Social creeds taught that people were poor due to their own vices, including laziness. To give those on relief the illusion of working for their relief payments, governments created makeshift jobs known as "boon-doggling." The town of New Toronto, Ontario, for example, required relief workers to haul large stones to vacant lots, where they were smashed and used for road construction. In Prince Edward Island, road machines sat idle so that more men could be hired to do roadwork manually. Rumours abounded of some municipalities that had "relief men" dig holes one day and fill them in the next, simply to keep them occupied.

To avoid drifters coming into town for assistance, most municipalities had lengthy residence requirements to qualify for relief. New immigrants faced a hostile reception. The Immigrant Act allowed for the deportation of immigrants on relief especially if they happened to belong to socialist organizations. Consequently, some municipalities provided the authorities with lists of immigrants who were receiving government assistance. Between 1930 and 1935, Ottawa returned 30,000 immigrants to Europe. The fear of the "enemy alien" and the "dangerous foreign agitator" continued into the 1930s. As criticism mounted against the capitalist system, people sought alternatives. Socialism and the left in general gained momentum.

Relief Camps

By 1932, the Great Depression had deepened. More than 1.5 million Canadians (15 percent of the nation's population) depended on relief, and the country seemed ripe for social unrest. Of particular concern to the authorities were unemployed single men, many of whom "rode the rails" across Canada in search of work, begged for food and clothing, camped in shantytowns on the outskirts of cities, and lined up at soup kitchens and hostels for food and shelter. General Andrew McNaughton, chief of the Army General Staff, and Charlotte Whitton, prominent social worker, proposed the establishment of relief camps to offer temporary work and prevent dissidence and violence. Beginning in 1932, the federal government established numerous camps across the country, usually in isolated areas distant from major population centres and under military supervision.

During the four-year period that they existed, an estimated 100,000 single, homeless male "volunteers" worked long hours at menial jobs designed simply to keep them busy, for a meagre 20 cents a day. Intolerable living conditions in these make-work camps, combined with the fact that these angry young men were gathered in one location, created ideal situations for labour organizers. Not surprisingly, the camps were infiltrated by radical organizations such as the Single Unemployed Workers' Association, an organization funded by the Communist Party of Canada. Such "infiltration," however, should not be exaggerated, and most relief camp workers welcomed such support and organization. The government, on the other hand, was paranoid about this "radical infiltration" and shrugged off the legitimate complaints of the relief camp workers as the result of troublemaking communists.

The On-to-Ottawa Trek

In the spring of 1935, as the men were preparing to return to the relief camps, they decided to strike. The Relief Camps Strike was staged in Vancouver, British Columbia, where many of the men spent the winter. They took control of city hall, and the strike was deemed so successful that the organizers decided to take their demands for "work for wages" all the way to Ottawa and Prime Minister Bennett himself. They hopped onboard CPR boxcars and began riding the rails eastward through the interior of British Columbia and into Alberta. Bennett assumed that the On-to-Ottawa Trek would lose momentum long before it reached Ottawa. He was mistaken. Instead, as the Trek wound its way through the West, it gained momentum. Single, unemployed men joined the Trekkers; citizens came out to cheer the men on and bring them food and supplies. Picnics were held as the Trek moved through the various towns and cities along the main CPR line. The Trek leaders gave speeches on the injustices of their plight.

By the end of June, Bennett was concerned. At one point, the leaders travelled ahead of the Trek to Ottawa to meet with the prime minister. The discussions failed, however, and Bennett dismissed the leaders as rabble-

The Regina Riot, Dominion Day, 1935. One plainclothes policeman was killed and numerous strikers and police officers were injured.

Source: City of Regina Archives Photograph Collection, CORA-RPL-B-393.

rousing communists. The prime minister was worried about the Trek reaching Winnipeg, deemed the most radical city and the site of the General Strike of 1919. Regina was home to the RCMP depot and Saskatchewan was home to the partisan Liberal government of Jimmy Gardiner. The Trek would go no farther. The prime minister accused the Trekkers of trespassing on government property by riding the CPR. About 2000 Trekkers reached Regina before the federal government ordered the RCMP to break it up.

On July 1, 1935, while the Trekkers were picnicking at the Exhibition Grounds in Regina and listening to speeches, the RCMP moved in to arrest the leaders. The ensuing confrontation, the Regina Riot, left one plainclothes policeman dead and numerous strikers and police officers injured. The police arrested 120 of the Trekkers and convicted 8 of them. In many ways, the Regina Riot and On-to-Ottawa Trek came to symbolize the hopelessness, the frustration, and the failure of the economic and political systems in Canada during the Depression.

Canada's millionaire prime minister also came to represent the callous indifference of the rich to the suffering of the unemployed and destitute. People spoke of "Bennett buggies," engine-less cars pulled by horses because the owners could not afford gas; "Bennett boroughs," the makeshift shantytowns for homeless men; and "Bennett blankets," the newspapers under which transients slept on park benches. Bennett was even ridiculed in a parody of the Lord's Prayer:

> *Our Father, who art in Ottawa, Bennett be thy name. Give us this day our bowl of soup and forgive us our trespasses on the CPR and the CNR as we forgive the bulls from chasing us. Lead us not into the hands of the RCMP, nor yet to the relief camp, for thine is the kingdom the power and glory, until there's an election— Amen.*

R.B. Bennett's legacy was inevitably shaped by the Depression. To a large extent, he was the victim of bad timing. The Conservative policies that stressed fiscal orthodoxy and balanced budgets, and sought to avoid

A "Bennett buggy" was a car pulled by a horse or oxen because the owner could not afford gas.

Source: Glenbow Archives/NA-2434-1.

further strains on the federal treasury by resisting entering provincial jurisdiction and relief spending, were no different than the Liberals' policies. Mackenzie King, it turned out, was fortunate to lose the election of 1930. By handing power to the Tories, the Liberals avoided the taint of the Depression. While in opposition, the Liberals offered no innovative alternatives to handling the economic crisis. Instead, they allowed the Depression to do its damage and awaited their inevitable re-election.

While history has not been kind to Bennett, his government did enact a number of measures that, over time, strengthened Canada's economy and became permanent structures. In 1935 he established a central bank—the Bank of Canada—to "promote the economic and financial welfare of the Dominion." The Bennett government passed the Natural Products and Marketing Act, which set up a federal marketing board with authority over all "natural products of agriculture and of the forest, sea, lake or river" exported or sold across provincial boundaries. His government also introduced the Canada Grain Board Act, which gave Ottawa control of the marketing of coarse grains, including wheat.

In 1934, Bennett appointed the Royal Commission on Price Spreads to investigate the buying practices of major department stores and the labour conditions in certain industries. Out of that commission came legislation to institute unemployment insurance and to regulate wages and working hours. Both bills, however, were struck down by the Judicial Committee of the Privy Council as unconstitutional. In 1940, however, the federal government succeeded in implementing an unemployment insurance plan, after the BNA Act was amended to allow for Ottawa's intervention into this traditional field of provincial jurisdiction.

Bennett's "New Deal"

Bennett realized that his party had little chance of being re-elected. As the election of 1935 approached, he decided to imitate the example of the highly popular American president, Franklin D. Roosevelt. In a series of radio addresses in January, Bennett announced his "New Deal," a program of reform that his party would introduce if the Conservatives were re-elected. It came as a complete surprise, even to his cabinet members, who had not been consulted about the reform package. The prime minister went so far as to announce that there was a "crisis in capitalism." The spate of reforms included health and unemployment insurance, a maximum work week, financial assistance to farmers to enable them to stay on their farms, and the creation of the Economic Council of Canada to advise the government. The New Deal broadcasts were relatively radical, particularly coming from the Conservatives. Because they crossed over into provincial jurisdiction, in order to be implemented, they would require a constitutional amendment.

Many Canadians were sceptical of Bennett's sudden conversion to reform, especially since none of the legislation was prepared going into the election. The departure from Conservative philosophy seemed too convenient and too contrived. While expediency certainly helps explain the New Deal broadcasts, they were also indicative of a party in crisis. The old Tory Party of John A. Macdonald and even Robert Borden now seemed anachronistic. The failed attempts to use tariffs and a return to British imperial trade to solve the Depression were symptomatic of a party in need of a makeover.

The voting public expressed its skepticism and its criticism of the Conservatives in the election of 1935. It returned Mackenzie King's Liberal Party to power with a majority government (173 for the Liberals, 39 for the Conservatives, 17 for Social Credit, and 7 for the CCF) but with almost the same percentage of votes as in 1930. The Liberal campaign slogan of "King or Chaos" indicated the lack of policy alternatives. The Liberal victory was more a rejection of Bennett than an endorsement of King. Indeed, in the popular vote, more than 25 percent of Canadians rejected both of the mainline parties to vote for one of the new parties that entered the election.

Third Parties

The Co-operative Commonwealth Federation

Two of these new parties began on the Prairies. The Co-operative Commonwealth Federation (CCF) emerged from the ashes of the Progressive Party and had its beginnings at a national convention in Calgary in August 1932. The CCF drew together dissident groups from a broad spectrum of Canadian society, including farmers, labourers, socialists, academics, and disenchanted Liberals. At the convention the party chose Labour MP J.S. Woodsworth as its leader.

The CCF distanced itself from the two mainline parties by offering a social democratic program to deal with the Depression. The party agreed with Bennett that there was a "crisis in capitalism." Woodsworth asked the League for Social Reconstruction (LSR), an organization of left-wing intellectuals who were mostly, although not exclusively, from universities, to draft a "manifesto" for the new party. University of Toronto historian Frank Underhill and McGill University law professor F.R. Scott did so. The "Regina Manifesto," adopted at the party's second annual convention in Regina in 1933, set out a ten-point program for the CCF to follow in its effort to "eradicate capitalism" and create a cooperative commonwealth in Canada. The CCF favoured government control of the economy through the nationalization of the means of production, distribution, and exchange. It also worked for a more equitable distribution

The federal CCF caucus meets with its secretary J.S. Woodsworth, standing in the centre. On the extreme left sits Tommy Douglas, later premier of Saskatchewan—the first leader when the CCF changed its name to the New Democratic Party.

Source: Library and Archives Canada/PA 167544.

of wealth, the creation of a welfare state, and the pursuit of international peace through the League of Nations.

The CCF had learned lessons from the Progressive experiment. The new party was not populist; it was firmly situated to the left of the political spectrum. It would not sit as a pressure group in Parliament, trying to exist and act outside the political system; it was a party vying for office. But the CCF faced some of the same serious obstacles to its election; most importantly, it remained a political party distinctly associated with one region of the country, the West.

The CCF entered its first federal election in 1935 in high hopes of becoming a major party. Those expectations were dashed when it won only 7 seats, all from the West, although the party did win 8.8 percent of the popular vote. Two of those elected—M.J. Coldwell and T.C. "Tommy" Douglas—later became national party leaders. Although weak in representation, the party did come to acquire the reputation of being "the conscience of the House of Commons." Provincially, the CCF did better. The party became the official opposition in British Columbia in 1933, in Saskatchewan in 1934, and in Ontario in 1943. But its real breakthrough came in the midst of World War II, when in 1944 Tommy Douglas led the party to victory in Saskatchewan. It was the first "socialist" government to be elected in North America.

Social Credit

In Alberta, a party quite different from the CCF—the Social Credit Party—also began in the midst of the Depression. Major C.H. Douglas, a Scottish engineer, first enunciated the theory of Social Credit in the 1910s. Douglas was concerned about the waste and underutilization of resources in the capitalist system ("poverty in the midst of plenty"). He did not blame the capitalist system, which he admired, but rather the financial institutions that hoarded money, preventing consumers from buying the abundant goods that the system produced. Douglas's solution was for governments to inject more money into the economy and give it to the people to spend. He used his "A plus B Theorem" to explain his reasoning. "A" represented the wages, salaries, and dividends paid to individuals; "B" represented all other costs involved in making an item, such as raw materials and bank charges. Together, the two costs would give the "just price" of an item. The problem, Social Credit theorists argued, was that individuals only got the "A" portion. To make up the difference (the "B" portion), a Social Credit government would provide a "national dividend" to every individual to enable him or her to purchase essential goods. To people without sufficient money to buy even the necessities of life, the theory was appealing. When presented as A plus B, it seemed remarkably simple.

C.H. Douglas's theories awaited a popular leader and Alberta provided one: the charismatic William "Bible Bill" Aberhart. Born in Ontario, Aberhart came west in 1910. A high school principal in Calgary, he also served as a lay preacher in a local Baptist Church. In 1925, the radio station CFCN invited him to give Sunday sermons on their "Voice of the Prairie" program. This opportunity enabled Aberhart to use the new technology and communication medium to reach an estimated 350,000 people across the Prairies and mid-western United States with his religious message. With financial contributions from listeners, the evangelist built the Prophetic Bible Institute in Calgary, which he later used to distribute Social Credit material.

Aberhart "converted" to Social Credit in the summer of 1932 after the suicide of one of his best students as a result of the Depression. He introduced his own altered version of C.H. Douglas's Social Credit economic theory into his weekly sermons. Wrapped in religion, the population, already desperate and seeking solutions, was attracted to Aberhart's confident, simplistic, and hopeful politics. The message became more attractive when Aberhart blamed the economic crisis on the "big interests," including the banks and the federal government. Initially, "Bible Bill" hoped one of the established political parties would adopt Social Credit. When they failed to do so, he began his own party on the eve of the 1935 provincial election in Alberta. He promised every citizen a $25-a-month "basic dividend" to purchase necessities. Helping the party to gain popularity was a sex scandal involving the United Farmers of Alberta (UFA) premier John Brownlee, which destroyed his career.

In the 1935 provincial election, Social Credit swept Alberta, winning 56 of the 63 seats. Once in power, the new premier and his party found they could not implement their election promises because the promises were outside provincial jurisdiction. Premier Aberhart brought in legislation in an attempt to control the banks and even the press. The federal government challenged the constitutional legality of a province issuing its own currency. The federal power of disallowance, now a rarely used device, was used for the last time in Canadian history. Aberhart responded by vilifying Ottawa for preventing the implementation of Social Credit theory and discriminating against Alberta. The federal government allowed Alberta to go bankrupt in 1935 (the only province to do so) while propping up Saskatchewan and Manitoba. The party also lacked parliamentary expertise, since the majority of its candidates were political neophytes. Only after the outbreak of war, and especially after the discovery of oil in 1947, did the party become well established under Aberhart's protégé, Ernest Manning, who took over after Aberhart's death in 1943. The Social Credit Party would remain in power until 1971, further establishing Alberta's reputation as a one-party province.

The Reconstruction Party

H.H. Stevens, a British Columbia member of the Bennett government and head of the Select Committee and then of the Royal Commission on Price Spreads, resigned from the cabinet in October 1934 to begin his own party, the Reconstruction Party. He promised "to re-establish Canada's industrial, economic and social life for the benefit of the great majority." In the 1935 election, the Reconstruction party won over 8 percent of the popular vote but elected only one candidate, Stevens. The party reduced Conservative support in various constituencies across the country. It disappeared after the election.

Communists and Fascists

Extreme left- and right-wing political movements, such as the Communist Party and fascist groups, grew during the interwar years, reflecting what was occurring on the international scene. The Communist Party of Canada, founded in 1921 in Guelph, Ontario, thrived in the crisis conditions of the Depression, especially among immigrants threatened with deportation. It modelled itself after the Soviet Communist Party. Government repression of the party occurred frequently in the 1930s by invoking section 98 of the Criminal Code, which made it illegal to advocate "governmental, industrial or economic change within Canada by the use of force, violence or physical injury to persons or property, or by threats of such injury" even if the accused did nothing to bring about such changes. In one crackdown in August 1931, party leader Tim Buck and seven others were arrested. As a result of an attempt on Buck's life in Kingston Penitentiary a year

Communist-organized May Day parade in Toronto, May 1, 1934. Note the sign, "Release Tim Buck." The Communist Party of Canada leader had been tried and convicted of sedition. Imprisoned in the Kingston Penitentiary in 1932, he gained his release later in 1934.

Source: City of Toronto Archives, Fonds 1266, Globe and Mail Collection, item 33196.

later, the "Toronto Eight," as they became known, emerged as the embattled underdogs. They won sympathy from a number of Canadians who believed in the democratic right of left-wing dissident groups to express their views.

Most Canadians who wanted change during the Depression preferred the peaceful, democratic approach of the CCF to the violent, revolutionary change advocated by the communists. On the eve of World War II, the Communist Party had 16,000 members. But when the Soviet Union signed a non-aggression pact with Adolf Hitler that summer, many members quit the party in protest. In June 1940, the Canadian government used the opportunity offered by the War Measures Act and declared the Communist Party illegal.

Even though World War II would be fought against fascism, no action was taken against fascist groups in Canada during the Depression. It was assumed that fascists were less numerous and less dangerous than communists. The Deutscher Bund Canada, for example, founded in 1934 and led by German Canadians, never had more than 2000 members, while the Canadian Nationalist Party, founded by right-wing militants, and the allied Swastika clubs, added a few thousand more. It was also assumed that communists were more of a sinister threat to the established order.

But the influence of the fascists was real, and this manifested itself in numerous forms. Swastika clubs tried to stop Jews from visiting Kew and Balmy Beaches in east Toronto. In Quebec, Adrien Arcand patterned his National Social Christian Party along Nazi lines. He claimed to represent the last stand of Roman Catholicism against communists and other "atheist" groups. While Arcand remained a marginal and eccentric character, anti-Semitism found support among nationalist movements in the province, such as the Jeune-Canada and the Ligue d'action nationale. The Catholic Church was staunchly opposed to communism and in this struggle often found a ready ally in fascist groups.

Thousands of persecuted Jews fleeing Nazi Germany found Canada's doors firmly closed. Sadly, the anti-Semitic views of fascist groups also often found a welcome audience in Canada. At McGill University in Montreal, officials conspired to turn away Jewish applicants. A leading member of the Canadian immigration department summarized the government's view toward Jewish immigrants: asked how many Jews would be let into Canada, he responded "None is too many." Only a few Canadian leaders, such as Cairine Wilson, Canada's first woman senator and chairperson of the Canadian National Committee on Refugees, denounced Nazi atrocities and urged a liberalization of Canadian immigration regulations. Immigration in total reached an all-time low in the 1930s: only 149,000 immigrants were allowed in during the entire decade, and only 5000 of them were Jews.

An anti-Semitic poster at Sainte-Agathe, a resort area in the Laurentians north of Montreal, 1939.

Source: Library and Archives Canada/PA-107943. Reprinted with permission of *The Gazette*, Montreal.

Federalism and Dominion–Provincial Relations

The Great Depression not only signalled a crisis in capitalism, it demonstrated a crisis in Canadian federalism. The federal structure created at the time of Confederation in 1867 proved inadequate during such a time of crisis. As a result of modernization and an array of new expenses (including roads, urban infrastructure, unemployment, and health costs), municipalities and provinces were unable to meet their financial obligations and to provide an equal level of services to their citizens across the various regions of Canada. The nation was clearly divided into the "haves" and "have nots." Provinces faced bankruptcy, thereby damaging the financial status of the nation. Dominion–provincial relations became the most contentious quagmire in Canadian politics.

The unpopularity of the Bennett Conservatives tainted the provincial Tory parties. By the time of the federal election in October 1935, there were no Conservative governments left in the provinces. The united stand against Bennett was made evident when almost every provincial premier appeared alongside Liberal Leader Mackenzie King at an election rally at Maple Leaf Gardens in Toronto in 1935.

Newfoundland and the Maritimes

Various problems beset Newfoundland in the 1930s. The most important was the falling price of fish as a result of the Depression. In 1932, Sir Richard Squires, the Liberal premier, narrowly escaped being lynched by a mob infuriated by disclosures of scandal, as well as by the government's tough relief policies when almost half of the island's labour force was out of work. The British navy had to be called in to assist local police in controlling rioters. A new government, the United Newfoundland Party, took power after the election of 1932. It obtained further bank loans by arguing that the money was needed to ward off "grave threats of insurrection." A royal commission reviewed the economic crisis and recommended the dissolution of the legislature. Newfoundland, which was a dominion at the time, reverted to the status of a British colony, and London was obliged to pay off the colony's debts.

In Nova Scotia, Angus L. Macdonald, a former law professor, became premier in 1933. Practising an activist style of government, "Angus L." implemented old-age pensions and began paving provincial roads. He also appointed a royal commission to investigate Nova Scotia's position in Confederation. The three-person commission, including University of Toronto historian Harold Innis, argued for additional compensation for Canada's poorer provinces, since their disadvantageous position resulted from their role in Confederation.

In both New Brunswick and Prince Edward Island, the Liberals came to power on promises of economic and social reform. In New Brunswick, Allison Dysart's government introduced old-age pensions, created public works projects, and pressured timber companies into activating their leases or else losing them. In Prince Edward Island, Thane Campbell's government had the distinction of being the first to win every seat in a provincial election. In office, Campbell established a permanent civil service and supported cooperative organizations and marketing boards as its response to the Depression.

All three Maritime provinces, however, lacked the revenues to complete promised reforms. New Brunswick, for example, borrowed heavily to finance its massive public works program. Inevitably, other priorities suffered. Education and health services declined to barely half the national average by the end of the 1930s, and illiteracy and infant mortality rates in the province were the highest in the country.

Quebec

In Quebec, the new Union nationale Party under the leadership of Maurice Duplessis arose from an alliance between a nationalist branch of the provincial Conservative Party and a dissident group of Liberals who had already left to create the Action libérale nationale (ALN). This nationalist alliance lasted only long enough to defeat the long-standing Liberal government in

Quebec premier Maurice Duplessis meets Ontario premier Mitch Hepburn around 1935.

Source: Library and Archives Canada/C-19527.

1936, in power since 1897, at which point the right-wing Duplessis purged his government of the ALN faction.

With the strong backing of the Catholic Church, Duplessis attacked a number of dissident groups in the province, including socialists, communists, and trade unionists. In 1937 he introduced the "Padlock Law," which made it illegal for any group to use a house or hall "to propagate communism or bolshevism" or to publish or distribute literature "tending to propagate communism." As the bill did not define "communist," it gave the premier a weapon with which to attack any left-wing or dissident organization he wished. Duplessis used the law to lock premises suspected of being used for communist activities, to ban publications, and, on a couple of occasions, to arrest opponents. He attacked union leaders, denouncing them as "dangerous agitators," when unions refused to comply with Quebec's labour laws. Most notably, the law was used to crack down on such groups as Jehovah's Witnesses.

Ontario

In Ontario in 1934, voters ousted the Conservatives, who had been in office since 1923. They elected the Liberals under their flamboyant leader, "Mitch" Hepburn, whose oratorical skills and quick wit served him well on the political hustings. At one country rally, Hepburn gave his speech from the only available stage, a manure spreader. He remarked that it was the first time he had given an address on a Conservative platform.

Although initially seen as a reformer, Hepburn soon proved to be reactionary. He sided with industrialists against labourers in a bitter sixteen-day strike against General Motors in Oshawa in 1937. He denounced the United Auto Workers union as "communist inspired," and sent in a government-supported police force, dubbed "Hepburn's Hussars" or "sons of Mitches," to break up the strike. Two of his cabinet ministers, Arthur Roebuck and David Croll, resigned in disgust. Croll proclaimed his "place was marching with the workers rather than riding with General Motors."

The Prairies

The government in Manitoba continued to be led by John Bracken. It is difficult to attach a party label to the administrations because Bracken mastered the art of coalition government. Upon taking office in 1922, Bracken led the United Farmers of Manitoba (UFM). As a Progressive, however, Bracken disdained party labels as interfering with "effective" government and advocated "nonpartisanship." Over the years, and in order to stay in power, Bracken formed coalitions with almost every other political group. The formula worked—the Manitoba government was the only one in the country to enter the Depression in office and emerge from the crisis intact.

Saskatchewan was unique among the Prairie provinces in not falling to the Progressive wave in the 1920s. Instead, the Liberal Party distanced itself from its federal counterpart in the 1920s under Premiers W.M. Martin and Charles Dunning. Premier Jimmy Gardiner reunited the two wings of the party toward the end of the decade but lost to the Conservatives under J.T.M. Anderson at the beginning of the Depression. The Liberals returned to office in 1934, but politics in Saskatchewan was changing. The Conservatives were destroyed and the new opposition to the Liberals took the form of a labour–farmer coalition; "the contest was framed as a battle between liberalism and socialism."[2]

Politics in Alberta proved a frustrating mystery to federal politicians. The political culture in the province was dominated by one-party contests. The Liberals were in office from 1905 until 1921, when they were replaced by the United Farmers of Alberta. While the Progressives returned to their Liberal roots in the other provinces, they remained a distinct and independent group in Alberta. But while maintaining their stance on nonpartisanship, grassroots democracy, and effective government, their political philosophy gradually shifted from left to right. When the UFA finally seemed to be disintegrating by the time of the provincial election of 1935, it seemed the Liberals would make their long-awaited breakthrough in Alberta. The sweeping victory of William Aberhart and his Social Credit Party dashed these hopes.

British Columbia

In British Columbia, another flamboyant and self-assured provincial Liberal leader, T.D. "Duff" Pattullo, became premier in the midst of the Depression. Pattullo had won and lost fortunes in a business career in the Yukon and northern British Columbia before entering politics. He won the election of 1933 on the promise of "work and wages." His program became known as the "little New Deal," which promised a provincial health-insurance plan, reduced taxes on lower incomes, public works, unemployment insurance, and an economic council with labour representation to study the problem of unemployment. He also believed in injecting money into the economy by spending on major public works projects, such as the bridge that bears his name and the Alaska Highway. According to historian Robin Fisher, "the first Pattullo administration offered the most vigorous political response to the depression of any government in Canada."[3] But as in Alberta's case, the government of British Columbia lacked the tax base to make these changes. Pattullo looked to the federal government for loans to help his government fight the "war on poverty." When the Conservative, and then Liberal, administrations in Ottawa refused funding requests, Pattullo failed to follow through on many policies. Nevertheless, he managed to get re-elected in 1937. His government remained in power until 1941, when it was replaced by a Liberal–Conservative coalition.

Labour in the Depression

Workers became more militant amid the desperate conditions of the Depression and the crisis in capitalism. "Red" trade unions grew and some were affiliated with the Communist Party of Canada. For example, the Workers' Unity League (WUL) was born out of a directive from Moscow that communist-led unions should separate from "reformist" unions, like the All-Canadian Congress of Labour (ACCL), and prepare for the coming world revolution. After signing up workers in mines and shops, the WUL declared strikes to obtain union recognition and better wages and working conditions. At its peak in 1932, the WUL had an estimated 40,000 members. It claimed leadership of most of the strikes across the country in the early 1930s. The WUL also organized the unemployed by establishing workers' councils in various cities and by circulating a petition, eventually signed by 300,000 people, calling for a national non-contributory unemployment-insurance scheme.

Violent confrontation occurred between police and strikers or between strikebreakers and strikers. The worst was in Estevan, Saskatchewan, in 1931, when 600 coal-mine workers walked out of the mines. The owners denounced the strike as "Communist-led," ensuring the support of the politicians and the RCMP. The police opened fire during a strikers' parade, killing three unarmed strikers.

The CIO in Canada

In 1935 a new union, the American-based Congress of Industrial Organizations (CIO), emerged in Canada to "organize the unorganized." The CIO's greatest success in Canada occurred in 1937, when the United Auto Workers led the strike at the General Motors factory in Oshawa, Ontario. Premier Hepburn intervened to break the strike because he feared a CIO victory would encourage unionization and strikes elsewhere in the province. The CIO also organized Montreal's female garment workers, as well as coal miners in Nova Scotia.

Despite some successes and much publicity, however, the CIO made little headway elsewhere in Canada in the 1930s. Strong opposition came from business and the crafts-dominated Trades and Labor Congress (TLC), which in 1939 expelled the CIO affiliates. The CIO then merged with the weaker All-Canadian Congress of Labour in 1940 to form the Canadian Congress of Labour (CCL).

Women in the 1930s

In the 1930s, women's wages fell dramatically and working conditions deteriorated. Initially, the Depression benefited women who wanted to work because they could be hired at half a man's wages. Then came the backlash. Men were seen as the "breadwinners," and women were blamed for taking jobs away from unemployed men who had wives and families to support. CCF member Agnes Macphail pointed out that the economic system, not women, was to blame for unemployment. She added that many women needed to work if they and their families were to survive. As historian Katrina Srigley points out, however, this did not mean that women did not continue to work:

> Despite the gender expectations that surrounded employment, women had long worked for money and, by the interwar years, were working in greater numbers than ever before. In fact, wage earning had become an expected stage in women's lives between schooling and marriage.[4]

Women faced difficulties getting relief even if they were eligible. In addition, many municipalities opposed giving relief to women. Authorities reasoned that single, unemployed women posed no threat to society, as did single, unemployed men. Furthermore, they assumed that these women would be cared for by their families. Authorities feared that relief to women would contribute to the breakdown of the family by threatening the breadwinner model. Some married women assumed the dual responsibilities of breadwinner and sole head of the family, because their husbands left home in search of work or simply deserted their families. Destitute single mothers in Ontario could apply for the Mothers' Allowance, implemented in 1920, but the amount was meagre and the recipients became, in essence, wards of the state. Young women took on work to help supplement the family income.

Emphasis was placed on women being wives and mothers. Over 90 percent of women eventually married, although many delayed doing so during the Depression. Once married, they were expected to give up their jobs and take up domestic duties. Often, they kept working regardless.

Family size declined in the 1930s. Infant mortality still remained high, due to several factors. Babies born in the winter months had to survive the poor heating in even the best-built residences. Infants also faced a wide range of "childhood diseases"—measles, mumps, scarlet fever, and whooping cough—illnesses that proved deadly due to a lack of public-health programs and antibiotics.

Birth control was seldom an option women could consider, although by 1937 birth-control clinics existed in Toronto, Hamilton, and Windsor, Ontario. A.H. Tyrer's *Sex, Marriage and Birth Control* (1936) was a surprise bestseller. But the popular belief of the day was expressed by Dr. Helen MacMurchy, director of the Dominion Division of Child Welfare, who described birth control among those of British background as "race suicide." French-Canadian nationalists used the same argument in Quebec. The idea of eugenics—the selective breeding of the fittest and the compulsory sterilization of those considered inferior—gained popularity in the 1930s. Heading the movement was A.R. Kaufman, a wealthy manufacturer who believed that the "inferior" working class was producing over half of the nation's children. Among them were the "irresponsible, criminal and mentally deficient" who were the source of "most of our social liabilities." His solution was to distribute birth-control information and devices, and even to perform sterilization to restrict or prevent reproduction among certain groups.

A few doctors provided birth-control information and devices, but they did so at the risk of losing their medical licence. Dr. Elizabeth Bagshaw, for example, operated a birth-control clinic for working-class women in Hamilton, Ontario. Dorothea Palmer was arrested in a French-Canadian suburb of Ottawa for distributing contraceptive information. At her trial, where both Tyrer and Kaufman lent support, the judge acquitted her because he believed she had acted "for the public good." The poor, he stated, "are a burden to the taxpayer. They crowd the Juvenile Court. They glut the competitive labour market." For some women, self-induced miscarriages seemed to be the only alternative to unwanted children or children they simply could not afford.

Support for birth control tended often to come from left-wing groups. Some women socialists believed that the capitalist system encouraged large families to have a cheap source of labour for its factories and cannon fodder for its armies. In 1924, British Columbia socialists founded the Canadian Birth Control League to educate working-class women. In 1929, the Saskatchewan section of the United Farmers of Canada recommended the establishment of birth-control clinics staffed by trained doctors.

The First Nations People in the 1930s

First Nations and Métis communities faced numerous challenges. "Conditions on Indian reserves in practically every area—social services, health, education, and living facilities—had deteriorated in the years since the signing of the treaties."[5] The Indian Act's tight regulations remained in full force. But a ray of hope emerged in this decade: political organization. British Columbia led the way with the formation of the Allied Tribes of British Columbia in 1915, replaced by the more powerful Native Brotherhood of British Columbia in 1931. Fred Loft's League of Indians of Canada, founded after World War I, briefly became the first pan-Indian political organization extending across Canada in the early 1920s. It contributed to the formation of the Indian Association of Alberta in 1929, which also publicized Aboriginal issues.

Liberal Policies

The election of Mackenzie King's Liberals in 1935 resulted in little change in federal policy dealing with the Depression. King shared Bennett's desire to balance budgets and avoid federal responsibility for costs dealing with unemployment. But like the Conservatives, the Liberals were forced to accept important changes within Canadian federalism, and indeed the state's role in society, whether they agreed with them or not. Despite his bitter opposition during the first half of the decade, King maintained many of Bennett's policies.

The prime minister continued the Conservatives' policy of aid to the drought-stricken farmers of western Canada. This included maintaining the Prairie Farm Rehabilitation

Administration (PFRA), an act passed by the Bennett government that provided money to experiment with new farming methods, especially in the dry-belt area of the Palliser Triangle. The experimental farms in the region applied the latest scientific knowledge to attempt to get the soil to regain its productivity. Two innovations followed: first, the Noble plough, invented by Charles Noble of Nobleford, Alberta, which cut the roots of weeds without turning over the topsoil to expose it to sun and wind; and second, "trash farming"—instead of ploughing and harrowing their fields to make them look neat and clean, farmers were encouraged to leave the dead plants and grain stubble on the field to prevent wind erosion. The PFRA also provided money to build dugouts for spring runoff water for cattle, helped reseed vacant and pasture land, and, in the case of destitute farm families in the Palliser Triangle area, assisted with relocation to better farming areas to the north.

The Liberals supported the Bank of Canada (created by the Bennett Conservatives in 1935) as an essential stabilizing force in times of financial crisis. After the government purchased a majority of the bank's stock, King made its governor responsible to Parliament for monetary policy. Part of the reason for the policy crossover was that the experts now working in the civil service continued in their positions, despite the change in government. The best examples of these "Ottawa Men" who wielded considerable influence in policy were O.D. Skelton in external affairs and Clifford Clark in finance.

In 1936, the federal government reorganized the Canadian Radio Broadcasting Commission, founded in 1932 to control radio under federal government jurisdiction, into the Canadian Broadcasting Corporation (CBC). According to Graham Spry, whose Canadian Radio League had fought for such an institution, the choice was between "the State or the United States." The government mandated the CBC to regulate private broadcasting and to develop its own network across the country with Canadian content in both official languages. The CBC was "the 20th-century parallel to Macdonald's railway."[6] In 1937, the Liberals also established Trans-Canada Air Lines (TCA), the forerunner of Air Canada, as a Crown corporation.

The King government maintained policy initiatives that saw the state intervene in the realms of public works and housing. The Municipal Improvements Assistance Act authorized $30 million in federal loans at 2 percent interest for special municipal public-works projects. The National Housing Act (NHA), meanwhile, brought the government into the housing industry by backing mortgages. With the Depression making it difficult for people to purchase homes, the NHA provided $30 million worth of mortgages. It also allowed potential homeowners to borrow at least 60 percent of value for up to 20 to 25 years, and combined repayment of both interest and principal under a system of blended payments. The legislation, however, was primarily designed to aid the middle class and did little to alleviate the slum conditions facing the working class. This new financing arrangement was "a key development in suburb development" by allowing more people to buy a home.[7]

The Liberals did, however, alter the Conservatives' high tariff policy. Charles Dunning, the finance minister and former premier of Saskatchewan, negotiated low tariff agreements with both Britain and the United States. The tariff, however, was no longer the central issue in Canadian politics and economics. It had been replaced by unemployment.

Like Bennett, King was forced to deal with the relief question. On the heels of the On-to-Ottawa Trek, the Liberals discontinued the relief camps. The federal government established the National Employment Commission to re-examine and restructure the administration of direct relief. In 1867, relief had been a very minor matter, assigned in the BNA Act to the provinces and municipalities. The Royal Commission made two important recommendations: first, that the federal government take over unemployment payments because this was too expensive an undertaking for municipal or provincial governments; and second, that the government adopt a policy of deficit financing to provide additional relief and stimulate economic growth. Like Bennett,

King hesitated in accepting federal responsibility for unemployment and relief, responsibilities that would increase the federal debt load. He also resisted the Keynesian monetary policy of deficit financing, which went against his traditional liberal policies of laissez-faire and balanced budgets.

WHERE HISTORIANS DISAGREE

The Welfare State

The Great Depression marked a turning point in the relationship between Canadians and the state. Between 1930 and 1945, the role and influence of the state reached unprecedented levels. After suffering the economic ravages of the postwar recession, the Depression, and then World War II, the appetite for social welfare programs seemed insatiable. In September 1943, the Co-operative Commonwealth Federation (CCF), a social-democratic party, scored higher in the polls than either the Conservatives or the Liberals. The CCF called for centralized economic planning and governmental management. Liberal Prime Minister Mackenzie King realized the need to embrace an expanded role for the state.

The shift away from the old economic orthodoxy of balanced budgets and minimal governmental intervention was labelled "Keynesianism," after British economist and monetary theorist John Maynard Keynes. It promoted government spending as a means of shoring up consumer spending, curbing inflation, promoting employment, and using governmental funds to keep the economy "pump-primed" even during a recession. Keynesian budgets were evident in Canada as early as 1937.

This new approach demanded an activist government that applied economic and managerial techniques to ensure that economic catastrophes could be averted. The Liberal government took a step to the left and introduced social policies designed to undercut the growing popularity of the CCF, including Family Allowances (known as the "Baby Bonus") in 1944 and the "Green Book" proposals (extended social security benefits and the creation of new federal departments of health and welfare and postwar reconstruction) in 1945.

Historian Doug Owram argued that the interwar period saw a dramatic change in the way Canadian intellectuals viewed the role of the state in economic life. He argued that the group of intellectuals who came of age during World War I and staffed Mackenzie King's bureaucracy formed a transitional generation that rejected an older Victorian idealism of public virtue and embraced a new political individualism based on the emerging social sciences. The government bureaucracy became staffed by university-trained "experts" who formed a "government generation."[1]

Barry Ferguson studied four prominent Canadian social scientists (all from Queen's University) whose work covered the tumultuous first quarter of the twentieth century. These men worked for the federal government during their careers, while also holding academic posts. They questioned the wisdom of an economic order that put the functioning of the market economy above the well-being of the individual citizen, and they saw government as an instrument for extending social and economic benefits. According to Ferguson, it created a "new liberalism" that made possible the development of the Canadian welfare state.[2]

Part of this "new liberalism" was the rise of what J.L. Granatstein has called "the Ottawa Men." This small group of elite-trained bureaucrats staffed Ottawa's key governmental agencies. For twenty years, a small, closely knit group of intellectuals provided the federal government with what Granatstein believes was perhaps the best civil service in the world. These men distinguished themselves by helping Canada produce its own foreign, economic, and social policies during an era of depression and war, and ensured that the country entered the postwar world victorious, autonomous, and with a solid economy. In Granatstein's words, these men made the civil service "a model of policy innovation and efficiency" and brought to their country the interventionist state.[3]

Perhaps no man better exemplified the talent and work ethic of the Ottawa Men than the deputy minister of finance, William Clifford Clark. Robert Wardhaugh has argued that Clark acted as recruiter, leader, and source of inspiration for the civil service and produced a record of achievement without parallel. During his seventeen-year career in Ottawa, Clark was instrumental in dealing with the Depression, creating the Bank of Canada, orchestrating monetary policy, guiding dominion–provincial relations, leading the wartime economy, and forging Canada's new role in international economic organizations. He also helped build the welfare state. But despite Clark's achievements during this "golden age" of the bureaucracy, Wardhaugh took some of the sheen off the Ottawa Men by arguing that they often pushed the acceptable limits of their influence by advancing their own agendas.[4]

According to Robert Campbell, the Great Depression and World War II created a "rupture" with Canada's past and opened the door to new approaches to government and economic policy. The adoption of Keynesian methods was a watershed moment, because the relationship between the citizenry and the state was fundamentally reshaped. Citizens came to view the federal government as responsible for ensuring their social security and promoting full employment. They believed that governmental planning could forestall economic destabilization. Nevertheless, the success of Keynesianism, was largely an illusion. Keynesian methods were not actually applied as widely and systematically as previously thought.[5]

James Struthers has claimed that welfare "is our most complex, least understood, and most unpopular social program."[6] Welfare critics usually argue that increased social assistance undermines the work ethic and creates a culture of dependency. In provinces such as Ontario, as in the federal government, it was assumed that welfare could be adequately provided by technical expertise, often through the efforts of social workers. This technical and administrative approach to welfare delivery and anti-poverty programs failed because the political culture significantly limited the ability of the state to act. The primary flaw in welfare delivery in Ontario, according to Struthers, was the managerial approach—at the expense of building a political base of support.

Nancy Christie has challenged the assumption that welfare state programs were gender-neutral. The male bread-winner family was the state's model for the Canadian family. Policymakers possessed a rigid definition of gender and its relationship to citizenship and market participation. Social scientific methodologies, designed to modernize welfare administration, did not challenge this assumption. The result was that women were to remain in the home, while working fathers were expected to earn the family income. It was deemed in the national interest to guarantee men the breadwinner role because "welfare reformers saw social forces as but a reflection of familial relationships."[7]

Jennifer A. Stephen agrees that views on gender, race, and class influenced the social, economic, and manpower policies implemented by Ottawa during and after the war. The federal civil service responded to a political climate favourable toward governmental direction by implementing policies designed to control or "manage" the labour market. The civil service used social scientific methods of mental hygiene and intelligence screening to decide the fitness of potential workers, which led to discrimination against women. Tests vaunted by the government for their objectivity actually worked to discriminate against women,

particularly those of different races and ethnicities and from the working class. According to Stephen, the policies issued by the state were not based on objective standards but reflected prejudices that were historically contingent and attuned to the values of Ottawa's governing elite.[8]

Shirley Tillotson has challenged the distinction between public and private spheres in Canadian political life that was at the heart of the male breadwinner model. She argues that public welfare policies and private charitable fundraising did not exist in two separate spheres but were closely intertwined. Private fundraising organizations were staffed by people who worked in private business as well as public life, and their involvement in both spheres ensured that government welfare policy was influenced by the role of private charities in Canada.[9]

The abundance of historical scholarship on the creation of the Canadian welfare state is indicative of what is being called the "new political history." It emphasizes the role of the state and power relations rather than politicians and parties.

---

1   Doug Owram, *The Government Generation: Canadian Intellectuals and the State 1900–1945* (Toronto: University of Toronto Press, 1986).

2   Barry Ferguson, *Remaking Liberalism: The Intellectual Legacy of Adam Shortt, O.D. Skelton, W.C. Clark, and W.A. Mackintosh, 1890–1925* (Montreal/Kingston: McGill-Queen's University Press, 1993).

3   J.L. Granatstein, *The Ottawa Men: The Civil Service Mandarins, 1935–1957* (Toronto: Oxford University Press, 1982), p. 18.

4   Robert A. Wardhaugh, *Behind the Scenes: The Life and Work of William Clifford Clark* (Toronto: University of Toronto Press, 2010).

5   Robert Malcolm Campbell, *Grand Illusions: The Politics of the Keynesian Experience in Canada, 1945–1975* (Peterborough, ON: Broadview Press, 1987).

6   James Struthers, *The Limits of Affluence: Welfare in Ontario, 1920–1970* (Toronto: University of Toronto Press, 1994), p. 261.

7   Nancy Christie, *Engendering the State: Family, Work, and Welfare in Canada* (Toronto: University of Toronto Press, 2000), p. 17.

8   Jennifer A. Stephen, *Pick One Intelligent Girl: Employability, Domesticity, and the Gendering of Canada's Welfare State, 1939–1947* (Toronto: University of Toronto Press, 2007).

9   Shirley Tillotson, *Contributing Citizens: Modern Charitable Fundraising and the Making of the Welfare State, 1920–66* (Vancouver: UBC Press, 2008).

The Royal Commission on Dominion–Provincial Relations

The crisis in federalism led Prime Minister King to establish the Royal Commission on Dominion–Provincial Relations in 1937 to explore all aspects of relations between the two levels of government in the light of the current economic crisis. Heralded as the most important royal commission in Canadian history, the Rowell–Sirois Commission—as it was named, after lead commissioners N.W. Rowell of Ontario and Joseph Sirois of Quebec—was sweeping in its breadth. Its mandate included studying the history of Canadian federalism since 1867 in order to understand how the system had broken down during the Depression and how such crises might be avoided in the future. But the decision to launch the commission ran into strong provincial opposition from some of the era's most powerful and vocal premiers, including Hepburn in Ontario, Aberhart in Alberta, Patullo in British Columbia, and Duplessis in Quebec. These premiers were fighting bitter jurisdictional battles with Ottawa.

The Rowell–Sirois report was massive and contained an impressive storehouse of ideas to restructure Canadian federalism. But World War II intervened. As a result, the report did not appear until 1940. Meanwhile, the War Measures Act gave the federal government licence to increase its powers without provincial consent. While the recommendations of Rowell–Sirois were not followed, Ottawa took over taxation powers of the provinces while using the report and the war as justification. The result was the most centralist and powerful federal government the nation had ever experienced.

Religion

Religion continued to play an essential role in the individual lives of Canadians and in the reform agenda of the nation. Many Canadians turned to religion for solace and direction amid the suffering and uncertainty of the Depression. Some socially minded Protestants looked to the Fellowship for a Christian Social Order, founded by members of the United Church, for answers to the economic crisis. Fellowship members insisted that realizing the kingdom of God on earth meant replacing a bankrupt capitalist system with socialism. Critics of the group complained that too many of its members were more committed to the teachings of Karl Marx than those of Jesus Christ.

Student activists turned to the Student Christian Movement (SCM), an organization begun in 1920 by the YWCA and YMCA. The SCM provided study groups on most Canadian university campuses in the 1930s to discuss social issues and advocate social change. For young girls, the Canadian Girls in Training (CGIT), an organization founded by the YWCA and the Protestant churches in 1917 to train young girls to improve both their lives and those of others, reached its peak of popularity during the Depression, when it had an estimated 40,000 members.

Conservative and fundamentalist groups flourished in the 1930s. Church leaders promised that if people could not find salvation in this world, they could still find hope in the afterlife. Disciples of the British spiritual organization Oxford Group toured Canada, delivering a message of "revelation, not revolution" to overflow audiences, which on one occasion included R.B. Bennett and his entire cabinet, at the prime minister's request.

In Quebec, many viewed the Depression as evidence of divine punishment for the sins of humankind—

A Canadian Girls in Training (CGIT) meeting, probably in Toronto, around 1920. The Young Women's Christian Association and the major Protestant denominations established the organization in 1915 to promote the Christian education of girls aged 12 to 17.

Source: Canadian Girls in Training Collection/Library and Archives Canada/PA-125872.

including communism, materialism, urbanization, and even capitalism. They supported a back-to-the-land movement as the best means to combat both unemployment and "moral decrepitude."

The Antigonish Movement

Still others, particularly those in the Maritimes, looked to cooperatives as the answer. In 1931, Pope Pius XI issued his encyclical *Quadragesimo anno*, in which he attacked the competitive nature of capitalism as heartless and cruel, and advocated cooperation instead. His appeal found a receptive audience in the cooperative movement in eastern Canada.

Beginning in the late 1920s and throughout the 1930s, Moses Coady, director of the extension department at St. Francis Xavier University in Antigonish, Nova Scotia, and Jimmy Tompkins, a fellow priest, worked to improve the lives of poor farmers, miners, fishers, and their families. A representative of this young cooperative movement would visit a community and, using local contacts, call a public meeting. A study group would follow to assess the community's economic strengths and weaknesses. After the group's meetings concluded, one or more cooperatives would form to remedy the identifiable weaknesses. The cooperatives might be credit unions, or perhaps cooperatives for selling fish or farm produce. Accused of being too left-wing, Father Coady replied: "I'm not a leftist; I'm where the righteous ought to be."

Culture in the 1930s

Popular culture continued to flourish, despite the Depression. New forms of entertainment—radio, for instance—allowed a greater choice of escapes from the realities of the crisis. Owners of radio sets listened to the comedy show *Amos 'n' Andy,* the most popular program of the decade. *Hockey Night in Canada,* with Foster Hewitt, was also a regular favourite. Such recording artists as Willie Eckstein, Percy Faith, and Guy Lombardo and His Royal Canadians had their start on Canadian radio, although by 1940 both Faith and Lombardo had left Canada for larger dance floors in the United States. Lombardo's famous version of "Auld Lang Syne" had its origins in the Scottish communities of Ontario where he played, but it became synonymous with the American New Year's Eve celebration. Don Messer began playing his "old time" fiddle music on radio in the 1930s, and formed "The Islanders" for CFCY radio in Charlottetown in 1939. In Quebec, people enjoyed the immensely successful serials written specifically for radio, such as *Le curé de village* and *La pension Velder*. Radio variety shows were equally popular programs in Quebec. The songs of "La Bolduc" (Mary Travers-Bolduc) enjoyed enormous popularity.

The birth of the Dionne quintuplets near Callander, Ontario, in May 1934, the first quintuplets to have survived through infancy, attracted worldwide attention, and brought over 3 million people for a glimpse at a special hospital set up to care for them under the auspices of the Ontario government—a government that quickly appreciated the profit to be made from this "tourist attraction." Even this real-life event was a form of escape for many.

Novels

In the 1930s, Morley Callaghan's three novels—*Such Is My Beloved* (1934), *They Shall Inherit the Earth* (1935), and *More Joy in Heaven* (1937)—stood out as examples of realistic novels, a reaction to the sentimental and romantic literature of an earlier generation. Irene Baird's *Waste Heritage* (1939) dealt with labour unrest and unemployment in Vancouver during the Depression. In Quebec, the book *Trente arpents* by Ringuet (a pseudonym for Philippe Panneton) was a realistic work that graphically depicted the transition from rural to urban life. Breaking with literary tradition by describing the French-Canadian farmer as tragic, it traces the fall of Eucha-riste Moisan from initial prosperity on his farm to existing as a broken man in a New England factory town.

Theatre

During the 1930s in Quebec, several of the best-known French-Canadian playwrights, such as Gratien Gélinas, learned their trade by writing scripts for radio productions, especially for the Canadian Broadcasting Corporation. But criticism arose once again concerning the propriety of theatre. When a Parisian company performed the popular but risqué operetta *Phi-Phi* at Montreal's St.-Denis theatre, a judge declared it indecent, closed it down, and levied $15 fines on each of the actors, their agents, and even the orchestra leader.

Although the Catholic Church opposed public theatre for entertainment purposes, the clergy did support amateur theatre for educational purposes. In 1937 Father Émile Legault founded a troupe of young actors at Montreal's Collège de Saint-Laurent that from 1938 to 1952 wrought a theatrical renaissance in Quebec. With his encouragement, the group moved from an early emphasis on religious theatre to one on classical and contemporary plays. Félix Leclerc, the famous Quebec singer, songwriter, playwright, and actor, acted with these Compagnons de St. Laurent in the early 1940s.

In general, professional theatre languished in the depressed atmosphere of the 1930s. Most theatre groups, barely able to hold on even during good times, folded.

Sport

Sport became another form of popular entertainment and a distraction during the Depression. In winter, hockey dominated. Hockey stars became household names among sports-minded families: the Toronto Maple Leafs' famous "Kid Line" of Charlie Conacher, Joe Primeau, and Busher Jackson; the legendary Eddie Shore of the Boston Bruins, known for his speed and scoring flair; Francis "King" Clancy of the Toronto Maple Leafs, who once played every position on the ice in a single game; and Howie Morenz of the Montreal Canadiens, who, with his speed and flashy stickhandling, was easily the greatest hockey superstar of the 1930s. Shortly after Morenz's tragic death on January 28, 1937, as a result of injuries received in a game, thousands of Montrealers filed past his bier, placed at centre ice in the Montreal Forum.

In summer, baseball continued to be Canada's most popular sport. Most communities had a local team, and the larger towns and cities enjoyed franchises in minor professional leagues. As well, Canadians followed American big-league baseball as though it were their own "national" sport and cheered the successes of the legendary Babe Ruth. Canadian baseball fans gathered in front of the newspaper offices to watch the World Series—it was recorded on a scale-model baseball diamond while an announcer described the game as it came in over the wire service.

SUMMARY

The Great Depression marked the worst economic crisis the Western world had ever experienced. Canada was hard-hit, and the crisis affected all aspects of society. Out of desperation, people turned to the state for aid. Governments, in turn, reluctantly accepted new economic and social responsibilities, while admitting that there was a "crisis" in both capitalism and federalism. The political system was further disrupted, and new political parties appeared, each offering its own solution to the Depression. It was a difficult period for ethnic groups as the doors of immigration closed, and those already within the gates faced growing persecution amid escalating tension throughout the world. Women and labourers also faced difficulties making gains, particularly with spiralling unemployment and the entrenchment of the male breadwinner model. It would take the onset of another world war to pull Canada from the economic turmoil.

NOTES

1. John Herd Thompson with Allen Seager, *Canada, 1922–1939: Decades of Discord* (Toronto: McClelland & Stewart, 1985), p. 194.

2. Robert Wardhaugh, *Mackenzie King and the Prairie West* (Toronto: University of Toronto Press, 2000), p. 181.

3. Robin Fisher and David J. Mitchell, "Patterns of Provincial Politics Since 1916," in Hugh J.M. Johnston, ed., *The Pacific Province: A History of British Columbia* (Vancouver: Douglas & McIntyre, 1996), p. 259.

4. Katrina Srigley, *Breadwinning Daughters: Young Working Women in a Depression-Era City, 1929–1939* (Toronto: University of Toronto Press, 2010), pp. 3–4.

5. Stan Cuthand, "The Native Peoples of the Prairie Provinces in the 1920's and 1930's," in Ian A.L. Getty and Donald B. Smith, eds., *One Century Later: Western Canadian Reserve Indians Since Treaty 7* (Vancouver: University of British Columbia Press, 1978), p. 41.

6. Jack McLeod, "Taking a Leaf from Sir John's Good Book," *The Globe and Mail*, January 11, 1997, p. D-5.

7. Richard Harris, *Creeping Conformity: How Canada Became Suburban, 1900–1960* (Toronto: University of Toronto Press, 2004), p. 11.

BIBLIOGRAPHY

A popular account of the 1930s is Pierre Berton, *The Great Depression, 1929–1939* (Toronto: McClelland & Stewart, 1990). For a more scholarly account, see John Herd Thompson with Allen Seager, *Canada, 1922–1939: Decades of Discord* (Toronto: McClelland & Stewart, 1985). For a good, brief synthesis, see Michiel Horn's booklet *The Great Depression of the 1930s in Canada* (Ottawa: Canadian Historical Association, 1984). A.E. Safarian analyzes economic developments in *The Canadian Economy in the Great Depression* (Toronto: University of Toronto Press, 1959). The stock-market crash of 1929 is discussed in Doug Fetherling, *Gold Diggers of 1929: Canada and the Great Stock Market Crash* (Toronto: Macmillan, 1979).

On the response of Canadians to the Depression, see R.D. Francis and H. Ganzevoort, eds., *The Dirty Thirties in Prairie Canada* (Vancouver: Tantalus Research, 1980); Michiel Horn, ed., *The Dirty Thirties: Canadians in the Great Depression* (Toronto: Copp Clark, 1972); James Gray, *The Winter Years* (Toronto: Macmillan, 1990 [1966]), and his *Men Against the Desert* (Saskatoon: Western Producer Prairie Books, 1967); and L.M. Grayson and Michael Bliss, eds., *The Wretched of Canada: Letters to R.B. Bennett, 1930–1935* (Toronto: University of Toronto Press, 1971).

Some good material exists on politics on the Depression, but much of it is now also dated. H. Blair Neatby provides an overview in *The Politics of Chaos: Canada in the Thirties* (Toronto: Macmillan, 1972). On R.B. Bennett, consult Larry A. Glassford, *Reaction and Reform: The Politics of the Conservative Party Under R.B. Bennett, 1927–1938* (Toronto: University of Toronto Press, 1992) and P.B. Waite, *In Search of R.B. Bennett* (Montreal/Kingston: McGill-Queen's University Press, 2012). Federal financial measures are studied in Robert B. Bryce, *Maturing in Hard Times: Canada's Department of Finance Through the Great Depression* (Toronto: Institute of Public Administration of Canada, 1986). On the founding of the Bank of Canada, see Douglas H. Fullerton, *Graham Towers and His Times* (Toronto: McClelland & Stewart, 1986). On the New Deal, see J.R.H. Wilbur, ed., *The Bennett New Deal: Fraud or Portent* (Toronto: Copp Clark, 1968).

For the Canadian experience of the Spanish Civil War, see Michael Petrou, *Renegades: Canadians in the Spanish Civil War* (Vancouver: UBC Press, 2008); and Patricia Rae, "Between the White and Red: Remembering Canadians in the Spanish Civil War," *Queen's Quarterly*, 115(3) (2008): 389–400.

How Canada dealt with jobless or "radical" immigrants is discussed in Barbara Roberts, *Whence They Came: Deportation from Canada, 1900–1935* (Ottawa: University of Ottawa Press, 1988). See Patryk Polec, *Hurrah Revolutionaries: The Polish Canadian Communist Movement, 1918–1948* (Montreal: McGill-Queen's University Press, 2015) for a specific case study of radicalized immigrants. James Struthers has studied the relief question in *No Fault of Their Own: Unemployment and the Canadian Welfare State, 1914–1941* (Toronto: University of Toronto Press, 1983), and, for Ontario, his *The Limits of Affluence: Welfare in Ontario, 1920–1970* (Toronto: University of Toronto Press, 1994). See as well Raymond B. Blake and Jeff Keshen, eds., *Social Welfare Policy in Canada: Historical Readings* (Toronto: Copp Clark, 1995); Cynthia R. Comacchio, *"Nations Are Built of Babies": Saving Ontario's Mothers and Children, 1900–1940* (Montreal/Kingston: McGill-Queen's University Press, 1993); Lara Campbell, *Respectable Citizens: Gender, Family, and Unemployment in Ontario's Great Depression* (Toronto: University of Toronto Press, 2009); and Raymond Blake, *From Rights to Needs: A History of Family Allowances in Canada, 1929–1992* (Vancouver: UBC Press, 2008).

On the Depression in the Prairies, see Bill Waiser, *All Hell Can't Stop Us: The On-to-Ottawa Trek and the Regina Riot* (Calgary: Fifth House, 2003). On the relief camps, see Laurel Sefton MacDowell, "Relief Camp Workers in Ontario during the Great Depression of the 1930s," *Canadian Historical Review*, 76(2) (June 1995): 205–28. Greg Marchildon has a series of articles dealing with governmental responses to both the Dust Bowl and crop failures of the 1930s. See Gregory P. Marchildon, "The Prairie Farm Rehabilitation Administration: Climate Crisis and Federal–Provincial Relations during the Great Depression," *Canadian Historical Review*, 90(2): 275–301; Gregory P. Marchildon, J. Pittman, and D.J. Sauchyn, "The Dry Belt and Changing Aridity in the Palliser Triangle, 1895–2000," *Prairie Forum*, 34(1): 31–44; and Gregory P. Marchildon, "Institutional Adaptation to Drought and the Special Areas of Alberta, 1909–1939," *Prairie Forum*, 32(2): 251–271. For additional work on environmental history in the Prairie West, see Christopher Armstrong et al., *The River Returns: An Environmental History of the Bow* (Montreal/Kingston: McGill-Queen's University Press, 2009). On politics in the West, see Robert Wardhaugh, *Mackenzie King and the Prairie West* (Toronto: University of Toronto Press, 2000).

Much material on Canada's socialists is available. Walter Young, *The Anatomy of a Party: The National CCF* (Toronto: University of Toronto Press, 1969), is a good analysis. See also Michiel Horn, *The League for Social Reconstruction: Intellectual Origins of the Democratic Left in Canada, 1931–42* (Toronto: University of Toronto Press, 1980). Biographical works on J.S. Woodsworth include Grace McInnis, *J.S. Woodsworth* (Toronto: Macmillan, 1953); and Kenneth McNaught, *A Prophet in Politics* (Toronto: University of Toronto Press, 1959). More recently, see James Naylor, *The Fate of Labour Socialism: The Co-Operative Commonwealth Federation and the Dream of a Working-Class Future* (Toronto: University of Toronto Press, 2016). Three studies in intellectual history are David Laycock, *Populism and Democratic Thought in the Canadian Prairies, 1919–1945* (Toronto: University of Toronto Press, 1990); Allen Mills, *Fool for Christ: The Political Thought of J.S. Woodsworth* (Toronto: University of Toronto Press, 1991); and R. Douglas Francis, *Frank H. Underhill: Intellectual Provocateur* (Toronto: University of Toronto Press, 1986).

On Social Credit, see David R. Elliott and Iris Miller, *Bible Bill: A Biography of William Aberhart* (Edmonton: Reidmore Books, 1987); and Alvin Finkel, *The Social Credit Phenomenon in Alberta* (Toronto: University of Toronto Press, 1989). Two recent studies have examined anti-Semitism in Social Credit: Bob Hesketh, *Major Douglas and Alberta Social Credit* (Toronto: University of Toronto Press, 1997); and Janice Stingel, *Social Discredit: Anti-Semitism, Social Credit, and the Jewish Response* (Montreal/Kingston: McGill-Queen's University Press, 2000). Both C.B. Macpherson's and John Irving's books remain classics on the subject. See C.B. Macpherson, *Democracy in Alberta: Social Credit and the Party System* (Toronto: University of Toronto Press, 1962); and John Irving, *The Social Credit Movement in Alberta* (Toronto: University of Toronto Press, 1959). Bradford Rennie's edition on the premiers of Alberta offers studies of both William Aberhart and Ernest C. Manning: see Bradford J. Rennie, ed., *Alberta Premiers of the Twentieth Century* (Regina: University of Regina, Canadian Plains Research Center, 2004). See also Brian Brennan, *The Good Steward: The Ernest C. Manning Story* (Calgary: Fifth House, 2008).

On the Communist Party, see Norman Penner, *Canadian Communism: The Stalin Years and Beyond* (Toronto: Methuen Publications, 1988). For a reconsideration of leftist history in Canada, see Ian McKay, *Rebels, Reds, Radicals: Rethinking Canada's Left History* (Toronto: Between the Lines, 2005). Extreme right-wing movements are examined in Martin Robin, *Shades of Right: Nativist and Fascist Politics in Canada, 1920 to 1940* (Toronto: University of Toronto Press, 1991). Esther Delisle discusses anti-Semitism in Quebec in *The Traitor and the Jew: Anti-Semitism and Extreme Right-Wing Nationalism in Quebec from 1929 to 1939* (Montreal: R. Davies, 1993).

On Quebec, see Richard Jones's booklet, *Duplessis and the Union Nationale Administration* (Ottawa: Canadian Historical Association, 1983); and the relevant chapters in Paul-André Linteau et al., *Quebec Since 1930* (Toronto: James Lorimer 1991). On the history of the Union nationale Party, consult H.F. Quinn, *The Union Nationale*, rev. ed. (Toronto: University of Toronto Press, 1979). For a look at Quebec Social Credit, see Michael B. Stein, *The Dynamics of Right-Wing Protest: A Political Analysis of Social Credit in Quebec* (Toronto: University of Toronto Press, 1973).

For Ontario, see John T. Saywell, *"Just Call Me Mitch": The Life of Mitchell F. Hepburn* (Toronto: University of Toronto Press, 1992). On Duff Pattullo in British Columbia, consult Robin Fisher, *Duff Pattullo of British Columbia* (Toronto: University of Toronto Press, 1991). For studies of Depression-era politics in Saskatchewan and Manitoba, see Gordon L. Barhart, ed., *Saskatchewan Premiers of the Twentieth Century* (Regina: Canadian Plains Research Centre, 2004); and Barry Ferguson and Robert Wardhaugh, eds., *Manitoba Premiers of the Nineteenth and Twentieth Centuries* (Regina: Canadian Plains Research Centre, 2010).

On the social impact of relief, consult Dennis Guest, *The Emergence of Social Security in Canada* (Vancouver: University of British Columbia Press, 1980). For a personal memoir, see James Gray, *The Winter Years* (Toronto: Macmillan, 1966). Irving Abella and Harold Troper, *None Is Too Many: Canada and the Jews of Europe, 1933–1948*, 3rd ed. (Toronto: Lester, 1991), is a poignant account of Canada's treatment of Jewish refugees. On the growth of suburbia in Canada, see Richard Harris, *Creeping Conformity: How Canada Became Suburban, 1900–1960* (Toronto: University of Toronto Press, 2004).

Labour in the interwar years is discussed in Bryan D. Palmer, *Working-Class Experience: Rethinking the History of Canadian Labour, 1800–1991* (Toronto: McClelland & Stewart, 1992). On the 1930s, see Evelyn Dumas, *The Bitter Thirties in Quebec* (Montreal: Black Rose Books, 1975), and Stephen L. Endicott, *Raising the Workers' Flag: The Workers' Unity League of Canada, 1930–1936* (Toronto: University of Toronto Press, 2012).

On women in the 1930s, see Katrina Srigley, *Breadwinning Daughters: Young Working Women in a Depression-Era City, 1929–1939* (Toronto: University of Toronto Press, 2009); and the relevant chapters in Alison Prentice et al., *Canadian Women: A History*, 2nd ed. (Toronto: Harcourt Brace, 1996); as well as Veronica Strong-Boag, *The New Day Recalled: Lives of Girls and Women in English Canada, 1919–1939*, rev. ed. (Toronto: Copp Clark Pitman, 1993). The equivalent study for Quebec women is Andrée Lévesque, *Making and Breaking the Rules: Women in Quebec, 1919–1939* (Toronto: McClelland & Stewart, 1994). Consult, as well, articles in Linda Kealey and Joan Sangster, eds., *Beyond the Vote: Canadian Women and Politics* (Toronto: University of Toronto Press, 1989). On gender and the welfare state, see Nancy

Christie, *Engendering the State: Family, Work, and Welfare in Canada* (Toronto: University of Toronto Press, 2000); and Margaret Jane Hillyard Little, *"No Car, No Radio, No Liquor Permit": The Moral Regulation of Single Mothers in Ontario, 1920–1977* (Toronto: University of Toronto Press, 1998).

Birth control is the subject of Angus McLaren and Arlene Tigar McLaren, *The Bedroom and the State: The Changing Practices and Politics of Contraception and Abortion in Canada, 1890–1980* (Toronto: McClelland & Stewart, 1986); Mary F. Bishop, "Vivian Dowding: Birth Control Activist," in Veronica Strong-Boag and Anita Clair Fellman, eds., *Rethinking Canada: The Promise of Women's History* (Toronto: Copp Clark Pitman, 1986), pp. 200–07; and Diane Dodd, "The Canadian Birth Control Movement on Trial, 1936–37," *Histoire sociale/Social History*, 16 (November 1983): 411–28. On the Dionne quintuplets, see the special issue *Journal of Canadian Studies*, 29(4) (Winter 1995).

For First Nations in western Canada in the 1930s, two works provide good starting points: Hugh A. Dempsey, *The Gentle Persuader: A Biography of James Gladstone, Indian Senator* (Saskatoon: Western Producer Prairie Books, 1986); and Norma Sluman and Jean Goodwill, *John Tootoosis: A Biography of a Cree Leader* (Ottawa: Golden Dog Press, 1982). Laurie Meijer Dress's chapter "The Origins of the IAA," in the *Indian Association of Alberta: A History of Political Action* (Vancouver: UBC Press, 2002), pp. 9–27, provides a good overview of the 1930s in Alberta. For Ontario, see Robin Jarvis Brownlie, *A Fatherly Eye: Indian Agents, Government Power, and Aboriginal Resistance in Ontario, 1918–1939* (Toronto: Oxford University Press, 2003). J.L. Taylor has written *Canadian Indian Policy During the Interwar Years, 1918–1939* (Ottawa: Department of Indian Affairs and Northern Development, 1984). Murray Dobbin's *The One-and-a-Half Men: The Story of Jim Brady and Malcolm Norris, Métis Patriots of the Twentieth Century* (Vancouver: New Star Books, 1981), is a good study of Métis developments in western Canada in the 1930s.

University education in the 1930s is the subject of Paul Axelrod's *Making a Middle Class: Student Life in English Canada during the Thirties* (Montreal/Kingston: McGill-Queen's University Press, 1990).

On religion, see Nancy Christie and Michael Gauvreau, *A Full-Orbed Christianity: The Protestant Churches and Social Welfare in Canada, 1900–1940* (Montreal/Kingston McGill-Queen's University Press, 1996); Nancy Christie and Michael Gauvreau, *Christian Churches and Their Peoples, 1840–1965* (Toronto: University of Toronto Press, 2010); Michael Gauvreau, *The Evangelical Century: College and Creed in English Canada from the Great Revival to the Great Depression* (Montreal/Kingston: McGill-Queen's University Press, 1991); W.E. Mann, *Sect, Cult and Church in Alberta* (Toronto: University of Toronto Press, 1955); Richard Allen, *The Social Passion: Religion and Social Reform in Canada, 1914–1928* (Toronto: University of Toronto Press, 1971); and David B. Marshall, *Secularizing the Faith: Canadian Protestant Clergy and the Crisis of Belief, 1850–1940* (Toronto: University of Toronto Press, 1992).

On cultural nationalism in the 1930s, see Mary Vipond, *The Mass Media in Canada*, rev. ed. (Toronto: James Lorimer, 1992). For painting, see J. Russell Harper, *Painting in Canada: A History*, 2nd ed. (Toronto: University of Toronto Press, 1977); and Dennis Reid, *A Concise History of Canadian Painting*, 2nd ed. (Toronto: Oxford University Press, 1988). On music, see George A. Proctor, *Canadian Music of the Twentieth Century* (Toronto: University of Toronto Press, 1980). On theatre in Quebec, see Elaine F. Nardocchio, *Theatre and Politics in Modern Quebec* (Edmonton: University of Alberta Press, 1986); and Jean Hamelin, *The Theatre in French Canada (1936–66)* (Quebec: Department of Cultural Affairs, 1968). On working-class theatre, see Richard Wright and Robin Endres, eds., *Eight Men Speak and Other Plays from the Canadian Workers' Theatre* (Toronto: New Hogtown Press, 1976). On sport, see the relevant section in Colin D. Howell, *Blood, Sweat, and Cheers: Sport and the Making of Modern Canada* (Toronto: University of Toronto Press, 2001); and for women and sport, M. Ann Hall, *The Girl and the Game: History of Women Sport in Canada* (Peterborough: Broadview Press, 2002).

Chapter Thirteen

CANADA IN WORLD WAR II

TIME LINE	
1931	Japan invades Manchuria
1933	Adolf Hitler becomes chancellor of Germany
1935	Italian dictator Benito Mussolini invades Ethiopia
1936	Spanish Civil War begins
1937	Mackenzie King visits Hitler in Berlin
1938	Munich Crisis occurs
1939	Germany invades Poland World War II begins Canada declares war on Germany
1940	Federal government begins unemployment insurance Canada and United States sign Ogdensburg Agreement Liberals win election under Mackenzie King
1941	Hyde Park Declaration signed Canadian Women's Army Corps established
1942	Plebiscite on conscription held in April Canadian troops participate in Dieppe Raid
1943	Canadian troops join Allied forces in invasion of Italy
1944	Family Allowance Act comes into effect Green Book proposals advanced at conference Canadian troops participate in invasion of Normandy Conscription decreed
1945	Germany surrenders Atomic bombs dropped on Hiroshima and Nagasaki Japan capitulates Canada joins United Nations Strike at Ford Motor plant in Windsor, Ontario Liberals win election under Mackenzie King

The interwar period witnessed significant advances in Canada's role on the world stage. While still very much part of the British Empire, Canada gained increased autonomy in international affairs through the Balfour Declaration and the Statute of Westminster. But the world was becoming a more dangerous place. The rise of totalitarianism threatened world peace, and even though it was difficult to fathom, another world war loomed on the horizon. Only twenty years after the "War to End All Wars," the world again teetered on the edge of the abyss.

Canada's autonomy in international affairs reflected the forces of nationalism at work but they also reflected a growing sense of isolation from Europe. Canada was becoming a North American nation. The United States was rising as the new global power and its neighbour to the north used this growing power as a counterweight to the influence of the British Empire. But Canada was still a British nation. The "eldest daughter of Empire" continued to mature but she was not quite ready to leave home.

When Britain declared war on Germany in September 1939, there was no doubt that Canada would fight alongside the mother country. This second war, however, would be fought and handled very differently from the first. Important lessons had been learned. Yet the same divisions and threats to national unity remained. The debates would be no less stormy. As with World War I, Canada emerged from the crisis with a new sense of itself.

The Canada of 1945 differed significantly from the country that had embarked on war in 1939. The heavy demands of war production catapulted the nation out of economic depression and into rapid growth. The Great War was a disaster for Western economies. Governments were intent on not making the same mistakes in World War II, such as allowing inflation to spiral out of control. Costs had to be controlled and the war had to be paid for by the generation fighting it. Only the state could exercise the necessary controls. As people crowded into the cities in search of jobs, the state continued on the path it had followed since early in the century, and took an increasingly active role in providing social services. Canada moved toward the creation of a modern welfare state.

The war also had profound, although in part temporary, implications for Canadian women. The government needed women to participate in war-related activities, to alleviate labour shortages in the war industries, and to support men in the armed forces. It remained a question as to whether these gains would again be temporary or have more lasting implications for gender relations. The war also produced the same ethnic cleavages. Internment camps were again set up, this time to house German, Italian, and Japanese Canadians. Once again, the rest of Canada accused Quebec of not doing its share for the war effort.

With the power of the state increasing, the war had enduring effects on Canadian federalism. The pendulum of power swung toward Ottawa, as the central government mobilized the economy and controlled national finances to further the war effort. The federal government was aided in this endeavour by an impressive cadre of university-trained "experts." This "brain trust" known as the "Ottawa Men" built the modern civil service in Canada. To an extent, they wielded more power in shaping the nation than the elected officials. The provinces fought back against the forces of centralization, but as the Depression had made clear, the federal structure of Canada was inadequate. The onset of World War II may have ended the Depression in Canada but it continued to advance centralization. The federal government that emerged in 1945 was the most centralized and powerful the nation had ever witnessed.

World War II did not cause the same havoc to Canada's political system as occurred in the Great War. Canada's Liberal government under Mackenzie King successfully weathered war-related problems, including another conscription crisis. Canadians had no deep affection for their aging prime minister but they seemed to recognize his political astuteness and ability to keep the nation united. The successful handling of the war would be King's crowning achievement.

World War II ended dramatically and symbolically with the dropping of the atomic bombs on Hiroshima and Nagasaki, Japan. Nothing would ever be the same again. The nuclear age had arrived, the world found itself in the grip of a new "Cold War," and Canada emerged with the status of a middle power.

Isolationism in the 1930s

In the 1930s, Canada used its newly won autonomy in foreign affairs to avoid entanglements overseas. Prime Minister Mackenzie King was well aware of the threat to national unity posed by such commitments, not to mention the consequences for his own party. The solution seemed to be to avoid them at all costs. This tactic fit well with King's cautious and noncommittal brand of brokerage politics. But even under the Conservatives and R.B. Bennett, Canada avoided commitments on the international stage. When, for example, Japan invaded Manchuria in 1931, Canada under Bennett refused to endorse sanctions at the League of Nations. Indeed, the Canadian delegate made a speech judged so pro-Japanese that Japan's diplomatic representative in Ottawa thanked the Canadian government. Similarly, after Italian dictator Benito Mussolini invaded the independent African kingdom of Abyssinia (Ethiopia) in October 1935, Canada's two major political leaders, then in the midst of a federal election campaign, agreed in spite of political differences that Canada should not become involved.

Nevertheless, events in 1935 soon forced the Canadian government to respond to this major test of the League's ability to curb aggression. Walter Riddell, Canada's advisory officer at the League's headquarters in Geneva, personally favoured strong economic sanctions against Italy. Before receiving specific orders from Ottawa, he proposed including oil and other strategic materials on the embargo list. On the advice of O.D. Skelton and Ernest Lapointe, King's minister of justice and his Quebec lieutenant, the prime minister repudiated the "Canada proposal." In his own words, he gave Riddell "a good spanking." Britain and France saved Riddell from further embarrassment when, in exchange for peace, they offered Mussolini the territory he had already overrun in East Africa. A few weeks later, King claimed in the House of Commons that Canada had saved Europe from war. The forces of appeasement were well entrenched in Canada.

The Rise of Nazi Germany

Adolf Hitler posed the greatest threat to world peace. Systematically, the Nazi leader, who became chancellor in 1933, set out to re-establish, consolidate, and increase Germany's power. First, he reoccupied the hitherto demilitarized zone of the Rhineland in March 1936, in violation of the Treaty of Versailles and the Locarno agreements. Then, in March 1938, he forced the *Anschluss* (union) upon Austria. Next, he seized the Sudetenland (the western region of Czechoslovakia), a conquest that Britain and France, in their desire to avoid war, accepted at the Munich conference in the fall of 1938. In March 1939, the German leader annexed what remained of Czechoslovakia. Throughout all these acts of aggression, Canada supported Britain and France's policy of appeasement.

Mackenzie King visited Adolf Hitler in June 1937. The Canadian prime minister, convinced of his own divine mission as international peacemaker, described the Führer as a man "who truly loves his fellow-men, and his country, and would make any sacrifice for their good." In March 1938, King still held out hope that Hitler was "a man of deep sincerity and a genuine patriot":

> *I believe the world will yet come to see a very great man. . . . Hitler . . . will rank someday with Joan of Arc among the deliverers of his people, & if he is only careful may yet be the deliverer of Europe.*

Despite being taken with Hitler's charisma and wanting to believe that conflict could be avoided, King told the German dictator that in the event of war, Canada would support Britain.

Reasons for Appeasement

It is easy in hindsight to condemn those who advocated appeasement. It is important to remember, however, that only twenty years earlier the world had endured the horrors of the Great War. To consider repeating that experience was more than most people could fathom. In addition, many supporters of appeasement in Canada saw Hitler and Mussolini as bulwarks against the spread of communism, defenders of order in an era of chaotic revolution. They viewed General Francisco Franco, the fascist leader who won power in Spain in 1939 after a bitter civil war against a democratically elected leftist government, in the same light. The Roman Catholic Church, led by the Vatican, was sympathetic to the fascist's struggle against communism. Rodrigue Cardinal Villeneuve, Archbishop of Quebec, reminded his clergy in May 1937 that "dictatorship is better than revolution." To the embarrassment of the King government, which wanted to avoid involvement in Spain, 1250 Canadian volunteers formed the Mackenzie–Papineau battalion to fight for the Spanish republic against Franco's fascists.

Other explanations exist for Canada's support of appeasement. King and his foremost advisers, like O.D. Skelton, favoured appeasement out of fear that British policies might undermine Canadian autonomy and draw the country into imperial conflicts, as they had in the past. With his sure political instincts, King also knew that another war risked the unity of the nation, his government, and his own party.

Furthermore, isolationist sentiment ran deep in Canada, as it did in the United States, which had never even joined the League of Nations. Frank Underhill put it bluntly when he asserted that "all these European troubles are not worth the bones of a Toronto grenadier." Canadian politicians and civil servants wanted Canada to take a "back seat" in the international "lunatic asylum." Despite the unpopularity of the position, there were those in Canada who were convinced that Hitler and a rearmed Germany had to be confronted sooner or later. The most influential newspaper editor in the nation, J.W. Dafoe, wrote editorial after editorial in the Winnipeg *Free Press* warning Canada of the futility of appeasement.

Similar to 1914, the nation again entered a major military conflict completely unprepared. Under King's leadership, Canada disarmed during the interwar period. In 1938–39, the country's total budget for the armed forces was barely $35 million. The navy had fewer than a dozen fighting ships, and the air force, at best, only 50 modern military aircraft. The professional army had just 4000 troops; the navy, 3000; and the air force, only 1000. Despite the impressive showing in the Great War, twenty years of neglect seriously weakened Canada's defences. The nation could not even defend its own coasts, let alone dispatch fully equipped and trained forces to Europe.

Canada Declares War

On September 1, 1939, German troops invaded Poland. On September 3, Britain and France declared war on Germany. Canada followed a week later, a somewhat belated gesture that symbolically demonstrated the nation's newly acquired sovereignty. A small number of Canadians opposed the war on moral grounds. These included pacifists in the Women's International League for Peace and Freedom and in the CCF. But there was never any real possibility that Canada would remain neutral, as the United States chose to do until the Japanese attacked Pearl Harbor in December 1941. Canada's emotional and political ties with Britain remained strong.

Trainee pilots walk along the tarmac in front of Curis P-36 aircraft stationed at the Little Norway training centre, Toronto Island. The British Commonwealth Air Training Plan was a massive undertaking and a significant part of Canada's wartime commitment in World War II.

Source: National Film Board of Canada/Canada Department of National Defence/Library and Archives Canada/ PA-136047.

A War of "Limited Liability"

The period from September 1939 until the Fall of France in June 1940 became known as the "phoney war" due to the lack of major military operations. This period, however, came as a blessing to Canada, because it allowed the unprepared nation to rearm while gearing up its economy for wartime production. Prime Minister King intended to fight a war of "limited liability," meaning that Canada's role was to supply the Allies with war materials while avoiding combat operations and ensuing casualties. This strategy was intended to avoid another conscription crisis.

As part of this strategy, Canada negotiated the British Commonwealth Air Training Plan (BCATP) in late 1939. The plan involved using Canada as a training ground for pilots from across the Commonwealth. By the end of the war, the BCATP had trained 130,000 aviators, nearly half the Commonwealth's air crews. The plan also gave a tremendous boost to the aeronautics industry and, as a result of the more than $2 billion spent, to the Canadian economy in general. On a local level, many communities hosted the handsome young men in uniform from Australia, New Zealand, and Britain. The young women in these communities were asked to entertain the pilots at dances and other events.

Negotiations with Britain to establish the terms of Canada's involvement proved arduous, even rancorous. As historian Desmond Morton observed, "King's attachment to England did not always extend to Englishmen."[1] But the negotiations also demonstrated Canada's increasing sovereignty. Mackenzie King assembled what was likely the strongest cabinet in Canadian history, including the likes of Ernest Lapointe, C.D. Howe, J.L. Isley, Charles Dunning, Jimmy Gardiner, and T.A. Crerar. In addition, Canada's civil service was filled with what had become an impressive mandarin class, the "Ottawa Men," including O.D. Skelton, Norman Robertson, Clifford Clark, and Bob Bryce. These individuals were adamant that Canada would emerge from this war with its economy intact and its place on the world stage secure. The King Liberals won the election of 1940 with 179 seats—to only 36 for the Conservatives now under Robert Manion, 8 for the CCF under J.S. Woodsworth, and 7 for Social Credit under John Blackmore.

The War Effort, 1940–42

The Nazis' unexpected invasion of neutral Denmark, Norway, and the Low Countries in the spring of 1940 transformed the war. The rapid German advance led to the near-capture of the entire British Expeditionary Force at Dunkirk. The darkest day of the war, however, occurred when France fell in June, leaving Britain and its dominions to stand alone against the German and Italian aggressors. Overnight, Canada became Britain's chief ally. Until the German invasion of the Soviet Union in June 1941 and the Japanese attack on the United States naval base at Pearl Harbor that December, it remained so. During these dark months, Britain's surrender seemed likely.

> *["The Fall of France" — "The Allies' Darkest day" — when FR fell in June leaving BRIT alone against GER + ITALY — handwritten marginal notes]*

The Fall of France was a terrible blow for the Allies. Canada was placed in the seemingly unfathomable position of preparing for Britain's fall. Preparations were made to coordinate the defence of North America with the United States. The situation also forced Canada to abandon its strategy of fighting a war of "limited liability." It built up a much larger army, constructed dozens of warships and hundreds of aircraft, and converted the entire economy to war production. In response to Britain's dire wartime financial needs, Canada lent, and then gave, it huge sums of money—more than $3 billion—through mutual-aid agreements, although most of the money was spent in Canada on war materials destined for Britain.

Combat for Canadian troops occurred first in the Pacific theatre. The federal government offered to reinforce British troops in Hong Kong with two infantry battalions and a brigade headquarters (almost 2000 personnel). The largely untrained force arrived in the highly vulnerable British colony in November 1941, a foolish decision in the eyes of most historians: Mackenzie King's "comprehension of strategy and logistics was not very profound and in this essentially military situation his customary political insight deserted him."[2] Although a state of war did not yet exist, Japan attacked Hong Kong and captured it on Christmas Day, 1941. More than 550 Canadians perished, either in the attack or afterward in the harsh conditions of Japanese slave labour camps. Later, in the Pacific war, Canada played a relatively minor role. Three RCAF squadrons did see action in Southeast Asia, but plans to increase Canada's air and sea participation in the Pacific theatre in the summer of 1945 were cancelled after the Americans dropped atomic bombs on two Japanese cities.

Canadians in Europe experienced their baptism by fire in August 1942, in the ill-conceived Allied raid on the French coast at Dieppe. By this time, pressure (both at home and from Allied Command) was mounting on the Canadian government to get its troops into action. Canadian soldiers had been training in England for months and they were frustrated as they watched the British ship off to the battlefields while they were left

A convoy near Halifax, 1941. During the war the Royal Canadian Navy played a major role in defending Allied convoys that transported troops and supplies to Britain.

Source: Library and Archives Canada/DND PA-105344.

A HISTORICAL PORTRAIT

Sir Frederick Banting and Pilot Joseph Mackey[1]

Sir Frederick Banting is known as the discoverer, with Charles Best, of insulin, used in the treatment of diabetes. Joseph Mackey was an American pilot, one of several hundred pilots and crew who worked for Ferry Command, an enterprise set up by the British in Montreal and responsible for flying more than 9000 planes across the Atlantic for delivery in Great Britain.

The first flights began in February 1941. Banting, wanting to go to England, sought space on an aircraft as a passenger. He was assigned to the Lockheed Hudson piloted by Mackey. After bad weather finally cleared, Mackey took off from Gander airport in Newfoundland. Shortly after takeoff, the left engine of Mackey's plane failed. The pilot turned back. Then the right engine lost power and the plane crashed near Musgrave Harbour, Newfoundland. Mackey was injured, but not seriously. The other two crew members were killed. Banting suffered a concussion and internal bleeding. He died a few hours later despite Mackey's efforts to save his life. Three days later, Mackey was finally spotted by a plane and rescued. He later sold his story to a Toronto newspaper and then donated the proceeds to the family of his deceased radio officer.

More than 500 airmen lost their lives while working for Ferry Command, often in crashes of large Liberator bombers used to bring the crews home. About 50 passengers were killed, as well. Banting was the first.

1   Carl A. Christie, *Ocean Bridge: The History of RAF Ferry Command* (Toronto: University of Toronto Press, 1995), pp. 62–72.

in the wet, damp conditions of camp. But pressure was also coming from Allied Command to get the Canadians into battle. Russia entered the war when Germany broke their non-aggression pact in 1941. Joseph Stalin was pushing for the opening of a western front to take pressure off the eastern front. British and American commanders wanted the German defences of occupied France tested to prepare for an eventual invasion. Recent research indicates that there was also an ulterior motive for the bold attack: British commandoes were sent on a top secret "pinch" mission to capture one of the new German four-rotor Enigma code machines. Success could help the Allies decode the Germans' communications.

The Dieppe Raid was a military disaster. The Germans learned of the assault and rained hell on the Canadian and British troops as they landed on the beaches. In a few terrible hours, more than 60 percent of the 5000 Canadian participants were killed or captured. The Germans used their documentary film of the slaughter of Canadians on the beach to boost the morale of their own soldiers. In the aftermath, Allied leaders justified the failed assault as providing essential information on German defences.

For long months after the tragedy at Dieppe, Canadian troops continued garrison duty in Britain. They were not completely inactive: indeed, thousands of marriages between Canadian servicemen and British women took place. One Montreal journalist commented that the Canadian army was "the first formation in the history of war" in which the birth rate exceeded the death rate. Many of these "war brides" would immigrate to Canada when the war was over.

Canadian–American Relations

Canadian–American relations had steadily improved after the end of the Great War. World War II inevitably drew Canada even closer to the United States. The improving relationship was symbolically highlighted in August 1938, when President F.D. Roosevelt came to Kingston, Ontario, where he pledged that the United States would not stand "idly by" if domination of Canadian soil was threatened by any other empire. This statement pleased Prime Minister King, who considered himself good friends with the president. It demonstrated, however, that Canada was very much within the American orbit of influence.

The Ogdensburg Agreement

When France fell and the Battle of Britain commenced, Canada and the United States prepared to stand together against an eventual German invasion. As early as 1938, the two countries began exchanging military information. In the summer of 1940, King pushed for talks on common defence planning. In August, King and Roosevelt signed the Ogdensburg Agreement, which created the Permanent Joint Board on Defence (PJBD), responsible for discussing military questions of mutual interest. When Roosevelt proposed the PJBD, King agreed, although he had doubts about making the board permanent.

Historian Donald Creighton claimed that by signing the Ogdensburg Agreement, Canada fell increasingly under American control. King "behaved like a puppet which could be animated only by the President of the United States."[3]

In contrast, J.L. Granatstein and Norman Hillmer have argued that King "wanted to protect Canada and to help Great Britain as much as possible, and he understood and accepted that this obliged him to seek even closer relations with Roosevelt's America."[4] Other historians assert that rather than being manipulated by the charming Roosevelt, King used his friendship to protect Canadian interests at a very dark time in the war.[5]

There is no doubt, however, that Mackenzie King enjoyed his relatively close relationship with Roosevelt. The Canadian prime minister felt that he could use quiet diplomacy with his American friend and that the relationship could bring dividends by smoothing negotiations. King also enjoyed what he considered his "lynchpin" role that he played between Britain and the United States. British Prime Minister Winston Churchill wanted pressure exerted on the United States to enter the war. King became the source of this pressure. For example, King won important modifications to the American Neutrality Act, enabling Canada and Britain to purchase military supplies while the United States remained neutral. King knew the limits of his influence, however, and also the limits of an American president's powers in the face of a Congress jealous of its prerogatives.

The Hyde Park Declaration

King and Roosevelt signed a second agreement, the Hyde Park Declaration, at Roosevelt's Hudson River estate on a "grand Sunday" in April 1941. It proved an even more important milestone in Canadian–American relations than the Ogdensburg Agreement.

Canada's wartime economic relations with both Britain and the United States led to the Hyde Park Declaration. Since 1939, Britain had ordered ever-increasing amounts of war supplies from Canada and the United States, but it lacked the dollars to pay for them. Meanwhile Canada accumulated huge deficits in its American trade, largely because of its enormous defence purchases in the United States for equipment destined for Britain. When in 1941 the United States passed the Lend-Lease Act, which exempted Britain from making cash payments on its orders for war materials, Canada worried that it would now lose British business. Britain, for its part, used the threat of shifting orders to the United States to pressure Canada into better terms.

King successfully negotiated a satisfactory agreement. The United States promised to increase its defence purchases in Canada substantially, enabling Canada to make its own purchases of war equipment in the United States. Britain could continue buying Canadian goods and Canada could even get relief, through Lend-Lease, for its American purchases of war supplies to be sent via Canada to Britain. The agreement ended Canada's dollar shortage in 1942.

The Ogdensburg and Hyde Park agreements effectively coordinated continental military and economic relations during wartime. After Hyde Park, however, Canada's influence with the United States diminished. The American entry into the war in December 1941 following the Japanese attack on Pearl Harbor substantially changed American perspectives. Relinquishing its isolationism, the United States became more concerned with global rather than hemispheric issues. Canada lost its special status and became a junior partner in the Anglo–American–Russian alliance to defeat the Axis powers.

Reflecting on his wartime service at the Canadian embassy in Washington, external-affairs officer Lester B. Pearson put it bluntly: "We were not consulted about plans and decisions at high levels unless our agreement was essential, and this was seldom." At the outset of the war, Pearson worried that Canada might be squeezed *between* the United States and Britain. As time went on, he became convinced that the main problem Canada faced was simply being squeezed *out*. Even at the two Allied wartime conferences held in Quebec City that brought together the British and the American war leaders, Winston Churchill and Franklin D. Roosevelt, Canada acted merely as host. King's presence was largely confined to the official photos.

The Wartime Economy

The worst years of the Great Depression were over by 1939, but it was the onset of war that finally ended the economic crisis. On the eve of war, more than half a million Canadians—one out of five members of the workforce—lacked jobs. Barely a year later, full employment was a reality. Canada produced 4000 airplanes a year, as well as ships, tanks, and huge quantities of shells and guns. Investment in industry doubled between 1939 and 1943. War materials had priority over civilian goods, whose production was severely curtailed.

Just as during World War I, the burgeoning economy generated inflationary pressures. But the lessons of the Great War loomed large and the federal government was intent on avoiding a repeat performance. By 1940 Ottawa was already planning for postwar reconstruction. It was assumed that the war would be followed by a recession as had happened in 1918. The wartime budgets therefore imposed exceedingly heavy taxes. As the deputy minister of finance noted, the argument for high taxes was "based on the fundamental fact that the *real* costs of war must be borne by the generation which fights it.… We, and not the post-war generation … must make those sacrifices today."

In the spring of 1941, prices increased at an annual rate of more than 12 percent. In response, Ottawa implemented drastic wage and price controls. The government also resorted to so-called voluntary measures. It exhorted homemakers to put their savings into Victory Bonds, and merchants to offer customers their change in war savings stamps. The government used the revenue from the bonds and stamps to purchase arms and build bombs. And that—as one patriotic poster proclaimed—was how homemaker "Mrs. Morin bombarded Berlin." Women also established branches of the Consumers Service that, among other activities, denounced merchants who violated the law. Because of such measures, the cost of living went up very little during the remainder of the war.

Rationing

The Interwar Era was one of consumerism

The scarcity of consumer goods led to rationing. The government issued books of coupons and recruited thousands of female volunteers to distribute them to shoppers. Sugar became the first product to be rationed. Later, tea, coffee, butter, meat, and gasoline were added to the list. Merchants complained about the paperwork required to administer the coupons. As well, a black market in unused coupons flourished, and some farmers sold produce illegally for a good price. Some people hoarded scarce goods, in spite of the threat of fines. Occasionally, shortages provoked an outcry. When brewers could not supply enough of their favourite beverage, Ontario workers threatened to boycott the sale of Victory Bonds. "No beer, no bonds!" was their warning. The interwar era was one of consumerism and this did not cease with the onset of war.

Fitting the guns on a 25-tonne tank at Montreal Locomotive Works, Montreal, around 1942.

Source: Photograph Collection and Library Services Canada/Science and Technology Museum, Image CN 001876.

The lack of automobiles and of the gasoline to make them run, together with full employment, explains the substantial increase in the use of urban public transport. During the war, buses and trams were often overcrowded. Mothers shopping for food had to compete with commuters for space. The media urged shoppers to avoid travelling at peak hours. Women frequently faced sexual harassment as men complained about "feminine intrusion into their cultural privacy and social space," particularly "their" smoking section at the rear of the bus.[6] Gender relations were changing as a result of the war.

Members of the business community improved their public image, tarnished during the Depression years, by helping the federal government organize the country's war production. Hundreds of them trooped off to Ottawa to work, often for a symbolic annual salary of one dollar. Many worked for the powerful C.D. Howe, minister of munitions and supply, the department in charge of all war procurement. Howe set up numerous Crown corporations and adopted the techniques of private enterprise. He also avoided the accusations of graft and profiteering that plagued Robert Borden's government during World War I. Business leaders admired Howe's efficiency.

Women and the War Effort

According to the breadwinner model, married women belonged in the home. Men worked and played in the public realm, while the private realm was the domain of women. This breadwinner model was supported by the increasingly powerful state through new social programs. War needs, however, altered women's roles. At war's end, pressure for women to return to their domestic occupations intensified. But it would not be a case of "one step forward, two steps back" as in the Great War. The progress made by women laid the foundation for the revolution in gender relations to come in the 1960s and 1970s.

Many women, particularly younger, unmarried women, worked outside the home long before the war, generally in low-paying occupations such as teaching, office work, retail sales, factory labour in textile and clothing mills, and as domestics. Now, in response to the general labour shortage created by the war, many more women entered the civilian workforce, mainly in war-related industries. Through the National Selective Service, set up to coordinate the mobilization of Canada's labour power, the federal government encouraged female recruitment. Department of Labour advertisements urged women to "roll up [their] sleeves for victory"; the men overseas needed support and women had to "back them up—to bring them back."

Women often did what was traditionally perceived as men's work. When a plywood factory opened in Port Alberni on Vancouver Island in 1942 to supply plywood for ammunition boxes and other uses, 80 percent of the workers hired were women. Many of these affectionately nicknamed "plywood girls" had brothers in the armed forces.

To attract women to factories from small towns and rural areas, industry and government provided incentives. Employers offered women relatively attractive wages, particularly in war industries. Wages for women increased more quickly during the war years, although they still remained substantially lower than those of men. Ottawa temporarily amended the income tax laws to make it possible for husbands to continue to enjoy a full married exemption while their wives earned wages.

At first, the government sought only unmarried women and married women without children, but by 1943 a chronic lack of "manpower" made it essential to recruit mothers, at least for part-time, low-paying service jobs. Child care often caused problems for working women. Most left their children in the care of relatives and friends, but a modest number of government-funded nurseries began operating by 1943, on a temporary basis, in Ontario and Quebec.

Patriotic appeals drew thousands of women into volunteer work. They collected and recycled such items as paper, metal, fat, bones, rags, rubber, and glass. They also collected clothes for

Women war workers return home after shift change, Edmonton, 1943.

Source: Library and Archives Canada/National Film Board of Canada fonds/PA-116122.

free distribution and prepared parcels to be sent overseas. Together with their unpaid labour in the home, women's voluntary efforts constituted, in the words of historian Ruth Roach Pierson, "far and away the largest contribution made by Canadian women to the war effort."[7]

Women in the Armed Services

For the first time, women served in the armed services. By the end of the war, 50,000 women had enrolled, but these "Jill Canucks" were not "pistol-packing Mommas" and they did not hurl grenades.[8] The armed services assigned them positions considered appropriate to their gender and always paid them less than males. They remained subordinate to men of the same rank, and they commanded only other women. A special Canadian Women's Army Corps (CWAC), created in 1941 and incorporated into the Canadian Army (Active) in late winter 1942, supplied female support staff to release men for combat training and other duties. Auxiliary women's units also existed in the air force and the navy. Unilingual French-speaking women were not accepted, because training facilities were available in English only.

Efforts to achieve fairness and equality did not permeate all aspects of life in the services. Male dominance meant a double standard when it came to sexual morality. Literature on vene-real disease, for example, warned servicemen to beware of "diseased, predatory females," but women received no similar advice regarding "loose men." Pregnancy was cause for an immediate discharge on medical grounds.

By the end of the war, 3000 members of CWAC had served overseas. Largely because of how they were deployed, none were killed due to enemy action.

The First Nations and the War

The University of Toronto and Yale University Conference on the North American Indian met in Toronto in early September 1939. To an extent, it symbolized the transition from the old to the new Canada on Aboriginal issues. The conference, organized by University of Toronto's Dr. Tom McIlwraith, the first academic anthropologist employed at a Canadian university and the curator of ethnological collections at the Royal Ontario Museum, was designed "to reveal the conditions today of the white man's Indian wards, and in a scientific, objective and sympathetic spirit, plan with them for their future." Over 70 Canadian and American government officials, missionaries, and academics attended. It was the first conference ever held to discuss First Nations welfare and the first scholarly meeting to include Indigenous delegates.

For nearly two weeks, the conference delegates discussed North American Aboriginal cultures, reserve economics, health, and education. Perhaps the most revealing information about the First Nations in Canada came from federal government officials who pointed out that, beginning in the mid-1930s, the status-Indian population reversed its previous decline and was increasing annually by 1 percent, due to an increase in the birth rate, a decline in the death rate, and advances in medical care, which were finally beginning to reach Aboriginal populations. The conference papers presented assimilation as still both inevitable and desirable. On the last day, delegates passed resolutions urging greater attention to "the psychological, social, and economic maladjustments of the Indian populations of the United States and Canada."

Then a dramatic event occurred. The Aboriginal delegates broke from the main group and met separately to pass their own resolutions. They objected to government officials, missionaries, and non-Aboriginal sympathizers speaking for them:

> We hereby go on record as hoping that the need for an All Indian Conference on Indian
> Welfare will be felt by Indian tribes, the delegates to such a conference be limited to bona

> *fide Indian leaders actually living among the Indian people of the reservations, and reserves,*
> *and further, that such a conference remain free of political, anthropological, missionary,*
> *administrative, or other domination.*

Unfortunately, their appeal went largely unheard by a Canadian public totally preoccupied by the entry of Canada into World War II. But in retrospect, the conference was a symbolic turning point.

According to the records of the Indian Affairs Branch, over 3000 status Indians enlisted in World War II. Most joined the army. Indeed, until 1943, navy regulations required that enlistees be "British born subjects, of a white race." Some 200 First Nations soldiers died in service. These figures do not include the Métis, Inuit, or non-status Indians. Military service files provided no information on ethnicity, except in the case of Aboriginal people covered by the Indian Act.

As in the Great War, Canadian society offered no gratitude for the service of the First Nations. Indeed, during the war the status-Indian population experienced increased oppression. In violation of the treaties, the federal government initially tried to include status Indians among those eligible for overseas military conscription. Other arbitrary wartime measures included the seizure of reserve lands, the moving of reserve populations, and the revision of band membership lists. When, for example, the federal government decided in 1942 that it needed a military training facility on Lake Huron, it invoked the War Measures Act to appropriate Ontario's Stoney Point Reserve to establish Camp Ipperwash. The Stoney Point people had to live in the territory of their Kettle Point neighbours.

Financial exigency during the war also contributed to First Nations resentment. To save money and promote self-sufficiency, the Indian Affairs Branch unilaterally proposed a centralization plan designed to remove status Mi'kmaq in Nova Scotia from nineteen small reserves to two large inland ones—one at Eskasoni, 50 kilometres southwest of Sydney, and the other at

The delegates to the Yale–Toronto Conference on the North American Indian, September 1939. This was the first conference held in Canada to discuss Aboriginal peoples' welfare and the first scholarly conference to include First Nations delegates. The photo was taken on the lawn at the back of the Royal Ontario Museum.

Source: Pringle and Booth/Courtesy of Ken Kidd, a delegate at the conference.

Shubenacadie, 65 kilometres northwest of Halifax. The abandoned reserves were to be sold. Only mounting First Nations' opposition led to the cancellation of the proposal.

In northern Alberta, Malcolm McCrimmon, an Indian Affairs Branch official, created havoc in 1942 when he revised the membership lists in the Lesser Slave Lake agency to trim 700 individuals who he claimed were not "true Indians." He argued that anyone added to the membership list after 1912 needed to prove that his or her father was a "full blood Indian." His action revitalized the already existing First Nations political organization the Indian Association of Alberta, which had been founded in 1939. These actions undermined the Branch's credibility among the First Nations, as did the fact that its 65 members included only 2 First Nations persons in 1944. Moreover, few of the non-Native Branch officials had any previous experience in Aboriginal affairs.

In general, the war years demoralized the First Nations. Their people served in significant numbers in the war, but they were denied benefits given to the other veterans. Furthermore they continued to be legal "wards of the state," without the right to vote. First Nations communities had no control over their reserve land or money from the sale of their land. Still, the war years contributed to a greater political consciousness.

Private Huron Eldon Brant, member of the Tyendinaga Mohawk community, receiving the Military Medal for bravery at Grammichele, Italy, 1943, from General Bernard Montgomery. One year later he was shot and killed during an attack near Rimini.

Source: Captain Frank Royal/Library and Archives Canada/ PA-130065.

Culture and the State

The interwar period was an era of cultural development and autonomy for Canada. The nation emerging from the Great War was imbued with a sense of self. This cultural nationalism was evident in the development of Canadian sport and the arts, and was expressed through the work of writers and painters. World War II continued this movement. Increasingly, the state came to play a significant role in fostering and developing Canadian culture. The National Gallery of Canada sent thousands of reproductions of artists' works to Canadian military establishments in the hope that soldiers' morale would be boosted when they contemplated familiar scenes. Artists and writers also organized associations to work for a postwar "cultural reconstruction" in which the state recognized the importance of assisting the arts community. In 1945, however, neither Ottawa nor the provinces were ready to include culture in their postwar plans. That would soon change.

The War and National Unity

As with World War I, the state moved quickly to control propaganda under the War Measures Act. This time, however, the newspapers were not censured to the same extent but were instead expected to cooperate voluntarily with the war effort and the government's policies. The National Film Board (NFB), founded in 1939, produced "progressive film propaganda" designed to enhance Canadians' faith in their country. In the same year, Ottawa set up the Bureau of Public Information to promote patriotism and "Canadianism" among all ethnic groups in English Canada.

The need to emphasize Canadian participation was brought home when American newsreels playing in Canadian theatres portrayed the Dieppe Raid, in which so many Canadians lost their lives, as primarily an American action. The bureau published hundreds of pamphlets, arranged for news stories, magazine articles, and radio broadcasts, and subsidized "loyal" segments of the foreign-language press.

Wartime Treatment of Ethnic Groups

World War I was marked by nativist sentiments that translated into the persecution of certain ethnic groups in Canada. World War II repeated the injustices. The federal government established the Nationalities Branch of the Department of National War Services, apparently to combat anti-immigrant attitudes during the war, but with its staff of two, the branch was scarcely an adequate response to a very real problem. As the Wartime Information Board reported in 1943, "It is obvious that prejudice against 'foreigners' in general and Jews in particular has grown."

While focusing on keeping the country united, the King government meted out harsh treatment to members of ethnic groups whose homelands were at war with Canada, on the justification that they constituted a danger to the state. Under the War Measures Act, the federal government interned hundreds of German Canadians, although the RCMP found no evidence of domestic subversion. Upon Italy's entry into the war, the RCMP began a "mop-up of Italians," as the *Montreal Star* described the operation. It fingerprinted and photographed thousands of Italian Canadians, and arrested some 700, including tailors, miners, shopkeepers, a United Church minister, and almost all doctors. Businessman James Franceschini was one of those interned at Camp Petawawa. He saw his businesses placed in the hands of the Custodian of Alien Property and the equipment sold off at fire-sale prices to his Montreal competitors. Franceschini's lawyer claimed that these business rivals even intervened to hinder his client's release. A few members of the clergy and university professors questioned the arrests. Most Canadians appeared, by their silence, to acquiesce. Indeed, in Cape Breton, coal miners laid down their tools to force their employer to ban Italians from the mines.

More than any other group, Japanese Canadians bore the brunt of Canadians' animosity. British Columbia, in particular, had witnessed a long history of racism against Asians, including the Chinese, Japanese, and East Indians. The war, and the threat to Pacific security posed by the Japanese Empire, provided justification for the harsh treatment of the Japanese community, including people who had lived in Canada for generations. As a visible minority, the Japanese were particularly vulnerable to discrimination.

After the Japanese surprise attack on Pearl Harbor in December 1941, which brought fears of an invasion of the Pacific coast, the federal government evacuated the more than 20,000 Japanese Canadians living in coastal British Columbia. Ottawa was far away from this perceived threat, so the government relied heavily on the advice of British Columbia politicians. Evacuees were first housed in the exhibition buildings in Hastings Park, Vancouver, where wooden bunks were installed in horse stalls in the livestock barns. Later, most were transported to camps in the interior of the province, but several hundred males deemed "dangerous" were placed under armed guard at a camp in the Lake Superior bush country. Those interned saw their property confiscated and auctioned off. Families wishing to stay together had to agree to go to sugar-beet farms in Alberta and Manitoba, where they had to perform the backbreaking labour of sugar-beet topping. After the war, Ottawa resettled the Japanese Canadians across Canada and even attempted to deport thousands—many of whom were Canadian citizens—to Japan. Although the federal government abandoned these plans in 1947, hundreds of Japanese Canadians, embittered by life in Canada, chose to return to Japan.

Most historians view wartime government policy toward the Japanese in Canada as the result of long-standing racial hostility toward this group. According to Peter Ward, "the threat of Japanese

Japanese Canadians being "relocated" to camps in the interior of British Columbia. More than 20,000 Japanese and Japanese Canadians were moved, and their property confiscated and auctioned off, after the Japanese attack on Pearl Harbor in December 1941 and throughout the duration of the war.

Source: Tak Toyota/Library and Archives Canada/C-46350.

subversion was created by the union of traditional racial attitudes and perceptions shaped by the fears and anxieties conjured up by war."[9] A hostile public easily convinced federal politicians to act. Historians Patricia Roy and others, however, have argued that Ottawa carried out the evacuation of the Japanese "as much for their own protection, and, by implication, the protection of Canadians in Japanese hands."[10] Forty years later, the federal government apologized to Japanese Canadians for their wartime treatment and offered financial compensation.

French Canada and the War

The Mackenzie King government was focused on preserving national unity and this entailed dealing with Quebec. Memories of the 1917 election and conscription crisis haunted the prime minister. He had remained loyal to Laurier during the crisis and his government relied heavily on Quebec support, mainly through the powerful personage of his Quebec lieutenant, Ernest Lapointe. This war, however, was different from the first: the enemy was much more recognizable and easier to demonize. Not just an imperial war, it was a struggle against a very real evil. Although French Canadians generally accepted participation, as in World War I, they remained adamantly opposed to compulsory military service for overseas operations.

Prime Minister King and his Quebec cabinet ministers closely monitored the province and its response to the war. During the 1930s, many French-Canadian intellectuals showed sympathy for Franco and Mussolini, because the fascist leaders portrayed themselves as stalwart opponents

[handwritten margin note: French Canadians remained adamantly opposed to compulsory military service for overseas operations]

[handwritten note: (Italy)]

of communism. The Catholic Church was virulently anti-communist. Any support for fascism, however, diminished when the war started.

The King government was concerned with how the provincial government of Maurice Duplessis would cooperate with Ottawa in coordinating a united war effort. The powerful premier was already resisting King's attempts to examine and likely reframe the federal system through the Royal Commission on Dominon–Provincial Relations. Duplessis found an unlikely ally in the premier of Ontario, Mitchell Hepburn. Both premiers were well aware that during wartime, the powers of the federal government would be increased. The cause of provincial autonomy in Quebec was intertwined with French-Canadian nationalism.

Two weeks after the declaration of war in September 1939, Duplessis called a provincial election in Quebec. King realized that a Duplessis government during wartime would be a constant thorn in his side. The prime minister met with the Quebec members of his cabinet and formulated a strategy to intervene in the provincial election and defeat Duplessis' Union nationale. Breaking normal protocol, the Quebec ministers entered the campaign, warning Quebeckers that a Union nationale victory would translate into a want of confidence in themselves as federal ministers representing the province. It would cause them to withdraw from cabinet, leaving the province unrepresented at a time when the issue of conscription would inevitably arise. The federal Liberals took direct charge of the provincial Liberal campaign, including organization and finances. The federal intervention and manipulation succeeded. The Union nationale was defeated by the Liberals under Adelard Godbout. The Godbout government served as a puppet of the King Liberals throughout most of the war, until Duplessis was returned to office in 1944.

Quebec's support for the war effort hinged on the conscription issue. Realizing the importance of national unity at such a tenuous time, both the Liberals and the Conservatives promised that military enlistment would be voluntary. There would be no conscription.

The Plebiscite of 1942

In the first few years of the war, it appeared that the conscription bogeyman would indeed be avoided. The "phoney war" and the war of "limited liability" produced few casualties for Canada. As the war dragged on, however, and military leaders demanded reinforcements, the calls for conscription became louder. As in World War I, English Canadians claimed that Quebec was not doing its fair share. For one Toronto Conservative member of Parliament, conscription was the only way to get the "disloyal bloody French" to fight.

Mackenzie King was ardent in his opposition to conscription. Politically, the Liberals had come to rely heavily on its Quebec base for support. But they could not lose the other regions of Canada in the meantime. The prime minister moved cautiously. In mid-1940, his government decreed national registration, which provided that men be called up for compulsory military training but for home service only. When voluntary recruitment for overseas service lagged in 1941, Ottawa decided to retain the conscripts, known as "zombies," for the duration of the war, in the hope that volunteers in home defence units would agree to serve overseas. When few signed up, and pressure mounted for King to send more troops, the prime minister decided to hold a plebiscite on conscription in April 1942.

Nationalists in Quebec accused King of breaking his promises. In preparation for the plebiscite, they formed the Ligue pour la défense du Canada to encourage French Canadians to vote "non." But the plebiscite was vintage King. The wily prime minister realized that some action had to be taken to relieve the pressure, yet he could not be seen to be breaking his promises to Quebec. By staging a referendum to seek the people's opinion directly, he would create the appearance of action without being bound by its results. And as with all referendums, the framing of the question was critical. The plebiscite question deliberately

[handwritten margin note: The plebiscite question deliberately avoided mentioning the word "conscription"]

avoided even mentioning the word "conscription." Instead, it asked Canadians: "Are you in favour of releasing the Government from any obligations arising out of any past commitments restricting the methods of raising men for military service?" Whatever the result, the government promised no specific action. A "yes" vote would provide King with the democratic justification of breaking his promises, if necessary, in the future. The results of the vote on April 21, 1942, revealed the deep division between Quebec and the rest of Canada. While 72 percent of Quebeckers answered "no," 80 percent of the electorate of the other provinces responded "yes."

Still, Mackenzie King delayed. When asked if the time had come to implement conscription, he replied evasively with a phrase that would become his mantra: "Conscription if necessary, but not necessarily conscription." Remembering the disastrous consequences of the conscription crisis of 1917 for national unity and for the Liberal Party, King hoped that conscription would never be necessary. In order to further alleviate pressure and give the appearance of action on the plebiscite result, the government did go one step closer to conscription in the fall of 1942 when it amended the National Resources Mobilization Act (NRMA) to permit the dispatch of conscripts overseas by order in council. Until late 1944, however, Canada continued to rely on voluntary enlistments.

[handwritten margin note: Mackenzie King feared the same Disastrous consequences of the conscription crisis of 1917 for national unity]

The Right Honourable W.L. Mackenzie King voting in the plebiscite on the introduction of conscription for overseas military service. King was haunted by the spectre of conscription after it split the country during the World War I.

Source: Library and Archives Canada/C-022001.

A Montreal demonstration against conscription.
Source: Library and Archives Canada/*The Gazette* (Montreal) fonds/ PA-107910.

Canada Intensifies Its War Effort

One of Canada's most important roles during the war was escorting supply ships from North America to Britain through the Atlantic corridor. The Royal Canadian Navy (RCN) enlisted 100,000 men and 6500 women during the conflict. The job was dangerous. Moreover, living conditions on the escorting corvettes were often terrible, as seawater penetrated continually during bad weather. "The smell just got worse and worse," one sailor remembered. "The ship was a floating pigpen of stink. You couldn't get away from it. The butter tasted of it…. The bread smelled of feet and armpits." In the first years of the war, Allied naval losses were staggering. By spring 1943, German submarines in the North Atlantic had sunk more than 2000 ships, and shipyards were unable to build replacements fast enough. Initially, the Canadian navy had few successes in the anti-submarine war, as a result of inexperience, poor crew training, and deficient technical equipment. But once properly trained and equipped, Canadians played a significant role in the Battle of the Atlantic by sinking, or helping to sink, many German U-boats.

One boat sunk by torpedoes fired from a German submarine was the *City of Benares*, en route from England to Canada in September 1940. Among the 400 passengers and crew aboard were 90 English children whose parents had decided to send them to Canada for safety from German bombardments. Only 13 children survived the sinking, half of them on an overcrowded lifeboat that drifted on the stormy North Atlantic for seven days.

Canadian troops were late getting into the action on land, but after July 1943 combat was constant. The Allied forces were pushing back the Germans but the process would take time and cost casualties. In the mistaken hope that casualties would be light, King pressured British Prime Minister Churchill to allow Canadian forces to join in the Allied invasion of Sicily.

In British General (later Field-Marshal) Bernard Montgomery's view, the Canadians behaved "magnificently." Nearly 100,000 Canadian troops took part in the lengthy Italian campaign that followed. Some 6000 Canadian soldiers lost their lives, another 20,000 were wounded, and untold numbers became neuropsychiatric casualties. The fierce battle to capture the strategic Italian town of Ortona alone cost the Canadians 700 dead: they fought from doorway to doorway, from courtyard to courtyard, from rooftop to rooftop, sometimes even moving from house to house without going outside, through a technique of breaking through the walls between houses known as "mouse-holing."

Although they faced Germans who were often better armed, the Canadians relentlessly pushed north, breaching the imposing German fortifications of the Gothic Line in September

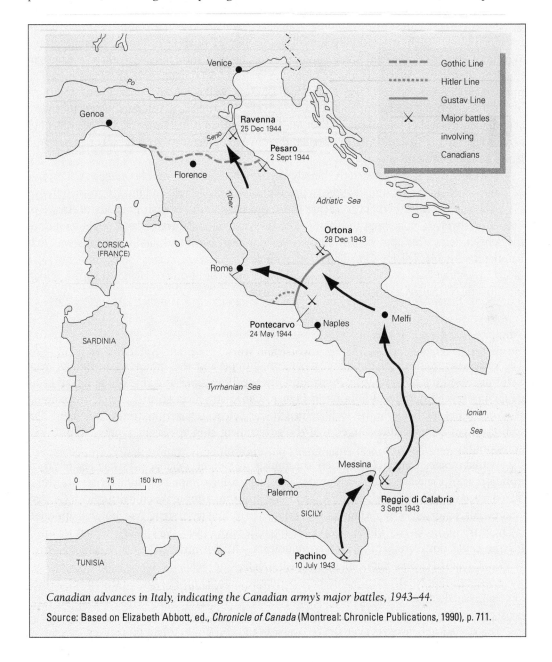

Canadian advances in Italy, indicating the Canadian army's major battles, 1943–44.

Source: Based on Elizabeth Abbott, ed., *Chronicle of Canada* (Montreal: Chronicle Publications, 1990), p. 711.

1944. American journalist Martha Gellhorn noted a special sadness in this bloody combat, which she witnessed: "It is awful to die at the end of summer or in the gentle days of the new autumn when you are young and have fought a long time … and when you know that the war is won anyhow."

After playing the major role in testing the North Atlantic defences at Dieppe, Canadians also played a significant role in the Normandy invasion of June 6, 1944. Assisted by the RCN, Canadian troops took an entire German-held beach. The Canadian division suffered greater casualties than the British formations, but it also advanced farther inland than any other Allied division on D-Day. Initial successes were made possible by far superior Allied airpower and by the failure of the Germans to mount an immediate counterattack.

Over the next few weeks, the Canadian army's progress deeper into France was slowed by several costly failures. In possibly the Canadians' worst reversal, a complete battalion, the Canadian Black Watch, was virtually annihilated on July 25 in an unsuccessful attempt to take Verrières Ridge, south of Caen. Allied bombing errors brought substantial Canadian casualties in the days after the Normandy landings. Moreover, at least 150 Canadian deaths were, in reality, murders by German soldiers of the Hitler Youth Division, well behind the lines. In one notorious incident, a group of Canadian prisoners was marched to the Abbaye d'Ardennes, where they were shot in the garden after interrogation. Kurt Meyer, the German commander held responsible, did serve some time in prison—first in Canada, then in West Germany—but he was released to a hero's welcome in Germany.

The Canadians also organized the bloody sieges of the French towns of Boulogne, Calais, and Le Havre. Then, in the autumn of 1944, in dreadful conditions of cold and mud, Canadian troops played a major role in the fight to secure the approaches to the Belgian port city of Antwerp. One effort involved an attempt to dislodge the Germans on Walcheren Island, at the mouth of the Scheldt delta. This approach by land was over a long, bleak rock-and-earth causeway that became a veritable hell for Canadian attackers raked by intense enemy bombardment. After heavy losses, the Canadians managed to establish a bridgehead on the island; then the British modified their strategy and decided to attack elsewhere.

The Conscription Crisis

The heavy involvement of Canadian troops in Europe and the mounting casualties once again increased the pressure for conscription. By late 1944, after one year of the Italian campaign and several months of fighting in France, Canadian officers overseas were demanding reinforcements, particularly the well-trained home defence conscripts, or NRMA men. The Conservatives, in opposition, urged that the government stop appeasing Quebec and decree conscription.

Within cabinet, Colonel J.L. Ralston, the minister of national defence, who had just returned from a tour of Canadian forces in Europe, also pushed for compulsory military service. King feared a possible cabinet revolt over the issue. The prime minister replaced Ralston with General Andrew McNaughton, who promised to continue the voluntary system. As Churchill appealed for fresh troops in the face of the German counteroffensive in late 1944, McNaughton reported that he could not recruit the necessary volunteers. On November 22, just as several of his English-Canadian cabinet ministers prepared to resign, King yielded. Canada would again introduce conscription; NRMA men would now be sent to Europe. King's Quebec lieutenant, Ernest Lapointe, had died, but several French-Canadian cabinet ministers resigned. As in the Great War, conscription was implemented in Canada near the end of the conflict.

Few Canadian conscripts ever served overseas and conscription had little effect. In spite of the criticism from both supporters and opponents, and perhaps because the criticism came from

Members of the Fusiliers Mont-Royal Regiment in Falaise, France, just after the Normandy invasion. A Canadian Sherman tank offers the tired infantrymen protection in the narrow streets of this Norman town, August 1944.

Source: Library and Archives Canada/PA-115568.

both ends of the spectrum, King was able to portray himself as a moderate. But he was also able to portray himself to Quebec as having done everything possible to avoid conscription. In one of his most emotional speeches, King turned his back on the opposition and spoke directly to his Quebec members:

> *If there is anything to which I have devoted my political life, it is to try to promote unity, harmony, and amity between the diverse elements of this country. My friends can desert me, they can remove their confidence from me, they can withdraw the trust they have placed in my hands, but never shall I deviate from that line of policy.*

To a large extent, Quebec had little option but to stay with the Liberal Party. At the time, there was no French-Canadian nationalist alternative and the province was not going to turn to the pro-conscriptionist Tories. The Liberal Party survived the crisis intact. Mackenzie King emerged at war's end with the nation united.

An Evaluation of Canadian Participation

During the last months of the war, in the late winter and early spring of 1945, Canadian troops

The town of Leeuwarden, during the liberation of the Netherlands by Canadian troops, April 16, 1945.

Source: Donald I. Grant/Library and Archives Canada/PA-131566.

[handwritten margin note:] After King introduced conscription, he was able to portray himself to QC as having done everything possible to avoid conscription

participated in the liberation of the Netherlands and in the final offensive against Germany. By war's end, 250,000 troops had served in the Canadian army in northwestern Europe; more than 11,000 of them died. In addition, from 1942, Canadian aviators conducted thousands of perilous night-bombing missions that destroyed most of Germany's large cities. Canadians eventually made up about a quarter of Bomber Command's crews.

More than 17,000 of the nearly quarter-million Canadians who served in the RCAF lost their lives. All told, more than 1 million Canadians out of a total population of 11.5 million saw military service in Canada and overseas during World War II. Approximately 42,000 were killed, and nearly 55,000 were wounded. Many of these would never recover.

The war caused innumerable personal tragedies, as thousands of Canadians lost a husband, father, son, brother, or fiancé. Sometimes the news came with harsh abruptness. One Canadian woman wrote to her soldier boyfriend in France, and after a few weeks the letter came back stamped "Killed in action." The soldiers' return—at a time before posttraumatic stress disorder was recognized and accepted as legitimate, and in some cases after five years of absence—provoked poignant emotions. Time brought change, and lengthy absences often altered perceptions of relationships. The soldiers had to relearn how to be civilians. The divorce rate increased substantially.

Young Canadians, operating under extremely stressful conditions, fulfilled Canada's part in the strategic bomber offensive against Germany. Bomber aircrew suffered the highest wartime casualty rates of all of the branches in Canadian military service.

Source: © All rights reserved. PL-30121 reproduced with the permission of DND (2016).

WHERE HISTORIANS DISAGREE

Canadian Participation in Northwestern Europe

In the early 1990s, as the media marked the fiftieth anniversary of the events of World War II, Canadian historians showed new interest in the conflict and, in particular, in the role Canadians played in combat in northwestern Europe.

The tragedy at Dieppe in August 1942 has been the subject of several studies and sits at the centre of an emotional debate. Can the raid be justified or was it a military blunder? In *Unauthorized Action: Mountbatten and the Dieppe Raid*, Brian Loring Villa assigned responsibility for having ordered the raid to Lord Louis Mountbatten, British Chief of Combined Operations. Villa stated that Canadian newspaper magnate Lord Beaverbrook minced no words when he encountered Mountbatten later at a dinner party: "You have murdered thousands of my countrymen.... They have been mown down and their blood is on your hands."[1] But Villa also noted that General A.G.L. McNaughton, commander of Canadian forces in Britain, had delivered numerous bellicose statements. When, at last, an opportunity to use Canadian troops presented itself, McNaughton could scarcely decline the offer. Nor, in spite of his typical caution, could Prime Minister King refuse his authorization. He had to take into account the rising criticism of Canadians who wanted to see their country's troops take a more active part in the struggle.

J.L. Granatstein laid the blame on General H.D.G. Crerar, who commanded the 1st Canadian Corps. Crerar, he said, "had come to England convinced that the army had to see action soon, both for its own morale and for domestic Canadian consumption."[2] After Dieppe, Crerar's approach was to rationalize the raid by speaking of lessons learned, an approach that Granatstein said "may even be right." Peter Henshaw also believed that the Canadian commanders were primarily responsible for the Dieppe fiasco: "Their struggle for autonomy, and for a leading Canadian role in raids, interacted with British interservice rivalries in a way that was decisive for the progress of the planned raid."[3]

Denis and Sheilagh Whitaker, the former a captain at Dieppe, blamed British Prime Minister Winston Churchill, who needed to prove to Soviet dictator Joseph Stalin that it was impossible in 1942 to open a second front against the Germans. They argued that Churchill's strategy "was successful, no matter how high the costs." Moreover, the Allies gained essential experience at Dieppe in preparation for D-Day. The lessons learned, they said, "saved countless lives as a result of their far-reaching influence on the success of future operations."[4]

W.A.B. Douglas and Brereton Greenhous agreed. Because of Dieppe, the Allies realized that "objectives must be more realistic, tactics more sophisticated, and training more rigorous. Communications must be more comprehensive, equipment more appropriate, and, most of all, fire support by sea and air must be overwhelming."[5] Timothy Balzer studied how Dieppe was presented to the public. He noted that allied authorities planned in advance to portray any failure as success and to manipulate the press to further this claim. For example, communiqués were to stress the lessons learned before any lessons were learned.[6]

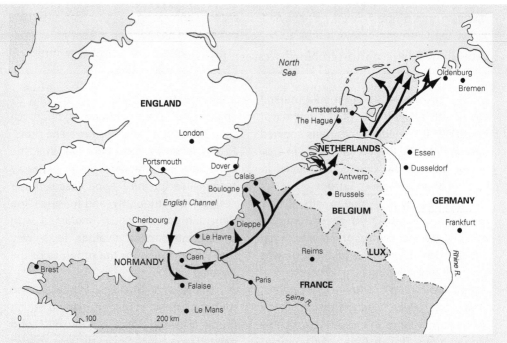

Canadian troop movements in northwestern Europe, 1944–45.

Source: From Fielding / Evans. *Canada: Our Century, Our Story*, 1E. © 2001 Nelson Education Ltd. Reproduced by permission. www.cengage.com/permissions.

An intriguing new twist on the Dieppe Raid has been offered by David O'Keefe who uncovered documents indicating that one of the raid's objectives—perhaps even its main one—was to "pinch" one of the new German four-rotor Enigma code machines being used in the coastal town. O'Keefe argued that the raid was intended to provide cover and act as a distraction for the top-secret mission undertaken by British commandos.[7] The breaking of the code later in the war allowed the Allies access to German communications and served as a significant factor in winning the war.

Canadians participated actively in the invasion of Normandy in June 1944 and in the lengthy campaign in northwestern Europe that followed. Canadian casualties were high. Indeed, in John English's view, "the lives of many soldiers were unnecessarily cast away." Who should be blamed? To English it was "those who left them exposed in open wheatfields to be harvested like so many sheaves. . . . The

responsibility must rest with the high command."[8] English argued that when large-scale training exercises finally began for Canadian soldiers garrisoned in England, senior officers had little idea of how to direct a modern army in field operations. Although many Canadian battalions and armoured regiments were well led and proved successful in battle, at the divisional and brigade levels, command was often given to regular army officers of doubtful professional competence.

Historian Terry Copp refuted this interpretation of Canada's military performance in Normandy. He disagreed that Canadian soldiers were poorly led and poorly trained. While they did suffer heavier casualties than other Allied units, they spent more time in close combat. Their performance was extraordinary, Copp concluded, and they made an important contribution to the defeat of the Germans.[9]

In autumn 1944, Allied troops advanced into Belgium but halted at Antwerp, failing to secure the Scheldt estuary and giving the Germans precious time to set up defences and regroup. It was "one of the war's most costly blunders" and it had a direct bearing on extending the war by many months.[10] Certainly the Canadians paid dearly, sustaining more than 6000 casualties before routing the enemy and clearing the estuary. During these final months of war, Canadians experienced both successes and failures. There was no "ascending learning curve."[11]

In January 1992, *The Valour and the Horror*, a television series on Canada's role in World War II broadcast by the CBC and Radio-Canada, provoked bitter controversy. The three-part series focused on the role of Canadians in the Battle of Hong Kong, the aerial bombardment of German cities by Bomber Command, and the Normandy campaign. The series was particularly critical of Canada's role by highlighting the poor training of its troops, incompetent leadership, the killing of civilians, and even war crimes committed against German prisoners. War veterans and several historians accused the writer–producers, Brian and Terence McKenna, of extreme bias and distortion of history. In particular, they felt that the presentation maligned military commanders. A Senate subcommittee held hearings on the series—a gesture some media attacked as a threat to freedom of expression.

S.F. Wise and David J. Bercuson reviewed the series in the framework of an evaluation done by the CBC ombudsman. Both judged the series to be "bad history." Wise took issue with the filmwriters' contention that Canadian atrocities in Normandy were equivalent to those perpetrated by German troops. He also refuted the film's portrayal of Canadian generalship. Bercuson, while affirming a general belief that "the Canadian Army as a whole did not acquit itself well in the Normandy fighting," decried the "failure" to put events in Normandy into a broader context and maintained that British and American units were not well prepared either. The ombudsman's report concluded that the series had indeed failed to "measure up to the CBC's demanding policies and standards."[12]

Perhaps historian Graeme Decarie's words of caution were wisest: "The truth ... as this committee seems to be seeking it, does not exist. History is bound to have imbalance, incompleteness and error ... because historians are always selective in the information they use."[13]

---

1   Brian Loring Villa, *Unauthorized Action: Mountbatten and the Dieppe Raid*, 2nd ed. (Toronto: Oxford University Press, 1994), p. 18.

2   J.L. Granatstein, *The Generals: The Canadian Army's Senior Commanders in the Second World War* (Toronto: Stoddart, 1993), p. 102.

3   Peter Henshaw, "The Dieppe Raid: A Product of Misplaced Canadian Nationalism?," *Canadian Historical Review*, 77 (1996): 252.

4   Denis and Sheilagh Whitaker, *Dieppe: Tragedy to Triumph* (Toronto: McGraw-Hill Ryerson, 1992), p. 290.

5   W.A.B. Douglas and Brereton Greenhous, *Out of the Shadows: Canada in the Second World War*, rev. ed. (Toronto: Dundurn Press, 1995), p. 128.

6   Timothy Balzer, "'In Case the Raid Is Unsuccessful ...': Selling Dieppe to Canadians," *Canadian Historical Review*, 87 (2006): 409–30.

7   David O'Keefe, *One Day in August: The Untold Story behind Canada's Tragedy at Dieppe*, (Toronto: Alfred A Knopf Canada, 2013).

8 John A. English, *The Canadian Army and the Normandy Campaign: A Study of Failure in High Command* (New York: Praeger, 1991), p. 256.

9 Terry Copp, *Fields of Fire: The Canadians in Normandy* (Toronto: University of Toronto Press, 2003).

10 Denis and Sheilagh Whitaker, *Tug of War: The Canadian Victory That Opened Antwerp* (Toronto: Stoddart, 1987), p. 373.

11 Terry Copp, *Cinderella Army: The Canadians in Northwest Europe 1944–1945* (Toronto: University of Toronto Press, 2006), p. 287.

12 S.F. Wise and David J. Bercuson, *The Valour and the Horror Revisited* (Montreal/Kingston: McGill-Queen's University Press, 1994), pp. 10, 51, 72.

13 Quoted in Graham Carr, "Rules of Engagement: Public History and the Drama of Legitimation," *Canadian Historical Review*, 86 (2005): 338.

Canadian Fatalities in the Two World Wars

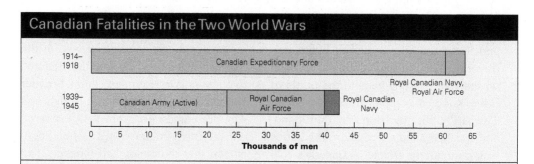

Source: Christopher A. Sharpe, "Military Activity in the Second World War," Plate 47 of Donald Kerr and Deryck W. Holdsworth, eds., *Historical Atlas of Canada*, vol. 3 (Toronto: University of Toronto Press, 1990). Reprinted with permission of the publisher.

Military Fatalities in World War II, Selected Countries

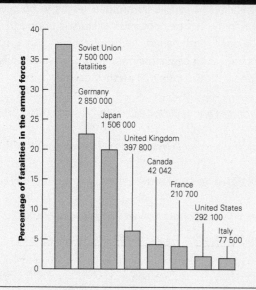

In all, the terrible bloodbath between 1939 and 1945 claimed the lives of nearly 60 million civilians and soldiers.

Source: Christopher A. Sharpe, "Military Activity in the Second World War," Plate 47 of Donald Kerr and Deryck W. Holdsworth, eds., *Historical Atlas of Canada*, vol. 3 (Toronto: University of Toronto Press, 1990). Reprinted with permission of the publisher.

The Expansion of Unions

On the home front, organized labour made significant gains in the war years. The labour surplus of the 1930s became a shortage in the early 1940s. As employment increased, so too did union membership, particularly in the new industrial unions, which combined all workers in a particular industry in a single union. Between 1940 and 1945, union membership doubled to more than 700,000.

Although the war brought jobs and, in general, higher wages, grievances remained. Employers fiercely resisted union attempts to impose collective bargaining and many bitter strikes resulted from unions' efforts to ensure recognition. In one case, 3000 shipyard workers in Halifax ceased work for one month in 1944 when their employer refused the automatic checkoff of union dues, a right gained by unions in Nova Scotia in 1937. Sometimes militant workers rebelled against their own union leadership, which they judged too conciliatory. When Cape Breton miners struck unsuccessfully for five months in 1941 for better wages and working conditions and more control over the work process, their rallying cry was "Down with Hitler and [United Mine Workers officer] Silby Barrett."[11]

The federal government intervened constantly to prevent strikes that might interfere with war production. When workers occupied an aluminum plant in Arvida, Quebec, during a work stoppage in July 1941, Ottawa sent in troops to end the strike. To subvert union demands for wage increases, it applied wage controls that labour denounced as inequitable. The government felt it necessary, for political reasons, "to conciliate business, its wartime ally in developing the war economy."[12] Business representatives sat on government policy boards; labour did not. Compulsory conciliation often involved interminable delays, a situation that favoured employers. The unions believed that employers alone benefited from this imposed cooperation.

Industrial Conflicts

Workers' growing resentment contributed to a wave of industrial conflicts that peaked in 1943. That year, one union member in three went out on strike and 1 million working days were lost. A lengthy and very bitter gold-miners' strike in Kirkland Lake, Ontario, in particular, led the archrivals the Trades and Labor Congress (TLC), an association of skilled craft unions, and the Canadian Congress of Labour (CCL), the leading industrial union, to make joint demands for legislative remedies. Labour's increasing support for the CCF worried Prime Minister King.

The government responded to labour unrest with Order in Council P.C. 1003, which recognized the right of workers in industries under federal jurisdiction to join unions and to bargain collectively. It established certification procedures, set out penalties for unfair labour practices by which employers commonly interfered with workers' attempts to set up unions, and established a labour-relations board to administer the law. After the war the federal government adopted new legislation similar to P.C. 1003, and most provinces passed comparable laws.

A strike at the Ford Motor plant in Windsor, Ontario, in 1945 also highlighted the issue of labour security, among others. The union wanted an agreement specifying that all employees had to belong to the union and that the company had to deduct union dues from wage cheques—"union shop and checkoff" was the workers' demand. Ford adamantly refused, although across the river, in Dearborn, Michigan, the company had acquiesced on these issues in 1941. To ensure a tight picket line, militant strikers set up a massive automobile blockade in the streets around the plant, imprisoning the vehicles of hundreds of commuters. Federal and provincial authorities as well as the CCL itself intervened, without success.

Finally, the two sides agreed to accept binding arbitration. Justice Ivan Rand of the Supreme Court of Canada proposed what became known as the Rand Formula: since all employees benefited from union activities, all should pay union dues, to be collected by the company and remitted to the union. Workers need not join the union, however. Rand also recommended the establishment of a grievance procedure, as well as heavy penalties for unauthorized, or "wildcat," strikes. Although he admitted that a strike was not a "tea party," Rand strongly condemned the workers' motor blockade. He also made a plea for democratic control of unions and for "enlightened leadership at the top."

The late 1940s saw more dramatic confrontations between labour and management, often in provinces whose governments sided openly with employers. Still, unions felt more secure as the war years ended. The relative labour peace of the 1950s resulted, in part, from these wartime gains.

The State's New Role

The war changed Canada in other ways as well. After the Depression, Canadians sought economic security. Although the war eliminated unemployment and restored a degree of prosperity, it exacted heavy financial sacrifices from the public. By 1943, as war fatigue set in and increasing Allied success pointed the way to victory, Canadians reflected on the postwar society they wanted to build. In particular, many wanted governments to introduce measures that would help those in need and establish greater equality within society. The memories of the Great Depression seared a generation determined never to repeat it.

In 1940, with provincial consent and after making a requisite amendment to the British North America Act, the federal government adopted an unemployment-insurance plan whose provisions covered about half the workforce. King supported the project, because he was "anxious to keep Liberalism in control in Canada [and] not let third parties wrest away from us our rightful place in the matter of social reform." Although the Conservatives tried to project a reformist image with a new leader (John Bracken), a new name (the Progressive Conservatives), and proposals for such reforms as a national health scheme, King felt little threat. The left, however, troubled him. By September 1943, chiefly as a result of urban support, the CCF had reached 29 percent in the polls—ahead of each of the two major parties by 1 percentage point.

Social Welfare Measures

A report presented in 1943 by Leonard Marsh, research director for the government's Committee on Reconstruction, urged the creation of a full welfare state. It recommended a comprehensive system of social security, including measures to assist the unemployed, a national health-insurance scheme, old-age pensions, and children's allowances. The federal government, fearful of the costs involved, adopted a cautious and piecemeal approach. In 1944, it introduced a family allowance program that initially provided monthly payments of $6–$8 to help Canadian mothers support their children. King hoped that the measure would diminish the CCF's popularity. Certain Conservatives, such as Ontario premier George Drew, denounced the project as a "baby bonus" designed to benefit Quebec with its high birth rate, while nationalists in Quebec condemned it as an infringement on provincial autonomy. Business reacted favourably; it hoped that the allowances would diminish pressure to raise wages. The government's acceptance of these social welfare measures reflected its desire to avoid a postwar recession and create economic stability. They were primarily designed to aid the middle classes rather than alleviate the suffering of the lower classes.

One of the best examples of this approach was in housing policy. Housing was a serious problem during the Depression, and the federal government intervened with a policy that aided the middle class in obtaining mortgages. Housing remained a problem for increasing numbers of urban Canadians during the war years. As migrants flocked to cities to work in war-related industries, many families lived in garages, empty warehouses, shacks, chicken–coops, "and indeed, in anything that will hold a bed," as one report put it. The influx of military and civilian war workers strained housing facilities in Halifax. By 1943, Montreal needed 50,000 new dwellings. Unscrupulous landlords gouged tenants, despite the imposition of rent controls.

As the war ended, Canada's rental-controls administrator noted that the country was attempting to solve its shelter problem by "compressing more and more people into the same cubic space." He estimated that at least 200,000 Canadian households were now living "doubled up" or even "tripled up." Ottawa ignored pleas for public intervention to provide low-rental housing. Instead, the federal government revised its national housing policy, reducing down payments and guaranteeing mortgages, in order to stimulate the building of new homes and enable families with moderate incomes to purchase property. It also showed considerable interest in the future of returning soldiers, whom it sought to resettle on small farms by means of the Veterans' Land Act of 1942.

Women at the End of the War

In the middle of the war, Ottawa established a special subcommittee to study the role of women in postwar Canada. The members, all women, assumed that many female workers would return to the home. For those who remained employed outside the home, the subcommittee's report recommended expanded employment opportunities, equal pay, better working conditions, and the granting of children's allowances.

These proposals stirred up substantial opposition. Concerned about postwar unemployment, government planners wanted women out of the workforce to make room for returning soldiers and workers in shut-down war industries. Unions did not want to see women competing for scarce jobs with their fathers, sons, husbands, or fiancés. Polls showed that most Canadians—women as well as men—wanted women back in the home after the war. Regardless, the House of Commons paid little attention to the report, tabled in early 1944. Other "more pressing" problems had arisen. The subcommittee's report was "pigeon-holed and forgotten."[13]

Life seemed to return to "normal" at the end of the war. Women in the armed services were demobilized. Many of the barriers blocking women from the workforce went back up again. The "plywood girls" of the Port Alberni plywood factory, for example, now became "plywood bags," a derogatory term often used by other women to express their disapproval of young female workers who were occupying jobs that, in their view, should rightfully be given to returning veterans.[14] The proportion of women working outside the home plummeted. Although women slowly began to return to the workforce in the early 1950s, not until the 1960s would the proportion of female workers return to the 27 percent it had been in 1944.

The 1945 Election

King's cautious yet reformist approach to social problems proved politically sound. The timing of the federal elections did not hurt either. An election was held in 1940, and the Liberals rode to victory on the wave of nationalist propaganda that followed the start of the war. By the midpoint of the war, the Liberals had fallen heavily in the polls, and their spate of wartime measures—from high taxes to wage and price controls—were highly unpopular. But the next election was held in 1945, timed perfectly to take advantage of the, euphoria and jubilation of victory. King won the election in 1945 with 118 seats and 40 percent of the vote, while the Progressive Conservatives won 67, the CCF 28, and Social Credit 13.

The Liberals faced a weak Tory opposition that was in the process of remaking itself. Decades as a high-tariff and pro-British party now created the image of an anachronistic party lost in a past that no longer existed. The Conservatives tried to refashion its image (and its strength in western Canada) through the selection of the Progressive John Bracken as leader and a name change to the Progressive Conservative Party. The attempt failed. Appealing to the West was not going to impress Quebec. While the CCF gained support during the war, by 1945 Canadians seemed to want security, stability, and prosperity. The Liberals and Mackenzie King were known commodities. ↑

Relations with the Provinces

The first half of the twentieth century—marked by a major depression and two world wars—demonstrated that the Canadian federal structure was insufficient to handle such challenges and crises. The Depression restricted the autonomy of the provinces, forcing them to rely increasingly on Ottawa for financial assistance. The wars created conditions that furthered centralization, as the federal government took the dominant role in organizing the Canadian economy and, indeed, the lives of Canadians.

The Rowell–Sirois Report

The Rowell–Sirois Commission on Dominion–Provincial Relations, set up by the King government in 1937, made public its report in May 1940. With the objective of stabilizing provincial finances and giving equal services to all Canadians, the commissioners recommended that Ottawa collect all income taxes and succession duties and, in return, make unconditional grants to the provinces. Disadvantaged provinces should receive special subsidies to enable them to offer social and educational services equivalent to those of other Canadian provinces without having to tax more heavily than the Canadian average. The federal government should also assume all provincial debts.

Provincial autonomists condemned the report as a veritable centralizer's "Bible." They ignored the chief recommendation—the national adjustment grant—and instead argued that its recommendations would place provincial treasuries at Ottawa's mercy, and that the federal government would determine provincial activities by what it was willing to pay out. Premier Mitchell Hepburn of Ontario—a province that would not benefit from the special adjustment grants—attacked the report as "the product of the mind of a few college professors and a Winnipeg newspaperman [John Dafoe] who has had his knife in Ontario ever since he was able to write editorial articles."

Most newspapers reacted favourably to the report. Federal ministers and bureaucrats also endorsed the recommendations strongly, particularly those relating to money. Ottawa wanted to ensure control over fiscal policy to pay for the war as well as to diminish inflationary pressures. But the report was released during the war and, as a result, its recommendations were lost amid a desire to gain control of the provinces' taxes. Even though it was not what the Rowell–Sirois report recommended, the federal government urged the provinces to "rent" their tax fields to the federal government. Ottawa took on new powers and the report was used as the justification.

With no illusions about the outcome, King invited the premiers, in January 1941, to discuss the proposals. While some provinces insisted on the need for further study, others rejected Ottawa's plans outright. The conference collapsed in deadlock. Ottawa, however, pressed ahead. It promised, as a "temporary wartime expedient," that the provinces would have to surrender their income taxes only for the duration of the war, and it proposed to compensate the provinces more generously. All the provinces yielded, although some did so reluctantly.

After 1943, the economic planners in Ottawa, many of whom were disciples of British economist John Maynard Keynes, set forth their designs for the immediate postwar era. They feared that a depression might result from the reconversion of the economy to peacetime conditions, just as it had after World War I. Moreover, they wanted to make certain that Ottawa could assume the heavy financial responsibilities and increased debt charges resulting from the war. Ottawa, they urged, should thus act as the "balance wheel" of the economy. If it kept its hand firmly on taxation, it could combat cyclical tendencies, either deflationary busts or inflationary booms; it could maintain high and stable employment; and it could offer costly social-security measures to all citizens, thus supporting consumer buying power. For these civil servants, economic, political, and humanitarian objectives dictated that the federal government take charge.

The Dominion–Provincial Conference on Reconstruction

In August 1945, immediately before Japan's surrender, Ottawa convened the Dominion–Provincial Conference on Reconstruction. Prime Minister King, pushed by the department of finance and the influential "brain trust" of mandarins, assured the provinces that he did not want to weaken or subordinate them but rather wished to ensure their "effective financial independence." He intended to do this by convincing them to continue to allow Ottawa to levy all income taxes in return for increased provincial grants, with no strings attached. As part of the *Green Book Proposals*, the federal government also offered to pay part of the cost of a comprehensive health-insurance plan and of old-age pensions, and to expand the coverage of federal unemployment insurance.

Although most provinces reacted positively, the premiers of Ontario, Quebec, and Alberta objected to what they saw as the concentration of financial and administrative powers in the federal government's hands. Historian Alvin Finkel suggested that King actually hoped that the premiers would oppose his ideas so that he would have the "necessary excuse" to abandon plans for costly social programs.[15] Ottawa eventually managed to reach agreement on the tax proposals. For the next decade, Canadian federalism remained highly centralized.[16]

Regional and Provincial Developments

The war and the after-effects of the Depression fostered the continued uneven development of Canada's regional economies. This reality was highlighted by the findings of the Rowell–Sirois Commission, and the report's proposed national adjustment grants were designed to deal with the lack of balance. But this aspect of the report was ignored.

Manufacturing and Resources

The war diversified Canada's manufacturing capacity, as well as further promoting its resource-based industries. Quebec, British Columbia, and especially Ontario made dramatic advances. In Quebec, industries such as chemical products and aluminum refining expanded rapidly. In Ontario, factory employment increased greatly and the exploitation of the province's huge iron-ore deposits began at Steep Rock Lake north of Lake Superior. On the Pacific coast, the port of Vancouver prospered. Its shipyards and those of Victoria employed 30,000 workers at their peak. Prince Rupert became an important supply centre for American bases in Alaska, particularly after the Americans built the Alaska Highway through British Columbia. The military buildup on the West Coast also stimulated British Columbia's economy. By 1943, British Columbians had the highest per capita income of all Canadians. In spite of the war, tourism continued to contribute to Vancouver's development, and wartime promotion ensured that the sector would be poised for rapid postwar expansion.

The Northwest

In 1942, the United States Army Corps of Engineers coordinated the construction teams that built, for defence purposes, a 2500-kilometre highway from Dawson Creek in northeastern British Columbia to Fairbanks, Alaska. The next year the Public Roads Administration, an American civilian agency, directed the transformation of the rough military road into a permanent civilian highway, widening it, extending branch roads to the airstrips, and completing a telegraph line along this American highway built on Canadian soil.

The attack on Pearl Harbor led American defence planners to worry about the threat to energy supplies in the North; oil tankers now appeared vulnerable to Japanese submarine attack. As a result, the Canadian Oil (Canol) project was begun to pipe oil from the Imperial Oil Company's field at Norman Wells, on the Mackenzie River. The Americans made large-scale expenditures to build a pipeline to Whitehorse, a refinery, and a whole host of subsidiary facilities. This dependable source of oil could then be used in the Pacific theatre. For three years, thousands of men worked on this second American project on Canadian soil. When the Japanese threat in the Pacific ended, the completed Canol pipeline, now unneeded, was shut down.

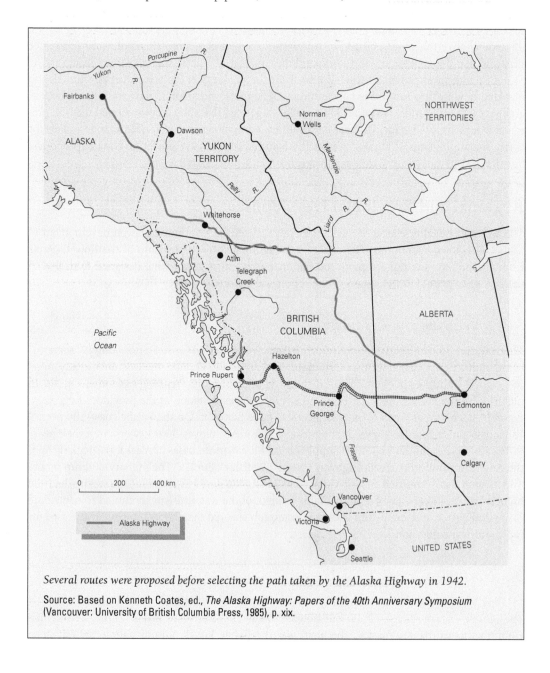

Several routes were proposed before selecting the path taken by the Alaska Highway in 1942.

Source: Based on Kenneth Coates, ed., *The Alaska Highway: Papers of the 40th Anniversary Symposium* (Vancouver: University of British Columbia Press, 1985), p. xix.

Quebec

In Quebec, the Liberal government of Adélard Godbout nationalized the private electric power companies and created Hydro-Québec, a publicly owned hydroelectric utility. To boost educational levels, it made school attendance obligatory until age 14, a measure hitherto opposed by the Catholic clergy, who argued that parents, not the state, should decide how long children went to school. In the Quebec Labour Relations Act, the government set out the rules governing collective bargaining. The bill, supported by the unions, was intended to force companies to negotiate with their unionized employees. In 1940, women in Quebec finally obtained the right to vote provincially. Suffragist Idola Saint-Jean argued forcefully for this right:

> We vote in federal elections as intelligently as women in neighbouring provinces. Why shouldn't we be concerned with problems debated in the provincial parliament? Don't housing, public health and education concern us much more directly than the problems of federal politics?

The legislative assembly finally agreed, despite the vigorous objections of the church and conservative groups.

Ontario

In Ontario, the impetuous Mitchell Hepburn appeared mainly interested in pursuing a vendetta against his federal Liberal counterpart, Mackenzie King. Debates over federalism lay at the base of the dispute between the nation's prime minister and the most influential province's premier, but stark personality differences also increased antagonism. The ever-opportunistic King used his feud with Hepburn to claim the premier was thwarting a united war effort and to call a federal election in 1940.

At the same time, the provincial CCF attracted support in Ontario, largely in urban working-class districts. In the 1943 provincial election, the CCF, with one-third of the popular vote, placed second, just behind George Drew's Conservatives. While Premier Drew denounced the socialists, he energetically pursued reform policies, notably in health, education, and housing. Provincial planning became important in areas such as forest conservation, industrial development, and water use. Drew also wanted to boost immigration from Britain. He established the War Brides Bureau in London to counsel British wives coming to Canada with their soldier husbands. Drew's enthusiastic salesmanship caused Canadian-born British press magnate Max Aitken, now Lord Beaverbrook, to comment: "Look George, is Ontario a part of Canada or Canada a part of Ontario?"

The CCF proved much less threatening in the Ontario election of 1945. Declining in the cities and lacking a rural base, it became the victim of fierce denunciations of "state socialism." Party leader E.B. Jolliffe's sensational "revelations," that Drew was maintaining in Ontario "at this very minute, a secret political police, a paid spy organization, a Gestapo" to keep himself in power, backfired. Drew won a majority and Ontario settled into what would become more than forty years of Conservative government.

The Maritimes and Newfoundland

The war brought fewer economic benefits to Canadians in the three Maritime provinces. On the one hand, the rise in food prices and the growing demand for minerals and pulp and paper aided the region's economy. War spending also helped. By 1943, some 75,000 men and women were building and repairing vessels in Maritime shipyards, even at night under floodlights. Halifax became Canada's major port for shipping munitions and other supplies to Western Europe.

After the war an "army" of 40,000 war brides (mainly British) with their 20,000 children, most under the age of 3, arrived in Canada.

Source: H.B. Jefferson Collection/Nova Scotia Archives and Record Management/N-820.

But the impact of Ottawa's war policies on the Maritimes overall was "largely negative." While the government did "generate economic activity, it created relatively little new industry in the region and even less of a permanent nature."[17] Federal Minister of Munitions and Supply C.D. Howe believed it was more efficient to develop industry along the St. Lawrence and in the Great Lakes region. Nor did provincial governments succeed in obtaining federal funds for necessary infrastructure or private investment in industry. In general, at the war's end, the region appeared ill-equipped to undertake any substantial industrial expansion.

Economic weakness meant that Maritime governments lacked funds for investment in health and education. In 1945, Prince Edward Island had only half the number of doctors needed to meet the national standard of 1 doctor per 1000 people. New Brunswick had Canada's highest infant and maternal death rate, and Nova Scotia followed closely. In Prince Edward Island, the great majority of schools had only one room; many needed repair or were beyond repair. Teachers were often poorly qualified and salaries were low. New Brunswick had Canada's highest illiteracy rate, affecting particularly the province's French-speaking Acadian population. Only after 1940 did the provincial government authorize the use of French-language texts in public schools and recognize the importance of making French the language of instruction in Acadian schools.

Newfoundland's case was somewhat unique. At the outbreak of war, low fish prices and uncertain markets left the population of the outports in poverty. The relief rolls overflowed. At first, the war worsened the situation, resulting in increased taxes and decreased services. Eventually, however, it created a temporary boom in employment through the construction and maintenance of large American defence projects, especially the bases at Argentia, Gander, and Stephenville. After the British-appointed Commission of Government developed costly plans for postwar reconstruction, Britain came to an understanding with the Canadian government to encourage the island's eventual entry into Canada. Not everyone in the federal government was excited at the thought of Newfoundland joining as the tenth province. Some saw the island as a "little Ireland."

The West

The Prairie provinces, hard hit by the Depression of the 1930s, recovered slowly. Although war spending brought relatively few jobs to the region, farmers increased their incomes substantially due to higher prices, caused largely by the much-increased demand for wheat in Europe, and to improved harvests, made possible by better weather conditions. Farm incomes remained much lower than other workers' wages. Most rural homes had no indoor plumbing or electricity, and farm villages enjoyed few services. The provinces looked to expand their social services while also diversifying their economies.

The war boosted crude-oil production in Alberta, at least until the Turner Valley field near Calgary went into decline after 1942. Coal mines prospered and in Prairie cities the construction industry flourished. But the war did not create the diversified economy that many felt the region needed.

Politically, third parties on the Prairies grew stronger, although they tended to moderate their ideology. Social Credit in Alberta was led by William Aberhart until his death in 1943, and then for a quarter-century after by his protégé Ernest Manning. The government denounced socialism and centralization, promised able, businesslike administration, and gently laid Social Credit doctrine to rest.

The CCF made inroads in the West but scored its first victory in Saskatchewan in 1944. Although it had attenuated the socialism of the Regina Manifesto, its ambitious program promised public ownership of natural resources, security of land tenure for farmers, collective bargaining for workers, educational reform, and social services, including a universal socialized health plan. Baptist preacher and CCF leader Tommy Douglas denounced the economic system that he likened to a cream separator: the farmer pours in the milk, the worker turns the handle, and the capitalist, because he owns the machine, "sits on a little stool with the cream spout fixed firmly in his mouth while the farmer and the worker take turns on the skim milk spout." Once in power, the CCF launched major reforms, particularly during its first two years in office, but financial and other factors soon forced it to make pragmatic policy adjustments.

Manitoba maintained its image as a bastion of stable, efficient, and group government. The war was certainly no time to make changes. Reminding the opposition parties that he "had never

The family of Private Louis Zarowny welcomes him home, at Mewata Stadium in Calgary, in July 1945. Wounded twice, Zarowny served with the Loyal Edmonton Regiment in Italy and Northwestern Europe.

Source: Glenbow Archives, Calgary, Canada/Herald Collection/NA-2864-3448.

Canada's Minister of External Affairs, Louis St. Laurent, and Prime Minister Mackenzie King at the General Assembly of the United Nations Conference on International Organization, San Francisco, May 8, 1945.

Source: Library and Archives Canada/C-22720.

looked upon party politics in provincial affairs with any favour," Premier John Bracken formed a coalition with the Conservatives and CCF. In 1942, however, Bracken abandoned his safe position to enter the raucous and uncertain realm of federal politics.

In British Columbia, the old political order also changed. When the Liberals failed to gain a majority in the 1941 election, party members favouring coalition with the Conservatives ousted their leader, Duff Pattullo, whom they sharply criticized for his feuding with Ottawa, his road-building policy, and his abrasive style. The CCF then formed the opposition to the new Liberal–Conservative alliance.

Toward a New Internationalism

The war in Europe ended when Germany surrendered in May 1945. By September, Japan also capitulated after atomic bombs were dropped on two of its cities, Hiroshima and Nagasaki. Peace brought with it new problems and, in particular, the difficult question of how to maintain it. In contrast to its position after World War I, Canada was ready to accept responsibility in world affairs. Like the other Allied countries, Canada supported the necessity of establishing an international organization comparable to, but more effective than, the League of Nations. Canada thus participated in the founding conference of the United Nations in San Francisco in April 1945, where it worked to ensure that both the United States and the Soviet Union became members.

Canada also pushed for world economic and social cooperation. In late 1945, Lester Pearson chaired the founding meeting of the United Nations Food and Agriculture Organization in Quebec City. As a member of the United Nations Relief and Rehabilitation Administration, Canada became a major supplier of aid to war-torn countries, although it had great difficulty convincing the Americans of its right to participate in determining the operations of the association. Canada also joined the International Monetary Fund, as well as the International Civil Aviation Organization, whose headquarters came to Montreal. As external-affairs officer John Holmes commented later, Canada "moved with the tide," trying to avoid letting the Great Powers control everything.[18] Conscious of its position as a rising middle power, Canada attempted, with some success, to get recognition for states like itself. Canada was now in the vanguard pushing for a more "multilateral" world.

Canada's position as a rising middle power

SUMMARY

World War II changed Canada at home and abroad. The war created an economic boom that instilled hope among Canadians for a better life. Trade-union organizations made notable gains, as governments enacted legislation establishing a new framework for the conduct of industrial relations. The entry of large numbers of women into the workforce announced a substantial change in their role. In the aftermath of the Nazi atrocities, a new spirit of tolerance seemed to grip the postwar world, and it was hoped that it would pervade Canada's treatment of its minorities. With the nation's new federal social programs, Canadians took a significant step in the direction of the welfare state. In federal–provincial relations, Ottawa reasserted a pre-eminence that endured for two decades. The nation had managed to avoid national disunity over the conscription issue. In Ottawa, Canadians continued to support the Liberal government of Mackenzie King, perhaps because he was, in historian Frank Underhill's words, the leader "who divides us least."[19]

The war ended the isolation of the 1930s. Involvement in world affairs as a middle power brought benefits but carried a price. Despite Canada's attempts to develop relationships with multilateral associations of states, such involvement meant closer ties to the United States. For supporters of the *rapprochement*, the closer links brought security and economic prosperity through trade and investment. For critics, the triumphant move toward nationhood in the interwar years appeared to have abruptly ended, with Canada being relegated once more to colonial status—this time, as a colony of the United States.

NOTES

1. Desmond Morton, *Canada and War: A Military and Political History* (Toronto: Butterworths, 1981), p. 106.

2. W.A.B. Douglas and Brereton Greenhous, *Out of the Shadows: Canada in the Second World War*, rev. ed. (Toronto: Dundurn Press, 1995), p. 111.

3. Donald Creighton, *The Forked Road: Canada, 1939–1957* (Toronto: McClelland & Stewart, 1976), p. 43.

4. J.L. Granatstein and Norman Hillmer, *For Better or for Worse: Canada and the United States to the 1990s* (Mississauga, ON: Copp Clark Pitman, 1991), p. 144.

5. James Eayrs, *In Defence of Canada*, vol. 2, *Appeasement and Rearmament* (Toronto: University of Toronto Press, 1965), p. 191.

6. Donald F. Davis and Barbara Lorenzkowski, "A Platform for Gender Tensions: Women Working and Riding on Canadian Urban Public Transit in the 1940s," *Canadian Historical Review*, 79 (1998): 442–43.

7. Ruth Roach Pierson, *"They're Still Women After All": The Second World War and Canadian Womanhood* (Toronto: McClelland & Stewart, 1986), p. 33.

8. Ruth Roach Pierson, "'Jill Canuck': CWAC of All Trades, But No 'Pistol-Packing Momma,'" *Historical Papers/Communications historiques* (1978): 106–33.

9. W. Peter Ward, *White Canada Forever: Popular Attitudes and Public Policy Toward Orientals in British Columbia* (Montreal/Kingston: McGill-Queen's University Press, 1978), p. 146.

10. Patricia Roy et al., *Mutual Hostages: Canadians and Japanese during the Second World War* (Toronto: University of Toronto Press, 1990), p. 215.

11. Michael Earle, "'Down with Hitler and Silby Barrett': The Cape Breton Miners' Slowdown Strike of 1941," *Acadiensis*, 18 (1988): 56–90.

12. Laurel Sefton MacDowell, "The Formation of the Canadian Industrial Relations System During World War Two," *Labour/Le travail*, 3 (1978): 186.

13. Gail Cuthbert Brandt, "'Pigeon-Holed and Forgotten': The Work of the Subcommittee on the Post-War Problems of Women, 1943," *Histoire sociale/Social History*, 15 (1983): 239–59.

14. Susanne Klausen, "The Plywood Girls: Women and Gender Ideology at the Port Alberni Plywood Plant, 1942–1991," *Labour/Le travail*, 41 (1998): 199–235.

15. Alvin Finkel, "Paradise Postponed: A Re-examination of the Green Book Proposals of 1945," *Journal of the Canadian Historical Association*, 4 (1993): 128.

16. R.M. Burns, *The Acceptable Mean: The Tax Rental Agreements, 1941–1962* (Toronto: Canadian Tax Foundation, 1980), p. 35.

17. Ernest R. Forbes, *Challenging the Regional Stereotype: Essays on the 20th Century Maritimes* (Fredericton: Acadiensis Press, 1989), p. 195.

18. John W. Holmes, *The Shaping of Peace: Canada and the Search for World Order, 1943–1957*, vol. 1 (Toronto: University of Toronto Press, 1979), pp. 235–36.

19. Frank Underhill, "The End of the King Era," *Canadian Forum* (September 1948); reprinted in F.H. Underhill, *In Search of Canadian Liberalism* (Toronto: Macmillan, 1960), p. 127.

BIBLIOGRAPHY

C.P. Stacey's survey of Canadian foreign policy remains useful, *Canada and the Age of Conflict: A History of Canadian External Policies*, vol. 2, *1921–1948: The Mackenzie King Era* (Toronto: University of Toronto Press, 1981). R.D. Cuff and J.L. Granatstein review aspects of Canadian–American relations in *Ties That Bind: Canadian–American Relations in Wartime from the Great War to the Cold War*, 2nd ed. (Toronto: Samuel Stevens Hakkert, 1977). On the Canadian–American relationship, see also John Herd Thompson and Stephen J. Randall, *Canada and the United States: Ambivalent Allies*, 4th ed. (Montreal/Kingston: McGill-Queen's University Press, 2008); and Galen Roger Perras and Katrina E. Kellner, "A Perfectly Logical and Sensible Thing: Billy Mitchell Advocates a Canadian–American Aerial Alliance Against Japan," *Journal of Military History*, 72(3) (2008): 785–823. J.L. Granatstein, *Canada's War: The Politics of the Mackenzie King Government, 1939–1945* (Toronto: University of Toronto Press, 1975, 1990), is useful on foreign and domestic policy, as are the relevant chapters in Robert Bothwell, Ian Drummond, and John English, *Canada, 1900–1945* (Toronto: University of Toronto Press, 1987). See also Robert Bothwell and Jean Daudelin, eds., *Canada Among Nations: 100 Years of Canadian Foreign Policy* (Montreal/Kingston: McGill-Queen's University Press, 2008). Norman Hillmer et al., eds., present several articles on Canada on the eve of war in *A Country of Limitations: Canada and the World in 1939* (Ottawa: Canadian Committee for the History of the Second World War, 1996). See also Christopher McCreery and Arthur Milnes, ed., *The Authentic Voice of Canada: R.B. Bennett's Speeches in the House of Lords, 1941–1947* (Montreal/Kingston: McGill-Queen's University Press, 2009).

In addition to works mentioned in this chapter's Where Historians Disagree box, books on Canada's participation in the war include David J. Bercuson, *Maple Leaf Against the Axis: Canada's Second World War* (Toronto: Stoddart, 1995); J.L. Granatstein and Desmond Morton, *A Nation Forged in Fire: Canadians and the Second World War, 1939–1945* (Toronto: Lester & Orpen Dennys, 1989); and appropriate chapters in J.L. Granatstein, *Canada's Army: Waging War and Keeping the Peace* (Toronto: University of Toronto Press, 2002). The soldiers' stories are recounted in Ted Barris and Alex Barris, *Days of Victory: Canadians Remember, 1939–1945* (Toronto: Macmillan, 1995); Desmond Morton and J.L. Granatstein, *Victory 1945: Canadians from War to Peace* (Toronto: HarperCollins, 1995); George G. Blackburn, *The Guns of*

Victory: A Soldier's Eye View, Belgium, Holland, and Germany, 1944–45 (Toronto: McClelland & Stewart, 1996); and Blake Heathcote, *Testaments of Honour: Personal Histories of Canada's War Veterans* (Toronto: Doubleday, 2002).

The Hong Kong debacle is described in Brereton Greenhous, *C-Force to Hong Kong: A Canadian Catastrophe, 1941–1945* (Toronto: Dundurn Press, 1996); and Oliver Lindsay, *The Battle for Hong Kong, 1941–1945: Hostage to Fortune* (Montreal/Kingston: McGill-Queen's University Press, 2006). Books on the Italian campaign include Daniel G. Dancocks, *The D-Day Dodgers: The Canadians in Italy, 1943–1945* (Toronto: McClelland & Stewart, 1991); Mark Zuehlke, *The Gothic Line: Canada's Month of Hell in World War II Italy* (Vancouver: Douglas and McIntyre, 2003); and Lance Goddard, *Hell and High Water: Canada and the Italian Campaign* (Toronto: Dundurn Press, 2007). For studies on the infantry, see Robert Engen, *Canadians Under Fire: Infantry Effectiveness in the Second World War* (Montreal/Kingston: McGill-Queen's University Press, 2009); David J. Bercuson, *The Fighting Canadians: Our Regimental History from New France to Afghanistan* (Scarborough, ON: Harper Collins Canada, 2008); and Bernd Horn, *Establishing a Legacy: The History of the Royal Canadian Regiment, 1883–1953* (Toronto: Dundurn Press, 2008). Paul Jackson discusses the homosexual military experience in *One of the Boys: Homosexuality in the Military during World War II*, 2nd ed. (Montreal, Kingston: McGill-Queen's University Press, 2010).

Canada's military leaders are studied in J.L. Granatstein, *The Generals: The Canadian Army's Senior Commanders in the Second World War* (Toronto: Stoddart, 1993); and Bernd Horn and Stephen Harris, eds., *Warrior Chiefs: Perspectives on Senior Canadian Military Leaders* (Toronto: Dundurn Press, 2001). Terry Copp and Bill McAndrew study one particular type of battle casualty in *Battle Exhaustion: Soldiers and Psychiatrists in the Canadian Army, 1939–1945* (Montreal/Kingston: McGill-Queen's University Press, 1990). Three books look at the fate of Canadian prisoners of war: Jonathan Vance, *Objects of Concern: Canadian Prisoners of War Through the Twentieth Century* (Vancouver: University of British Columbia Press, 1994); Howard Margolian, *Conduct Unbecoming: The Story of the Murder of Canadian Prisoners of War in Normandy* (Toronto: University of Toronto Press, 1998); and David McIntosh, *Hell on Earth: Aging Faster, Dying Sooner: Canadian Prisoners of the Japanese during World War II* (Toronto: McGraw-Hill Ryerson, 1996). Spencer Dunmore discusses air-force pilot training in *Wings for Victory: The Remarkable Story of the British Air Training Plan in Canada* (Toronto: McClelland & Stewart, 1994). Articles concerning the rehabilitation of returning veterans may be found in Peter Neary and J.L. Granatstein, eds., *The Veterans Charter and Post-World War II Canada* (Montreal/Kingston: McGill-Queen's University Press, 1998) and Peter Neary, *On to Civvy Street: Canada's Rehabilitation Program for Veterans of the Second World War* (Montreal-Kingston: McGill-Queen's University Press, 2011). Carolyn Gossage has written a popular history of women in the armed services, *Greatcoats and Glamour Boots: Canadian Women at War, 1939–1945*, rev. ed. (Toronto: Dundurn Press, 2001). On Native participation in the war, see Janice Summerby's illustrated brochure, *Native Soldiers; Foreign Battlefields* (Ottawa: Minister of Supply and Services, 1993), and R. Scott Sheffield, *The Red Man's on the Warpath: The Image of the "Indian" and the Second World War* (Vancouver: UBC Press, 2004).

The history of the Royal Canadian Navy is told in Marc Milner, *North Atlantic Run: The Royal Canadian Navy and the Battle for the Convoys* (Toronto: University of Toronto Press, 1985); Tony German, *The Sea Is at Our Gates: The History of the Canadian Navy* (Toronto: McClelland & Stewart, 1990); and Donald E. Graves, *In Peril on the Sea: The Royal Canadian Navy and the Battle of the Atlantic, 1939–1945* (Toronto: Robin Brass Studio, 2003). Among books recounting the RCN's battle against German U-boats are Michael L. Hadley, *U-Boats Against Canada: German Submarines in Canadian Waters* (Montreal/Kingston: McGill-Queen's University Press, 1985); and Marc Milner, *The U-Boat Hunters: The Royal Canadian Navy and the Offensive Against Germany's Submarines* (Toronto: University of Toronto Press, 1994). The story of the child evacuees from England bound for Canada is told in Tom Nagorski, *Miracles on the Water: The Heroic Survivors of a World War II U-Boat* (New York: Hyperion, 2006). David Zimmerman describes the technical problems encountered by the RCN in developing better-quality radar in *The Great Naval Battle of Ottawa* (Toronto: University of Toronto Press, 1989). Donald Avery studies Canada's contribution to Allied defence research in *The Science of War: Canadian Scientists and Allied Military Technology During the Second World War* (Toronto: University of Toronto Press, 1998). For the role of the RCAF, the major work is Brereton Greenhous, Stephen J. Harris, William C. Johnston, and William G.P. Rawling, *The Crucible of War, 1939–1945: The Official History of the Royal Canadian Air Force*, vol. III (Toronto: University of Toronto Press, 1994).

The most thorough study on conscription is J.L. Granatstein and J.M. Hitsman, *Broken Promises: A History of Conscription in Canada*, rev. ed. (Toronto: Copp Clark Pitman, 1985). For an explanation of Quebec's reaction, see Richard Jones, "Politics and Culture: The French Canadians and the Second World War," in Sidney Aster, ed., *The Second World War as a National Experience* (Ottawa: Canadian Committee for the History of the Second World War, 1981), pp. 82–91; and Andre Laurendeau, *La crise de la conscription* (Montreal: Éditions du jour, 1962). See also Michael D. Stevenson, *Canada's Greatest Wartime Muddle: National Selective Service and the Mobilization of Human Resources During World War II* (Montreal/Kingston: McGill-Queen's University Press, 2001). The mobilization of natural resources is examined in Matthew Evenden, *Allied Power: Mobilizing Hydro-Electricity during Canada's Second World War* (Toronto: University of Toronto Press, 2015). Wartime censorship is treated in Claude Beauregard's excellent study, *Guerre et censure au Canada, 1939–1945* (Sillery, QC: Septentrion, 1998). The work of Canadian historians who chronicled the story of the war is described in Tim Cook, *Clio's Warriors: Canadian Historians and the Writing of the World Wars* (Vancouver: UBC Press, 2006).

Social security is discussed in a special issue of the *Journal of Canadian Studies* on "Leonard Marsh and Canadian Social Policy" (vol. 21, 1986). On family allowances see Nancy Christie, *Engendering the State: Family, Work and Welfare in Canada* (Toronto: University of Toronto Press, 2000). Doug Owram examines the evolution of ideas concerning the role of the modern state in *The Government Generation: Canadian Intellectuals and the State, 1900–1945* (Toronto: University of Toronto Press, 1986). Studies on food and rationing during the war include Ian Mosby, *Food Will Win the War: The Politics, Culture, and Science of Food on Canada's Home Front* (Vancouver: UBC Press, 2014). For a look at soldiering and citizenship, see Deborah Cowen, *Military Workfare: The Soldier and Social Citizenship in Canada* (Toronto: University of Toronto Press, 2008). Carman Miller looks at the effects of war on the Maritimes in "The 1940s: War and Rehabilitation," in E.R. Forbes and D.A. Muise, eds., *The Atlantic Provinces in Confederation* (Toronto: University of Toronto Press, 1993). Material on Newfoundland may be found in Peter Neary, *Newfoundland in the North Atlantic World, 1929–1949* (Montreal/Kingston: McGill-Queen's University Press, 1988).

On women in wartime, see Ruth Roach Pierson, *"They're Still Women After All": The Second World War and Canadian Womanhood* (Toronto: McClelland & Stewart, 1986); Melynda Jarratt, *War Brides: The Stories of the Women Who Left Everything Behind to Follow the Men They Loved* (Toronto: Dundurn Press, 2009); Jennifer A. Stephen, *Pick One Intelligent Girl: Employability, Domesticity, and the Gendering of Canada's Welfare State, 1939–1947* (Toronto: University of Toronto Press, 2007); and Cynthia Toman, "Front Lines and Frontiers: War as Legitimate Work for Nurses, 1939–1945," *Histoire sociale/Social History*, 40(79) (2007): 45–74. For one Toronto woman's experience, see Gunda Lambton, *Sun in Winter: A Toronto Wartime Journal, 1942–1945* (Montreal/Kingston, McGill-Queen's University Press, 2003). Jeffrey A. Keshen analyzes the war's negative social ramifications in *Saints, Sinners, and Soldiers: Canada's Second World War* (Vancouver: UBC Press, 2004). Maria Tippett examines culture in wartime in *Making Culture: English-Canadian Institutions and the Arts Before the Massey Commission* (Toronto: University of Toronto Press, 1990). Aspects of union activity are examined in Desmond Morton with Terry Copp, *Working People: An Illustrated History of the Canadian Labour Movement*, 3rd ed. (Toronto: Summerhill Press, 1990). On the impact of the war on labour–management relations, consult Laurel Sefton MacDowell, *Remember Kirkland Lake: The Gold Miners' Strike of 1941–42*, rev. ed. (Toronto: Canadian Scholars' Press, 2001). The impact of war on the labour movement and ethnic workers is examined in Carmela K. Patrias, *Jobs and Justice: Fighting Discrimination in Wartime Canada, 1939–1945* (Toronto: University of Toronto Press, 2011), and Wendy Cuthbertson, *Labour Goes to War: The CIO and the Construction of a New Social Order, 1939–45* (Vancouver: UBC Press, 2013).

Literature on ethnic groups during the war traditionally focuses on discrimination and internment. On the treatment of Japanese Canadians, consult Ann Gomer Sunahara, *The Politics of Racism: The Uprooting of Japanese Canadians During the Second World War* (Toronto: James Lorimer, 1981); Peter Ward, *White*

Canada Forever: Popular Attitudes and Public Policy Toward Orientals in British Columbia, 2nd ed. (Montreal/ Kingston: McGill-Queen's University Press, 1990); and Mona Oikawa, *Cartographies of Violence: Japanese Canadian Women, Memory, and the Subjects of the Internment* (Toronto: University of Toronto Press, 2011). The internment of Italian Canadians and German Canadians is discussed in Franca Iacovetta, Roberto Perin, and Angelo Principe, eds., *Enemies Within: Italian and Other Internees in Canada and Abroad* (Toronto: University of Toronto Press, 2000), and Robert H. Keyserlingk, "The Canadian Government's Attitude Toward Germans and German Canadians in World War II," *Canadian Ethnic Studies* 16, no. 1 (1984). Some historians have attempted to justify the necessity of internment. For this view, consult Patricia Roy et al., *Mutual Hostages: Canadians and Japanese during the Second World War* (Toronto: University of Toronto Press, 1990). More recently, historians have studied the experiences of ethnic Canadians with an emphasis on agency over victimhood. See, for example, Stephanie Bangarth, *Voices Raised in Protest: Defending North American Citizens of Japanese Ancestry, 1942–1949* (Vancouver: UBC Press, 2007). See also Aya Fujiwara, *Ethnic Elites and Canadian Identity: Japanese, Ukrainians, and Scots, 1919–1971* (Winnipeg: University of Manitoba Press, 2012), and Elliot Worsfold, "Cast Down, But Not Forsaken: The Second World War Experience and Memory of German-Canadian Lutherans in Southwestern Ontario," *Ontario History* CVI, no. 1 (2014): 57–76. Ivana Caccia traces the origins of Canadian multiculturalism to World War II in *Managing the Canadian Mosaic in Wartime: Shaping Citizenship and Policy, 1939–1945* (Montreal/ Kingston: McGill-Queen's University Press, 2011). Pacifism is examined in Tom Socknat, *Witness Against War: Pacifism in Canada, 1900–1945* (Toronto: University of Toronto Press, 1987). Larry Hannant, *The Infernal Machine: Investigating the Loyalty of Canada's Citizens* (Toronto: University of Toronto Press, 1995), deals with the questions of internal security and civil liberties.

Part 4

MODERN CANADA, 1945 TO THE PRESENT

INTRODUCTION

Canada emerged in the second half of the twentieth century as an important industrial nation and a respected global middle power. Overall, Canadians enjoyed one of the highest standards of living of any country in the world, although certain groups within society remained less favoured and some regions of the country experienced fewer advantages than others. But the post-1945 era witnessed attempts to create a more equal, accepting, and tolerant Canada.

Internationally, Canada emerged from World War II prepared to play a more active role on the world stage. But the world was a different place. The dawn of the nuclear age arrived and the threat of world annihilation cast its dark shadow over the planet. The United States superseded Britain as the new empire, but the rise of the Soviet Union created a balance of power and a world divided between two armed camps. This global struggle took on ideological dimensions and was pitched as a struggle between communism and capitalism, East and West, totalitarianism and freedom.

Caught in the middle of this Cold War, Canada wanted to play the role of middle power. But the ideological confines of the Cold War, along with Canada's traditional ties to the West and its geographical proximity between the United States and the Soviet Union, meant that in reality, Canada was always an American and British ally. But the desire for autonomy continued to shape Canada's domestic and international policies, as well as its search for an identity.

Politically, the Liberal Party became known as "the government party," and led Canada for three-quarters of the period since the end of World War II. The Progressive Conservatives struggled in their efforts to reforge their own identity and place on the Canadian political scene. Third parties played an increasingly significant role. These parties reflected the regionalized character of the nation. The Co-operative Commonwealth Federation (CCF), which became the New Democratic Party (NDP) in 1961, became the voice of the left in Canada, pushing the Liberals to the middle and the Progressive Conservatives to the right. Despite a powerful central government intent on creating one unified Canadian identity, the forces of regionalism, particularly in the West and Quebec, challenged national leaders to find consensus.

Beginning in the 1970s, the forces of globalization transformed Canada. While the nation struggled to find its identity and resist American hegemony, changes in communications and transportation made the world an increasingly small place—in the words of the Canadian philosopher Marshall McLuhan, a "global village." The Cold War ended in 1991 and for a brief hiatus, Canada seemed to have few international enemies. That changed on September 11, 2001, with the emergence of the "War on Terror."

Source: Library and Archives Canada/Credit: Richard Harrington/National Film Board of Canada fonds/Acc. no. 1971-271 NPC/PA-111390.

Chapter Fourteen

TOWARD A MORE AFFLUENT SOCIETY: 1945–60

TIME LINE

1946	Joint House and Senate Committee begins hearings to consider revision of the Indian Act
1947	Oil gushes from the first well in the Leduc oil field in Alberta
1949	Liberals win federal election under Louis St. Laurent
	Newfoundland enters Confederation
	Canada joins North Atlantic Treaty Organization
	Quebec asbestos workers strike for five months
1950	Outbreak of Korean War
1951	Parliament passes new Indian Act
1952	Canada's first television station begins broadcasting in Montreal
1953	Liberals win federal election under Louis St. Laurent
	Opening of Stratford (Ontario) Shakespearean Festival
1954	Construction begins on International Seaway and Power Project on the St. Lawrence River; work is completed in 1959
1956	Founding of Canadian Labour Congress
1957	Lester Pearson wins Nobel Peace Prize
	North American Air Defence Command (NORAD) founded
	Public hospital-insurance program established
	Liberals defeated by John Diefenbaker's Progressive Conservatives in federal election
	Founding of Canada Council, in support of culture and the arts
1958	Conservatives win huge majority in federal election
1959	Newfoundland loggers' strike

(1929 - 1939)

After a decade of economic depression and six years of war, Canadians wanted to make up for lost time and look toward a bright future. Workers sought stable jobs and better wages. Consumers wanted cars, household appliances, adequate housing, and more leisure time. Yet modest family budgets, limited availability of goods (particularly in the immediate postwar years), and fears that prosperity would not continue forced them to be patient and prudent. In addition, the insecurity of the recent past made Canadians look increasingly to governments to provide an array of health, educational, and social services as a safety net against misfortune. When they looked beyond the nation's borders, they took pride in Canada's respected role in international organizations, and in the welcome their country extended to immigrants from war-torn and economically ravaged Europe.

Looked to gov't to provide: health/ educational/ social services as a safety net against misfortune

Traditional values and beliefs continued to govern the behaviour of a majority of Canadians. Although more women worked outside the home, long-held notions concerning the role of women in society loosened only gradually. By the late 1950s, however, the old mentality was changing. Slower growth with rising unemployment disrupted the postwar boom. People grew tired of unimaginative politicians who boasted of past successes and talked in platitudinous generalities. A new generation was ready for new ideas and new solutions.

Unexpected Prosperity

Postwar Canada prospered. The federal government had performed admirably in preventing a postwar recession through its handling of wartime finances. The lessons of World War I had been learned. The economic situation was aided by the need to rebuild Europe. *Fortune* magazine called Canada a "businessman's country." Construction boomed. Total industrial output rose by half in the 1950s, and productivity soared due to technological innovation. The lighting of the flame on the first Leduc oil well in a farmer's field near Edmonton on a cold February day in 1947 signalled large-scale job creation and rapid population growth in Alberta. The discovery of large deposits of base metals in northern New Brunswick boosted hopes for significant job creation in that province. In Ontario, demand for a wide array of goods stimulated industrial expansion. The government-owned Polymer Corporation in Sarnia, Ontario, produced 10 percent of the world's synthetic rubber, used by the rapidly expanding automobile industry.[1] By 1951, 10 percent of the Canadian labour force had jobs related to motor vehicles, mostly in southern Ontario. That same year, the Ford Motor Company announced the construction of a huge plant in the small town of Oakville, just west of Toronto. For a time, Oakville's residents enjoyed the highest per capita incomes in Canada.

The average worker had reason to feel satisfied. Rapid economic growth meant that unemployment rates remained low: between 2.8 and 5.9 percent. Pay packets for factory workers doubled between 1945 and 1956. In spite of significant increases in the prices of food and consumer goods, workers saw their living standards improve. They also worked less, as the 40-hour week became the norm. In addition, federal transfer payments, such as family allowances and old-age pensions, put more money into consumers' pockets.

The Age of the Consumer

The era of the consumer and technological advancements introduced a new lifestyle. In towns, the iceman with his horse-drawn cart lost his remaining customers as people gradually discarded their iceboxes and equipped their kitchens with electric refrigerators. Coal merchants' *to →* sales tumbled as homeowners bought electric ranges and switched to cleaner and more efficient gas and oil heat. Families acquired a variety of new appliances, such as washing machines and barbeques, intended to reduce the drudgery of housework. Sales of new automobiles

Supermarkets became a symbol of postwar prosperity. Woodward's department store, Vancouver, was one of the first in Canada. It included in-store home economists and baby seats in the shopping carts.

Source: Vancouver Public Library/25644.

increased in the 1950s as Canadians bought sleek American Fords and Chevrolets, or slim British Morrises and Austins.

Subdivisions proliferated around major cities. According to historian Doug Owram, "the rise and triumph of low-density residentially oriented communities was the single most significant urban event of the postwar decades."[2] A million new homes were built between 1945 and 1960. Canadians could buy a bungalow for $15,000 and then borrow the money to pay for it at a fixed rate of just over 4 percent for twenty-five years. Proud new home-owners hurried to vary the colour of the trim or to plant shrubs in order to distinguish their dwelling from similar constructions on all sides. Roofs acquired an important new use—as supports for forests of television antennas. Shopping centres sprang up, the first appearing in a Toronto suburb in 1946.

The Environment

The prosperity posed new threats to the environment. In search of new outdoor recreational opportunities, more mobile urban dwellers invaded provincial and national parks. Existing parks quickly became saturated. In response to this demand, Ontario, for example, embarked on a major program of park expansion: the number of parks grew from only 8 in 1954 to 94 in 1967. By the late 1950s, however, conservationists worried that increased outdoor recreation threatened the survival of natural areas and they called for the establishment of nature preserves. In 1959, Ontario adopted the Wilderness Areas Act, which set aside areas of natural, historic, and scenic importance. Conservation practices had not yet influenced the operations of the forest industry. Harvesting aimed at maximum profits. Clearcutting, facilitated by the mechanization of the industry, was the primary method employed, because it permitted lower labour costs while increasing logging volumes.

The Less Advantaged

Yet Canadians were often unhappy when they compared themselves, as they often did, with their neighbours to the south. Magazines and newspapers featured articles that delved into the revenues and expenses of "typical" Canadian and American families. In 1950, Canadian per capita income was still 40 percent below American levels. Canadians complained that refrigerators costing $400 could be purchased for only $275 in the United States. Canadian entertainers, researchers, and engineers migrated south, while those who remained behind bemoaned the "brain drain."

Many Canadians saw no prosperity at all. Few men and far fewer women held the university diplomas that guaranteed good jobs. Salaries were often low, especially for non-unionized workers, immigrants, and women. In the immediate postwar years, most people limited themselves to what historian Magda Fahrni calls the "cautious consumption of necessities."[3] Memories of the Great Depression and wartime rationing were still very fresh.

[margin handwriting: Before 1950, only a minority of homes had electricity]

In rural Canada before 1950, only a minority of households had electricity. The 1951 census revealed that half of Canadian families still did not own an electric refrigerator or a vacuum cleaner, 60 percent had no car, 40 percent had no telephone, and 25 percent did not have an electric washing machine. Indeed, one dwelling in three did not have hot and cold running water. Thousands of small farmers, incapable of earning a living, abandoned their land. Incomes of residents of the Atlantic provinces remained nearly 40 percent below the Canadian average. New Brunswick was sharply divided into the impoverished north and east, largely Acadian, and the more favoured south, mostly English-speaking. Thousands of Montrealers with incomes below the poverty line lived in the tenements of St. Henri, which were portrayed poignantly by Gabrielle Roy in her novel *Bonheur d'occasion* (which in English was called *The Tin Flute*). In Quebec, anglophones enjoyed income levels twice those of francophones and one-third higher than those of bilingual francophones. In the West, Winnipeg suffered from the decline of old industries and the relocation of Canadian Pacific Airlines to Vancouver in 1948, which cost the city many jobs.

Disadvantaged provinces offered social services of inferior quality. When Newfoundland entered Confederation in 1949, two-thirds of its schools had only one room and lacked electricity and running water. Rural areas of richer provinces were scarcely better equipped. In Quebec, the wages of primary school teachers, often barely $600 a year, did little to attract talented personnel into the teaching profession. Throughout Canada, the underprivileged, whether unemployed or sick, handicapped or elderly, could not count on the array of social welfare benefits.

Mrs. Hawkins of Ottawa doing the washing with a traditional labour-intensive wringer washer, 1947. Today young people may have heard the expression "through the wringer" but do not know its origin. Hawkins is putting her laundry through the wringer in order to squeeze out the excess water. Modern automatic washers were as yet rarely seen in Canadian homes.

Source: Library and Archives Canada/PA-115254.

A HISTORICAL PORTRAIT

Betty and Ruby

At the conclusion of World War II, many working women left the workforce and became homemakers for their bread-winner husbands and full-time mothers for their children. The gendered division of labour seemed normal and natural. The happiest women were supposedly those whose husbands were able to purchase a modest bungalow on a separate lot in one of the dozens of suburbs that sprang up around Canada's cities in the 1950s. Their husbands went to work each day while the children went to school, leaving the women to use their new appliances to clean the home, bake, and tend to the flower gardens. They now had the leisure time to shop, socialize with other women in the neighbourhood, and undertake hobbies. These myths of suburban bliss, however, and their portraits of the con-tented suburban woman, are now under scrutiny by historians.

Betty's husband bought a bungalow in Cooksville, Ontario, a west Toronto suburb. Betty, a white Anglo-Saxon woman, who had a B.A. in music and had worked until her marriage, now settled in as a full-time homemaker. Some modern appliances made her work easier. In 1950, she already had an automatic washing machine. Historian Joy Parr showed that, in this regard, Betty, an American immi-grant, was not typical of her Canadian neighbours, the majority of whom used labour-intensive wringer washers until the mid-1960s. Such washers cost much less, they consumed far less water, and they enabled users to assert more control over the washing process; the wringers, however, did pose some dangers to chil-dren's hands.[1]

Betty's husband, Dick, commuted to work in downtown Toronto. He did not have a job, he had a "vocation." The distinction signified that Dick viewed his work as socially important and that he had to devote virtually all his time to it. Betty was thus often home alone with the chil-dren because Dick was away on business. She was convinced that she was doing what was expected of her. "A woman's place is in the home," she repeated. Dick agreed. He was sure that women working outside the home were a cause of divorce and of juvenile delinquency.

One day Betty decided to begin giving piano lessons at home. Perhaps she merely wanted some extra spending money of her own; perhaps she felt that her musical talents were being wasted; perhaps she was simply bored and lonely. Earnings from the job were modest; indeed, Dick often belittled his wife's efforts. At the same time he did not hesi-tate, over Betty's protests, to delve into the piano money box when he needed some spare change.

Ruby was another Ontario homemaker in the 1950s. Her sister, Edna Staebler, edited the letters that Ruby wrote to mem-bers of her family. Ruby worried about her appearance—she constantly complained about being overweight and not being able to buy nice clothes. She talked a lot about her children, which, of course, were expected, along with her husband, to be the focus of her existence. She also got a job outside the home. In a letter to sister Kay, she expounded on her decision.

I'm so thrilled and so nervous I don't know what to do. I won't sleep a wink tonight I'll bet. You know I've been talking about getting a job for so long because Fred wasn't earning enough and I guess he got sick of hearing about it.... I finally got up enough nerve to go down to the employment office to see what they could do for me.... I'm to go to Musser's store on Monday afternoon and start selling gloves. I'm so scared. I'll have to make change and fit people and be on my feet all those hours—and what will Fred say when he comes home tonite and I tell him?

Gosh, why did I do it? I could be so comfortable here just watching TV and working on my rug and I wouldn't need many clothes.... If I

work ... I'll always be in a rush with my housework and have to make dinner at noon. And I won't be home when the kids get here from school.... [But] it would be good training. And I could use the extra money for so many things we need around here....[2]

The stories of Betty and Ruby were common in the immediate postwar period, and they highlight the gendered realities of the household in suburban Canada. Idealized versions of their lives were portrayed in the American sitcoms of the era, such as *I Love Lucy* and *My Three Sons*. "Home dreams" did not fully meet the aspirations of all Canadian women after 1945, as historian Veronica Strong-Boag concluded.[3]

---

1   Joy Parr, *Domestic Goods: The Material, the Moral, and the Economic in the Postwar Years* (Toronto: University of Toronto Press, 1999), Chapter 10.

2   Edna Staebler, ed., *Haven't Any News: Ruby's Letters from the Fifties* (Waterloo, ON: Wilfrid Laurier Press, 1995), p. 58.

3   Veronica Strong-Boag, "Home Dreams: Women and the Suburban Experiment in Canada, 1945–60," *Canadian Historical Review*, 72 (1991): 504.

Canada had many second-class citizens. French Canadians suffered a linguistic disadvantage, even within Quebec. Women did not enjoy the same employment opportunities as men. Discrimination also afflicted Canada's First Nations peoples as well as African Canadians, recent immigrants, and Jews. In 1948, Pierre Berton, a young reporter for *Maclean's*, set out to investigate anti-Semitism. When he attempted to reserve a room at summer resorts north of Toronto, he had much more success using the name "Marshall" than when he identified himself as "Rosenberg." When he replied to a job advertisement as "Greenberg," he was frequently told that the vacancy had been filled. When he telephoned later and said his name was "Grimes," the job was still available. To help combat such discrimination through education, the newly founded Canadian Council of Christians and Jews instituted Brotherhood Week, a major program, in 1948. At the same time, various interest groups urged governments to take action to defend minority rights. In 1947, Saskatchewan became the first province in Canada to adopt a comprehensive bill of rights.

Society in this era emphasized family and reproductive heterosexuality. Psychologists warned that overprotective mothers and absent fathers risked provoking homosexual tendencies in their sons. Gays and lesbians faced social stigma as "perverts" and "sex deviates," as well as job discrimination. Immigration law prevented homosexuals from even entering Canada. In 1953, lesbian practices were criminalized for the first time. Gay men were often viewed as potential child molesters and, in the climate of the Cold War, as security risks to be purged from government service. By the mid-1960s, RCMP files reportedly contained the names of 7500 homosexuals.

Aparthcid – institutionalized racial segregation

Most homosexuals hid their sexual orientation, except perhaps from a few persons close to them. Yet gay and lesbian networks expanded in Canadian cities. Gay men met in bars, parks, and theatres; indeed newspapers reported frequent arrests in such places. Lesbians socialized at bars that women could frequent and at house parties.

The inequalities suffered by many Canadians engendered increasing discontent. For many Canadians, the war had been fought against such inequalities and to prevent abuse of minority groups. As historian Franca Iacovetta has shown, "many Canadians, including ordinary women and men, assumed the role of sympathetic gatekeepers in early Cold War Canada." They sought to help European refugees rebuild their shattered lives, and "guide the newcomers' adjustment to middle-class Canadian social, cultural, moral, and political norms." In doing so, however, they also "took efforts to contain or remove the newcomers' more threatening or undesirable ways and reshape their behaviour according to 'Canadian standards.'" These "newcomers" were grateful for the opportunities offered by their new country but they were not complacent. They were active agents in reshaping the contours of postwar Canada. For example, they helped transform the major immigrant cities, such as Toronto, Montreal, and Vancouver.[4]

The First Nations

The most glaring evidence of inequality in Canada was found in the condition of the country's Aboriginal peoples. As late as 1932, Diamond Jenness, a distinguished Canadian anthropologist, made the casual observation that "Doubtless all the tribes will disappear. Some will endure only a few years longer, others, like the Eskimos, may last several centuries."[5] The growing realization after World War II that the Aboriginal peoples were not "vanishing" gradually forced the dominant society to re-evaluate the role and position of the First Nations in Canada. The strategies of assimilation that shaped government policy had failed; society's desire to push these peoples away onto remote reserves until they disappeared had failed. Both government and society were suddenly facing a growing population with no plan as to what to do with it. Ottawa was left with a racialized population living in Third-World conditions under an apartheid system of reserves.

Starvation deaths of caribou Inuit

From the 1930s onward, a new group of politically conscious Aboriginal leaders made their voices heard. After making a substantial contribution to the fighting of both world wars, the First Nations believed that they deserved a say in the nation they had fought and died to defend. The end of World War II and the move toward decolonization highlighted Canada's treatment of its racial minorities, particularly its First Nations.

The war ended the isolation of many First Nations, Métis, and Inuit in Canada's North. Thousands of armed-service personnel and civilians established military airstrips and radio stations in the North. Small communities arose around these posts. Furthermore, in the late 1940s, with the collapse of the fur market and the unexpected failure to meet the migrating caribou herds, Inuit depended on the federal government for help. Ottawa responded by flying starving families to fur trading posts, where food supplies existed. The federal government also became active in the North in other ways. It brought in nurses and doctors to look after the Inuit refugees coming off the land, and it built hospitals and schools, as well as living quarters. As soon as these non-Native medical personnel, administrators, and teachers arrived, even on a semi-permanent basis, the federal government built permanent installations, such as power plants, water and sewer systems, and roads. The small non-Native bureaucracy that administered the social-assistance programs gained control over the Inuit.

For those Inuit who had tuberculosis or other communicable diseases, the government provided medical assistance, such as X-rays and immunization. Those patients requiring immediate hospitalization were sent south by plane or boat. By the 1950s, hundreds had been hospitalized, and the Department of Health and Welfare succeeded in lowering substantially the high mortality rate among the Inuit.

Ottawa now viewed its task as bringing the northern First Nations to a level comparable to that of the Inuit in the eastern Arctic. In the Mackenzie valley, the Indigenous peoples had not experienced the same economic collapse as the Inuit after World War II. Moreover, they already lived in semi-permanent camps or cabins around Hudson's Bay Company posts and Christian missions. Ottawa replaced the mission schools with public schools and provided the same medical services and administrative help as in the eastern Arctic. The government clashed, however, with local chiefs and elders, who up to this point had run their own affairs and resented this intrusion into their communities.

Canadians, in general, began a gradual re-evaluation of the Aboriginal peoples, for several reasons. First, social scientists discredited social Darwinism—the pseudoscientific race theory of the late nineteenth and early twentieth centuries that had held certain "races" to be inherently inferior. Second, many Canadians learned through the press and radio, and, in the 1950s, through television, of the impoverished health and living conditions of the northern First Nations and Inuit. Improvements in water and especially air transportation brought even the most remote regions of the Arctic into much closer contact with southern Canada, creating greater awareness of northern conditions. Third, the expansion of the natural-resources frontier took southern Canadians into Aboriginal territory (a situation that brought Aboriginal land claims throughout northern Canada to the public's attention). Fourth, the decolonization movement in Asia and Africa, and later the civil-rights movement in the United States in the 1950s and 1960s contributed to a new consciousness of injustices to minorities, including the Indigenous peoples. Most importantly, Aboriginal leaders made their opinions known. First Nations political leaders demanded recognition of their civil rights. Modern technology enabled the new Aboriginal leadership to communicate more easily. First Nations were set to force their way back onto the pages of Canadian history.

After 1945, the Indian Association of Alberta campaigned to have Parliament review the Indian Act. This single piece of legislation from 1876 epitomized Canada's historical mistreatment of its First Nations. Designed to control the Aboriginal population, it laid out a blueprint for assimilation. It also defined who and who was not "Indian." Whenever the federal government wanted to alter the design, it simply amended the Indian Act. As a result, the Act had been amended over 100 times to include some of the most draconian measures taken against the First Nations, including imposing the pass system and banning Indian rituals following the 1885 Rebellion.

The Indian Association of Alberta and other provincial Indian organizations participated in the hearings of the Joint Committee of the House of Commons and the Senate on the Indian Act, held from 1946 to 1948. Out of these deliberations came a new revision of the Indian Act in 1951. The new Act allowed band councils more authority. Women gained the vote in band council elections. Bans on the potlatch and the Sun Dance were lifted. Compulsory enfranchisement for status-Indian males was removed. Yet the underlying goal remained assimilation. It made it easier for individuals to give up their Indian status. It also included new provisions to allow the placement of First Nations children in integrated provincial schools. In addition, the new Act gave provincial authorities responsibility for the welfare of status-Indian children.

Prosperity and Trade

The federal government, buttressed with an impressive team of civil servants, had been preparing for postwar reconstruction almost since World War II began. This careful preparation paid off. After demobilization, the federal government worked to convert the Canadian economy back to

[handwritten note at top: Marshall Plan - US gave + 12B in economic assistance to help rebuild Western European economies after WWII.]

a free-enterprise system and to avoid a repetition of the severe recession that followed the Great War. To achieve this objective, C.D. Howe, Canada's manager of wartime production and now in charge of the country's postwar reconstruction, sold war plants for a fraction of their cost, on condition that they reopen for business. Officials in the department of finance and the Bank of Canada pushed their American and British counterparts for the creation of a multilateral trading world. Never again could the world return to protectionism. They advanced open markets and liberalized trade through such international organizations as the IMF (International Monetary Fund) and the GATT (General Agreement on Tariffs and Trade).

Canada's trade expanded, albeit unevenly. From the late 1940s, the country had a persistently negative trade balance as imports increased faster than exports. The trade balance would have been even worse if prices for Canada's forest products and minerals had not remained high. In real terms, Canada exported less in the mid-1950s than at the end of the war. Most Canadian-made manufactured products could not compete in international markets. Production costs remained high because Canadian companies manufactured a wide variety of products in small quantities, and they often relied heavily on imported American components.

As Britain sought to increase its purchases in Europe after the war, its imports from Canada declined. Canada moved to establish closer economic ties with the United States. Indeed, by 1947, as imports from the United States increased sharply and British regulations made it impossible for Canada to convert into dollars the pounds it earned in trade with Britain, Canada experienced a severe shortage of American dollars.

One solution was to negotiate a free trade agreement with the United States, in an attempt to boost exports. Free trade agreements with the United States, despite the long history of fearing American annexation, had long been the economic pot at the end of the rainbow for Canada. When the "Ottawa Men" indicated that the United States was prepared for such an agreement in 1948, it was assumed to be a done deal. But Prime Minister Mackenzie King, nearing retirement, was now reticent. He had played a major role throughout his long career in advancing Canadian autonomy within the Empire and then the Commonwealth. He advanced close ties with the United States through his relationship with President Roosevelt. But now, in the early years of the Cold War, with Britain clearly declining and the United States rising, the prime minister doubted Canada's future. He feared lest Canada had slipped too far into the American orbit, and so, at the last minute, he balked at the proposed free trade deal. "The long objective of the Americans," he wrote, "was to control this Continent. They would want to get Canada under their aegis."

A safer move was to try to convince the Americans to permit European countries receiving American aid through the Marshall Plan to use a portion of it to buy Canadian goods. The Americans agreed, thus resolving the dollar crisis. Ottawa also hoped that the GATT would come to its aid. This multilateral trade agreement, signed in Geneva in 1947, aimed at stimulating world trade by reducing tariffs. It included accords between Canada and its two principal trading partners, the United States and Britain.

An Investment Boom

Regardless of Canada's rejection of free trade, continental economic integration proceeded apace. Foreign capital poured into Canada, particularly during the Korean War from 1950 to 1953. The Americans sought Canada's resources, as production of some important minerals declined in the United States. Moreover, to gain access to a Canadian market protected by high tariffs, American multinational corporations established, especially in central Canada, branch plants that manufactured consumer products and industrial goods.

[handwritten note in left margin: branch plants]

Keynesian economics- a Stabalization policy; argues for ↑ gov't expenditures + lower taxes to raise demand + pull world output + employment out of their

The Royal Commission on Canada's Economic Prospects *Depression slump.*

Most Canadians assumed that, despite closer economic links with the United States, Canada could maintain its political sovereignty. Some provinces, in their quest for jobs, actively encouraged the entry of foreign capital by keeping taxes and labour costs down. Nevertheless, some observers worried about the "complacency" with which Canadians sold out the country's resources. The Royal Commission on Canada's Economic Prospects recommended in 1956 that Canada control foreign investment.

Advocates of North American integration argued that multinationals gave jobs to Canadians and helped the country's balance of payments by reducing imports. C.D. Howe protested in a speech in 1956 that "had it not been for the enterprise and capital from the United States … our development would have been slower, and some of the spectacular projects of which we are so proud … would still be in the future." He called the Royal Commission's preliminary report "bullshit."

Investment money (both Canadian and foreign) financed several important development projects. Pipelines carried oil and gas from Alberta to markets in Ontario and the United States. A railway nearly 600 kilometres long, running north from Sept-Îles, Quebec, opened up ore-rich Labrador. The construction of the St. Lawrence Seaway and the Trans-Canada Highway began.

Then the boom ended. By 1958, sluggish growth raised unemployment to nearly 10 percent. Automation eliminated jobs. When railways switched to diesel engines, for example, they needed fewer machinists, blacksmiths, and firemen. The high-valued Canadian dollar, which brought a premium when exchanged for an American dollar, damaged exports.

A Government of Efficient Administrators

In the late 1940s and early 1950s, voters wanted politicians to manage the country efficiently and achieve greater prosperity. They also called upon the state to protect them from the risks of unemployment, illness, and poverty. The generation that had suffered the Great Depression believed that only careful administration, planning, and control could avoid such a calamity from ever occurring again. Keynesian financing became the new fiscal orthodoxy. Pump-priming a sluggish economy through state-controlled investment displaced traditional theories of reduced spending and balanced budgets. Government and spending increased apace. The Liberal Party, known as the "Government Party" because it had successfully manoeuvred the middle of the political spectrum and held office for so long, fulfilled this need.

When William Lyon Mackenzie King finally retired in 1948, he had led the Liberal Party for nearly thirty years, and could boast of having been the longest-serving prime minister in the history, not just of Canada, but of the entire British Commonwealth. His political record was remarkable, particularly written against the backdrop of one of the most difficult times in the nation's history. The poet and intellectual F.R. Scott, who objected indignantly to King's being given credit for everything but putting the oil under Alberta, attributed the prime minister's success to his blandness: "He will be remembered wherever men honour ingenuity, ambiguity, inactivity, and political longevity."

Yet many observers of Canadian politics admired King for his accomplishments, even though they disliked him personally and found him uninspiring. It was difficult to argue with political success. Nevertheless, Mackenzie King had—like Macdonald and Laurier before him—held the country together effectively through difficult times.

The St. Laurent Governments

Louis St. Laurent, chosen as King's successor in 1948, was a former corporation lawyer from Quebec City and the second French-speaking (though fluently bilingual) prime minister.

Louis St. Laurent:
- King's Successor
- a former Corporation lawyer
- a Federalist who supported Conscription

Denounced in his home province during the war for his approval of conscription, he was a federalist. On constitutional questions he opposed the provincial autonomists in Quebec and elsewhere. In foreign affairs, he was less concerned with autonomy and more in favour of Canada playing an influential role on the world stage and being a dependable ally of the United States in the Cold War.

But the new prime minister followed his predecessor's accommodative approach, acting only after consensus was achieved. While the Progressive Conservatives suffered from their links with the "Bay Street interests," and the CCF suffered from their associations with socialism (particularly damaging during the Cold War), the Liberals continued to occupy the centre of the political spectrum and thus established the consensus apparently so necessary to govern Canada. Prosperity facilitated their task.

The transition from Mackenzie King to Louis St. Laurent demonstrated another example of the successful brand of politics offered by the Liberals. King's emphasis on consensus went beyond Canada's diverse regions and provinces to within the ranks of his own party. He surrounded himself with talented cabinet ministers and this team approach reaped dividends. Most importantly, the party remained united, and any serious divisions or factionalism were kept behind closed doors. The Liberals won the federal election of 1949 with 191 seats to the Progressive Conservatives' 41; the CCF won 13 and Social Credit 10. In 1953, the Liberals won 169 seats, the PCs 51, the CCF 23, and Social Credit 15. It was an era of Liberal domination.

Newfoundland Enters Confederation

In 1949, soon after the St. Laurent government took office, Newfoundland became Canada's tenth province. On April 1, the *St. John's Evening Telegram* observed, "Newfoundland slipped as quietly into Confederation last midnight as the grey mist which settled over the capital early this morning."

Confederation for Newfoundland, however, was preceded by months of bitter struggle, and the aftermath produced years, if not decades, of continuing bitterness. Joey Smallwood, leader of the confederationist forces, campaigned tirelessly, at times from an old seaplane equipped with loudspeakers, to prove that Newfoundlanders "would be better off in pocket, in stomach, and in health" within Canada. Reminiscent of the campaigns in the Maritimes in the 1860s, anti-confederationists denounced those who would "lure Newfoundland into the Canadian mousetrap." They called Smallwood a "Judas" who belittled Newfoundland's good name and lamented that at least Iscariot had the decency to hang himself.

The referendum held in June 1948 allowed Newfoundlanders to choose among three options: Confederation, favoured by both Britain and Canada; responsible government or dominion status, perhaps leading to economic union with the United States; and the unpopular existing system, by which a commission of British-appointed officials governed

Louis St. Laurent (left) and Prime Minister Mackenzie King (centre) at the national Liberal convention of 1948, at which St. Laurent was chosen to succeed King as Liberal leader and prime minister. In the background is a portrait of former Liberal leader and prime minister Wilfrid Laurier.

Source: William Lyon Mackenzie King Collection/Library and Archives Canada/C-23278.

Newfoundland. Responsible government won and Confederation placed second. But since no clear majority emerged, a second referendum was held in July in an atmosphere of sectarian bitterness.

Most Roman Catholics, fearing loss of their denominational schools, spoke against Confederation, while many Protestants favoured it. In general, the urban commercial classes opposed Confederation, fearing the competition of the big Canadian department stores (such as Eaton's) and the mail-order companies. The confederationists won narrowly this time, with a majority of 52 percent. Amid accusations of blackmail, bribery, and election manipulation, Newfoundlanders were clearly divided on the question of joining Canada. But a majority, however narrow, was viewed as a majority, and once the decision was made, there was no turning back. Canadians and Newfoundlanders now set about negotiating the final terms of union.

Historian David Alexander argued that the decline of the fishing economy, which fell victim to tumbling prices and oversupply, "led Newfoundlanders reluctantly into Confederation."[6] Poverty was endemic: in 1949, the island's citizens had incomes only one-third as high as those of Canadians. Death rates for diseases associated with poverty stood two to three times higher than Canadian rates. Canada's safety net of social programs looked inviting. Canada seemed to offer the path to modernity.

In addition, Britain clearly desired to quit Newfoundland. In the words of historian Peter Neary, Britain arranged its departure "with a hard logic and clinical precision she would not manage in other parts of her far-flung but now crumbling empire."[7] Yet Canada also wanted Newfoundland. During the war, federal civil servants and politicians had discovered the island's strategic and economic importance. Canadians also worried that the United States might seek to strengthen its ties with the island after using it to establish military bases during the war.

Newfoundland's entry into Canada proceeded rapidly. Immediately upon joining Confederation, family allowances and other federal social programs were ready to function. Income levels improved. Yet the federal government did little to favour the province's economic development, and as historian Raymond Blake observes, the province simply "shifted its dependence from London to Ottawa."[8]

Federal–Provincial Tensions

In the postwar era, the Liberal government's preoccupation with maintaining a buoyant economy had serious implications for Canadian federalism. Civil servants and politicians in Ottawa believed that the federal government should maintain, and even strengthen, the fiscal and legislative pre-eminence that it had acquired during the wartime emergency. Disadvantaged provinces had benefited financially. New Brunswick, for example, reaped substantial increases in its revenues when it ceded to Ottawa its right to collect income taxes. But several provinces objected to Ottawa's aggressive centralization. Nova Scotia premier Angus L. Macdonald complained that federal subsidies destroyed provincial independence and transformed the provinces into "mere annuitants of Ottawa." Ontario insisted on its right to formulate its

A Newfoundland woman votes in the referendum of 1948. Although Newfoundlanders in this referendum opted for responsible government over union with Canada, the indecisive results forced a second referendum, which the confederationists won. On March 31, 1949, Newfoundland joined Confederation as Canada's tenth province.

Source: C.F. Marshall/Centre for Newfoundland Studies, Queen Elizabeth II Library, Memorial University of Newfoundland.

own economic priorities and programs. In Quebec, Maurice Duplessis, now back in government, feuded with Ottawa over federal tax and spending policies. The province's Royal Commission of Inquiry on Constitutional Problems (the Tremblay Commission) called in 1954 for an end to federal "imperialism" and a return to "true federalism."

Toward a Welfare State

The centralization of Canada's federal structure was also driven by the nation's path toward the welfare state. The Depression and wars left the populace feeling vulnerable; Canadians were willing to embrace an even more interventionist state. The populace was particularly critical of the old-age pensions program instituted by Ottawa in 1927 by which the elderly had to prove need in order to benefit. It was felt that the means test stigmatized the poor and penalized those who had saved. In 1951, after all the provinces had agreed to the requisite constitutional amendment, federal legislation authorized sending old-age-security cheques in the amount of $40 a month to all Canadians over the age of 70 and to needy Canadians over 65. Family allowances, also a universal program covering all children, now took second place. For the government, the family allowances, instituted in 1944, had served their purpose: workers' wages increased, there was no postwar depression, and the CCF no longer posed a threat. The government's failure to increase the value of the allowances meant that, with higher living costs because of inflation, their impact on family budgets diminished.

The government also adopted other measures concerning health and welfare. In 1948, Ottawa enacted the National Health Program, which provided for federal grants to each province in the fields of hygiene and health. Unemployment insurance coverage was extended to new categories of workers such as Atlantic fishers. In 1956, after a national publicity campaign by the Canadian Welfare Council, Parliament enacted the Unemployment Assistance Act, a shared-cost program designed to assist employable persons on welfare. Provinces also spent significantly more on welfare as case numbers increased. Yet such aid failed to take into account increased housing and clothing costs. For historian James Struthers, in Ontario "the poor went hungry to pay the rent."[9]

Most Canadians who became ill in the 1950s knew the prohibitive cost of health care. One Montreal businessman, after paying the bills resulting from his wife's serious illness, commented wryly: "There are two things that can send you to the poorhouse: hospital bills and borrowing from loan sharks. And 90 percent of the borrowing from loan sharks is to pay hospital bills!" Many Canadians tried to cover eventual health costs at least partially by participating in Blue Cross or other doctor-sponsored insurance plans, but at least half of Canadians had no direct coverage for medical care.

Calls for a national health plan were heard increasingly. Anxious doctors warned that such a plan would rob them of their independence and interfere with the intimate doctor–patient relationship. They did not, however, oppose a plan that would cover only hospital care. Several provincial premiers, especially those from the western provinces, most of which had already established hospital insurance, pressured Ottawa into acting. Finally, in 1957, Parliament adopted the Hospital Insurance and Diagnostic Services Act, which provided federal financial assistance to provinces willing to set up a publicly administered hospital-insurance program with universal coverage.

The Golden Age of Canadian Diplomacy

After 1945, Canada had to adapt to a new world order. The geopolitical situation in the world had changed. To offset growing American power, particularly in the context of the Cold War and the expectation that Canada would be a dependable ally against communism, the nation worked to build strong multilateral institutions. Canada looked to use its growing influence internationally as a counterweight to American influence, while using this place on the world stage to offer its own voice.

Canada in the Cold War Era

Even before World War II was over, the lines of a new struggle were being drawn as the Allies jockeyed to divide Europe between East and West, communism and capitalism. In the words of British Prime Minister Winston Churchill, an "Iron Curtain" fell across the continent. Europe, indeed the world, was divided into two armed camps. The Soviet Union, so recently an ally, was now an enemy to be regarded with the utmost suspicion. At the Paris Peace Conference of 1946, Canada hoped to play a role in the European settlement commensurate with its contribution to the war effort. The country went virtually unnoticed.

As relations between the United States and the Soviet Union soured, Canadian officials feared that the often bellicose attitude of the United States would only make matters worse. In the view of external affairs official John Holmes, the American position was to refuse to negotiate with the Soviet "devil," while Canadians wanted only to make him behave.[10]

The reality of the Cold War came to Canada suddenly and unexpectedly. On September 5, 1945, Igor Gouzenko, a cipher clerk at the Soviet embassy in Ottawa, defected. Carrying 109 stolen top-secret documents, Gouzenko arrived at the offices of the RCMP late on a Friday afternoon. The officers on duty did not believe his story. Now panicking, certain he was being followed, and fearing for the lives of him and his family, Gouzenko went to the *Ottawa Journal* newspaper, which was also not interested. He then went to the Department of Justice, where he could find no one to help him. He returned to his apartment and hid his family in the apartment across the hall for the night. Gouzenko watched through the keyhole as a group of Soviet agents broke into his apartment. They left only when confronted by Ottawa police. When Gouzenko finally convinced the RCMP to listen, his disclosures sent shockwaves across the Western world. That a Soviet espionage network could exist in "sleepy little Ottawa" convinced governments that the Red Menace could be anywhere. Gouzenko's evidence resulted in the conviction of 18 Canadians, including Fred Rose, the only communist ever elected as a member of Parliament.

The intensification of the Cold War led Canada into ever-closer relations with the United States. Britain's own decline left Canada little choice. "London's impotence," historian Jack Granatstein argued, compelled Canadian governments to seek "shelter within Uncle Sam's all-encompassing embrace."[11] Mackenzie King, always the autonomist, warned of American influence. He tried to steer Canadian policy away in his last years, but his influence was waning. King was replaced by a new generation of politicians and diplomats who were "Cold Warriors," including Louis St. Laurent, Lester Pearson, Norman Robertson, and Brooke Claxton.

Fears of the Soviet Union and paranoia of communism also led to increased police surveillance of Canadians deemed sympathetic to left-wing causes in general. For example, the RCMP surveilled Tommy Douglas, the Saskatchewan politician who later became leader of the federal New Democratic Party, for thirty years. Some people were censored for their ideological beliefs or unjustly dismissed from their jobs because they were labelled subversives.

The North Atlantic Treaty Organization

As people questioned whether the United Nations could assure world peace through collective security, the Canadian government pushed for an Atlantic alliance for mutual self-defence. The Americans and the British showed interest in the proposal. By December 1948, work began on a draft treaty to form the North Atlantic Treaty Organization (NATO). The United States envisaged

The Commonwealth- 53 countries, incl.CAN, that were once part of the British Empire

a purely military pact, but Canada sought cooperation in other sectors that might eventually unite the Atlantic nations into a closely knit community. Canada fought for the inclusion in the draft treaty of an article indicating general economic and social aims.

Canada's interest was clear. Links with Western Europe would strengthen Canada in its relationship with the militarily dominant Americans. The so-called "Canadian article" did get into the treaty, in spite of the adamant opposition of the Americans to this product of "typical Canadian moralizing." In March 1949, the House of Commons approved the treaty, and on April 4, NATO came into existence. Rising East–West tensions, especially the outbreak of war in Korea in 1950, turned NATO into an almost exclusively military alliance, soon placed under the American nuclear umbrella. Even so, as historian David Bercuson has shown, Canada did indeed make a significant difference to NATO in the alliance's early years "in both the quantity and the quality of its military contribution."[12] Then, as defence spending fell and Canada's priorities became continental, its influence declined.

New Interest in the North

As had long been the case, Canadian interest in the remote North waxed and waned depending on the region's practical use and importance. With the development of the Cold War in the late 1940s, the North became an area of vital strategic interest to both Canada and the United States. Acting together, the two countries worked to provide a warning system in the event of a Soviet nuclear attack on Canadian and American cities. A chain of more than 40 Distant Early Warning (DEW) radar stations was built in the 1950s across the Arctic, from Alaska to Baffin Island. The DEW Line allowed for four to six hours' warning of a manned Soviet bomber attack across the North Pole. Begun in 1954 and completed in 1957, the system remained in full operation for nearly a decade, until intercontinental ballistic missiles largely replaced the bomber threat. With the warning time now calculated in minutes, the DEW Line lost much of its effectiveness. In 1957, Canada and the United States signed the North American Air Defence Agreement (NORAD), which formally coordinated the two countries' air forces. NORAD, however, was clearly under American military command, and in times of crisis, it was questionable how much autonomy Canada would have, even over its own military forces.

The DEW Line and other American proposals revived fears about Canada's sovereignty in the Arctic. Recognizing the surest grounds for Canada's claim would be effective occupation, the federal government in 1953 arranged to relocate about ten Inuit families from northern Quebec and Baffin Island nearly 2000 kilometres away, to Cornwallis and Ellesmere islands in the high Arctic. The migrants lost contact with their communities and, the government's promises aside, found themselves in a much more inhospitable environment than the one they had left behind.

The Commonwealth

In keeping with its desire to balance closer links to the United States with an increased international participation, Canada looked with hope to the evolving British Commonwealth of Nations. Mackenzie King, however, maintained the position he had held throughout the 1920s and opposed the idea of a uniform Commonwealth foreign policy. Moreover, the Commonwealth was changing, with the addition of new members such as India, Pakistan, and Sri Lanka (then Ceylon). In the era of decolonization, the Commonwealth would no longer be made up of only the white self-governing dominions. Canada helped move the Commonwealth in directions that made it an acceptable organization for these new states. It also supported and contributed to the Colombo Plan, which was set up at a meeting of Commonwealth foreign ministers in 1950 to promote economic development in Commonwealth countries in Asia.

The Quest for Middle-Power Status

Canada searched for its own voice on the world stage. The nation viewed itself as a rising middle power and looked to maintain its role as mediator, performed so effectively between Britain and the United States during the war. Other nations, however, continued to view Canada as a Western ally and, in many cases, a puppet of either Britain or the Americans. In 1950, when communist North Korea invaded capitalist South Korea in an attempt to reunite the country, and the United Nations Security Council (which the Soviet Union was boycotting) denounced this act of aggression, Canada contributed a brigade to fight alongside mostly American troops in the name of collective security. Canada ultimately sent 26,000 troops and eight destroyers to the 1950–53 Korean War. Although it was officially a UN conflict, it was in reality an American war.

Five hundred Canadians lost their lives in the fighting. As the war moved toward a stalemate, Lester Pearson, then Canada's secretary of state for external affairs, helped to restrain the "overzealous" Americans from actions that risked bringing China and the Soviet Union into the war. But at the same time, as historian John Price has shown, Pearson proved himself to be a "cold warrior par excellence"[13] in his pragmatic support for the pro-American regime in South Korea. Then, in 1954, Canada agreed, with considerable apprehension, to join Poland and India in a three-country International Control Commission to supervise the peace in Indochina where France, the occupying colonial power, had just been defeated by the Vietnamese, who were fighting for their independence.

Finally, in 1956, came what many considered to be Canada's greatest contribution internationally. In October, despite strong American opposition, Israel, together with Britain and France, invaded Egypt in response to Egypt's nationalization of the Suez Canal. The Americans viewed the aggressiveness of Britain and France as consistent with their imperial pasts. Canada was caught in a quandary: Would the nation support its old mother country or its new global superpower neighbour? Wary of the dangerous split developing in the Western alliance, Lester Pearson, a Liberal diplomat turned politician, proposed the creation of a multinational United Nations emergency peacekeeping force in the region. He lobbied to have the plan accepted by the General Assembly. For his successful efforts, he won the Nobel Peace Prize in 1957. According to biographer John English, Pearson's initiative "strengthened the United Nations, moderated the tensions between Washington and London, and helped to maintain both the Commonwealth and NATO."[14] The crisis was averted, and Canada's reputation as a mediator and a peacekeeper was secured.

Canadian members of the United Nations Emergency Force (UNEF) patrol the border between Egypt and Israel. In addition to Lester Pearson's initiatives in the United Nations, the Canadian military played a major logistical role during the deployment of UNEF.

Source: Canada Department of National Defence/Library and Archives Canada/PA-122737.

The Winds of Political Change

By the mid-1950s, the Liberals had held power in Ottawa since 1935. When Canadians went to the polls in 1957 to select a government, another Liberal victory seemed likely. Most political observers were shocked when the Progressive Conservatives, under their new leader, John Diefenbaker, won a narrow victory with 112 seats and 38.5 percent of the vote. The Liberals under St. Laurent won 105 seats and 40.5 percent of the vote. Stunned Liberals, as cabinet minister J.W. Pickersgill later put it, wondered why they had to suffer a Tory government once in every generation. The CCF, which had restated its original aims in less revolutionary fashion in its Winnipeg Declaration of Principles in 1956, felt bitterly disappointed over its failure to arrest its decline in popularity. It won 25 seats in the federal election of 1957 while Social Credit won 19.

Although the Liberals boasted during the election campaign that voters would not "shoot Santa Claus," not all Canadians were prosperous in 1957. Residents of the Prairies and the Maritimes complained of their regions' underdevelopment. Many senior citizens endorsed Conservative assertions that old-age pensions not protected against inflation were scandalously insufficient. Other voters agreed with Diefenbaker's denunciations of the "dictatorial" tactics employed by the Liberals during the pipeline debate in 1956. The government wanted to make an important loan to Trans-Canada Pipe Lines, a private company formed by American and Canadian business interests, to assist in building the western section of a pipeline to carry Alberta gas to central Canadian markets. The debate was reminiscent of the decision to build the transcontinental railway in the 1870s. The Progressive Conservative and CCF parties united to oppose the deal on the basis of American involvement, but their voices were quickly muted. In a hurry and running against a deadline, Minister of Trade and Commerce C.D. Howe pushed the bill through the House of Commons, unamended, by imposing closure and cutting off debate at each stage. To an electorate already ready for a change, the arrogance and complacency of the Liberals was too much.

The "Diefenbaker Party"

The Progressive Conservatives found an unlikely hero to play David against the Liberal Goliath. John Diefenbaker was a small-town lawyer from Saskatchewan. Prior to finally winning the leadership of the federal Conservatives, he had established one of the most losing records in

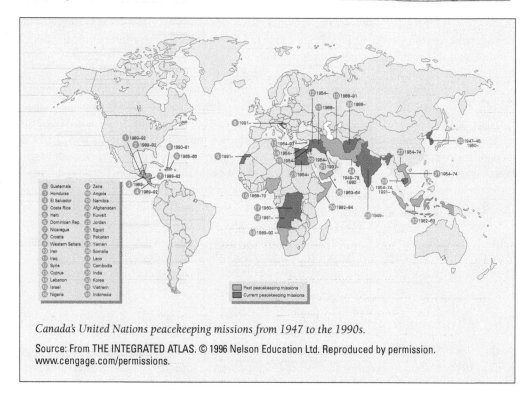

Canada's United Nations peacekeeping missions from 1947 to the 1990s.

Source: From THE INTEGRATED ATLAS. © 1996 Nelson Education Ltd. Reproduced by permission. www.cengage.com/permissions.

Canadian politics. Diefenbaker lost bids to become the mayor of Prince Albert, Saskatchewan, the provincial and the federal representative of the area, as well as the leadership of the provincial and federal Progressive Conservatives. As the party's new leader in 1956, he sought to change the image of the Tories. He wrested control of the party from the Toronto business elite, the "Bay Street Boys." His oratorical talents outshone anything the Liberals could muster. At Massey Hall in April 1957, the "modern-day Jeremiah" proclaimed his message: "This party ... has an appointment today with destiny, to plan and to build for a greater Canada ... one Canada, with equality of opportunity for every citizen and equality for every province." Diefenbaker appeared as the ideal leader to defeat the old, tired, arrogant, and complacent Liberals.

The new Liberal leader, Lester Pearson, was more comfortable dealing with international issues than domestic politics. "Mike," as he preferred to be called, with his academic overtones and signature bow tie, was no match in parliamentary debate with the fiery Diefenbaker. When Pearson suggested that the surprising election results were a mistake and simply a gesture by Canadians to teach the Liberals a lesson, and that the Progressive Conservatives should now move aside and allow the "natural" governing party in Canada to retake control, Diefenbaker seized his opportunity. The new government barely had time to adopt a few popular measures designed to assist the unemployed, Prairie farmers, and Maritimers before the new prime minister, anxious to form a majority government, called another election in March 1958.

In the 1958 election campaign, Diefenbaker presented his "vision of opportunity" for Canada, a vision based on the development of resources and of the North. Liberal newspapers like the *Toronto Star* mocked the prime minister's program as "humbug and flapdoodle served up with an evangelistic flourish." Pearson attempted to brush off what he termed the "oracular fervour and circus parades." The result was a Diefenbaker landslide, with the Progressive Conservatives winning the greatest majority in Canadian electoral history to that time: 208 of the 265 seats in the House of Commons, including 50 seats from Quebec, and 54 percent of the vote. If the Liberals were scolded by the electorate for their arrogance in 1957, they received a proper spanking in 1958. They won only 48 seats, while the CCF was reduced to 8 and Social Credit disappeared.

From the start, however, the Conservatives had difficulty governing. So long had they sat in the political wilderness that all the new ministers lacked experience. In many cases, they questioned the loyalty of civil servants accustomed to a close working relationship with Liberal politicians. The Senate, not surprisingly, was filled with Liberal appointees. For most Quebec Tory MPs, the triumph of 1958 was their first—and last—electoral victory. Their unilingual leader from Saskatchewan knew little about Quebec and entrusted no senior cabinet portfolios to the province. As a result, Diefenbaker's success in Quebec was more a reaction against the Liberals than a sign of strong support for the Conservatives.

The situation was made worse by Diefenbaker's personality and leadership style. His paranoia of Liberal influence caused him to see conspiracies taking shape all around. Typical of other Tory leaders, Diefenbaker was not a team player, preferring to keep power in his own hands. His vision of northern development, of "opening Canada

A campaign poster. John Diefenbaker with his hero, Sir John A. Macdonald.

Source: Diefenbaker Centre poster collection, Diefenbaker Centre, University of Saskatchewan.

Populism - a belief in the power of regular people + their right to have control over their govt rather than a small group of political insiders / wealthy elites

to its polar reaches," did not capture the imagination of southern Canadians. Liberals mocked what they called a program of "roads from igloo to igloo." Diefenbaker did, however, remain highly popular in the West. He was a charismatic stump speaker and a dangerous opponent in Parliament. As "Saskatchewan's native son," his populist approach and willingness to stand up to the vested interests in his party, the nation, and even on the world stage, gained him popularity.

The Conservative government's major problem in 1958, however, was the country's deteriorating economic situation. Ottawa responded to rising unemployment with winter works programs, subsidies, and welfare benefits for seasonal workers. As expenses increased and government receipts declined, budgetary deficits grew and the business community complained of financial mismanagement. Once again, the Conservatives had finally won power only to be assailed by an economic recession. Lady Luck, it seemed, remained at the beck and call of the Liberals.

Labour Relations in Times of Prosperity

Postwar economic growth gave a powerful boost to the unions. In 1950, union membership passed the 1 million mark, or 30 percent of the workforce. "Elite" unions in sectors such as heavy manufacturing enjoyed strong bargaining power and succeeded in negotiating high wages. They had frequent recourse to strikes, particularly in the late 1940s. In 1946, for example, one worker in six went on strike, resulting in a total loss of 4.5 million workdays. These strikes aimed at forcing employers to recognize union rights, improve working conditions, and increase salaries. In retaliation, companies frequently hired strikebreakers, and violent confrontations sometimes ensued. Provincial governments supported employers directly through anti-union legislation and the use of the police and the courts.

Industrial Unrest

Although most workers signed contracts without going on strike, and although sickness resulted in far more loss of work time than did strike activity, certain sensational confrontations earned a place in the annals of Canadian working-class history. In one dramatic encounter in 1946, Steel Company of Canada (Stelco) management used airplanes and boats to avoid picket lines and to transport food and supplies to strikebreakers inside its plant in Hamilton, Ontario. In the same year, textile workers, many of them women, struck in Valleyfield, Quebec. Led by Madeleine Parent and Kent Rowley, the strikers obtained recognition for their union only after bloody skirmishes with police. Parent was then convicted of seditious conspiracy and had to wait until 1954 before being acquitted after a new trial.

In 1947, Nova Scotia fishers went on strike against National Sea Products, the monopoly conglomerate, in an attempt to gain union recognition. The company waged a fierce anti-labour campaign and, with assistance from the courts and the provincial government, broke the strike. A year later, the Prince Edward Island government seized a Canada Packers plant during a strike, hired non-union labour, and reopened the plant. It then adopted legislation prohibiting labour affiliation with any union organization outside the province.

In 1949, 5000 Quebec asbestos workers struck for five months to improve wages and working and health conditions. The Duplessis government defended the companies, decertified the union, and sent in special police squads. Some members of the clergy, including Archbishop Joseph Charbonneau of Montreal, defied the government and sided openly with the strikers, one of whose supporters was a young Montreal lawyer, Pierre Elliott Trudeau. Although the settlement gave workers no significant material gains, the strike itself took on symbolic value: Quebec sociologist Jean-Charles Falardeau even viewed it as a "quasi-revolution."[15]

Conflict continued into the 1950s—a period of consolidation for labour, now that union recognition was more generally assured. Major strikes occurred among loggers, fishers, government employees, and longshoremen in British Columbia; building-trades workers in Halifax

CCL – for 16 years the CCL was in the forefront of CAN union activity + organization

and Vancouver; gold miners in Ontario and Quebec; and automobile workers and employees of the International Nickel Company (Inco) in Ontario. In August 1950, 130,000 employees of Canada's two major railways left their jobs, but the government, declaring that "the country cannot afford a railway strike," ordered the workers back. Textile workers at Louiseville, Quebec, went out for ten months in 1952, while copper workers at Murdochville, Quebec, struck for seven months in 1957 in a violent but vain confrontation. In 1959, Newfoundland loggers, members of the International Woodworkers of America (IWA), went on strike. They wanted better wages, a shorter workday, and camp amenities. Violence broke out when the company recruited fishers to replace strikers. In one skirmish, a policeman suffered fatal injuries. In an effort to break the IWA, Premier Joseph Smallwood set up a union and had the legislature outlaw the IWA in the province. The federal government refused to send the RCMP reinforcements that Smallwood demanded, but the strike nonetheless failed.

Workers versus Workers

Economic prosperity worked to the benefit of workers and unions, but the atmosphere of the Cold War proved a detriment. Struggles within unions at times were particularly bitter as conservative members were pitted against the more radical. These struggles had long taken place, but the anti-communist and paranoid atmosphere made it easy and convenient to condemn the "pinkos." On the left, communists and democratic socialists battled each other.

Anti-communists in the Canadian Congress of Labour (CCL) insisted that, to fight the bosses, "we must get rid of the communists." The CCL thus manoeuvred to oust certain affiliate unions whose executives it charged with being "complete vassals of uncle Joe Stalin." The communist-led Canadian Seamen's Union (CSU) was crushed when the Canadian and American governments combined with the shippers and Trades and Labor Congress (TLC) officers to replace the CSU with the rival Seafarers' International Union (SIU). After a judicial inquiry later found the SIU guilty of racketeering and a host of other improper practices, Ottawa placed the union under a government trusteeship. Its director, Hal Banks, who had boasted of his ambition to control "everything that floats," forfeited bail and fled to the United States. Some Canadian unionists thought that the battle against communists merely permitted American unions to reinforce their hold in Canada. According to historian Irving Abella, the communist purge did little to strengthen the union movement and, in hindsight, was probably "neither necessary nor wise."[16]

Increased labour unity came in 1956, when the TLC and the CCL formed the Canadian Labour Congress (CLC). This union followed the merger in 1955 of the American labour congresses: the AFL and the CIO. The costly raids by TLC and CCL unions on each other, with no total gain in membership, then ended. Claude Jodoin, a well-known Quebec labour leader and president of the TLC, became president of the new million-member CLC. Many of the CLC unions were affiliated with the American AFL–CIO, and they remained subject to American influence. Most Canadian workers, who were employed by American branch companies, found nothing unusual in belonging to American-dominated unions. This, however, was one of the reasons that the Quebec-based CTCC refused to join the CLC.

Although unions made major gains in the postwar period, much work remained. Collective agreements generally left managers with complete authority over the work process on the shop floor. Union organizers had yet to reach vast numbers of workers, especially in the service sector. An attempt to unionize the 12,000 mainly female employees of Eaton's, Canada's largest department store and third-largest employer, failed. The increasing bureaucratization of the union movement, fostered by the "excessively legalistic and rigid framework" that came to characterize industrial relations, tended to exclude the rank and file from decisions.[17] Labour legislation in several provinces was unsympathetic to unions. Automation made job security an increasingly serious issue. Worker safety also caused concern: accidents on the job caused nearly 5 million injuries and more than

12,500 deaths between 1945 and 1959. When fire killed 5 Italian labourers laying a water main in the Hogg's Hollow district of Toronto, the coroner denounced management's "callous attitude" toward worker safety and noted that "almost all the safety regulations … were violated at one time or another, and many of the regulations were violated continuously."

The Status of Women

After 1945, society expected women to abandon the paid labour force and return to the domestic sphere. The state certainly promoted this move, and the social security measures adopted by the federal government reinforced the model of the male breadwinner and the nuclear family. Churches stressed family life as a means of countering juvenile delinquency, illegitimate births, and other social ills.

Women who continued in paid employment outside the home still had to perform all the domestic and family chores. As one female journalist explained, "A man whittles himself down to less of a man by consistently performing women's work." Cultural stereotypes reinforced the traditional role of women: school textbooks depicted men in interesting careers while portraying women as staying at home, cooking meals, and scolding children. Women's magazines such as *Chatelaine* and the *Canadian Home Journal* contained many articles on sewing, homemaking, gardening, and fashion, but very few on such areas under male control as politics or business. Women were paternalistically excluded from sports judged unsuitable for them. Public recreation programs funded hockey and softball far more generously than "activities for women" such as arts and crafts. In the conservative atmosphere of the postwar era and the Cold War, it seemed that women, as had occurred after World War I, had taken "one step forward, two steps back."

Women in the Workforce

Slowly, however, female participation in the workforce increased. The prosperity opened up new opportunities, rather than creating a situation in which women had to leave to make way for returning veterans. In 1951, one paid worker in four was a woman, usually unmarried. During the 1950s the proportion of married women workers also increased, as mothers rejoined the workforce after their youngest children enrolled in school. Most worked as secretaries, nurses, sales personnel, and clerks. As late as 1960, only a handful of women were professionals; they accounted for just 7 percent of doctors, 3 percent of lawyers, and a mere 1 percent of engineers.

For female workers, inequality was everywhere. Men generally received higher wages for performing the same tasks. This so-called "wage differential" was justified by men's role as family breadwinners. Universities paid female professors less than male professors of the same rank and experience. Nor did women have equal opportunity for promotions, even in female-dominated sectors such as teaching. Across Canada, men had a far greater chance of becoming school principals. Minimum wage rates, fixed by governments, were usually lower for women than for men. Wage parity (equal pay for performing the same task) was only beginning to be an issue when Ontario's Female Employees Fair Remuneration Act was passed in 1951. Although the legislation had obvious political value, historian Shirley Tillotson argued that it had little tangible effect; the opposition CCF Status of Women Committee called it "a toothless ghost of a real equal pay bill."[18]

Churches such as the United Church of Canada, which accepted women as ministers, nevertheless placed numerous obstacles in the paths of those seeking ordination. United Church moderator James Mutchmor gave Lois Wilson, a minister's wife, reasons for objecting to her ordination: Who would "wear the pants" in the family? Who would have priority in the use of the car? Wilson succeeded in gaining ordination because prominent men supported her. She later became the United Church's first female moderator.

Only a few women held positions of influence in business or politics in the 1950s. Between 1930 and 1960, the federal government named only 7 women senators, while more than 250 men received the lifetime appointment. Few women ran in elections. Those who did generally ran as their party's sacrificial lambs in impossible races. Only in 1957 did a prime minister, John Diefenbaker, appoint a woman to a federal cabinet post—Ellen Fairclough, from Hamilton, Ontario. Fully aware of widespread discriminatory behaviour against women, Fairclough was determined not to let herself be co-opted as an "honorary man." Many observers saw this nomination as only a modest beginning. Charlotte Whitton, Ottawa's feisty mayor, predicted that women were growing so impatient with "the man-made messes of a man-made world" that they would soon insist on a much larger voice in public affairs.

WHERE HISTORIANS DISAGREE

Women and Unions in Postwar Canada

By 1964, 30 percent of hired workers were women, employed mainly in non-unionized sectors of activity, such as clerical and domestic work. Of the barely 16 percent of union members who were women, most worked in industry. What did unionized women seek to obtain from their unions? Did they see themselves simply as workers who, like the men, wanted to improve wages and working conditions? Or did they see themselves primarily as women with objectives that were different from, and at times contradictory to, those of men? And how did men react to the entry of women into "their" workplace?

Labour historians, preoccupied with labour's battles against employers, did not at first ask these questions, particularly as they pertain to the postwar years. Bryan Palmer described the rise of the communist-led United Electrical, Radio and Machine Workers' Union (UE), whose expansion was fostered by enormous consumer demand for electrical products. The union waged a number of bitter strikes in 1946. Although Palmer noted that a significant part of the UE's membership was female (25 percent by 1954), he did not view their struggle as anything other than a workers' struggle against the bosses.[1]

Craig Heron stated that industrial unions of these years had difficulty eliminating the segregation of women into low-wage job ghettos, and then commented, revealingly, that "even if the male unionists' pride had allowed more equity, most men still assumed that women should be at home, supported by a male wage."[2]

In her study of working women in Peterborough, Ontario, Joan Sangster showed how unions and labour disputes have been arenas of both gender conflict and class solidarity.[3] Looking at the UE, she noted that union leadership endorsed gender equality, partly in order to gain women workers' support for the UE's struggle against a rival union. The UE also tried to focus on grievances that could unite men and women, such as more equal pay rates, because men feared the substitution of female for male labour. On other issues, notably the contentious question of merging male and female seniority lists, the union equivocated. Sangster noted also how difficult it was for women to become involved in union activities. While the union itself gave pre-eminence to class rather than to gender, separate organizations for women within unions eventually provided an innovative means for women to demand better working conditions and wages.

Julie Guard also studied the experience of women within the UE. Like Sangster, she showed that the union was interested primarily in the class struggle, not in women's rights. It made slow progress in endorsing equal pay for women, in spite of women's attempts to prove that low pay for women put a brake on male wages. She too noted that few women participated in union leadership, a fact that men attributed to personal choice rather than to the "inherent gender bias of union structure and culture."[4]

Joy Parr examined the effect of gender on strike action against a textile company in Paris, Ontario, in 1949. About one-half of the workers were women and, although women were less inclined to join the union than were men, female militancy on the picket line was considerable. Yet, whereas the union itself whipped up male strikers' militancy, female militancy was "forged and sustained in family and neighbourhood relationships" rather than through union organization.[5]

In her study of the United Auto Workers in Canada, Pam Sugiman argued that the traditional view of the UAW as a progressive union that gave vocal support to women's rights in society was only partly true; the UAW also showed persistent gender bias and allowed blatant inequalities to persist in the working environment.[6] Male union officials were reluctant to view the special concerns of female dues-paying members as legitimate union issues. In the immediate postwar years, women did not generally challenge gender ideologies, separate seniority lists, and large pay differentials. Even in the 1950s, women still did not "openly contest their subordination as a sex" although they did develop "a stronger self-identification as wage earners and as unionists."[7] Due to improving economic conditions, women became bolder and made use of grievance procedures to protest inadequate wages and to try to improve working conditions.

Gillian Creese studied the white-collar union at BC Hydro. Although women constituted nearly one-half of the union's membership in the 1950s, union leadership was increasingly dominated by men and contract negotiations represented male concerns and assumptions. Creese argued that the union did confront discrimination on an individual level, but that "systematic differentiation that resulted in better jobs and career prospects and higher pay for men was simply not recognized as a form of discrimination."[8] It was only in the late 1970s that a Women's Committee was formed and that many women (but not all) began to challenge masculine privilege and emphasized so-called "women's issues" such as sexual harassment, pay equity, and day care.

Were female unionists as militant as male unionists? Or did they follow the leadership of their husbands at home and their male co-workers? Robert Ventresca examined the behaviour of women workers, many of them Italian immigrants, in two industrial conflicts in Welland, Ontario. During the lengthy strike at the Lanark auto parts plant in 1964, some women did cross the picket lines; the majority did not. Ventresca contended that most Italian workers demonstrated only weak support for unionization. He concluded that the union focused on "class struggle," not gender. Further research will be necessary to understand the "structural and cultural constraints which have historically conditioned labour militancy."[9]

Ester Reiter also viewed industrial unions as having functioned traditionally as protectors of male privilege. Yet during the strike against Lanark, the union gave "strong support" to women workers even though it knew that its chances of winning were slight.[10] Reiter argued that workingmen's class interests led them in this case to support women's struggles. Both the UE and the UAW were engaged in a bitter struggle against a rival union that had been ousted from the Lanark plant by the UE. They supported the Lanark workers, mostly women, because of union interests, not because, or in spite of the fact that, most of the workers were women. As for the women themselves, Reiter concluded: "Their energies in this strike were directed against their unfair treatment as workers, rather than the particular injustices they suffered as women workers."[11]

1　Bryan Palmer, *Working Class Experience: Rethinking the History of Canadian Labour, 1800–1991*, 2nd ed. (Toronto: McClelland & Stewart, 1992), p. 287.

2　Craig Heron, *The Canadian Labour Movement: A Short History*, 2nd ed. (Toronto: James Lorimer, 1996), p. 78.

3　Joan Sangster, *Earning Respect: The Lives of Working Women in Small-Town Ontario, 1920–1960* (Toronto: University of Toronto Press, 1995), p. 167.

4　Julie Guard, "Fair Play or Fair Pay? Gender Relations, Class Consciousness, and Union Solidarity in the Canadian UE," *Labour/Le travail*, 37 (1996): 176.

5　Joy Parr, *The Gender of Breadwinners: Women, Men, and Change in Two Industrial Towns, 1880–1950* (Toronto: University of Toronto Press, 1990), p. 108.

6　Pam Sugiman, *Labour's Dilemma: The Gender Politics of Auto Workers in Canada, 1937–1979* (Toronto: University of Toronto Press, 1994), pp. 4–5.

7　Ibid., p. 99.

8　Gillian Creese, *Contracting Masculinity: Gender, Class, and Race in a White-Collar Union, 1944–1994* (Toronto: Oxford University Press, 1999), p. 141.

9　Robert Ventresca, "'Cowering Women, Combative Men?' Femininity, Masculinity and Ethnicity on Strike in Two Southern Ontario Towns, 1964–1966," *Labour/Le travail*, 39 (1997): 141 and 142.

10　Ester Reiter, "First-Class Workers Don't Want Second-Class Wages: The Lanark Strike in Dunnville," in Joy Parr, ed., *A Diversity of Women: Ontario, 1945–1980* (Toronto: University of Toronto Press, 1995), p. 170.

11　Ibid., p. 194.

The Baby Boom

Prosperity pushed down the average age for marriage. In the aftermath of Depression and war, young adults tended to marry earlier—age 22 for women and only a little older for men. For many, it seemed that life had been put on hold for so long. Now, it was a time to enjoy the prosperity, get educated, and set off on new career paths. It was also time to get married, buy a home, and raise a family. With good times, a higher proportion of young adults married. As historian Mary Louise Adams explains,

> Marriage was a legitimate avenue of sexual expression for those men and women who felt caught between the incitement to sex in the culture at large and the proscriptions against their own engagement in it. Early marriage was one way to bring changes in sexual behaviour into line with the established moral order.[19]

It would not be long, however, before a new generation would challenge that moral order and usher in a sexual revolution.

A wonderful shot of an Edmonton couple by a 1940s car with a handwritten sign: "Just Married Watch Edmonton Grow!" A perfect photo to make the point about the post-World War II baby boom—or is it? Buyer beware! This "perfect photo" apparently predates the post-World War II baby boom: if you look closely at the licence plate, you can see that the expiry date reads March 31, 1942.

Source: City of Edmonton Archives/EA-160-898.

Meanwhile, a veritable "baby boom" occurred. By 1947, the birth rate had increased to nearly 29 per thousand, and the average family had 3 or 4 children. This large contingent of youth had significant repercussions on Canadian society. The precise nature of the impact altered with time, as the baby boomers went through childhood, adolescence, young adulthood, middle age, and retirement. The baby boom led to a rapid increase in Canada's population. During the 1950s, births exceeded deaths by 3 million. Including immigration, Canada's annual growth rate exceeded 3 percent.

Higher Education

Few Canadians attended colleges or universities in the 1950s. In 1951, Canada's institutions of higher learning had only 60,000 students, barely 4 percent of the eligible age group. Only about one university student in four was female. Most female students enrolled in programs in education or the liberal arts; few entered the sciences or the professional schools. In Quebec, until 1960, the provincial government denied women's classical colleges the state funds that were made available to all-male colleges. Religious authorities encouraged Quebec women to attend "family institutes," euphemistically nicknamed "schools of happiness," where they would learn to take up the challenges of life in the home. In Toronto, the elite University of Toronto Schools (whose graduates almost all went on to university) admitted no women, even though it was largely state-supported.

In 1951, the Royal Commission on National Development in the Arts, Letters and Sciences, chaired by Vincent Massey, declared that Canadian universities faced "a financial crisis so great as to threaten their future usefulness." The Massey Commission recommended direct federal financial support. Then, in 1956, while the first cohorts of the baby boom generation were still in elementary school, the National Council of Canadian Universities warned that enrolments would soon dramatically increase. The Soviet launching of *Sputnik*, the first space satellite, in 1957, proved an unforeseen boon to Canadian universities. The fear of Soviet scientific superiority convinced many Canadians that governments should invest much more in higher education. Provincial authorities loosened the purse strings and the federal government instituted a system of grants. Facilities for higher education expanded, as several new universities came into being in the late 1950s.

Culture: Canadian versus American

While the fear of American annexation had long been a dominant theme in Canadian history, in the postwar era, this perceived threat took on a new form. The physical threats of American domination, in the form of military or economic annexation, were replaced by a more subversive threat: culture. Canadian nationalists increasingly felt the dangers of dependence on American culture. The pervasive influence of the rising global superpower was flooding across the border through shifting mediums of communication. Print media, in the form of books, newspapers, and magazines, were difficult enough to control, but the new technologies of radio, and soon television, with their invisible airwaves, seemed unstoppable.

The federal government, however, was prepared to play the role of cultural defender. But some argued that the fight had already been lost. Reduced funding for the Canadian Broadcasting Corporation (CBC) threatened to undermine public broadcasting. Private broadcasters, who wanted to offer more American-produced commercial programming, resented the CBC's regulatory role. The federal government also reduced the National Film Board's budget after the war, and private filmmakers sought to obtain the Board's work. Institutions such as the Public Archives of Canada and the National Museum of Canada suffered from lack of coordination, while the country still had no national library. After three-quarters of a century, the National Gallery of Canada still remained in borrowed space.

Cultural associations that enjoyed strong cabinet support convinced the government to establish the Massey Commission. As historian Paul Litt has shown,

Zoologist William Rowan lecturing at the University of Alberta, Edmonton, before 1956. Beginning in the 1960s, class sizes would expand to the bursting point with the arrival of the baby boomers at universities.

Source: University of Alberta Archives/Acc. no. 82-29-37.

these associations influenced the commission to obtain the recommendations they wanted.[20] The commissioners agreed that the CBC should retain its supervisory powers over broadcasting. In 1959, however, the Conservative government created instead an independent regulatory body for broadcasting: the Board of Broadcast Governors.

The Massey Commission, in 1951, recommended the establishment of a national arts-funding body, free of partisan and bureaucratic control. Finally, six years later, the Liberals founded the Canada Council. It gave financial assistance to a multitude of arts organizations, among them ballet companies, theatre troupes (including the Stratford Shakespearean Festival), and orchestras. The council also gave grants to writers and scholarships to graduate students. Critics denounced what they viewed as extravagant expenditures financed by ordinary folk to support longhair, highbrow misfits and freeloaders. But the state was now playing the role of cultural defender. In doing so, it played an influential part in constructing and fostering its own desired version of Canadian nationalism.

Popular Culture

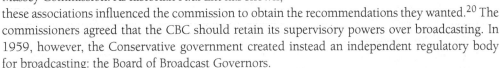

Prosperity enabled many Canadians to spend more on entertainment. They purchased the new long-playing records, often of poor quality and relatively costly. In the late 1940s, they flocked to movie theatres. The real revolution in the entertainment industry, however, came in the early 1950s with television. Canadians living close to the American border rushed to buy television sets with the standard ten-inch black-and-white screen, at first a status symbol because of the relatively high cost. By 1952, Canada's own television broadcasting began in Toronto and Montreal. It quickly expanded to other cities. Critics warned that television might destroy conversation and make thinking obsolete. The CBC and the French-language Radio Canada countered by airing many news programs, including René Lévesque's current affairs program, *Point de mire*. Canadian public broadcasting also presented numerous cultural programs, which attracted small audiences.

The advent of television increased popular interest in sport. Watching *Hockey Night in Canada* became a popular pastime on Saturday night. Fans avidly discussed the feats of Syl Apps, Maurice "Rocket" Richard, and Gordie Howe, and celebrated the Stanley Cup triumphs of the Toronto Maple Leafs in the late 1940s and of the Montreal Canadiens in the late 1950s. From 1942 to 1967, the National Hockey League (NHL) remained a six-team league. The NHL made numerous changes to make television viewing easier. It had ice surfaces painted white and lighting improved, and it dressed on-ice officials in striped jerseys. Canadian performance in international sport brought much less satisfaction, as Canadian teams suffered ignominious defeats in world and Olympic hockey, and sometimes attracted attention for boorish behaviour.

English Canadians enjoyed newspaper supplements such as the *Star Weekly* and *Weekend*, while French Canadians read a variety of tabloid newspapers. By the end of the 1950s, however, American mass-circulation magazines, among them *Time* and *Reader's Digest* and its French edition, *Sélection du Reader's Digest*, accounted for 75 percent of the Canadian general-interest magazine market.

Most movies watched in Canada were American-made, although some came from Britain or, in the case of the Quebec market, France.

Although the CBC presented Canadian variety shows such as *Showtime*, which featured dance, song, music, and comedy, it also imported popular American variety shows to boost its ratings and increase its commercial revenues. On Sunday evenings, Canadians watched the most

The Schiefners, a farm family living outside Milestone, Saskatchewan, on a Saturday evening in 1956. Hockey Night in Canada: Toronto versus Detroit *would be broadcast at 9 p.m.*

Source: Library and Archives Canada/Credit: Richard Harrington/National Film Board of Canada fonds/Acc. no. 1971-271 NPC/PA-111390.

famous and longest-lasting of these, *The Ed Sullivan Show.* Sullivan introduced Elvis Presley and his hip gyrations to Canadians in September 1956. He also boosted the fortunes of Canadian comedians Johnny Wayne and Frank Shuster. Both CBC and private television imported popular American comedies such as *I Love Lucy* and *The Jackie Gleason Show*, and presented contemporary American singers such as Perry Como and Dinah Shore. Baby boom children watched Roy Rogers, Lassie, Walt Disney programs, and the popular American puppet show *The Howdy Doody Show.*

French-language television had more local content. While it beamed a French-speaking *Hopalong Cassidy* (and many other programs dubbed in French) into Quebec living rooms and kitchens, it also carried original productions, such as the Wednesday-night series adapted from novelist Roger Lemelin's *La famille Plouffe*. Children watched a captivating Quebec-made puppet show called *Pépino*. The CBC's very successful variety show *Music Hall*, produced in Montreal, featured French stars such as Edith Piaf, Maurice Chevalier, and Charles Aznavour. By 1957, television production in Montreal, historian Susan Mann writes, was "third in the world to New York and Hollywood and second to none in French."[21]

English-Canadian Literature

Canadian literature in both languages came into its own, but only gradually, in the postwar era. In Montreal, Hugh MacLennan published his celebrated novel *Two Solitudes,* with its theme that Canada's two major linguistic communities needed to demonstrate more mutual tolerance. In Vancouver, Earl Birney, a professor of English at the University of British Columbia and part of a new generation of Canadian poets, published his collection of poems, *Now Is Time*. In *The Mountain and the Valley*, Ernest Buckler wrote of a Nova Scotia boy who found his creativity stifled by his deep attachment to rural life. Throughout the 1950s, Saskatchewan's W.O. Mitchell wrote his masterful *Who Has Seen the Wind* and produced his highly successful "Jake and the Kid" stories for magazine and radio.

Mordecai Richler's *The Apprenticeship of Duddy Kravitz*, a portrait of a young Montreal Jewish entrepreneur, established the Montreal novelist. Adele Wiseman's first novel, *The Sacrifice*, was strongly influenced by the experiences of her Russian Jewish parents. In 1951, Morley Callaghan's highly acclaimed *The Loved and the Lost*, set in Montreal, appeared. Robertson Davies gained early recognition as an essayist and novelist. Poet Dorothy Livesay won governor general's awards for *Day and Night*, in 1944, and *Poems for Peace*, in 1947, while the versatile and flamboyant Irving Layton produced numerous volumes of love poems and prose.

French-Canadian Literature

At the same time, an "aesthetic thaw" came slowly to Quebec. In *Refus global*, a manifesto written in 1948, Paul-Émile Borduas and other signatories condemned Quebec's asphyxiating orthodoxy. The artist's cry for the right to total freedom of expression cost him his teaching job at the École du meuble in Montreal. He left first for New York, then later settled in Paris.

Novelists in Quebec cast aside traditional themes of religion and rurality. Some, such as Roger Lemelin in *Au pied de la Pente douce*, used urban working-class settings. Others, such as Anne Hébert in *Le torrent* and André Langevin in *Poussière sur la ville*, portrayed personal dramas. Yves Thériault won international fame with *Agaguk, a novel about the Inuit*. Professional theatre troupes proliferated, with some of their repertories supplied by Quebec playwrights. The play *Tit-Coq*, by Gratien Gélinas, met with spectacular success. The film that followed attracted 300,000 ticket buyers. Quebec culture seemed to have attained new vibrancy, despite the province's tiny market and few public libraries and bookstores.

Books in Canada were often censored, particularly when they described sex scenes too explicitly. Censorship in all provinces regulated movies. The British Columbia Moving Pictures Act, for example, outlawed films "considered injurious to morals or against public welfare, or which may offer evil suggestions to the minds of children." Alberta's censors watched carefully for "any materialistic, undemocratic, un-Christian propaganda disguised as entertainment."

Religion

Religion "stands out as one of the great gulfs" separating the 1950s from today, according to historian Doug Owram.[22] In the immediate postwar era, the majority of Canadians attended church or the synagogue regularly. Indeed, a higher proportion of Canadian Protestants belonged to churches and enrolled their children in Sunday schools than had done so in the 1930s. Religion was present in most schools across the country, even in so-called public schools.

Nevertheless, the forces of secularization were at work. The influence of religion often appeared superficial and practices were often linked more to socialization than to faith. The *United Church Observer* frequently bemoaned the limited commitment of many adherents. The churches seemed powerless against the forces of modernization, and the opportunities and temptations it offered, particularly through the new communications mediums. Under the influence of the more liberal attitudes of women in Catholic Action movements and against the teachings of the church's hierarchy, Quebec women were coming to see marriage as linked to personal fulfillment rather than uniquely directed toward procreation.[23] Even the sanctity of Sundays, the proverbial day of rest, came under attack. The citizens of Toronto voted in favour of Sunday sports in a plebiscite in 1951.

Across English Canada, provincial drinking restrictions that determined who could drink, where they could drink, and under what conditions, were increasingly challenged. In British Columbia, for example, citizens voted in 1952 to authorize the sale of liquor and wine by the glass in cocktail lounges that would be frequented by a well-behaved middle-class clientele. The beer parlours, often viewed as indecent working-class centres of excess, continued to exist, however, with separate sections for men, and for ladies and escorts.[24]

SUMMARY

In the late postwar era, Canadian consumers had more money to spend and new products to spend it on. Workers in most regions of the country easily found jobs, and pay scales increased substantially. Governments went about the task of managing economic growth. For a time, Canada's postwar prosperity camouflaged the poverty and inequalities that remained the lot of many Canadians, in spite of the appearance of new social programs. When, by the late 1950s, the postwar boom appeared to have run its course, new tensions emerged in society. Canadians increasingly believed that it was time for change.

NOTES

1. Matthew J. Bellamy, *Profiting the Crown: Canada's Polymer Corporation, 1942–1990* (Montreal/Kingston: McGill-Queen's University Press, 2005), p. 89.

2. Doug Owram, "Canadian Domesticity in the Postwar Era," in Peter Neary and J. L. Granatstein, eds., *The Veterans Charter and Post–World War II Canada* (Montreal/Kingston: McGill-Queen's University Press, 1998), p. 213.

3. Magda Fahrni, *Household Politics: Montreal Families and Postwar Reconstruction* (Toronto: University of Toronto Press, 2005), p. 11.

4. Franca Iacovetta, *Gatekeepers: Reshaping Immigrant Lives in Cold War Canada* (Toronto: Between the Lines Press, 2006), pp. 290–92.

5. Diamond Jenness, *The Indians of Canada* (Ottawa: King's Printer, 1932), p. 264.

6. David G. Alexander, *Atlantic Canada and Confederation: Essays in Canadian Political Economy* (Toronto: University of Toronto Press, 1983), p. 32.

7. Peter Neary, *Newfoundland in the North Atlantic World, 1929–1949* (Montreal/Kingston: McGill-Queen's University Press, 1988), p. 359.

8. Raymond Blake, *Canadians at Last: Canada Integrates Newfoundland as a Province* (Toronto: University of Toronto Press, 1994), p. 6.

9. James Struthers, *The Limits of Affluence: Welfare in Ontario, 1920–1970* (Toronto: University of Toronto Press, 1994), p. 180.

10. John W. Holmes, *The Shaping of Peace: Canada and the Search for World Order, 1943–1957*, vol. 2 (Toronto: University of Toronto Press, 1982), p. 36.

11. J.L. Granatstein, *How Britain's Weakness Forced Canada into the Arms of the United States* (Toronto: University of Toronto Press, 1989), p. 3.

12. David J. Bercuson, "Canada, NATO, and Rearmament, 1950–1954: Why Canada Made a Difference (But Not for Very Long)," in John English and Norman Hillmer, eds., *Making a Difference? Canada's Foreign Policy in a Changing World Order* (Toronto: Lester, 1992), p. 104.

13. John Price, "The 'Cat's Paw': Canada and the United Nations Temporary Commission on Korea," *Canadian Historical Review*, 85 (June 2004): 323.

14. John English, *The Worldly Years: The Life of Lester Pearson*, vol. II, *1949–1972* (Toronto: Knopf Canada, 1992), p. 145.

15. J.-C. Falardeau, *Bulletin des relations industrielles*, 4 (1949), quoted in Fraser Isbester, "Asbestos 1949," in Irving Abella, ed., *On Strike: Six Key Labour Struggles in Canada, 1919–1949* (Toronto: James, Lewis & Samuel Publishers, 1974), p. 163.

16. Irving Abella, *Nationalism, Communism, and Canadian Labour: The CIO, the Communist Party, and the Canadian Congress of Labour, 1935–1956* (Toronto: University of Toronto Press, 1973), p. 221.

17. Peter S. McInnis, *Harnessing Labour Confrontation: Shaping the Postwar Settlement in Canada, 1943–1950* (Toronto: University of Toronto Press, 2002), p. 13.

18. Shirley Tillotson, "Human Rights Law as Prism: Women's Organizations, Unions, and Ontario's Female Employees Fair Remuneration Act, 1951," *Canadian Historical Review*, 72 (1991): 532–57.

19. Mary Louise Adams, *The Trouble with Normal: Postwar Youth and the Making of Heterosexuality* (Toronto: University of Toronto Press, 1997), pp. 105–106.

20. Paul Litt, *The Muses, the Masses, and the Massey Commission* (Toronto: University of Toronto Press, 1992).

21. Susan Mann, *The Dream of Nation: A Social and Intellectual History of Quebec* (Montreal/Kingston: McGill-Queen's University Press, 1982, 2002), p. 284.

22. Doug Owram, *Born at the Right Time: A History of the Baby-Boom Generation* (Toronto: University of Toronto Press, 1996), p. 103.

23. Michael Gauvreau, "The Emergence of Personalist Feminism: Catholicism and the Marriage-Preparation Movement in Quebec, 1940–1966," in Nancy Christie, ed., *Households of Faith: Family, Gender, and Community in Canada, 1760–1969* (Montreal/Kingston, McGill-Queen's University Press, 2002), p. 321.

24. Robert A. Campbell, *Sit Down and Drink Your Beer: Regulating Vancouver's Beer Parlours, 1925–1954* (Toronto: University of Toronto Press, 2001).

BIBLIOGRAPHY

A general study of this period is Robert Bothwell, Ian Drummond, and John English, *Canada since 1945: Power, Politics, and Provincialism*, rev. ed. (Toronto: University of Toronto Press, 1989). Doug Owram, *Born at the Right Time: A History of the Baby-Boom Generation* (Toronto: University of Toronto Press, 1996) deals with the baby boomers. Postwar consumerism is discussed critically in Joy Parr, *Domestic Goods: The Material, the Moral, and the Economic in the Postwar Years* (Toronto: University of Toronto Press, 1999); and Magda Fahrni, *Household Politics: Montreal Families and Postwar Reconstruction* (Toronto: University of Toronto Press, 2005). Material on economic development can be found in Kenneth Norrie and Douglas Owram, *A History of the Canadian Economy*, 3rd ed. (Toronto: Nelson Thomson, 2002).

Aspects of the welfare state are discussed in Alvin Finkel, *Our Lives: Canada After 1945* (Toronto: James Lorimer, 1997); and James Struthers, *The Limits of Affluence: Welfare in Ontario, 1920–1970* (Toronto: University of Toronto Press, 1994). The Quebec experience is discussed in Dominique Marshall, *The Social Origins of the Welfare State: Quebec Families, Compulsory Education, and Family Allowances, 1940–1955* (Waterloo, ON: Wilfrid Laurier University Press, 2006). Housing is studied in Richard Harris, *Creeping Conformity: How Canada Became Suburban, 1900–1960* (Toronto: University of Toronto Press, 2004); and John R. Miron, *Housing in Postwar Canada: Demographic Change, Household Formation, and Housing Demand* (Montreal/Kingston: McGill-Queen's University Press, 1988).

Conservation and the environment in the postwar years is examined in George M. Warecki, *Protecting Ontario's Wilderness: A History of Changing Ideas and Preservation Politics, 1927–1973* (New York: Peter Lang, 2000); and Alan MacEachern, *Natural Selections: National Parks in Atlantic Canada, 1935–1970* (Montreal/Kingston: McGill-Queen's University Press, 2001). On the construction of the St. Lawrence Seaway, see Daniel Macfarlane, *Negotiating a River: Canada, the U.S., and the Creation of the*

St. Lawrence Seaway (Vancouver: UBC Press, 2014) and Joy Parr, *Sensing Changes: Technologies, Environments, and the Everyday, 1953–2003* (Vancouver: UBC Press, 2009).

Dale C. Thomson presents a biography of Canada's prime minister, 1948–1957, in *Louis St. Laurent, Canadian* (Toronto: Macmillan, 1967). J.L. Granatstein examines the role of federal bureaucrats in *The Ottawa Men: The Civil Service Mandarins, 1935–57* (Toronto: University of Toronto Press, 1998). See also Robert Wardhaugh, *Behind the Scenes: The Life and Work of William Clifford Clark* (Toronto: University of Toronto Press, 2010). Studies of provincial politics of this era include Richard Gwyn, *Smallwood: The Unlikely Revolutionary*, rev. ed. (Toronto: McClelland and Stewart, 1972, 1999); Roger Graham, *Old Man Ontario: Leslie M. Frost* (Toronto: University of Toronto Press, 1990); and P.E. Bryden, *"A Justifiable Obsession": Conservative Ontario's Relations with Ottawa, 1943–1985* (Toronto: University of Toronto Press, 2013). A. W. Johnson, *Dream No Little Dreams: A Biography of the Douglas Government of Saskatchewan, 1944–1961* (Toronto: University of Toronto Press, 2004); and, on Alberta, Ted Byfield, ed., *Manning and the Age of Prosperity, 1946–1963* (Edmonton: United Western Communications, 2001). Among several books that examine Newfoundland's entry into Confederation is David MacKenzie, *Inside the Atlantic Triangle: Canada and the Entrance of Newfoundland into Confederation, 1939–1949* (Toronto: University of Toronto Press, 1986), and Corey Slumkoski, *Inventing Atlantic Canada: Regionalism and the Maritime Reaction to Newfoundland's Entry into Canadian Confederation* (Toronto: University of Toronto Press, 2011).

On Canadian foreign policy of the late 1940s and 1950s, see Robert Bothwell, *Alliance and Illusion: Canada and the World, 1945–1984* (Vancouver: UBC Press, 2007); Adam Chapnick's myth-debunking *The Middle Power Project: Canada and the Founding of the United Nations* (Vancouver: UBC Press, 2005); Reg Whitaker and Steve Hewitt, *Canada and the Cold War* (Toronto: James Lorimer, 2003); Norman Hillmer and Adam Chapnick, eds., *Canadas of the Mind: The Making and Unmaking of Canadian Nationalisms in the Twentieth Century* (Montreal/Kingston: McGill-Queen's University Press, 2007); Robert Bothwell and Jean Daudelin, eds., *Canada Among Nations, 2008: 100 Years of Canadian Foreign Policy* (Montreal/ Kingston: McGill-Queen's University Press, 2008); and Greg Donaghy, ed., *Canada and the Early Cold War, 1943–1957/Le Canada au début de la guerre froide, 1943–1957* (Ottawa: Department of Foreign Affairs and International Trade, 1998).

In *Pragmatic Idealism: Canadian Foreign Policy, 1945–1995* (Montreal/Kingston: McGill-Queen's University Press, 1998), Costas Melakopides looks at Canada's involvement in peacekeeping, arms control, and human rights. Critical studies of Canada's participation in the Korean War include William Johnston, *A War of Patrols: Canadian Army Operations in Korea* (Vancouver: UBC Press, 2003); David Bercuson, *Blood on the Hills: The Canadian Army in the Korean War* (Toronto: University of Toronto Press, 1999); and Brent Byron Watson, *Far Eastern Tour: The Canadian Infantry in Korea, 1950–1953* (Montreal/ Kingston: McGill-Queen's University Press, 2002). Joseph Levitt examines Canada's role as a "junior partner" in arms-control talks in *Pearson and Canada's Role in Nuclear Disarmament and Arms Control Negotiations, 1945–1957* (Montreal/Kingston: McGill-Queen's University Press, 1993). On the emergence of Canadian military intelligence, see Kurt Jensen, *Cautious Beginnings: Canadian Foreign Intelligence, 1939–1951* (Vancouver: UBC Press, 2008); and Martin Rudner, "The Historical Evolution of Canada's Foreign Intelligence Capability: Cold War SIGINT Strategy and Its Legacy," *Journal of Intelligence History*, 6(1) (2006): 67–83. Postwar trade issues are discussed in B.W. Muirhead, *The Development of Postwar Canadian Trade Policy: The Failure of the Anglo-European Option* (Montreal/Kingston: McGill-Queen's University Press, 1992).

For Canadian–American relations in the defence sector, see Joseph T. Jockel's study, *No Boundaries Upstairs: Canada, the United States and the Origins of North American Air Defence, 1945–1958* (Vancouver: University of British Columbia Press, 1987); Joseph T. Jockel, *Canada in NORAD, 1957–2007* (Montreal/ Kingston: McGill-Queen's University Press, 2007); James G. Ferguson, *Canada and Ballistic Missile Defence, 1954–2009* (Vancouver: UBC Press, 2010); Frances Jewel Dickson, *The DEW Line Years: Voices from the Coldest Cold War* (East Lawrencetown, NS: Pottersfield, 2007); John Herd Thompson and Stephen J. Randall, *Canada and the United States: Ambivalent Allies*, 4th ed. (Montreal/Kingston: McGill-Queen's University Press, 2008); and Mark Davidson, "Preparing for the Bomb: The Development of Civil Defence Policy in Canada, 1948–1963," *Canadian Military History*, 16(3) (2007): 29–42. For

Canada's relations with India and Britain, see Ryan M. Touhey, *Conflicting Visions: Canada and India in the Cold War World, 1946–76* (Vancouver: UBC Press, 2015).

Craig Stewart looks at one failed Canadian defence initiative in *Shutting Down the National Dream: Avro and the Tragedy of the Arrow* (Toronto: McGraw-Hill Ryerson, 1988). The history of Canada's atomic energy program is discussed in Brian Buckley, *Canada's Early Nuclear Policy: Fate, Chance, and Character* (Montreal/Kingston: McGill-Queen's University Press, 2000). Andrew Richter studies Canada's defence thinking in *Avoiding Armageddon: Canadian Military Strategy and Nuclear Weapons, 1950–63* (Vancouver: UBC Press and Canadian War Museum, 2002). Issues linked to internal security are examined in Amy Knight, *How the Cold War Began: The Gouzenko Affair and the Hunt for Soviet Spies* (Toronto: McClelland & Stewart, 2005); and Reg Whitaker and Gary Marcuse, *Cold War Canada: The Making of a National Insecurity State, 1945–1957* (Toronto: University of Toronto Press, 1994). David MacKenzie's historical booklet, *Canada's Red Scare, 1945–1957* (Ottawa: Canadian Historical Association, 2001), paints a brief portrait of the context.

On human rights campaigns, see Ross Lambertson, *Repression and Resistance: Canadian Human Rights Activists, 1930–1960* (Toronto: University of Toronto Press, 2005). For a look at activism during the Cold War, see Nigel Roy Moses, "Canadian Student Movements on the Cold War Battlefield, 1944–1954," *Histoire sociale/Social History*, 39(78) (2006): 363–404; and Magda Fahrni and Robert Rutherdale, eds., *Creating Postwar Canada: Community, Diversity, and Dissent, 1945–1975* (Vancouver: UBC Press 2007). And for an examination of Commonwealth relations postwar, see Francine McKenzie, "In the National Interest: Dominions' Support for Britain and the Commonwealth after the Second World War," *Journal of Imperial and Commonwealth History*, 34(4) (2006): 553–76; and Christian Champion, "Courting 'Our Ethnic Friends': Canadianism, Britishness, and New Canadians, 1950–1970," *Canadian Ethnic Studies*, 38(1) (2006): 23–46.

A good business history is Matthew J. Bellamy, *Profiting the Crown: Canada's Polymer Corporation, 1942–1990* (Montreal/Kingston: McGill-Queen's University Press, 2005). For a general presentation of unions of this period, see Bryan D. Palmer, *Working-Class Experience: Rethinking the History of Canadian Labour, 1800–1991*, 2nd ed. (Toronto: McClelland & Stewart, 1992). Peter S. McInnis examines postwar labour–management relations in *Harnessing Labour Confrontation: Shaping the Postwar Settlement in Canada, 1943–1950* (Toronto: University of Toronto Press, 2002).

For a look at women in the workplace, see Donica Belisle, "Negotiating Paternalism: Women and Canada's Largest Department Stores, 1890–1960," *Journal of Women's History*, 19(1) (2007): 58–81. On the history of the Canadian Autoworkers, see Charlotte Yates, *From Plant to Politics: The Autoworkers Union in Postwar Canada* (Philadelphia: Temple University Press, 1993). The history of another famous union is told in Andrew Neufeld and Andrew Parnaby, *The IWA in Canada: The Life and Times of an Industrial Union* (Vancouver: IWA Canada/New Star Books, 2000). For an overview of the emerging "car culture," see Dimitry Anastakis, *Car Nation: An Illustrated History of Canada's Transformation Behind the Wheel* (Toronto: James Lorimer, 2008). British Columbia's labour movement is chronicled in Benjamin Isitt, *Militant Minority: British Columbia Workers and the Rise of a New Left, 1948–1972* (Toronto: University of Toronto Press, 2011).

Two general syntheses of women's history are Micheline Dumont et al., *Quebec Women: A History* (Toronto: Women's Press, 1987); and Gail Cuthbert-Brandt et al., *Canadian Women: A History*, 3rd ed. (Toronto: Nelson Education, 2011). For Canadian women and political life, consult Brian T. Thorn, *From Left to Right: Maternalism and Women's Political Activism in Postwar Canada* (Vancouver: UBC Press, 2016). Patricia T. Rooke and R.L. Schnell, *No Bleeding Heart: Charlotte Whitton, A Feminist on the Right* (Vancouver: University of British Columbia Press, 1987), examines the career of a famous mayor of Ottawa. The issue of female clergy is addressed in Valerie J. Korinek, "No Women Need Apply: The Ordination of Women in the United Church, 1918–65," *Canadian Historical Review*, 74 (1993): 473–509. Joan Sangster studies how the justice system dealt with women in *Regulating Girls and Women: Sexuality, Family, and the Law in Ontario, 1920–1960* (Toronto: Oxford University Press, 2001). Veronica Strong-Boag examines the life of suburban women in "Home Dreams: Women and the Suburban Experiment in Canada, 1945–60," *Canadian Historical Review*, 72 (1991): 471–504. On women and work, see Joan Sangster, *Transforming*

Labour: Women and Work in Postwar Canada (Toronto: University of Toronto Press, 2010); and Jennifer A. Stephen, "Balancing Equality for the Postwar Woman: Demobilising Canada's Women Workers After World War II," *Atlantis*, 32(1) (2007): 122–32. Valerie Korinek studies a women's magazine in *Roughing It in the Suburbs: Reading Chatelaine Magazine in the Fifties and the Sixties* (Toronto: University of Toronto Press, 2000). The world of fashion is discussed, and abundantly illustrated, in Alexandra Palmer, *Couture and Commerce: The Transatlantic Fashion Trade in the 1950s* (Vancouver: UBC Press, 2001). Several essays on aspects of women's life in Ontario in this period may be found in Joy Parr, ed., *A Diversity of Women: Ontario, 1945–1980* (Toronto: University of Toronto Press, 1995). For a look at masculinity postwar, see Christopher Dummitt, *The Manly Modern: Masculinity in Postwar Canada* (Vancouver: UBC Press, 2007). Tarah Brookfield looks at how the Cold War shaped women and families in Canada in *Cold War Comforts: Canadian Women, Child Safety, and Global Insecurity* (Waterloo: Wilfrid Laurier University Press, 2012). For studies on youth and gender, see Christopher J. Greig, *Ontario Boys: Masculinity and the Idea of Boyhood in Postwar Ontario, 1945–1960* (Waterloo: Wilfrid Laurier Press, 2014), and Sharon Yvonne Wall, "Some Thought They Were 'in Love'": Sex, White Teenagehood, and Unmarried Pregnancy in Early Postwar Canada," *Journal of the Canadian Historical Association*, no. 1 (2014): 207–241.

Psychology's place in the postwar Canadian family is studied in Mona Gleason, *Normalizing the Ideal: Psychology, Schooling, and the Family in Postwar Canada* (Toronto: University of Toronto Press, 1999). On heterosexuality and homosexuality, see Mary Louise Adams, *The Trouble with Normal: Postwar Youth and the Making of Heterosexuality* (Toronto: University of Toronto Press, 1997); Gary Kinsman, *The Regulation of Desire: Homo and Hetero Sexualities*, 2nd ed. (Montreal: Black Rose Books, 1996); and Richard Cavell, ed., *Love, Hate, and Fear in Canada's Cold War* (Toronto: University of Toronto Press, 2004). For a study of sexuality, see Becki L. Ross, *Burlesque West: Showgirls, Sex, and Sin in Postwar Vancouver* (Toronto: University of Toronto Press, 2009). For an examination of immigration in Cold War Canada, see Franca Iacovetta, *Gatekeepers: Reshaping Immigrant Lives in Cold War Canada* (Toronto: Between the Lines Press, 2006); and Royden Loewen and Gerald Friesen, *Immigrants in Prairie Cities.* (Toronto: University of Toronto Press, 2009).

William Kaplan recounts the struggle for rights of Jehovah's Witnesses in *State and Salvation: The Jehovah's Witnesses and Their Fight for Civil Rights* (Toronto: University of Toronto Press, 1989). The changing attitudes of Canadians toward alcohol are examined in Robert A. Campbell, *Sit Down and Drink Your Beer: Regulating Vancouver's Beer Parlours, 1925–1954* (Toronto: University of Toronto Press, 2001).

Paul Litt tells the story of the Massey Commission in *The Muses, the Masses, and the Massey Commission* (Toronto: University of Toronto Press, 1992). Paul Rutherford looks at television fare in *When Television Was Young: Primetime Canada 1952–1967* (Toronto: University of Toronto Press, 1990); and for a look at conservative thought and the commission, see Philip A. Massolin, *Canadian Intellectuals, the Tory Tradition and the Challenge of Modernity, 1939–1970* (Toronto: University of Toronto, 2001).

Useful maps and charts on Canada in the World War II and postwar period appear in Donald Kerr and Deryck W. Holdsworth, eds., *Historical Atlas of Canada*, vol. 3, *Addressing the Twentieth Century, 1891–1961* (Toronto: University of Toronto Press, 1990).

Source: Provincial Archives of Alberta/J127/1, reproduced with permission of the *Edmonton Journal.*

Chapter Fifteen

PROTEST AND REFORM: THE 1960s

TIME LINE	
1960	York University opens in Toronto Diefenbaker government adopts Bill of Rights First Nations people obtain right to vote in federal elections without giving up Indian status
1961	The CCF becomes New Democratic Party (NDP); Tommy Douglas chosen as leader
1962	Progressive Conservatives under John Diefenbaker win minority government Opening of Trans-Canada Highway from St. John's to Victoria Medicare introduced in Saskatchewan
1963	Liberals under Lester Pearson win office Royal Commission on Bilingualism and Biculturalism begins hearings
1964	Beatles tour Canada
1965	Maple Leaf replaces the Red Ensign as Canada's national flag Auto Pact agreement signed Canada Pension Plan established
1966	Ottawa provides grants to provinces for postsecondary education Canada Assistance Act passed
1967	Canada celebrates centennial Expo 67 held in Montreal, welcomes 50 million visitors Royal Commission on Status of Women appointed National Health Insurance Program (Medicare) comes into being
1968	Pierre Elliott Trudeau replaces Pearson as Liberal leader and prime minister
1969	Parliament adopts Official Languages Act The Liberals introduce "White Paper" on Indian Affairs but later withdraw it due to protest

Canada, along with much of the Western world, experienced profound social and cultural upheavals in the rebellious decade of the 1960s. A new generation of young people, in particular, challenged authority. "A new student class has emerged, aware of its power, ready to act," *Maclean's* proclaimed in November 1967. The universities became centres of protest as demonstrations erupted on campuses. The youth rejected traditional social and cultural values, and sexual taboos weakened.

In the atmosphere of the often-violent civil rights movement in the United States, and spurred by the "Year of the Barricades" in 1968 in Western Europe, minority groups in Canada emerged to have their voices heard. The women's movement shifted from what is now called first-wave feminism to a second wave; maternal feminism was replaced by a search for gender equality. The "New Left," buoyed by decolonization and the move to finally break the hold of the old empires, was more prepared to accept violent means if necessary to break the chains of the capitalist establishment. Racial inequality took centre stage in the United States, and Canada's treatment of its ethnic and racial minorities could no longer be ignored. In the relative context of the "black power" and "red power" movements in the United States, Canadian attention was increasingly focused on the plight of the Aboriginal peoples and the Third-World conditions in which they lived.

[handwritten margin note: Maternal feminism replaced by gender equality.]

In Quebec a new nationalist movement emerged, one that was more aggressive and intent on putting the Quebecois in control of their own fate. The old empires were being dismantled but amid the Cold War, new ones were clearly emerging. Many Canadians became increasingly critical of American hegemony as evidenced by the Vietnam War. A powerful peace movement made its presence felt.

Ironically, at the time when Canada was celebrating its centennial in 1967, the nation's sense of itself seemed to be unravelling. The old Canadian identity based on an attachment to Britain no longer fit the times. But Canadians searched for a sense of self that was also distinct from the United States. A host of new interest groups, with various agendas, entered the political forum. No longer could a small group of middle-aged men, primarily of British origin and speaking only English, rule Canada politically. Diversity became an essential characteristic of the newly constructed Canadian identity.

The economic stability of the postwar years was shaken in the 1960s. As the decade opened, Canada faced the highest unemployment levels since the Great Depression. Although prosperity returned, rapidly rising prices became a worry. Economic difficulties focused attention on social inequality.

Secularization

Canadian society in the 1960s became more secular. In Quebec, the influence of the Roman Catholic Church waned as church attendance declined, and the institution lost its historic role in society to the state. Many clergy left the church's religious orders, and new recruitment fell rapidly. But the process of secularism did not occur overnight. The forces that created the "Quiet Revolution" in Quebec had their roots in intellectual movements going back decades. Catholicism, so long a pervasive force in Quebec, did not disappear in the face of secularism. It declined but it also changed with the times.

Elsewhere in Canada, the major Protestant denominations also lost ground. Sunday school attendance in the Protestant churches fell precipitously. In his book *The Comfortable Pew*, historian Pierre Berton attacked the churches for their lack of relevance, as they vainly attempted to combat the supporters of beer parlours, Sunday movies, and Sunday sports. Rev. James Mutchmor, the head of the United Church's board of evangelism and social service, and later moderator, denounced the new trends. The "voice against vice" became the most-quoted churchman in Canada in the mid-1960s. Mutchmor's critics mocked: "Let's have much less of Mutchmor!"

Orthodoxy – authorised/ generally accepted theory/ doctrine/ practice,

As churches attempted to come to terms with change, their congregations often represented a wide spectrum of opinion. Liberal Catholics applauded the decisions of the Vatican II Council, which modernized certain religious practices while conservative adherents feared the loss of essentials to the faith. Many Protestants who felt that the traditional denominations had become too liberal joined conservative fundamentalist groups such as the Pentecostals.

Youth Protest

Age and generation usually play a significant role in challenges to tradition and order. The youth of the Great War generation, for example, challenged the orthodoxy of the era, ushering in important political, social, and cultural change and shaping the interwar period. But "generation" became a catchword for the protest movements of the 1960s and the "baby boomers" identified as a generation. The youth culture of this generation of mass media and culture was visible as never before. High school boys put away their hair oil and let their hair grow, while their mothers remonstrated with them in vain and barbers lost business. "Flower children" dressed in fringes and beads and displayed psychedelic colours. Blue jeans became the uniform of a generation. The youth denounced age and experience, and promised to stay young.

Perhaps most significantly, Canada, along with other Western nations, experienced a sexual revolution. Sexual repression, so long at the centre of social control and regulation, was finally challenged. These challenges led to fundamental questionings about morality, ownership and control of human bodies, interracial relationships, patriarchy and the subordination of women, homosexuality and homophobia, and sexual freedom and expression. In challenging sexual norms, the youth culture threw down the gauntlet to the twin pillars of society—the church and state.

The youth found other ways to challenge the establishment. "Rock and roll" music with its free-moving and sexualized style of dancing shocked the older generation. It was only the beginning. The use of "recreational" drugs became another means to challenge and protest against the establishment. Experimentation with drugs was not new but its social acceptance certainly was. Student associations called for the legalization of certain drugs such as marijuana; medical opinion was divided over the issue. As historian Marcel Martel has shown, groups such as the police forces had more success than others in shaping public debate and in imposing their choice of policy, which was to keep the status quo.[1] Regardless, "sex, drugs, and rock 'n' roll" became the catchphrase of a generation.

"Peace and Love"

In an era of mass communications and mass culture, music became a source and medium of protest. As with novelists, poets, and artists, Canadian singers and musicians made their mark in the American- and British-dominated industries. While Canadians empathized with the peace-and-love message of American folk singers such as Bob Dylan and Joan Baez, Canadian folk singers, including Ian and Sylvia Tyson, Gordon Lightfoot, and Joni Mitchell, also achieved an international reputation. The Tysons became popular in the United States at the start of the folk revival in the 1960s, paving the way for other Canadian performers at a time of limited recording opportunities in Canada. Gordon Lightfoot from Orilla, Ontario, began his career in coffee houses and bars. As composer of such pieces as "Early Morning Rain" and "For Lovin' Me," he soon drew crowds to his performances at the Mariposa folk festival and elsewhere. As the decade advanced and interest in folk music waned, Lightfoot enlarged his public by making the transition to pop and country music.

In Quebec, young people flocked to listen to the *chansonniers* who sang, accompanied only by their guitars or the piano, in the *boîtes à chansons* that sprang up across Quebec in the early 1960s. Félix Leclerc and Raymond Lévesque pioneered this form of entertainment. At first, the lyrics dwelt on apolitical themes such as love and nature. Later, as a powerful nationalist current surged through the province, new themes bearing on the historical experience of Quebec identity appeared. Gilles Vigneault, who came from Natashquan, a tiny hamlet on the lower north shore of the St. Lawrence River, became one of the most well-known singer–songwriters of the era. His "Mon pays" became the anthem of nationalist youth.

But despite the state's desire to foster Canadian artists as representative of a constructed Canadian culture and identity, the pervasive influence of mass culture permeated national borders. Young Canadians were much more influenced by the emergence and impact of Buddy Holly, Elvis Presley, and the Beatles. They fell victim to Beatlemania, especially during the shaggy-haired foursome's tour of Canada in September 1964. On September 8, the *Toronto Star* headlined: "200 Girls Swoon in Battle of the Beatles." Vancouver's Empire Stadium saw even greater hysteria during a concert by the "Fab Four," as hundreds of fans rushed the stage and screams drowned out the singing. Beatle products inundated the market. As the decade advanced, a multitude of Canadian rock bands sprang up, usually modelled on British and American groups. But because of the popularity of foreign groups, few Canadian rock-music records appeared. Canadian singers received a substantial boost in 1970, when the Canadian Radio-television and Telecommunications Commission (CRTC) established Canadian-content rules for broadcasters.

A psychedelic party at Toronto's Rochdale College to raise funds for U.S. draft dodgers. Students in both the foreground and background are applying body paint. Rochdale was a free student-run cooperative in which students and teachers cohabited to share knowledge. It had difficulty meeting its operational costs and was closed in 1975 because of concerns over drug use and crime.

Source: York University Libraries, Clara Thomas Archives & Special Collections, Toronto Telegram fonds, ASC04620.

Student Revolt

The 1960s constituted "the moment in history that forever defined the baby boom as a distinct generation."[2] The boomers' centres of activity were the university campuses (although the majority of boomers never went to university), which became centres of protest in the 1960s. Infused with the spirit of "peace and love," Canadian students, like American and Western youth in general, picketed in favour of a wide range of reformist causes, and especially against the increasingly bloody war in Vietnam, in which the United States had greatly expanded its military campaign in an effort to prevent Communist-dominated North Vietnam from dislodging the pro-American and highly corrupt regime in South Vietnam. In an era when the old European empires were finally disintegrating, excuses for American imperialism (regardless of the Cold War rhetoric and justifications) rang hollow. Protest took root and flourished, often tended closely by university professors. Academics in the social sciences, particularly in Toronto, prepared research studies to show the extent to which Canada had become an American colony, and proposed measures for buying or taking it back. In Quebec's universities,

This protest march on Jasper Avenue in Edmonton, October 22, 1967, was aimed mostly at American involvement in Vietnam, but other placards suggest agendas for social justice.

Source: Provincial Archives of Alberta/J127/1, reproduced with permission of the *Edmonton Journal*.

Cultural survival was still the end goal, but language and not religion was now the issue of contention,

equal fervour was applied to proving that Quebec was a Canadian colony and to devising plans for liberating it.

University protest had political repercussions. In Quebec, it contributed to the rise of a new French-Canadian nationalism. This version was not based on the defensive traditionalism of the past, rooted in an agrarian and Catholic identity. Instead, it was an assertive nationalism that urged the Quebecois to wrest economic control from the English. Quebeckers were second-class citizens in their own homeland. Cultural survival was still the end goal, but language and not religion was now the issue of contention. The new nationalism assisted the rise of the Parti Québécois led by René Lévesque. Federally, Pierre Elliott Trudeau, who appeared to challenge the establishment and who brought new ideas to the fore, won the Liberal leadership and the federal election of 1968.

Students abandoned classes and occupied administrative offices, demanding more active participation in the university community and the recognition of students' rights. At the University of Toronto, for example, students protested against recruiting on campus by Dow Chemical Corporation,

The University of Lethbridge, main building, designed by famed architect Arthur Erickson. Construction was completed in 1971.

Source: Courtesy of the University of Lethbridge.

a manufacturer of napalm used by the American military during the Vietnam War. Such protests were all the more visible, in part, because students were now far more numerous. University enrolments doubled during the 1950s, then tripled during the 1960s and 1970s. The parents of baby boomers, many of whom had never finished high school, preached the virtues of a university degree as the key to a bright future.

The Role of Universities

Provincial governments, convinced that higher education would bring economic benefits to society, increased spending on universities and established a host of new institutions. British Columbia Premier W.A.C. Bennett told the chairman of BC Hydro in 1963: "I want you to be the chancellor of a new university. Select a site and build it and get it going." As a result Simon Fraser University opened in 1965, atop Burnaby Mountain, with 2500 students. In Ontario, York University admitted its first 75 students in 1960; a year later the province gave York 200 hectares in northwest Toronto for the building

The Montreal campus of the Université du Québec, one of the new universities that sprang up during the 1960s. To build the campus, a church and a convent were torn down. The architects integrated parts of the church's facade into the new structure. Today the Université du Québec has regional affiliates across the province.

Source: Bibliothèque et Archives nationales du Québec, à Montréal Fonds E6, S7, cote: p800063. Auteur: Adrien Hubert.

of a campus. Laurentian, Trent, Brock, and Lakehead Universities were also set up, as well as Erindale and Scarborough Colleges, affiliated with the University of Toronto. Quebec established the public Université du Québec à Montréal with several regional affiliates. The University of Alberta, Calgary branch, became the separate University of Calgary in 1966, while Alberta's third university, the University of Lethbridge, opened in 1967. New Brunswick's francophones obtained their own university, the Université de Moncton, in 1963. Regional and community colleges began operations in several provinces. The federal government, which had been making grants directly to the universities since 1951, began in 1966 to make contributions to provincial governments for the financing of postsecondary education. In all, government spending on universities increased sevenfold during the 1960s.

As a result of their rapid growth, universities faced serious shortages of professors and they recruited heavily on American campuses. Many American academics took jobs in Canada as a way to "dodge the draft" and avoid fighting in Vietnam. By 1968, fewer than half of the university professors in Canada were Canadians. In that same year, only one of every eight positions filled went to a Canadian. Critics accused universities of ignoring Canadian university graduates in their hiring policies, and called for the Canadianization of faculties.

Pushing Back on the State

Although university professors and students were among the loudest voices calling for change and criticizing the establishment, Canadians in general endorsed increased state intervention as a necessary tool for reform and stability. The state seemingly rescued society from the trials of the Depression and the world wars. It ushered in the era of the welfare state. But the voices calling for change were now conflicted. While the state helped alleviate some of the worst inequalities and injustices, it was now the main obstacle in advancing progressive change. These voices demanded that provincial governments invest heavily in elementary and secondary education, building schools and hiring teachers as enrolments burgeoned due to the baby boom generation
(increased)

A HISTORICAL PORTRAIT

The Student Radicals at Sir George Williams University

The late 1960s witnessed protests against many aspects of the established order. The most vigorous protesters were university students in France, the United States, and elsewhere, particularly in 1968—"the Year of the Barricades." They spoke out on a wide variety of issues, from the oppressiveness of university campuses, to banning the bomb, to the war in Vietnam. Preferred methods were strikes, sit-ins, teach-ins, and occupations of buildings.

Canada was no exception. The events of February 11, 1969, at Sir George Williams University (today Concordia University) in Montreal appeared to mark a watershed. "Police rout SGWU militants; $1 million computer centre wrecked," read *The Montreal Star's* headline that day. The damage figure was revised upward the next day to $2 million.

In December 1968, students had levelled charges of racism against a biology professor at the university. In early February, protesters occupied the Faculty Club in the nine-storey Henry Hall Building. At first they succeeded in generating sympathy. Over time, however, the students lost support as they seemed more content to be protesting than focusing attention on the issue of racism. One of the leaders proclaimed

that he didn't really care about the charges of racism against the professor. "All we want to do is burn down the university. We want the police to come, we want violence."

The protesters broke into the cafeteria on the seventh floor and hurled chairs and tables down escalators, stairwells, and elevator shafts. As police moved against the crowd, occupants turned on fire hoses against them, then retreated to the computer centre on the ninth floor. When police attempted to evict them from the centre, the protesters threw computers, punchcards, tapes, and furniture onto the street, and then set fire to the centre. Police made 90 arrests, including 30 protesters who were not Sir George Williams students.

The events at Sir George Williams provoked a backlash. Although *The Montreal Star* argued that university administrations were frequently guilty of a lack of responsiveness to reasonable demands, it denounced what it termed "an indefensible act by student anarchists." When the Quebec student union declared its support for the rioters, SGWU students quit its ranks. For Doug Owram, the SGWU episode, because of the degree of violence and destruction, "foreshadowed the end of the 1960s era."[1]

---

1   Doug Owram, *Born at the Right Time: A History of the Baby-Boom Generation* (Toronto: University of Toronto Press, 1996), p. 286.

and immigration. In Ontario, spending increases on education became an explosive political issue as property taxes, largely to pay for schools, soared. In Alberta, revenues from sales of oil and gas enabled the government to spend more money per capita, notably on health and education, than any other province.

Reformers also wanted governments to take measures to protect society's weaker elements, such as the unemployed, older Canadians, people needing expensive medical care, and those living in disadvantaged regions of the country. Citizens urged the state to act to protect consumers, promote the equality of women, and combat discrimination against minority groups. They pressured municipal governments to improve the quality of life in cities by controlling the heights of buildings, curtailing expressway expansion, expanding urban transit, improving parks and libraries, protecting established neighbourhoods, and fighting urban blight. The cultural lobby requested financial aid to assist Canadian cultural development, while sport organizations urged Ottawa to fund amateur sport and to work to improve Canadian athletes' performances in international competitions.

The First Nations

First Nations youth were not enjoying the same "liberation" as their white counterparts. As if the federal program of residential schools was not damaging enough, in the 1960s the provinces took Aboriginal children from their families and communities, and placed them in protective care, in what became known as the "Sixties Scoop." In 1955 in British Columbia Native children constituted 1 percent of the children in care; by 1964 that figure had risen to over 34 percent. Thousands of Indigenous children were removed and settled into foster and adoptive homes.

Driving to the Suburbs

In response to calls for action, governments intervened, at least modestly, to supply disadvantaged Canadians with low-income housing. In the late 1940s, large areas of Cabbagetown, a working-class area in Toronto, were cleared and replaced with three-storey brick apartment buildings with open spaces and playgrounds. The 1960s saw the construction of large apartment buildings but with much less space, a situation that gave rise to a variety of social problems. Vancouver's Strathcona area, Halifax's Uniacke Square, and Montreal's Jeanne Mance Park saw similar developments.

Most Canadians, however, dreamed of owning a house in the suburbs. Federal government programs made low-cost mortgages available, provincial governments built roads, and local authorities installed services. The Don Mills community of Toronto, built in 1952–62, served as the prototype of a planned corporate suburb. Around a core area containing a shopping centre and a high school at the intersection of two arterial roads, developers built small apartment buildings and townhouses. Beyond them were four low-density neighbourhood units. Edmonton had its own planned suburb, Mill Woods. Developers made plans for a population of 100,000 people, who were to live in 23 neighbourhoods that were focused on a town-centre complex containing the necessary services. All large Canadian cities witnessed suburban expansion in the 1960s.

The development of suburbia was possible only through changes in transportation. Urban transit systems expanded in Canadian cities to allow "commuters" to travel from home in the suburbs to work in the downtown. But the prosperity of the postwar era finally allowed the automobile revolution to occur, a development that began in the interwar period but was

Many Canadians dreamed of owning a house in the suburbs. This photo shows children at play in the then unfinished wartime home development of Winston Park, now a part of Toronto, in 1945.

Source: City of Toronto Archives fonds 1266, item 98646.

thwarted by the Depression and World War II. Many citizens could finally afford to own vehicles. This trend made suburbia traversable and accessible.

Population Trends

Demographic upheaval also characterized the 1960s as the baby boom of the late 1940s and 1950s fizzled into a "baby bust." In a single decade, the rate of growth of Canada's population dropped by nearly half. Newfoundland's birth rate remained the highest, at 24.3 births per thousand people in 1970, but its rate declined also in the following decade.

Quebec went from having one of the highest birth rates of all the provinces in 1960 to having the lowest rate in 1970, at just 16.1 per thousand. The two-child family—the minimum to maintain the current size of the population—became the norm in Canada. Single-child or childless families became more ordinary.

The decrease in family size was correlated with rising affluence. A century earlier, large families were necessary. On farms, for example, children meant additional workers and, in general, the extended family cared for its elderly members. In Canada's modern social welfare state, the aged relied less on adult children for financial assistance. Canadians wanted fewer children and they wanted them later in life.

Religious commentators attributed the decrease in family size to the secularization of society and indeed one of the main factors was the availability of better contraceptive methods, particularly the birth-control pill, which became available in Canada in 1966. In 1961, Barbara and George Cadbury founded Planned Parenthood of Toronto, an information and referral service; they opened a Canada-wide equivalent two years later. Only in 1969, however, did Parliament amend Canada's Criminal Code to permit the distribution of birth-control information and devices. The availability of the pill was likely the most revolutionary development ever to occur to Canadian women. It gave them more control of their own bodies and their sexuality. It also occurred at a time when women were seeking to enter the workforce and have careers. The advancement of women in society inevitably affected the birth rate.

1969 – Parliament ammended CAN criminal code to permit distribution of birth control info / devices.

Changing Family Patterns

A general revolution in family patterns began in the 1960s. Traditional marriage had long served as a patriarchal institution in which women were generally viewed as part of the domain of their husbands. With no financial autonomy, they were often powerless to leave. Both the church and the state conspired to keep women in the domestic realm. The growth of gender equality inevitably affected such traditional institutions as marriage. A social movement against the establishment caused youth to question the expected path toward marriage and children. After 1968, when Parliament modified Canadian laws, divorce became more frequent in Canada. By the 1970s, Canada registered one divorce for every three marriages. The trend was particularly apparent in Quebec, where, as in Newfoundland, divorce had been rare.

The sexual revolution also changed family patterns. Traditional sexual taboos relaxed as society became more liberal and tolerant. As it became less taboo to have sex out of wedlock, the need for marriage was further diminished. While homophobia remained deeply entrenched in Canadian society, gay and lesbian themes appeared in literature and films. Quebec writer Michel Tremblay introduced gay characters into his plays, while in English-speaking Canada Jane Rule published her first novel, *The Desert of the Heart*, with a lesbian theme. Same-sex relationships became more open after the federal government, declaring it had no place in the bedrooms of

CHAPTER FIFTEEN PROTEST AND REFORM: THE 1960s

the nation, legalized homosexual practices between consenting adults in private in 1969. Many parliamentarians who were favourable to the legislation nevertheless expressed the view that homosexuals were deviants who needed psychiatric help rather than prison cells. Most Conservative members denounced the changes on religious and moral grounds. While the Canadian Bar Association supported decriminalization, the Canadian Association of Police Chiefs vigorously opposed the legislation, asserting that it would lead to "depravity, robbery, and murder." In spite of their apparent victory, gays and lesbians worried that their concerns had now been reduced to narrow issues of criminal-law reform. A coalition of gay and lesbian liberation groups stated that, in spite of the reform, "we are still confronted with discrimination, police harassment, exploitation and pressures to conform which deny our sexuality."

Young people in general began to experiment with different types of living arrangements. For a time, communes were in fashion, although few lasted long. "Living together," or common-law marriage, hitherto frowned upon socially, gained popularity. Some women favoured living together, because they opposed marriage in principle as a form of economic servitude—women working without pay—disguised by the myth of romantic love. In most cases, for both women and men, convenience was also a compelling factor in favour of such unions.

WHERE HISTORIANS DISAGREE

Gay and Lesbian Activism

Gay and lesbian history in Canada is an expanding field. Emerging out of the new social history of the 1970s, gay and lesbian historians began "coming out" in academia. The 1969 Stonewall Riots in New York City, a particularly violent series of demonstrations resulting from a police raid on a gay bar, served as a catalyst for the gay liberation movement and consequently "queer" history. Local grass-roots historians as well as young academics in the United States began to trace the history of gay and lesbian persecution, identity, and community formation. Jonathan Ned Katz and John D'Emilio were pioneers in the field through their research into the history of homosexual community development in the United States.[1]

In Canada, a similar trend emerged. Sociologist Gary Kinsman wrote *The Regulation of Desire* in 1987, which was the first monograph to focus on the history of sexuality in Canada. He argued that "sexuality is not some natural essence which has been repressed; it is socially produced and regulated." Sexuality, according to Kinsman, is a social construction. Although Kinsman provided a close analysis of sexual regulation in Canada, he did not discuss the discursive roots of heterosexual hegemony. Kinsman's work remains the only monograph to trace gay and lesbian sexuality throughout the history of Canada.[2]

Historians Tom Warner, Becki Ross, and Valerie Korinek each studied the gay and lesbian liberation movement in Canada. Warner focused on activism over the past three decades, arguing that gay liberation "is the defiant response to pervasive, systematic homophobia and heterosexism."[3] Ross focused specifically on lesbian activism in Toronto and emphasized the gendered differences between the two groups: "Lesbians have been and are subject to gender oppression as women, but also to sexual oppression as perverts and queers. Clearly, lesbians have stood and continue to stand in a different social position with regard to official sexual discourse, legislation and police practices than have gay men."[4]

Valerie Korinek also challenged the historiography, and in particular, the urban-centric approach to the study of gay and lesbian liberation. Activism existed outside large urban areas, and groups were able to use the "small town ethos" to their advantage by creating lobbying networks with the heterosexual community.[5] While the dynamics differed, gay and lesbian liberation was not only an urban phenomenon. Queer historians in Canada are demonstrating the complex nature of the liberation movement by analyzing gendered and regional differences.

Other Canadian historians have studied gay and lesbian community development prior to the Stonewall Riots in 1969. Following the lead of American historian George Chauncey, Steven Maynard and Elise Chenier focus on the emergence of gay and lesbian subcultures in Toronto. Maynard argues that gay communities developed in the early twentieth century through alternative uses of public spaces. Men in Toronto developed cruising grounds throughout the city in public parks, lavatories, movie theatres, and bathhouses. These public spaces, according to Maynard, facilitated the development of a gay subculture.[6]

Chenier, in a similar fashion, studied the development of a lesbian bar culture in Toronto during the 1950s. Chenier argued that these women were able to negotiate their position in bars through alliances with heterosexual men. By accompanying straight men into bars, lesbian women were able to create a community centered on these establishments in working-class Toronto districts. Chenier and Maynard both connected the development of these subcultures to large urban environments, specifically Toronto. Gay men and lesbian women developed interconnected communities prior to the liberation movement.[7]

Queer history in Canada remains in its infancy. While impressive work has been done on the liberation movement, subcultures, and large urban environments, many avenues remain unexplored.

---

1   Jonathan Ned Katz, *Gay American History: Lesbians and Gay Men in the U.S.A.* (New York: Crowell, 1976); and John D'Emillio, *Sexual Politics Sexual Communities: The Making of a Homosexual Minority in the United States, 1940–1970* (Chicago: University of Chicago Press, 1983).

2   Gary Kinsman, *The Regulation of Desire: Sexuality in Canada* (Quebec: Black Rose Books, 1987), p. 15.

3   Tom Warner, *Never Going Back: A History of Queer Activism in Canada* (Toronto: University of Toronto Press, 2002), p. 14.

4   Becki L. Ross, *The House that Jill Built: A Lesbian Nation in Formation* (Toronto: University of Toronto Press, 1995), p. 6.

5   Valerie Korinek, "'The Most Openly Gay Person for at Least a Thousand Miles:' Doug Wilson and the Politicization of a Province, 1975–1983," *Canadian Historical Review* (2002): 520.

6   For information on the development of homosexual subcultures in Toronto at the turn of the twentieth century, see Steven Maynard's "Horrible Temptations: Sex, Men and Working-Class Male Youth in Urban Ontario, 1890–1935," *Canadian Historical Review*, 78(2) (June 1997): 191–236; "Through a Hole in a Lavatory Wall: Homosexual Subcultures, Police Surveillance and the Dialectics of Discover, Toronto, 1890–1930," in Joy Parr and Mark Rosenfeld, eds., *Gender and History in Canada* (Toronto: Copp Clark, 1996); and "'Without Working?': Capitalism, Urban Culture, and Gay History," *Journal of Urban History*, 30 (March 2004): 378–98.

7   Elise Chenier, "Rethinking Class in Lesbian Bar Culture: Living the 'Gay Life' in Toronto, 1955–1965," *Left History*, 9(2) (2004): 85–118.

Women: The Long Road

The desire for smaller families symbolized a more general desire by women for a change in their condition. In this era of protest, women's groups demanded that governments intervene, at both the federal and the provincial levels, to promote equality. Thus began the "second wave" of the women's movement.

Many women disagreed about the nature of the "ideal woman." Historian Valerie Korinek describes a contest created by *Chatelaine*, Canada's only mass-market women's magazine and a publication that contained numerous feminist articles and editorials. The goal of the contest was to discover Canada's foremost homemaker, "Mrs. Chatelaine," a stay-at-home wife and mother who also did volunteer work and could serve as a role model for readers. Some women, however, proposed other models. One suggested setting up a "Mrs. Slob contest," and named herself as winner. She admitted that she did not always serve nourishing meals, she liked fish and chips, she entertained only when her neighbours came in to gab, and she did not find time to do much volunteer work. She offered her philosophy: "Be happy, don't worry. You do what you can with what you've got when you feel like it."[3]

Canadian Voice of Women in a demonstration for peace, 1960s.

Source: Canadian Voice of Women for Peace.

As the 1960s began, women increasingly made their voices heard on national affairs. When *Toronto Star* journalist Lotta Dempsey lamented what appeared to be the increasing danger of nuclear war and wondered where the voice of women was, she hit a raw nerve: hundreds of women turned out for a public meeting at Massey Hall. The Voice of Women was born, and its membership grew to 10,000 in less than a year. Although it was soon racked by internal disputes, the organization had "a 'multiplier effect' on Canadian society out of all proportion to its size and the middle-class character of its membership."[4] Many of its participants later became activists in other women's associations.

Convinced that much more needed to be done, Laura Sabia, president of the Canadian Federation of University Women, called together delegates from 32 women's organizations across Canada who agreed in 1966 to form a new group dedicated to advancing the cause of women. Representatives from this nonpartisan Committee for the Equality of Women in Canada then met members of the federal cabinet to press for the creation of a royal commission on the status of women in Canada. Thérèse Casgrain and other members of the Fédération des femmes du Québec also attended in order to demonstrate that francophone women were making the same demands. Ottawa finally agreed, the following year, to set up a commission, but only after the committee threatened to organize a huge march on the national capital. In general, the media responded negatively to the appointment of the commission, portraying it as a waste of taxpayers' money.

The Royal Commission on the Status of Women, chaired by professional broadcaster Florence Bird, held hearings across Canada and received nearly 500 briefs. Issued in September 1970, the "Bird Report," which one journalist called "a bomb, already primed and ticking," called for a societal change in the attitude toward women. It proposed dozens of recommendations concerning women in the workplace, in political life, in education, and in family life.

Women in the Paid Workforce

Male-dominated legislatures adopted some laws that improved the lot of women. They made divorce simpler and maternity benefits more generous, and they granted tax deductions for child-care expenses. However, women's major demands for change—and, indeed, the changes themselves—occurred in the workplace. In 1961, only one married woman in five was in the labour force, often in part-time employment. Public attitudes still strongly disapproved of married mothers taking paid employment. By 1971, however, as increasing numbers of married women sought jobs outside the home, the proportion had risen to one in three. By 1981, it reached one in two.

Women who worked outside the home needed to find some type of day care for their small children. Until the 1960s, it was expected that they would make their own arrangements. Then feminists began to call for affordable state-supported day care that could enable women to exercise their right to work. It would be necessary to wait until the 1970s, however, before even modest state subsidies for provincial day-care centres became available.

Sex segregation in the workplace, resulting in "pink-collar ghettos," still remained the norm. As retail stores proliferated in a consumer-oriented society, many women found jobs as sales clerks. The expansion of health care and education also created traditional employment for women as teachers and nurses. Expanding governments hired large numbers of women for office clerical work. Indeed, in the late 1960s, the federal government became the largest employer of women in Canada. Eighty percent of its female employees worked in office or administrative-support jobs. Men dominated in the higher-level, better-paying managerial positions.

Ontario innovated in 1963 by establishing a women's bureau within the provincial Department of Labour. Although primarily responsible for research and public relations, the bureau became interested by the late 1960s in policy development and antidiscrimination initiatives. It helped bring about the adoption of the Women's Equal Employment Opportunity Act in 1970. In spite of many loopholes, the law provided for legal unpaid maternity leave and banned the firing of women upon marriage. Business complained that maternity leaves would eventually lead to paid leaves, a kind of "reward for pregnancy"; unions with largely male memberships also showed little enthusiasm for measures to counter discrimination against women.

Women disagreed over the means to effect necessary changes and, indeed, over the changes that they should seek. Some shared the liberal view that legislative reform would give women more equal opportunities. Younger, more radical feminists, inspired by theorists such as the American Kate Millett and the Australian Germaine Greer, believed that only a fundamental transformation of the economic and social structures that perpetuated the dominance of men would end female oppression. This group regarded the Bird Report as far too conservative and many feminists distrusted the political process itself. From the late 1960s, they waged a campaign for women's liberation through demonstrations and rallies, organized discussions, and in newspapers and other printed literature. Feminists were particularly active on university campuses where they established women's caucuses of Students for a Democratic Union. In Quebec, the Front de libération des femmes du Québec sought national independence.

Labour

In the 1960s, criticism of large multinational corporations increased. They were accused of being the principal villains in society and the prime forces of conservatism. Critics castigated business in general for its unquenchable thirst for profits, and for its failure to display any social or environmental conscience. Developers were accused of destroying old "character" neighbourhoods to build luxury highrise apartment buildings and office towers. In an age of rising inflation and of concern for consumers' rights, companies were denounced for gouging consumers by endlessly raising prices.

While these criticisms were not new, the voices of the left were now contained within more influential political organizations. Attacks on business and "the establishment" came from reformist political parties such as the Parti Québécois and the New Democratic Party (NDP), launched in 1961, the beneficiary of considerable union support. The major organized assault on business, however, came from unions.

Unions

Canadian workers became increasingly restive during the 1960s. The labour force grew younger as the first cohorts of baby boomers reached the workplace. Many of these new workers had high expectations, which they hoped to realize quickly. As well, in the late 1960s, rising consumer prices made it imperative for workers to obtain generous wage settlements. But more generally, the criticisms of society posited by labour no longer seemed as isolated and radicalized. They were no longer voices in the wilderness. Labour could now join with other voices to form a chorus of protest.

The union rank and file vigorously attacked authority. Workers frequently rebelled against their more conservative leaders by launching wildcat strikes (illegal work stoppages). A lengthy wildcat strike by Inco workers in Sudbury brought miners the highest wages in North America. Another clash at the Stelco plant in Hamilton, with considerable violence and destruction of property, enabled steelworkers to obtain substantial wage increases. During an illegal work stoppage on the railways, one striker explained that the "young guys" were "fearless. They don't give a damn for the company or the government or the union. It's a new generation.... We're our own boss now."

Many unionized workers were women. In contrast to the 1950s, when women often hesitated in their resistance to discriminatory practices in the workplace, they now waged "a more concerted and organized campaign for gender equality." In this regard, their actions became part of the emerging women's rights movement in the wider society. Results came slowly, however, because while they were quick to condemn class inequality, male union members were usually slow to condemn gender inequality. The breadwinner model worked to the benefit of male workers. Fighting for women's rights at the workplace seemed to threaten male jobs as well as the role of women in the home. In 1968, women at General Motors with six years' seniority were being laid off while the company continued to hire new men. One woman vented her frustration with a poem in the newspaper of the local United Auto Workers, to which she belonged:

> I read that whole darn paper and never make the grade;
>
> Do they just count the females when union dues are paid?
>
> We wait on recognition and it better show up soon,
>
> I feel more isolated than the men that walked the Moon.
>
> So all you fancy journalists, here's one thing to remember:
>
> I'm classed as just a female, but I'm still a union member.[5]

Workers (often women) in the rapidly growing public sector—teachers, hospital workers, civil servants, municipal employees, and others—also sought to improve salaries and working conditions. They successfully lobbied governments to place them on an equal footing with workers in the private sector, to recognize their right to form unions and, in many cases, to strike.

Public-sector unions soon became the largest in Canada and among the most militant. Lengthy work stoppages in the post office, for example, beginning with the postal workers' illegal walkout in 1965, became notorious.

Unlike the American-controlled international unions to which many private-sector workers belonged, public-sector unions were entirely Canadian. Indeed, in the climate of rising nationalism that characterized the 1960s and 1970s, some Canadian sections of international unions withdrew and formed their own Canadian unions.

A Cultural Renaissance

The social upheaval forced Canadians to rethink their relationship to the nation and to reconsider their identity. This process was already under way as a result of Canada's new place on the world stage and vis-à-vis its relationship with Britain and the United States. Questions of nationalism and national identity were mainstays in Canadian history. They were present at the time of Confederation in 1867; they were present during the tumultuous events of the first half of the twentieth century; not surprisingly, they were present when Canadians came to celebrate the nation's 100th birthday.

Both English and French cultural expression underwent a transformation in the 1960s. Universal education increased the potential market for cultural products, and higher disposable incomes and more leisure time made it possible for people to enjoy them. The appeal of mass culture, however, worried those in government who served as architects for the construction of a Canadian identity. They worried that hegemonic influences from the United States, for example, would undermine the development of this identity. Federal and provincial grant agencies gave considerable assistance to cultural endeavours, funding both organizations and individual artists. The Canada Council, for example, helped to finance the activities of the Montreal and Toronto symphony orchestras, several ballet companies, the Stratford Shakespearean Festival, and the Shaw Festival at Niagara-on-the-Lake. Most provinces invested substantially in libraries, museums, theatres, and concert halls. But how many Canadians could afford to participate in such high cultural displays? How did these lofty endeavours influence the average Canadian who was much more shaped by the forces of popular and mass culture that the state was railing against?

Literature

The 1960s saw the rapid growth of vibrant and diverse literature in both English and French, due in part to Canada Council grants and other federal and provincial government support programs. By 1970, most universities in Canada offered courses in Canadian literature. New literary periodicals such as *Canadian Literature* and *Liberté* were established to publish and critique Canadian writing. Several new publishing houses also appeared. Jack McClelland took over his father's publishing company in 1961. Under his leadership, McClelland and Stewart promoted Canadian literature and became a home for a new generation of writers.

Many of the most popular writers of the decade were women. Margaret Laurence, who spent her early life in Neepawa, Manitoba, and then lived in Africa and England for many years, wrote *The Stone Angel*, *A Jest of God*, and *The Diviners*. These novels were set in the fictitious town of Manawaka, which bore a close resemblance to Neepawa. Alice Munro, in some of her short stories set in Ontario's Huron County, examined the difficulties experienced by an adolescent girl in coming to terms with her family and with life in a small town. Margaret Atwood, who began her literary career as a poet in 1966 with the publication of *The Circle*

Game, published her first novel, *The Edible Woman*, in 1969, on the theme of women's alienation in a modern consumer society. These female novelists, however, faced difficulties not only in gaining recognition in their own nation but also in trying to make ends meet as both writers and mothers. The Canada Council Grants were essential in allowing these women to continue writing.

A sense of place and identity was important for many novelists. Ernest Buckler situated his *Ox Bells and Fireflies* in Nova Scotia. Robert Kroetsch, who grew up in rural Alberta, published an "Out West" series of novels before moving mainly into poetry. Rudy Wiebe, a Mennonite from the Prairies, set out to explore the tensions between pacifism and war in *Peace Shall Destroy Many*. The diversity of Canada, from small town to city, region to region, was manifest in the novels.

A new generation of poets also made their mark. Indeed, a volume on Canada's fifteen most outstanding poets in 1970 featured only three who were well known before 1960. Irving Layton was a Romanian Jew whose family settled in an impoverished immigrant district in Montreal. His provocative views on Israel, anti-Semitism, and other subjects attracted much attention. Al Purdy chronicled the geographical and historical complexities of Canada in such volumes as *The Cariboo Horses*, which he wrote after a trip to Baffin Island. Milton Acorn's populist poetry featured left-wing causes. In 1964, Acorn helped found the underground magazine *Georgia Straight* in Vancouver. Leonard Cohen of Montreal, with his brilliant lyrics and unique voice, gained an international reputation as a poet and as a singer and songwriter.

Nationalism played an important role in Quebec poetry. Fernand Ouellette dwelt on the alienation and oppression of the Québécois in *Le soleil sous la mort*, while Jacques Ferron's short stories dealt with the problems of maintaining Quebec's cultural identity.

Nationalism, however, formed only part of the general theme of liberation being experienced in Quebec during these years. Many novelists examined the emancipation of the individual in relation to society. *Une saison dans la vie d'Emmanuel*, which presented a sombre portrait of a tyrannical Quebec family, brought novelist Marie-Claire Blais a wide international audience. Feminist concerns permeated Françoise Loranger's *Encore cinq minutes*, while themes of war, sexual repression, and exploitation of the weak were central to Roch Carrier's highly acclaimed *La guerre, Yes Sir!*

A growing awareness and concern for Aboriginal rights inspired much of the work of Quebec novelist Yves Thériault. In his *Ashini*, the hero, a Montagnais (or Innu), commits suicide in the hope that his death will awaken his people from their apathy and bring them to claim their ancestral lands. Playwrights Marcel Dubé and Michel Tremblay made major contributions to French-language theatre. Tremblay's *Les belles-soeurs* violated traditional codes by being the first play to be written entirely in *joual*, French working-class slang.

Filmmaking

Canada's film industry underwent substantial development in the 1960s. The National Film Board (NFB), working on a mandate "to interpret Canada to Canadians and to other nations," began producing films in French as well as English, and even relocated its headquarters to Montreal. Quebec cinema flourished in both critical and box-office terms; in 1970, for example, one-third of the province's population went to the movies to see Claude Fournier's *Deux femmes en or*. English-Canadian film struggled much more in the shadow of an American industry that controlled film distribution. The creation of the Canadian Film Development Corporation in 1967 signalled the desire to maintain and develop a domestic film industry in the face of Hollywood's dominance.

Politics in the Age of Mass Media

Canadian politics in the 1960s also felt the winds of change. In the age of mass media, the cult of celebrity emerged and made the politics of personality much more important. The differences among political parties were more obvious in the period prior to 1945. It was clear what Liberals, Conservatives, and the CCF stood for and against. In the postwar era, however, the political spectrum narrowed considerably. It is doubtful that Mackenzie King would have enjoyed longevity in the age of mass media.

The advent of television in the 1950s increased this focus on personalities. In many ways, it changed politics by replacing traditional political picnics, public speeches, and tours. Television became a rapid and effective means of communicating information. Through the news and televised events such as leadership conventions and election debates, it brought politicians into the living rooms of Canadians. At the same time, television inhibited the thoughtful exposition of policies and promoted "simple and flashy promises and one-line put-downs of the opposition."[6] The media stressed conflict and confrontation in their coverage, emphasizing sensational and exciting occurrences rather than important policy initiatives. Prime Minister Lester Pearson once complained that "when we do discuss policies seriously … reporters do not even appear to listen, until we say something controversial or personal, charged with what they regard as news value." Television began to play a major role in moulding the images—favourable and unfavourable—of politicians.

Politics in Disarray

It did not help, however, that federal politics in the early 1960s promoted cynicism among many voters. The country faced serious problems. At the beginning of the decade, more Canadians were out of work than at any time since the Depression. Canada also incurred large deficits in foreign trade. The increasing cost of living provoked costly demands from unions. Relations with the provinces were often difficult, while growing discord also characterized ties with the United States. Voters wondered, however, whether either Progressive Conservative leader John Diefenbaker or Liberal leader Lester Pearson had the vision or strength to change the situation.

On four occasions these two politicians faced each other on the electoral battlefield; only in the first encounter, in 1958, was the result decisive. In 1962, 1963, and again in 1965, neither won enough seats in the House of Commons to form a majority government. Each made numerous—and costly—promises in attempts to rally more voter support. Some of their techniques elicited mockery and disdain. The Liberals, for example, published colouring books portraying Diefenbaker riding backward on a rocking horse. They also formed a "truth squad" to pursue the Conservatives relentlessly across the country to make sure they told the truth. The squad lasted three days. The results of these ploys were disastrous for the Liberals and

John Diefenbaker at the opening of Parliament, May 12, 1958.

Source: Cameron, Duncan/Library and Archives Canada/PA-112693.

only increased the skepticism of the electorate. Once elected, Canada's politicians devoted themselves to discussing a seemingly endless succession of alleged scandals. In his memoirs, Pearson gave the title "Politics in Disrepute" to a chapter on the years 1964 and 1965. While these political trends frustrated, annoyed, and alarmed voters, they were portents of things to come.

The Diefenbaker Government (1957–63)

When the decade of the 1960s opened, the Progressive Conservatives led by John Diefenbaker were in government in Ottawa. Diefenbaker first came to power in 1957 with a minority government; then, in an election called in 1958, he won a landslide victory. At first, "Dief the Chief" benefited from a very positive image. Different from many previous Conservative leaders in his populist appeal and image as the "Prairie's favourite son," Diefenbaker promised to champion the rights of ordinary Canadians. He was also a fiery orator, able to captivate audiences. Yet by 1960, his popularity had nosedived. In elections held in 1962, Diefenbaker barely managed to retain power with a minority government. A year later the Diefenbaker government was defeated and the Conservatives returned to the opposition benches for another long spell in the political wilderness.

Diefenbaker's Economic Policies

To some extent, the controversial prime minister became a victim of circumstance. After twenty-two years in opposition, the Conservatives had no experience with the art of governing, nor could they count on the support of many Ottawa bureaucrats whose loyalties lay with the Liberal Party. In 1961, a public dispute (which came to be known as the "Coyne Affair") between Diefenbaker and the Governor of the Bank of Canada James Coyne, demonstrated the lack of trust that existed between the prime minister and civil servants. Coyne wanted to battle inflation, while Diefenbaker, realizing that strategy would not be popular, instead wanted the Bank to infuse money into the economy. Coyne was forced out of the position, but not before releasing correspondence in an attempt to embarrass the government.

The severe recession of 1960–61, Canada's most serious since the Dirty Thirties, was not Diefenbaker's fault any more than the Depression had been R.B. Bennett's. But sharply rising unemployment posed serious challenges for the government, compromised its ability to launch new development policies, and undermined Diefenbaker's popularity. Industry encountered increased difficulty in selling goods to foreign markets and laid off workers as a result. Worldwide overproduction and declining prices of agricultural products hit Prairie farmers particularly hard.

Canada's surplus grain was purchased by China, the Soviet Union, and eastern Europe. Farm income on the Prairies increased significantly, and Conservative popularity in the region remained strong. The decision to sell to these communist countries resulted in criticism from the United States. The Diefenbaker government followed the traditional Conservative line and raised tariffs, but protectionism in the postwar era of multilateralism made the prime minister seem out of touch with the times. With increased trade to the United States, the higher tariffs were unpopular with consumers who found it more expensive to buy American goods.

As the Depression had shown, protectionism was not a solution to an economic downturn. To make matters worse, unemployment was rising and the issue brought back bitter memories to a generation raised in the 1930s. The federal government remained committed to Keynesian financing and kept spending in an attempt to pump-prime the economy. The decision provoked the business and financial community, already skeptical of the populist prime minister. The minister of finance even had to resort to austerity measures and to arrange emergency credits with the International Monetary Fund.

Even more controversially, in 1962, with the Canadian dollar falling in value, the government fixed it at a relatively low (for that era) 92.5 cents (U.S.). It was hoped that the measure would reduce Canada's trade deficit with the United States. The decision brought both outright condemnation by importers and enthusiastic approval by exporters. The Liberals protested that "devaluation" would mean higher prices for consumers. They printed thousands of so-called "Diefenbucks"—92.5-cent dollars adorned with the prime minister's likeness—which they used effectively during the election campaign of June 1962. The dollar's devaluation did indeed stimulate exports, but Canada's balance of payments with the United States remained negative as Canadian subsidiaries of American companies sent back dividends to the United States and Canadian visitors spent heavily.

The Canadian economy continued to weaken and Diefenbaker's critics charged him with economic mismanagement. They found an easy target when pointing out that Conservative governments were consistently matched with economic recessions. Although Atlantic and western Canada continued to endorse the Conservatives, Ontario and Quebec, and especially the cities, opposed him. By 1962, even traditionally Conservative newspapers such as the Toronto *Globe and Mail* and the Montreal *Gazette* were calling for a Liberal government to "get us out of the abyss."

In the election of 1962, the PCs won 116 seats with a popular vote of 37 percent. The Liberals won 99 seats with the same percentage of the popular vote, while a reorganized Social Credit won 30 seats and the NDP won 19. The Diefenbaker Tories tried to maintain government with a minority. Internal division, however, plagued Diefenbaker's cabinet and he faced attempts to remove him as leader as well as resignations. The government fell on two confidence votes in February that sent the nation into another election in 1963. Aside from the economy, the issue that caused Diefenbaker so much trouble was Canada's relationship with the United States.

Strained Relations with the United States

While this issue proved the nail in the coffin for his government, to an extent Prime Minister Diefenbaker represented the concerns of many Canadians. Diefenbaker worried about Canada's increasing economic dependence upon the United States. Like R.B. Bennett, he wanted to maintain closer ties with the Commonwealth and he promised to divert trade from the United States to Britain. But also like Bennett, he failed to realize or accept the difficulties in altering the direction of trade against the powerful forces of continentalism.

Regardless, Britain was seeking to boost trade links with Europe and not the Commonwealth. Indeed, the renewal in 1959 of Canada's defence production treaty with the United States had the effect of stimulating trade, especially in arms. And when the United States imposed controls on oil imports in support of domestic producers, Canada obtained an exemption from Washington, and Alberta oil continued to flow south. Diefenbaker also hoped to reduce American investment in Canada by applying a tax on interest, dividends, and profits sent to nonresidents. In practice, the measure had little effect other than to increase the prime minister's reputation for being anti-American.

If trade issues indicated a cooling of the Canadian–American relationship, the government's defence policy demonstrated a chill. The problem for Diefenbaker was that while he was championing Canadian nationalism by resisting American domination, the Cold War atmosphere made it impossible. The world was supposedly in a battle against the menacing spread of communism. Canada was expected to do its share and play the role of American ally. As a result, issues linked to continental defence embittered relations with the United States, who increasingly viewed Canada and its difficult prime minister as obstructive and untrustworthy.

Shortly after the 1957 election, Diefenbaker personally committed Canada to the North American Air Defence Command (NORAD)—the continental air-defence alliance headed by an American air force general. Then, in 1962–63, in a reversal of his original position, the prime minister refused to accept the nuclear warheads that the Americans wanted installed in their anti-aircraft missiles on Canadian soil. Spurred by his minister of foreign affairs, Howard Green, Diefenbaker became an opponent of nuclear weapons. Again, while his position was in sync with the sentiments of many Canadians, his critics accused him of waffling and being indecisive. When the government fell in February 1963, it was just one day after Douglas Harkness, the minister of national defence, resigned over the issue.

Diefenbaker's relationship with the United States was characterized by his tumultuous relationship with the highly popular President John F. Kennedy. The two politicians could not have been more different. Kennedy represented a golden age for American culture and politics. His charisma fit perfectly with the new age of television and the cult of celebrity. Diefenbaker, on the other hand, seemed tired, and out of touch with the pervasive youth culture. The two men disliked each other intensely and made little attempt to hide their disdain. Lawrence Martin, at the time *The Globe and Mail*'s Washington correspondent, wrote that Canadian–American relations were plunged into what was, up until then, their "worst state of disrepair in the century."[7]

The Avro Arrow affair symbolized the deteriorating relationship, as well as Diefenbaker's waffling. In 1953 the St. Laurent government agreed to fund the production of CF-105 Avro Arrows, airplanes designed to intercept Soviet nuclear bombers; they were at the time considered to be an advanced technical and aerodynamic achievement for the aviation industry. Almost immediately, however, the project ran into difficulties due to rising costs and delays that made the technology increasingly obsolete. Senior Canadian military officials questioned the viability of the aircraft and the overall project, particularly when the American Bomarc surface-to-air missile was developed. The Liberal government considered scrapping the project but decided to move forward. As a result, in 1957 Diefenbaker inherited what was already a military problem and a potential public relations nightmare. As the economy tanked, the potential for problems increased. After delaying for too long, Diefenbaker finally made the decision to scrap the Arrow.

By the early 1960s, Diefenbaker was squabbling with the United States over Canada's role in NATO. Aside from reversing his stance on storing American nuclear weapons on Canadian soil, he opposed NATO's policy of nuclear deterrence. His reputation in American circles deteriorated. The relationship between Diefenbaker and Kennedy hit an all-time low during the Cuban Missile Crisis of 1962. When the Americans learned that the Soviets were constructing missile installation sites in Cuba, President Kennedy threatened a nuclear response if the process was not halted. The United States established a naval blockade. NORAD automatically went on alert and moved to DEFCON 3 (defensive condition, a series of five alert stages moving toward a nuclear strike). The Americans assumed that Canada would follow the directive but Diefenbaker was opposed. Instead, he called for the United Nations to mediate the dispute. Meanwhile, NORAD forces moved to DEFCON 2 despite the opposition of the Canadian government. As a result of the poor relationship between Diefenbaker and Kennedy, Canada was kept largely in the dark about what was transpiring. The prime minister argued that the issue highlighted the lack of Canadian sovereignty and an American bullying attitude, but the vast majority of Canadians sided with President Kennedy. In the end, the Soviets responded to the game of "chicken" and withdrew. The world had never come so close to all-out nuclear war.

The Diefenbaker government seemed disorganized and rife with dissension, particularly regarding economic issues and relations with the United States. A paranoid Diefenbaker complained that enemies from within were plotting to "deliver up my head on a silver platter."

The Conservatives and Quebec

Diefenbaker's troubles were also tied to his party's lack of support in Quebec. Despite a seeming breakthrough in the province, the electoral support was a temporary backlash against the governing Liberals. The Conservatives had a weak party organization in Quebec, and Diefenbaker had little understanding or sympathy for the province. The prime minister's attempts at speaking French were often the subject of ridicule, even though Mackenzie King had never spoken French. In particular, Diefenbaker's attachment to the British monarchy and his championing of "unhyphenated Canadianism" alienated Quebeckers.

Third Parties, Right and Left

The rapid decline of federal Conservative strength in Quebec coincided with the rise of a third party in that province. Since the 1930s, when the party burst onto the scene by winning office in Alberta, Social Credit remained a fringe group in Quebec. Then, in the 1962 federal election, to the surprise of most observers, it won one-quarter of the popular vote and 26 seats in Quebec.

Social Credit's success may be explained partly by a desire for change. A vote for the créditistes was a way of striking back against the establishment. Leader Réal Caouette, an automobile salesman from Rouyn, in northern Quebec, joined Social Credit in 1939. In 1962, he carried his crusade through rural and small-town Quebec. He promised a national dividend to all citizens to raise consumers' buying power. He pledged help for the aged, the unemployed, and large families. Most of all he assured voters that they had nothing to lose by trying Social Credit. Cauoette delivered the same message to weekly television audiences. Social Credit's success had a considerable impact on federal Liberal fortunes by reducing the party's strength in Quebec, likely costing it the election in 1962 while ensuring that it could form only a minority government in 1963 and again in 1965.

Less spectacular was the reconstitution of the national Co-operative Commonwealth Federation. After its poor showing in the federal election of 1958, the CCF decided to cooperate with the Canadian Labour Congress and left-wing organizations to form a broad-based movement for social reform. In 1961 these groups launched the New Democratic Party (NDP), choosing Tommy Douglas, then premier of Saskatchewan, as leader. The party program called for jobs, health insurance, free education, and, in a break with the CCF's past tendency to favour a powerful central government, a policy of "cooperative federalism." Financial and organizational difficulties quickly put an end to the euphoria of the new party's initial moments. Electoral results during the 1960s at both the federal and provincial levels proved disappointing.

The Pearson Years (1963–68)

In the election of 1963, the Pearson Liberals promised a new Canadian flag, a reformed health-care program, and a new public pension plan. The Liberals won 128 seats (and 42 percent of the vote), while the PCs won 95, Social Credit 24, and the NDP 17. But the Liberals still had only a minority government. Fortunately for the Liberals, however, economic recovery seemed well under way. Unemployment dropped to about 5 percent as sales increased and companies began hiring more employees. Even the usually despondent *Globe and Mail* expressed optimism: "Where gloom and doom about the future of Canada has been the governing mood in recent years, there is now buoyancy and optimism." But by 1966, a new worrisome trend became evident: prices were rapidly rising.

Canadians battled inflation in various ways. Angry shoppers boycotted specific super-markets, accusing them of price gouging. The members of strong unions in key sectors of the economy, such as transportation, sought significant pay increases. Seaway workers demanded a 35 percent raise over two years and obtained 30 percent. Railway workers struck and won 24 percent, spread over three years. Air Canada's machinists went out in support of their demand for 20 percent in one year. These large increases, although important for workers, added to inflationary pressures. In 1967, while inflation showed no signs of abating, the economy slowed down noticeably. Economists coined a new word—*stagflation*—to describe the phenomenon of inflation at a time of slow economic growth.

Liberal Economic Policies

The Liberals failed to curb inflation. To little avail, the government urged companies to restrain price increases. It also raised some taxes in an effort to dampen consumer demand. The PC financial critic complained, boldly comparing the Liberal mini-budget to then-fashionable mini-skirts: "Taxes are getting higher and higher and covering less and less." Most Canadians strongly disagreed with the economists' explanation that inflation was caused by the fact that consumers had too much money to spend.

Rebuilding Relations with the United States

While the Pearson government struggled to improve the economy, it was successful in rebuilding Canada's relationship with the United States. Trade between the two countries continued to expand. The best example of this close economic relationship was the Automotive Products Agreement, signed in 1965. It provided for free trade among the manufacturers. Canadian drivers could not, however, bring automobiles duty-free from the United States. Most economists agree that the "Auto Pact," accompanied by a lower Canadian dollar, brought increased prosperity to southern Ontario, where Canada's automobile industry and most of its automotive parts industry were concentrated. Manufacturers now rationalized their production. Canadian plants specialized in producing relatively few models.

Increased trade with the United States spurred nationalist concerns and Canadians pas-sionately debated the issue of American ownership of Canadian industries. Walter Gordon, the Liberal finance minister, announced a tax on takeovers of Canadian firms by foreigners, but the ensuing protests from the U.S. government as well as from Canadian business leaders forced him to retract the proposal. Undaunted, Gordon published in 1966 *A Choice for Canada*, in which he argued that the country would have to choose between political and economic independence or colonial status in the American empire. He also set up a task force on the structure of Canadian industry, chaired by University of Toronto economist Mel Watkins, to study "the significance—both political and economic—of foreign investment."

The war in Vietnam also demonstrated the difficulties of maintaining good relations with the United States. Canada's involvement in the Vietnamese conflict dated to 1954. A long struggle against French imperialism resulted in the division of Vietnam into the communist North and the pro-Western South. Canada participated in a tripartite commission to supervise the truce. As the communist presence within South Vietnam intensified, however, the United States exerted pressure on Canada to defend Western and American interests on the com-mission. As North Vietnam continued its incursions in an attempt to reunite the country, the United States began to bomb North Vietnam and to boost substantially its military presence in the South. Public opposition to American intervention in the war mounted in Canada (and in the United States). Pearson refused American requests to send Canadian troops.

War in Vietnam—Pearson refused American requests to send Canadian troops.

Prime Minister Lester B. Pearson visits President John F. Kennedy, spring 1963.

Source: AP Images/The Canadian Press.

In April 1965 Prime Minister Pearson made a speech at Temple University in Philadelphia that was critical of American policy and urged the United States to stop bombing North Vietnam. At a meeting with Pearson that evening at Camp David, a furious President Lyndon B. Johnson reportedly seized Pearson by the lapels of his jacket and shouted: "Don't you come into my living room and piss on my rug." As the war escalated, so did Canadian criticism of American actions in Vietnam. But strong domestic opposition to the war now preoccupied the Johnson government far more than foreign criticism.

The contradiction within the Pearson government over Canada's relationship with the United States reflected a contradiction being experienced nationwide. It was a push–pull, love–hate relationship. On the one hand, Canadians were willing to join with their global superpower neighbour in combating communism and fighting the Cold War; they were more fond of American presidents than their own leaders; they hungrily purchased American consumer goods and embraced American culture; and they were jealous of American prosperity. On other hand, the traditional fear of domination loomed larger as American influence increased globally; Canadians sought their own national identity and balked when compared to Americans; and they demanded their own distinct voice on the world stage.

The Welfare State

The economic downturn reminded Canadians of the Depression, and both Progressive Conservative and Liberal governments responded by bolstering the welfare state. The Diefenbaker government increased old-age pensions; now Ottawa moved to improve its social-security programs for the poor. In 1966 the Canada Assistance Act—a coordination of largely existing provincial measures designed to aid persons unable to work or ineligible for unemployment insurance— was passed. Although the Pearson government turned down proposals to establish a national guaranteed income for all Canadians, it did make low-income pensioners eligible for a guaranteed income supplement.

The most significant programs launched by the Liberals concerned pensions and medical care. In 1965, Ottawa established the Canada Pension Plan, a compulsory and completely portable contributory plan paid for by workers and employers. Negotiations with the provinces proved arduous and Quebec chose to set up its own provincial plan.

Canadians increasingly called for universal medical care. The Liberals introduced hospital insurance in 1957 and, by 1961, the Diefenbaker government helped finance provincial plans across Canada. The Saskatchewan NDP government led the way in insuring the costs of medical services by establishing a health-insurance plan in 1962. In response, doctors in the province staged a bitter three-week strike before finally capitulating. Debate over constitutional issues and lack of agreement within the federal government slowed action on a Canada-wide program. Only in 1968 did Ottawa enact into law the National Health Insurance Program, also known as Medicare—a national health scheme that provided for financial

1968 - National Health Insurance Program

contributions to provincial plans, all of which had to be universal, comprehensive, portable, and publicly administered. But social and health programs proved costly: health expenses alone nearly doubled from $3.3 billion in 1965 to $6 billion in 1970. The federal government registered what would be its last budgetary surplus for nearly thirty years in 1969–70, a year after Pearson's departure from office.

Pearson's Legacy

The legacy of the Pearson government was based around conciliation and compromise. In this way, he followed the traditional Liberal path set by Laurier and King. In addition to his government's social and health legislation, Pearson initiated a series of federal–provincial conferences on the Canadian constitution and the issue of patriation, based around what he called "cooperative federalism." In answer to Quebec's claims for linguistic equality, he set up the Royal Commission on Bilingualism and Biculturalism in 1963 to study the issue and make recommendations. Also, after weeks of debate in the House of Commons, the Pearson government gave Canadians a national flag.

But Canadian nationalists accused Pearson of doing little to counter the forces of Americanization. Legislation designed to assist Canadian magazines contained important exemptions for the two biggest American magazines in the country, *Time* and *Reader's Digest*. Even though Diefenbaker had been lambasted for reversing his position regarding nuclear weapons, Pearson also waffled on the issue. The winner of the Nobel Peace Prize in 1957 revised his earlier position and authorized nuclear warheads for American missiles in the country. Canadians hotly debated the issue of American ownership of the Canadian economy but the Pearson government did little to control foreign investment.

Quebec nationalists argued that Pearson was resisting their legitimate demands, while strong centralists declared that his concessions to Quebec and the other provinces were balkanizing the country and whetting the appetites of separatists. Monarchists censured him for tolerating creeping republicanism, while French Canadians and new Canadians favoured a loosening of Canada's ties with the British crown. Residents of the Atlantic provinces claimed he was doing little to alleviate regional disparities and westerners judged him ill attuned to their interests. In sum, Pearson endeared himself to virtually none of the regions or major interest groups.

A Changing Economy

The country's economy underwent major structural changes during the 1960s. Services, such as those provided by governments, schools, hospitals, the communications industry, retail trade, and financial institutions, constituted the largest sector of employment. Manufacturing placed second. Primary industries, including agriculture, came last—a complete reversal of the Canada of 1867.

Such sectors as transportation and communications developed as a result of new technologies. Often they had difficulty finding the highly trained personnel required. In several other sectors, workers faced painful adjustments in the wake of job losses. Although employees in traditional "soft" industries such as footwear and textiles, hard hit by lost markets and cheap imports, suffered particularly, other industries also faced problems. Shipbuilders, for example, laid off thousands of workers as the federal government reduced subsidies and Canadian shipyards remained internationally uncompetitive.

Declining prices for their products and fierce competition from abroad led Canada's natural-resource industries to modernize in order to reduce costs. Technological change and market forces led to new challenges in agriculture. Large farms, with the equipment necessary to work more land and boost yields, became the norm. Small farmers lacked the means to make the necessary adjustments. In eastern Canada, for example, as dairies forced farmers to switch from cans to expensive bulk-storage equipment, farmers who kept only a few cows were forced out of business. Many abandoned the land that their families had farmed for generations.

Unequal Growth

Some regions of Canada—southern Ontario and parts of western Canada—prospered during the 1960s. Others, including the Atlantic provinces, much of Quebec, and parts of the Prairies, saw increased unemployment and poverty. Regional disparities had always been a product of the Canadian federation but these tensions increased to new levels.

regional disparities

On the 56th floor of the Toronto-Dominion Centre, Toronto, April 1966. Constructed from 1963 to 1969, this building was designed by the German-American architect Mies van der Rohe, and reflected the International style of architecture. Skyscrapers like this one came to dominate cityscapes from the 1960s onward.

Source: Photo by John McNeill/*The Globe and Mail*/The Canadian Press.

Prosperity in Ontario

The 1950s and 1960s were good for Ontario. Demand for a wide variety of goods stimulated industrial expansion, especially in the south, an area that became known as the "golden horseshoe." Services—banking, merchandising, education, health, and government—multiplied. The construction industry prospered due to strong demand for housing. Governments at all levels invested heavily in building highways and urban expressways. They also promoted urban transit, sponsored electric-power projects, including nuclear-power plants, and completed work on the St. Lawrence Seaway. This intense activity explains the province's generally low unemployment rate (below 4 percent from 1945 to 1970).

Western Canada

In the West, the development of natural resources continued apace during the 1960s, but as a result the region generally lacked economic diversification. To an extent, Manitoba was the exception. Manitoba's government invested heavily in northern development, where it favoured hydroelectric projects such as the huge installations on the Nelson River, and it attempted to attract private capital through loans and other concessions. Some projects such as the rich Inco mine at Thompson proved successful. Others failed: for instance, the Churchill Forest Industries complex at The Pas, which involved a government loan of $100 million, was halted when the owners disappeared with most of the money.

Saskatchewan relied heavily on agriculture but some experiments in diversification were successful. The province attracted private capital to develop its natural resources, including potash and pulp and paper. Alberta, however, proved to be the Canadian Cinderella story. It went from being the only province to declare bankruptcy during the Depression to being flush with oil money by the 1950s. Alberta's oil production increased when, in 1961, the Diefenbaker government acted to prevent Montreal refineries, using less expensive crude oil from Venezuela, from entering the Ontario market. This policy forced Ontario to buy oil from the West.

In British Columbia, the Social Credit government assisted large corporations in consolidating their control of the resource sector by offering tax concessions, low stumpage rates for timber, and cheap hydroelectricity. It improved highway, maritime, and rail transportation. It extended, at heavy cost, the Pacific Great Eastern Railway, linking the northern interior to the rest of the province. It nationalized the giant B.C. Electric Company and undertook hydroelectric projects. One of these, the gigantic Peace River Dam, built across the Rocky Mountain Trench, created Williston Lake, the province's largest body of water. Premier W.A.C. Bennett also successfully battled with the federal government over the terms of the Columbia River Treaty signed between Canada and the United States in 1961. The premier wanted to sell British Columbia's power allotment from the Columbia dams to the United States, while Ottawa opposed the sale.

The Maritime Provinces

Economic growth was slow in the Atlantic region. From 1951 to 1971, 15 percent of the population left the region in search of work. In Prince Edward Island, for example, the traditional "island way of life" disappeared as many small farmers, unable to compete because of low potato prices, abandoned farming.

Ottawa paid some heed to the region's complaints. In 1962, the government set up the Atlantic Development Board to fund projects and improve the region's infrastructure. Political and patronage considerations, however, often determined its choices. This initiative, together with equalization grants and other subsidies, facilitated the creation of jobs, albeit often temporary ones, and ensured that the area could offer its citizens services similar to those provided by wealthier provinces. In 1969, the newly established federal Department of Regional Economic Expansion (DREE) offered incentives to encourage companies to locate in less-favoured areas of the country, such as the Maritimes. The department spent money on highway construction, schools, and municipal services, and also attracted some new industry.

The provincial governments also sought to stimulate economic growth. Nova Scotia's Conservative government created Industrial Estates Limited, with well-known businessman Frank Sobey as its first president, to invest in local enterprises. Serious losses, however, followed the investment company's initial successes. New Brunswick's Liberal government led by Louis Robichaud—the province's first elected Acadian premier—intervened actively in resource development. When pulp and paper companies failed to use Crown lands they held under long-term lease, the government cancelled their licences and awarded them to other companies. When an American mining company reduced operations in its lead and zinc mine near Bathurst, Robichaud engineered a buyout by Canadian investors, including native son K.C. Irving, who set about building a huge smelter complex. Irving hired his own companies to perform the construction work on the smelter complex, but delays and ballooning costs caused the provincial government to allow a takeover by Noranda. Although the value of the mineral industry increased in the 1960s, the industry did not have the desired transforming effects on local economies.

The Robichaud government also created the Equal Opportunity Program, aimed at improving the lot of the province's poorer citizens, often French-speaking Acadians who lived in rural areas in the north and east. The government expanded health, social, and educational services. These measures generated fierce opposition among anglophones

New Brunswick Premier Louis Robichaud, the province's first elected Acadian premier. His administration in the 1960s built many hospitals, schools, and public buildings.

Source: Provincial Archives of New Brunswick/P57-15.

in the south, who regarded them as proof of a costly Liberal plot to "rob Peter to pay Pierre." In spite of the opposition, the Robichaud government moved to adopt the Official Languages Act, which aimed to provide linguistic equality to the province's francophones.

Newfoundland and Labrador

After Newfoundland entered Confederation in 1949, the federal government failed to restructure the fishing industry, especially the inshore fishery. Ottawa extended unemployment insurance coverage to seasonal fishers, a measure that helped increase the workforce at a time when the continued health of the industry necessitated significant downsizing.

Joey Smallwood, premier from 1949 until 1972, hoped to carry out an "industrial revolution" to create thousands of new jobs, stem emigration, and drag the province "kicking and screaming into the twentieth century." He encouraged foreign investment and sponsored projects to develop the province's natural resources, such as iron and pulpwood, as well as Labrador's vast hydroelectric potential at Churchill Falls. How successful was he? He dedicated a chapter of his memoirs to his twenty-three greatest failures in his twenty-three years in office, saying they "aren't even 10 per cent of the total; they are only the most serious ones."

A HISTORICAL PORTRAIT

Newfoundland Fishers

Culture transmits, through its diverse forms, the experiences that mark human life. In a plan to fight the poverty rife in Newfoundland's outports, the Smallwood government, mainly during the 1960s, had 250 smaller communities totally evacuated in household resettlement programs involving nearly 30,000 people. Many inhabitants were moved against their will.

Newfoundland artist David Blackwood memorialized the experience in his paintings. One work, titled *Resettlement*, showed an outport family in a boat piled high with their belongings. The painting captured the profound despair of people who had lost all control over their own destiny. Artist Gerry Squires also did several works on the same theme, including *The House Where Nobody Lives*, which showed one of the thousands of abandoned dwellings: "I still see the fear and the tears when people realized they could never come back."

The experience of relocation was also transmitted through songs that revealed the deep sadness of people at being separated from traditional livelihoods and familiar surroundings:

> No more we'll watch the caplin as they wash upon the sand,
>
> The little fish they used for bait, to fertilize their land;
>
> No more they'll watch their gardens grow or their meadows full of hay,
>
> Or walk the roads in their working clothes in the good old-fashioned way.[1]

The new communities into which outport residents were transplanted did not offer what had been promised. Songs often revealed the bitterness and frustration of those who had been uprooted and transplanted:

> To a place called Placentia, some of them went
>
> And in finding their new homes their allowances spent
>
> So for jobs they went looking, but they looked all in vain

> For the roof had caved in on the Government Game.
>
> It's surely a sad sight, their moving around
>
> Wishing they still lived near the codfishing ground
>
> But there's no going back now, there's nothing to gain
>
> Now that they've played in the Government Game.[2]

1   Reproduced with permission of Ernie Wilson. © Ernie Wilson.

2   Reproduced with permission of Pat Byrne and Al Pittman. © Pat Byrne and Al Pittman. SingSong Inc.

Environmental Concerns

Although most Canadians still took their environment for granted in the 1960s, an increasingly vocal minority realized the effects of industrial development. Critics pointed to pulp and paper companies, and to smelters in particular, as major polluters of the nation's air and water. They urged governments to force such companies to bear some of the huge costs of cleaning up the production process. In Ontario, environmentalists focused their attention on water quality in heavily industrialized areas of the province. *The Hamilton Spectator* complained in 1962 that "Sewage, detergents, sludges, chemicals, oil … they all pour into the harbour." Detergent manufacturers vied with each other to create the longest-lasting suds for washing machines and dishwashers. These suds eventually piled up along the shores of lakes and rivers. In the face of public outcry, the industry regulated itself and developed more biodegradable detergents.

By the late 1960s, concern was growing about the health of the Great Lakes. Algae proliferated, depleting oxygen levels and killing multitudes of fish. The cause was phosphates, again from detergents. At the University of Toronto, antipollution campaigners founded Pollution Probe, staging such events as a mock funeral for Toronto's "dead" Don River. After 1970, governments agreed to take steps to cut phosphate use dramatically in an effort to improve water quality.

First Nations Issues   Franchise - the right to vote,

Spurred by the civil rights movement, the dominant society showed more sensitivity to Aboriginal issues in the 1960s. Gradually, the provinces granted the provincial franchise to status Indians. Until 1960, First Nations people on reserves (approximately three-quarters of the Aboriginal population) could not vote in federal elections, but that year Ottawa extended the right to vote in federal elections to all status Indians unconditionally. The federally appointed Hawthorn Commission reported in the mid-1960s that it found that the First Nations occupied the lowest rung on Canada's economic ladder. The report concluded that "in addition to the normal rights and duties of citizenship, Indians possess certain additional rights as charter members of the Canadian community." After the publication of the report, Prime Minister Lester Pearson committed his government to revising the Indian Act, after consultation with First Nations people.

Prime Minister John Diefenbaker with Plains Cree at Maple Creek, Saskatchewan, during the 1965 federal election.

Source: © Government of Canada. Reproduced with the permission of the Minister of Public Works and Government Services Canada (2011). Location: Library and Archives Canada/Photograph by Bill Cadzow PA-154863.

The federal government also allowed more band autonomy. In 1960, for example, the Walpole Island band council in southwestern Ontario assumed responsibility for road improvements and other public works on the reserve. Five years later, the same band council gained control over the administration of its own local affairs. By 1966, approximately one-third of all bands in Ontario administered their own welfare services. Other bands created their own police forces, as Walpole Island did in 1967.

Beginning of the Trudeau Era

For many Canadians, the Diefenbaker–Pearson years marked the end of an era in Canadian politics. The shift from black-and-white television to colour seemed to symbolize a new, flashy style of politics. Canadians had only to look south to the United States to find a more attractive alternative. Diefenbaker may have been a powerful stump speaker but he was ill-suited to the politics of the television era. This became abundantly clear during the first televised leader's debates when the PC leader was visibly uncomfortable. Pearson was little better. His characteristic bow ties were hardly stylish. In the world of mass communications and popular culture that seemed increasingly built around youth, and with the American example of the Kennedys looming large, Canadian politics seemed in desperate need of a makeover. The public longed for a new style, a new type of leadership, an imaginative and refreshing approach to the complex issues of the day. In 1968, many believed that they found it in Pierre Elliott Trudeau.

It was not apparent who might succeed Lester Pearson when the Liberal leader announced his resignation in late 1967. Pierre Elliot Trudeau, the young and dynamic justice minister, attracted attention at the constitutional conference in early 1968 when he jousted with Quebec premier Daniel Johnson over the role of the federal government. He also endeared himself with youth when he supported policies that liberalized divorce laws, birth control, and homosexuality. His views on sexuality were articulated by his declaration that "the state has no place in the bedrooms of the nation."

The Path to a Political Career

Trudeau was a political rookie. He had been elected for the first time in 1965 when Pearson convinced him, along with labour leader Jean Marchand and journalist Gérard Pelletier, to enter the House of Commons to help renew Quebec's presence in Ottawa. Prior to that period, Trudeau favoured the NDP and its predecessor, the CCF. During the Duplessis years, Trudeau was a bitter critic of the Union nationale regime and, with Pelletier, he established a small-circulation magazine called *Cité libre* to give a voice to liberal-minded Quebeckers. He studied at Harvard and the London School of Economics and gained a reputation as a handsome, rich, womanizing globetrotter whose family wealth made it unnecessary for him to grow up and settle down.

Nevertheless, Trudeau's style and background intrigued delegates at the Ottawa leadership convention in 1968. As *The Globe and Mail* put it: "He is the man we all would like to be: charming, rich, talented, successful." This image was certainly at the basis of the wave of "Trudeaumania" that swept the nation during the Liberal leadership race and reached its height during the June 1968 federal election. The Liberals won easily with 154 seats (and 45 percent of the vote) to the PC's 72 seats, the NDP's 22, and Social Credit's 14. Trudeau was treated like a celebrity. Canada had found its John F. Kennedy.

Trudeau's Program

Trudeau's program differed from that of Pearson and Diefenbaker. In the 1968 campaign, he made few specific promises. He could afford to be confident and nonchalant due to his overwhelming popularity. Instead, he focused on broad but alluring messages, such as the search for a "just society," a society whose personal and political liberties were ensured by a charter of rights, a society in which minorities would be sheltered from the caprices of majorities, in which regions and social groups who had not participated fully in the country's material abundance would have greater opportunities. Trudeau appealed to participatory democracy, claiming that he wanted to have a conversation with Canadians about their country's future. He promised a complete revision of Canada's foreign policy in an effort to reorient and reinvigorate Canada's reputation and standing abroad.

Trudeau was a strong federalist who believed in a powerful central government and that Ottawa had allowed the provinces to erode federal power. When he asked for a strong mandate to oppose the Quebec government's ambitions to play a role in international affairs, Toronto newspapers congratulated him for his "firmness." He vigorously attacked new Conservative leader Robert Stanfield's implicit support for the "two nations" doctrine of a more decentralized Canada. Trudeau ardently supported a bilingual and bicultural vision for Canada. He promised Quebec that he would promote bilingualism in Canada, notably in the federal civil service, and that he would give Quebec a major role in federal politics. Trudeau's triumphant victory in the 1968

The election of Pierre Elliott Trudeau as Liberal Party leader, spring 1968.

Source: © Library and Archives Canada (LAC). Reproduced with the permission of LAC. Location: LAC/Credit: Duncan Cameron/Duncan Cameron fonds/PA-111214.

Expo 67, Montreal 1967—an exciting celebration of Canada's centennial year. Canada put forward its very best and invited the world. Some 50 million visitors attended.

Source: © Government of Canada. Reproduced with the permission of the Minister of Public Works and Government Services Canada (2011). Location: Library and Archives Canada/Centennial Commission fonds/C-0018536.

election suggested that he might succeed in building a new consensus among Canadians if he could overcome the Liberals' weakness in the West.

The Canadian Centennial, 1967

The 1960s were a time of celebration as well as confrontation. The highlight of the decade was the celebration of Canada's centennial in 1967. Provinces and municipalities vied in organizing festivities to mark the nationalistic event. Still, typically subdued Canadians gave vent to few of the effusions of American-style patriotism, and many wondered whether the country was going to succeed in holding itself together.

One centennial activity was not restrained: Expo 67, staged on an island in the St. Lawrence River at Montreal. The international showpiece event brought together more than 60 nations to celebrate the theme "Man and His World." Fifty million visitors passed through the turnstiles.

The federal government, now having adopted a more supportive role toward the Aboriginal peoples, helped to build a pavilion for the First Nations at Montreal's Expo 67. The Indigenous organizers of the pavilion used the building to tell Aboriginal Canada's story to non-Natives. At the entrance, a message greeted visitors: "The Indian people's destiny will be determined by them and our country, Canada, will be better for it." Inside, visitors saw, in bold script, statements such as "Give us the right to manage our own affairs" and "Help us preserve the moral values, the meaningful way of life, the inheritance of our forefathers." The anti-assimilation messages announced the First Nations' political agenda for the remainder of the century.

SUMMARY

The Canada of 1970 differed greatly from the country that had timidly embarked on an era of change in the late 1950s. Materially, most Canadians were better off than they had been a decade earlier. They were also better educated and more liberal in their views. The civil rights movement had a profound impact. Minority groups defended their interests more vigorously and found that society was more attentive to their claims. A cultural revolution occurred as the youth protested the stifling confines of tradition and convention. This revolution contained fundamental changes to attitudes toward gender and sexuality.

But the revolution was only just beginning and there was much work to be done. Divisions according to class, gender, race, ethnicity, sexual orientation, and region still marked Canadian society. In many ways, the 1970s would see a continuation of this era of rapid change as the nation faced a new series of challenges.

NOTES

1. Marcel Martel, *Not This Time: Canadians, Public Policy, and the Marijuana Question, 1961–1975* (Toronto: University of Toronto Press, 2006), pp. 198–208.

2. Doug Owram, *Born at the Right Time: A History of the Baby-Boom Generation* (Toronto: University of Toronto Press, 1996), p. 159.

3. Valerie J. Korinek, "'Mrs. Chatelaine' vs. 'Mrs. Slob': Contestants, Correspondents and the *Chatelaine* Community in Action, 1961–1969," *Journal of the Canadian Historical Association/Revue de la Société historique du Canada*, 7 (1996): 266.

4. Barbara Roberts, "Women's Peace Activism in Canada," in Linda Kealey and Joan Sangster, eds., *Beyond the Vote: Canadian Women and Politics* (Toronto: University of Toronto Press, 1989), p. 299.

5. Pamela Sugiman, *Labour's Dilemma: The Gender Politics of Auto Workers in Canada, 1937–1979* (Toronto: University of Toronto Press, 1994), p. 136.

6. Frederick J. Fletcher, "Playing the Game: The Mass Media and the 1979 Campaign," in Penniman, ed., *Canada at the Polls, 1979 and 1980: A Study of the General Elections* (Washington, DC: American Enterprise Institute for Public Policy Research, 1981), p. 319.

7. Lawrence Martin, *The Presidents and the Prime Ministers: Washington and Ottawa Face to Face: The Myth of Bilateral Bliss, 1867–1982* (Toronto: PaperJacks, 1983), p. 193.

BIBLIOGRAPHY

Overviews of the 1960s include Bryan D. Palmer, *Canada's 1960s: The Ironies of Identity in a Rebellious Era* (Toronto: University of Toronto Press, 2009). More dated studies include Robert Bothwell, Ian Drummond, and John English, *Canada since 1945: Power, Politics, and Provincialism*, rev. ed. (Toronto: University of Toronto Press, 1989); and J.L. Granatstein, *Canada, 1957–1967: The Years of Uncertainty and Innovation* (Toronto: McClelland & Stewart, 1986). Social history is available in Alvin Finkel, *Social Policy and Practice in Canada: A History* (Waterloo, ON: Wilfrid University Press, 2006). Doug Owram studies the baby boom's effects in *Born at the Right Time: A History of the Baby-Boom Generation* (Toronto: University of Toronto Press, 1996). On Canada's centennial, a highlight of the 1960s, see Gary Miedema, *For Canada's Sake: Public Religion, Centennial Celebrations, and the Remaking of Canada in the 1960s* (Montreal/Kingston: McGill-Queen's University Press, 2005).

David Cameron provides much material on universities in the 1960s in *More Than an Academic Question: Universities, Government, and Public Policy in Canada* (Halifax: Institute for Research on Public

Policy, 1991). On the role of women in advancing education in Canada, see Kristina R. Llewellyn, *Democracy's Angels: The Work of Women Teachers* (Montreal/Kingston: McGill-Queen's University Press, 2012). Drug policy is discussed in Marcel Martel, *Not This Time: Canadians, Public Policy, and the Marijuana Question, 1961–1975* (Toronto: University of Toronto Press, 2006). RCMP espionage on university campuses is treated in Steve Hewitt, *Spying 101: The RCMP's Secret Activities at Canadian Universities, 1917–1997* (Toronto: University of Toronto Press, 2002). For a look at foreign policy and defence policy in this era, see Norman Hillmer and Adam Chapnick, eds., *Canadas of the Mind: The Making and Unmaking of Canadian Nationalisms in the Twentieth Century* (Montreal/Kingston: McGill-Queen's University Press, 2007); and Joseph T. Jockel, *Canada in NORAD, 1957–2007* (Montreal/Kingston: McGill-Queen's University Press, 2007). For domestic concerns during Cold War Canada, consult Andrew Burtch, *Give Me Shelter: The Failure of Canada's Cold War Civil Defence* (Vancouver: UBC Press, 2012).

On environmental concerns of the 1960s and the resultant rise of environmentalism, see Ryan O'Connor, *The First Green Wave: Pollution Probe and the Origins of Environmental Activism in Ontario* (Vancouver: UBC Press, 2015); Jennifer L. Bonnell, *Reclaiming the Don: An Environmental History of Toronto's Don River Valley* (Toronto: University of Toronto Press, 2014); and Frank S. Zelko, *Make It a Greenpeace! The Rise of Countercultural Environmentalism* (New York: Oxford University Press, 2013).

The evolution of Canada's welfare state is discussed in Jacqueline S. Ismael, ed., *The Canadian Welfare State: Evolution and Transition* (Edmonton: University of Alberta Press, 1987); Keith Banting, *The Welfare State and Canadian Federalism*, 2nd ed. (Montreal/Kingston: McGill-Queen's University Press, 1987); and Allan Moscovitch and Jim Albert, eds., *The 'Benevolent' State: The Growth of Welfare in Canada* (Toronto: Garamond Press, 1987). On the 1960s in particular, see Penny E. Bryden, *Planners and Politicians: The Liberal Party and Social Policy, 1957–1968* (Montreal/Kingston: McGill-Queen's University Press, 1997). John R. Miron, ed., studies housing in *House, Home, and Community: Progress in Housing Canadians, 1945–1986* (Montreal/Kingston: McGill-Queen's University Press, 1993). For an examination of Medicare, see Gerard W. Boychuk, *National Health Insurance in the United States and Canada: Race, Territory, and the Roots of Difference* (Washington, DC: Georgetown University Press, 2008). For a classic study of the role of social class and power in Canadian society, see John Porter, *The Vertical Mosaic* (Toronto: University of Toronto Press, 1965).

For further study of Canadian literature, W.H. New, ed., *Encyclopedia of Literature in Canada* (Toronto: University of Toronto Press, 2002); and Eugene Benson and William Toye, *The Oxford Companion to Canadian Literature*, 2nd ed. (Toronto: Oxford University Press, 1997), are good sources. See also Branko Gorjup, ed., *Northrop Frye's Canadian Literary Criticism and Its Influence* (Toronto: University of Toronto Press 2009). Gary Evans, *In the National Interest: A Chronicle of the National Film Board of Canada from 1949 to 1989* (Toronto: University of Toronto Press, 1991), describes the activity of an important cultural institution. More recent scholarship includes Thomas Waugh, Michael Brendan Baker, and Ezra Winton, eds., *Challenge for Change: Activist Documentary at the National Film Board of Canada* (Montreal/Kingston: McGill-Queen's University Press 2010); and Zoe Druick, *Projecting Canada: Government Policy and Documentary Film at the National Film Board* (Montreal/Kingston: McGill-Queen's University Press, 2007).

Paul Rutherford offers a lengthy description of television programs of the era in *When Television Was Young: Primetime Canada, 1952–1967* (Toronto: University of Toronto Press, 1990). Ted Magder studies the history of Canadian filmmaking in *Canada's Hollywood: The Canadian State and Feature Films* (Toronto: University of Toronto Press, 1993). Sport history in this period is discussed in Colin Howell, *Blood, Sweat, and Cheers: Sport and the Making of Modern Canada* (Toronto: University of Toronto Press, 2001).

For syntheses of women's history, see the bibliography of this book's Chapter 14. Books that study the role of women in politics include Sydney Sharpe, *The Gilded Ghetto: Women and Political Power in Canada* (Toronto: HarperCollins, 1994); and Sylvia Bashevkin, *Toeing the Lines: Women and Party Politics in English Canada*, 2nd ed. (Toronto: Oxford University Press, 1993). Judith Fingard and Janet Guildford examine women's issues in Halifax in *Mothers of the Municipality: Women, Work, and Social Policy in Post-1945 Halifax* (Toronto: University of Toronto Press, 2005). Tarah Brookfield situates women and families in the context of the *Cold War in Cold War Comforts: Canadian Women, Child Safety, and Global Insecurity* (Waterloo: Wilfrid Laurier Press, 2012). For lesbian women, see Liz Millward, *Making a Scene: Lesbians and Community across Canada, 1964–1984* (Vancouver: UBC Press, 2015). For debates around birth control, see Katrina Ackerman, "In Defense of Reason: Religion, Science, and the Prince Edward Island Anti-Abortion Movement, 1969–1988," *Canadian Bulletin of Medical History* 31, no. 2 (2014); and Christabelle Sethna, "The Evolution of the *Birth Control Handbook* From Student Peer-Education Manual to Feminist Self-empowerment Text, 1968–1975," *Canadian Bulletin of Medical History* 23, no. 1 (2006) 89–118.

How the media responded to the feminist movement is discussed in Barbara Freeman, *The Satellite Sex: The Media and Women's Issues in English Canada, 1966–1971* (Waterloo, ON: Wilfrid Laurier University Press, 2001). On birth control, consult Angus McLaren and Arlene Tigar McLaren, *The Bedroom and the State: The Changing Practices and Politics of Contraception and Abortion in Canada, 1880–1980* (Toronto: McClelland & Stewart, 1986). Issues linked to homosexuality are presented in Gary Kinsman, *The Regulation of Desire: Homo and Hetero Sexualities*, 2nd ed. (Montreal: Black Rose Books, 1996); and Bruce MacDougall, *Queer Judgments: Homosexuality, Expression, and the Courts in Canada* (Toronto: University of Toronto Press, 2000). For a "feel" for the era, see Gerry Kopelow, *All Our Changes: Images from the Sixties Generation* (Winnipeg: University of Manitoba Press 2009); M. Athena Palaeologu, ed., *The Sixties in Canada: A Turbulent and Creative Decade* (Montreal: Black Rose Books, 2009); Dimitry Anastakis, ed., *The Sixties: Passion, Politics, and Style* (Montreal/Kingston: McGill-Queen's University Press, 2008); and Stuart Henderson, *Making the Scene: Yorkville and Hip Toronto in the 1960s* (Toronto: University of Toronto Press, 2011).

For works that chronicle postwar labour and the emergence of the New Left in Canada, see Ian Milligan, *Rebel Youth: 1960s Labour Unrest, Young Workers, and New Leftists in English Canada* (Vancouver: UBC Press, 2015), and Benjamin Isitt, *Militant Minority: British Columbia Workers and the Rise of a New Left, 1948–1972* (Toronto: University of Toronto Press, 2011). On Aboriginals in the postwar economy see Mary Jane Logan McCallum, *Indigenous Women, Work, and History, 1940–1980* (Winnipeg: University of Manitoba Press, 2014); Mary-Ellen Kelm, *A Wilder West: Rodeo in Western Canada* (Vancouver: UBC Press, 2011); and James Kenny and Bill Parenteau, "'Each year the Indians flexed their muscles a little more': The Maliseet Defence of Aboriginal Fishing Rights on the St. John River, 1945–1990," *Canadian Historical Review* 95, no. 2 (2014): 187–216. Janis Thiessen looks at how Mennonites reconciled their theology with Canadian capitalism in *Manufacturing Mennonites: Work and Religion in Post-War Manitoba* (Toronto: University of Toronto Press, 2012). For a broader look at religion, see Kevin N. Flatt, *After Evangelicalism: The Sixties and the United Church of Canada* (Montreal/Kingston: McGill-Queen's University Press, 2013).

A detailed survey of the economy can be found in Kenneth Norrie and Douglas Owram, *A History of the Canadian Economy*, 4th ed. (Toronto: Nelson, 2008). Dimitry Anastakis, *Auto Pact: Creating a Borderless North American Auto Industry, 1960–1971* (Toronto: University of Toronto Press, 2005) examines a major economic development of the day. Among syntheses of labour history containing material on the 1960s are Craig Heron, *The Canadian Labour Movement: A Short History*, rev. ed. (Toronto: James Lorimer, 2012); Desmond Morton, *Working People: An Illustrated History of the Canadian Labour Movement*, 5th ed. (Montreal/Kingston: McGill-Queen's University Press, 2007); and Bryan D. Palmer, *Working-Class Experience: Rethinking the History of Canadian Labour 1800–1991*, 2nd ed. (Toronto: McClelland & Stewart, 1992).

Works on John Diefenbaker include Garrett Wilson and Kevin Wilson, *Diefenbaker for the Defence* (Toronto: James Lorimer, 1988); and Denis Smith, *Rogue Tory: The Life and Legend of John G. Diefenbaker* (Toronto: Macfarlane Walter & Ross, 1995). Peter Newman offers a "striptease contribution" (in Pearson's words) of the Diefenbaker–Pearson rivalry in *The Distemper of Our Times*, rev. ed. (Toronto: McClelland & Stewart, 1990). On the Bank of Canada and the "Coyne Affair," see James Powell, *The Bank of Canada of James Elliot Coyne: Challenges, Confrontation, and Change* (Montreal/Kingston: McGill-Queen's University Press, 2009).

On Pearson, consult the diplomat-politician's *Mike: The Memoirs of the Right Honourable Lester B. Pearson*, 3 vols. (Toronto: University of Toronto Press, 1972–75); as well as John English's biography, *The Worldly Years: The Life of Lester Pearson*, vol. 2, *1949–1972* (Toronto: Knopf Canada, 1992). A critical examination of Pearson's legacy may be found in Norman Hillmer, ed., *Pearson: The Unlikely Gladiator* (Montreal/Kingston: McGill-Queen's University Press, 1999).

Pierre Elliott Trudeau's early career is presented in John English, *Just Watch Me: The Life of Pierre Elliott Trudeau, 1968–2000* (Mississauga, ON: Random House 2009); and Stephen Clarkson and Christina McCall Newman, *Trudeau and Our Times*, vol. 1, *The Magnificent Obsession* (Toronto: McClelland & Stewart, 1990). For an examination of the politics of Robert Stanfield, see Richard Clippingdale, *Robert Stanfield's Canada: Perspectives of the Best Prime Minister We Never Had* (Montreal/Kingston: McGill-Queen's University Press, 2008). See also Claude Morin, *Mes premiers ministres: Lesage, Johnson, Bertrand, Bourassa et Levesque* (Montreal: Boreal, 1991).

Maurice Pinard analyzes the Social Credit phenomenon in Quebec in *The Rise of a Third Party: A Study in Crisis Politics* (Montreal/Kingston: McGill-Queen's University Press, 1975). On the NDP, see Desmond Morton, *The New Democrats, 1961–1986: The Politics of Change* (Toronto: Copp Clark Pitman, 1986). See also William Christian and Colin Campbell, *Political Parties and Ideologies in Canada* (Toronto: McGraw-Hill Ryerson, 1995). English Canada's changing identity is discussed in Philip Buckner, ed., *Canada and the End of Empire* (Vancouver: UBC Press, 2005); and José E. Igartua, *The Other Quiet Revolution: National Identities in English Canada, 1945–71* (Vancouver: UBC Press, 2006).

On aspects of Canada's international relations, see Robert Bothwell, *Alliance and Illusion: Canada and the World, 1945–1984* (Vancouver: UBC Press, 2007); and John English and Norman Hillmer, eds., *Making a Difference? Canada's Foreign Policy in a Changing World Order* (Toronto: Lester, 1992). Studies of Canadian–American relations with material on the 1960s include J.L. Granatstein and Norman Hillmer, *For Better or for Worse: Canada and the United States to the 1990s* (Toronto: Copp Clark Pitman, 1991); John Herd Thompson and Steven Randall, *Canada and the United States: Ambivalent Allies*, 4th ed. (Montreal/Kingston: McGill-Queen's University Press, 2008 for economic issues, Bruce Muirhead, *Dancing Around the Elephant: Creating a Prosperous Canada in an Era of American Dominance, 1957–1973* (Toronto: University of Toronto Press, 2005); and Jessica Squires, *Building Sanctuary: The Movement to Support Vietnam War Resisters in Canada, 1965–73* (Vancouver: UBC Press, 2013). On Canada's relationship with Britain and India, see Ryan M. Touhey, *Conflicting Visions: Canada and India in the Cold War, 1946–76* (Vancouver: UBC Press, 2015).

For a provocative essay on the subject of nationalism, see a new edition of George Grant's classic of the 1960s, *Lament for a Nation: The Defeat of Canadian Nationalism* (Montreal/Kingston: McGill-Queen's University Press, 2005); see also Hugh Donald Forbes, *George Grant: A Guide to His Thought* (Toronto: University of Toronto Press 2007); and Robert C. Sibley, *Northern Spirits: John Watson, George Grant, and Charles Taylor—Appropriations of Hegelian Political Thought* (Montreal/Kingston: McGill-Queen's University Press, 2008). On the flag debate, see C.P. Champion, "A Very British Coup: Canadianism, Quebec, and Ethnicity in the Flag Debate, 1964–1965," *Journal of Canadian Studies*, 40(3) (2006): 68–99. On Canada's involvement in the war in Vietnam, consult Douglas Ross, *In the Interests of Peace: Canada and Vietnam, 1954–1973* (Toronto: University of Toronto Press, 1984).

The best overview of the Atlantic provinces is E.R. Forbes and D.A. Muise, eds., *The Atlantic Provinces in Confederation* (Toronto: University of Toronto Press, 1993). A general survey of Ontario is available in Randall White: *Ontario, 1610–1985: A Political and Economic History* (Toronto: Dundurn Press, 1985); the province's economy is studied in K.J. Rea, *The Prosperous Years: The Economic History of Ontario, 1939–75* (Toronto: University of Toronto Press, 1985). For federal–provincial relations during this time period, see P.E. Bryden, *'A Justifiable Obsession': Conservative Ontario's Relations with Ottawa, 1943–1985* (Toronto: University of Toronto Press, 2013); and Raymond Blake, *Lions or Jellyfish: Newfoundland–Ottawa Relations since 1957* (Toronto: University of Toronto Press, 2015).

Overviews of western Canada include Gerald Friesen, *The Canadian Prairies: A History* (Toronto: University of Toronto Press, 1984); John Thompson, *Forging the Prairie West: The Illustrated History of*

Canada (Don Mills, ON: Oxford University Press, 1998); and John F. Conway, *The West: The History of a Region in Confederation*, 3rd ed. (Toronto: James Lorimer, 2006). Alberta and British Columbia are studied in Howard and Tamara Palmer, *Alberta: A New History* (Edmonton: Hurtig, 1990); and Jean Barman, *The West Beyond the West: A History of British Columbia*, 3rd ed. (Toronto: University of Toronto Press, 2007), respectively.

Chapter Sixteen

THE MAKING OF MODERN QUEBEC

TIME LINE

1959	Maurice Duplessis dies
1960	Quebec Liberals defeat Union nationale and usher in Quiet Revolution
1963	Nationalization of all electric companies in Quebec under Hydro-Québec The Royal Commission on Education presents report
1966	The Metro (subway) system in Montreal begins service
1967	De Gaulle proclaims "Vive le Québec libre" during a speech from the balcony of Montreal's City Hall
1968	Parti Québécois founded through amalgamation of Mouvement souveraineté-association and the Ralliement national
1969	The huge Manic-5 Dam on Manicouagan River inaugurated Trudeau government passes Bill C-120, making French and English official languages of Canada FLQ terrorists bomb Montreal Stock Exchange
1970	October Crisis in Quebec; War Measures Act invoked
1976	Election of the Parti Québécois led by René Lévesque
1977	Bill 101, the Charter of the French Language, adopted Quebec becomes first Canadian province to protect gays and lesbians from discrimination
1980	Referendum on sovereignty-association defeated
1985	Lévesque resigns as head of Parti Québécois; Liberals back in power
1987	Quebec's National Assembly ratifies Meech Lake Accord
1990	Meech Lake Accord dies in Manitoba's Legislative Assembly Bouchard resigns from Mulroney cabinet; founds Bloc Québécois
1995	Referendum on sovereignty is defeated by narrow margin
1998	A major ice storm deprives three million Quebeckers (and many Canadians elsewhere) of electricity
2003	Quebec Liberal Party defeats Parti Québécois and forms government Quebec Court legalizes same-sex marriage in province
2007	Jean Charest's Liberals win election with the ADQ forming opposition and relegating Parti Québécois to third place
2008	Quebec City celebrates 400th anniversary Charest's Liberals win slim majority but Parti Québécois returns as official opposition

Quebec underwent an era of rapid change in the years after 1960, as the province evolved into a more modern and secular society. In many ways, Quebec became more like other regions of North America. Yet, at the same time, many French-speaking Quebeckers (or Québécois, as Quebec francophones now began to style themselves) pushed their society to reinforce its unique linguistic and cultural character. This era, dubbed the "Quiet Revolution," was marked by reform and a new, aggressive French-Canadian nationalism.

The processes of modernization began well before 1960. Despite the utopian desires of the influential Catholic Church to have Quebec remain largely agrarian and rural, the province was an industrial and urban society by the end of the nineteenth century. But the influence of the church working closely with the provincial government, worked against the forces of modernization. These forces proved impossible to stop. As a result, the image created by church and state was out of step with the reality in Quebec. Young French Canadians were educated in a traditional but outdated system; they were taught that the cities were corrupting places and that business was the domain of les anglais. The situation allowed the English minority to maintain considerable control of Quebec's economic levers. It also allowed American investment considerable influence. This era, characterized by the political leadership of the colourful but iron-fisted premier, Maurice Duplessis, later became known by critics as the grande noirceur or "Dark Ages."

Change in Quebec was brought about by the death of Duplessis in 1959 and the readiness of a new government to implement important reforms. An increasingly interventionist Quebec state became a catalyst for change in nearly all sectors of activity, from the economy and education to health and culture. At the same time, as elsewhere in the Western world in the 1960s, many Quebeckers demanded and welcomed change.

English Canada observed Quebec with increasing concern. The resurgence of nationalism in the province had implications for the rest of the country. But this was not the traditional Catholic nationalism of such influential figures as the priest and historian Lionel Groulx, based upon the land, the parish, and the family; it was not the pan-French-Canadian nationalism of Henri Bourassa, based upon a bicultural, two-nations foundation; this was an aggressive secular nationalism based upon the city, the language, and the state. Francophones in Quebec complained of being second-class citizens, and sought control of their own province and recognition for their language. Religion was pushed aside as language became the essential medium for la survivance of the French Canadians in North America. When various political movements and parties vied with one another in claiming greater political autonomy for Quebec—and even independence— Canada's future as a united nation appeared to be in doubt. The aspirations of many Quebeckers appeared threatening to the rest of Canada.

During the 1995 Quebec referendum debate, Charles Jefferson of Ottawa raised a Canadian flag over a street sign in Montreal. The street, once named Dorchester, a British governor after the conquest, was renamed Boulevard René-Lévesque, for the late Quebec premier, one of the founders of the mainstream separatist movement in Quebec.

Source: CP PHOTO/Robert Galbraith.

Quebec after World War II

Maurice Duplessis and his conservative Union nationale Party first took power in Quebec in 1936 during the Great Depression. Canadian federalism was in crisis as evidenced by the bitter battles between Ottawa and the provinces. The federal government took over areas of provincial jurisdiction because the provinces were in financial difficulty, with some even facing bankruptcy. In Quebec, the moves toward centralization and a more interventionist state were resisted because they threatened the role of the provincial government in defending culture. Duplessis became a thorn in the side of the Mackenzie King government. His government held power with the strong support of the Catholic Church, and his Union nationale Party was strongest in the rural areas of the province.

When war broke out in 1939, Duplessis made it clear that he would continue to oppose the federal Liberals in Ottawa. Prime Minister King used the patriotic fervour created by the war to take the questionable step of interfering in the Quebec election and helping defeat Duplessis. He threatened Quebec by arguing that if the Union nationale was elected, the influential Quebec ministers in his government, including the popular Ernest Lapointe, would resign, leaving the province without influence in the face of a potential conscription issue. The ploy worked and Duplessis was defeated. During the war, Quebec was administered by the Liberal government of Premier Adélard Godbout. It was widely viewed as a puppet of Ottawa, however, and lost support over issues linked to the federal Liberals, such as conscription and increasing centralization. With Duplessis' return to power in 1944, the Union nationale began an unbroken sixteen-year reign.

During the period from 1945 to 1960, Quebec's demography changed, much as Canada's as a whole did. The province's population increased rapidly, by more than 25 percent in the 1950s. Although 400,000 immigrants settled in the province in these years, most of the rise in population stemmed from an increased birth rate. Also affecting the province's demography, large numbers of rural inhabitants moved to the cities in search of work.

Quebec also underwent rapid economic growth as investment—much of it foreign—accelerated. The United States not only provided a market, it also supplied development capital for resource industries such as mining. Employment in the principal manufacturing industries also increased significantly, but the major gains in jobs came in the service industries. Due to the booming economy, Quebeckers who like other Canadians had endured the sacrifices of depression and war, now enjoyed greater prosperity.

Traditional ideas and values gave way. Religious practice declined, particularly in Montreal. Radio and, especially, television introduced new ideas, norms, and values from beyond Quebec's borders. "Television brought the world, no longer filtered by press, priest, or politician, into Quebec's kitchens and living rooms."[1]

Amid these changes, the conservative Duplessis, supported by traditional elites, continued to emphasize the importance of religious values and respect for the established order. His government favoured private enterprise, encouraged the entry of foreign (largely American) capital, and kept taxes low. It built roads and bridges, especially in election years, and aided small-scale farmers, from whom it derived its electoral support.

Labour Unrest

Duplessis was a bitter opponent of the unions. He tolerated the Catholic unions in Quebec but was adamant in preventing incursions by the more militant organizations from outside the province. As a result, his government designed labour legislation to limit strikes, and provincial labour boards showed a pro-employer bias. At times the government used the provincial police to protect strikebreakers or break up demonstrations. It set a low minimum wage for non-unionized workers, which affected large numbers of working women and immigrants. Other glaring inequalities, which the government did little to alleviate, also cast a pall over the general atmosphere of prosperity. Average wages of French Canadians as a group were lower than those of most other ethnic groups in the province. The strident opposition of the Catholic Church to socialism and communism helped create a stifling atmosphere in Quebec.

Opposition to Duplessis

In the 1950s, Duplessis' opponents became increasingly vocal. They included political foes, union leaders, liberal members of the clergy, and the newspaper *Le Devoir*, as well as intellectuals such as Pierre Elliott Trudeau, who, with Gérard Pelletier, published *Cité libre*, a reformist magazine hostile to the Union nationale. Several university professors, among them Dominican priest Georges-Henri Lévesque, dean of the Faculty of Social Sciences at Université Laval, also risked criticizing the government. Although all wanted a more liberal, more modern Quebec, these critics differed considerably in their views on nationalism. Some, like Trudeau, viewed nationalism as conservative and reactionary, resulting only in ethnic bitterness and conflict. Others, among them journalist André Laurendeau, who later was co-chair of the Royal Commission on Bilingualism and Biculturalism, saw nationalism as a potentially progressive force.

Duplessis' adversaries also attacked the Union nationale's corrupt political and electoral behaviour. They highlighted how the party machine extorted money from commercial establishments and entrepreneurs throughout the province, and then used it to buy political support. They pointed to electoral abuses such as stuffed ballot boxes, police intervention in favour of government candidates, and "telegraphs," whereby electors voted under false identities.

Premier Maurice Duplessis, third from left at the front, at the dedication of Ste-Thérèse Bridge, August 18, 1946. To Duplessis' left, the Most Reverend Joseph Charbonneau. Church and state cooperated to mutual benefit.

Source: Library and Archives Canada/*The Gazette*/C-53641.

These practices demonstrated, according to journalist and future politician Pierre Laporte in a series of articles after the election of 1956, that Duplessis did not win his elections "by prayers alone."

Progressive elements inside and outside the Catholic Church grew restive as the hierarchy uncritically supported Duplessis in return for subsidies for church schools, hospitals, and social agencies. As well, critics censured the government for "reactionary" attitudes in labour relations, education, and health. They denounced the common practice of choosing civil servants primarily for their political loyalty. Some critics claimed that the government's economic development policies resulted in a virtual giveaway of the province's natural resources to foreigners. Others blamed Duplessis for his obstinate refusal to accept federal money to finance necessary social and educational programs. They also decried the Union nationale's neglect of urban Quebec, a failure made possible by the government's refusal to revise an outdated electoral map that blatantly favoured rural areas. By 1956, some urban ridings had more than 100,000 voters, while many rural ridings counted fewer than 10,000.

Anti-Duplessis forces also deplored *le chef*'s vendetta against opposition groups. Duplessis sought to discredit opponents by linking them with communism in the era of Cold War paranoia. His government applied the notorious "padlock law" of 1937 that authorized police to lock premises from which alleged communist activities were conducted. In other attacks on civil liberties, the government brought hundreds of Jehovah's Witnesses before the courts for distributing brochures on the streets and had them fined and imprisoned. Moreover, Duplessis often ran the legislative assembly as a personal fiefdom, with total disregard for parliamentary procedure.

A Re-evaluation of the Duplessis Era

While Duplessis deserves criticism, it is important to note that most early assessments were made by his political enemies. Duplessis was opposed by an intelligentsia who, after the Quiet Revolution, took over the halls of power. Their interpretation dominated the historical record. In their harsh assessment, the critics ignored mitigating circumstances. Patronage, although rife in the Duplessis regime, was endemic in Canadian political life. The premier's refusal of federal funds for roads, universities, and other programs appeared negative, but how else could he fight Ottawa's intrusions into areas of provincial jurisdiction? Even Pierre Trudeau supported Duplessis' refusal to accept federal grants for higher education. Duplessis welcomed foreign capital, just as his Liberal predecessors had done. Such investment provided jobs and opened up new areas of the province for development. The government's spending policies were admittedly conservative but they made it possible to keep taxes and debts low. At the same time, the government substantially boosted spending on social services and education. Most importantly, Duplessis was successful in defending Quebec's interests.

Even more telling is the fact that the Union nationale enjoyed public support, winning four consecutive elections between 1944 and 1956. Fifty percent of all Quebeckers and more than 60 percent of French-speaking electors voted for the party. Even in 1960, a minor shift of votes would have assured the Union nationale's re-election. Yet, by this time, Duplessis (who died in 1959) and Paul Sauvé (his popular, reform-minded successor, who died after three months in office) were gone, and the once-powerful party appeared a spent force compared with the Liberals, who offered a capable new leader, a dynamic team, and a revitalized program. Many of those who, in the midst of the Quiet Revolution, emphasized the sombre realities of the Duplessis era did so to lend greater credence to their own heady visions and ambitious aspirations.

The Quiet Revolution

tonnerre = thunder

The term "Quiet Revolution" describes the years from 1960 to 1966, during which Liberal Premier Jean Lesage and his *équipe du tonnerre* brought rapid but nonviolent change to Quebec. In fact, the major changes all occurred before 1964. Nevertheless, the Union nationale continued the reforms when it returned to power in 1966, as did the Liberals under Robert Bourassa after 1970. The Parti Québécois also had an agenda of reform that it implemented from 1976 to 1980. Thus, it might be said that the Quiet Revolution, in spite of pauses, lasted for two decades.

The Liberals campaigned under the slogans *Il faut que ça change* ("Things have to change") and *Maîtres chez nous* ("Masters of our own house"), phrases coined by *Le Devoir* editor André Laurendau. Although the Liberals came to power with numerous plans for reform in 1960, they had little idea of how much they would be able to accomplish. Lesage's cabinet contained such progressive individuals as René Lévesque and Paul Gérin-Lajoie. It also harboured many solid conservatives who, while they accepted the need for change, did not want to revolutionize Quebec society. When, for example, the Union nationale attempted in 1960 to discredit its opponents by pointing out that the Liberals threatened the Catholic Church's role in Quebec life, the Liberals countered by publishing biographical sketches of their own candidates that emphasized the number of priests, nuns, and brothers among their relatives. Jean Lesage, for example, was presented as having fought, as a federal minister, for Roman Catholic schools for the "Eskimos" and as having had an audience with Pope Pius XII.

Liberal Reforms

Once in power, the Liberals worked to end electoral corruption. They also cleaned up much of the petty patronage practised by the Union nationale, although in so doing they alienated many supporters who wanted a share in the spoils now that their party had at last taken power. Early in its mandate, the government set up a royal commission, chaired by Monseigneur Alphonse-Marie Parent of Université Laval, to examine Quebec's educational system. Whereas English Canada experienced progressive reforms in education that led to a more modern and practical school system, Quebec resisted change. The system remained under the control of the church and emphasized a traditional humanities education. The result was a lack of vocational and business education. The Liberal government established a provincial ministry of education. As minister, Paul Gérin-Lajoie reorganized the province's hundreds of school commissions into 55 regional districts. The government built large, "polyvalent" (comprehensive) secondary schools, improved teacher training, revised curricula, and broadened access to educational facilities. The church had little choice but to retreat, since it did not possess the financial and human resources that had to be devoted to schooling in the wake of Quebec's postwar population boom. The recruitment of new clergy, both male and female, declined noticeably during the 1950s, and many clergy left the ministry.

Although educational reforms constituted an important part of the Quiet Revolution, changes were occurring in other areas as well. In 1962, after heated cabinet debate, René Lévesque convinced Lesage to nationalize the province's private electrical power companies and to merge them with the Crown corporation Hydro-Québec. The giant utility company contributed to the province's development. The government also set up the Société générale de financement to serve as a holding company that would acquire small companies in difficulty. This was but one of a series of initiatives taken to promote a more dynamic francophone presence in an economy dominated by capital from outside the province.

Executives from Shawinigan Water and Power taking French lessons after the Liberals nationalized the private hydroelectric companies in Quebec.

Source: Archives d'Hydro-Québec. Fonds Commission hydroélectrique de Québec 1944-1963 (H2). H2/701644. Ressources humaines, formation: cours de français délivré aux employés de la Compagnie d'Électricité de Shawinigan, 1964. Image no. 32188-2.

The government improved the financial situation of Quebec's municipalities and established a ministry of cultural affairs with a modest budget. It revised the labour code and granted most employees in the public sector, with the exception of police officers and firefighters, the right to strike. Progressive but costly measures in the field of health care included the establishment of a provincial hospitalization insurance plan—one of the Liberals' major electoral promises in 1960. Henceforth Quebeckers could receive hospital care without regard to ability to pay.

Quebec–Ottawa Relations

In his dealings with Ottawa, Lesage's position was consistent with that of past governments. He adopted the traditional Quebec stance of resisting incursions by the federal government into areas deemed of local jurisdiction. Shortly after coming to power, Premier Lesage promised to put an end to conditional subsidies, by which the federal government paid for part of the cost of a program in an area of provincial concern, in return for setting its conditions. Lesage now demanded financial compensation for those federal programs in which Quebec did not participate. He also insisted that Ottawa turn more tax money over to Quebec in view of the province's "prior needs." After the Pearson government in Ottawa unveiled its proposals for the Canada Pension Plan in 1963, Lesage responded with a separate plan for Quebec—one that allowed the province to invest the enormous sums of money generated by such a scheme as it saw fit. The Caisse de dépôt et placement du Québec became Canada's largest investment fund. It sponsored the expansion of numerous Quebec firms and helped increase francophone involvement in the province's economy.

The Quiet Revolution altered the face of Quebec but to a large extent the process of modernization, so long thwarted in the province, was inevitable. It was also rapid. These years produced a cultural transformation beyond the structural reforms because basic attitudes and values changed significantly.[2] The changes announced the end of what remained of traditional clerical society. Talented authors, musicians, and other artists captured the new spirit in their works (see Chapter 15). But as historian Michael Gauvreau has pointed out, the "revolution" was not so black and white. The process did not begin in the 1960s, and the Catholic Church should not be viewed as a one-dimensional conservative structure that resisted change until the end. The roots of change can be found in the 1930s, when organizations under the auspices of the church began to transform Quebec society. The switch from a religious to a secular society was also not as stark as is often portrayed.[3]

The change in French-Canadian nationalism, however, was stark. Francophones acquired a new confidence that encouraged them to challenge inequalities. They strongly criticized a Canada in which the federal bureaucracy spoke only English, in which French enjoyed no official recognition in the nine other provinces, and in which, even in Quebec, French-speakers carried little economic weight. Here were the makings of a new nationalism.

Critics of the Quiet Revolution

Many in the urban middle class viewed the Quiet Revolution as the birth of a modern Quebec, "the reappearance of a spirit of independence that had frozen in the course of the long winter that had endured for more than a century."[4] For this group, the Quiet Revolution signified needed reforms in the important sectors of education, political life, the social services, the civil service, and the economy. A more modern Quebec offered obvious advantages to both them and their children.

The breathless pace of change, however, upset many conservative Quebeckers. In rural Quebec, where hundreds of small schools were closed and children were transported long distances by bus to large, impersonal institutions, discontent was rife. Many people felt ignored and grew nostalgic for the Duplessis era. Disadvantaged citizens in French-speaking districts of Montreal also felt bypassed by the major thrust of the Quiet Revolution, as large-scale spending on education and the rapid growth of the civil service did little for them. For some Quebeckers, state interference in the school system meant that religion was being ruthlessly driven out. "Give Jean Lesage breeches and a beard and he'll be a Castro," Union nationale opposition leader Daniel Johnson warned.

The Quiet Revolution engendered big government and bureaucracy, which was deemed technocratic and often insensitive to the needs of the individual. Higher spending and increased taxes won Lesage the nickname of *Ti-Jean la taxe* (Little John, the taxman). Public-sector labour unions made use of their newly acquired right to strike. The press increasingly criticized Lesage for his "arrogance," a characteristic that came to the fore during the election of 1966, when he campaigned virtually alone.

A small but vocal minority on the left also attacked Lesage. The Quiet Revolution was driven by an intelligentsia representative of the middle class. Reforms were based around education, health, and nationalization of industries. There was little in it for the working classes. Some urban Quebeckers doubted the government's continuing commitment to reform, especially after 1964. Hardline nationalists viewed Lesage's objective of greater autonomy for the province as insufficient. They favoured separation, with the creation of an independent, more interventionist, French-speaking state, as outlined in the program of Pierre Bourgault's Rassemblement pour l'indépendance nationale (RIN). They viewed Quebec's progress as part of the larger process of decolonization. Quebeckers had to throw off the yoke of English-Canadian and American imperialism.

By 2000 historical analyses became more critical, and the almost mythical status given the Quiet Revolution became hotly contested. Critics argued that institutions not linked to the state suffered too much erosion. Citizens became too dependent on an interventionist government, just as they had been in earlier times on an interventionist church. The origins of many of the problems that Quebec faced in the new millennium, it was argued, could be linked to the failures of the reforms implemented. Education was democratized, but its quality was often doubtful. The church ceased to intervene in family affairs, but the family as an institution was increasingly fragile. The government intervened vigorously in the economy, but failures were numerous and costly for taxpayers. It was in this atmosphere that the historical reputation of the arch villain in the story, Maurice Duplessis, was rejuvenated.

Return of the Union Nationale to Power

Led by Daniel Johnson, the Union nationale regained power in 1966, thanks to strong support in rural Quebec. In addition, the fact that the leftist RIN took votes mostly from the Liberals enabled the Union nationale to win in several close races. Surprisingly, perhaps, the Union nationale under Johnson, and then under Jean-Jacques Bertrand (who became premier after Johnson's sudden death in September 1968) did not attempt to undo the Liberals' reforms. In the field of education, Johnson applied the recommendations of the Parent commission and established the Collèges d'enseignement général et professionnel (called CEGEPs), the junior colleges that allowed Quebec students to enrol in occupational programs or to prepare for entrance into the universities. It also established a fourth French-language university, the public Université du Québec, which opened campuses in regional centres throughout the province.

During the late 1960s, the polarization of Quebec society between left and right over issues such as labour–management relations increased. Strike activity, notably in the public sector, grew dramatically, and, as elsewhere in the Western world at the time, protests shook colleges and universities. But the protest movements in Quebec took on a national and cultural hue. Before winning power, Johnson published a manifesto in which he warned that if Quebec could not achieve equality within Canada, it must seek independence. He wanted more than linguistic equality; he also sought greater autonomy for the province. Pointing out that Quebec—the home of more than 80 percent of French-speaking Canadians—represented one of Canada's two major ethnic communities or "nations," Johnson argued that a new constitution should recognize this fact through an appropriate division of powers.

Ottawa and most of the other provinces appeared willing (although not enthusiastic) to discuss the Constitution, but Pierre Trudeau, Canada's prime minister after 1968, warned that he opposed any reduction of federal authority. To Trudeau, the federal government represented all Canadians and he believed Ottawa could, and should, act to further linguistic equality across the country. However, many Canadians opposed Quebec's demands from the outset and felt that federal politicians had long been too focused on the "Quebec question."

The Debate over Language

Conflict over language was inevitable in Quebec after the Quiet Revolution. Most Quebeckers felt that their language did not occupy the position it deserved, even in their home province. While elsewhere in Canada most francophones learned English, most English-speaking Quebeckers knew little French. Communication in Quebec was usually carried on in the language of the minority. The powerful Montreal business establishment included few French Canadians.

Many stores in downtown Montreal failed to offer service to customers in French. Commercial signs in Montreal were usually only in English.

Quebec's English-speaking minority possessed its own institutions, including schools, universities, newspapers, hospitals, churches, and municipal councils. Quebec was the only province where the linguistic minority could function entirely in its own language. Moreover, census statistics confirmed that French Canadians in most regions outside Quebec were losing their battle against assimilation. In 1971, approximately one-third of Canadians whose mother tongue was French used English as the main language in the home. Only in a few areas of Canada could French-speakers be assured of getting at least part of their education in French. In addition, the language of the workplace in the other provinces was almost always English.

Since Confederation, Quebec residents enjoyed the right or privilege of choosing whether their children would be educated in French or English. In practice, however, the great majority of immigrants to Quebec since 1945 saw little reason to learn French. They enrolled their children in English schools to assure their integration into the English-speaking community and to equip them to take advantage of career opportunities in an increasingly English world. Demographers warned that if current trends continued, Montreal would soon have an English-speaking majority. For Quebeckers concerned about the survival of their language, "free choice" of the language of education represented a serious threat. It also demonstrated the "threat" of immigration.

Conflict over English-Language Schools

Conflict over the language of education first erupted in the Montreal Island community of St. Leonard, when the Catholic school board's French-speaking majority voted in 1967 to convert an English-language school, attended mainly by children of Italian origin, into a French-language school. The issue symbolized the determination of many Quebeckers to ensure that children of non-English origin enrolled in French schools. It also demonstrated to the English community that traditional free choice of the language of education was threatened. Each group pressured the government to support its position. The Union nationale government ruled against obligatory French schools. While Bill 63—which recognized the right of Quebeckers to enrol their children in English-language schools—pleased the non-French population, it unleashed storms of protest among Quebeckers. Language became a volatile political issue.

A Polarized Quebec

The FLQ and the October Crisis

The 1970s were turbulent for Quebeckers. Issues such as language, separatism, inflation and other economic problems, union unrest, and generational conflict divided the province. In 1970, in the midst of an economic downturn, the Liberals, led by Robert Bourassa, won power.

The new government soon found itself stumbling from crisis to crisis. Shortly after assuming power, it was confronted with the "October Crisis." Since 1963, the Front de libération du Québec (FLQ) had been involved in over 160 acts of terrorism, including bank robberies, thefts of dynamite, and bombings. The revolutionary socialist group opposed "Anglo-Saxon imperialism" and was influenced by leftist movements in Algeria, Vietnam, and Cuba. It was dedicated to the establishment of an independent, socialist Quebec. In February 1969, the FLQ detonated a bomb in the Montreal Stock Exchange, injuring 27 people and causing extensive damage. In September, the home of Montreal Mayor Jean Drapeau was bombed.

In October 1970, members of the FLQ kidnapped James Cross, a British trade representative in Montreal, and, five days later, Pierre Laporte, a Quebec cabinet minister. The nation was shocked by the bombings and kidnappings. The RCMP (Canada's intelligence service at the time) scrambled to gain information about this little-known group. The FLQ demanded that its manifesto be broadcast nationally on CBC television. Laporte was subsequently found murdered. Federal cabinet minutes released in 2001 revealed that certain federal ministers, overwhelmed by events and fearing that Quebec might secede from Canada, wanted to "use the situation in Quebec and the death of Mr. Laporte ... to reinforce Canadian unity." Thus, when Premier Bourassa hesitated and seemed to favour negotiations with the terrorists, Ottawa intervened. The Trudeau government agreed to dispatch 8000 heavily armed soldiers to Quebec, to guard public buildings and well-known personalities. The following day, on October 16 at 4 a.m., it invoked, for the first time in peacetime, the War Measures Act, which enabled police to arrest more than 500 "suspects" on the mere suspicion of being sympathetic to the revolutionaries. Nearly all those arrested were eventually released, with no charges laid. In the end, a negotiated solution brought the Crisis to an end. The five known FLQ kidnappers of Cross were allowed to flee to Cuba.

While the October Crisis heightened French–English tensions in Canada and the sight of armed soldiers on street corners caused widespread panic, it was an anomaly. Spurred by the movement toward decolonization, particularly in northern Africa, the FLQ was an extremist group that advocated violent resistance against perceived English-Canadian imperialism. The FLQ "cells" represented a disorganized organization of angry youth, and the threats they posed to society were exaggerated by the press and government. Intelligence on the FLQ remained scant and the seriousness of the threat was never clear. Regardless, Prime Minister Trudeau's decision to invoke the War Measures Act and suspend the civil liberties of Canadians was also extreme and remains highly controversial. Most Canadians at the time, however, applauded Trudeau's strong leadership as well as his famous response to a journalist. When asked how far he would go to suppress the threat posed by the FLQ, he replied "Just watch me."

The Constitution

As he had during the FLQ crisis, Premier Bourassa appeared equally hesitant in 1971 when, after lengthy discussions on the Constitution, he rejected the Victoria Charter—a package of constitutional proposals assembled by the federal government, which included an amending formula and a bill of rights. By the 1970s, Canada had not yet patriated its Constitution. Constitutional amendments still had to be passed by the British Parliament. The issue had been discussed by federal governments in Canada since the 1930s, and Britain was prepared to act, but provincial agreement on an amending formula proved arduous. How many provinces had to agree to amend the Constitution? Did agreement have to be unanimous? Was a simple majority required? Due to their size and influence, Quebec and Ontario expected a veto on constitutional change. Moreover, Quebec took the position that it was not a province like the others; it was not simply one of ten. Prime Minister Trudeau diverted from the stance taken by St. Laurent and Pearson, and made it clear he was not out to accommodate Quebec. Hopes for a renewed federalism dissipated.

Bill 22

Bourassa could not avoid dealing with the language question. His solution, Bill 22, was aimed at increasing the use of French in the workplace, mainly through pressure. The bill gave access to

English-language schools to children whose mother tongue was English and to those children of non-French origin who could pass a language test. It also created enrolment quotas for English schools in each school district. In the end, Bill 22 pleased no one. Nationalists complained that the law would do little to bring immigrants into French schools. The anglophone community and ethnic groups bitterly denounced the measure as arbitrary and even totalitarian. The issue cost Bourassa support in the election of 1976, which he lost to the Parti Québécois.

WHERE HISTORIANS DISAGREE

The Quiet Revolution

Quebec's "Quiet Revolution" led to significant changes in the province's education system, its use of natural resources, its economic structure, and the provision of its health care and social services. For observers outside Quebec, these changes appeared suddenly. Within Quebec, however, the actions of the Lesage government reflected ongoing concerns over the direction and modernization of society. The causes and effects of Quebec's rapid change after 1960 are the subject of considerable debate, and historians continue to disagree over the role of nationalism, liberalism, modernity, and religion.

Early commentaries were written by those who experienced the Quiet Revolution first-hand. As a result, they reflected the liberal biases of those trying to reform Quebec government and society. They praised the policies of Premier Jean Lesage, seeing them as the end of the *Grande noirceur* of the Duplessis era. These supporters included, among others, young French-Canadian journalists and intellectuals, such as René Lévesque, André Laurendeau, Gerard Pelletier, and Pierre Trudeau. Together this group worked to promote the idea that Quebec was a "normal" society, no different from any other in the Western world.

In the aftermath of the Quiet Revolution, René Lévesque came to believe that the province could best achieve modernization by reforming along national lines and separating from Canada. In contrast, Pierre Trudeau believed that Quebec needed no special accommodation and was strong enough to forge a reforming path within Canada. He was highly critical of the nationalist approach, arguing that "good government is a damned good substitute for national self-determination."[1] Despite their disagreements, these commentators, described by later historians as neo-nationalists and neo-liberals, were equally critical of former and long-time Quebec premier Maurice Duplessis. Both groups argued that the Quiet Revolution represented a clear break from the Catholic conservatism that had dominated Quebec society for decades.

This interpretation influenced a new generation of historians led by Paul-André Linteau and Normand Séguin. They embraced the idea that Quebec was a normal society and interpreted the Quiet Revolution as a political movement. They also rejected earlier approaches to Quebec history that focused on the role of the church and the importance of the conquest as the pivotal event in the province's history. Instead, these revisionist historians highlighted the secular history of Quebec and its normal and rational characteristics.

The liberal-secular approach to the Quiet Revolution remained dominant until well into the 1990s.[2]

Historians began challenging the view that Quebec's liberalism emerged only in the postwar period, particularly after 1960 with the election of the Lesage government. Antonin Dupont, Bernard L. Vigod, and Patricia Dirks pushed back the dates of Quebec's liberalism.[3] Nonetheless, these works remained political in nature and did not fundamentally alter understandings of the Quiet Revolution. But since the 1980s, disagreement has emerged among historians. The most divergent arguments are those between Michael Behiels and Michael Gauvreau.

Behiels examined the Quiet Revolution as a postwar phenomenon in Quebec. His approach built on the liberal-secular interpretation, and identified two groups that challenged French-Canadian nationalism—the neo-liberals, or Cité librists (named for the journal *Cité libre*), and the neo-nationalists (associated with the newspaper *Le Devoir* and the organization *L'Action nationale*). Behiels argued that neo-nationalists tried to modernize Quebec nationalism by updating and expanding its intellectual foundations to better reflect the economic and social realities of postwar Quebec. Cité librists, in contrast, called for more dramatic changes. According to Behiels, they desired a "sociopsychological revolution" leading to secularization and the eradication of the "cancer of clericalism."[4]

Gauvreau disagreed and argued that the intellectual roots of the Revolution can be found in the early 1930s. Moreover, he rejected the liberal-secular view, focusing instead on the movement's Catholic origins. Gauvreau presented a social history of the Quiet Revolution that engaged an international dialogue on religion and its responses to modernity and secularism in the twentieth century. His study attempted to decouple the "orthodox liberal" and "revisionist" master narratives of Quebec's Quiet Revolution. Gauvreau explained how Catholic youth groups, such as Catholic Action, motivated young Quebeckers to reconsider their place in society. Although they rejected much of Quebec's clericalism, the youth remained influenced by Catholic teachings. Moreover, he argued that the church embraced modernity by providing people—especially the working classes and women—with practical approaches to everyday concerns like "youth sociability, marriage preparation, and family life."[5]

Behiels and Gauvreau saw further differences in the legacy of the "liberal project" of the Cité librists. Behiels interpreted their policies along political and economic lines. The neo-liberals were a failure because of their misguided political objectives. Rather than criticizing from the sidelines, Behiels felt the Cité librists should have assisted the Liberal Party's reform wing to build their ideal democratic and rational society. This failure ensured the conversion of many in Quebec to neo-nationalism.

Gauvreau, however, differentiated himself from earlier scholarship by arguing for a more complex understanding of the liberal/nationalist binaries. He saw the Quiet Revolution as more than a shift from Catholicism to secularism. Instead, it encompassed broader (at times contradictory) changes whereby Quebeckers embraced new identities. For Cité librists such as Trudeau, family-focused approaches to reform championed by Catholic Action were defective. They threatened an ideal culture "based upon rationality, professionalism, and education." The neo-liberal's rejection of this approach reflected socio-religious *conservatism*. The result? A more complicated sociocultural view of the Quiet Revolution, experienced as much by the women and the middle classes as the province's political and economic elites.

1 Pierre Elliott Trudeau, "New Treason of the Intellectuals," in *Federalism and the French Canadians* (Toronto: Macmillan, 1968), p. 154.

2 Ronald Rudin, *Making History in Twentieth-Century Quebec* (Toronto: University of Toronto Press, 1997), p. 175.

3 Antonin Dupont, *Les relations entre l'église et l'état sous Louis-Alexandre Taschereau* (Montreal: Guerin, 1972); Bernard L. Vigod, *Quebec Before Duplessis: The Political Career of Louis-Alexandre Taschereau* (Montreal/Kingston: McGill-Queen's University Press, 1986); and Patricia Dirks, *The Failure of L'Action Liberale Nationale* (Montreal/Kingston: McGill-Queen's University Press, 1991).

4 Michael Behiels, *Prelude to Quebec's Quiet Revolution: Liberalism Versus Neo-nationalism, 1945–1960* (Montreal/Kingston: McGill-Queen's University Press, 1985), pp. 5, 6, 272.

5 Michael Gauvreau, *The Catholic Origins of the Quiet Revolution, 1931–1970* (Montreal/Kingston: McGill-Queen's University Press, 2008), pp. 12, 354–5.

The Growth of Nationalism

Quebec nationalism was becoming more aggressive with calls for constitutional reform, stricter language legislation in Quebec, more bilingualism in the federal government, an increased francophone presence in Quebec's economy, and even separation from Canada. Some English-Canadian journalists blamed a few individuals for this heightened nationalism, accusing Jean Lesage and Daniel Johnson of undermining the loyalty of Quebeckers through their aggressive stance in relations with Ottawa. They also criticized French President Charles de Gaulle for adding fuel to the fire when he appeared to give support to the cause of Quebec independence in his celebrated cry of "Vive le Québec libre!" during a speech from the balcony of Montreal's City Hall during the Expo 67 celebrations.

The new nationalists tended to be members of the middle class, including teachers, civil servants, and journalists; some came from the business and professional communities. Critics pointed out that these groups had a vested interest in nationalist causes. A bilingual civil service in Ottawa, for example, would create job openings for francophones. But these nationalists also came from the youth and from the left. They resented the inferior position that French speakers occupied in Canada and, to a certain extent, in Quebec itself. Events elsewhere in the world also influenced them. The movements of national liberation in Africa and Asia, and the struggle of African Americans for civil rights, reminded many French Canadians of what they perceived to be their own inferior condition. In one poignant autobiographical account, *Nègres blancs d'Amérique* (titled *White Niggers of America* in English translation), journalist and FLQ

"Vive la France! Vive le Québec! Vive le Québec libre!" The crowd roared with approval when French President Charles de Gaulle voiced his support for an independent Quebec at Montreal's City Hall, July 24, 1967.

Source: The Canadian Press/Chuck Mitchell.

theorist Pierre Vallières portrayed French-Canadian workers as cheap labour, as exploited second-class citizens who had no control over their own society and economy. The global culture of student protest so prevalent in the late 1960s, which symbolized deep societal and generational shifts, also lent momentum to the Quebec nationalist movement.

The Rise of the Parti Québécois

In 1967, René Lévesque, dissatisfied with the Liberals' constitutional policies, quit the party. The following year, he founded the Parti Québécois (PQ). As a former war correspondent in Korea, host of a highly popular television news program, and then a provincial cabinet minister responsible for such successes as the nationalization of Hydro-Québec, Lévesque had the prestige and stature needed to rally the majority of nationalists.

The rise of the PQ was striking. Quickly realizing that only a small minority of Quebeckers considered themselves unconditional independentists, party leaders set out to convince more moderate federalist nationalists that independence would improve their lot. While in opposition, the PQ successfully linked nationalism to a variety of progressive social causes, enabling it to build a broad base of support. Unions, increasingly hostile to the Bourassa government, now came to see an independent Quebec as one in which workers would be better treated. Many in the women's movement found common cause with nationalists.[5] Both sought more status and desired greater autonomy. For many feminists, an independent socialist Quebec was the key to the liberation of women. The Parti Québécois, with so many reformist measures written into its program, seemed the tool to help bring this about.

The electoral gains of the *péquistes* (as members and supporters of the Parti Québécois were known) confirmed the success of this strategy. The party won one-quarter of the vote in the first election it contested in 1970. When Bourassa's promises to create jobs fell flat, support for the PQ increased. Three years later, although the Liberals took virtually all the seats in the National Assembly, PQ support increased to one-third. Then, in 1976, with slightly more than 40 percent of the vote, the PQ won the election on the promise of a referendum in Quebec on separation, or what was termed "sovereignty association." The rest of Canada was stunned to wake up the morning following the election to find a government in Quebec committed to separating from Canada.

Many péquistes saw their victory as a vote for independence, the first step in the march toward national liberation. Certainly, the "happening" in the Paul Sauvé Arena in Montreal on the night of November 15, as party militants savoured victory, demonstrated that hopes were high. Other observers, however, saw the PQ success simply as a vote for good government and against the scandal-ridden Bourassa regime. The PQ had, after all, promised that it would not try to separate until the decision was approved in a referendum. Many voters therefore believed that they had voted only for a change in government, and that the stunning election results would be enough in themselves to show the rest of Canada that they were serious about the need for change.

Quebec under the Parti Québécois

The new PQ government pursued reforms that continued the Quiet Revolution of the 1960s. In order to democratize Quebec politics and prevent powerful interests from "buying" favourable legislation, it overhauled the electoral law to prohibit large—mainly corporate—contributions to political parties. The government also introduced a no-fault system of automobile insurance, covering all personal injuries sustained; private companies continued to insure drivers for damage to vehicles. It brought in agricultural zoning legislation designed to protect increasingly scarce good farmland, much of which had disappeared due to urban sprawl since World War II. It set up a dental care plan for children, adopted new legislation to protect consumers, and froze tuition fees for university students at the lowest levels in Canada. It also supported unions through an anti-strikebreaking law, a move that management bitterly opposed. In 1977, it amended the Quebec Charter of Rights to make Quebec the first Canadian province to protect gays and lesbians from discrimination.

Bill 101

In contrast to Bourassa's vacillation on the language question, the stance of the Parti Québécois seemed clear. In 1977, the government adopted Bill 101, a charter of the French language, which was intended to make Quebec as overwhelmingly French as Ontario was English. This controversial legislation opened English-language schools only to children who had at least one parent educated in English in Quebec. This criterion was used because of the impossibility of verifying a child's mother tongue, one of the conditions used by Bourassa's Bill 22, to determine admission.

René Lévesque at the Paul Sauvé Arena, Montreal, on the night of the Quebec election, October 29, 1973. His recently created Parti Québécois won 33 percent of the popular vote in that election, but only six seats. By 1976, the party would be in power.

Source: © Library and Archives Canada. Credit: Duncan Cameron/Duncan Cameron fonds/PA-115039.

French, with a few exceptions, was to become the language of the workplace, and professionals were required to have knowledge of French. Most signs were to be posted in French only. The Parti Québécois hoped to obtain by law for French in Quebec what the "free market" and "free choice" assured English elsewhere in Canada.

The new minority status of Quebec anglophones necessitated often painful adjustments. Although the federal commissioner of official languages commented in 1978, after the adoption of Bill 101, that "Quebec's anglophones are much better off than their francophone counterparts in other provinces," many Anglo-Quebeckers, including a large proportion of young adults convinced that they could have a better future elsewhere, left the province. At the same time, a large number of corporate head offices in Montreal, complaining of the language legislation, high taxes, the dangers of separatism, and poor relations with unions, decided to move out, mainly to Toronto.

Among the English-speakers who chose to stay in Quebec, bilingualism increased significantly. By 2001, fully 66 percent of this group was bilingual. At the same time, Quebec's "Frenchness" was attenuated by the fact that nearly 40 percent of the majority French-language group reported that they could also speak English; this figure was even higher for younger age groups. In addition, half of those Quebeckers whose mother tongue was neither French nor English said that they were trilingual. Nationally, however, rates of bilingualism remained low, making up about 17 percent of the population. A significantly higher number of francophones, about 43 percent, were bilingual, compared to only 9 percent of anglophones and allophones. Within Quebec, rates of bilingualism stood at about 40 percent, compared to a rate of 10 percent outside of the province.

With considerable federal support, some anglophones in Quebec responded to Bill 101 by launching or supporting legal challenges to several of its clauses. Court rulings, as well as amendments to the law introduced by both the Parti Québécois and, after 1985, the new Quebec Liberal government under Robert Bourassa, weakened the legislation. While many anglophones judged the amendments insufficient and, indeed, wanted an end to all language legislation, francophones continued to worry over the fragility of the status of French.

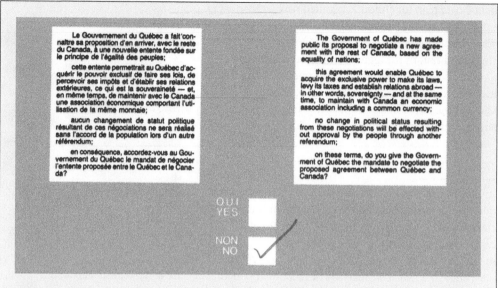

The Quebec referendum ballot, May 20, 1980. The Parti Québécois asked only for the right to negotiate political sovereignty within an economic association with the rest of Canada, not for immediate independence.

Source: Le directeur général des élections du Québec.

The 1980 Referendum

Of even greater interest to Canadians than the language question was Quebec's referendum on political sovereignty, which would decide Quebec's—and Canada's—future. The Levesque government promised a referendum during its term in office. It waited until the end of that mandate and a time when the possibilities of a victory seemed greatest. As with all referendums, the government shrewdly worded the question. The Parti Québécois government asked voters for a mandate to negotiate political sovereignty within an economic association with the rest of Canada. In hopes of obtaining majority support, the government asked only for the right to *negotiate*. No unilateral declaration of independence would follow a positive vote. The campaign debate was fierce, dividing families and friends. Claude Ryan, Robert Bourassa's successor as the Quebec Liberal leader, led the *non* forces. Prime Minister Trudeau intervened late in the campaign, promising unspecified constitutional change if Quebeckers voted *non*.

On May 20, 1980, Quebeckers defeated the referendum proposal by a 60–40 margin. While most of the non-French-speaking Quebeckers voted no, the French-speaking population split virtually in half. Analyses of the vote showed that the older age groups, the economically disadvantaged, and those with relatively little education tended to vote *non*. Those in the younger age groups and people with more education and higher incomes more often answered *oui*.

The Pessimism of the 1980s

The mood in Quebec during the early 1980s was pessimistic. The defeat of the referendum came as an emotional blow to the separatists. It was visible on Levesque's face and in his speech the night of the referendum. But while a reprieve had been won by the federalists, the battle was not over, as indicated by Levesque's prophetic parting comment: "*à la prochaine fois*" (until next time).

The pessimism deepened along with the 1981–82 recession, which dramatically cut employment in the resource and manufacturing industries. Unions suffered membership losses as well as rising unpopularity among a public weary of strikes and agitation. Universities reeled beneath the government's stringent cutbacks in financing.

The outcome of the constitutional debate further dampened spirits in Quebec. Prime Minister Trudeau indicated during the referendum campaign that he would interpret a rejection of separatism as a mandate to renegotiate federalism with Quebec. But the federal government's subsequent proposals gave Quebec none of the powers that its provincial governments had consistently claimed since 1960. The era of "cooperative federalism" ushered in by Pearson was cast aside and replaced by Trudeau's adamant refusal to concede Quebec "special status" in Confederation.

Frustrated by provincial opposition, Trudeau made plans to patriate the Constitution unilaterally, without provincial consent. He backed down from this approach under pressure from the provinces and the Supreme Court, and again opened negotiations. Debate erupted, particularly in Quebec, over the proposed amending formula (Quebec lost its veto) and the proposed charter of rights and freedoms (Quebec felt it was losing its special status in Confederation). Moreover, Ottawa managed to isolate Quebec by playing it off against the other nine provinces. At first the western provinces aligned with Quebec against Trudeau's centralizing approach, because they had their own battles with Ottawa over control of natural resources. But the West and Quebec had always made strange bedfellows. In November 1981, Trudeau hosted a provincial conference as a final attempt to negotiate a constitutional resolution.

After days of unsuccessful talks, an agreement was hashed out late on the final night between Canada and nine provinces—but with Quebec unaware the private negotiations had continued. Quebec claimed it had been "betrayed," and dubbed this the "Night of the Long Knives." In slightly amended form, the constitutional proposals became law despite Quebec's objections. Neither Premier René Lévesque nor opposition leader Claude Ryan attended the celebrations on April 17, 1982, when Queen Elizabeth II proclaimed the new Constitution. Quebec was legally bound by its terms, but the document lacked moral legitimacy in the province.

Quebec responded to the "betrayal" by re-electing the Parti Québécois in 1981. But the PQ proved unprepared to move forward in the post-referendum atmosphere, particularly when the economy was in such dire straits. The harsh recession and a severe budget crisis forced the government to reduce services and increase taxes. Its harsh measures to recover part of the salary increases that had been granted to public service workers alienated the unions. Moreover, the era of large-scale spending and government interventionism had passed as budget deficits increased and a new conservative (neoconservative) mood, emphasizing free-market capitalism, gained strength throughout the Western world, including Quebec.

Nationalism in Decline

Nationalist sentiment weakened after the defeat in the referendum of 1980. The now-middle-aged champions of yesterday's nationalist causes became disillusioned, and younger Quebeckers worried more about finding jobs. The growing unpopularity of the PQ led some observers to predict nationalism's demise. Sensing the waning of nationalist fervour in the face of the stinging defeats of 1980 and 1982, René Lévesque decided to put aside, at least for the foreseeable future, the issue of sovereignty, a decision that provoked a dramatic revolt within the party and, in 1985, Lévesque's own resignation. In the elections held in December 1985, the party lost power to the Liberals under their resurrected leader, Robert Bourassa.

In the years following the recession of the early 1980s, Quebec's rapid economic growth made it a leader among Canada's provinces. Reassured by the new political stability and by the reduced level of government interference, investment accelerated and business flourished. The provincial government held spending in check and reduced certain taxes.

While the Bourassa government prided itself on offering competent administration, it failed to exercise leadership with regard to environmental issues. Paper mills, aluminum manufacturing plants, and other industries continued to foul water and air with chemical pollutants, often in flagrant violation of existing regulations. Agricultural wastes, fertilizers, and pesticides fouled the province's rivers. Critics worried that the huge new hydroelectric megaprojects planned for Quebec's north would go forward without adequate study of the potential threats to the environment. Several incidents involving fires deliberately set in toxic waste and tire dumps dramatized both the dangers of pollution and the government's ecological neglect. While it was no worse than that of other provinces, Quebec's environmental record gave its citizens, reputed by polls to be among the most environmentally conscious of Canada's citizens, little cause for satisfaction.

The Revival of Nationalism

Those who had proclaimed nationalism's demise in the early 1980s proved poor prophets. By the end of the decade, both the language issue and Quebec's future links with Canada again became important public topics. The language issue emerged with renewed force in late 1988 over the issue of public signs. When the Supreme Court of Canada found Quebec's sign law (which required French-only) to be in violation of the freedom of expression provisions of both the federal and the Quebec charters of rights, Bourassa had to act. The Supreme Court admitted that signs solely in English could be prohibited and that the government could require "the predominant display of the French language, even its marked predominance." Bourassa's solution was to invoke the Constitution's "notwithstanding clause" (which enables a province to suspend certain rights for five-year periods) and to introduce legislation requiring French-only signs outdoors, while authorizing bilingual signs within certain stores. Anglophones across the country protested vehemently, and three English-speaking ministers resigned from Bourassa's cabinet.

Supporters of French-only signs argued that Quebec needed a French "face" in order to persuade new immigrants to integrate into the francophone community. They added that the influence of English in the North American context could be counterbalanced only by legislation protecting the French majority. The debate became rancorous. Passions cooled over time and, when the five-year period ran out in 1993, the Bourassa government adopted more liberal legislation.

In spite of the weakening of Bill 101's clause on the language of signs, Montreal in the mid-1990s was considered more French than it had in 1970. By 1990, almost all immigrant children were enrolled in French schools, but, in many of these, they constituted an overwhelming majority and had little contact with Quebeckers whose mother tongue was French. Due in part to the exodus of many anglophones, more francophones now held upper-level positions in business. More workers earned their living in French, but language legislation did not cover small enterprises, and many employers insisted that their French-speaking personnel be able to serve anglophones in English. Adversaries of Bill 101 warned that language legislation would hurt economic development and tarnish Quebec's reputation, since the media gave abundant publicity to anglophone complaints.

It would have been impossible to promote the use of French without undermining the important role of English in Quebec, particularly in the province's economy. According to the 2006 census, while nearly half of Montrealers claimed French as their mother tongue and 17 percent claimed English, a full 33 percent claimed neither language as a mother tongue, indicative of the waves of immigration the city witnessed in recent decades.

Meech Lake

The Constitution had been patriated in 1982, but with Quebec, one of the country's founding provinces, refusing to take part, the constitutional issue seemed unfinished. Meeting in Edmonton in August 1986, the provincial premiers agreed to undertake a "Quebec round" of negotiations to bring about "Quebec's full and active participation in the Canadian federation." Quebec put forth five conditions. They involved constitutional recognition of Quebec as a "distinct society," a constitutionally secured provincial role in immigration, a provincial role in Supreme Court appointments, limitations on the federal power to spend in areas of provincial jurisdiction, and an assured veto for Quebec in any future constitutional amendments.

In June 1987, Conservative Prime Minister Brian Mulroney and the ten provincial premiers met in Ottawa and, after arduous all-night negotiations, gave unanimous assent to an accord amending the Constitution. Premier Robert Bourassa proclaimed that Quebec could now adhere to the Canadian Constitution "with dignity and honour."

In the months that followed, the federal government and eight provinces, beginning with Quebec, ratified the proposals. Then the accord began to unravel as newly elected premiers in the two remaining provinces, New Brunswick's Frank McKenna and Manitoba's Gary Filmon, argued that they were not bound by their predecessors' signatures and demanded substantial modifications. Subsequently, a third premier, Clyde Wells of Newfoundland, had his province rescind its approval. Groups representing women, Aboriginal peoples, ethnic associations, and northerners objected that their own concerns had not been addressed. Other critics, including former Prime Minister Pierre Trudeau (who emerged from the shadows of retirement), argued that the Meech Lake Accord would seriously weaken federal authority and promote linguistic ghettos within Canada. In addition, while the agreement's opponents in English Canada feared that the accord would confer unwarranted additional powers on Quebec, some Quebeckers were convinced that their province would in fact obtain too little by virtue of the agreement.

As the three-year period for approval of the accord drew to a close in June 1990, protracted negotiations among the premiers produced an add-on agreement that included promises to work for a revamped Senate that would represent regional interests more effectively. Then, under intense pressure, the premiers of Manitoba and Newfoundland promised to submit the accord to their respective legislative assemblies. Developments in the final moments were unexpected. With the support of Aboriginal leaders from across Canada, Elijah Harper, a Cree NDP member of the Manitoba legislature, denounced the Meech Lake Accord for ignoring the rights of Canada's First Nations, and signalled his intention to use the rules of parliamentary procedure to kill it. On June 23, 1990, as the deadline for approval expired, the Meech Lake Accord died.

Many Canadians outside Quebec felt relief at the failure of the accord; polls showed that a growing majority opposed it. Those who had worked behind the scenes negotiating the accord mournfully pointed out that perhaps the best and only chance to get a deal done was now lost. In Quebec the failure of this new episode of constitutional reform had grave repercussions. Nationalists, including many federalists, perceived the death of the agreement as signifying English Canada's refusal to accommodate the province's minimal concerns. Independence now seemed the only possible choice for those who could not accept the status quo. The words of Premier Jean Lesage in 1965 came hauntingly back: "If ever Confederation collapses, it will not be because Quebec, the native land of French-Canadians, will have separated. It will be because the means of keeping Quebec in the fold will not have been found."

Several federal members of Parliament from Quebec quit their parties to join a new group, the Bloc Québécois, headed by former Conservative cabinet minister Lucien Bouchard. To deflect criticism of his government, Robert Bourassa set up a nonpartisan commission to study Quebec's constitutional future, and promised to hold a referendum.

A large Canadian flag carried by pro-Confederation Canadians at a "No" rally during the referendum on Quebec sovereignty in 1995.

Source: CP PICTURE ARCHIVE/Ryan Remiorz.

Constitutional Impasse

After the "failure of Meech," the Mulroney government decided to reopen the constitutional issue, this time by holding consultations across Canada. One of the main criticisms of Meech was that it was a backroom deal, negotiated by white male leaders. It lacked public involvement and consensus. First Nations, among other groups, played a far more important role in the ensuing discussions. Quebec, however, refused to participate in the talks until the final round of negotiations, held in Charlottetown.

Quebeckers reacted with little enthusiasm to the ensuing agreement. Premier Bourassa claimed it was the best he could do, while his political adversaries asserted that he had accepted much less than the Meech Lake Accord had offered. In a referendum held in October 1992, voters in six provinces, including Quebec, rejected the Charlottetown agreement and constitutional negotiations ceased.

The Referendum of 1995

The seeming impossibility of reaching any constitutional agreement with the rest of Canada led to an increase in nationalist sentiment in Quebec. Within thirty minutes of receiving the referendum result that Canada had rejected the Charlottetown Accord, the leaders of the federal Bloc Québécois and the provincial Parti Québécois declared that the campaign for separation had begun. More importantly, Jean Chrétien, who had been a minister under Trudeau and became Canada's prime minister in 1993 after the Liberal electoral victory, was perceived by even

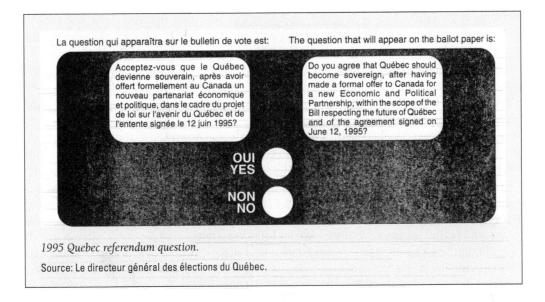

La question qui apparaîtra sur le bulletin de vote est: The question that will appear on the ballot paper is:

Acceptez-vous que le Québec devienne souverain, après avoir offert formellement au Canada un nouveau partenariat économique et politique, dans le cadre du projet de loi sur l'avenir du Québec et de l'entente signée le 12 juin 1995?

Do you agree that Québec should become sovereign, after having made a formal offer to Canada for a new Economic and Political Partnership, within the scope of the Bill respecting the future of Québec and of the agreement signed on June 12, 1995?

OUI
YES

NON
NO

1995 Quebec referendum question.

Source: Le directeur général des élections du Québec.

moderate nationalists as rigidly opposed to Quebec's claims for greater autonomy. In that same election, the nationalist Bloc Québécois proved far more popular than Chrétien's Liberals within the province. The return to power of the Parti Québécois in 1994 made a new referendum certain.

In this referendum, held on October 30, 1995, the provincial government asked electors if they wanted Quebec to become "sovereign," after having formally offered Canada a new economic and political partnership. Over 93 percent of the eligible electorate voted. The contest could not have been closer and the momentum swayed back and forth during referendum night as the results came in. At one point, it seemed the separatists had won. In the end, however, the federalist *non* won a razor-thin victory, with only 50.6 percent. Lucien Bouchard's prominent role in the campaign helped explain the strong showing of the *oui* forces, favoured by well over 60 percent of French-speaking voters. Anglophones, allophones, and members of First Nations communities supported the *non* option with near-unanimity. Premier Jacques Parizeau's accusatory comments in which he blamed the defeat on *"l'argent et le vote ethnique"*—"money and the ethnic vote"—cast another shadow over referendum night.

English Canada Reacts

The separatist forces were again defeated but there was little jubilation. The affection shown toward Quebec by large numbers of English Canadians, who invaded Montreal just before the referendum for an enthusiastic pro-Canada demonstration, evaporated rapidly after the vote. Many Canadians reacted with bitterness to the

Lucien Bouchard (left) and Jacques Parizeau (right) in Quebec City on October 2, 1995, shortly before the referendum. Premier Parizeau resigned after the referendum; Lucien Bouchard replaced him.

Source: CP PHOTO/Jacques Boissinot.

outcome of the referendum, feeling that separation was now inevitable and that it was time to drive a hard bargain with Quebec. One commentator described English Canada's reaction as a "national psychosis."[6]

In Ottawa, the Chrétien government adopted a hard-line approach toward Quebec and sought legal means to block future referendums and what seemed like inevitable separation. In 1998, in an advisory opinion, the Supreme Court of Canada affirmed unanimously that no province enjoyed a legal right to secede unilaterally. If, however, Quebeckers repudiated the existing constitutional order unambiguously in regard to the question asked and to the support received, then all parties had an obligation to negotiate constitutional change in good faith.[7] The Court thus recognized that Quebec's constitutional future was a political question. In 1999, the Chrétien government adopted legislation that sought to give Ottawa the right to determine unilaterally the conditions under which it would recognize the result of any future referendum. Quebec responded to the "Clarity Act" by asserting the right of its citizens to determine their own political future, and judged the law unconstitutional and antidemocratic.

During these years, Ottawa invested millions of dollars in programs designed to increase Ottawa's visibility in Quebec. Lucrative contracts went to Montreal advertising agencies that were generous donors to the Liberal Party. When the RCMP launched an investigation into allegations of political favouritism and mismanagement of public funds, Prime Minister Chrétien dismissed evidence of impropriety with an appeal to patriotism: maintaining Canadian unity was well worth "the theft of a few million dollars." In 2004, when a federal commission inquired into the "sponsorship scandal," detailed revelations of money laundering and false accounting tarnished the Liberal Party. It led to a sharp decline in Liberal support in Quebec.

Yet the support for independence was clearly diminished in Quebec. One analyst described the sovereigntist movement as "declining for the moment, not necessarily forever."[8] Commentators found an explanation for the apparent demobilization of the most ardent sovereigntists: they were aging and a new generation did not feel as they did.[9] As support for separatism receded, so did support for the Parti Québécois. Concern for health and social services and other issues came to the fore.

Regardless, relations between Ottawa and Quebec remained testy. Blessed with huge budget surpluses as a result of a surging economy, the federal government undertook new initiatives in such fields of provincial jurisdiction as education and health. In Quebec's case particularly, Ottawa wanted to assure a more active federal presence, through scholarships to students, research chairs to universities, and grants to municipalities. A 2010 poll revealed a diminished appetite for sovereignty, with nearly 60 percent of respondents claiming that the movement had run its course and only 14 percent believing that Quebec would achieve sovereignty in the next thirty years. A full 40 percent of respondents, however, continued to support sovereignty in theory (about the same number of *oui* votes in the 1980 referendum), showing that the debate on the future of Quebec in Canada is far from over.

Contemporary Politics

Support for the Parti Québécois weakened in the provincial election of 1998, and the governments of Lucien Bouchard and then Bernard Landry stated that no referendum would be held unless a victory for independence was certain. In spite of an improved economy, voters blamed the government for failing to improve health care, for forcing the amalgamation of cities and suburbs (Montreal expanded to comprise the entire island of Montreal in 2002), and for doing little to promote the economic development of outlying regions. For a time electors looked with interest at a new party, a more populist conservative grouping called Action démocratique du Québec (ADQ). In elections held in 2003, however, the more centrist and strongly federalist

Liberals, led by former Progressive Conservative MP Jean Charest, gained power, promising to improve health care, authorize the secession of suburbs from the new cities, reduce taxes, and lessen the role of the state.

By 2007, many voters expressed dissatisfaction with the Charest government. The government failed to honour its promises to lower taxes. In spite of increased spending on health care, Quebeckers generally felt that services had not improved. Plans to reform and streamline the provincial civil service were abandoned after resistance by unions. Urban infrastructure was crumbling.

Dissatisfaction with Charest did not boost the fortunes of the Parti Québécois and its new leader, André Boisclair. Most Quebeckers did not want a new referendum on independence (a major promise of the PQ) and saw immediate problems, particularly health care, as more important. More socially conservative francophones now preferred the ADQ, with its populist anti-elite electoral platform, shorn of the more radical proposals it had espoused earlier. On constitutional issues, the ADQ took a vaguely autonomist stance, supporting neither independence nor unconditional federalism.

Charest won re-election in 2007 but with only a minority of seats in the National Assembly, most of them in districts with large numbers of anglophone voters. While the ADQ formed the official opposition and saw itself as a government in waiting, the Parti Québécois won its lowest percentage of the popular vote since 1970, placing third. Boisclair resigned and was replaced by Pauline Marois, who now became the first woman to head a major Quebec political party.

After losing in 2007 and 2008 provincial elections, the PQ won in 2012 and Pauline Marois became premier with a minority government. The scandal-plagued Liberals took second place and the balance of power was held by the newly formed Coalition Avenir Québec led by François Legault. With only a minority, however, the PQ was unable to pursue its dream of an independent Quebec.

Two years into the PQ's mandate, polls indicated that the party could win a majority. Marois took a political risk and proposed the Quebec Charter of Values, which, if adopted, would prohibit public-sector employees from wearing or displaying conspicuous religious symbols, including kippahs, turbans, hijabs, niqabs, and larger crosses and religious pendants. While the charter fit in with Quebec's increasing secularism, it was criticized throughout Canada as running against such fundamental Canadian values as freedom of religion and multiculturalism. The premier took another risk when she accepted the nomination of star-candidate Pierre Karl Péladeau, the president and CEO of media conglomerate Quebecor. Péladeau's anti-union history alienated leftist PQ supporters and his attempts to resurrect the issue of Quebec independence fell flat.

The Liberals returned to power in the election of 2014 under Philippe Couillard. Support for the PQ fell to a level not seen since 1970. The Quebec Charter of Values died and the separatist movement again shrank into the background.

Quebec's Economy since 1990

Economic recession in the early 1990s provoked a substantial rise in Quebec's unemployment rate. Many jobs in inefficient, formerly tariff-protected industries such as textiles and furniture disappeared in the face of competition from low-wage developing nations. For a time, Montreal was afflicted with the highest jobless rate of any major Canadian city.

Then, in the mid-1990s, economic conditions improved. Free trade stimulated exports, 60 percent of which now went to the United States. The unemployment rate, which hit highs of 14 percent in 1992, dropped to 8 percent in 2002. By 2000, per capita revenues reached 86 percent of Ontario levels, up from only 74 percent in 1960. The increasing productivity of the Quebec workforce (due to improved technology, research and development, and educational advances) helped explain the province's improved performance.[10]

After 2000, Montreal's economy underwent expansion, boosted by growth in such sectors as aeronautics, biotechnology, information technology, pharmaceuticals, and telecommunications. Publicly owned Hydro-Québec increased its profits, half of which it then remitted to its sole shareholder, the Quebec government. Other industries did not do as well. In spite of Quebec's promises of new investments, General Motors closed its plant in Boisbriand, north of Montreal, the only automobile plant in the province.

After 2005, the province's economy again encountered serious weaknesses. The rising Canadian dollar (from 62 cents in American currency in 2002 to near par and beyond after 2008), stimulated by the huge American demand for western Canada's oil and gas, in combination with a slowing of the American economy, harmed exports. The forest industry, with its innumerable small local sawmills and its lack of value-added wood products, was hit especially hard. Textile and furniture manufacturers continued to close their doors. Bright spots in the economy included new hydroelectric projects in the north, government spending on public transportation, the construction of methane gas port facilities on the St. Lawrence River, and, in Montreal, the creation of many new jobs in information technologies and video-games publishing.

Public Finances

Public finances, and hence government spending on health, education, and other services, depended on the state of the economy. Budget deficits burgeoned, in Quebec as in other provinces, through the early 1990s, not only because of lower tax revenues but also as a result of Ottawa's own major spending cuts. In response, Quebec increased taxes and cut services. In the universities, for example, declining provincial subsidies combined with low tuition costs to produce a severe crisis. By 1999, the province balanced its budget, in part by sending hundreds of medical personnel into early retirement, and then even lowered taxes, earning the approval of bond rating agencies, the business establishment, and undoubtedly of taxpayers, but displeasing those who found services less accessible. In 2012, university students held mass protests against the Charest government's proposed tuition hikes.

Yet balanced budgets did not prevent the province's debt, already high, from increasing by several billion dollars each year. Quebec's auditor general blamed the provincial government's artful accounting for the discrepancy. Another worsening problem, faced by all provinces, was the ever-increasing portion of the budget—nearly 45 percent of Quebec's spending in 2007—that had to be devoted to health care, and health costs for a rapidly ageing population were rising each year at well above the rate of inflation.

Population

Demographic trends have long raised concerns for Quebec's future. The 2011 census showed that Quebec was still growing, although at a slower rate than five other provinces, including all of those in the West. In 2008, Quebec's fertility rate, at 1.74, was higher than the Canadian average of 1.59, but it was below the replacement fertility rate of 2.1 (the rate that demographers consider necessary to maintain a stable population size). This is significant compared to Quebec's rate of fertility in the 1950s, when its rates were among the highest of any industrial society.

In addition, more people continued to leave Quebec than entered it, but the difference, in the years 2006–2011 still constituted a significant improvement over the 1990s. Quebec put considerable effort into attracting immigrants from abroad, particularly from French-speaking countries, and then integrating them. Yet as a French-speaking province in English-speaking North America, Quebec suffered from a competitive disadvantage in regard to neighbouring Ontario.

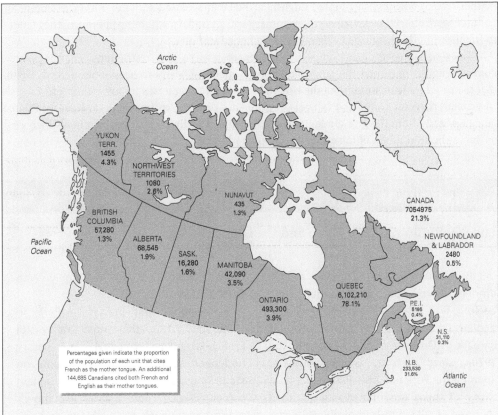

Canada's francophone population, 2011. Note the French-speaking community's strong majority position in Quebec, but minority status (less than 5 percent of the total population) in all other provinces and territories, with the exception of New Brunswick.

Source: Statistics Canada, 2011 Census, Highlights Tables, Mother Tongue: Canada, Provinces, Territories.

In hopes of boosting the number of births, the Bourassa government established a system of baby bonuses in 1987. Birth rates increased. While a study by the C.D. Howe Institute affirmed that the policy had positive effects, other observers thought that the bonuses simply encouraged couples to have children earlier. The Parti Québécois replaced the program in 1997 with tax-supported day-care services at $5 per day, with the objective of helping young couples conciliate work and family. A program of lengthy parental leaves after the birth of a baby also appeared to contribute to a slight rise in the birth rate.

Language and Culture in Quebec

Almost four decades after the adoption of Bill 101, a large majority of francophones still felt that the survival and development of the French language in Quebec remained under threat. They complained that many companies forced workers to use English-language manuals and tended to advertise virtually all positions as necessitating the ability to communicate in English. The language of work of many small businesses remained English, exempted from the language-of-work stipulations of Bill 101. Some reports signalled a marked deterioration in the use of French in Montreal, especially among immigrants. Large numbers of newcomers whose mother tongue was neither French nor English adopted English as the language used at home. Although immigrant children were obliged by law to do their primary and secondary schooling in French, they tended to frequent English-language institutions of higher education.

The Quebec government refused, however, to impose new restrictions. For many new-comers, English remained the language of social mobility. Many francophones agreed, feeling that increased trade relations with the United States meant that it was important to learn English. In general, they supported the Liberal government's decision to introduce mandatory English language study from the first grade, in 2006. Enrolment in English-language schools increased, as francophone children of mixed marriages entered them.

A HISTORICAL PORTRAIT

Luc Plamondon, Céline Dion, and the Global Village

In the 1950s, several Quebec artists, among them poet and singer Félix Leclerc, first achieved fame abroad, particularly in Paris, before continuing their careers in Quebec. In the 1960s and the 1970s, stars such as Gilles Vigneault, Jean-Pierre Ferland, and Pauline Julien, many of them ardent nationalists, rose to fame in Quebec, although on occasion they performed abroad. Since the 1980s, however, many of Quebec's most talented artists have quite literally gone global, working in New York, Toronto, Los Angeles, Las Vegas, Paris, London, and elsewhere. Luc Plamondon and Céline Dion epitomized this new tendency.

Luc Plamondon grew up in modest circumstances in a small town in Quebec's Eastern Townships. He first built a career in Quebec, then extended his activities to France, notably as a songwriter for popular singer Diane Dufresne. France offered possibilities that Quebec, with its small population, could not. As Plamondon put it, "the Paris region contains 12 million potential spectators, twice the entire population of Quebec." And yet Plamondon built his major shows, the rock opera *Starmania* and the musical production *Notre-Dame de Paris*, based on Victor Hugo's celebrated novel, largely with Quebec talent.

Starmania first played in Paris in 1979; by 2002, the most successful French-language musical in history had been seen by 3 million people on stage and had sold more than 5 million copies. French radio played the show's major songs, such as "Le blues du businessman" and "Les uns contre les autres," morning and night. The pop opera *Notre-Dame de Paris*, which opened in Paris in 1998, attracted tremendous success, with performances always sold out well in advance. Its dazzling choreography, its seductive and romantic music, and its songs, such as the enormously popular "Belle" and "Le temps des cathédrales," sung by Quebecker Bruno Pelletier, thrilled audiences. The show then took to the road to perform elsewhere in Europe and in Quebec. Plamondon, who promised himself in 1960 that he would create for the French-speaking world a musical hit that would be what *Hair* was to the English-speaking world, could boast of his contribution to a living French language, as his contemporary hits even managed to push American successes off the airwaves in France.

Céline Dion

Source: AP Photo/Express-News, Kevin Geil/The Canadian Press.

Céline Dion, another superstar with unpretentious roots, first became a child star in Quebec in the 1980s. In 1984, she sang for Pope John Paul II at Olympic Stadium in Montreal. In 1988, she won first place at the annual Eurovision competition, Europe's Olympics of song contests. The year 1992 saw her win awards for her CD containing songs written by Luc Plamondon, a recording that was hugely successful in Quebec and France. Then, in 1993, she won Juno awards in Toronto, singing in recently learned English and, in the words of gushing critics, bridging the cultural gap between Canada's "two solitudes." In 1997, she performed two songs for the Academy Awards to an audience that reportedly numbered 1 billion people. She also picked up two Grammy Awards in New York City. In her acceptance speech, she addressed Quebeckers in French, a gesture that one *Globe and Mail* columnist thought worth more than "a trillion distinct society clauses."

By 2000, Dion, whom *Time* magazine proclaimed a "global diva," had sold more than 130 million albums, with 26 megahits, including "Falling into You" and "Let's Talk About Love." Biographer Barry Grills saw her as building cultural bridges from Quebec to the rest of the planet; she occupied "a huge international territory, while still maintaining a direct connection to the culture where, for her, it all began."[1] Yet in an interview Dion once said, "I am very much Americanized." In this regard, she seemed to voice the attraction to the American dream that many Quebeckers have felt throughout their history. In 2002, "Canada's biggest cultural export," as *The Globe and Mail* styled Dion, came out of retirement and released a new English-language CD, *A New Day Has Come*; thanks in part to lavish publicity, it immediately became a top hit. A *New York Times* critic hypothesized that Dion's success came from her never being specific: the more general and abstract her message, the more people were able to relate what was said to the particularities of their own experience. Here undoubtedly was globalization in action. Dion then settled in Las Vegas. For much of the past decade, she has been a resident entertainer at Caesar's Palace, performing approximately 1000 shows.

1   Barry Grills, *Falling into You: The Story of Céline Dion* (Kingston, ON: Quarry Press, 1997), pp. 9–10.

The Environment

In the early 1990s, interest in the environment reached a low ebb. Reflecting this decreased interest, the Quebec government created no new land-based parks during the decade. Acid rain, most of it originating from industries and coal-fired electric power stations in Ontario and the American Midwest, continued to degrade Quebec's lakes and forests, and worsened the problem of urban smog. Agricultural pollution of water remained a grave problem, but governments feared that new regulations on farm practices would alienate rural voters. Industrial pollution of the St. Lawrence River and its tributaries also continued, but polluting industries were also important employers. As in many parts of North America, Quebec cottage owners despoiled the lakes they loved by letting fertilizers, wastewater, and sediment from erosion run into them. And, as in many parts of North America, good-quality Quebec farmland was swallowed up by suburban development.

By the end of the 1990s, the pendulum began to swing back toward greater concern for environmental degradation. Environmentalists warned that the province's forests were being cut down at a rate substantially in excess of their capacity to regenerate. In 1999, well-known pop singer Richard Desjardins even produced a film, *L'erreur boréale*, denouncing what he saw as the collusion between timber companies and the government that allowed clearcutting of huge tracts of land to go ahead with no concern for the survival of forest ecosystems. Finally, after a government-commissioned report called for a substantial reduction of logging quotas, the provincial government did impose lower limits, but had to face substantial opposition from companies and workers who blamed government policy and environmentalists, rather than a declining resource, for their plight.

Like people elsewhere, Quebeckers discussed climate change and ways to reduce the production of greenhouse gases. The Liberal government of Jean Charest launched a plan, financed largely with federal money, whose objective was to enable Quebec to respect the objectives fixed by the 2001 international agreement on the reduction of greenhouse gases, the Kyoto Protocol. Quebec's contribution to gas emissions was already far below the Canadian average, since the province had no oil or gas industry and depended almost entirely on hydroelectricity. Although the government invested in public transport to encourage commuters to leave their cars home, it promised, at the same time, to build a new bridge across the river from Montreal to Laval, as well as more expressways. Nor was it willing to risk the wrath of drivers by imposing the mandatory inspections of automobiles necessary to remove aged and highly polluting vehicles from the roads. Quebec also encouraged the establishment of wind-power farms, although some citizens complained that the huge turbines might have a negative impact on the spectacular scenery that attracted so many tourists.

In the name of conserving biodiversity, the government promised to create new protected areas from which logging and mining operations would be excluded, mostly in northern forests, but it delayed acting in the face of strong opposition from industrial lobbies; in any case, its much-renewed promise to protect 5 percent of Quebec's territory was far below the Canadian average of 10 percent and the international norm of 12 percent. It adopted legislation (later rescinded after heavy public pressure) to amputate one famous existing park of part of its territory so that commercial activities could proceed in the newly privatized sector. Environmentalists also urged Quebec to act to protect the province's remaining wetlands, which perform enormous services as filters and sponges for water. Nearly three-quarters of the wetlands of southern Quebec had been destroyed since 1975. Yet governments, particularly municipal, tended to heed the wishes of developers, interested in draining and building, in view of the additional tax monies that new housing, shopping centres and industrial parks would procure. Environmental organizations themselves were frequently accused of attempting to block important development projects that could create jobs and wealth.

SUMMARY

The history of Quebec since 1945 has been tumultuous. While the Quiet Revolution, in many ways, turned Quebec into a society much like the rest of the country, it also highlighted the distinct status of the French in Canada. While the October Crisis was an anomaly in the history of the province, the rise of a new, aggressive French-Canadian nationalism was not. Religion gave way to language as the major issue dividing French and English Canadians; the personalities and approaches of Pierre Elliott Trudeau and René Lévesque reflected the divisions between the federalist and separatist options for Quebec. After two referendums, Quebec remains part of Canada, but to assume that the question is settled would be naïve.

NOTES

1. Susan Mann, *The Dream of Nation: A Social and Intellectual History of Quebec* (Montreal/Kingston: McGill-Queen's University Press, 2002, 1982), p. 284.

2. Guy Rocher, *Le Québec en mutation* (Montreal: Hurtubise, 1973), p. 18.

3. Michael Gauvreau, *The Catholic Origins of Quebec's Quiet Revolution, 1931–1970* (Montreal/Kingston: McGill-Queen's University Press, 2005).

4. Marcel Rioux, *La question du Québec* (Paris: Seghers, 1969), p. 104.

5. Susan Mann, *The Dream of Nation*, pp. 318–20.

6. Maryse Potvin, "Some Racist Slips About Quebec in English Canada Between 1995 and 1998," *Canadian Ethnic Studies*, 32 (2000): 1–26.

7. John T. Saywell, *The Lawmakers: Judicial Power and the Shaping of Canadian Federalism* (Toronto: University of Toronto Press, 2002), p. 306.

8. Maurice Pinard, quoted by Lysiane Gagnon, "Sovereignty Is Not Dead, Just Sleeping," *The Globe and Mail*, November 11, 2002.

9. Gilles Gagné and Simon Langlois, *Les raisons fortes: Nature et signification de l'appui à la souveraineté du Québec* (Montreal: Presses de l'Université de Montréal, 2002).

10. Pierre Fortin, "L'évolution de l'économie depuis 1960: Le Québec a comblé la moitié de son retard sur l'Ontario," *Le devoir*, March 27, 2000.

BIBLIOGRAPHY

Although considerable scholarly material on Quebec exists in English, students wanting exposure to a full range of often controversial viewpoints need a reading knowledge of French. Two useful general syntheses are Susan Mann, *The Dream of Nation: A Social and Intellectual History of Quebec*, 2nd ed. (Montreal/Kingston: McGill-Queen's University Press, 2002); and John Dickinson and Brian Young, *A Short History of Quebec*, 4th ed. (Montreal/Kingston: McGill-Queen's University Press, 2008). Recent research on modern Quebec is summarized in English translation in Paul-André Linteau et al., *Quebec Since 1930* (Toronto: James Lorimer, 1991). A general analysis is available in Kenneth McRoberts, *Quebec: Social Change and Political Crisis*, 3rd ed. with a postscript (Toronto: Oxford University Press, 1999). Ramsay Cook presents his interpretations in *Canada, Québec, and the Uses of Nationalism*, 2nd ed. (Toronto: McClelland & Stewart, 1995), and in *Watching Quebec: Selected Essays* (Montreal/Kingston, McGill-Queen's University Press, 2005). David Chennells offers a useful synthesis in *The Politics of Nationalism in Canada: Cultural Conflict since 1760* (Toronto: University of Toronto Press, 2001). See also Ronald Rudin's provocative analysis of Quebec historiography, *Making History in Twentieth-Century*

Quebec (Toronto: University of Toronto Press, 1997). See also Jessica van Horssen, *A Town Called Asbestos: Environmental Contamination, Health, and Resilience in a Resource Community* (Vancouver: UBC Press, 2016).

On the Duplessis years see Conrad Black, *Render Unto Caesar: The Life and Legacy of Maurice Duplessis* (Toronto: Key Porter, 1998); Herbert F. Quinn, *The Union Nationale: Quebec Nationalism from Duplessis to Lévesque*, 2nd ed. (Toronto: University of Toronto Press, 1979); and, for a brief sketch, Richard Jones's booklet *Duplessis and the Union Nationale Administration* (Ottawa: Canadian Historical Association, 1983). Michael Behiels, *Prelude to Quebec's Quiet Revolution: Liberalism Versus Neo-Nationalism, 1945–1960* (Montreal/Kingston: McGill-Queen's University Press, 1985), examines the ideological conflicts among Duplessis' opponents. Recent research on Quebec society during the Duplessis years is available in Louise Bienvenue, *Quand la jeunesse entre en scène: L'action catholique avant la Révolution tranquille* (Montreal: Boréal, 2003); Michael Gauvreau, *The Catholic Origins of Quebec's Quiet Revolution, 1931–1970* (Montreal/Kingston: McGill-Queen's University Press, 2005); Dominique Marshall, *The Social Origins of the Welfare State: Quebec Families, Compulsory Education, and Family Allowances, 1940–1955* (Waterloo, ON: Wilfrid Laurier University Press, 2006); and Alain-G. Gagnon and Michel Sarra-Bournet, *Duplessis: Entre la Grande noirceur et la société libérale* (Montreal: Québec Amérique, 1997).

Dale C. Thomson studies the early 1960s in *Jean Lesage and the Quiet Revolution* (Toronto: Macmillan, 1984). Marcel Martel studies relations between Quebec and French-speaking minorities in *French Canada: An Account of Its Creation and Break-up, 1850–1967* (Ottawa: Canadian Historical Association, 1998). Critical views of the Quiet Revolution can be had in Gilles Paquet, *Oublier la révolution tranquille: Pour une nouvelle socialité* (Montreal: Liber, 1999); and E.-Martin Meunier and Jean-Philippe Warren, *Sortir de la grande noirceur: L'horizon personnaliste de la Révolution tranquille* (Quebec: Septentrion, 2002). For Quebec's relationship with France, consult David Meren, *With Friends Like These: Entangled Nationalisms and the Canada–Quebec-France Triangle, 1944–1970* (Vancouver: UBC Press, 2012). For a journalistic account of the Bourassa years, see L. Ian MacDonald, *From Bourassa to Bourassa: Wilderness to Restoration*, 2nd ed. (Montreal/Kingston: McGill-Queen's University Press, 2002). On the independentist movement in general, consult William D. Coleman, *The Independence Movement in Quebec, 1945–1980* (Toronto: University of Toronto Press, 1984). Graham Fraser studies the Parti Québécois in *René Lévesque and the Parti Québécois in Power*, 2nd ed. (Montreal/Kingston: McGill-Queen's University Press, 2002). Philosopher Charles Taylor proposes an original analysis of French–English relations in Guy Laforest, ed., *Reconciling the Solitudes: Essays on Canadian Federalism and Nationalism* (Montreal/Kingston: McGill-Queen's University Press, 1993). See also Guy Laforest and Roger Gibbins, eds., *Beyond the Impasse: Toward Reconciliation* (Montreal: Institute for Research on Public Policy, 1998).

On the referendum of 1980, see Gertrude Robinson, *Constructing the Quebec Referendum: French and English Media Voices* (Toronto: University of Toronto Press, 1998). Constitutional issues are examined extensively by Edward McWhinney in two books: *Quebec and the Constitution, 1960–1978* (Toronto: University of Toronto Press, 1979), and *Canada and the Constitution, 1979–1982: Patriation and the Charter of Rights* (Toronto: University of Toronto Press, 1982). For Quebec viewpoints, see Christian Dufour, *A Canadian Challenge: Le défi québécois* (Lantzville, BC: Oolichan Books, 1990); Louis Balthazar, Guy Laforest, and Vincent Lemieux, *Le Québec et la restructuration du Canada, 1980–1992: Enjeux et perspectives* (Sillery, QC: Septentrion, 1991); Alain-G. Gagnon, *Québec: État et société* (Montreal: Québec Amérique, 1994); and Robert A. Young, *The Secession of Quebec and the Future of Canada*, rev. ed. (Montreal/Kingston: McGill-Queen's University Press, 1998). Alan Cairns, *Charter versus Federalism: The Dilemmas of Constitutional Reform* (Montreal/Kingston: McGill-Queen's University Press, 1992), offers a thoughtful essay.

Among the many publications bearing on the Meech Lake Accord, see Michael D. Behiels, ed., *The Meech Lake Primer: Conflicting Views of the 1987 Constitutional Accord* (Ottawa: University of Ottawa Press, 1989); Andrew Cohen, *A Deal Undone: The Making and Breaking of the Meech Lake Accord* (Vancouver: Douglas & McIntyre, 1990); Jean-François Lisée, *The Trickster: Robert Bourassa and the Quebeckers, 1990–1992* (Toronto: James Lorimer, 1994); Guy Laforest, *Trudeau and the End of a Canadian Dream* (Montreal/Kingston: McGill-Queen's University Press, 1995); and Patrick J. Monahan, *After Meech Lake: An Insider's View* (Kingston: Institute of Intergovernmental Relations, Queen's University, 1990). A fine overview of English-Canadian reaction to Quebec nationalism is provided by Kenneth McRoberts, *Beyond Quebec: Taking Stock of Canada* (Montreal/Kingston: McGill-Queen's University Press, 1995); see also his *Misconceiving Canada: The Struggle for National Unity* (Toronto: Oxford University Press, 1997), a study highly critical of Pierre Trudeau's policies for national unity. Constitutional developments after Meech are examined in Kenneth McRoberts and Patrick Monahan, *The Charlottetown Accord: The Referendum, and the Future of Canada* (Toronto: University of Toronto Press, 1993); and Robert A. Young, *The Struggle for Quebec: From Referendum to Referendum* (Montreal/Kingston: McGill-Queen's University Press, 1999). Brian Mulroney presents his point of view on the constitutional debate in *Memoirs 1939–1993* (Toronto: Douglas Gibson Books, 2007).

Analyses of the language question include articles by Richard Jones and William D. Coleman in Michael D. Behiels, ed., *Quebec since 1945: Selected Readings* (Toronto: Copp Clark Pitman, 1987), pp. 223–62; Pierre Godin, *La poudrière linguistique: La Revolution tranquille, 1967–1970* (Montreal: Boréal Express, 1990); Michel Plourde, ed., *Le français au Québec: 400 ans d'histoire et de vie* (Quebec: Conseil de la langue française, 2000); and Graham Fraser, *Sorry, I Don't Speak French: Confronting the Canadian Crisis That Won't Go Away* (Toronto: McClelland & Stewart, 2006). Works on Quebec's English-speaking minority include Ronald Rudin, *The Forgotten Quebecers: A History of English-Speaking Quebec, 1759–1980* (Quebec: Institut québécois de recherche sur la culture, 1985); Josée Legault, *L'invention d'une minorité: Les anglos-québécois* (Montreal: Boréal Express, 1992); Martha Radice, *Feeling Comfortable? The Urban Experience of Anglo-Montrealers* (Quebec: Presses de l'Université Laval, 2000); and Garth Stevenson, *Community Besieged: The Anglophone Minority and the Politics of Quebec* (Montreal/Kingston: McGill-Queen's University Press, 1999). For English Canada's reaction to the language question, see Matthew Heyday, *So They Want Us to Learn French: Promoting and Opposing Bilingualism in English-speaking Canada* (Vancouver: UBC Press, 2015).

Cultural development is examined in Richard Handler, *Nationalism and the Politics of Culture in Quebec* (Madison: University of Wisconsin Press, 1988). A summary of Martin Pâquet's important study of immigration is available in a brochure, *Toward a Quebec Ministry of Immigration* (Ottawa: Canadian Historical Association, 1997). Quebec's response to immigrants is further examined in Sean Mills, "Quebec, Haiti, and the Deportation Crisis of 1974," *Canadian Historical Review* 94, no. 3 (2013): 405–35. Lucia Ferretti chronicles religious history in *Brève histoire de l'Église catholique au Québec* (Montreal: Boréal, 1999), as does Gregory Baum in *Truth and Relevance: Catholic Theology in French Quebec since the Quiet Revolution* (Montreal/Kingston: McGill-Queen's University Press, 2014). Pierre Anctil, Ira Robinson, and Gérard Bouchard, eds., *Juifs et canadiens français dans la société québécoise* (Sillery, QC: Septentrion, 2000), examines relations between Jews and French Canadians. For a study of the postwar generation in Quebec, see François Ricard, *The Lyric Generation: The Life and Times of Baby Boomers* (Don Mills, ON: Stoddart, 1994). The experience of women in Quebec is covered in Micheline Dumont et al., *Quebec Women: A History* (Toronto: Women's Press, 1987); a revised version of this study, in French only, is available. Danielle Lacasse examines a social problem in *La prostitution féminine à Montréal, 1945–1970* (Montreal: Boréal, 1994).

Denis Monière's *Ideologies in Quebec* (Toronto: University of Toronto Press, 1981) is a useful intellectual history, while Sean Mills situates Montreal protests in the context of the world's decolonization movements in *The Empire Within: Postcolonial Thought and Political Activism in Sixties Montreal* (Montreal/Kingston: McGill-Queen's University Press, 2010). On labour history, see Jacques Rouillard, *Histoire du syndicalisme au Québec* (Montreal: Boréal, 1989). Studies of Quebec society include Fernand Dumont, ed., *La société québécoise après 30 ans de changements* (Quebec: Institut québécois de recherche sur la culture, 1990); the same author's *Genèse de la société québécoise* (Montreal: Boréal, 1993); and Simon Langlois et al., *Recent Social Trends in Quebec, 1960–1990* (Montreal/Kingston: McGill-Queen's University Press, 1992).

Sylvie Vincent and Garry Bowers have edited a collection of essays on the first James Bay hydroelectric project: *Baie James et nord québécois: Dix ans après/James Bay and Northern Quebec: Ten Years After* (Montreal: Recherches amérindiennes au Québec, 1988). Richard F. Salisbury's *A Homeland for the Cree: Regional Development in James Bay, 1971–1981* (Montreal/Kingston: McGill-Queen's University Press, 1986) is another analysis of the project's impact on the Cree. See also Hans M. Carlson, "A Watershed of Words: Litigating and Negotiating Nature in Eastern James Bay, 1971–75," *Canadian Historical Review*, 85 (2004), pp. 63–84. Studies of Quebec-based businesses include Maurice Chartrand and René Pronovost, *Provigo: An Outstanding Entrepreneurial Success* (Scarborough, ON: Prentice-Hall, 1989); Peter Hadekel and Ann Gibbon, *Steinberg: The Breakup of a Family Empire* (Toronto: Macmillan, 1990); and Larry MacDonald, *The Bombardier Story: Planes, Trains, and Snowmobiles* (Toronto: J. Wiley Publishers, 2001).

Source: CP PHOTO/Frank Gunn.

Chapter Seventeen

IMMIGRATION AND MULTICULTURALISM

TIME LINE	
1946	Postwar European refugees begin arriving in Canada
1947	Parliament repeals Chinese Exclusion Act adopted in 1923
1948	UN Declaration of Human Rights issued by UN General Assembly
1956	Hungarian refugees enter as immigrants
1962	Racial discrimination officially ends in immigration regulations
1966	Department of Manpower and Immigration established
1967	"Points system" for immigrants introduced
1971	Ottawa adopts multiculturalism policy
1976	New Immigration Act passed
1982	The Charter of Rights and Freedoms accords constitutional protection to multiculturalism
1986	Employment Equity Act comes into effect
1988	Mulroney government acts to stem illegal immigration Canadian Multiculturalism Act passed, making Canada first nation to enshrine multiculturalism in law
1993	Parliament adopts new legislation on immigration to attract the highly educated
2003	Statistics indicate 18.4 percent of population are immigrants
2007	Ottawa increases annual immigration target to highest level in twenty-five years

Canada's history is a story of migration. It is a story of the movement of peoples and their experiences. From the pre-contact migrations of the First Nations across thousands of years, to the arrival of the French onto the continent, to the waves of immigration during the Loyalist and Napoleanic eras, to the opening of the West, to the post-World War II era, and into the new millennium, the history of immigration is a central theme to Canadian history. But the particular story in each of these periods differs significantly.

The history of Canada's immigrants since 1945 involves three intertwined elements: the federal government's immigration policy; the response of Canadians to these newcomers; and the experiences of the immigrants themselves. Discussion of these experiences gives rise to several important questions: Where did the immigrants come from and why? How did they react and adapt to their new environment? How did the host society respond? How were immigrant communities transformed and what impact did they have on Canadian society?

After the western immigration boom at the turn of the twentieth century, Canada's doors were largely closed to new peoples. Two world wars and a Depression were not conducive to immigration. But when World War II ended, the nation experienced another significant entry of peoples. As usual, the federal government attempted to control the gates of entry in order to shape society. But amid a new atmosphere of internationalism espoused by such organizations as the United Nations, which issued its universal Declaration of Human Rights in 1948, attitudes toward race and ethnicity were changing. These attitudes were further transformed during the civil rights movement of the 1960s. Those citizens not part of Canada's charter groups (French and English) questioned their place in Canadian society. They expressed reservations about the concept of two nations and two founding peoples, which, besides ignoring the existence of the Aboriginal peoples, gave special treatment to Canadians of French and British origin.

By the early 1970s the elusive search for Canada's national identity increasingly focused on the theme of immigration. The federal government's multiculturalism policy, announced in 1971, accorded minority ethnic groups an official status they had not enjoyed in the past. The Canadian Constitution of 1982 gave additional recognition to ethnic minorities. These political acts served as recognition of how Canada, in one century, had become a multiethnic and multicultural society, one in which those of backgrounds other than English or French made up nearly one-third of the total population, a proportion that continues to increase. The story, however, was not so welcoming. As historian Franca Iacovetta demonstrates, the host society also served as vigilant "gatekeepers."[1]

Postwar European Immigration, 1945–57

In 1946, millions of destitute refugees from war-torn areas of Europe remained crowded in camps, awaiting a permanent home. Over the course of the war, the world learned of atrocities on levels never before witnessed. The horrors of the Holocaust, and the genocide perpetrated by the Soviet Union against its own peoples, deeply unnerved the Europeans, making Canada appear as a safe haven from the uncertainties of the postwar world. Canada's record in serving as a sanctuary, however, was poor. As historians Irving Abella and Harold Troper indicate, the doors to Jews fleeing the Nazis during the war were closed.[2] The country had received few immigrants during the preceding fifteen years. As far as most Canadians were concerned, the nation had its own children to look after. Furthermore, economists worried that the war's end would bring on another depression, as it had immediately after World War I. A wave of new arrivals risked swelling the ranks of the unemployed.

European Refugees

Prime Minister Mackenzie King sensed Canadians' hesitancy about immigration. He saw little electoral advantage to opening the doors to Europe's homeless. Pressure, however, continued to mount as the full horror of the Nazi atrocities, and the full extent of Europe's refugee crisis, were revealed. In the House of Commons, a few MPs, mainly CCF, denounced the government's "shameful" vacillation and insisted on Canada's "moral and Christian duty" toward the victims of war. Certain religious groups and ethnic associations also spoke in favour of the refugees. Finally, after hearings in the spring of 1946, the Senate Committee on Immigration and Labour recommended that immigration offices be opened in Europe to process as many displaced persons and refugees as the country could absorb.

The Canadian government moved cautiously. The first refugees to arrive in 1946 were 4000 Polish veterans who had fought with British military units in the war. Hugh Keenleyside, deputy minister of mines and resources (the department responsible for immigration), believed Canada must act quickly to select the best immigrants. By admitting a few thousand displaced persons immediately, he argued, Canada could obtain good candidates, improve the country's international image, and encourage other nations to follow suit. John Holmes, an external-affairs officer, claimed that Canada selected refugees "like good beef cattle, with a preference for strong young men who could do manual labour and would not be encumbered by aging relatives."[3] By the fall of 1948, 40,000 refugees had reached Canadian shores. Although the numbers then began to decrease, about 165,000 refugees had come to Canada by 1953. Upon arrival, many of them applied to bring in their close relatives.

One of these refugees was Ann Kazimirski, a Jew born in eastern Poland. After the German invasion of her region in June 1941, the Nazis murdered most of her family. In 1942 she married a local dentist and, because dentists were needed to treat German troops, the couple was allowed to live outside the Jewish ghetto. As Nazi killings of Jews increased, a friend of the Kazimirskis agreed to hide the couple in an attic. One night troops rounded up most of the town's Jewish population of 18,000, took them away in trucks to the outskirts of town, and shot them. Shortly afterward, Ann's mother was captured and murdered before her eyes. The Kazimirskis escaped through the town's sewers, and hid in the surrounding countryside. In 1949 they reached Canada. Ann later testified in Germany during the trial for war crimes of the Nazi district administrator, identified by Ann as the person in charge of the killings; he was acquitted. Kazimirski returned to Canada and founded a choir group in Montreal, convinced that, while there was much to cry about, there was even more to sing about. She told her story in a book, *Witness to Horror*.[4]

Maria Redekop Wall was another refugee. At the age of 47, she reached Canada with her six children and her meagre belongings in September 1948. Historian Marlene Epp recounts that Wall was part of a group of 8000 Mennonites, a majority of whom were women, who immigrated to Canada in the years 1947–52.[5] Wall lived in a Mennonite village in the Ukraine. In 1938, her husband, like numerous other Mennonite men, was arrested by Soviet police and disappeared. In 1941, Hitler's armies occupied Ukraine. When the Germans were forced to retreat in September 1943, Wall and her co-religionists, as ethnic Germans, had no choice but to follow. After an arduous four-month trek in horse-drawn vehicles, they reached Poland, where the remaining men were conscripted into the German army. With the Soviet advance into Poland in 1944, the Mennonites were again uprooted. Most were taken prisoner by the Soviets; rape and suicides were common. Wall managed to reach a refugee camp in West Germany but spent many anxious months fearing she would be sent back to the USSR. Indeed, at the end of the war, the Red Army forcibly repatriated thousands of eastern Europeans behind the "Iron Curtain," often condemning them to prison, persecution, and death. After spending three years in the camp, Wall was finally chosen to go to Canada. She settled in the Fraser Valley in British Columbia and bought a berry farm. Adaptation to the new society was not without problems, however, and even within the Mennonite community divergent lifestyles and experiences often strained relations between more conservative Canadian Mennonites and women who had long been forced by extraordinary, and often tragic, circumstances to make difficult decisions and compromises.

A number of refugees were well-educated professionals or highly skilled workers. Often they concealed their training in order to better their chances with Canadian officials, who sought manual labourers. Industries in need of unskilled labour sponsored many of the refugee immigrants, who readily accepted almost any job, salary, and working conditions. Once in Canada, they fulfilled their contractual obligations on farms, in lumber camps, in mines, and often, in the case of women, in domestic service, before moving on to more suitable occupations.

Immigrant Labour

Employers frequently exploited new immigrants. One notorious scheme involved Ludger Dionne, an MP and owner of the Dionne Spinning Mill Company at Saint-Georges-de-Beauce, south of Quebec City. In 1947, Dionne obtained government authorization to recruit 100 Polish women for his mill. He paid them 20 cents an hour; after deductions of $6 a week for board, they were left with $3.60 weekly. Dionne assured parliamentarians that young women from Quebec City did not want to work in the small towns and that his working conditions were better than those in Toronto. He also accused his detractors of being propagandists for communism.

Many immigrants did well financially. By 1971, Latvians and Estonians, for example, had incomes that were 25 percent higher than the Canadian average. Such groups included unusually large numbers of educational, community, cultural, and political leaders.[6] Most, however, had to work hard and save frugally in the hopes that the next generation—their children—would have opportunities for education and careers their parents could only dream about.

Historian Franca Iacovetta has described the lives of many poor peasant farmers and rural artisans from southern Italy who settled in Toronto, where they faced considerable hardship before they were able to secure a stable life for themselves and their families.[7] Jobs were often dirty, disagreeable, and risky. Iacovetta also examined the personal histories of women refugees from elsewhere in Europe.[8] Eighteen-year-old Elena Krotz, for example, was recruited by Canadian officials in a displaced-persons camp in West Germany. She had fled her native Czechoslovakia when communist authorities sought to arrest her after she participated in a student protest. After staying for a few weeks at a government hostel, Krotz was sent to the home of a farm couple in southwestern Ontario, to work as a servant. She arrived with all her worldly belongings in two tiny bags: a blanket and one change of clothes. A drive to succeed, the encouragement and mutual support of the community, and the relative youth of the newcomers combined to help these immigrants adjust to their new environment.

Postwar Federal Immigration Policy

Since most prospective immigrants to Canada, even in the early postwar years, were not refugees, the country needed a general immigration policy. In a speech to the House of Commons on May 1, 1947, Prime Minister King attempted to satisfy both supporters and opponents of immigration. Canada would benefit by boosting its population, he claimed, and immigration would make the country more prosperous and secure. At the same time, he put forth the nebulous notion of Canada's "absorptive capacity" (the notion of how many immigrants Canada could successfully admit and integrate), promising that the government would "ensure the careful selection and permanent settlement" of only as many immigrants as could "advantageously be absorbed in our national economy." The number admitted could vary from year to year, in an alternating open-door/closed-door approach.

King's comments revealed Canadian attitudes toward race and ethnicity. Responding to those who denounced racial distinctions in immigration policy, the prime minister asserted Canada's right to choose its future citizens. The government did repeal the blatantly discriminatory Chinese exclusion law of 1923 but it continued to apply severe restrictions on Asian immigration since, in King's words, the "massive immigration from the orient would alter the fundamental composition of the Canadian population" and "give rise to social and economic problems."

Canadian Responses to Postwar Immigration

Canadians debated the issues of how many immigrants the country needed and who should be admitted. Some business and financial leaders lobbied for substantial immigration. They argued that a larger population would benefit the economy and yield per capita savings in areas such as transportation and administration. Ethnic associations and several religious groups also favoured increased immigration.

Many Canadians, however, were reluctant to receive any sizable influx of immigrants. By 1954, only 45 percent of Canadians favoured increased immigration, down from 51 percent in 1947. A general fear and distrust of outsiders, and a belief they would have a negative impact on society, were prominent among Canadians. Workers often viewed immigrants as competitors willing to work for lower wages. Unions wanted immigrants to be carefully selected and prepared to occupy less desirable jobs in remote regions that Canadians did not want. As the economy began to slow in the late 1950s, a majority of Canadians felt the country was accepting too many immigrants. Even MP David Croll, an enthusiastic advocate of higher immigration, joked: "If you put pants on a penguin, it could be admitted to this country." After 1957, the new Progressive Conservative government substantially reduced immigration levels.

French-Speaking Immigrants

In 1947, the birth rate of French Canadians remained high, yet large-scale immigration of non-French-speakers into Quebec risked undermining this natural increase. Concern for the survival of the French-Canadian culture created a particularly hostile atmosphere for immigrants to Quebec. Francophones often perceived immigrants as a threat because most joined the ranks of the English-speaking minority.

In the fall of 1948, the federal government, in hopes of satisfying Quebec members of the Liberal caucus as well as French-Canadian public opinion, put French nationals on an equal legal footing with British subjects and American citizens for purposes of entry into Canada. Civil servants, however, immediately thwarted the new policy for alleged "security" reasons, arguing that a large proportion of would-be French immigrants might be either communists or former Nazi collaborators.[9]

Ottawa's policy on French immigration had only a slight effect: between 1946 and 1950, fewer than 5000 French immigrants came to Canada. Although authorities in France did not encourage emigration, prospective immigrants besieged Canadian consular offices in Paris. While the Canadian consul in Paris made urgent requests for more staff and more office space, Hugh Keenleyside advised the deputy minister of labour to channel "all efforts in the same direction, that is to say, the encouragement of British immigration to Canada."

The Canadian government preferred British immigrants over all others. "We put forth much more effort in the United Kingdom than in any other country," J.W. Pickersgill, minister of citizenship and immigration, admitted in 1955. It was only natural, he asserted, that Canada favour British immigration since it was easier to transplant individuals into "similar soil." Although he viewed the massive influx of new arrivals in 1956–57—40 percent of whom were British—as "too big for Canada to digest," he added candidly that any attempt to stem the tide of British immigration "would be the finish of the Liberal party in many Anglo-Saxon constituencies."

Immigration from France did increase in the 1950s and 1960s, before declining again. In the years 1945–80, between one-half and two-thirds of immigrants to Canada were English-speaking, whereas French-speakers numbered only about 3 percent, and bilingual English-French 4 percent. The remainder soon learned English. By 2000, although Canada's major sources of immigrants were no longer European, more than half of new immigrants—many of them from India—still spoke English, whereas fewer than 5 percent spoke French. The census of 2011 showed that immigration was the primary factor in explaining the relative decline of Quebec's population in regard to Canada's total population. About 12.4 percent of Quebeckers are foreign-born, as compared to about 20.6 percent of all Canadians.

An overwhelming majority of these new Quebeckers, as is the case in much of Canada, chose to settle in larger urban centres, with nearly 87 percent choosing Montreal. Most spoke English instead of French. Immigration reinforced the numerical strength of English-speaking Canada linguistically, although diversifying it racially, ethnically, and culturally.

An Evaluation of Postwar Immigration Policy

This first wave of postwar immigration, which brought 1.7 million immigrants to Canada, ended in the late 1950s when rising unemployment led the Canadian government to reconsider its policy. The year 1957, however, witnessed a boom before the bust, with 282,000 arrivals—a figure that still paled in comparison with the 400,000 immigrants who came in 1913. Some 37,000 of these new arrivals were Hungarians who fled their homeland in 1956 as Soviet armies crushed an uprising. Among them were most of the student body and faculty of a Hungarian school of forestry. Transported across Canada on a "freedom train," they were relocated at the University of British Columbia.

Canadians believed their country was generously offering liberty and opportunity to victims of persecution. In practice, economics and prevailing notions of race and ethnicity dictated how many and which immigrants came to Canada. Ottawa sought immigrants possessing certain skills and initiated bulk labour schemes. Federal authorities directed many immigrants, once in Canada, to farms and to unattractive jobs in remote resource regions. Once they fulfilled their contracts, however, many immigrants soon left for the cities.

Racial bias explains why few immigrants gained entrance from outside Europe and the United States. In

Jack Pickersgill (right), the federal minister responsible for immigration in the St. Laurent government, greets the dean of the faculty of forestry engineering at the University of Sopron, Hungary, in Montreal, 1957. Some 37,000 young and highly skilled Hungarians, including much of the teaching staff and 200 students of this faculty, arrived in Canada during and immediately after the Hungarian uprising of 1956.

Source: Champlain Marcil/Library and Archives Canada/ PA-147725.

1958, the director of the Immigration Branch explained why "coloured British subjects" from the Caribbean were excluded from Canada: "They do not assimilate rapidly and pretty much vegetate to a low standard of living." The introduction of quotas, which remained in effect until 1967, also limited immigration from the Indian subcontinent. The location of immigration offices and the nature of government promotional literature also helped ensure that the majority of immigrants came from Britain and the European continent, as well as from the United States.

Emigration

New immigrants experienced the worst of the economic downturn of the late 1950s and early 1960s. Disappointed with the lack of opportunities in Canada and embittered by what they considered false promises, many (particularly British) returned home. From the early 1950s to the early 1970s, one in every three or four immigrants to Canada either returned home or moved to the United States.

More worrisome was the movement southward of 800,000 native-born Canadians in the period 1952–71. Approximately one-tenth of this group consisted of professionals and managers—what was described as a "brain drain." Estimates indicated that in 1963, 8000 graduates of the University of Toronto lived in the United States and that 800 of these taught in American colleges. Historian Arthur Lower conjectured that this loss of talent helped keep Canada "in that state of low water which has always been the object of the Yankee's good-natured scorn."[10] After a temporary reversal of the brain drain in the 1960s and early 1970s, at the time of the Vietnam War and the race riots in the United States, the movement to the south resumed in the late 1970s and 1980s. In the mid-1980s, 50,000 Canadians departed annually, attracted largely by the buoyant American economy and southern sunshine.

The problem continued in the 1990s, when some 275,000 Canadians took up residence in the United States. In certain years, the number of nurses and physicians who emigrated represented the equivalent of about one-half of the number of graduates from Canada's training programs. Many engineers, scientists, teachers, and managerial workers also joined the trek south, attracted to the United States by the prospect of better working conditions and higher salaries. The cost to Canada was substantial, as emigrants took with them skills they had developed in largely publicly financed postsecondary schools.

The Haim Abenhaim family, Sephardic Jewish immigrants from Morocco, arriving in Montreal, 1960. In the early 1970s, immigrants from developing countries began to come to Canada in significant numbers.

Source: Canadian Jewish Congress National Archives/PC 2/1/7 A.4.

The Immigrant Experience in the 1960s and 1970s

Due to an economic slowdown, the Diefenbaker years (1957–63) witnessed a slump in immigration. Fewer agents staffed Canadian immigration offices abroad. Unions exerted pressure to decrease immigration, and most parliamentarians were at best indifferent. Even Diefenbaker, despite favourable public pronouncements in speeches aimed at ethnic groups based on his own German background, appeared to have little interest in the question.

Sometimes immigration made sensational headlines. The press reported numerous cases of foreign seamen who jumped ship in

Canadian waters and then hurriedly married Canadian women in order to remain in Canada. Large-scale illegal Chinese immigration, promoted by a Hong Kong-based group that bought and sold false identities, also appeared to overwhelm the government. Ottawa promised to grant amnesty to most illegal migrants who would come forth and declare themselves (many thousands did), but the program did not eliminate the illegal immigration rings.

Toward a Colour-Blind Immigration Policy

The Diefenbaker Conservatives did, however, introduce new regulations in 1962 that ended the use of race and national origin as reasons for exclusion from Canada. The old discriminatory provisions were increasingly embarrassing in an era that discredited racism. In 1960, Diefenbaker proudly presented the Canadian Bill of Rights, which rejected discrimination by reason of race, national origin, colour, religion, or sex. Economic factors also contributed to the reversal of the former policy: Canada could no longer obtain the labour it needed from the "old countries." For a time, southern Europe supplanted Britain and northern Europe as the area of origin of most immigrants to Canada. Then, immigration diminished from these countries as well, as the economies of southern Europe stabilized in the 1960s, creating less impetus toward out-migration. By the 1970s, Asia and the Caribbean supplanted Europe as the major sources of immigrants to Canada.

This 1955 poster questions the colour code applied to immigrants from within the British Commonwealth.

Source: Jewish Labour Committee of Canada/Library and Archives Canada/PA-139579.

A New Wave of Immigrants

Assisted by the return of economic prosperity in the early 1960s, the Pearson government (1963–68) instituted structural changes designed to increase immigration. In 1966, it established the Department of Manpower and Immigration to relate immigration to the needs of the labour market, while the Department of the Secretary of State obtained responsibility for the integration of immigrants into Canadian society.

In 1967, new immigration regulations set up a points system for selecting independent immigrants. Criteria included education and training, personal qualities, occupational demand, and age and linguistic capacity. Sponsored dependants and, particularly, non-dependent relatives now found it more difficult to gain admittance. The government also set up the independent Immigration Appeal Board, which was almost immediately overwhelmed with appeals from alleged "visitors" who had applied to stay but had been refused and ordered deported.

The gradual elimination of racial discrimination from Canada's immigration policy, the decline of European sources of immigrants, and the expansion of the network of immigration offices around the world transformed the face of Canadian immigration. In 1966, for example, 87 percent of immigrants were of European origin; only four years later, 50 percent came from other regions. The West Indies, Haiti, Guyana, India, Hong Kong, the Philippines, and the Indochinese nations all figured among the major suppliers of immigrants in the 1970s.

Immigrant Settlement

Newcomers to Canada were not distributed evenly across the country. More than one-half settled in Ontario, especially in the south of the province. Good employment opportunities, large urban centres, and the region's prosperous image, along with already well-established ethnic communities with religious centres, clubs, welfare organizations, newspapers, and professional and other services, proved attractive. Quebec received fewer than 15 percent of new arrivals—about the same proportion as British Columbia. Alberta, especially during oil booms, attracted many immigrants, although most newcomers arrived from other provinces. The oil boom of the early 2000s led to substantially increased immigration into both Alberta and Saskatchewan, finally reversing a long and steady population decline in the latter province. The Atlantic provinces, for their part, experienced little immigration. The region was usually a source of immigrants for the resource sectors of western Canada.

In all regions, immigrants settled mainly in major metropolitan areas. As many as one-half of all immigrants to Ontario chose Toronto, which, with the rise of Asian immigration during the 1990s, became North America's most ethnically diverse city. Of the 1.16 million newcomers to Canada between 2006 and 2011, almost 40 percent chose Toronto as their point of destination. This group of newcomers made up almost 9 percent of the city's population, and the total foreign-born population of the Greater Toronto Area was 46 percent. Toronto, along with Vancouver and Montreal, remain the destinations of choice for nearly two-thirds of all newcomers to Canada. This demographic trend highlighted a dichotomous relationship between (largely white) rural and (more racially diverse) urban areas of Canada.

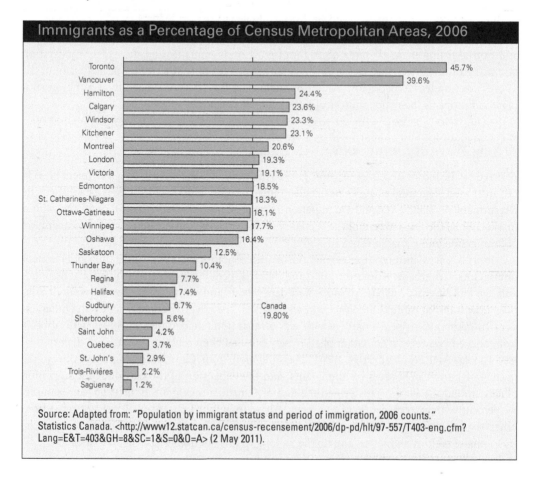

Immigrants as a Percentage of Census Metropolitan Areas, 2006

Area	Percentage
Toronto	45.7%
Vancouver	39.6%
Hamilton	24.4%
Calgary	23.6%
Windsor	23.3%
Kitchener	23.1%
Montreal	20.6%
London	19.3%
Victoria	19.1%
Edmonton	18.5%
St. Catharines-Niagara	18.3%
Ottawa-Gatineau	18.1%
Winnipeg	17.7%
Oshawa	16.4%
Saskatoon	12.5%
Thunder Bay	10.4%
Regina	7.7%
Halifax	7.4%
Sudbury	6.7%
Sherbrooke	5.6%
Saint John	4.2%
Quebec	3.7%
St. John's	2.9%
Trois-Rivières	2.2%
Saguenay	1.2%

Canada 19.80%

Source: Adapted from: "Population by immigrant status and period of immigration, 2006 counts." Statistics Canada. <http://www12.statcan.ca/census-recensement/2006/dp-pd/hlt/97-557/T403-eng.cfm?Lang=E&T=403&GH=8&SC=1&S=0&O=A> (2 May 2011).

Immigration in Recent Years

The deep recession of the early 1980s again caused immigration to decline. Economic problems contributed to an anti-immigrant backlash, as many Canadians viewed immigrants as competitors for scarce jobs or believed they were crowding the welfare rolls.

Most studies on the relationship between immigration and employment, however, demonstrate that immigrants do not increase unemployment but rather help create a larger, more flexible, and more adaptable labour force. Immigrants often work at jobs that Canadians cannot or will not do. For some time after arrival, they may require more social services; yet a report produced by the Economic Council of Canada in 1992 concluded that the proportion of welfare recipients among recent immigrants is not significantly different from that of the native-born. Moreover, through their need for housing, food, clothing, and other consumer goods, immigrants increase the size of the domestic market and thereby assist in boosting growth. "The objective evidence does not support the view that the relation between immigration and unemployment is a major problem."[11] Most immigrants obtain jobs soon after arrival and many end up working in jobs for which they are overqualified.

Regardless, racist and nativist sentiments often shape public opinion more than statistics and evidence do. When Canada faced new economic problems in the early 1980s, the Progressive Conservative government of Brian Mulroney revised each year's immigration quotas downward, according to its vague predictions of what the economy could bear. Immigration declined to its lowest levels in more than two decades. After 1986, the government did, however, facilitate the entry into Canada of several thousand "business class" immigrants—wealthy entrepreneurs, especially from Hong Kong. These individuals agreed to invest their capital in Canada, set up businesses, and hopefully create jobs for Canadians. Most immigrant investors chose to settle in British Columbia, Quebec, and Ontario.

How Many Immigrants and From Where?

In the late 1980s, Ottawa gradually raised the ceiling on immigration from 100,000 to 200,000. But taking into account annual emigration of at least 50,000, the net immigration figure was substantially lower. Then, in 1990, the federal government announced further increases—a politically risky decision as the economy slowed again and as certain groups, such as the Reform Party, based in western Canada, attacked immigration and multiculturalism policies. An average of nearly 220,000 immigrants was nonetheless admitted to Canada each year from 1992 to 1999.

By the 1990s, Sri Lanka and Taiwan replaced the Caribbean nations as major homelands of arriving immigrants. In the years immediately preceding Hong Kong's cession to China in 1997, the former British colony was Canada's major source of immigrants. Some 200,000 of these returned to Hong Kong after obtaining Canadian citizenship following three years of residence in Canada. Since 2000, annual arrivals have fluctuated between 225,000 and 250,000. Almost one-third of newcomers to Canada now came from just three countries: the Philippines, China, and India. Pakistan, Iran, and Korea were also major source countries. Outside Asia, many immigrants came from the United States and the United Kingdom (although many people from Britain were of Indian origin), as well as Colombia, France, Romania, and Russia.

As a result of Caribbean and then Asian immigration, so-called "visible minorities" became an important part of Canada's social fabric. While only 12,000 West Indians lived in Canada in 1961, the figure climbed to 225,000 in 1986. The number of Canadians of Chinese origin increased from 60,000 to nearly 350,000 in the same period, and then to 1 million by 2001. In 2011, such minorities made up 19 percent of the country's population and more than 45 percent of the populations of Vancouver and Toronto.

Leading Source Countries of Immigrants, Selected Years

1960	1976	1984	1991–1995	1996–2000	2001–2006
Italy	Britain	Vietnam	China	China	China
Britain	United States	Hong Kong	India	India	India
United States	Hong Kong	United States	Hong Kong	Philippines	Philippines
Germany	Jamaica	India	Philippines	Pakistan	Pakistan
Netherlands	Lebanon	Britain	Sri Lanka	Hong Kong	United States
Portugal	India	Poland	Poland	Iran	South Korea
Greece	Philippines	Philippines	Vietnam	Taiwan	Romania
France	Portugal	El Salvador	United Kingdom	United States	Iran
Poland	Italy	Jamaica	United States	Sri Lanka	United Kingdom
Austria	Guyana	China	Jamaica	South Korea	Colombia

Source: Adapted from: "Place of birth for the immigrant population by period of immigration," 2006, Statistics Canada. <http://www12
.statcan.ca/census-recensement/2006/dp-pd/hlt/97-557/T404-eng.cfm?Lang=E&T=404&GH=4&GF=1&SC=1&S=1&O=D> (2 May 2011).

Immigrants and Canada's Economy

In 1968, 75 percent of immigrants belonged to the so-called "economic class" in which one
family member, the principal applicant, was seen as a potential investor in the Canadian
economy or assessed for skills deemed in demand. In the early 1990s, fewer than 40 percent
of immigrants belonged to this group. By far the majority of immigrants admitted to Canada
now belonged to the other two categories of "family class" (i.e., close relatives of Canadian
residents) and refugees. In response to critics who urged the government to link immigration
more closely to economic needs, Ottawa adjusted its rules in 1993 to favour more highly
educated newcomers, and the number of immigrants with university diplomas rose sharply.

By 2001, as a result of new selection criteria, more than 60 percent of immigrants were
independent workers (including their dependants) and investors, chosen with the objective of
responding to labour market requirements. About 30 percent were family relatives, and some
10 percent were refugees. Revised rules set out in 2002 favoured educated applicants with work
experience and a confirmed job offer, people judged to be adaptable and to have "flexible and
transferable skills" for the "knowledge economy."

Still Canada's immigration system showed signs of strain. In its search for highly educated and
well-trained immigrants, Canada had to work to compete with several other countries, including
the United States and Australia. Construction companies begged the government to admit the
skilled tradespeople they needed and to regularize the status of the thousands of undocumented
immigrants it employed, allegedly often for less than the minimum wage.

However, in 2006 Ottawa refused an amnesty that risked encouraging more illegal immigration. Moreover, many workers selected because of their high qualifications had difficulty
having their foreign credentials recognized in Canada. As one Toronto newspaper commented,
"Foreign-trained engineers may make wonderful taxi drivers, but they also deserve a chance,
if their credentials stand up to scrutiny, to be wonderful engineers." Ontario, which received
more than half of Canada's immigrants, attempted to force self-governing professions to
maintain fair, clear, and open licensing processes. At the same time, the province's economy
appeared unable to absorb the large numbers of immigrant engineers who arrived every year,
and many immigrants were not covered since they were in non-regulated professions. Not
surprisingly, a Statistics Canada survey showed that poverty rates among immigrants, despite

their high levels of education, remained high. In addition, 40 percent of economic immigrants left Canada within ten years.

Business, with its demands for more skilled workers to alleviate worrying labour shortages, was not alone in seeking high numbers of immigrants. Policy analysts, including demographers, warned that due to current low fertility rates (Canadian women were expected to have on average 1.5 children), the country's population would begin to contract in the medium term, even at present levels of immigration. Some middle-aged Canadians began to worry about who would pay for their old-age pensions and future health care.

Adaptation

Adapting to a new society is a difficult process. Even though most immigrants found their new life in Canada a considerable material improvement, the transition was never easy. For most, there was no opportunity to return home, even if they so desired. Governments and community associations attempted to assist the new arrivals. Mutual aid and support among families and kinship networks remained important.

Despite the rhetoric of tolerance and multiculturalism, assimilation remained an underlying (if no longer official) social strategy. Immigrants faced the upsetting necessity of coming to terms with Canadian customs. Studies of South Asian immigrants (from India, Pakistan, Bangladesh, and Sri Lanka) indicate that "only a small proportion" of homeland cultural practices survived the settlement process.[12] Culinary habits and cultural celebrations tend to be maintained in those cities where immigrant groups are sufficiently numerous.

Sod-turning for Edmonton's Hindu Centre, 1976.

Source: Provincial Archives of Alberta.

A HISTORICAL PORTRAIT

The Immigrant Experience

For many immigrants who have come to Canada, material betterment has been accompanied by a sense of cultural loss. Historian Hugh Johnston recorded the story of Tara Singh Bains, a Punjabi who arrived in Vancouver in 1953 and has since made many journeys back to the land of his origin. Bains, a man of strong religious convictions, told Johnston he deplored what he saw as the erosion of spiritual values among members of his community. Bains testified, "Materialism has created so many doorways to attract human thinking towards luxury, enjoyment, and selfishness, and in Western society ... the guidance of the family, the school and the church has fallen away."[1] Bains's lament might also be echoed, however, by adherents of traditional Christian sects as well, in whom the lures of materialism, and the emphasis on individualism, have also eroded religious observance.

Serious generational conflicts among members of ethnic communities, as among Canadians in general, have been frequent. Sociologist Edite Noivo has studied the life histories of members of three generations of Portuguese Canadians living in Montreal. These stories reveal sharp tensions.

Noivo found, for example, that many first-generation parents objected to a son's wish to marry, because his departure represented a serious financial loss. One father reported that he told his son that "we couldn't afford it now and that he had to wait a couple of years more." Although the son at first agreed to abide by his father's will, he later, in the father's words, "got impatient and started to make a big fuss ... so I allowed him to get married." Sons saw marriage as an advantage because it would bring financial independence. One explained, "I had been handing over my weekly pay since the age of fourteen.... By the time I was 22, I still didn't have a penny for myself.... So I figured that I had to get married.... If I got married I'd keep my paycheque."[2]

A young third-generation Portuguese Canadian adapted in a different fashion to parental constraints in matters concerning relations with the opposite sex. He reported, "None of the Portuguese girls I know are allowed to go to parties.... I can go, but my sister and cousins never do.... I can't take them along, my parents and their parents don't trust me.... Of course, none of my girl-friends are Portuguese, but they're just for fun. Like my mother says, a girl who is not a virgin at marriage is no good; I mean, she can't be trusted.... Sure I'll want to get married... to someone Portuguese like myself."[3]

Noivo herself had to face her respondents' disapproval of her own lifestyle. One first-generation male told her that she was only "half a woman.... One cannot be a full woman unless one is married and a mother." A second-generation female migrant made the same comment "in a more acrid and distasteful tone."[4]

---

1   Tara Singh Bains and Hugh Johnston, *The Four Quarters of the Night: The Life Journey of an Emigrant Sikh* (Montreal/Kingston: McGill-Queen's University Press, 1995), p. 227.

2   Edite Noivo, *Inside Ethnic Families: Three Generations of Portuguese-Canadians* (Montreal/Kingston: McGill-Queen's University Press, 1997), pp. 67–68.

3   Ibid., p. 119.

4   Ibid., p. 39.

Furthermore, the clash between contemporary Canadian values and those of the country of origin has frequently caused painful problems for immigrants and raised controversial issues within Canadian society. Parental authority has weakened in the context of Canada's much more permissive and liberal society. In South Asia, for example, parents tend to choose marriage partners for their children, and dating is a foreign practice. In Canada, the generation gap between immigrant parents and their children has often deepened into a gulf as children become Canadianized through the schools, television, and socialization.

Discrimination

Despite the multicultural rhetoric in Canada, many immigrants, especially members of visible minorities, suffered discrimination. In the 1970s and 1980s, the media gave wide publicity to certain cases, such as one in which "white" and South Asian members of a railway crew in Daysland, Alberta, clashed with bottles and axes. In numerous instances, Sikhs were attacked and had their turbans forcibly removed. Blacks were frequently harassed or physically assaulted. In Montreal, a taxi company fired its Haitian drivers, claiming that it was losing business to companies that employed only white drivers. (Haitians responded by buying the city's second-largest taxi company.) Incidents of police shootings of young African Canadians in Montreal and Toronto sparked widespread demands for inquiries into alleged racism in police forces. The War on Terror following the attacks on the World Trade Center on September 11, 2001, drastically increased Islamophobia and ethnic profiling.

Historian Stanley Barrett's research on a suburban Toronto community in the early 1990s highlighted the existence of widespread racism against visible minorities. He suggested that South Asians saw racism as inevitable, and sought to defend themselves by fostering strong links with their own ethnic communities. African Canadians, more in contact with the "white" community, often felt bitterness and anger in the face of what they perceived as rejection by their neighbours.[13]

Most complaints about discrimination concerned employment and housing. A study done in Toronto in 1985 found that when immigrants from South Asia or the Caribbean with the same qualifications as white applicants applied for job openings, they learned, in two cases out of five, that the opening no longer existed. In some instances, the same employer on the same day then interviewed white candidates for the same position. One survey showed that three-quarters of West Indians judged employment discrimination in Toronto to be "very serious." Surveys in eleven other Canadian cities repeated the same finding. Arabs spoke of having to confront deep mistrust. Provincial human-rights commissions did receive numerous complaints of discrimination. Yet most victims failed to report incidents, believing that nothing would be done or, worse, fearing retaliation. Human-rights defence groups criticized the courts for their slowness and their leniency, and have denounced existing laws for their lack of severity.

Reactions to Immigration

Canadians have had mixed reactions to new arrivals, particularly from developing nations. Religious and civic groups strongly urged the admission of refugees, such as the Vietnamese "boat people" in the late 1970s, refugees from Kosovo in 1999, and Syrian refugees in 2015. Yet many Canadians, at times even a majority, believed that Canada accepted too many newcomers, regardless of the desperate situation from which they fled or the relatively small number of immigrants actually admitted. What is more surprising, perhaps, is that these attitudes were shared by other recent immigrants.

The rise of <u>international terrorism</u> brought more debate about Canada's immigration policy. Critics accused Ottawa of <u>not sufficiently screening new immigrants</u>, thus permitting the entry into the country of militants who favoured the use of <u>violence</u> to promote the causes they espoused. As evidence, they cited several incidents, among them the <u>bombing in 1985 of an Air India airplane,</u> which resulted in the death of 329 people, most of them Canadian citizens of Indian origin. It was <u>Canada's worst mass murder.</u> Police and prosecutors blamed <u>Sikh militants,</u> but were unable to solve the crime and obtain convictions. In 2006, the Conservative government launched a commission of inquiry to study the investigation of the bombing. In September 2010, Inderjit Singh Reyat, one of the plotters of the bombing, was convicted of perjury, ending the longest terrorism probe in Canadian history. In other instances, investigative journalists linked Canadian-based militants of various national origins with participation in terrorist activities abroad.

The arrival in Canada, particularly in <u>Vancouver,</u> of a relatively <u>large number of wealthy Chinese immigrants from Hong Kong</u> in the late 1980s provoked strong reactions. Government and business leaders appreciated the large financial investments a number of newcomers made. But some Canadian residents spoke with derision of the "<u>yacht people</u>," criticizing what they perceived as <u>ostentatious displays of wealth</u>, such as the construction of "<u>monster homes.</u>" A booming Chinese economy by the early 2000s led to an increase in home purchases in cities such as Vancouver and complaints that this population was increasing real estate values and pushing the cost of homes out of reach for most residents.

The <u>role of women</u> in the family and in society, particularly in certain Asian and Middle-Eastern cultures, has generated considerable debate in Canada. The <u>conservatism of these cultures in terms of gender relations</u> often clashes with Canada's more <u>liberal values.</u> This clash raises a fundamental question about <u>cultural relativism:</u> should Canadians be tolerant toward immigrant values if they run counter to those of Canada, and, more importantly, if they are deemed sexist and harmful? Ontarians discussed whether Muslims could establish religious courts to decide issues of family law; the Ontario government decided they could not. <u>Quebeckers debated</u> the meaning of "reasonable accommodation" of religious differences. To this end, the province proposed <u>legislation requiring that all Muslim women wearing the niqab (a full-face covering)</u> would be <u>required to remove it in order to receive government services, to see a doctor, or to attend classes in colleges and universities.</u> A 2010 survey revealed that 80 percent of Canadians approved of this measure, signifying that expectations of cultural adaptation on certain issues remain strong among "the gatekeepers." In 2015 the federal government of Stephen Harper challenged the right of women to wear the niqab at citizenship ceremonies. The Supreme Court upheld a woman's right to wear whatever she chose but the issue became divisive during that year's election campaign, contributing to the Conservative defeat. Canadians in general have attempted to define so-called "<u>Canadian values</u>" that, they feel, should not be compromised; these include <u>democracy, freedom, tolerance, and equality.</u>

Refugees

Much of the criticism directed at federal immigration policy <u>since 1980</u> concerned refugees. Around the world, <u>millions of human beings became refugees</u>, fleeing <u>war and persecution in their homelands.</u> Canada was not immune to such mass movements. Humanitarian and refugee-advocacy groups, as well as ethnic communities favouring more immigration from their home countries, judged Canada's refugee quotas to be unreasonably low. They also denounced the government's cumbersome procedures for studying the cases of refugee-status claimants, resulting in backlogs that grew larger each year.

During this period, public opinion became notably less sympathetic to the cause of refugees: surveys showed that nearly half of all Canadians thought Canada had no moral obligation to open its doors to persons fleeing persecution in other lands. Many critics were undoubtedly influenced by the large numbers of would-be immigrants who entered Canada illegally—so-called "queue jumpers"—and who claimed refugee status, but whose reasons for emigrating seemed to be primarily economic. Indeed, the hearing that virtually all refugee-status claimants requested—an unforeseen consequence of earlier legislation—became "a routine channel for evading the normal admission requirements and getting easy access to Canada."[14] In 1986, the dramatic arrival of a large group of Tamil immigrants from Sri Lanka on the shores of Newfoundland and, the following year, of a group of Sikhs from India on the coast of Nova Scotia, was sufficient proof for many Canadians that Ottawa had lost control over entry into the country. The 2010 arrival of nearly 500 Tamil migrants off the coast of British Columbia, which again brought forth charges of "queue jumping" refugee claimants, precipitated a renewed debate on Canada's refugees policies, and proved that Canadian attitudes toward migrant, and particularly refugee, arrivals remains slow-changing.

Public pressure led the Mulroney government to act against illegal immigration in 1988, by which time government efforts to clear the huge backlog of refugee-status claimants had become bogged down. In addition, immigration officials had to study the applications of new refugees who arrived at Canada's borders and airports. The number of new claimants declined, and the government declared that it had succeeded in driving off unfounded claims. New legislation in 1993 further limited the right of rejected applicants to appeal, resulting in a further drop in the number of claimants arriving in Canada. Through the 1990s, the acceptance rate of refugee claimants declined from about 75 percent to about 50 percent—admittedly a much higher rate than existed in most Western countries. Refugee lawyers blamed "compassion fatigue." Panel members, they said, were becoming hardened to stories of abuse and persecution. Religious and ethnic groups feared that the measures also discouraged true political refugees.

The terrorist attacks of September 11, 2001, in the United States brought new and tighter immigration rules, which took effect in 2003. In response to American accusations that Canada admitted too many refugees without proper security vetting, Canada decided to turn back claimants arriving at Canadian land borders and invited them to seek asylum in the United States, whose rules were reputedly more restrictive. Critics maintained that henceforth more refugees would seek to enter Canada illegally, in order to make their claim from inside Canada. Newspaper reports asserted that claimants still enjoyed far too many possibilities for appeal and that economic migrants were displacing genuine refugees. In 2006 Canada began a new system for processing certain refugee applications. The change provided for the acceptance en masse of large groups of displaced people including Sudanese, Somalis, and Afghans.

The issue of Syrian refugees fleeing civil war at home became an international issue in 2015. The projected arrival of thousands of Syrians to Canada was one of the main issues in the Canadian federal election of that year. Despite the publicized suffering of this largely Muslim population, some Canadians opposed allowing the refugees entry for security reasons.

Multiculturalism

Canadians have often taken pride in the image of their country as a "cultural mosaic" rather than an American-style "melting pot." Official policy no longer favours rapid assimilation and instead emphasizes integration or acculturation. In his first speech in the Senate in 1964, Senator Paul Yuzyk, born in Manitoba of Ukrainian origin, discussed the emergence of what he termed a "third force," consisting of Canadians of neither French nor British descent. The Royal Commission on Bilingualism and Biculturalism widened its scope to include a study of the cultural contributions of other ethnic groups.

In October 1971, Prime Minister Trudeau told the House of Commons that the government "accepts the contention of other cultural communities that they, too, are essential elements in Canada and deserve government assistance in order to contribute to regional and national life in ways that derive from their heritages." Multiculturalism—but not multilingualism—was to be encouraged. The new Canadian Constitution of 1982 provided additional, though somewhat vague, protection to multiculturalism by declaring that the Canadian Charter of Rights and Freedoms "shall be interpreted in a manner consistent with the preservation and enhancement of the multicultural heritage of Canada." Still, various ethnic associations denounced what they termed the unacceptable primacy that the Charter accorded English and French in Canada. In 1988, a revised Multiculturalism Act provided new funds for promoting cultures and reducing discrimination.

By the mid-1980s, the federal government invested modestly in multiculturalism, funding ethnic day-care centres, heritage-language classes, cultural festivals, and conferences, and providing grants for the preparation of histories of the major Canadian ethnic groups. Money was made available to complete the revitalization of Vancouver's Chinatown and to transform this ethnic neighbourhood into a shining symbol of Canada's new multicultural nature and, at the same time, a valuable tourist attraction. By 2000, however, Vancouver's Chinatown was in decline.

Canadian hockey legend Willie O'Ree, the first black player in the NHL, chats with children at the Harmony Brunch in East Preston, Nova Scotia, held to commemorate International Day for the Elimination of Racial Discrimination.

Source: Nova Scotia Human Rights Commission.

Several provincial governments also contributed financially to support multicultural policy. The Ontario government, for example, used its Wintario lottery funding program to create a research institute, the Multicultural History Society of Ontario. Many school boards set up courses in non-official languages. In Edmonton, for example, immersion schooling could be had in Arabic, Chinese, Hebrew, Ukrainian, and German. Such policies had practical relevance. Already by the late 1980s, English was *not* the mother tongue of 50 percent of the children enrolled in Toronto public schools nor of 40 percent of those enrolled in Vancouver schools.

Increasingly, observers of multiculturalism expressed fears that the official emphasis on maintaining cultural diversity impeded the integration of newcomers. They cited the tendency of immigrant groups, particularly South Asians and Chinese, to live in self-segregated, often middle-class "ethnic enclaves," defined by Statistics Canada as communities with 30 percent of their population from one visible minority group. In such communities, contacts with the host society were reduced. Market researcher Allan Gregg commented, "In Canada, we may live in a multicultural society, but the evidence suggests that fewer and fewer of us are living in multicultural neighbourhoods."[15]

Where Historians Disagree

Evaluating Canada's Multicultural Policy

The arrival in Canada of large numbers of immigrants, first from Europe and since the late 1960s from the Caribbean, Latin America, Asia, and Africa, diversified Canada's population. Until the 1950s, the federal and the provincial governments espoused a policy of rapid assimilation of newcomers into the "Canadian mainstream." But many immigrants and their descendants attempted to conserve at least part of their ethnic heritage. As interest in the rights of minorities grew throughout the Western world during the 1960s, these groups sought government intervention to help attain their goals. In response, the federal government elaborated, in 1971, a policy of multiculturalism. Since then, governments and public agencies at all levels have launched programs favouring the retention of national cultures.

Official federal policy views multiculturalism as "a powerful bonding agent" that "helps unite us and identify us, while at the same time allowing every element of our society to retain its own characteristics and cultural heritage."[1] Observers have generally been somewhat suspicious of these stated intentions. In 1988, Howard Palmer described federal policy as, at least in part, an attempt to win the ethnic vote in urban Ontario and to temper western Canada's rising opposition to the policy of bilingualism.[2] Jean Burnet has criticized the "ambiguous conceptualization" of multiculturalism, but believes that its basic aims are a valid response to the Canadian situation.[3]

Regardless of the inevitable political considerations underlying the policy, has multiculturalism been worth pursuing? Norman Buchignani believed it has, and felt that federal policy has helped groups such as the South Asians feel "comfortable about being South Asian and Canadian at the same time."[4] He also viewed multicultural policy as heightening awareness among native-born Canadians of the new communities that have recently established themselves in their midst. Elliot L. Tepper agreed. In his view, multiculturalism "fosters acceptance of the reality that Canada is a nation of

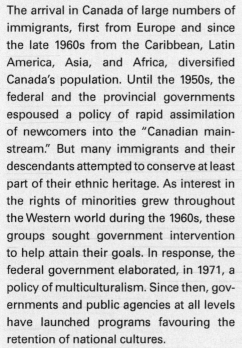

immigrants."[5] Lance W. Roberts and Rodney A. Clifton argued that the policy at least has symbolic value, permitting members of ethnic groups to "participate and benefit as members of a complex industrial society while retaining the sense that they belong to a smaller, more intimate community."[6]

Other observers expressed doubt. C. Michael Lanphier and Anthony H. Richmond argued that it is likely impossible to reconcile equality of opportunity and integration with "the maintenance of separate identities and cultural pluralism."[7] Gilles Paquet agreed. He saw multiculturalism as having heightened the belief among "other" Canadians that they do not have to adapt their mores while, at the same time, the "dominant cultures" have remained dominant. "The gap between expectations and realities has generated much ... frustration."[8] Peter S. Li and B. Singh Bolaria held a similar opinion. Multiculturalism is "the failure of an illusion, not of a policy."[9] The illusion is that a cultural solution, such as multiculturalism, could solve problems such as ethnic inequality and racial discrimination, whose roots are political and economic.

Wenona Giles asserted that multiculturalism—which she saw as a major component of Canadian nationalism—will not facilitate access to education and other basic resources "unless it is linked to more broadly based struggles against racism, and gender and class inequities."[10] Novelist Neil Bissoondath, who refuses the role of "ethnic" which would have him labelled an "East Indian-Trinidadian-Canadian-Quebecker," argued in a controversial book that the policy of official multiculturalism, by encouraging immigrants to focus on "There" (the ancestral homeland) rather than on "Here" (the new homeland), actually highlights the differences that divide Canadians rather than the similarities that unite them. To focus on what you were as compared to what you have become, he believed, "is to stultify the personality, creating stereotypes, stripping the individual of uniqueness."[11]

Regardless of the disagreements, Robert A. Harney argued there is merit even in engaging the debate. Multiculturalism is part of Canada's search to define itself. "Survival lies in traveling toward an identity, and we will all be better served if that traveling itself remains our identity."[12]

---

1   *Multiculturalism ... Being Canadian* (Ottawa: Secretary of State for Multiculturalism, 1987), p. 9.

2   Jean R. Burnet with Howard Palmer, *"Coming Canadians": An Introduction to a History of Canada's Peoples* (Toronto: McClelland & Stewart, 1988), p. 176.

3   Jean Burnet, "Multiculturalism Ten Years Later," in Jean Leonard Elliott, ed., *Two Nations, Many Cultures* (Scarborough, ON: Prentice-Hall, 1983), p. 241.

4   Norman Buchignani and Doreen M. Indra with Sam Srivastiva, *Continuous Journey: A Social History of South Asians in Canada* (Toronto: McClelland & Stewart, 1985), p. 227.

5   Elliot L. Tepper, "Immigration Policy and Multiculturalism," in J.W. Berry and J.A. Laponce, eds., *Ethnicity and Culture in Canada: The Research Landscape* (Toronto: University of Toronto Press, 1994), p. 95.

6   Lance W. Roberts and Rodney Clifton, "Multiculturalism in Canada: A Sociological Perspective," in Peter S. Li, ed., *Race and Ethnic Relations in Canada* (Toronto: Oxford University Press, 1990), p. 133.

7   C. Michael Lanphier and Anthony H. Richmond, "Multiculturalism and Identity in 'Canada Outside Quebec,'" in Kenneth McRoberts, ed., *Beyond Quebec: Taking Stock of Canada* (Montreal/Kingston: McGill-Queen's University Press, 1995), p. 314.

8   Gilles Paquet, "Political Philosophy of Multiculturalism," in J.W. Berry and J.A. Laponce, eds., *Ethnicity and Culture in Canada: The Research Landscape* (Toronto: University of Toronto Press, 1994), p. 63.

9 Peter S. Li and B. Singh Bolaria, *Racial Minorities in Multicultural Canada* (Toronto: Garamond Press, 1983), introduction.

10 Wenona Giles, *Portuguese Women in Toronto: Gender, Immigration, and Nationalism* (Toronto: University of Toronto Press, 2002), p. 110.

11 Neil Bissoondath, *Selling Illusions: The Cult of Multiculturalism in Canada*, rev. ed. (Toronto: Penguin Canada, 2002), p. 222.

12 Robert A. Harney, "'So Great a Heritage as Ours': Immigration and the Survival of Canadian Policy," in *Daedelus* 117 (Fall 1988), p. 93.

Indeed, ethnic communities themselves have questioned whether the federal and provincial governments fund the right programs, or whether they have preferred short-term, highly visible manifestations of what has been labelled "ethnic exotica." Perhaps rather than keeping immigrants "singing and dancing and talking their own language," as one journalist put it, the federal government should address "real" problems such as ethnic inequality in the Canadian labour market. Certain groups such as Ukrainians have vigorously proposed the recognition of minority-language rights. Other students of multiculturalism doubt that English–French dualism and ethnocultural pluralism can really be reconciled, or that the vastly diverse multicultural third force has the power to assure changes in the traditional bases of Canadian society. Further attempts to foster ethnic and linguistic heterogeneity might facilitate national unity or, conversely, might make unity more difficult to attain.

Non-official Languages

Heritage-language programs emphasize retention of the mother tongue and are seen to have moral and psychological value. However, immigrants and their offspring, in order to integrate into Canadian society, have had to learn English or, in Quebec, French. And although such groups as the Portuguese, the Greeks, and the Chinese have had considerable success in retaining the language of the country of origin, assimilative trends generally become more pronounced over time and the retention of non-official languages diminishes sharply. As ethnolinguist Joshua Fishman noted, "for 95 percent of the third generation, the language of the cradle is the language of the streets."[16] Indeed, the 2011 census revealed that one Canadian in five had a mother tongue that was neither English nor French; yet about one-third of this group rarely or never spoke their mother tongue and had adopted an official language, generally English.

Less than 30 percent of Ukrainian Canadians, for example, speak Ukrainian as a home language, and intermarriage has hastened the pace of assimilation. Historian Varpu Lindstrom-Best viewed second- and third-generation Finns as having become an "indistinguishable part" of Canadian society, although they will still attach a Finnish flag

Welcoming Syrian refugees, 2015.

Source: Stacey Newman/iStock/Thinkstock.

Top Ten Countries of Birth for Recent Immigrants and All Immigrants, 2006

RECENT IMMIGRANTS*	NUMBER	%
People's Republic of China	155,105	14
India	129,140	11.6
Philippines	77,880	7
Pakistan	57,630	5.2
United States	38,770	3.5
South Korea	35,450	3.2
Romania	28,080	2.5
Iran	27,600	2.5
United Kingdom	25,655	2.3
Colombia	25,305	2.3
Subtotal	600,615	
All other countries[†]	509,365	
Total	**1,109,980**	**100.1**

*Immigrants counted in 2006 who came to Canada between 2001 and 2006.
[†]Major "other" countries include Sri Lanka, the Russian Federation, France, Mexico, Afghanistan, Algeria, and Ukraine.

ALL IMMIGRANTS*	NUMBER	%
United Kingdom	579,620	9.4
People's Republic of China	466,940	7.5
India	443,690	7.2
Philippines	303,195	4.9
Italy	296,850	4.8
United States	250,535	4
Hong Kong	215,430	3.5
Germany	171,405	2.8
Poland	170,490	2.8
Pakistan	133,280	2.2

*All people counted in 2006 not born in Canada.
Source: Adapted from "Place of birth for the immigrant population by period of immigration, 2006," Statistics Canada, *2006 Census Highlight Tables* <http://www12.statcan.ca/census-recensement/2006/dp-pd/hlt/97-557/T404-eng.cfm?Lang=E&T=404&GH=4&GF=1&SC=1&S=1&O=D> (2 May 2011).

to their bumper.[17] Dutch Canadians have also become "invisible ethnics."[18] In a study of Poles in Canada, Henry Radecki concluded that ethnic identification will have to depend on knowledge of Poland's culture and history rather than on "rapidly declining" mastery and use of the language in Canada.[19] Of Toronto's half-million-strong Italian community, fewer than 150,000 (belonging generally to the original immigrant generation) in 1984 were "active in Italian institutions."[20] Large numbers of Italians have deliberately broken their ethnic links and taken refuge in "Anglo conformity" because of the prejudice they have faced. Studies carried out by sociologist Jeffrey Reitz suggest that linguistic assimilation leads to destruction of the cohesive ethnic community.[21] While the prognosis for linguistic survival looks bleak for older ethnic communities from Europe, the number of Canadians speaking such languages as Chinese, Spanish, Punjabi, Tagalog, and Arabic is increasing rapidly as immigration rejuvenates these groups.

The Impact of Immigration

Immigrants have had an immeasurable impact on Canada. Since the late 1970s, for example, the number of non-British, non-French writers in Canada has grown substantially, and Canadian literature has become increasing diversified. Indeed, Canada became part of the literary global village as many novels written by new Canadians featured settings that often had little to do with

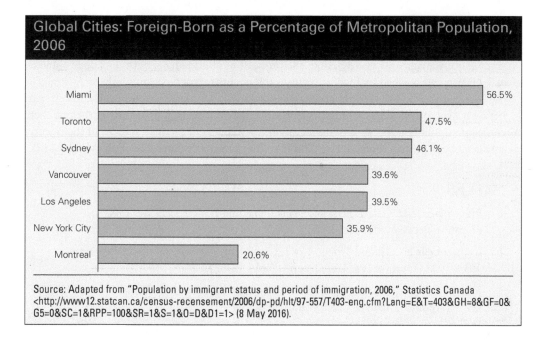

Global Cities: Foreign-Born as a Percentage of Metropolitan Population, 2006

City	Percentage
Miami	56.5%
Toronto	47.5%
Sydney	46.1%
Vancouver	39.6%
Los Angeles	39.5%
New York City	35.9%
Montreal	20.6%

Source: Adapted from "Population by immigrant status and period of immigration, 2006," Statistics Canada <http://www12.statcan.ca/census-recensement/2006/dp-pd/hlt/97-557/T403-eng.cfm?Lang=E&T=403&GH=8&GF=0& G5=0&SC=1&RPP=100&SR=1&S=1&O=D&D1=1> (8 May 2016).

Canada. Austin Clarke, born in Barbados, set *The Polished Hoe*, a poignant account of injustice, on an imaginary West Indian island in the 1950s. This novel, his ninth, won him the Giller Prize in 2002. Indian-born Rohinton Mistry used India as his setting for *A Fine Balance* and *Family Matters*, while Michael Ondaatje, from Sri Lanka, set his fourth novel, *The English Patient*, in Tuscany, Italy, in the closing moments of World War II. Filmmaker Deepa Mehta, also born in India, has produced critically acclaimed and controversial films such as *Fire* and *Heaven on Earth* that examine both the inherent tensions in Hindu culture and the clash of Indian and Western cultures.

Immigrants have brought new political questions to the fore in such areas as education and social policy, and the "ethnic vote" has become significant in many constituencies. Whereas, typically, ethnic groups supported the Liberal Party because they entered the country under Liberal governments and they were largely liberal in philosophy, their support has more recently fluctuated between the Liberals and the Conservatives. Many of these groups are now seen as conservative on such issues as law and order, and social and family issues.

Immigration has enabled urban Canada to acquire a much more diverse and vibrant cultural life. Demographically, immigration has boosted Canada's population. From 1981 to 1986, net immigration represented one-fifth of the country's population growth; from 1986 to 1996, it represented more than half; and from 1996 to 2006, it accounted for two-thirds.

Immigration brought much of the blue-collar labour that the country needed for large-scale industrial and resource development in the 1950s. By 1961, 12 percent of the country's workforce, and 20 percent of Ontario's, was composed of postwar immigrants. Immigration also provided many of the skilled workers and professionals that the country needed. In the 1960s, for example, hundreds of American university professors entered the country, permitting the rapid expansion of the Canadian university system but also setting the stage for the nationalist outcry against American domination in the early 1970s. Bringing in educated immigrants at that time helped ease the pressure on an already overburdened educational system in Canada, a country with a much higher proportion of young people than most European nations. Ironically, for a country that has often complained of suffering a brain drain to the United States, Canada has been criticized by some developing countries for attracting the highly qualified people that those developing nations so desperately need to keep at home.

SUMMARY

Immigration and multiculturalism continue to be issues of debate, just as they have been throughout Canada's history. By 2006, the proportion of Canadians born outside of Canada, at 19.8 percent, reached its highest point in the postwar period, second only to Australia in the Western world. The integration of immigrants will continue to be painful, and relations between new arrivals and the host society will raise controversial issues. Nevertheless, there can be no doubt that, because of immigration, the Canada of the first decades of the twenty-first century is a much more diverse land than the country that emerged from World War II.

NOTES

1. Franca Iacovetta, *Gatekeepers: Reshaping Immigrant Lives in Cold War Canada* (Toronto: Between the Lines Press, 2006).

2. Irving Abella and Harold Troper, *None Is Too Many: Canada and the Jews of Europe, 1933–1948* (Toronto: Lester & Orpen Dennys, 1982).

3. John W. Holmes, *The Shaping of Peace: Canada and the Search for World Order 1943–1957*, vol. 1 (Toronto: University of Toronto Press, 1979), p. 101.

4. This story is told by M. J. Stone in "Ann Kazimirski, Music Teacher 1922–2006," *The Globe and Mail*, November 3, 2006.

5. Marlene Epp, *Women Without Men: Mennonite Refugees of the Second World War* (Toronto: University of Toronto Press, 2000).

6. Karl Aun, *The Political Refugees: A History of the Estonians in Canada* (Toronto: McClelland & Stewart, 1985).

7. Franca Iacovetta, *Such Hardworking People: Italian Immigrants in Postwar Toronto* (Montreal/Kingston: McGill-Queen's University Press, 1992).

8. Franca Iacovetta, "Remaking Their Lives," in Joy Parr, ed., *A Diversity of Women: Ontario, 1945–1980* (Toronto: University of Toronto Press, 1995), pp. 135–67.

9. The subject of postwar French immigration is examined in Richard Jones, "Spécificités de l'immigration française au Canada au lendemain de la deuxième guerre mondiale," *Revue européenne des migrations internationales*, 2 (1986): 127–43.

10. Arthur Lower, quoted in Christina McCall Newman, "The Canadian Americans," *Maclean's*, July 27, 1963, p. 10.

11. Quoted in Henry Aubin, "Do Immigrants Steal Jobs or Create New Ones?," *The Gazette* (Montreal), January 10, 1985.

12. Norman Buchignani and Doreen M. Indra with Ram Srivastiva, *Continuous Journey: A Social History of South Asians in Canada* (Toronto: McClelland & Stewart, 1985), p. 163.

13. Stanley R. Barrett, *Paradise: Class, Commuters, and Ethnicity in Rural Ontario* (Toronto: University of Toronto Press, 1994), p. 235.

14. Gerald E. Dirks, *Controversy and Complexity: Canadian Immigration Policy during the 1980s* (Montreal/Kingston: McGill-Queen's University Press, 1995), pp. 79–80.

15. Allan Gregg, quoted in Marina Jimenez, "Do Ethnic Enclaves Impede Immigration?," *The Globe and Mail*, February 8, 2007, p. 8.

16. Joshua Fishman, quoted in Robert Harney, "'So Great a Heritage as Ours': Immigration and the Survival of the Canadian Policy," *Daedelus*, 117 (Fall 1988): 83.

17. Varpu Lindstrom-Best, *The Finns in Canada* (Ottawa: Canadian Historical Association, 1985), p. 18.

18. Herman Ganzevoort, *A Bittersweet Land: The Dutch Experience in Canada, 1890–1980* (Toronto: McClelland & Stewart, 1988), p. 127.

19. Henry Radecki with Benedykt Heydenkorn, *A Member of a Distinguished Family: The Polish Group in Canada* (Toronto: McClelland & Stewart, 1976), p. 106.

20. Robert Harney, quoted in Margot Gibb-Clark, "'Italian Community's a Myth,' Historian Says," *The Globe and Mail*, October 20, 1984, p. 14.

21. Jeffrey G. Reitz, "Language and Ethnic Community Survival," in Jay E. Goldstein and Rita M. Bienvenue, eds., *Ethnicity and Ethnic Relations in Canada* (Toronto: Butterworths, 1980), p. 122.

BIBLIOGRAPHY

Two comprehensive overviews of Canada's immigration policy are available: Ninette Kelley and Michael Trebilcock, *The Making of the Mosaic: A History of Canadian Immigration Policy* (Toronto: University of Toronto Press, 2010); and Donald H. Avery, *Reluctant Host: Canada's Response to Immigrant Workers, 1896–1994* (Toronto: McClelland & Stewart, 1995). The 1980s in particular are examined in Gerald E. Dirks, *Controversy and Complexity: Canadian Immigration Policy during the 1980s* (Montreal/Kingston: McGill-Queen's University Press, 1995). Questions relating to immigration are discussed in Peter S. Li, *Destination Canada: Immigration Debates and Issues* (Toronto: Oxford University Press, 2003). On refugees, see the early study by Gerald E. Dirks, *Canada's Refugee Policy: Indifference or Opportunism?* (Montreal/Kingston: McGill-Queen's University Press, 1977). For a look at the federal–provincial relationship on immigration policy, see Chris Kostov, "Canada–Quebec Immigration Agreements (1971–1991) and Their Impact on Federalism," *American Review of Canadian Studies*, 38(1) (2008): 91–104.

Critical works on Canadian immigration policy include Daniel Stoffman, *Who Gets In: What's Wrong with Canada's Immigration Policy—And How to Fix It* (Toronto: Macfarlane Walter & Ross, 2002); Victor Malarek, *Haven's Gate: Canada's Immigration Fiasco* (Toronto: Macmillan, 1987); Reg Whitaker, *Double Standard: The Secret History of Canadian Immigration* (Toronto: Lester & Orpen Dennys, 1987). Journalist Stewart Bell has penned a serious indictment of Canadian immigration and refugee policies in *Cold Terror: How Canada Nurtures and Exports Terrorism Around the World*, rev. ed. (Mississauga, ON: John Wiley & Sons, 2006). An analysis of the costs and gains of immigration is available in Don J. DeVoretz, ed., *Diminishing Returns: The Economics of Canada's Recent Immigration Policy* (Toronto: C.D. Howe Institute, 1995).

On the influx of European immigrants in the postwar period, see Noula Mina, "Taming and Training Greek 'Peasant Girls' and the Gendered Politics of Whiteness in Postwar Canada: Canadian Bureaucrats and Immigrant Domestics, 1950s–1960s," *Canadian Historical Review* 94, no.4 (2013): 514–39; Laura Madokoro, "'Slotting' Chinese Families and Refugees, 1947–1967," *Canadian Historical Review* 93, no. 1 (2011): 25-56; and Howard Margolian has written *Unauthorized Entry: The Truth About Nazi War Criminals in Canada, 1946–1956* (Toronto: University of Toronto Press, 2000). For a critical reading of how the federal government promoted cultural assimilation, see Franca Iacovetta, *Gatekeepers: Reshaping Immigrant Lives in Cold War Canada* (Toronto: Between the Lines, 2006). Christian P. Champion looks at immigration promotion in "Courting 'Our Ethnic Friends': Canadianism, Britishness, and New Canadians, 1950–1970," *Canadian Ethnic Studies*, 38(1) (2006): 23–46.

Social histories of postwar refugees include Milda Danys, *DP: Lithuanian Immigration to Canada After the Second World War* (Toronto: Multicultural History Society of Ontario, 1986); Morton Beiser, *Strangers at the Gate: The 'Boat People's' First Ten Years in Canada* (Toronto: University of Toronto Press, 1999); Marlene Epp, *Women Without Men: Mennonite Refugees of the Second World War* (Toronto: University of Toronto Press, 2000); Lubomyr Y. Luciuk, *Searching for Place: Ukrainian Displaced Persons, Canada,* and the Migration of Memory (Toronto: University of Toronto Press, 2000); and Hans Werner, Imagined Homes: Soviet German Immigrants in Two Cities (Winnipeg: University of Manitoba Press, 2007). Elizabeth McLuhan, ed., Safe Haven: The Refugee Experience of Five Families (Toronto: Multicultural History Society of Ontario, 1995) personalizes the immigrant experience.

For broader overviews of ethnicity in Canada, see Peter S. Li, ed., Race and Ethnic Relations in Canada, 2nd ed. (Toronto: Oxford University Press, 1999); Augie Fleras and Jean Leonard Elliott, Unequal Relations: An Introduction to Race, Ethnic and Aboriginal Dynamics in Canada, 7th ed. (Scarborough, ON: Prentice-Hall Allyn Bacon, 2012); Leo Driedger, ed., Multi-ethnic Canada: Identities and Inequalities (Toronto: Oxford University Press, 1996); Raymond Breton et al., Ethnic Identity and Equality: Varieties of Experience in a Canadian City (Toronto: University of Toronto Press, 1990); and Raymond Breton and Jeffrey Reitz, The Illusion of Difference: Realities of Ethnicity in Canada and the United States (Toronto: C.D. Howe Institute, 1994). Informative essays on all immigrant groups can be found in Paul Robert Magocsi, ed., Encyclopedia of Canada's Peoples (Toronto: Multicultural History Society of Ontario and University of Toronto Press, 1999).

Howard Palmer and Tamara Palmer, eds., Peoples of Alberta: Portraits of Cultural Diversity (Saskatoon: Western Producer Prairie Books, 1985) is a good study of one province's ethnocultural groups. Dutch immigration and assimilation are described in Herman Ganzevoort, A Bittersweet Land: The Dutch Experience in Canada, 1890–1980 (Toronto: McClelland & Stewart, 1988). The Scottish experience is examined in Lucille H. Campey, An Unstoppable Force: The Scottish Exodus to Canada (Toronto: Dundurn Press, 2008). On the English, see Marilyn Barber and Murray Watson, Invisible Immigrants: The English in Canada since 1945 (Winnipeg: University of Manitoba Press, 2015).

The Chinese experience is examined in Peter S. Li, The Chinese in Canada, 2nd ed. (Toronto: Oxford University Press, 1998). See also Wing Chung Ng, The Chinese in Vancouver, 1945–80: The Pursuit of Identity and Power (Vancouver: UBC Press, 1999); Katie Sluser, "The Yellow Peril Revisited: Prejudice and the Immigrant Experiences of Chinese Canadians," Mirror, 28 (2008): 77–92; and Kenneth M. Holland, "A History of Chinese Immigration in the United States and Canada," American Review of Canadian Studies, 37(2) (2007): 150–60. Recent works include Lily Cho, Eating Chinese: Culture on the Menu in Small Town Canada (Toronto: University of Toronto Press, 2010).

On Asian immigrants more broadly, see Norman Buchignani et al., Continuous Journey: A Social History of South Asians in Canada (Toronto: McClelland & Stewart, 1985); and Patricia E. Roy, The Triumph of Citizenship: The Japanese and Chinese in Canada, 1941–1967 (Vancouver: UBC Press 2007). Studies of Italian immigrants include Nicholas DeMaria Harney, Eh Paesan!: Being Italian in Toronto (Toronto: University of Toronto Press, 1998); and Kenneth Bagnell, Canadese: A Portrait of Italian Canadians (Toronto: Macmillan, 1989). Franca Iacovetta studies one important Italian community in Such Hardworking People: Italian Immigrants in Postwar Toronto (Montreal/Kingston: McGill-Queen's University Press, 1992). On Portuguese immigrants, see Carlos Teixeira and Victor M.P. Da Rosa, eds., The Portuguese in Canada (Toronto: University of Toronto Press, 2000).

Scholarly works on the Jewish community include Robert J. Brym, William Shaffir, and Morton Weinfeld, eds., The Jews in Canada (Toronto: Oxford University Press, 1993); Alan T. Davies, Antisemitism in Canada: History and Interpretation (Waterloo, ON: Wilfrid Laurier University Press, 1992); Gerald Tulchinsky, Canada's Jews: A People's Journey (Toronto: University of Toronto Press, 2008); David J. Azrieli, et al., Rekindling the Torch: The Story of Canadian Zionism (Toronto: Key Porter Books, 2008); and Alan Mendelson, Exiles from Nowhere: The Jews and the Canadian Elite (Toronto: Robin Brass Studio, 2008). Harold Troper and Morton Weinfeld examine problems of intergroup relations in Old Wounds: Jews, Ukrainians and the Hunt for Nazi War Criminals in Canada (Markham, ON: Viking, 1989). On Jewish refugees after the World War II, see Adara Goldberg, Holocaust Survivors in Canada: Exclusion, Inclusion, Transformation, 1947–1955 (Winnipeg: University of Manitoba Press, 2015).

For a look at the Ukrainian experience, see also Rhonda L. Hinther and Jim Mochoruk, eds., Re-Imagining Ukrainian-Canadians: History, Politics, and Identity (Toronto: University of Toronto Press 2010). The immigration of draft dodgers is studied in John Hagan, Northern Passage: American Vietnam War Resisters in Canada (Cambridge: Harvard University Press, 2001). Immigrant adjustment is studied in Shiva S. Halli and Leo Driedger, eds., Immigrant Canada: Demographic, Economic, and Social Challenges (Toronto: University of Toronto Press, 1999); Norman Hillmer and J.L. Granatstein, The Land Newly Found: Eyewitness Accounts of the Canadian Immigrant Experience (Markham: Allen Publishers, 2006); and Vic Satzewich and

Lloyd Wong, eds., *Transnational Identities and Practices in Canada* (Vancouver: UBC Press, 2006). On political and cultural activism among immigrant communities, see Houda Asal, "Les premieres mobilisations d'immigrants arabes au Canada, à travers l'exemple du journal *The Canadian Arab*, 1945–1948," *Journal of International Migration and Integration*, 9(1) (2008): 1–19; and Xiaoping Li, *Voices Rising: Asian Canadian Cultural Activism* (Vancouver: UBC Press, 2006).

For historical perspectives on multiculturalism, see Howard Palmer, "Reluctant Hosts: Anglo-Canadian Views on Multiculturalism in the Twentieth Century," in Gerald Tulchinsky ed., *Immigration in Canada: Historical Perspectives* (Toronto: Copp Clark Longman Ltd., 1994), 297–333; Aya Fujiwara, *Ethnic Elites and Canadian Identity: Japanese, Ukrainians, and Scots* (Winnipeg: University of Manitoba Press, 2012); Christopher Alcantara et al., "Canadian First Ministers' Conferences and Heresthetic Strategies: Explaining Alberta's Position on Multiculturalism at the 1971 Victoria Conference," *Journal of Canadian Studies* 48, no. 2 (2014): 99–121; Andrew Cardozo and Louis Musto, eds., *The Battle over Multiculturalism* (Ottawa: Pearson-Shoyama Institute, 1997); Richard J.F. Day, *Multiculturalism and the History of Canadian Diversity* (Toronto: University of Toronto Press, 2000); and Augie Fleras and Jean Leonard Elliott, *Engaging Diversity: Multiculturalism in Canada*, 2nd ed. (Toronto: Nelson Thomson Learning, 2002). Critiques of this policy can be found in Reginald Bibby, *Mosaic Madness: The Poverty and Potential of Life in Canada* (Toronto: Stoddart, 1990); Neil Bissoondath, *Selling Illusions: The Cult of Multiculturalism in Canada*, rev. ed. (Toronto: Penguin Canada, 2002); Wenona Giles, *Portuguese Women in Toronto: Gender, Immigration, and Nationalism* (Toronto, University of Toronto Press, 2002); and Keith Banting, Thomas J. Courchene, and F. Leslie Seidle, ed., *Belonging? Diversity, Recognition and Shared Citizenship in Canada* (Montreal: Institute for Research on Public Policy, 2007).

Racism and discrimination are studied in Evelyn Kallen, *Ethnicity and Human Rights in Canada*, 2nd ed. (Toronto: Oxford University Press, 1995); B. Singh Bolaria and Peter S. Li, *Racial Oppression in Canada*, 2nd ed. (Toronto: Garamond Press, 1988); Frances Henry, *The Caribbean Diaspora in Toronto: Learning to Live with Racism* (Toronto: University of Toronto Press, 1994); Gerald A. Archambeau, *A Struggle to Walk with Dignity: The True Story of a Jamaican-Born Canadian* (Victoria: Trafford Publishing, 2008); Eleanor Laquian et al., *The Silent Debate: Asian Immigration and Racism in Canada* (Vancouver: Institute of Asian Research, 1998); Frances Henry et al., *The Colour of Democracy: Racism in Canadian Society*, 4th ed. (Toronto: Harcourt Brace, 2010); Leo Driedger and Shiva S. Halli, *Race and Racism: Canada's Challenge* (Montreal/Kingston: McGill-Queen's University Press, 2000); Jeffrey G. Reitz and Rupa Banerjee, *Racial Inequality and Policy Issues in Canada* (Montreal: Institute for Research on Public Policy, 2007); and Dirk Hoerder, "'Of Habits Subversive' or 'Capable and Compassionate': Views of Transpacific Migrants, 1850s–1940s," *Canadian Ethnic Studies*, 38(1) (2006):1–22. Studies of black migrants in postwar Canada include Karen Flynn, *Moving Beyond Borders: A History of Black Canadian and Caribbean Women in the Diaspora* (Toronto: University of Toronto Press, 2011), and David Austin, *Fear of a Black Nation: Race, Sex, and Security in Sixties Montreal* (Toronto: Between the Lines Press, 2013). On the discussion of temporary workers and immigration, see Austina Reed, "Canada's Experience with Managed Migration: The Strategic Use of Temporary Foreign Worker Programs," *International Journal*, 63(2) (2008): 469–84. For a look at immigrant community adjustment in the modern urban environment, see Royden Loewen and Gerald Friesen, *Immigrants in Prairie Cities: Ethnic Diversity in Twentieth Century Canada* (Toronto: University of Toronto Press, 2009); and Feng Hou, "Spatial Assimilation of Racial Minorities in Canada's Immigrant Gateway Cities," *Urban Studies*, 43(7) (2006): 1191–1213. Frances Swyripa also surveys how immigrants shaped the landscape in *Storied Landscapes: Ethno-Religious Identity and the Canadian Prairies* (Winnipeg: University of Manitoba Press, 2010).

Language retention is discussed in J.G. Reitz, *The Survival of Ethnic Groups* (Toronto: McGraw-Hill Ryerson, 1980); Ronald Wardhaugh, *Language and Nationhood: The Canadian Experience* (Vancouver: New Star Books, 1983); and Edward N. Herberg, *Ethnic Groups in Canada: Adaptations and Transitions* (Scarborough, ON: Nelson, 1989). Ethnic groups in politics is the subject of a study prepared for the Royal Commission on Electoral Reform: Kathy Megyery, ed., *Ethnocultural Groups and Visible Minorities in Canadian Politics: The Question of Access* (Toronto: Dundurn Press, 1992). The political activities of the Canadian Ethnocultural Council are examined in Leslie A. Pal, *Interests of State: The Politics of Language, Multiculturalism, and Feminism in Canada* (Montreal/Kingston: McGill-Queen's University Press, 1993).

the Organization of Petroleum Exporting Countries (OPEC) manufactured an energy crisis by increasing oil prices substantially, in 1973 and again in 1979; gas prices climbed seemingly without end. Motorists complained bitterly. But they also slowed down to conserve gasoline, and for a time, some abandoned their roomy, high-powered American automobiles in favour of smaller, more efficient, imported vehicles, mostly from Japan.

The prime minister's popularity, so evident with Trudeaumania, soon dissipated. The failure to curb inflation, however, only partially explains the rising popular discontent with the government. Within four years, the seemingly modest Trudeau—who had wanted to "dialogue" with Canadians and promote a "just society"—was seen as arrogant, remote, and temperamental. The prime minister's hard-line federalist position with Quebec pleased much of English Canada but alienated many francophones. His dream of making Canada a bilingual nation angered many in English Canada, particularly the West. The government's apparent inability to handle economic and social issues—not only inflation, but also unemployment, welfare, strikes, and high taxes—galvanized voter disaffection.

The First Nations and the White Paper of 1969

The civil rights movement of the 1960s forced issues of race and ethnicity onto the Canadian agenda. Trudeau responded by attempting to deal with the tragic condition of the First Nations. The Hawthorn Report had recommended that Aboriginal people be treated as "citizens plus." Lester Pearson had promised that the Indian Act would be revised after prior consultation with the First Nations population. Prime Minister Trudeau, however, decided that the best way to deal with the problem was simply to terminate the much-maligned and clearly racist Indian Act, as a means of removing all vestiges of colonialism. Legislation was drafted in the form of the White Paper on Indian policy in 1969.

Trudeau's policy fit with his views on the role of minority groups within Canadian society and was framed around his strategy in handling Quebec. No group, according to Trudeau, should be afforded special treatment. He agreed that the Indian Act was a symbol of injustice and mistreatment, and he wanted it terminated so the First Nations could enter society on an equal footing with other Canadians. In order to accomplish this goal, institutions of injustice, such as the reserves and the treaties, had to be eliminated. "It's inconceivable, I think," Trudeau told an audience in Vancouver in August 1969, "that in a given society one section of the society have a treaty with the other section of society."

In the White Paper, Minister of Indian Affairs Jean Chrétien called for the end, within five years, of the Department of Indian Affairs, the repeal of the Indian Act, the elimination of reserves, and the transfer to the provinces of many of the federal government's responsibilities for Indian affairs. In one fell swoop, the Liberal government was seeking to reforge the relationship between the Canadian state and the First Nations. The termination of these colonial vestiges was viewed as a progressive policy by most Canadians. The special recognition of Aboriginal peoples as wards of the state was paternalistic and mired in a racist past, so it seemed to make sense to leave it behind. Prime Minister Trudeau also announced his government's refusal to negotiate land settlements for the roughly one-half of the country that was not under treaty.

Trudeau and Chrétien, however, misread the First Nations population. They also misread Canadian history. As usual, plans were made without consulting the people most involved. But the First Nations were now more organized, and they were learning how to lobby and have their voices heard. Strong resistance to the proposals erupted immediately. While the White Paper would eliminate many of the official trappings of racism and whitewash the past by removing the colonial structures that created Indian status, the result would still be the assimilation of the First Nations. Aboriginal groups had lost their lifestyles, experienced traumatic transition,

Jean Chrétien, Minister of Indian Affairs, meeting with a delegation from the Indian Association of Alberta and other First Nations groups in Ottawa, June 1970. Prime Minister Trudeau is seated beside Jean Chrétien. The First Nations representatives have just presented the "Red Paper," their response to the government's controversial White Paper.

Source: © Library and Archives Canada (LAC). Reproduced with the permission of LAC. Source: LAC Credit: Duncan Cameron/Duncan Cameron Fonds/PA-170161.

surrendered their land through treaty, been isolated onto reserves, suffered the loss of their children to residential schools, and faced constant and continuing racial persecution. The goal was always assimilation. In return, the people at least were given their treaty rights, including some land, implements, an annuity, medicine, and education. Now, according to the White Paper, they were to surrender even these rights, forget the past injustices, and embrace white society on a basis of idealistic equality. Although unsatisfied with the colonial relationship imposed by the Indian Act, the First Nations leaders realized that the legislation at least recognized their special constitutional status. The First Nations had no intention of being treated as just another ethnic minority in Canada. The past would not so easily be cast aside.

Soon after the release of the 1969 White Paper, young, educated First Nations leaders joined ranks with Aboriginal elders. By presenting a united front, First Nations political organizations succeeded in convincing the Liberal government to withdraw the White Paper in March 1971. The provincial and territorial Aboriginal political associations representing status Indians in Canada and the National Indian Brotherhood (founded in 1968, and reorganized in 1982 as the Assembly of First Nations) worked next to secure the constitutional entrenchment of Aboriginal and treaty rights.

A Shock at the Polls

Trudeau's arrogance, along with economic problems, nearly cost him the election of 1972. The charismatic prime minister dismissed the need to campaign, assuming instead that because he was doing a good job and Canadians wanted him to govern, they would return him to power. The Liberals were punished on election night. They won 109 seats, the Progressive Conservatives won 107, the NDP won 31, and Social Credit won 15. The NDP, led by David Lewis, held the balance of power in a minority Liberal government. After conducting what is perceived as the worst campaign in Canadian electoral history, Trudeau spent the next two years trying to win back voter approval.

Pressured from the left by the NDP, Ottawa increased public spending on social programs and indexed income-tax brackets and exemptions to the cost of living in order to protect tax-payers from inflation. The federal government liberalized unemployment insurance access rules to aid the Maritime fishing industry. To win support in central Canada, the government promised to keep rising oil prices at levels substantially below world levels—a policy that infuriated the oil-producing provinces of western Canada. When PC leader Robert Stanfield argued for a wage and price freeze in 1974, labour hesitated, then gave its support to the Liberals, who declared their opposition to such a freeze. "Zap! You're frozen!" Trudeau mocked in one notorious bit of repartee.

In the federal election of 1974, the Trudeau Liberals won a majority government with 141 seats. The PCs elected 95, the NDP 16, and Social Credit 11. The next year the Liberals reversed themselves and adopted a wage and price freeze. These controls, which affected the public sector and large private companies, lasted three years. The rate of increase in prices did slow, but it took more than controls and guidelines to defeat inflation.

Economic Nationalism

By 1970, many Canadians, particularly in industrialized southern Ontario, expressed concern over the high degree of foreign (especially American) ownership of the Canadian economy. Journalist Peter Newman warned that "the end of the Canadian dream" was imminent. The "Waffle" faction within the NDP urged large-scale nationalization of foreign-owned businesses and resources. Even moderate nationalists called for a gradual buying-back of large enterprises. Others believed that actual ownership mattered little if Ottawa exercised stronger control over large foreign-owned corporations operating in the country.

In an effort to appease nationalist discontent, the Trudeau government set up the Foreign Investment Review Agency (FIRA) in 1971 to screen takeovers and determine whether they were of "significant benefit" to Canada. But FIRA did not prevent American investment in Canada. In 1980, the American ambassador himself expressed satisfaction with the agency's 90 percent approval rate.

Western Canada

While western Canada consisted of four very different provinces, they were united in their sense of alienation from the corridors of power and economic influence in central Canada. Westerners often felt that their voices were ignored in distant Ottawa and that the federal government focused too much on accommodating Quebec. Prime Minister Trudeau's apparent obsession with creating a bilingual nation increasingly angered the West, who realized that it was the votes of Quebec and Ontario that won elections. The roots of western alienation stretched back decades, but by the 1970s, buoyed by natural resource wealth, the western provinces demonstrated a new aggres-siveness in their dealings with Ottawa.

In British Columbia, disenchantment with the long-governing Social Credit government of W.A.C. Bennett favoured the election of the NDP in 1972, which promised greater economic and social equality. Under combative leader Dave Barrett, the NDP initiated controversial reforms (its opponents accused it of "legislating by thunderbolt") including public automobile insurance, a new innovative labour code, and an attempt to preserve agricultural land. Barrett's reforms, high spending, and new taxes led conservative forces to unite in reaction. An economic downturn assisted this new coalition in bringing the populist Social Credit Party back into power in 1975.

In neighbouring Alberta, Calgary lawyer Peter Lougheed revived the Progressive Conservative Party, infusing the province with the promise of both change and continuity. Strongly supported by Alberta, the Conservatives won power in 1971 and established a new political dynasty, sweeping Social Credit—which had governed the province for thirty-six years—almost out of political existence. The oil money flowing into the treasury allowed Albertans to enjoy high-quality social services while paying the country's lowest provincial income taxes and no provincial sales tax.

Saskatchewan's booming economy in the 1970s also generated increasing revenues, which enabled the province's NDP government, led by Allan Blakeney, to pursue an agenda of "province-building." The government nationalized a large American-owned potash company and launched a vigorous exploration and development program in uranium. It established an enterprise that served as a holding company for the province's state-owned companies—such as SaskTel, Sask-Power, and SaskOil—and bought large blocks of shares in private companies.

Agriculture, Saskatchewan's largest industry, remained subject to violent swings, depending on world wheat prices, export markets, and weather conditions. Low prices for grain and the high costs of technological innovation forced smaller and less efficient farmers to sell their land to larger operators and to migrate elsewhere in search of work. Between 1976 and 1996, Saskatchewan lost 14,000 farms. Unused grain elevators, abandoned rail lines, and closed hospitals symbolized the decline of small-town Saskatchewan.

The New Democratic Party also governed Manitoba for much of the 1970s. In these years of relative prosperity, the government of Ed Schreyer spent heavily on public housing and adopted major tax and social reforms. It also launched a second huge hydroelectric development project in the north. As in British Columbia and Saskatchewan, critics on the right denounced increased state intervention under the NDP.

First Nations Activism

The early and mid-1970s were marked by greater First Nations activism. In the United States the rise of the Red Power movement led to a series of confrontations, including the lengthy standoff of the American Indian Movement (AIM) with the FBI at the village of Wounded Knee in South Dakota in 1973. Canada also saw a new level of unrest. In late 1971, Alberta First Nations began a six-month sit-in at the Department of Indian Affairs offices in Edmonton to protest the inferior conditions at reserve schools. Throughout the decade, Ottawa phased out most of the residential schools (the last one closed in 1986) and integrated First Nations children into provincially controlled programs. But integrated schooling did not prove successful. Its shortcomings led a number of bands in the early 1970s to call for community control of their schools. Blue Quills, near St. Paul, Alberta, became the first band-controlled school in 1970. Others followed, and in 1973 the federal government endorsed First Nations-controlled schools.

Increasingly, however, land claims cases became the major battleground for First Nations rights in Canada. Anishinaabe occupied Anicinabe Park in Kenora, northwestern Ontario, in the summer of 1974, in a land-claims dispute. A Native caravan from Vancouver, several hundred strong, reached Parliament Hill in September 1974 to protest poor housing and social services on reserves, as well as to highlight land-claims issues.

The decision of the Supreme Court of Canada in the *Nisga'a* case of 1973 assisted the First Nations cause. Although its decision went against the Nisga'a on a legal technicality, the Supreme Court agreed that the First Nations held Aboriginal title to their lands. Thus the federal government was obliged to accept comprehensive claims in the areas of Canada where treaties had not been signed, as well as specific claims elsewhere. Specific claims usually related to demands for compensation or the restitution of land or money on the basis of the unfulfilled terms of an existing treaty or formal legal agreement with the government. In 1974, Ottawa established an Office of Native Claims, a branch of the Department of Indian Affairs and Northern Development, to rule on Aboriginal claims.

The first comprehensive land claim signed immediately after the enactment of the new federal policy was the James Bay and Northern Quebec Agreement in 1975. By this treaty, the Cree and Inuit surrendered their Aboriginal rights to over 1 million square kilometres of land, an area the size of British Columbia. In return, they gained ownership, in and around their communities, of over 14,000 square kilometres, as well as exclusive hunting, fishing, and trapping rights over 150,000 square kilometres. The agreement also awarded the Cree and the Inuit $225 million over a period of twenty-five years. In 2002, the Grand Council of the Cree and the Quebec government reached an understanding to extend the original 1975 agreement. In exchange for permitting further hydroelectric development on the Rupert and Eastmain Rivers, the Cree obtained a promise of payments valued at $3.5 billion over a fifty-year period. They also received important commitments relating to employment, land, and co-management of the region's resources.

Continuing Dissatisfaction

Between 1974 and 1979, support for the federal Liberals fluctuated. By 1979, with Canada again in a severe inflationary crisis, the business community worried about the economy and the rapidly rising federal deficit, which the government financed by borrowing heavily, even at historically high interest rates. Regional discontent increased as well. Alberta and Saskatchewan feuded with Ottawa over the pricing and taxing of natural resources. Frustrated wheat farmers, hurt by mounting world surpluses of wheat and sagging prices, exhorted the federal government to act, while an annoyed Trudeau asked rhetorically: "Why should I sell your wheat?"

In the federal election of 1979, the Trudeau Liberals were defeated. The Progressive Conservatives under Joe Clark won a minority government with 136 seats but only 36 percent of the popular vote. The Liberals won 114 seats and 40 percent of the vote, while the NDP under Ed Broadbent won 26 seats and Social Credit won 6. Pierre Elliott Trudeau resigned as Liberal leader.

A Conservative Interlude

The Conservatives, however, continued their historical traditions of poor timing and bad luck. Their narrow election victory in 1979 came at a time of sharp economic difficulties. The party also continued their tradition of infighting. The selection of the young Albertan Joe Clark as party leader caused internal dissension. Clark did not have the charisma or international reputation enjoyed by Trudeau. Journalist Jeffrey Simpson concluded that the Tories won the election of 1979 not because of Clark but in spite of him.

An energy crisis precipitated the collapse of Clark's brief minority government. Promoting a policy of "short-term pain for long-term gain," Clark's finance minister, John Crosbie, announced a 4-cent-per-litre excise tax on gasoline designed to bring billions of dollars into the federal treasury in order to attack the rising deficit. Defeated in the House of Commons, the government resigned. During the ensuing election campaign in 1980, Trudeau emerged from retirement and promised to revoke the immensely unpopular tax. When the votes were counted, the Liberals won a majority government with 147 seats. Clark and his PCs were reduced to 103 seats, while the NDP won 32.

The National Energy Program

Trudeau's final mandate began with a bitter crisis in relations between the federal government and Alberta. Strongly influenced by Ontario demands to have oil and gas considered "national commodities, belonging to all Canadians," the Trudeau government established the National Energy Program (NEP), with a "made-in-Canada" oil price that allowed Canadian consumers to pay prices lower than the world price. The producing provinces resented federal price controls that deprived them of billions of dollars. Alberta Premier Peter Lougheed, galled by the federal government's intention to appropriate a greater share of huge oil revenues for federal purposes, likened the plan to "having strangers take over the living room." Ottawa responded that too great a transfer of wealth to one province was upsetting the equilibrium of Confederation.

In response to Ottawa's measures, the Alberta government reduced the flow of crude oil to the East. A popular bumper sticker urged Albertans to "Let the Eastern bastards freeze in the dark!" Young boys sported ball caps decorated with a noose and a caption that read: "Trudeau Come West." Western anger increased and separatist parties urged westerners "to take to the lifeboat of independence before it's too late."

Prime Minister Pierre Trudeau and Alberta Premier Peter Lougheed, 1973, at the Western Economic Opportunities Conference in Calgary. Appearances can be deceiving— despite the cordiality evident in this photograph, animosity existed between the two leaders over the federal government's pricing of Alberta oil and gas.

Source: Herald Collection/Glenbow Archives, Calgary, Canada/NA-2864-23502.

A main objective of the National Energy Program was to Canadianize the petroleum industry by reducing the role of American oil companies. The Alberta government, however, also opposed this strategy, blaming it for the decline in investment in the oil fields. The western Canadian business community denounced Ottawa's intervention, while the U.S. trade representative, worried about the consequences of discrimination against American firms, threatened: "We have a quiver full of arrows and we are prepared to shoot them in self-defence if we must."

The NEP was ill-timed. Just when the federal government spent billions of dollars purchasing foreign oil companies and assisting exploration by Canadian companies, oil prices crashed dramatically. Canada's biggest corporate liability became Dome Petroleum, a creation of Liberal energy policies that had accumulated a debt of more than $6 billion by the mid-1980s. Ironically, it was then sold to an American oil company.

Recession

Recession struck the economy in 1981–82 and Canadians blamed federal policies. The recession resulted in part from government monetary policy, particularly high interest rates, designed to dampen inflationary pressures. It also stemmed from worldwide overproduction in the resource industries, in agriculture, and in secondary manufacturing. The daily press offered a sombre litany of factory closings, layoffs, and cutbacks. Magazine articles frequently evoked the Great Depression of the 1930s.

In the West, in particular, the recession undermined the heady confidence that people felt during the prosperous 1970s. The decline in demand for oil, followed by significantly lower oil prices in 1986, checked Alberta's growth and highlighted the fragility of its resource-based economy. Construction on huge synthetic-oil production and heavy-oil upgrading projects ceased. The province's jobless rate matched national levels; indeed, many unemployed workers returned home to eastern and central Canada. Real estate values fell sharply. The oil industry called upon both provincial and federal governments for assistance. Having denounced Ottawa's attempts to impose a ceiling on oil prices in 1980, it now urged the federal government to apply a floor price to provide some stability to the industry. At the same time, agriculture faced serious difficulties, as drought afflicted farmers in the province's southern region and declining world prices and increased costs wiped out profit margins. The departure from political life of Pierre Trudeau in 1984 removed the principal target of western anger.

The Constitutional Issue

Prime Minister Trudeau had more success with the constitutional issue, but here, also, his approach was highly controversial and divisive. For decades, the federal government searched for a way to patriate the Constitution. The tricky part involved negotiating an amending formula with the provinces by which Britain's formal consent would no longer be necessary whenever Canada amended its own Constitution. At the same time, Trudeau wanted to introduce a Charter of Rights and Freedoms. Although most Canadians approved of Trudeau's initiatives, in the end Quebec refused to sign the agreement, which was negotiated in its absence during what became known as the "Night of the Long Knives." Thus the province that, since 1960, had been most insistent on the need for constitutional change was not a party to the reformed Constitution. The failure to have Quebec on board shaped the political landscape for the next several decades.

The First Nations, meanwhile, used the constitutional issue to have their concerns placed on the national table. Native political organizations, including the National Indian Brotherhood (the first permanent national organization for status Indians), the recently formed Native Council of Canada (representing Métis and off-reserve and non–status Indians), and the Inuit Tapirisat of Canada (representing the Inuit), entered the constitutional debate. A strong campaign led to the inclusion of section 35(2) in the new Constitution of 1982, guaranteeing Aboriginal rights. The clause gave constitutional protection for the first time in Canadian history to the "existing Aboriginal and treaty rights of the Aboriginal peoples of Canada." Most importantly for the Métis, the new Constitution also identified them, for the first time, as Aboriginal people. Since 1885 the Métis had become "the forgotten people." They fell between the cracks of Canadian society, accepted by neither the whites nor the First Nations. They were not given "status" and therefore were not covered by the treaties. Now recognized as Aboriginal, the Métis commenced their own struggle in the courts to gain their rights.

The signing of the Canadian Constitution by Her Majesty Queen Elizabeth II, April 1982. Prime Minister Trudeau looks on. The Constitution ended the British Parliament's power to amend the British North America (BNA) Act, and also included a Charter of Rights and Freedoms.

Source: Library and Archives Canada/RG84, C-4, vol. 2377.

Trudeau's Legacy

Pierre Trudeau resigned briefly in 1979 after being defeated by Joe Clark. He returned in 1980 to lead the Liberals to victory in the federal election and the federalist forces in the Quebec referendum. He retired again in 1984 as another election approached. Even though he will go down in history as one of the most strong, charismatic, and intelligent prime ministers, the Trudeau years were replete with paradoxes.

Trudeau championed the Liberal theme of national unity at every election. Yet, during his terms in office, the country faced the most serious threats to its existence ever confronted. Trudeau promised to repair regional imbalances within Canada. Although measures such as increased equalization payments and other transfers helped reduce disparities, they had "little effect on their root causes."[1] Trudeau frequently denounced the dangers of nationalism, especially Quebec nationalism, but he imposed his own vision of a powerful federal government with special accommodation for none. He embraced an economic nationalism at a time when the forces of globalization were pushing for more open trade relations.

By the time of his death in 2000, Canadians believed the 1982 Charter of Rights and Freedoms to be Trudeau's greatest legacy, a defining element of the Canadian identity. Charter decisions changed the face of Canada by upholding minority and individual rights. Yet, during the FLQ crisis of October 1970, his government invoked the War Measures Act and thereby effectively suspended civil liberties, enabling the police to arrest hundreds of individuals and to hold them incommunicado for several days, without ever laying charges against the vast majority.

Trudeau was well respected on the world stage. He embraced Canada's role as "helpful fixer" and peacekeeper, while maintaining a policy of national self-interest. Canada increased its developmental assistance to Third-World nations significantly in accord with Trudeau's stated commitments to aid the "global south." Trudeau took an autonomist stance in his relationship with the United States. As the Americans adopted a hard line with the Soviet Union and its allies, which culminated in President Ronald Reagan's plans for the "Star Wars" satellite missile defence system, Trudeau resisted, emphasizing trade, diplomacy, and disarmament as the keys to ending the Cold War. He took an independent line from the Americans when it came to relations with such communist states as Cuba and China. But Trudeau's stance led to criticism that Canada was soft on communism and an untrustworthy ally and NATO partner.

Trudeau had long spoken of the need to build a "just society," and women gained equality of status in the Charter of 1982. But during the first Trudeau mandate (1968–72), the House of Commons had only one female member. A *Chatelaine* article commented bitterly that "there are 56 whooping cranes in Canada, and one female federal politician." Feminists complained that the political parties showed no interest in working to recruit female candidates. Although society's changing attitudes brought a gradual improvement, by 1980 only 15 women, representing three parties, had won seats in the House. A decade later, although more women were involved in the various phases of party activity, most continued, in political scientist Sylvia Bashevkin's words, to "toe the lines" and to fill "conventional maintenance roles."[2]

Trudeau's dream of a bilingual Canada at first enthused many Canadians. In 1968, New Brunswick gave official recognition to bilingualism. The Trudeau government adopted the Official Languages Act in 1969 in an effort to make government services more widely available in French. Manitoba authorized the use of French as a language of instruction in schools in 1971, thus restoring a right taken away in the nationalist frenzy of World War I. But the adoption of multiculturalism in 1971 seemed to contradict bilingualism. In the face of separatism and referendums and attempts to accommodate Quebec, Trudeau's bilingual policies soured in much of the country. In 1985, the Manitoba legislature abolished official bilingualism. The Supreme Court of Canada ruled that the province had violated the Constitution and ordered that thousands of public documents be translated into French. Francophone groups in the province proposed a compromise involving far less translation in exchange for new, more useful French-language services. The government agreed, but the provincial Conservative Party, then in opposition, appealed to the "underlying virulent racism" of anti-francophone populist groups and adamantly opposed any new "concessions."[3] The NDP government of Howard Pawley retreated. After the Conservatives came to power in 1988 under Premier Gary Filmon, they bitterly attacked new Quebec legislation that restricted the use of English on commercial signs, helping to turn opinion against the Meech Lake Accord (see Chapter 16).

New rights in the provinces as well as federal assistance to French-language minorities did not stem the decline through rapid assimilation of most French-speaking minorities outside Quebec. While the number of French-speaking Quebeckers able to converse in English increased to over 40 percent by 2001, the number of English-speaking Canadians outside Quebec able to speak French dropped. Between 2001 and 2011, bilingualism dipped slightly from 17.7 percent to 17.5 percent of Canadians. Except in Quebec, New Brunswick, and the greater Ottawa area, the promise of a bilingual Canada was floundering beneath the overwhelming pervasiveness of English.

The Mulroney Years

When Trudeau retired a second time in 1984, John Turner won the leadership of the Liberal Party and became prime minister. Turner held office for only 79 days before losing in a landslide election to Brian Mulroney and his Progressive Conservative Party. The campaign seemed to hinge on one "knockout" blow during the televised leadership debate when Mulroney castigated Turner for the patronage policies of the Trudeau years. In the federal election of 1984, Mulroney's PCs won 211 of the 282 seats in the House of Commons and 50 percent of the vote, including a majority of Quebec's ridings. It was the first genuine breakthrough in Quebec for the Conservatives since Louis Riel was executed in 1885. Although women still held fewer than 10 percent of the seats in the House, they made up one-fifth of Mulroney's first cabinet. The Liberals were reduced to 40 seats while the NDP won 30.

Canada in the mid-1980s differed noticeably from the country in the 1970s. As in much of the Western world, a conservative mood prevailed and there was a distinctive shift to the right. For many Canadians, the Liberal record of big government was now identified with big deficits, increasing taxes, and high unemployment.

The First Mulroney Government

Although business welcomed the new Progressive Conservative government, Mulroney's appeal was much wider. He swept to power on the promise of change and a new approach to governing. He promised an "era of national reconciliation," notably in federal–provincial relations. Mulroney appeased the West by dismantling the hated National Energy Program and the lawyer from Baie-Comeau satiated Quebec by promising to negotiate acceptance of the Constitution of 1982. Not since the governments of Mackenzie King had a party ruled based on support coming from the two seeming irreconcilables—Quebec and the West. Like King, however, Mulroney would find the balancing act difficult, if not impossible.

Mulroney also satisfied Nova Scotia and Newfoundland by yielding them control of offshore mineral resources. The discovery of gas and oil off the Atlantic coast raised hopes for an economic boom, and the premier of Nova Scotia proclaimed optimistically that exploitation of energy resources would end "going down the road" in search of jobs elsewhere. To stimulate the region's economy, Mulroney set up the Atlantic Canada Opportunities Agency, which, like earlier programs, offered grants to businesses operating in the Atlantic provinces. All told, federal grants to businesses in the region under Trudeau and Mulroney totalled more than $5 billion between 1970 and 1995, but they produced "no appreciable closing of the gap between have and have-not provinces as measured by per capita income or unemployment rates."[4]

The Progressive Conservatives blamed the Liberals for Canada's uneasy relations with the United States. Announcing that Canada was again "open for business," the Mulroney government defanged what it called "the FIRA tiger," transforming it into a new agency—Investment Canada—with a mandate to encourage foreign investment. In the course of Mulroney's two mandates, Canada–U.S. relations underwent "a revolutionary shift toward ideological and political convergence and a remarkable accommodation on a wide range of divisive issues."[5] Mulroney found a kindred spirit in American President Ronald Regan.

Other Conservative foreign-policy initiatives gained approval. Human-rights advocates praised Mulroney for his vigorous condemnation of racial discrimination and the apartheid regime in South Africa, and his support of sanctions. French Canada approved of Mulroney's efforts to forge closer links with *la francophonie*, a loose association of the world's French-speaking states. The government's quick response to the famine in Ethiopia in 1984–85 won international accolades. Mulroney maintained Canada's role in international peacekeeping, which was increasingly associated with Canadian identity.

The strong economic recovery also aided the Conservatives. Unemployment fell, although young people still found it difficult to find jobs. The decline in the inflation rate, from 12.5 percent in 1981 to only 4 percent in 1985, brought interest rates down, making it possible again for businesses and consumers to borrow. The omens appeared favourable for the construction of a new political consensus among Canadians.

Prime Minister Brian Mulroney greets American President Ronald Reagan on his arrival for the "Shamrock Summit" at Quebec City, 1985, during which both leaders made much of their Irish origins. Mulroney hailed the summit as the inauguration of a new, positive era in Canadian–American relations.

Source: CP PHOTO/Bill Grimshaw.

The Conservative honeymoon, however, proved brief. The Mulroney government's frequent bouts with scandal soon hurt its public image. The economic recovery was unequal and the forces of regionalism remained strong. While metropolitan Toronto and southern Ontario basked in near full employment, Quebec, the West, and the Atlantic provinces faced continued high jobless rates. The decline of oil and resource prices, coinciding with a severe farm crisis, damaged the economies of the western provinces.

The Federal Deficit

Although not of their creation, the Progressive Conservatives inherited problems from the Trudeau Liberals. In particular, Mulroney found it difficult to reduce Ottawa's budgetary deficit. In 1985, the government had a record shortfall of more than $38 billion. A newspaper item depicted a wailing infant above the caption: "Already $8000 in debt." That was each Canadian's share of the $200-billion-and-growing national debt. A decade later, the baby owed nearly $27,000 when rising provincial and municipal indebtedness was taken into account, and Ottawa devoted one-quarter of its revenues simply to paying the interest on its borrowings. Most economists and business leaders saw the deficit as a time bomb, ticking away. In 1986, Brian Mulroney promised Canadians: "Our determination to reduce it or eradicate it is, and will be, unyielding and successful."

In spite of such valiant declarations, the political necessity of maintaining federal expenditures hampered plans to control spending. Mulroney's policy initiatives were further restrained by a Liberal-dominated Senate. Beleaguered farmers pleaded for cash compensation to shield them from depressed world grain prices. After two Alberta bank ventures crashed resoundingly in 1985, investors successfully sought a multibillion-dollar bailout by the federal government. When refineries closed in impoverished east-end Montreal, pressures mounted for Ottawa to intervene. In areas of high unemployment, local potentates sought an array of subsidies and low-cost loans for business to help create new jobs or save threatened ones. The defence lobby demanded money to overhaul and improve the country's defence capability.

When Ottawa reduced grants to the provinces, provincial governments accused it of pushing its deficit onto them. Ordinary Canadians, especially the worried middle class, prevailed on the government to reaffirm its seemingly wavering faith in the universality of social programs such as old-age pensions. Indeed, when the Mulroney government expressed its intention to index old-age pensions only partially to cost-of-living increases, seniors mobilized and forced the government into a hasty retreat. After a study of unemployment insurance in 1987 recommended substantial changes to reduce costs, labour and the poorer provinces rallied to the defence of the much-maligned program. Ottawa clearly understood the political risks of effecting drastic cuts. "Rattlesnakes get warmer welcomes," the Montreal *Gazette* noted of the government's own reaction to the report. Rather than cutting expenses, the government found it easier to raise income and sales taxes substantially, and to continue to borrow.

The Free Trade Debate

The issue of free trade (or reciprocity) with the United States had long been a controversial topic in Canadian history. On the one hand, such agreements were consistently sought after by Canadian governments due to their economic benefits; on the other, they were just as adamantly opposed because they immediately raised the spectre of American domination. The conclusion of a comprehensive trade agreement with the United States became the Mulroney government's most passionately debated initiative.

The Great Depression had demonstrated the futility and foolishness of protectionism. After 1945, Canada emerged from World War II intent on pursuing a new spirit of multilateralism and international trade opportunities. At the same time, Canadian workers expected the government to negotiate agreements that would reduce imports and protect Canadian jobs in industries seen as unable to withstand competition from abroad. Throughout the 1970s, the government kept tariffs, especially on manufactured products, among the highest in the industrialized world. When multilateral trade negotiations in the framework of GATT discredited protective tariffs, Canada, like many other countries, erected a host of non-tariff barriers, such as quotas, in an effort to impede the entry of cheap imports of goods such as clothing and footwear. The downward slide of the Canadian dollar after 1976—the year it reached a high of US$1.04—helped less productive Canadian firms compete in foreign markets. It also meant that imports cost more.

Trade Relations

In line with its economic nationalism, the Trudeau governments advanced diversification in trade partners. Resisting continental integration and American economic domination, in 1972 Trudeau proposed a "Third Option," which implied stronger links with Europe and other countries. The new policy failed due to the size and influence of the neighbouring global superpower. By 1985, fully 80 percent of Canada's exports went to the United States, and 70 percent of its imports originated there. Nor did the numerous "Team Canada" trade missions to Asia, Europe, and Latin America, organized by Ottawa, have a fundamental impact on the country's trade relations.

By the mid-1980s, Prime Minister Brian Mulroney was arguing for even closer trade relations with the United States. He asserted that a free trade agreement with the United States would create jobs. Increased sales of goods in that market would also diminish Canada's burgeoning balance of payments deficit in relation to the flow of investment income, tourism, services, and interest payments to foreign lenders to finance the growing federal debt.

Support for free trade came from many sources. The Royal Commission on the Economic Union and Development Prospects for Canada strongly endorsed it in 1985. Many sectors of the business community had long favoured it. Polls showed that, in the early stages of the debate, a solid majority of Canadians backed it as well. Consumers were generally convinced that free trade would bring lower prices.

Opposition to Free Trade

As the debate heated up, public support for free trade cooled. American protectionist measures weakened Canadian enthusiasm, although at the same time they seemed to make some form of agreement even more urgent. Labour unions, farmers, the churches, the federal New Democratic and Liberal parties, and the government of Ontario (whose major export, automobiles, was already protected by the Auto Pact), warned that free trade would cost thousands of jobs. They argued that American companies might close their higher-cost branch plants in Canada and serve the Canadian market from their more cost-efficient American bases. Canada might also lose control over the pricing of resources and be forced to abandon transport subsidies. Anti–free traders further warned that a deal could endanger Canada's social programs. Worst of all—here were shades of the 1911 election and the reciprocity debate—free trade could jeopardize Canada's political sovereignty.

Liberal Party leader John Turner and Prime Minister Brian Mulroney debate free trade during the federal election campaign in 1988.

Source: THE CANADIAN PRESS/Fred Chartrand.

The Canada–U.S. Free Trade Agreement

Arduous negotiations culminated in an agreement in 1987. By its terms, tariffs would end gradually, and Canada would gain enhanced access to most sectors of the American market. Canada did not succeed in obtaining the much-sought-after "binding mechanism for dispute resolution." Instead the agreement created a less satisfactory bi-national review panel that would simply ensure that each country's trade agencies made decisions on the basis of existing law. As it turned out, the United States would later make frequent use of this measure to block or penalize imports from Canada in such sectors as lumber and agricultural products. In future, Canada could no longer bar most American takeovers of Canadian industries. Moreover, although Canada gained unrestricted access for energy exports to the United States, the deal also secured American access to Canadian supplies even in times of shortages. But Canada did obtain exemptions for its agricultural products sold through marketing boards and its threatened cultural enterprises. Negotiators left the delicate issue of trade-distorting subsidies, given by governments to favour agriculture and certain industries, for later discussion.

The Liberal-dominated Senate refused to pass the agreement and, in doing so, forced an election in late 1988. As it turned out, the decision to make free trade the election issue saved the Mulroney Tories, who had fallen sharply in the polls since their triumphant victory in 1984, due to scandals and the miserable state of the economy. Discussion of free trade became the major issue. When the votes were counted, the PCs won another majority with 169 seats and 43 percent of the vote to the Liberal's 83 seats and the NDP's 43 seats. The Conservative victory, albeit with a substantially reduced majority, ensured ratification of the agreement in early 1989.

As plant closures brought steep job losses in 1989 and 1990, the labour movement blamed free trade. Other observers placed the responsibility on high interest rates, a rising Canadian dollar, a relative decline in productivity, increased taxes, and a deteriorating international economic situation. The Progressive Conservative government pushed on. Shortly after the election, it agreed to sign a new treaty with the United States and Mexico forming a North American free trade zone.

The Changing Face of Canada in the 1970s and 1980s

After 1970, Canada's population growth slowed to a rate of about 1 percent a year. High levels of immigration now explained much of the country's growth (see Chapter 17). Provinces whose population continued to expand rapidly, such as Alberta in the 1970s and Ontario in the 1980s, were those whose vigorous economies attracted newcomers, both from abroad and from the other provinces. Urban Canada continued to grow after 1970, although more slowly than in the 1950s and 1960s.

The Birth Rate

By 1970, the population was no longer growing naturally. The average Canadian family soon shrunk to include only 1.6 children. Armed with both increased career and birth-control options, many women postponed having children and decided to have fewer in number. After 1970, recourse to new birth-control methods, in particular the availability of "the pill," allowed women significantly more control of their reproductive systems.

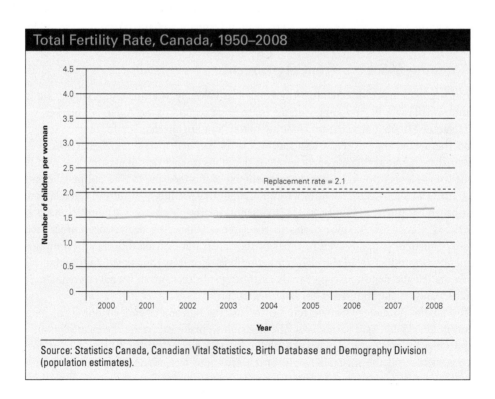

Total Fertility Rate, Canada, 1950–2008

Source: Statistics Canada, Canadian Vital Statistics, Birth Database and Demography Division (population estimates).

The issue of abortion provoked passionate debate in Canada. Under a law adopted by Parliament in 1969, abortions remained illegal except when continued pregnancy threatened a woman's life or health. Discontented with the arbitrariness of the law, and arguing that it took away their right to control their reproduction and bodies, women's groups mobilized to demand the decriminalization of abortion. The "pro-choice" movement was met head-on by the "pro-life" movement, fuelled by a resurgence of the "Religious Right" and neoconservatism in Canada. Toronto physician Dr. Henry Morgentaler, a prominent pro-choice advocate, was the target of death threats throughout the 1980s, which culminated in the firebombing of his clinic in 1992. In 1988, the Supreme Court of Canada found the abortion law to be unconstitutional. Although the Mulroney government attempted to recriminalize abortion in a new bill in 1990, the Senate defeated the measure. The number of therapeutic abortions increased in the 1970s, then further in the 1990s, before stabilizing at about 30 for every 100 live births in Canada. Abortion rates in Canada have declined steadily since 2004, a development accredited to the improved availability of contraceptives and better sexual education programs for young Canadians.

Changing Family Patterns

The changes in family patterns, begun in the late 1960s, continued into the 1970s and 1980s. Divorces became even more frequent, particularly after 1985, when new legislation made "marital breakdown" (evidenced by a year or more of separation or by adultery or cruelty) the sole grounds for divorce. Revised laws granting each spouse half of the property accumulated during the life of the marriage contributed to making divorce a viable financial option for the spouse who owned no property independently—most often, the woman. Moves toward gender equality in the workforce allowed women more financial independence and made them less reliant on marriage. With the decline of religion, divorce became less taboo. Common-law unions gained in popularity, especially in Quebec.

Changing family patterns ensured that child care became an important issue. Increasing numbers of dual-earner couples and single-parent families produced a "crisis of care" that made non-parental child-care arrangements essential.[6] In Toronto, for example, a coalition of women's groups, labour unions, and urban reformers convinced the city to make universally accessible child care available. Other Canadian cities and provinces followed. Quebec's 7$-a-day child-care system, however, would take the lead and become the envy of the nation.

Gays and Lesbians

Gays and lesbians worked for self-affirmation, liberation, and an end to homophobia in the 1970s. They denounced social stigmas and persecution, police harassment and repression, and demanded better protection from "gay-bashing" and other forms of violence. They rallied to such cries as "Out of the closets and into the streets," and "Gay is just as good as straight." Gay groups pursued agendas of political and social activism. Television series gradually broke new ground by portraying homosexuals in more open and less stereotypical terms. The responses, however, were often unfortunately stereotypical. In 1972, when French-language Radio-Canada broadcast an episode of the popular television series *Le paradis terrestre* in which two men were shown coming out of an elevator hand in hand, outraged spectators forced the show's cancellation. In 1977, Quebec became the first province to prohibit discrimination by reason of sexual orientation.

Canada's first Gay Pride celebration was staged discreetly in Toronto in August 1972 with activities and a picnic on Toronto Island. By 2015, nearly a million people attended the annual Pride Toronto, making it North America's largest such event. Pride Toronto, in fact, has become one of the largest and most recognized gay and lesbian gatherings in the world, and the city

Gay community activists in Toronto, protesting a speech by right-wing family values advocate Anita Bryant, 1978.

Source: Archives of Ontario/C193-3-0-3167, 78285-20, AO5290.

hosted World Pride in 2014, an international political and cultural event that promotes gay, lesbian, bisexual, and transgendered issues.

Attitudes toward gays and lesbians became more tolerant by the early 1980s but recurring episodes of homophobia demonstrated that the struggle would not be easy. Tolerance did not mean acceptance. Religious-based opposition to homosexuality grew more outspoken as homosexuality came out in the open. Many gays and lesbians knew that public knowledge of their sexuality could often still harm their career.

Changes for the First Nations

Before World War II, most First Nations lived in remote and isolated communities. In the decades that followed, many left the reserves for the cities. A long and painful history of colonialism and racism placed Aboriginal peoples at a disadvantage when they attempted to enter white society. Too many lived in Third-World conditions on reserves and then in urban ghettos in Canada's cities.

While the dominant society demanded and expected Aboriginal people to assimilate, it failed to welcome them as equal citizens. Racial discrimination remained rampant. The painful legacy of the residential schools scarred generations but even after the last schools closed, the impact was still felt by the children and grandchildren of survivors.

The definition of Aboriginal rights and the demand for self-government became the major constitutional questions for First Nations people in the 1980s and early 1990s. Section 35 of Canada's Constitution of 1982 recognized existing treaty and Aboriginal rights, as outlined in the Royal Proclamation of 1763. Yet in four subsequent First Ministers' Conferences on Aboriginal rights held between 1983 and 1987, political leaders and representatives of the First Nations failed

The Indian and Métis Friendship Centre in Winnipeg, 1960.

Source: Archives of Manitoba, Nan Shipley Collection 74.

to reach agreement on a definition of either "Aboriginal rights" or "Aboriginal self-government." In the end the federal and provincial governments refused to recognize that the Aboriginal peoples had an inherent right to self-government. These conferences did, however, bring Aboriginal issues to the forefront of public discussions. The House of Commons Committee on Indian Self-Government in 1983 endorsed in the Penner Report the concept of full Indian control over matters such as education, child welfare, health care, and band membership. For the first time in a federal document, the term "First Nation" was used.

With the end of the constitutional conferences on Aboriginal rights in 1987, the battleground between Indigenous groups and the federal government shifted back to the courts. From the mid-1980s onward, Supreme Court rulings provided an expanding interpretation of Aboriginal and treaty rights. In *Guerin* (1984) the court established the concept of a trust-like, or "fiduciary," relationship between the Crown and the Aboriginal peoples. This means that the federal government, as a trustee, is expected to act in the best interests of the First Nations. The following year the judges in *Simon* (1985) ruled that Indian treaties must be given a "fair, large and liberal interpretation." In 1990 in the *Sparrow* case, the Supreme Court drew on the Constitutional Act of 1982 to draw up rules to restrict to a minimum the government's infringement of Aboriginal and treaty rights. In 2003 the *Powley* case set precedent by defining Métis aboriginality.

In 1985, the Mulroney government passed Bill C-31 to amend the Indian Act and bring it in line with the Charter of Rights and Freedoms. The legislation had three objectives: to address gender discrimination in the Indian Act, to restore Indian status to those who were forcibly enfranchised in the past, and to allow bands to control their own membership lists as a step toward self-government. In particular, Bill C-31 restored status to Aboriginal women who married non-Indians and subsequently lost their status. It also gave status to their immediate descendants. Reinstatement as a status Indian entitled the individual to receive limited medical care, subsidies for higher education, and exemption from all federal and provincial taxation on monies earned on any reserve. Membership in a band provided a share of the band's assets, the right to reside on the band's reserve, hunting and fishing rights, eligibility for federal loans and grants to establish reserve businesses, and free schooling on the reserve.

Although the Mulroney government had assured First Nations that they would be consulted on constitutional matters, Bill C-31 was passed despite widespread opposition from chiefs who believed that it would have serious economic and social implications on their people's cultural identity, on the political balance of their elected councils, and on language preservation. Bill C-31 has had profound effect on the political power of Canadian First Nations – most immediately, by increasing the number of registered Indians by 115,000 between 1985 and 2001.

The Inuit

Beginning in the late 1960s, the northern First Nations and Inuit organized to place their concerns on the public-policy agenda. In 1973, the Yukon Native Brotherhood (which became the Council of Yukon Indians later that year) began formal talks with the federal government about Aboriginal rights.

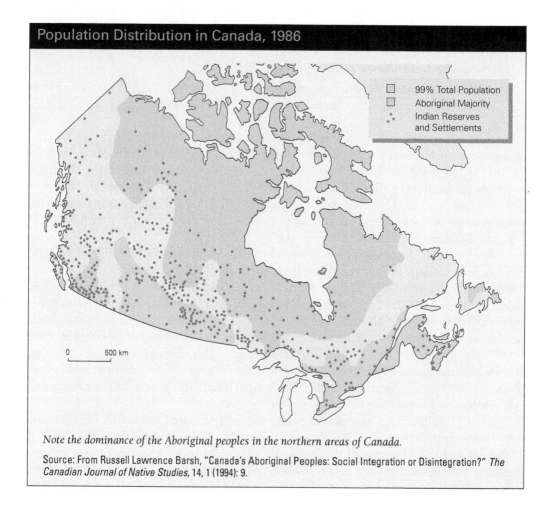

Population Distribution in Canada, 1986

99% Total Population
Aboriginal Majority
Indian Reserves and Settlements

0   500 km

Note the dominance of the Aboriginal peoples in the northern areas of Canada.

Source: From Russell Lawrence Barsh, "Canada's Aboriginal Peoples: Social Integration or Disintegration?" *The Canadian Journal of Native Studies*, 14, 1 (1994): 9.

John Amagealik (right), director of land claims for the Inuit Tapirisat of Canada, speaks to the Berger Commission in Ottawa on Thursday, June 3, 1976, as Mr. Justice Thomas Berger listens to his brief.

Source: CP PICTURE ARCHIVE/Fred Chartrand.

In 1968, the first territorial Aboriginal organization was formed in the Northwest Territories. In the following year, the Indian Brotherhood of the Northwest Territories, later called the Dene Nation, was formed. The Committee for the Original Peoples' Entitlement (COPE) was created in Inuvik two years later to protect the interests of the Inuit in the Mackenzie Delta—the Inuvialuit. In 1971, an Inuit organizing committee formed the Inuit Tapirisat of Canada (originally called the Eskimo Brotherhood), a pan-Inuit organization with a mandate to address questions of northern development and to work to preserve Inuit culture. COPE became one of the regional associations affiliated with the Inuit Tapirisat of Canada. Later, the Inuit of the eastern and central Arctic established the Tungavik Federation of Nunavut to represent specific regional concerns. In 1973, the Métis formed their own association, the Métis Association of the Northwest Territories, which joined with the Dene Nation to submit a joint land claim.

The Berger Inquiry of the mid-1970s provided a national audience to First Nations and Inuit concerns. In 1972, the building of a Canadian pipeline to carry American oil and gas from the vast Prudhoe Bay field on the northeastern coast of Alaska south through the Mackenzie valley seemed a certainty—until a commission was set up to investigate its feasibility. Judge Thomas Berger undertook a comprehensive environmental, social, and cultural impact study, holding community hearings not just in Yellowknife but also in 34 other settlements potentially affected by the pipeline. His final report in 1977 called for the settlement of Native land claims before proceeding and a ten-year delay on the development of the Mackenzie valley pipeline. The report conveyed the Aboriginal peoples' conviction that the North was their own distinct homeland, and not simply a resource frontier for southern Canada. The National Energy Board, the national regulatory body, also rejected the proposed development in the Mackenzie valley. The proposed pipeline was postponed. Several years later, in the early 1980s, a pipeline was built, but only halfway up the valley to Norman Wells.

The Changing Role of Women

The struggle for gender equality resulted in impressive victories during the "women's liberation" movement of the 1960s and 1970s. What came to be known as "second wave feminism" challenged gender boundaries in the home and the workplace, and was more aggressively focused on achieving equality. While significant gains were made, equality is an elusive goal and complacency can be dangerous. By the 2000s, a new generation of young women enjoyed the gains made by the previous generation, although the goal of full equality was still far from being achieved. Many young women came to feel that equality had been achieved; the struggle appeared to be over.

Institutionalized Feminism

When the federal government failed to act on the 167 recommendations of the Royal Commission on the Status of Women in 1970, an umbrella organization was created as a pressure group in 1971. The National Action Committee on the Status of Women (NAC) represented 700 widely disparate associations with more than 5 million members. Growing pressure led the Trudeau government to appoint a minister responsible for the status of women and to establish, in 1973, the Canadian Advisory Council on the Status of Women. Most provinces appointed similar advisory councils. Quebec's Conseil du statut de la femme, equipped with funds for research, produced a detailed plan for change, *Égalité et indépendance*. Women's groups organized a multitude of conferences and workshops during 1975, the year the United Nations decreed to be International Women's Year. But by the early 1990s, federal funding to the NAC was reduced. Cuts to spending continued until the organization ceased operations in 1998.

The Home

The home became a critical battleground for equality of the sexes. Change came slowly, and the role of homemaker continued to be viewed as women's work. This gendered division of labour was even more troublesome, because the role was not considered to be a "real job" or "productive" work. Polls suggested that Canadians in general wanted men to take responsibility for a greater share of the housework; men themselves were not so sure. A federal government poster published during International Women's Year extolled the homemaker's virtues by linking "women's jobs" in the home to prestigious occupations: nurse, teacher, accountant, plumber, chef. Women criticized the publicity for failing to mention a homemaker's less-prestigious occupations: janitor, launderer, dishwasher, waitress, taxi driver, and maid.

The 1980s brought to the fore the issue of violence against women. In 1982, a House of Commons report on violence in the family showed that as many as 10 percent of wives suffered beatings and noted that the numbers appeared to be increasing. Five years later, in response to another bleak report, *Battered but Not Beaten*, Ottawa announced major funding initiatives. Local women's groups opened shelters to assist homeless and battered women. They also set up rape crisis centres, fought for laws restricting pornography, and organized assistance for

Native women, immigrant and refugee women, and women on welfare. The murder of four-teen women at Montreal's École polytechnique in December 1989 proved a sad reminder that, as the 1990s dawned, much work remained in the prevention of misogyny and violence against women in Canada.

The Workforce

The workplace was another key battleground in the struggle for gender equality. The model of the male breadwinner had to be challenged if true equality was to be possible. In truth, women had long been forced by economic realities to work outside the private realm; they had never, however, been able to work on an equal playing field. But the notion of the "working woman" and "female breadwinner" further threatened the male-dominated house-hold and traditional family unit. Advancements for women were often viewed as threats to the traditional family. Critics decried an end to the family and chastised women for not being good mothers and wives. While men were often pleased to have a second income in the family, they were not as pleased to share household labour.

The labour movement in Canada won impressive gains for workers, but the gendered nature of work and the male breadwinner model usually pushed women's concerns to the background. Unionization improved working conditions and pay in some traditional female occupations, particularly in health care, education, and government service. In the 1970s, union membership grew four times more quickly among females than it did among males, although among workers, women were still less likely than men to belong to unions. Many of the unprotected worked in difficult-to-organize sectors such as banks, restaurants, offices, and retail stores. They often worked part-time as well.

Unions began to pay greater heed to women's needs. In 1979, women backed by the United Steel Workers filed a complaint for discrimination with the Ontario Human Rights Commission, to force Stelco to hire women for production jobs at its plant in Hamilton. Over the preceding two decades, Stelco received 300,000 job applications, including 30,000 from women; it had hired 33,000 men, but no women. The commission's verdict was favourable and Stelco began hiring women for these well-paid jobs. Massive layoffs in the late 1980s, however, eliminated almost all the women employed in production on the basis of seniority rules.

In Quebec, women's committees succeeded in convincing their unions to adopt policies on child care, maternity benefits, equal pay for work of equal value, job safety, sexual harassment, and discrimination. The myth of female docility evaporated rapidly as women-dominated organizations such as nurses' unions waged bitter, sometimes illegal, strikes against what they judged to be unsatisfactory working conditions. Although women remained underrepresented in union executives, particularly in international unions, they played a greater role, as symbolized by the election in 1975 of Grace Hartman as president of the Canadian Union of Public Employees (CUPE), Canada's largest union, and in 1986 of Shirley Carr as head of

Florence Bird, chair of the Royal Commission on the Status of Women.
Source: THE CANADIAN PRESS/Peter Bregg.

the Canadian Labour Congress. Yet Judy Darcy, elected president of CUPE in 1991, complained of the double standards that made many active women unionists feel guilty: guilty because their union work made them poor mothers, and guilty because their family responsibilities meant that they devoted less time to union duties.

By the 1970s, the principle of equal pay for men and women performing the same task gained wide recognition. Yet, in the 1980s, the average woman's wage remained at approximately 65 percent of the average man's. Although women's lesser work experience and the generally lower educational levels of older women explained part of this difference, the continued concentration of women in low-paying occupations appeared to be the principal factor. The situation appears to be changing, but slowly: in 2011, full-time working Canadian women still brought home only 73 cents for every dollar men earned.

In 1984, the federal Commission on Equality in Employment recommended mandatory employment equity programs, to be implemented through "affirmative action." Ottawa responded by requiring employers under federal jurisdiction, such as banks and national transportation companies, to give women and minorities better job opportunities. It also made affirmative action plans mandatory for all firms doing business with the government. While the aggressive policies paid dividends for women being hired, they often created bitterness in the generation of young men who felt they were being punished for the previous generation's advantages. The bitterness increased during the difficult economic times when jobs were even scarcer.

WHERE HISTORIANS DISAGREE

Shifting Historical Paradigms: Gender and Women's History

Prior to the 1970s, Canadian history was primarily the study of elite white men and rarely included women, ethnic/racial minorities, or working-class Canadians. The "second wave" feminist movement of the late 1960s (the "first wave" refers to the movement that struggled for suffrage and temperance in the late nineteenth and early twentieth centuries) began exploring women's historical past, intent on revealing "the ancient and enduring relationships that subordinate women to men, the antecedence of patriarchy to the rise of capitalism, and the salient feature of capitalism as a system run by and mainly to benefit some men."[1]

Feminist historians believed that studying women's history and patriarchy could undermine the structures and institutions that enforced men's oppression of women. Much of the new social history they wrote focused on the struggle for gender equality by highlighting the previously ignored contributions of women. But by the late 1980s, a "third wave" emerged that criticized the perceived failures of the previous movement and rejected an all-encompassing and "essentialist" feminist idea and objective. This wave urged women historians to embrace diversity related to race, ethnicity, class, and sexual orientation.

Although women's history is a rich academic field, some feminist historians are concerned that the field is straying from its original goals and losing its political edge. According to Judith Bennett, the political drive within women's history has waned, ironically, because of the field's successes. In order to gain respect and acceptance from their male colleagues, feminist historians have avoided important provocative questions in order to appear more mainstream.[2]

Increasingly, scholars are turning to gender studies as an alternative to women's history. Gender history, similar to women's history, recognizes that gender is socially constructed, but by also studying men, it is viewed as more inclusive. It rejects binary oppositional structures, and undermines the assumption that gender differences are biological rather than constructed by culture and society. Joan Scott has urged feminist historians to adopt a gendered analysis of conventionally male areas of history.[3] The absence of women from politics and government should not preclude gender as a tool of analysis in these areas of history. But the rise of postmodernism and poststructuralism (of which gender history was part) threatened the political goals of women's history—namely the quest for gender equality. Feminist historians were divided.

According to Monda Halpern, gender history abandons feminist politics; it examines the relationship between the two sexes instead of focusing on women's oppression by men. Joan Sangster recognizes that gender history enjoys a certain popularity based on its poststructuralist nuances and inclusiveness, but agrees that it downplays women's oppression in history. Furthermore, males continue to dominate every historical field except women's history. If women's history is replaced by gender history, there is a fear that women will lose the only space they

have created specifically for the study of women.[4]

Karen Dubinsky and Lynn Marks disagree. They argue that gender history and masculinity studies do not detract from feminist works, but actually strengthen them by undermining "masculine hegemony" and by understanding how it is maintained.[5] Joy Parr views gender studies as a necessary shift from women's history, because the latter tends to study women separately from "the social relationships which created her, and presumes that women existed in certain ways," while gender history "assumes that masculinity and femininity do not exist in isolation to each other."[6] Gender historians assert that it is historically problematic to analyze women independently from men, because gender relations are constantly evolving and are specific to time, place, and social position.

Some see women's and gender histories as naturally supporting and reinforcing one another. Veronica Strong-Boag recognizes gender analysis as part of a new movement in academe that encourages interdisciplinary approaches, especially between women's and gender history, "to foster dialogue and shared understandings; to develop, if we could, a common language; and to uncover, or rediscover, various constructions of our country."[7] Judith Bennett claims that both women's and gender history have more similarities than differences, and women's history usually includes the study of gender.

The future remains uncertain, but if the place and reputation of "feminism" in Canadian society is any indication, the future of women's history may be in doubt. Queen's University has replaced women's studies with gender studies, while the University of Guelph cancelled

the women's studies department altogether in 2009 due to budget cuts. Whether women's history will be subsumed
by gender history or remains as a
strengthened and vibrant field in its own
right remains to be seen.

---

1   Joy Parr, *The Gender of Breadwinners: Women, Men, and Change in Two Industrial Towns, 1880–1950* (Toronto: University of Toronto Press, 1990), p. 7.

2   Judith Bennett, *History Matters: Patriarchy and the Challenge of Feminism* (Philadelphia: University of Pennsylvania Press, 2006), p. 20.

3   Joan Wallach Scott, "Gender: A Useful Category of Historical Analysis," in Joan Wallach Scott, ed., *Feminism and History* (Oxford: Oxford University Press, 1996), p. 168.

4   Monda Halpern, "Sorting Through the Male: From Women's History to Gender History, and the Place of Women," presented at the University of Western Ontario conference "Roundtable: Future of the Past," March 15–17, 2002; Joan Sangster, "Reconsidering Dichotomies," *Left History*, 3(2) & 4(1) (1995–6): 239–48.

5   Karen Dubinsky and Lynne Marks, "Beyond Purity: A Response to Sangster," *Left History*, 3(2) & 4(1) (1995–6): 217.

6   Joy Parr and Mark Rosenfeld, *Gender and History in Canada* (Toronto: Copp Clark Ltd., 1996), p. 14.

7   Veronica Strong-Boag, Sherill Grace, Avigail Eisenberg, and Joan Anderson, eds., *Painting the Maple: Essays on Race, Gender and the Construction of Canada* (Vancouver: UBC Press, 1998), pp. 4–5.

Challenges for Labour

The numerous strikes in the public sector during the 1970s alienated public opinion and turned many Canadians against unions. Two of every three Canadian workers did not belong to unions. They, as well as many workers affiliated with small organizations, resented the attempts of the most powerful unions to secure a greater share of the national wealth for their members. Canada gained a negative image for the frequency of its strike activity—among developed nations, only Italy had a worse record. Yet, although 11 million workdays were lost to strikes in 1975 (a particularly bad year), that figure represented barely 1.5 percent of total working time. Accidents, illness, and general absenteeism affected productivity to a far greater extent.

The 1980s brought new challenges as Conservative governments moved to restrain wages and limit strikes. In Nova Scotia, for example, the government adopted anti-union legislation that, while embittering relations with labour, helped to create jobs by convincing Michelin Tire, a major employer in the province, to expand production. British Columbia's Social Credit government also adopted legislation to curb unions after a fierce confrontation with the public-sector unions.

Manufacturing industries and resource-sector companies laid off workers. Strong unions fought—sometimes quite successfully, as in the case of the autoworkers and the steelworkers—for job security and better pensions, and for wage protection against inflation and new taxes. Canadian autoworkers, favouring a less bureaucratic and more militant and democratic union, broke away from the American union in 1985 and then negotiated a made-in-Canada agreement with their employers. To reverse the decline in their numbers, unions signed up workers from outside their original jurisdictions. The steelworkers' union, for example, enrolled security workers, restaurant workers, and employees of fish-processing plants, promising that "if it moves or eats with a knife and a fork, we'll organize it."

Union strength increased to levels attained in the mid-1970s, about 37 percent of the non-farm workforce.

Education

During the 1970s, university expansion slowed. Student enrolments increased more modestly, although the proportion of women grew rapidly. In 1971, 68 percent of university students were male, but by 1991, gender parity had been reached. As of 2011, women made up 57 percent of full-time undergraduate students. They were far more numerous than men in university bachelor's and master's degree programs, although engineering, applied science, and mathematics faculties still represented a largely male domain. Men were still a majority in most doctoral programs.

A crisis in university financing appeared during the 1980s, as deficit-ridden provinces forced universities to accept cuts in spending. Ontario, in the face of intense public criticism of university spending, moved to get "more scholar for the dollar."[7] Significantly, not one new university opened its doors in Canada between 1980 and 1994, when the University of Northern British Columbia, in Prince George, began operations. Most provinces imposed higher tuition fees and turned enthusiastically to corporate benefactors for additional financing. The relationship between universities and business interests, however, threatened "a fundamental university objective, one that academic freedom is meant to protect, namely, the disinterested pursuit of knowledge."[8] The late 1990s saw some public reinvestment in universities; the federal government, now laden with budget surpluses, invested heavily in research and funded large numbers of university chairs. The prosperity lasted until 2008 when the bubble burst and a major global recession hit. Governments responded by scaling back heavily when it came to spending on higher education.

Tens of thousands of Sikhs walked in the annual Khalsa Day parade in Toronto on April 24, 2011.
Source: Vince Talotta/*Toronto Star*/ZUMA Press/Newscom.

Contemporary Religion

Immigration from Asia diversified Canada's religious demographics in the 1970s and 1980s, as sizable communities of Muslims, Buddhists, and Hindus became established. For most Canadians, however, the emphasis on individuality meant that religion became largely a personal matter. Many Canadians moved away from religions based on theology and denominational identification, and toward a view of religion as an inspiration for moral and ethical behaviour. The majority still expected to turn to organized religion for rites such as baptisms, weddings, and funerals but, with the notable exception of members of smaller Protestant conservative and evangelical churches, they attached diminishing importance to regular attendance at worship services. The majority of Roman Catholic Quebeckers, for example, went to midnight mass at Christmas, but malls were far more crowded than churches during the rest of the year. While two Canadians in three attended weekly religious services in 1946, only one in five did so in 2001. The baby boomers, in a collective existential crisis, turned in the 1990s to spiritual books and seminars. Canadians now wanted "religion 'à la carte,'" preferring to pick and choose beliefs, practices, programs, and professional services from increasingly diversified religious smorgasbords."[9]

Leisure

In the increasingly health-conscious 1970s and 1980s, many Canadians began to devote more hours to exercise. At the same time, however, they watched more television, with more channels. Access to personal computers by the end of the era ushered in the age of the video game, which also worked against the attention to health and fitness. The problem of childhood obesity increased as children spent less time playing outdoors and more time in front of their television and, increasingly, their computer screens. Canadians also became increasingly addicted to buying lottery tickets or to gambling in the casinos or on the video-lottery terminals that cash-starved provincial governments now approved.

Sports

Spectator sports remained an important aspect of popular culture and leisure. Athletes basked in glory as long as they scored goals, hit runs, or won races on the slopes in the winter and on the speedways in the summer, and as long as they avoided the steroids that proved to be widely used in certain sports. Hockey remained Canada's major sport, but it had to share the spotlight with football, baseball, and, increasingly, basketball. Big-league baseball came to Montreal in 1969, when the Expos began to play. Toronto had to wait until 1977 for its team, the Blue Jays, which became the most financially successful enterprise in any Canadian sport. The Ontario government invested huge sums in the building of an immense retractable-roof stadium in Toronto, the SkyDome, where the Jays entertained their loyal fans by winning the World Series in 1992 and 1993.

Hockey underwent an important expansion in the late 1970s as the National Hockey League took in four franchises from the failed World Hockey Association. Wayne Gretzky, undoubtedly the sport's brightest star of this era, demolished many scoring records and attained the crowning glory of being pictured on the cover of *Time*. By the end of the 1980s, however, the Edmonton Oilers relinquished their superstar to the Los Angeles Kings—an act akin to high treason in the eyes of many angry fans. As players' salaries soared and the Canadian dollar fell, without a salary cap, teams found survival more difficult in small Canadian markets.

The Canadian public strongly disapproved of proposals for government assistance to millionaire players and owners. Some owners then sought to sell their teams. The Quebec

Nordiques, for example, successful but playing in a small market, were transferred to Denver, Colorado, in 1995 where they promptly won the Stanley Cup. The 1996 loss of the Winnipeg Jets to Phoenix, Arizona, was yet another bitter pill for Canadian hockey fans to swallow.

In the late 1960s, Ottawa discovered the importance of sport as an instrument for promoting national unity and yielding political capital. The federal government began investing heavily in high-performance sports in order to produce more medal winners in international competitions. The Canada–Soviet hockey "Summit" series in 1972 showed that the return on such investments could be considerable. Watched by the largest Canadian television audience on record, Team Canada won the series in the last seconds of the dramatic final encounter with Paul Henderson's famous goal. One ecstatic Canadian university president suggested that the series probably did more to create a Canadian identity than ten years of Canada Council fellowships. Politicians saw a triumph for "Canadian virtues" and for capitalist liberal democracy.

Montreal hosted the summer Olympic Games in 1976, the first time the event took place in Canada. (In 1988, Calgary was the site of the winter Olympics, followed by Vancouver, which hosted the 2010 Winter Games.) Provincial and municipal taxpayers were uneasy at the prospect of new budget deficits, but Montreal mayor Jean Drapeau assured them there was no more possibility of incurring a deficit than there was

The most famous winning goal in Canadian hockey history, scored by Paul Henderson in Moscow in the final game of the 1972 Russia–Canada hockey series, with just 34 seconds of play remaining. On the twenty-fifth anniversary of the goal, in 1997, Paul appeared on a postage stamp issued by Canada Post.

Source: Frank Lennon/*Toronto Star* via Getty Images.

of his becoming pregnant. After the Olympic lottery, Olympic coins, Olympic stamps, and other promotional paraphernalia failed to prevent a massive deficit, delighted cartoonists drew sketches of a pregnant mayor. Only in 2006 did the city finally pay off the $1.5 billion tab for the Games, helped in part, ironically, by a special tax on tobacco. Journalists jested that Montreal had finally paid off the "Big Owe," a mocking reference to the nickname of the Olympic Stadium.

Cultural Industries

In the 1970s, cultural development became inextricably linked to the affirmation of national identity. For many English Canadians, the danger to survival came increasingly from the United States, and it came in the form of culture.

After 1970, the Americanization of Canadian broadcasting in English continued apace, although Canadian cultural industries did enjoy some protection through regulatory barriers. These determined, for example, how much non-Canadian programming could be broadcast on Canadian television stations. Then cable television enabled almost all Canadians to gain access to the major U.S. networks. The arrival of satellite dish services in the late 1990s made protection in this area virtually impossible.

Statistics highlighted the extent of foreign domination of Canada's cultural industries. By 1990, for example, foreign-owned publishers had acquired 80 percent of Canada's book market. To compete with the U.S. publishing industry, Canadian publishers relied on government grants. Nearly 85 percent of music recording sales were foreign, as were 80 percent of magazines sold in Canada. When Canada moved to protect Canadian magazine publishers, the United States immediately threatened economic reprisals.

In movie theatres, Canadian films had less than 5 percent of screen time, although a growing number of American producers, subsidized by the Canadian government, and lured by favourable exchange rates, filmed in Toronto and Vancouver, considered a "Hollywood North." Attempts on the part of the Canadian and Quebec governments to ensure a greater distribution in movie theatres of Canadian films provoked conflict with the major American distributors, forcing a Canadian retreat. Yet some critics insisted that while Canadians consumed and borrowed American cultural products, they also reconstituted them and imprinted them with Canadian values. Sometimes they even sold them back to the Americans. In this way, "The beaver can, and does, bite back."[10]

Ottawa also provided subsidies for artists in all fields and funded cultural infrastructures. The CBC continued to affirm its objective of preserving and enriching Canadianism. Yet, in the 1980s, just as new demands were made for public broadcasting to meet specific needs such as those of women, ethnic groups, Aboriginal peoples, and regions, the federal government reduced its financing. By the late 1980s, a former president of the CBC described government policy as "Americanization by importation, by privatization, and by fiscal deprival." The National Film Board (NFB), another important publicly supported institution, produced numerous high-quality documentaries, a field in which it excelled.

The late 1980s saw the production of several notable Canadian feature films. David Cronenberg's *Dead Ringers* proved a financial success, while several films by Atom Egoyan, among them *Speaking Parts*, earned him an international reputation. Canadian films in English generally played to small audiences. Most did not have the glossy production values of American successes, and modest budgets meant modest promotion and modest distribution.

Quebec films represented close to 70 percent of Canada's entire feature-film industry; they were the most successful in competing with American films. Claude Jutra's *Mon oncle Antoine*, a touching film on social life in Quebec's asbestos-mining region, illustrated the tensions between the nostalgia for bygone days and the need for change so much in evidence during the Quiet Revolution. Producer Denys Arcand portrayed decadent history teachers—surely an entirely fictional subject—in his *Decline of the American Empire*. François Girard's film *The Red Violin* captured the odyssey of a violin across four centuries and three continents.

Canadian Literature

After 1970, there were more Canadian writers and they wrote more. The growth of universities, as well as increased government funding, help explain this expansion. International acclaim gave many writers publicity, and established their reputations abroad as much as within Canada.

Literature mirrored Canadians' preoccupations, attitudes, and aspirations. Nationalist themes, for example, recurred frequently in novels in both English and French Canada, particularly during the 1970s. The works that secured Margaret Atwood's international reputation, including *Surfacing* and, later, *The Handmaid's Tale*, contained trenchant nationalist critiques. They were also feminist, and indeed much fiction of the contemporary period portrayed the everyday lives of women.

Many literary works explored the experience of minority groups such as First Nations peoples and immigrants. In his novel *The Temptations of Big Bear*, for example, Alberta writer Rudy Wiebe dwelt on the conflict between European and First Nations cultures provoked by the arrival of European settlers. Joy Kogawa, in *Obasan*, evoked the fate of Japanese Canadians during World War II. Other novels, such as those of Jane Rule and Gail Scott, and *The Wars* by Timothy Findley (which describes the growing madness of a young Canadian army officer) explored lesbian or gay themes.

Internationally acclaimed novelists Marie-Claire Blais and Réjean Ducharme were among those Quebec authors whose works sought to reveal the asphyxiating nature of traditional family relationships and religion. When Denise Boucher attacked the stereotypes of orthodox Roman Catholicism in *Les fées ont soif*, religious groups obtained an injunction forbidding public presentations of her play. The Supreme Court eventually decided in favour of the author.

Some writers set their works in small towns with closed societies. An example was Deptford, the scene of a powerful trilogy of novels by Robertson Davies featuring vivid central characters. Others dwelt on the realities of urban living. Quebec playwright Michel Tremblay's works, performed around the world, have featured a wide variety of Montrealers, including elegant upper-class ladies, drag queens, country singers, and very ordinary mortals from the working-class neighbourhoods he knew as a boy. Montreal served also as the setting of Yves Beauchemin's *Le Matou*, a fast-moving thriller that sold 1 million copies worldwide in the mid-1980s.

Canadian literature also continues to underline the important role that regions have played in Canadian life. Atlantic writer David Adams Richards wrote of poverty and pride in northeastern New Brunswick in *The Coming of Winter* and *Blood Ties*, while W.O. Mitchell's *Roses Are Difficult Here* chronicled a year in the life of an Alberta foothills town called Shelby. Prairie geography inspired Robert Kroetsch's poetry.

Health and Well-Being

In the 1970s and 1980s, Canadians became more conscious of the need to take preventive measures to ensure good health. The warnings were unpleasant: the Canadian Cancer Society estimated that one Canadian male in four and one female in five would die of cancer. Other studies highlighted the risks and causes of heart disease. Canadians began to heed appeals to eat less salt, sugar, and fat, and to consume more vegetables, fruit, and whole grains.

Automobile associations and victims of drunk drivers successfully lobbied governments to take measures to reduce carnage on the highways. The use of seatbelts also contributed to the steady decline in the number of Canadians killed in accidents on the roads. In addition, Canadians smoked less. Nonsmokers brought pressure to bear, legislative and otherwise, to force smokers to respect their air space. Those who did smoke paid more taxes and saw their packages covered with grisly health warnings showing black lungs and infected gums.

The rapid spread of the deadly AIDS (acquired immune deficiency syndrome) virus after 1980 finally brought health authorities to launch campaigns promoting "safe sex" or abstinence. The "free sex" era of the 1960s and 1970s was over. While promiscuity levels among youth would rise, there were now serious risks if "protection" was not used. At first the disease hit the gay community. Hysteria was aimed against the community and in the era of neoconservativism, homophobia increased. Then it spread among drug users, hemophiliacs, blood transfusion recipients, and heterosexuals. Warnings, such as those found in the lyrics of Bruce Cockburn's "Lovers in a Dangerous Time," demonstrated that the threat was now widespread. By 2000 the disease

A Covenant House poster draws attention to the plight of Canadian cities' homeless youth.

Source: Courtesy of Covenant House, Toronto.

had already killed more than 15,000 Canadians, but medical advances were helping to prolong the lives of those afflicted.

Poverty

In the face of rising rates of poverty, governments revamped social programs such as aid to families and pensions to seniors, taking away payments from higher-income Canadians but increasing assistance to the poorest. At the same time, spending cuts pushed Canadians on social assistance below low-income cutoff lines. The poor failed to come any closer to the rich in terms of income; in fact, the gap between rich and poor widened. Moreover, the middle class itself shrank. More workers had highly skilled, well-paid, stable jobs, but there were also additional workers in the lower-income category, often employed in part-time or temporary jobs in the traditional service sector.

Marital breakdown, together with the trend to reject the institution of marriage, resulted in large numbers of single-parent families, most of them headed by women. Their number doubled between 1971 and 1996, to 1 million. Many of these families had low incomes. In the past, such women often lived on welfare. By the end of the 1990s, however, welfare rolls had shrunk but poorly educated working mothers on low salaries still remained poor. Poverty rates remained stable at about one child in five. Despite a national economy that had grown by 50 percent in twenty years, child poverty rates remained unchanged. Children of new Canadians and single parents had the highest rates of poverty.

Crime

Rising crime rates became a serious social concern in the 1970s and 1980s. Many offences were drug-related. Although violent crime nearly doubled in the 1980s, rates for murder and armed robbery remained far lower than in the United States. Crime rates in Canada varied from one province to another, but they tended to increase steadily from east to west. Canadians wanted the courts to hand down more severe sentences, and many even favoured the return of capital punishment. After 1991, crime rates dropped steadily, returning to levels not seen since the 1970s.

But factors such as race, class, and ethnicity shaped the crime rates. Aboriginal Canadians faced much higher incarceration rates in jails, particularly in western Canada where they made up a higher percentage of the population and where they faced generally harsher conditions. Crime rates in western cities, such as Winnipeg, Regina, and Saskatoon, were the highest in the nation. Since the 1970s increased attention has been paid to the distinctive needs and participation of Aboriginal people in the justice system. Donald Marshall, Jr., for example, was a Mi'kmaq teenager wrongly convicted and imprisoned for murder in 1972. Marshall spent eleven years in prison until a re-examination of the case led to his acquittal in 1983. A judicial inquiry after his release revealed anti-Aboriginal prejudice embedded in every aspect of the justice system.

Race and ethnicity played a major role in shaping the gang cultures of the urban environments. In British Columbia, the influx and influence of "Asian gangs" caused considerable concern and employed significant resources and energies of law enforcement agencies.

The Environment

The centrality of environmental issues to human existence creeped up on Canadians in this era. Toronto hosted the international "Our Changing Atmosphere" conference in 1988, which launched the issue of climate change on the global policy agenda. At the conference, Canadian climatologist Kenneth Hare underlined his conclusion that global warming was "the central environmental problem of our times." But few Canadians at the time paid any attention.

Led by scientist David Suzuki and his ground-breaking television series *The Nature of Things*, environmental issues did gain increasing visibility after 1970 as Canadians discovered the negative aftermath of the unbridled, almost unregulated, development of past decades. They also learned that environmental issues were global in nature: the greenhouse effect, the depletion of the ozone layer, the pollution of air and water, and the destruction of tropical and temperate rainforests all involved worldwide responsibility, and solutions required international cooperation. During the 1980s and early 1990s, Canada signed several multilateral agreements on the environment, notably those concerning acid rain and ozone depletion.

More importantly, many Canadians came to see themselves as part of the problem. An expanding and wealthier population oriented toward consumption produced large quantities of wastes. It also made unsustainable demands on natural resources. The burning of fossil fuels to heat homes, to run automobiles, and to drive industries not only fouled the air: a growing consensus of scientists agreed that it also raised the global temperature by way of the greenhouse gases it produced. As numerous lakes and streams of the Canadian Shield became lifeless and as the surrounding vegetation showed increasing evidence of damage, Canadians realized the devastating effects of acid rain. Many industries also spewed chemical effluents into both air and water.

Prime agricultural land surrounding cities disappeared beneath low-density suburbs, roads, fast-food restaurants, shopping malls, and industrial parks. Since 1931, nearly one-third of southern Ontario's rich farmland has been lost to largely unplanned suburban sprawl. Agricultural methods, such as straightening streams and small watercourses, contributed to the erosion of topsoil and, through the abundant use of pesticides, herbicides, and fertilizers, to the pollution of water. Farmers and property developers drained ecologically sensitive wetlands for agricultural or residential purposes, logging companies prepared to harvest the country's last old-growth stands of timber, and untouched wilderness receded to their northern limits.

No easy solutions existed. Concerned citizens set up associations to publicize environmental dangers or to propose solutions. Some groups had international ramifications. The World Wildlife Fund, for example, had programs in Canada and in 100 other countries. Ducks Unlimited sought to conserve wetlands and waterfowl throughout North America. Other groups were Canadian creations. Greenpeace, a well-known environmental lobby, had its origins in Vancouver in 1970. Twenty years later the organization boasted 2.5 million members in 40 countries. The Canadian Parks and Wilderness Society worked to establish new parks. Its Ontario partner, the Algonquin Wildlands League, used the media and scientific research to fight for the protection of large tracts of woodland. The League won an important victory in 1973, when Quetico Park, on the north shore of Lake Superior, was reclassified as a primitive park from which all logging was banned. In the 1980s, Ontario doubled its park system, but here again debate raged on over the issue of allowing logging, mineral exploration, sport hunting, and commercial tourism in the parks.

Litigation also proved to be a useful weapon for environmentalists, Aboriginal peoples, and other concerned citizens. The Sierra Legal Defence Fund, founded in 1990, took governments to court to force them to respect their own laws and regulations concerning the environment, and to force offenders to obey environmental laws. The Nature Conservancy of Canada pursued another line of action: it sought to protect ecologically sensitive lands through outright land purchases paid for by donations.

Governments and the Environment

Public pressure forced governments to take an interest in the environment. In 1971, the federal government established the Department of the Environment, and most provinces soon followed suit. Governments established standards for clean air and clean water, and set up agencies to monitor compliance. They also provided for environmental assessments of important projects such as the construction of dams, but these proved difficult to carry out when powerful economic interests as well as provincial governments themselves supported the project, as was the case with the building of the Old Man River dam in southern Alberta.

Disposal of the millions of tonnes of wastes that Canadians produced annually proved increasingly onerous. In the early 1970s, landfill sites replaced open garbage dumps, but rural residents strenuously resisted having these sites in their "backyards." Some wastes could be incinerated, a costly process that produced dangerous gases. With the aid of provincial subsidies, municipal governments gradually instituted recycling programs for glass, metals, paper, and plastics. Tire dumps constituted a special problem, demonstrated in devastating fashion when a massive fire at Hagersville, Ontario, raged out of control for weeks in 1990. Even worse was the problem of storing or eliminating toxic wastes. A fire at a storage site for PCBs near Montreal necessitated the evacuation of an entire suburb.

Controlling air and water pollution meant difficult and prolonged negotiations with the United States, whose industries were major polluters of Canada's water and air. In 1987, Canada and the United States signed a tougher version of the Great Lakes Water Quality Agreement of 1978. Although the Americans were reluctant to force coal-burning thermal energy plants to reduce emissions of the sulphur dioxide responsible for acidifying Canadian lakes, the U.S. Congress finally added this stipulation to its Clean Air Act in 1990.

The battle for cleaner air and water involved tradeoffs. Publicly owned and heavily subsidized mines on Cape Breton Island produced high-polluting sulphurous coal, but closing them meant depriving miners of their livelihood. Pulp and paper mills polluted rivers and smelters poisoned the air, but they too provided jobs and revenues. In 1989, for example, Premier Bill Vander Zalm of British Columbia vetoed a cabinet proposal to reduce pulp and paper industry pollutants such as dioxins, declaring: "While I love the environment ... I also love those ... pulp mill workers and someone has to stand up for their jobs."

When provincial governments attempted to impose costly pollution controls, companies often resisted and threatened to shut down operations. When the Ontario government in the 1970s demanded that Inco, in Sudbury, reduce its acid rain-causing sulphur emissions (the region around Sudbury had come to resemble a lunar landscape), the company protested that jobs would be lost, production reduced, and investment postponed. Yet Inco installed new technology, reduced pollution substantially and, at the same time, became the world's lowest-cost nickel producer.

Conflicting economic and environmental preoccupations were also in evidence in regard to the problem of preserving what remained of Canada's wilderness. In the name of protecting biodiversity for future generations, the United Nations urged member states to set aside 12 percent of their territory as off limits for industrial and commercial activities; protected areas should be representative of all natural regions in each jurisdiction. The Canadian government took one important step in this direction in 1986 when it created the huge Ellesmere Island National Park Reserve, Canada's 32nd national park, thus protecting a biologically unique ecosystem situated close to the North Pole.

The 1960s have traditionally been viewed as a decade of rapid change. In many instances, however, changes begun in the 1960s continued and even accelerated during the 1970s and 1980s. The women's rights movement, for example, boasted important accomplishments in the course of these two decades. Gays and lesbians, linguistic minorities, and ethnic minorities also achieved greater equality in these years. But progressive change does not move in only one direction; progress is not inevitable. The liberalism of the 1960s and 1970s gave way to the conservatism of the 1980s.

SUMMARY

Political decisions brought significant change to Canadian society as well as to the country's economy. The Charter of Rights and Freedoms, part of the Canadian Constitution proclaimed in 1982, enabled women and minority groups to challenge laws that, in their view, prevented them from attaining greater equality. Free trade created even closer trade relations with the United States and, in particular, signified rapidly rising exports for many Canadian producers.

As the 1980s closed, new challenges presented themselves. Regional differences remained and exercised a significant influence on federal politics. Quebec had not signed onto the Constitution and until it did so, the threat of another referendum and separatism remained. The federal government, as well as most of the provinces, were borrowing heavily to finance spending that greatly exceeded revenues. As the 1990s opened, Canadians would be faced with the unpleasant realities of cuts in services as governments struggled to bring budget deficits under control.

NOTES

1. Paul Phillips, *Regional Disparities* (Toronto: James Lorimer, 1982), pp. 118–19.

2. Sylvia Bashevkin, *Toeing the Lines: Women and Party Politics in English Canada*, 2nd ed. (Toronto: Oxford University Press, 1993), p. vi.

3. Raymond M. Hébert, *Manitoba's French-Language Crisis: A Cautionary Tale* (Montreal/Kingston: McGill-Queen's University Press, 2004), p. 208.

4. Robert Finbow, "Atlantic Canada: Forgotten Periphery in an Endangered Confederation?," in Kenneth McRoberts, ed., *Beyond Quebec: Taking Stock of Canada* (Montreal/Kingston: McGill-Queen's University Press, 1995), p. 67.

5. John Herd Thompson and Stephen J. Randall, *Canada and the United States: Ambivalent Allies*, 3rd ed. (Montreal/Kingston: McGill-Queen's University Press, 2002), p. 274.

6. Rianne Mahon, "Child Care as Citizenship Right? Toronto in the 1970s and 1980s," *Canadian Historical Review*, 86 (2005): 285–315.

7. Paul Axelrod, *Scholars and Dollars: Politics, Economics, and the Universities of Ontario, 1945–1980* (Toronto: University of Toronto Press, 1982), pp. 141–78.

8. Michiel Horn, *Academic Freedom in Canada: A History* (Toronto: University of Toronto Press, 1999), p. 338.

9. Reginald Bibby, *Mosaic Madness: The Poverty and Potential of Life in Canada* (Toronto: Stoddart, 1990), p. 84.

10. David H. Flaherty and Frank E. Manning, eds., *The Beaver Bites Back? American Popular Culture in Canada* (Montreal/Kingston: McGill-Queen's University Press, 1993), p. 4.

BIBLIOGRAPHY

Many books presented in the bibliography of Chapter 15 are also pertinent to the 1970s and 1980s. Links between demography and the economy are discussed in David K. Foot and Daniel Stoffman, *Boom, Bust and Echo: Profiting from the Demographic Shift in the 21st Century* (Toronto: Stoddart, 2000). Trade issues are discussed in Michael Hart, *A Trading Nation: Canadian Trade Policy from Colonialism to Globalization* (Vancouver: UBC Press, 2002). Stephen High studies industry closures in Ontario in *Industrial Sunset: The Making of North America's Rust Belt, 1969–1984* (Toronto: University of Toronto

Press, 2003). Stephen Clarkson proposes a critical analysis of Canadian–American economic relations in *Canada and the Reagan Challenge*, 2nd ed. (Toronto: James Lorimer, 1985).

Concerning the free trade debate, see Michael Hart, *Decision at Midnight: Inside the Canada–US Free-Trade Negotiations* (Vancouver: UBC Press, 1994); Stephen J. Randall and Herman W. Konrad, eds., *NAFTA in Transition* (Calgary: University of Calgary Press, 1995); and Mel Hurtig, *The Vanishing Country: Is It Too Late to Save Canada?* (Toronto: McClelland and Stewart, 2002). L. Ian MacDonald, *Free Trade: Risks and Rewards* (Montreal/Kingston: McGill-Queen's University Press, 2000), offers contemporary viewpoints. See also Raymond Blake and Andrew Nurse, eds., *Beyond National Dreams: Essays on Canadian Citizenship and Nationalism* (Markham: Fitzhenry & Whiteside, 2008), for a wide-ranging discussion on Canadian nationalism.

Business history is presented in R.T. Naylor, *History of Canadian Business* (Montreal/Kingston: McGill-Queen's University Press, 2006). The energy question is discussed in G. Bruce Doern and Glen Toner, *The Politics of Energy* (Toronto: Methuen, 1985). On western agriculture, see Grace Skogstad, *The Politics of Agricultural Policy-Making in Canada* (Toronto: University of Toronto Press, 1987); and Barry Wilson, *Farming the System: How Politicians and Producers Shape Canadian Agricultural Policy* (Saskatoon: Western Producer Prairie Books, 1990). For a look at the automotive industry, see Dimitry Anastakis, "Industrial Sunrise? The Chrysler Bailout, the State, and the Reindustrialization of the Canadian Automotive Sector, 1975–1986," *Urban History Review*, 35(2) (2007): 37–50; and Jeremy Milloy, "Chrysler Pulled the Trigger: Competing Understandings of Workplace Violence during the 1970s and Radical Legal Practice," *Labour/Le Travail* 74 (2014): 51–88.

Writings on the environment include G. Bruce and Thomas Conway, *The Greening of Canada: Federal Institutions and Decisions* (Toronto: University of Toronto Press, 1994); Chad Gaffield and Pam Gaffield, eds., *Consuming Canada: Readings in Environmental History* (Toronto: Copp Clark, 1995); Kathryn Harrison, *Passing the Buck: Federalism and Canadian Environmental Policy* (Vancouver: University of British Columbia Press, 1996); Ken Drushka, *Canada's Forests: A History of Use and Conservation* (Montreal/Kingston: McGill-Queen's University Press, 2003); David Freeland Duke, *Canadian Environmental History: Essential Readings* (Toronto: Canadian Scholars' Press, 2006); and Alex C. Michalos, *Trade Barriers to the Public Good: Free Trade and Environmental Protection* (Montreal/Kingston: McGill-Queen's University Press, 2008).

Political issues are examined in Hugh G. Thorburn and Alain Whitehorn, eds., *Party Politics in Canada*, 8th ed. (Toronto: Prentice-Hall, 2001); and James Bickerton and Alain-G. Gagnon, *Canadian Politics*, 6th ed. (Peterborough, ON: Broadview Press, 2014).

A valuable biography of Trudeau is Stephen Clarkson and Christina McCall, *Trudeau and Our Times*, vol. 1, *The Magnificent Obsession*; vol. 2, *The Heroic Delusion* (Toronto: McClelland & Stewart, 1990, 1994). On Trudeau's early years, see John English, *Citizen of the World: The Life of Pierre Elliott Trudeau*, vol. I: *1919–1968* (Toronto: Knopf Canada, 2006). Guy Laforest, *Trudeau and the End of a Canadian Dream* (Montreal/Kingston: McGill-Queen's University Press, 1995), is a critical evaluation.

Journalist Jeffrey Simpson has written a well-documented study of Joe Clark's brief government: *Discipline of Power: The Conservative Interlude and the Liberal Restoration* (Toronto: University of Toronto Press, 1996). Richard Clippingdale has written a small book about the Progressive Conservative leader Robert Stanfield's politics entitled *Robert Stanfield's Canada: Perspectives of the Best Prime Minister We Never Had* (Montreal/Kingston: McGill-Queen's University Press, 2008). John Turner's career is examined in Paul Litt, *Elusive Destiny: The Political Vocation of John Napier Turner* (Vancouver: UBC Press, 2011).

Linda McQuaig offers a critical dissection of the Mulroney government in *The Quick and the Dead: Brian Mulroney, Big Business and the Seduction of Canada* (Toronto: Viking, 1991). Corruption and patronage are studied in Stevie Cameron, *On the Take: Crime, Corruption and Greed in the Mulroney Years* (Toronto: Macfarlane Walter & Ross, 1994). Mulroney tells his story in *Memoirs 1939–1993* (Toronto: Douglas Gibson Books, 2007). Stephen J. Ferris and Stanley N. Winer offer a comparative study of governmental size and administration in "Just How Much Bigger Is Government in Canada? A Comparative Analysis of the Size and Structure of the Public Sectors in Canada and the United States, 1929–2004," *Canadian Public Policy*, 33(2) (2007): 173–206.

Works on the Canadian left include John Richards, Robert Cairns, and Larry Pratt, eds., *Social Democracy Without Illusions: Renewal of the Canadian Left* (Toronto: McClelland & Stewart, 1991); and Alan Whitehorn, *Canadian Socialism: Essays on the CCF-NDP* (Toronto: Oxford University Press, 1992). Judy Steed proves a sympathetic biographer in *Ed Broadbent: The Pursuit of Power* (Markham, ON: Viking, 1988).

On the rising power of the Canadian west during this period, particularly Alberta, see Alan Hustak, *Peter Lougheed: A Biography* (Toronto: McClelland & Stewart, 1979); David G. Wood, *The Lougheed Legacy* (Toronto: Key Porter Books, 1985); Gordon Pitts, *Stampede: The Rise of the West and Canada's New Power Elite* (Toronto: Key Porter Books, 2008); and John Richards and Larry Pratt, *Prairie Capitalism: Power and Influence in the New West* (Toronto: McClelland & Stewart, 1979). For a look at the rise of petro-capitalism in the West, see Peter Foster, *The Blue-Eyed Sheiks: The Canadian Oil Establishment* (Don Mills, ON: Collins, 1979); and Alan MacFadyen and G. Campbell Watkins, *Petropolitics: Petroleum Development, Markets and Regulations, Alberta as an Illustrative History* (Calgary: University of Calgary Press, 2014). For a critical appraisal of the National Energy Program, dominion–provincial relations, and the politics of oil and gas, see James Laxer, *Oil and Gas: Ottawa, the Provinces and the Petroleum Industry* (Toronto: James Lorimer, 1983).

Books on federal–provincial relations include David Milne, *Tug of War: Ottawa and the Provinces Under Trudeau and Mulroney* (Toronto: James Lorimer, 1986); Garth Stevenson, *Unfulfilled Union: Canadian Federalism and National Unity*, 4th ed. (Montreal/Kingston, McGill-Queen's University Press, 2004); Richard Simeon and Ian Robinson, *State, Society, and the Development of Canadian Federalism* (Toronto: University of Toronto Press, 1990); P.E. Bryden, *'A Justifiable Obsession': Conservative Ontario's Relations with Ottawa, 1943–1985* (Toronto: University of Toronto Press, 2013); and Raymond Blake, *Lions or Jellyfish: Newfoundland-Ottawa Relations since 1957* (Toronto: University of Toronto Press, 2015).

Keith Banting and Richard Simeon, eds., *And No One Cheered: Federalism, Democracy and the Constitution Act* (Toronto: Methuen, 1983), presents a highly critical analysis of patriation. See also David Milne, *The Canadian Constitution: From Patriation to Meech Lake*, new ed. (Toronto: James Lorimer, 1989); and Howard Pawley, "Present at the Framing," *Canadian Issues* (Fall 2007): 12–15. On Ottawa–Edmonton relations in particular, see Paul Brunner, ed., *Lougheed and the War with Ottawa* (Edmonton: History Book Publications, 2003).

Robert Bothwell, *Alliance and Illusion: Canada and the World, 1945–1984* (Vancouver: UBC Press, 2007) is a recent study of Canada's foreign relations. J.L. Granatstein and Robert Bothwell, *Pirouette: Pierre Trudeau and Canadian Foreign Policy* (Toronto: University of Toronto Press, 1990), analyzes international affairs during Trudeau's tenure. On the Mulroney years, see Nelson Michaud and Kim Richard Nossal, eds., *Diplomatic Departures: The Conservative Era in Canadian Foreign Policy* (Vancouver: UBC Press, 2001). Defence-related issues are examined in Ernie Regehr and Simon Rosenblum, eds., *The Road to Peace: Nuclear Weapons, Canada's Military Policies* (Toronto: James Lorimer, 1988); and Albert Legault and Michel Fortmann, *Diplomacy of Hope: Canada and Disarmament, 1945–1988* (Montreal/Kingston: McGill-Queen's University Press, 1992).

On higher education, see Neil Tudiver, *Universities for Sale: Resisting Corporate Control over Canadian Higher Education* (Toronto: James Lorimer, 1999); and Paul Axelrod, *Values in Conflict: The University, the Marketplace, and the Trials of Liberal Education* (Montreal/Kingston: McGill-Queen's University Press, 2002).

Studies of Canada's culture include David H. Flaherty and Frank E. Manning, eds., in *The Beaver Bites Back? American Popular Culture in Canada* (Montreal/Kingston: McGill-Queen's University Press, 1993); and Ian Angus, *A Border Within: National Identity, Cultural Plurality, and Wilderness* (Montreal/Kingston: McGill-Queen's University Press, 1997). See also David M. Thomas, ed., *Canada and the United States: Differences That Count*, 2nd ed. (Peterborough, ON: Broadview Press, 2000). Daniel Francis explodes myths in his very readable *National Dreams: Myth, Memory, and Canadian History* (Vancouver: Arsenal Pulp Press, 1997).

On institutions designed to favour the development of Canadian culture, see Marc Raboy, *Missed Opportunities: The Story of Canada's Broadcasting Policy* (Montreal/Kingston: McGill-Queen's University Press, 1990); and Richard Collins, *Culture, Communications, and National Identity: The Case of Canadian Television* (Toronto: University of Toronto Press, 1990). Canada's film industry is studied in George Melnyk, *One Hundred Years of Canadian Cinema* (Toronto: University of Toronto Press, 2004).

Works of sports history include Donald Macintosh and David Whitson, *The Game Planners: Transforming Canada's Sport System* (Montreal/Kingston: McGill-Queen's University Press, 1990); Richard Gruneau and David Whitson, *Hockey Night in Canada: Sport, Identities, and Cultural Politics* (Toronto: Garamond, 1993); and Donald Macintosh and Michael Hawes, *Sport and Canadian Diplomacy* (Montreal/Kingston: McGill-Queen's University Press, 1994). Reginald W. Bibby proposes a provocative analysis of religion in the 1970s and 1980s in *Unknown Gods: The Ongoing Story of Religion in Canada* (Toronto: Stoddart, 1993).

On gays and lesbians, see Becki L. Ross, *The House That Jill Built: A Lesbian Nation in Formation* (Toronto: University of Toronto Press, 1995); Miriam Smith, *Lesbian and Gay Rights in Canada: Social Movements and Equality-Seeking, 1971–1995* (Toronto: University of Toronto Press, 1999); Tom Warner, *Never Going Back: A History of Queer Activism in Canada* (Toronto: University of Toronto Press, 2002); and Liz Millward, *Making a Scene: Lesbians and Community across Canada, 1964–1984* (Vancouver: UBC Press, 2015). Valerie J. Korinek's research on one pioneer gay man is available in "'The Most Openly Gay Person for at Least a Thousand Miles': Doug Wilson and the Politicization of a Province, 1975–83," *Canadian Historical Review*, 84 (2003): 515–50.

A synthesis on the history of women in Canada is Alison Prentice et al., *Canadian Women: A History*, 2nd ed. (Toronto: Harcourt Brace, 1996). A treatment of women in unions is Julie White, *Sisters and Solidarity: Women and Unions in Canada* (Toronto: Thompson Educational Publishing, 1993). Among works on Canadian feminism, see Nancy Adamson, Linda Briskin, and Margaret McPhail, *Feminist Organizing for Change: The Contemporary Women's Movement in Canada* (Toronto: Oxford University Press, 1988); Constance Backhouse and David H. Flaherty, eds., *Challenging Times: The Women's Movement in Canada and the United States* (Montreal/Kingston: McGill-Queen's University Press, 1992); Ruth Roach Pierson et al., *Canadian Women's Issues*, vol. 1, *Strong Voices*; vol. 2, *Bold Visions* (Toronto: James Lorimer, 1993, 1995); Sylvia B. Bashevkin, *Women on the Defensive: Living Through Conservative Times* (Chicago: University of Chicago Press, 1998); Wendy Robbins et al., eds. *Minds of Our Own: Inventing Feminist Scholarship and Women's Studies in Canada and Quebec, 1966–1976* (Waterloo: Wilfrid Laurier University Press, 2008); and Frank Trovato and Lalu Nirannanilathu, "From Divergence to Convergence: The Sex Differential in Life Expectancy in Canada, 1971–2000," *Canadian Review of Sociology and Anthropology*, 44(1) (2007): 101–22.

The evolution of Canada's welfare state is discussed in Raymond Blake and Jeff Keshen, eds., *Social Welfare Policy in Canada: Historical Readings* (Toronto: Copp Clark, 1995); and Raymond B. Blake, Penny E. Bryden, and J. Frank Strain, eds., *The Welfare State in Canada: Past, Present and Future* (Concord, ON: Irwin Publishing, 1997). Health-care issues are discussed in C. David Naylor, ed., *Canadian Health Care and the State: A Century of Evolution* (Montreal/Kingston: McGill-Queen's University Press, 1992); and Duane Adams, ed., *Federalism, Democracy, and Health Policy in Canada* (Montreal/Kingston: McGill-Queen's University Press, 2001). On housing, see Peter Ward, *A History of Domestic Space: Privacy and the Canadian Home* (Vancouver: UBC Press, 1999). Crime is addressed in D. Owen Carrigan, *Crime and Punishment in Canada: A History* (Toronto: McClelland & Stewart, 1991).

Chapter Nineteen

CONTEMPORARY CANADA

TIME LINE

1990	Oka Crisis occurs in Quebec
1991	Canadian troops participate in Gulf War
1992	Charlottetown Accord defeated in referendum Explosion at Westray mine in Pictou County, Nova Scotia, kills twenty-six miners
1993	Liberals under Jean Chrétien win federal election
1994	Canada, Mexico, and the United States sign the North American Free Trade Agreement (NAFTA)
1996	Royal Commission on Aboriginal Peoples issues report
1997	Liberals win federal election under Jean Chrétien Hibernia offshore oil platform begins drilling Opening of Confederation Bridge linking Prince Edward Island and New Brunswick
1998	British Columbia concludes treaty with Nisga'a First Nation Publication of *Gathering Strength: Canada's Aboriginal Action Plan* Federal budget announces first surplus in more than twenty-five years Nunavut becomes separate territory in eastern Arctic
2000	Liberals led by Jean Chrétien win federal election
2001	9/11 terrorist attacks on New York City and Washington, D.C.
2002	Canada sends combat troops to Afghanistan Canada ratifies Kyoto Protocol
2003	Toronto shaken by deadly outbreak of severe acute respiratory syndrome (SARS) virus Paul Martin replaces Chrétien as Liberal leader and prime minister
2004	Liberals led by Paul Martin win minority government
2005	Gomery report on sponsorship scandal released
2006	Conservative Party under Stephen Harper wins federal election with minority government
2008	Federal government offers official apology for residential schools Canada sets gold medal record at Vancouver Winter Olympic Games Bank failures in the United States lead to a global financial crisis Harper Conservatives win minority government in federal election
2011	Harper Conservatives win majority government in federal election Canada ends combat mission in Afghanistan
2014	Idle No More movement founded Terrorist attack occurs on Parliament Hill
2015	Truth and Reconciliation Commission issues report on Indian residential schools NDP wins majority government in Alberta Justin Trudeau's Liberals win majority government in federal election

The 1990s and 2000s witnessed significant changes to Canada's identity, both at home and abroad. Since 1945, Canada had carefully constructed a national identity based on an open, tolerant, friendly, peacekeeping, multicultural, and environmentally conscious society. By 2016, however, all of these attributes were in dispute. Canada's Medicare system was under scrutiny and widely viewed as unsustainable. The "War on Terror" created an atmosphere of fear and persecution against Muslim Canadians, and raised concerns about individual liberties and the treatment of minorities. Canada was a strong ally and supporter of American and Israeli policies in the Middle East and so became a target for terrorist attacks. The Canadian Airborne Regiment's killing of a Somalia teenager during a humanitarian effort in 1993, and Canada's subsequent combat roles in Kosovo, Afghanistan, and Syria diminished the nation's peacekeeping reputation. The federal government even went so far as to disdain the United Nations. As the world finally woke up to the serious threat of climate change, Canada emerged as a "leader" not only in terms of carbon emissions but also in obstructing international efforts to curb carbon production. To make matters worse, after a decade of prosperity, the bubble burst, and a global recession of massive proportions struck in late 2008.

But there were reasons for optimism. Canada handled the recession of the early 1990s with marked effectiveness. Other nations would subsequently turn to Canada as a model in dealing with crippling deficits. Canada's economy and trade diversified in the 1990s and 2000s. As the power and influence of the United States declined, Canada sought other markets, particularly in the new economic powers of China and India. When the real estate bubble burst in the United States, causing a serious bank failure and credit crunch, the American economy slid into its worst crisis since the Great Depression. Canada's banks, however, had not followed the U.S. banks' lax lending practices and proved remarkably resilient. While the nation inevitably followed its neighbour into recession, the shocks were lessened.

Even though the Progressive Conservative government of Brian Mulroney bore the brunt of public discontent during the recession of the early 1990s, its main economic policies to deal with the crisis were viewed favourably in hindsight. The much-maligned goods and services tax (GST) helped Canada climb out of the recession and the controversial Canada–U.S. Free Trade Agreement (FTA) aided the return to prosperity. But it would be the Liberal government of Jean Chrétien after 1993 that would reap the rewards of Conservative recession-bashing. The fact that the Liberals maintained both the GST and free trade (despite denouncing them in opposition) indicated the policies' success.

The election of 1988, fought primarily on the issue of free trade with the United States, and the failure of the Meech Lake and Charlottetown Accords highlighted the breakdown of political consensus in Canada. The Mulroney government's fortunes went from bad to worse. The Progressive Conservatives came to power in 1984 with support from both Quebec and the West. A decade later, two new regional parties—the Bloc Québécois and the Reform Party— transformed the political landscape. The result was the destruction of the PC Party, which lost a staggering 167 seats under the leadership of Kim Campbell, reducing the Tories to just 2 seats in the House of Commons. From 1993 to 2000, a divided and regionalized opposition helped the Chrétien Liberals win three consecutive majorities. After 1998, budgetary surpluses, the first in more than a quarter-century, made more activist government again possible. Then scandal, internal strife, and a resurgent and united Conservative opposition led by Stephen Harper undermined the Liberal governments of Chrétien and his successor, Paul Martin, paving the way for a Tory victory in 2006. The Conservatives won minority governments in 2006 and 2008, and then emerged with a majority in 2011. The NDP, riding an "orange wave," became the official opposition, while the Liberals were reduced to third place. In 2015, however, the Liberals under Justin Trudeau—the son of Pierre Trudeau—came from third place in the polls and won a surprise majority.

Despite the economic prosperity, there were portents of danger. As the numbers of elderly Canadians rose and young Canadians declined, health care became an ever more serious concern. Expenditures on health represented a constantly increasing share of provincial budgets. First Nations issues were not given proper attention, the condition of Aboriginal reserves deteriorated, and protests increased. Environmental issues worried Canadians and they heatedly discussed climate change and what they could do about it.

Fear of environmental dystopia mixed with a seeming technological utopia. The phenomenal development of the Internet linked Canadians and the rest of the world more closely. Companies and governments could now process and move data with speeds and efficiency unimaginable scarcely a few years earlier. Individuals could send messages electronically, obtain information on any subject, pay bills, purchase goods and services, and amuse themselves, all from their desktop, then laptop, then hand-held devices. The computer age also brought new and serious challenges to citizens' rights to privacy.

The Collapse of Consensus

The re-election of the Progressive Conservative government under Brian Mulroney in 1988 brought about leadership changes in the two opposition parties. The NDP chose Audrey McLaughlin to succeed Ed Broadbent; she became the first woman to lead a Canadian federal political party. Jean Chrétien, a Quebecker who occupied several cabinet posts under Trudeau, won the Liberal leadership in 1990, although his support in Quebec was weak due in part to his perceived insensitivity to the province's exclusion from the constitutional agreement of 1982.

The federal government faced the daunting task of slashing spending to reduce the deficit. The free trade debate had been divisive and scandals further tarnished the government's image. Better-off Canadians complained when the government "clawed back" their family allowances and old-age pensions. The harsh budget of 1989, with its tax increases and, even more, the government's decision to replace the hidden manufacturers' sales tax with a fully visible GST of 7 percent, to take effect in January 1991, provoked vehement opposition. Other measures, including cuts in subsidies to such national institutions as Via Rail and the Canadian Broadcasting Corporation (CBC), as well as the privatizing of Crown corporations, also generated criticism. The deepening crisis in public finances limited the government's ability to respond to the demands placed on it. The Progressive Conservatives plummeted to third place in the polls, and Prime Minister Mulroney joked that a small room now sufficed to bring together all of his supporters.

Ontario: The Engine That Drives Canada?

High interest rates and rising unemployment, particularly in central Canada, only compounded the prevailing discontent. Recession descended on Ontario in 1990 and the jobless rate rose dramatically, especially in manufacturing industries, construction, and retail sales. It would take until 1994 for the province to recover the jobs lost during the severe downturn. In 1990, the NDP in Ontario under Bob Rae won a stunning upset victory over the provincial Liberals. When the government brought down its first budget in 1991, the NDP opted for a massive deficit of nearly $10 billion in an effort to counteract the deleterious effects of the recession on Ontario's economy. Rapidly rising welfare and interest payments on the debt contributed to successive large budget deficits. Rae raised taxes and imposed a stringent restraint program designed to control public-sector wages while protecting jobs: employees were to take unpaid holidays, dubbed "Rae days." Unions condemned the measures. Popular support for the NDP collapsed, ensuring the government's defeat in 1995 by the Progressive Conservatives led by Mike Harris, who promised to implement a "Common Sense Revolution."

Ontarians also became increasingly critical of federal policies. The provincial government fought free trade. It asked Ottawa to share the cost of higher welfare payments. Now Ontarians asserted that they were doing more than their share of shouldering the "burden of unity," pointing out that their taxes paid a large portion of the cost of the equalization grants, unemployment insurance, farm subsidies, and industrial-development projects that the federal government bestowed on poorer provinces. Ontario was becoming a "not-so-friendly giant," with its own grievances to pursue, and its own interests to defend.[1]

The Reform Party and the Bloc Québécois

Despite the support for the Conservatives in the West and significant representation in cabinet, western Canadians came to view the Mulroney government, like the Trudeau government before it, as overly attuned to the interests of Quebec. The rise in popularity of the western-based Reform Party after 1987 provided evidence of a powerful wave of dissatisfaction with the mainstream parties. Proclaiming that "the West wants in," the new party, led by Preston Manning— son of former Alberta Premier Ernest Manning—condemned the federal government's financial mismanagement, its "welfare-state approach" to meeting social needs, its immigration policy, and its commitment to official bilingualism and multiculturalism.[2] Although the Reform Party toned down its West-oriented rhetoric in an effort to win support in Ontario and Atlantic Canada, its major successes occurred in Alberta and British Columbia in the federal elections of 1993 and 1997.

When Mulroney entered office in 1984, he had been intent on repairing the damage to national unity inflicted by Trudeau on the constitutional question. The boy from Baie-Comeau would return Quebec to the Canadian family. But the Meech Lake Accord failed (see Chapter 16). Within Quebec, support for sovereignty subsequently increased in response to what most Quebeckers perceived as a rejection of the province's legitimate aspirations by Canadians. In Ottawa, several Conservative MPs including Lucien Bouchard from Quebec quit their party and formed a new grouping, the Bloc Québécois, committed to Quebec's independence.

The Conservatives under Mulroney tried again to achieve an agreement on constitutional reforms in 1991–92. This time, wide consultations took place before the federal, provincial, and territorial first ministers and the leaders of First Nations organizations met in Charlottetown and agreed on proposals that attempted to respond to a host of agendas for change, including Senate reform and Aboriginal self-government. The October 1992 referendum on the Charlottetown Accord saw the voters of six provinces, including Quebec, reject the agreement. Constitutional change was dead for the foreseeable future.

The First Nations at National Councils

The Mulroney government also faced growing disenchantment from Canada's First Nations. In their view, the Meech Lake Accord had neglected to address Aboriginal concerns. Elijah Harper, an Aboriginal MLA in the Manitoba legislature, managed on a technical point to hold up Manitoba's ratification of the accord past the necessary deadline for its approval. Manitoba's and Newfoundland's failure to ratify it before the final deadline scuttled the Accord but the dominant image of the failure of Meech was Elijah Harper standing in the Manitoba legislature holding a lone eagle feather as a symbol of resistance.

The federal government's inability to settle the complex, two-centuries-old land claim of the Mohawk at Kanesatake (Oka) contributed to an outbreak of violence in the summer of 1990. The standoff was a pivotal event in the history of the relationship between the First Nations and the Canadian government. The Mohawk, who saw their land base sharply reduced over the years to a tiny fraction of its original size, resisted attempts by the town of Oka, 40 kilometres west of Montreal, to extend a golf course over disputed lands. Barricades led to a shootout in which a Quebec provincial police constable died, and then to a 78-day armed standoff between the Mohawk and the federal and Quebec governments.

The Oka Crisis became the catalyst for Ottawa's creation of the Royal Commission on Aboriginal Peoples, first promised at the time of the Meech Lake Accord. The federal government established the commission in April 1991. Four of its seven commissioners were Aboriginal. Its mandate was "to examine the economic, social and cultural situation of the aboriginal peoples." The commission continued for five and a half years.

The 1992 Charlottetown Accord promised to address the constitutional concerns of the First Nations. With Aboriginal leaders involved in the talks from the outset, the accord represented the new reality of Canada's relationship with its First Nations. It promised recognition of the inherent Aboriginal right of self-government within Canada, the acceptance of Aboriginal governments as one of Canada's three orders of government, and the opening up of the Senate and House of Commons to Aboriginal representation. But Canadians had grown weary of what Preston Manning called "constitutional wrangling." The Charlottetown Accord failed to win majority support in the referendum in 1992, even in First Nations communities.

Election of 1993

The federal election of 1993 underlined Canada's regional divisions. The Progressive Conservatives, now led by Kim Campbell, Canada's first female prime minister, met with a crushing defeat: only 2 were elected (one of them Jean Charest, soon to be Liberal premier of Quebec). The Liberals won a majority with 177 seats, thanks in large part to Ontario. Yet Prime Minister Jean Chrétien was the first French-speaking "old party" leader since Confederation to fail to win a majority of Quebec's seats. Voters in the province preferred to give their support to the Bloc Québécois, which became the official opposition in Parliament with 54 seats but only 14 percent of the national vote. Close behind came the West-based Reform Party with 52 seats and 19 percent. Finally, the unpopularity of provincial NDP governments in Ontario and British Columbia contributed heavily to the party's dismal performance of 9 seats and 7 percent of the vote.

Wilfrid Laurier took Canada into the twentieth century, and Jean Chrétien took Canada into the twenty-first.

Source: Tom Hanson/The Canadian Press.

The Chrétien Governments

Once in power, the Liberals accepted most of the Progressive Conservative deficit-cutting policies it had censured while in opposition. The Chrétien government did not repeal the GST but instead maintained the tax as a major form of revenue. After vehemently criticizing free trade during the campaign, it maintained the agreement and went further by signing the North American Free Trade Agreement (NAFTA) with the United States and Mexico in 1994.

In order to reduce the federal deficit that had climbed to a record $42 billion, the Liberal government made substantial cuts in grants to the provinces for health, education, and social welfare. It reduced unemployment benefits and tightened eligibility rules, provoking strong reaction among workers, particularly in eastern Canada. At the same time, it transferred into its general revenue fund most of the surplus that the employment insurance fund now accumulated because of high premiums and declining unemployment.

Government cuts to social programs signified the decline of the welfare state. The NDP blamed deficits not on excessive social spending but rather on the decreases in corporate taxation instituted by the Mulroney Conservatives and maintained by the Chrétien Liberals. Ottawa spent less elsewhere as well. It froze civil servants' wages, devoted less money to foreign aid, and slashed defence spending, making it necessary to cut short peacekeeping missions for lack of soldiers and equipment.

Land Claims

Because the process of contact and settlement had moved from east to west across North America, and had occurred over centuries, the First Nations on Canada's west coast faced the consequences relatively late. Their land was not originally coveted and, as a result, they were not involved in the signing of the numbered treaties to extinguish Aboriginal title to the Prairie West in the 1870s. Nor were they involved in the signing the Northern Treaties in the early decades of the twentieth century when the government sought control of mineral rights. From its entry into Confederation in 1871 British Columbia had not acknowledged that the Aboriginal peoples had any treaty rights or ancestral claims over traditional lands. This created a unique situation in the province where the First Nations had not surrendered title to their land through conquest or treaty.

In 1990, British Columbia made a historic change of policy and agreed to enter into treaty negotiations with the First Nations. The British Columbia Treaty Commission was established in 1993. Six years later, Parliament ratified the Nisga'a Treaty, the first comprehensive claim settled south of the Yukon and Northwest Territories since the James Bay Agreement in 1975. The Nisga'a obtained control over 2000 square kilometres of their territory, as well as nearly $120 million in compensation for their lost lands.

By the first decade of the new millennium, 50 First Nations in British Columbia (about two-thirds of all First Nations people in the province) were involved in negotiations. Progress was slow, however, and became bogged down in the courts. After 2007, a number of other British Columbia First Nations, including the Tsawwassen and the Xeni Gwet'in, commenced treaty negotiations with the provincial government. By 2014, the issue of land claims was complicated by struggles between British Columbia First Nations and governments over the issue of building gas and oil pipelines. A Supreme Court decision upheld a ruling that provided First Nations effective control over tracts of land that were outside their reserves but traditionally under their control. The decision meant that resource extraction and pipeline development required the explicit consent of First Nations.

In 1992 the federal government negotiated the $450 million Saskatchewan Treaty Land Entitlement Framework Agreement. It compensated for illegal losses of reserve lands in the province. This fund also allowed for the granting of additional lands to those communities entitled to larger land areas in their historic treaties. Saskatchewan led the way in the creation of urban reserves, or lands located in a municipality or Northern Administrative District, designed to provide urban locations for Aboriginal business. By 2005, 28 urban reserves had been initiated, 9 of them located in Saskatchewan cities.

In 1990, the First Nations and Métis of the Mackenzie valley area signed a tentative land-claims agreement. Had both Native groups ratified it, they would have received surface title to an area one-third the size of Alberta and $500 million in cash. Later in the year, however, some individuals rejected what is known as the extinguishment clause in the "agreement-in-principle," requiring them to give up all treaty and Aboriginal rights. In late 1990, the federal government announced that it would negotiate new claims with each of the regions in the Aboriginal territory separately. Parliament accepted the Gwich'in comprehensive land-claims agreement in late 1992, the Sahtu Dene and Métis land-claims agreement in 1993, and the Tlicho (Dogrib) Agreement in 2003, thus settling three of the five regions' land claims.

In the western Arctic in 1984, COPE, the political organization of the 2500 Inuvialuit, signed the first comprehensive settlement with the federal government in the Yukon and Northwest Territories. In return for surrendering their claim to the title of approximately 345,000 square kilometres of land, the Inuvialuit obtained title to about 90,000 square kilometres, including sub-surface mineral rights for 13,000 square kilometres of this area. They also received $152 million in financial compensation.

In the eastern and central Arctic, the Tungavik Federation of Nunavut and the federal government reached an agreement-in-principle in 1990. Three years later, they signed a land-claims settlement that gave the Inuit absolute ownership of land totalling approximately 350,000 square kilometres. They also received $580 million for relinquishing their Aboriginal claim to 2,000,000 square kilometres. In 1993, Parliament passed the Nunavut Land Claims Agreement.

In 1997, in the *Delgamuukw* case, the Supreme Court enlarged and clarified the definition of Aboriginal title in Canada. The court unanimously recognized in this British Columbia case that Aboriginal title could extend over large areas of traditional lands. The landmark decision also accepted the validity of using Aboriginal oral history and testimony from elders in cases involving Aboriginal title.

Another confirmation of the growing legal and political recognition of Aboriginal rights came in the Supreme Court's *Marshall* decision of 1999, in a case involving Mi'kmaq fishing rights initiated by Donald Marshall, Jr., the same individual acquitted in 1983 of a wrongful conviction of homicide. In 1999 the court in the second Marshall case ruled that the peace and friendship treaties made in 1760–61 between the Mi'kmaq and the British gave the Mi'kmaq a treaty right to a "moderate livelihood" in the Atlantic commercial fishery. Ottawa's continued attempts to try to regulate the Mi'kmaq fishery resulted in sporadic violence in the 2000 and 2001 fishing seasons, particularly at the Mi'kmaq community of Burnt Church, in New Brunswick's Miramichi Bay. The Supreme Court of Canada ruled in *Regina v. Van der Peet* in 1996 that Aboriginal practices are indeed protected, but only those practices that were present before European contact.

Election of 1997

In the federal election of 1997 the Chrétien Liberals again benefited from a fractured and region-alized opposition. They won the election with a majority government and 155 seats. Preston Manning's Reform Party took on the mantle of official opposition (with 60 seats) while the Bloc Québécois led by Gilles Duceppe maintained the support of Quebec (with 44 seats). The NDP, now under Alexa McDonough, won 21 seats and the PCs led by Jean Charest won 20 seats. In Quebec, after the referendum of 1995 on independence (see Chapter 16), sentiment for Quebec sovereignty waned.

The Royal Commission on Aboriginal Peoples

In late 1996, the Royal Commission on Aboriginal Peoples tabled its five-volume final report (roughly 3500 pages) in the House of Commons. The 440 recommendations covered a wide range of Aboriginal issues but focused on four major concerns: the need for a new relationship in Canada between Aboriginal and non-Aboriginal peoples; Aboriginal self-determination through self-government; economic self-sufficiency; and healing for Aboriginal peoples and communities. The report constituted the most in-depth analysis ever undertaken on Canada's First Nations.

The federal government waited fourteen months before issuing its reply. In January 1998, it presented it in a document entitled *Gathering Strength: Canada's Aboriginal Action Plan*. Although the statement committed the federal government to a new approach to Aboriginal policy in Canada, it replied directly to only a few of the recommendations. Ottawa accepted the treaty relationship as the basis for Canada's relationships with First Nations. This acceptance revealed the new spirit of the times—only thirty years earlier the Hawthorn Report of the mid-1960s and the 1969 White Paper considered treaties of marginal importance. Second, the federal government promised a more stable, long-term fiscal relationship with Aboriginal groups. Third, it promised to increase efforts to prepare First Nations for self-government. Fourth, additional access would be given to land and resources. Several months later, the federal government set aside $350 million to support community-based healing initiatives for First Nations people affected by the legacy of Indian residential schools.

WHERE HISTORIANS DISAGREE

Indian Residential Schools

For nearly a century a church/state-run system of residential schools worked to assimilate First Nations children into the dominant Euro-Canadian society. Each of the four Christian denominations responsible—the Anglicans, Presbyterians, Roman Catholics, and the United Church—have in recent years formally apologized for their role in this assimilation program. In 1998, the Chrétien government, in unveiling its Aboriginal Action Plan, also apologized for the government's part in developing and administering the schools. And in 2008, the Harper government made an even more direct and sweeping apology for the residential schools system:

> . . . Today, we recognize that this policy of assimilation was wrong, has caused great harm and has no place in our country. . . .
>
> . . . [There have been many] tragic accounts of the emotional, physical and sexual abuse and neglect of helpless children, and their

separation from powerless families and communities. . . .

. . . The government of Canada sincerely apologizes and asks the forgiveness of the aboriginal peoples of this country for failing them so profoundly.

We are sorry.

Historians, however, were slow to recognize the issue of residential schools, which were rarely mentioned in history classes. John Webster Grant, a religious historian, was one of the first academics to discuss the issue. Writing well before most Canadians had ever heard the term "residential school," he identified a number of the policy's failings. Grant noted that many First Nations people realized the injustice of residential schools and resisted their forced assimilation: "Resistance to enrollment was widespread, and school burnings were more common than mere accidents would explain." Financial handicaps, poor teachers, unhealthy

Assembly of First Nations Chief Phil Fontaine (right, wearing headdress) watches as Canadian Prime Minister Stephen Harper officially apologizes for more than a century of abuse and cultural loss involving Indian residential schools. The ceremony took place in the House of Commons in Ottawa, June 11, 2008.

Source: THE CANADIAN PRESS/Tom Hanson.

buildings, few amenities, all plagued the system. Yet, he argued, in the face of these difficulties, some schools performed well: "Despite its shortcomings, the residential school evidently met a need."[1]

As attention turned to the issue of residential schools in the 1980s, Celia Haig-Brown examined the record of the Kamloops Indian Residential School in central British Columbia, from the recollections of thirteen former students. From her study, rich in oral testimony, a fuller understanding of the schooling experience began to emerge. Reflecting vivid and painful memories, Haig-Brown emphasized "the injustice of the system which attempted to control and to transform." Yet, while it was easy and tempting to simply damn the entire process and system, she attempted to find some sense of balance: "Even with the controls already described well in place, the students found time and space to express themselves and to produce a separate culture of their own within the school."[2]

By 1990 the subject of residential schools permeated the general public's consciousness. With many of the schools' students still alive and court cases commencing against the churches for abuse, the issue became politicized. The statement by Phil Fontaine, then chief of the Assembly of Manitoba Chiefs, that he suffered sexual abuse as a student at a Manitoba residential school broke the silence of some other former students, who came forward to reveal their own stories of physical, sexual, and emotional abuse. Several years later, in 1996, J.R. Miller published *Shingwauk's Vision: A History of Native Residential Schools*. At the high point of the Indian residential school system in the early twentieth century, he observed, approximately one-third of the eligible Inuit and status Indians of school age attended: "It seems clear that the schools performed inadequately in most respects, and in a few areas, wrought profoundly destructive effects on many of their students."[3]

Through the ongoing hearings of the Royal Commission on Aboriginal Peoples in the mid-1990s, the public gained a greater awareness of the destructive policy. John S. Milloy, who wrote a report for the commission on residential schools, later published a full-length study in which he strongly criticized the church–state partnership for its assault on the well-being of the First Nations: "In thought and in deed the establishment of this school system was an act of profound cruelty rooted in non-Aboriginal pride and intolerance and in the certitude and insularity of purported cultural superiority."[4]

Canada's residential school policy was a tragedy. Some 150,000 Native children were forcefully removed from their homes and families, and sent away to one of over 130 schools across the country. Students were prohibited from speaking their language, wearing cultural dress, and pursuing their traditional spirituality.

Retribution to those who broke the rules was harsh. Many students experienced physical, emotional, and sexual abuse. The residential school system lasted until the 1960s but the last one closed only in the 1990s. In 2015, the Truth and Reconciliation Commission issued its report formally labelling the system as "cultural genocide."

1   John Webster Grant, *Moon of Wintertime: Missionaries and the Indians of Canada in Encounter since 1534* (Toronto: University of Toronto Press, 1984), pp. 179, 183.

2   Celia Haig-Brown, *Resistance and Renewal: Surviving the Indian Residential School* (Vancouver: Tillacum Library, 1988), pp. 88, 115.

3   J.R. Miller, *Shingwauk's Vision: A History of Native Residential Schools* (Toronto: University of Toronto Press, 1996), pp. 142, 418.

4   John S. Milloy, *"A National Crime": The Canadian Government and the Residential School System, 1879 to 1986* (Winnipeg: University of Manitoba Press, 1999), p. 302.

Nunavut and the North

In 1979, the Aboriginal majority in the legislative assembly of the Northwest Territories endorsed the proposed division of the territories. The government of the Northwest Territories held a plebiscite on the issue in 1982, in which 56 percent of the votes cast favoured division. Later that year, the federal government accepted the proposal in principle. An Inuit constitutional forum representing Nunavut (meaning "our land" in Inuktitut) and a second forum representing the western district, or Denendeh (meaning "land of the people" in Athapaskan), were formed to discuss how the territorial division might be accomplished. A major stumbling block became the proposed border between the two jurisdictions.

Despite blood ties with their fellow Inuit in the east, the Inuvialuit chose to keep their economic links with the west. The adherence of the western Arctic to Denendeh, rich in newly discovered oil and gas potential, pleased the Dene and the Métis. The addition of the 2500 Inuvialuit helped raise the Native population of Denendeh in 1982 to near-equality (15,000) with that of the non-Native population (17,000). On January 15, 1987, leaders of the two constitutional forums confirmed in Iqaluit the decision to divide the Northwest Territories. Subsequently the Northwest Territories legislative assembly and the federal government approved the territorial division, leading to the creation of Nunavut on April 1, 1999.

At division, the population of the Northwest Territories was approximately 40,000 people, split almost equally among Inuit and Inuvialuit, First Nations and Métis, and non-Natives; the population of Nunavut was approximately 25,000, of which 85 percent was Inuit and most of the remainder non-Native.

The creation of Nunavut strengthened Canada's sovereignty in the Arctic, because its claims to the Northwest Passage are based largely on the Inuit's use and occupancy of the area. The voyages through the waters of the Canadian Arctic Archipelago by the *Manhattan*, an American oil tanker, in 1969, and by the *Polar Sea*, an American icebreaker, in 1985, awakened Canadians to the uncertain status of their northern waters. The rapid advance of global warming has led to the thinning of the ice cover in the Northwest Passage and made the Passage a more viable commercial shipping route. It has also opened up new opportunities for oil extraction. For the Inuit, however, global warming is rapidly altering their traditional hunting-based lifestyle.

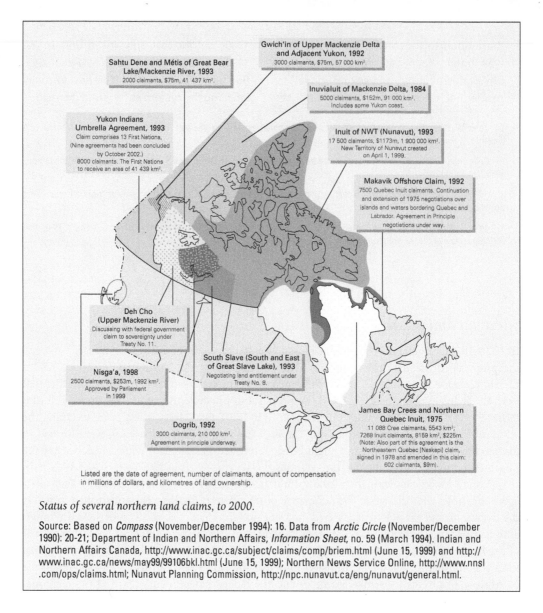

Gwich'in of Upper Mackenzie Delta
and Adjacent Yukon, 1992
3000 claimants, $75m, 57 000 km².

Sahtu Dene and Métis of Great Bear
Lake/Mackenzie River, 1993
2000 claimants, $75m, 41 437 km².

Inuvialuit of Mackenzie Delta, 1984
5000 claimants, $152m, 91 000 km².
Includes some Yukon coast.

Yukon Indians
Umbrella Agreement, 1993
Claim comprises 13 First Nations,
(Nine agreements had been concluded
by October 2002.)
8000 claimants. The First Nations
to receive an area of 41 439 km².

Inuit of NWT (Nunavut), 1993
17 500 claimants, $1173m, 1 900 000 km².
New Territory of Nunavut created
on April 1, 1999.

Makavik Offshore Claim, 1992
7500 Quebec Inuit claimants. Continuation
and extension of 1975 negotiations over
islands and waters bordering Quebec and
Labrador. Agreement in Principle
negotiations under way.

Deh Cho
(Upper Mackenzie River)
Discussing with federal government
claim to sovereignty under
Treaty No. 11.

South Slave (South and East
of Great Slave Lake), 1993
Negotiating land entitlement under
Treaty No. 8.

Nisga'a, 1998
2500 claimants, $253m, 1992 km².
Approved by Parliament
in 1999

James Bay Crees and Northern
Quebec Inuit, 1975
11 088 Cree claimants, 5543 km²;
7268 Inuit claimants, 8159 km², $225m.
(Note: Also part of this agreement is the
Northeastern Quebec (Naskapi) claim,
signed in 1978 and amended in this claim:
602 claimants, $9m).

Dogrib, 1992
3000 claimants, 210 000 km².
Agreement in principle underway.

Listed are the date of agreement, number of claimants, amount of compensation
in millions of dollars, and kilometres of land ownership.

Status of several northern land claims, to 2000.

Source: Based on *Compass* (November/December 1994): 16. Data from *Arctic Circle* (November/December 1990): 20-21; Department of Indian and Northern Affairs, *Information Sheet*, no. 59 (March 1994). Indian and Northern Affairs Canada, http://www.inac.gc.ca/subject/claims/comp/briem.html (June 15, 1999) and http://www.inac.gc.ca/news/may99/99106bkl.html (June 15, 1999); Northern News Service Online, http://www.nnsl.com/ops/claims.html; Nunavut Planning Commission, http://npc.nunavut.ca/eng/nunavut/general.html.

Conservative Disunity

The Chrétien Liberals continued to benefit from disunity on the right, where two parties vied for conservative support. On the one hand, the old Progressive Conservatives attempted to regain their popularity, led by such stalwarts as Joe Clark and others from the Mulroney era. On the other hand, the Reform Party replaced the Bloc as the official opposition in 1997 but, even reconstituted as the Canadian Alliance in 2000 under a new leader, it failed to expand its influence beyond the West.

Election of 2000

When Chrétien called a snap election in 2000 to take advantage of Conservative disunity, the result was another Liberal majority government and a gain of 17 seats. Party strife accompanied by a precipitous decline in membership resulted in the selection of a new leader for the Tories—Stephen Harper, a former Reform Party MP. While continuing to advocate fiscal conservatism, smaller government, and greater autonomy for the provinces, the Alliance also defended western and rural positions such as opposition to federal gun registration and to environmental controls that might hurt the petroleum industry in Alberta. Ontario, with its 103 seats, became the crucial electoral battleground.

Liberal Troubles

A long list of costly administrative failures and mismanagement of public monies provoked strong criticism of the Liberal government. The auditor general drew attention to billions of dollars of corporate taxes that went unrecovered, to questionable grants made by the Department of Human Resources, and to a firearms-registry program whose estimated $100 million cost climbed to $1 billion. In addition, the government and even the prime minister were faulted for questionable ethics and political patronage. Even though the Liberals claimed to be the only "national" party, their fortunes disappeared long ago in western Canada and they could stage no significant comeback in Quebec. By the early 2000s, a majority of the population was telling pollsters that the Liberals were "arrogant and corrupt."

Still, voters proved ready to pardon Liberal faults. Chrétien appealed to many English Canadians for his uncompromising stand in regard to Quebec sovereignty. A prosperous economy helped the party retain power. But the Liberal government could also boast of having finally brought order to government finances, certainly no mean feat after the economic records of Trudeau and Mulroney. Thanks to spending cuts and especially to increased revenues from high taxation rates and economic growth, the federal budget finally registered a surplus in 1998. Additional surpluses enabled Ottawa to reduce income taxes, and to begin to pay down accumulated debt, which had now reached $580 billion.

The Harper Governments

Chrétien's final months in power, as well as Paul Martin's brief minority Liberal government, were tarnished by the so-called "sponsorship scandal" (see Chapter 16). Daily revelations at a commission of inquiry both titillated and shocked observers. Although Martin denied knowledge of government corruption, voters, particularly in Quebec, were not inclined to pardon. Nor were conservative voters divided as they had been in previous elections. To make matters worse for the Liberals, the party broke with its tradition of maintaining a united front and seamlessly passing on the baton of leadership. A bitter feud between Chrétien and Martin revealed deep fissures within the party that would simmer for years to come.

A Reunited Right

While the Liberals were dividing, the Conservatives were reuniting. In 2003 the Progressive Conservative Party agreed to merge with Stephen Harper's Canadian Alliance to form a new Conservative Party. Harper's major challenge was to moderate conservative rhetoric and positions. As one biographer noted, Harper "has never been interested in implementing wrenching changes if it means doing lasting damage to Canadian conservatism's election chances."[3] In particular, the Conservative leader sought to appeal to voters in Ontario and even in Quebec, where the collapse of Liberal support offered new opportunities.

2004 Election

In the election of 2004, the Liberals under Paul Martin were reduced to a minority government with 135 seats and 37 percent of the vote. Harper's Conservatives won 99 seats while the Bloc won 54 seats and the NDP, now under Jack Layton, won 19. The result indicated the beginning of an era of minority governments. With the Conservatives reunited, the Liberals and NDP splitting the centre–left vote, and the Bloc holding strong in Quebec, there was little chance of any party winning a majority. It also meant that Canadians would face frequent elections.

2006 Election

In the campaign of 2006, Stephen Harper played to voters' anger at Liberal corruption, adopted a conciliatory stance in Quebec, and made just a few specific promises such as reducing the sales tax, providing money for child care, and adopting tougher laws against gun and gang violence in Canadian cities. He won the election and formed a minority government with 124 seats. The Martin Liberals won 103 seats, while the Bloc won 51 and the NDP, 29.

Seeking Consensus

Hoping to obtain a majority in the next election, Prime Minister Harper attempted to attract voters in populous central Canada without losing his base of support in the western provinces. He promised to redress the "fiscal imbalance" that, in the opinion of many provinces, was evidenced by huge federal surpluses and tight provincial budgets. In the federal budget of 2007, the government announced substantial spending increases, with more money for the equalization grants that enable poorer provinces to provide services comparable to those offered by richer provinces. These grants pleased Quebec, a major recipient of equalization, but displeased certain other recipient provinces, such as Nova Scotia and Newfoundland and Labrador, as well as Saskatchewan, which complained that Ottawa would not allow the province to keep all of its resource revenues without losing equalization.

Harper devoted more money to health, education, and welfare, to be granted on a per capita basis, and announced new spending for public transit, notably in Toronto. Moreover, the prime minister saw no urgent need to act to ensure a substantial reduction of climate-changing greenhouse gases; his reticence in this regard pleased the oil-producing provinces of Alberta and Saskatchewan.

Large budget surpluses enabled Harper to continue to pay down the national debt, with ensuing savings on interest payments. In addition, instead of reducing taxes for all taxpayers, he targeted in particular retirees and middle-income families in suburban Canada, groups often viewed as socially conservative. The Conservative Party made inroads among Asian Canadians, particularly the East Indian and Chinese communities, on the basis of its socially conservative platform. The Conservatives sought to build new strength in populous Quebec without producing a backlash in the rest of Canada. In 2006, Harper had Parliament adopt a resolution moving "That this House recognize that the Québécois form a nation within a united Canada."

The Harper government also reached out to First Nations. In November 2005, the Liberal government of Paul Martin signed an agreement-in-principle with the Assembly of First Nations to end 15,000 individual lawsuits of former residential school students and 21 class-action suits. The Conservative government subsequently approved the agreement to have former students obtain what has been termed a "common experience payment" of $10,000, in addition to $3000 for every year they attended the institutions. The estimated cost of the agreement was at least $1.9 billion. Further money was set aside to address claims of physical and sexual abuse.

In June 2008, Prime Minister Harper offered a formal apology to residential school survivors, when he addressed a packed House of Commons and uttered the historic words "We are sorry." In its commitment to right the wrongs of the residential schools system, the federal government committed $60 million to launch a truth and reconciliation commission on Indian residential schools to raise awareness and to help reveal the historical record. It travelled across Canada to hear and document stories from former pupils and teachers.

Meanwhile the Liberals chose a new leader, Stéphane Dion, a Quebecker who had assisted Jean Chrétien during his battle against Quebec separatism and who was known as a strong federalist. Harper's admission of the existence of a fiscal imbalance between Ottawa and the provinces, in contrast to the Liberals' refusal to do so, pleased Quebec. Harper hoped, as Mulroney before him, to attract so-called "soft nationalists" in Quebec, those who rejected both the federalist Liberals and the Bloc Québécois.

2008 Election

The Conservative efforts to make a breakthrough in Quebec failed in the election of 2008. Even though the election was a disaster for the Liberals under Stéphane Dion, Prime Minister Harper blundered when he made an offhand comment about government cuts to cultural programs, already a sensitive topic in Quebec. The result was another Conservative minority government, with Harper increasing his seats by 19. In the election aftermath that saw the Liberals lose 26 seats, Dion was replaced as Liberal leader by Michael Ignatieff, a Harvard academic whose father, George Ignatieff, had served as Canada's ambassador to NATO and the UN. The Bloc maintained support in Quebec, while the NDP gained an additional 8 seats. The environmentalist Green Party under Elizabeth May emerged onto the electoral scene. While the Greens failed to win a seat in Parliament, they won 7 percent of the vote and campaigned successfully to win a place in the all-important televised leaders' debates.

The global economic meltdown occurred just prior to the election. The Harper minority government spent the next two years focusing on the question of the economy and congratulating themselves for keeping Canada out of the worst of the disaster. A massive "stimulus package" was introduced to avoid recession. The opposition parties, for their part, refused to defeat the government based on their own fears of another election and opinion polls that indicated a likely Conservative majority. In the meantime, the Harper government was beset with scandals, corruption charges, and an increasing sentiment that it had little respect for democracy or parliamentary tradition.

2011 and 2015 Elections

The Canadian electorate grew tired of minority governments, and Stephen Harper's Conservatives finally won a majority in the election of 2011 with 163 seats. The Liberals under Michael Ignatieff suffered a crushing defeat, winning only 34 seats, the lowest number in party history. The NDP under Jack Layton, on the other hand, won the largest number of seats in its history with 103 seats and status as official opposition. The "orange wave" swept across Quebec where the party won 59 of 75 constituencies. The Bloc Québécois under Gilles Duceppe lost official party status with only 4 seats, while the Green Party won its first seat under Elizabeth May.

The election results indicated that Canadians were prepared to give the Conservatives a chance to fulfill their mandate. The result was significant changes to Canada's political culture. Despite its mantra to "clean up Ottawa," Harper's Conservatives ushered in a new era of corruption and scandals. And despite its mantras of grassroots democracy and accountability, Harper maintained power in his own hands and increased the influence of the prime minister's office. The prime minister refused to scrum regularly with the press and kept a tight rein on his cabinet ministers.

The government's message became highly controlled. Question period in Parliament was dominated by highly scripted questions and answers. Now armed with a majority, the Harper

Conservatives introduced vast amounts of legislation in "omnibus bills" to avoid debate on individual measures. Harper brought an end to meetings between the prime minister and the provincial premiers. Scientists working for government agencies complained that even they were censured. The government found itself at odds with the Supreme Court, losing a remarkable number of court decisions. These years were also marked by scandals in the Senate. By the federal election of 2015, all parties were calling for serious reform if not abolition of what most considered an outdated and unnecessary institution.

Harper took a hard-line approach to Canada's place on the world stage. Claiming that the nation's traditional "soft power" approach had failed, Canada redefined itself during the Conservative era and sent combat missions into Afghanistan and Syria. Canada backed Israel fully on dealings with the Palestinians and became a closer ally than even the United States. As Russian aggression increased in hot spots such as Ukraine, Harper's strong rhetoric against the regime of Vladimir Putin ramped up. The Conservative government regularly criticized the United Nations and reduced its aid programs; the UN responded by criticizing Canada's human rights record in dealing with its Indigenous peoples and with refugees.

The economy served as Harper's main ally. Polls consistently indicated that despite other issues, Canadians trusted the Conservatives with the handling of economic issues in uncertain times. Despite the global economic disaster of 2008, Canada's economy continued to perform well. The oil industry in particular kept Canada's economy buoyant and the Conservatives touted its record on reducing taxes and balancing budgets. By 2014, however, oil prices (and government revenues) fell dramatically.

When Stephen Harper called an election for October 2015, polls indicated a tight race. But the winds of change were blowing and Canadians were tired of divisive politics. The Liberals under Justin Trudeau came from third place and won a majority government with 184 seats. The Conservatives won 99 seats, while the NDP under Thomas Mulcair was sent back to third-party status with 44 seats. The Bloc Québécois won 10 seats, while the Green Party held onto its one seat.

Liberal Member of Parliament Justin Trudeau, after winning a charity boxing match in Ottawa against Conservative Senator Patrick Brazeau in March 2012. Three years later, Trudeau became prime minister.

Source: Jake Wright/The Canadian Press.

Canadian–American Relations

In the 1990s and early 2000s, Canada's trade links with the United States increased. Exports increased substantially—86 percent of Canada's exports went to the United States in 2000, stimulated by free trade and a depreciating Canadian dollar that, by 2002, fell to a mere US62 cents. Huge quantities of Albertan oil and gas flowed south. Several provinces exported electricity. The automotive industry in southern Ontario sent most of its production south. Foreign ownership increased, and even business leaders expressed concern about the loss of head-office jobs to the United States.

Despite free trade, some sectors of Canada's economy were injured by American protectionist measures that limited imports. In 2002, for the fourth time since 1982, the United States imposed punitive anti-dumping and anti-subsidy duties on softwood lumber imports from Canada. Although Ottawa won virtually all the decisions rendered by NAFTA's dispute settlement body on the issue, Washington simply ignored the rulings. In a settlement reached in 2006, the United States agreed to return most, but not all, of the duties it had collected illegally since 2002. Canada promised to cap lumber exports and to impose export taxes in certain cases. With considerable reticence, Canada's forestry industry accepted the agreement.

In spite of such disagreements, most Canadians supported trade liberalization. But critics contended that Canada had become dangerously dependent on the United States and had lost control over its own resources. Indeed, when British Columbia put a moratorium on bulk water exports in 1999, the California firm that wanted to import fresh water by tanker sued the federal government for $10 billion under NAFTA's investment provisions. Trade treaties with the United States signified that "the provincial and federal governments are handcuffed in all the policy fields of concern to U.S. corporate interests."[4] Mel Hurtig, a tireless advocate of an independent Canada, entitled a new book *The Vanishing Country*. But the emotion caused by the free trade issue dissipated in the era of globalization.

Globalization

The issue of globalization, however, met with vocal and at times violent criticism from around the world. Critics argued that globalization signified an era of global capitalism propelled by technological innovation. In their view, governments abdicated control to market forces through privatization, deregulation, and expenditure reduction. Multinational corporations now dwarfed many national governments in size. Increased global competition risked favouring reduced standards, resulting in increased poverty, diminished government services, weaker labour laws, swamped local cultures, and fewer environmental controls. Globalization, critics argued, ignored the real needs of citizens.

Canadian nongovernmental organizations (NGOs) played an important role in opposing globalization, often at international conferences where world trade and investment issues were discussed. These themes were given wide publicity in the protests and teach-ins held during the Free Trade Area of the Americas (FTAA) summit in Quebec City in April 2001. Police cordoned off a large part of the old city with a high security steel-and-concrete fence, and used tear gas and plastic bullets to disperse demonstrators. Mass protests became commonplace at international meetings of political leaders that symbolized the new global age. Meetings of the G8 and G20 nations, in particular, were targeted by protesters. When the two organizations met in Muskoka and Toronto in the summer of 2010, the costs for hosting the conference skyrocketed due to security concerns over the protests but also the threat of terrorist attacks.

Protesters at the G20 summit in Toronto, 2010, being "kettled"— encircled and detained—by police. Bystanders and members of the media were among the thousand people arrested at the summit, making this the largest mass arrest in Canadian history.

Source: THE CANADIAN PRESS/Chris Young.

Terrorism

On September 11, 2001, members of the Islamic terrorist group al Qaeda hijacked commercial airplanes and flew them into the twin towers of the World Trade Center in New York and the Pentagon in Washington, D.C.; a fourth airplane crashed in Pennsylvania. These attacks on the United States resulted in the deaths of some 3000 people including 25 Canadians, and had profound effects on Canada. When American media figures and politicians portrayed Canadian border security as lax, Ottawa felt a need to prove otherwise in order to protect jobs and investment. The federal government also wanted to demonstrate that Canada was standing strong alongside its American ally. This position was further strengthened when the Harper Conservatives came to power. The government's response was far-reaching and multifaceted. It improved aviation and airport security, and invested heavily in increased border security. It announced more spending on police and intelligence agencies, and adopted an antiterrorism bill that gave new powers of investigation and detention to law-enforcement authorities.

In 2002, while returning to Canada after visiting his family in Tunisia, Maher Arar was detained on suspicion of terrorism in the United States. He was deported to Syria, where he was tortured. A Canadian government commission of inquiry eventually cleared Arar of any wrongdoing. He has still to be exonerated in the United States, where his name remains on a terrorist watch list.

Source: REUTERS/Francois Lenoir.

Civil libertarians decried certain of its provisions, such as preventive detention and compulsive testimony during investigative hearings. These provisions were never used and the Conservatives failed to obtain Liberal support to renew them in 2007; they then accused the Liberals of being "soft on terrorism." In a related issue, the Supreme Court held that so-called security certificates, by which immigrants suspected of being involved in terrorist activities might be imprisoned indefinitely without trial while not being informed of the case against them, were unconstitutional. Critics asserted that the country's security laws were in need of wholesale revision to ensure that Canada could face eventual terrorist threats while still protecting civil liberties.

In one highly publicized case that showed how fears of terrorism might erode citizens' basic rights, Maher Arar, a Canadian born in Syria, was detained by American authorities while changing planes in New York in 2002. Instead of being sent to Canada (he was travelling on a Canadian passport), he was forcibly deported to Syria, where he was tortured and imprisoned in a tiny cell for almost a year. To justify their actions, American authorities invoked intelligence reports, later shown to be inaccurate, received from the RCMP. Canadian diplomats in Syria relayed the substance of Arar's purported confessions to Ottawa but made no reference to the fact that torture might be occurring. After Arar's return to Canada, some police and government officials attempted to smear Arar's reputation by leaking false information to the media. The Martin government then set up a public inquiry that absolved Arar of suspicion of any involvement in terrorist activities. The RCMP commissioner resigned in the face of contradictions in his own testimony, Arar was awarded compensation for his ordeal, and Prime Minister Stephen Harper issued an official apology on behalf of the Canadian government. For its part, the United States refused to admit any wrongdoing and kept Arar's name on a terrorist watch list.

In another high-profile case, the Harper government took a hard-line position against a 15-year-old Canadian by the name of Omar Khadr. The youth was accused of throwing a grenade in 2002 that killed an American soldier while defending a compound in Afghanistan. Khadr was seriously wounded in the American attack. He was imprisoned in American military prison in Guantanamo Bay, Cuba. Under torture, Khadr confessed to the crime, hoping he would be returned to Canada.

Despite Khadr being a minor and what critics called a "child-soldier," and despite the questionable legal processes that kept him detained without a trial, American and Canadian authorities colluded to keep the youth in Guantanamo Bay, claiming he was an enemy combatant and a murderer. Finally, in September 2012, despite the protestations of the Harper government, Khadr was repatriated to serve the rest of his sentence in Canada. He was released on bail in 2015.

Defence

Canadians continued to view peacekeeping as one of their country's core values. In 1991, Canada contributed fully 10 percent of peacekeeping troops to United Nations missions. Its armed forces possessed important expertise in peacekeeping. By the 2000s, this image was tarnished, as few Canadian peacekeepers remained. Canada shifted from a peacekeeper to a military belligerent. In 2006, the Conservative government announced that huge amounts of money would be spent to upgrade military equipment and increase the armed forces' capabilities. For the government, Canada's new military objective was to be able to fight terrorist insurgencies militarily and show leadership in the world community. "You can't lead from the bleachers," declared Prime Minister Harper.

The United States and its allies responded to the 9/11 attacks by invading Iraq and Afghanistan. In 2002, Canada agreed to deploy 850 combat troops to Afghanistan to serve under American control. By 2010, some 2500 of Canada's soldiers were fighting in that country, mostly in the perilous southern region of Kandahar. The costly deployment was Canada's largest since the Korean War, and over 150 soldiers lost their lives. Then, after minimal debate in Parliament, the Conservative government extended the mission to 2011. To mollify public opinion, it gave the assurances that Canadian troops also played humanitarian roles, delivering aid supplies, medical treatment, and other services, and it committed money for development projects.

The United Nations authorized the invasion of Afghanistan after the terrorist attacks in 2001. However, when American and British troops invaded Iraq in March 2003 without UN authorization, the Chrétien government refused to participate. Most Canadians, especially in Quebec, approved of the decision. When "weapons of mass destruction," the purported reason for the invasion, were not discovered in Iraq, the Canadian decision was further justified. Later, the Liberal government of Paul Martin announced that Canada would not participate in the anti-ballistic missile defence system that the United States wanted to set up. Relations with the United States improved with the election of the Harper Conservatives and Canada again became a strong supporter of American foreign policy, even as the government of Republican President George Bush became increasingly unpopular worldwide.

The election of Democratic President Barack Obama in 2008 ushered in a new stage in relations between Canada and the United States. While the United States was pleased to have Canadian military support for a war in Iraq and Syria against the Islamic State (ISIS) in 2014, Obama refused to cooperate with the Harper government's pipeline strategy, including the Keystone Pipeline project set to move oil from Alberta to Texas.

Regional Imbalances

The early 1990s were difficult years for almost all of the provinces; most suffered an economic recession that had a negative impact on their budgets. Severe cuts in federal transfers only exacerbated financial problems. Balancing budgets involved painful choices and unhappy voters often reacted negatively to declining services and higher taxes.

By the mid-1990s, the economies of most regions improved. Oil brought significant new revenues to Newfoundland and Nova Scotia. Central Canada's manufacturing firms churned out goods for the voracious American market. In the West, the exploitation and sale of natural resources brought prosperity. Then, after 2002, the rising Canadian dollar, described as a "petro-dollar" by economists because it was pushed upward mainly by higher oil prices, curtailed manufacturing exports by making them more expensive. Rising energy costs also hurt industry, offset to some degree by significant increases in manufacturing productivity. Major American automobile makers closed plants in Ontario, but losses were compensated for by gains from new factories opened by Toyota and other foreign manufacturers. Forestry registered significant job losses as a result of a decrease in home construction in the United States. Western Canada, for its part, basked in prosperity, thanks to expensive oil.

The financial crisis of 2008 crippled the American economy as well as the American dollar. The Canadian dollar rose to par and beyond. While the Canadian economy (supported by the Canadian banking sector) held up relatively well, the battering of the automotive industry hit southern Ontario particularly hard. When oil prices dropped dramatically in 2015, and the U.S. economy began to recover, the Canadian dollar again began a precipitous decline. Alberta and Saskatchewan were particularly hard hit. The expected boon to Canadian manufacturing, however, failed to materialize.

Newfoundland and Labrador

On May 9, 1997, politicians and business people gathered at Bull Arm, northwest of St. John's, to christen the new Hibernia offshore oil production platform, built with government and private money at a cost of $6 billion. The festive occasion was marred by a demonstration by hundreds of unemployed fishery workers, protesting against Ottawa's compensation program for the collapsed cod fishery. The event seemed to dramatize the contrast between the Newfoundland of yesterday, a province of low incomes and a slowly dying fishing industry, and the Newfoundland of tomorrow, richer and more developed.

Employment in the fishing industry attained a peak in 1988 of 90,000 jobs. Then, in the early 1990s, cod stocks, hitherto thought to be inexhaustible, declined as a result of domestic, foreign, and environmental factors. Destruction of the cod fishery was cited in international scientific literature as a classic example of a mix of biological catastrophe and environmental mismanagement. Ironically, Canada had been the first industrialized nation to ratify the United Nations Convention on Biological Diversity negotiated at the Earth Summit in Rio de Janeiro in 1992. From 1992 until 1998, Ottawa imposed a moratorium on catches. In 2003, as fish stocks did not recover, the federal government moved toward total closure of the fisheries. During the moratorium, Ottawa launched a five-year, $1.9 billion compensation plan to eliminate jobs. It later injected another $730 million into a program to buy back fishing licences. Layoffs reached 30,000. Shrimp and crab provided a lucrative replacement for a certain number of fishers. Others emigrated. Many in distant outports had only welfare to fall back on.

The exploitation of natural resources represented a substantial share of Newfoundland's economy. Major hydroelectric projects were planned in Labrador. Another megaproject involved the development of huge nickel deposits at Voisey's Bay in northern Labrador. In 2002, as nickel prices increased, agreement was finally reached between Inco and the province, whereby Inco promised compensation and jobs for Native communities, and agreed to build a smelter at Argentia to process ore within the province. Production began in 2007. It was estimated that the mine and the smelter would increase the province's gross domestic product by fully 80 percent and create 2400 jobs. Such jobs were welcome, but Newfoundland needed far more to put its population to work and end out-migration. High prices for oil and gas brought prosperity to Newfoundland and Labrador's economy but the bubble burst as prices slid in 2015. Resource revenues, when added to federal equalization payments, made it possible for the province to spend more per person on services than Ontario, whose wealth excluded it from equalization grants.

Maritime Provinces

High levels of unemployment also afflicted Nova Scotia, Prince Edward Island, and New Brunswick. Still, there were bright spots. In Nova Scotia, the building of the $2 billion Sable Island natural gas pipeline gave a strong boost to the construction industry, and offshore exploration continued. Prince Edward Island's economy benefited from the construction of the 13-kilometre-long Confederation Bridge, opened in 1997. The "fixed link" across Northumberland Strait to New Brunswick stimulated tourism, a major industry on the island, and local agriculture now benefited from lower transportation costs. Job creation was also a priority for New Brunswick's Liberal government, headed by Frank McKenna. In the early 1990s, expansion in the food-processing industry, new power plants, and more service-related jobs in sectors such as telecommunications helped compensate for employment losses in the forest industry and in federal government services. The new millennium saw many young Maritimers relocating—or, remarkably, commuting—to work in the oil sands of northern Alberta. Thanks to interprovincial migration and the fact that only a small proportion of immigrants choose the Maritimes as a new home, the region barely maintained its population and continued to decline relative to Canada as a whole.

Ontario and the "Common Sense Revolution"

Ontario's economy boomed after the mid-1990s due to low interest rates; a dynamic U.S. economy that imported goods made in Ontario, especially automobiles; and a low Canadian dollar that favoured exports. Conservative premier Mike Harris reduced provincial income taxes substantially—the highlight of his "Common Sense Revolution." To finance lower tax rates, he imposed severe spending cuts in education, health services, and welfare, as well as substantial increases in university tuition costs. These measures caused considerable protest. Then the province took control of public education funding, partly removing financing from municipally levied residential property taxes. In return, new responsibilities were devolved on municipalities, including welfare, child care, care for the elderly, social housing, health programs, and public transit. The government also introduced a new market-value property tax assessment system, and it ordered the merger of Metro Toronto's six municipalities. These measures provoked some of the most acrimonious debates in the province's history.

Business praised the Harris government for restoring competitiveness by lowering taxes and for favouring globalization and increased economic integration with the United States. Ontario was no longer a mere province; it had become "a North American region state."[5] But critics of the "Common Sense Revolution" accused the Conservative government of favouring the growth of business, while exacerbating social inequalities within the province and of dealing a harsh blow to the quality of public services.

The West

Free trade boosted Manitoba's exports to the United States in the 1990s. New markets opened for industrial products. Large construction projects also produced economic stimulus. By early 1999, Manitoba enjoyed Canada's lowest unemployment rate. Over the course of the next decade, Manitoba steadily improved its economic position by further diversifying its economy.

Saskatchewan boasted impressive economic growth in the 1990s, assisted by strong oil and gas prices. Then, in the late 1990s, the elimination of grain subsidies, in addition to low prices for grain and oil seed, provoked a serious farm crisis in both Saskatchewan and Manitoba. After repeated calls for help from angry grain farmers, Ottawa finally agreed to give $400 million in assistance in 2000. Drought and competition from heavily subsidized American farmers brought further difficulties. While oil revenues in the province contributed to a booming economy over the next decade, the province was aided by rising prices for grains and two bygone industries—uranium and potash. Saskatchewan went from a "have not" to a "have" province, demonstrated by its growing population and the dramatic rise in real estate prices.

Alberta's abundant oil revenues gave it financial latitude that other provinces lacked. The government reduced income taxes to a flat rate of 10 percent for all workers and, in 2005, gave every Albertan a "prosperity dividend" of $400, reflective of soaring oil prices. It eliminated the provincial debt. It increased public spending substantially, even subsidizing homes and businesses to protect them from increasing electricity and natural gas costs. It granted large wage increases to health and education personnel, thereby putting heavy pressure on neighbouring, less-favoured provinces. It earmarked billions of dollars for new schools, hospitals, bridges, and roads. By 2002, Alberta was spending more per capita on publicly financed programs than any other province. And still the province registered huge budget surpluses. It also boasted virtually full employment.

Alberta's boom did have a downside. A serious shortage of skilled labour threatened energy projects and drove up prices. Entrepreneurs in low-wage businesses found it difficult to find and retain workers. Real-estate prices made even Vancouver look affordable. Calgary's vacancy rate for rental accommodation was Canada's lowest. Growth also put tremendous pressure on infrastructure as well as on the environment. Alberta's major vulnerability, however, was one that has often faced Canadian provinces: overreliance on one resource and industry. This weakness showed itself in 2015, when the price of oil collapsed and Alberta found itself in serious economic difficulty.

In British Columbia, massive inflows of investment, as well as large numbers of new immigrants, mainly from Asia, helped maintain an economic boom after 1990, while the rest of Canada slid into recession. Trade with Asia increased rapidly. Economic diversification continued, as new service-sector jobs, many related to tourism, more than compensated for the loss of employment in the primary sector.

The late 1990s saw British Columbia struggle. Lost markets due to Asia's faltering economy, punitive American trade policies, rising international competition, and low prices brought sawmill closures and job losses. Fortunately tourism, the film industry, business services, and high-technology industries continued to show promise. Then, after 2000, soaring trade with China, especially the sale of natural resources such as coal, minerals, and lumber, brought new prosperity to the province.

Population

Continued high levels of immigration explained most of Canada's population growth after 1990. The census of 2011 showed that Canadians numbered 33.4 million, double the number of fifty years earlier. Canada grew more rapidly than any of the G8 countries in the preceding decade. Fully 80 percent of Canadians now lived in urban centres, and nearly one-half of them in just three areas: Toronto and the Golden Horseshoe region of southern Ontario, Montreal, and Vancouver. Many rural areas and centres based on the exploitation of resources lost population, as local sawmills and other industries closed. Alberta's population increased rapidly, as workers from other provinces flooded into the province in search of high-paying job opportunities. Indeed, in the space of just ten years, the province grew by 20 percent. The cost of housing climbed dramatically, and serious labour shortages developed in many occupations.

Cities and Suburbs

By 2016, Canada had become one of the more urbanized nations in the world. Many people chose to live in the condominiums and high-rise apartment buildings that altered the landscape of the

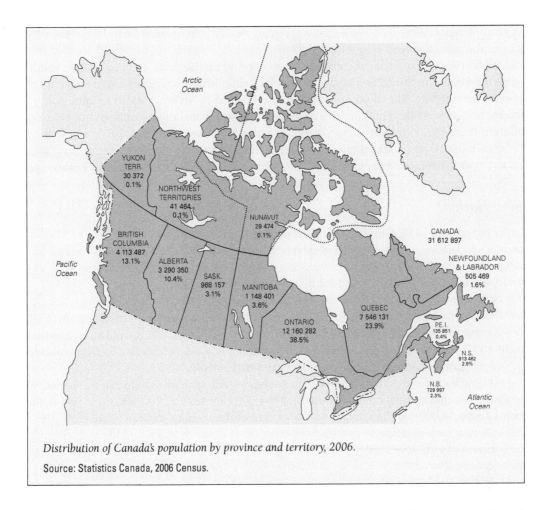

Distribution of Canada's population by province and territory, 2006.

Source: Statistics Canada, 2006 Census.

inner suburbs or formed part of huge redevelopment projects in once-derelict port and industrial districts, such as Vancouver's False Creek and Toronto's Harbourfront. But most preferred to inhabit the sprawling satellite communities that surrounded large cities. Costly infrastructures such as roads and sewer lines were necessary to serve these communities, and the use of automobiles was essential to commute to work or to find access to services. Most Canadians agreed that traffic was worsening. Vancouver's bridges and tunnels were famed for their spectacular traffic jams.

Toronto's expressways were often congested even at off-peak times, and the region had the country's longest average commute time. Dire predictions were made that by 2025, with 3 million new residents, drivers in the Greater Toronto Area would be facing total gridlock. The main arterial roads leading into Toronto were described as a "24-hour traffic jam." Mayors across Canada appealed for more government investment in buses, streetcars, subways, and light rail lines, but suburban sprawl made public transit inefficient and often prohibitively costly.

An Aging Population

While birth rates plummeted, advances in medicine and healthier lifestyles enabled Canadians to live longer. By 2015, female life expectancy reached 84 years, while that of males reached 80 years. Canadian society began to age rapidly. By 2009, the over-65s numbered 14 percent of the population—a figure well above the 8 percent criterion used by the United Nations to signify an aging population. Population changes by age group revealed Canada's greying future: while the number of preschoolers aged 0 to 4 decreased by 11 percent, seniors aged 70 to 79 increased by 27 percent, and older seniors by 41 percent.

In the 1990s, baby boomers embarked on a collective midlife crisis. In quest of their youth, some male boomers turned to Viagra and hair dye, while female boomers bought cosmetics to iron out the wrinkles. The "flower power" of the 1960s and 1970s now yielded to "grey power," forcing politicians to heed the concerns of seniors. Not surprisingly, more conservative attitudes asserted themselves. Education, emphasized so strongly in the 1960s and 1970s as the baby boomers passed through school now had to share much of the attention (and the funding) with issues of particular interest to older Canadians, among them pensions and especially health care.

First Nations

In the period after 1945, Canada's Aboriginal peoples—the Inuit, status Indians, and the Métis—became the fastest-growing population. The birth rate among the Inuit and status Indians was twice the national average. In 2011, Canada's native population topped 1.4 million, and was projected to rise to between 1.7 and 2.2 million within two decades.

Saskatchewan provided a good example of a growing Aboriginal population. Since the creation of the province in 1905, the number of First Nations people increased tenfold. In the 2001 census, just over 157,000 persons identified themselves as Aboriginal in the province, approximately 15.5 percent of Saskatchewan's total population. The First Nations and Métis population in Saskatchewan is considerably younger than the non-Aboriginal.

The number of individuals identifying themselves as Aboriginal has also increased. According to the 2011 census, there were approximately 851,000 Indians, 452,000 Métis and non-status Indians, and 59,000 Inuit in Canada, or 4.3 percent of the overall Canadian population. These were, in each case, significant increases from censuses of earlier decades, and likely represented both increases in the Aboriginal population and in the number of those who identify as Aboriginal.

Health Care

For most Canadians, universal publicly funded health care remains a defining feature that distinguishes Canada from the United States. It is also extremely expensive. In the early 1980s, increasing hospital user fees and extra billing by doctors led to fears that reasonable access to public health care was threatened. Canadians applauded the Canada Health Act, adopted by Parliament with all-party support in 1984, which penalized such practices. In the 1990s, in an effort to curtail sharply expanding health costs, some provinces sought to increase the role of the private sector. Private clinics offered tests to patients who agreed to pay cash.

Yet the health system was in a state of crisis. In the late 1990s and early 2000s, dissatisfaction mounted as waiting lists for diagnostic tests and surgery lengthened, hospital emergency wards were overwhelmed, drug costs soared, services were disinsured, and shortages of doctors and nurses developed. Improved public finances enabled governments to put more money into health care, but the crisis deepened. Asked by the federal government to report on the health-care system, Roy Romanow, former NDP premier of Saskatchewan, urged in 2002 that the public health-care system be retained, reinforced, and expanded. Private providers of medical services were to be excluded. Ottawa agreed to inject billions of dollars to fund primary care, home care, and catastrophic drug care, but sought to hold provinces accountable for how they spent federal monies. Later the Martin government folded all its payments into a Canada Health Transfer, and removed the requirement that provinces report.

By 2000, one-half of the adult population and one-third of children were considered by physicians as overweight. Sedentary and overweight Canadians increasingly fell victim to such chronic diseases as diabetes. By 2007, nearly one Canadian in ten, including large numbers of South Asian immigrants and Aboriginal Canadians, suffered from the illness.

An aging population also needed more care. Estimates indicated that the number of seniors would double within twenty-five years. Cancers occurred far more frequently among the elderly. Lung cancer in particular continued to kill large numbers of Canadians. The Canadian Cancer Society called for a national strategy to reduce prevalence of the disease, and asserted that half of all cancer deaths were preventable. Many elderly people fell ill with Alzheimer's disease, a degenerative disease of the brain that causes thinking and memory to become severely impaired. No cure existed, but nursing home care and medication for the half-million Canadians afflicted cost more than $5 billion each year.

Provincial health budgets increased, but chronic underfunding persisted. After a contaminated water supply made hundreds of residents sick and resulted in the deaths of seven persons in Walkerton, Ontario, in the summer of 2000, a judicial inquiry laid part of the responsibility on a lack of government controls due to spending cuts. Then, in 2003, an outbreak of the severe acute respiratory syndrome (SARS) virus in Toronto resulted in 44 deaths and had serious consequences for the city's and, indeed, Canada's economy. A commission of inquiry concluded that Ontario's public health system "lacked adequate resources, was professionally impoverished and was generally incapable of fulfilling its mandate." It was necessary to spend even more on health. The "swine flu" epidemic in 2009 again tested the system, but this time Canada was prepared.

Poverty

As unemployment grew during the recession of 1990, rising demand overwhelmed food banks in urban areas. The ranks of the homeless swelled. Increasingly, provincial spending cuts to welfare and social housing were seen as primary causes. In 1998, in a highly political move, the city of Toronto declared homelessness a national disaster and sought disaster-relief funds.

After 2000, economic growth and reduced unemployment contributed to the proportion of Canadians defined as poor, declining from nearly 16 percent in 1996 to 11 percent in 2004. Yet poverty remained very much present. Vancouver's Downtown East Side was plagued with Canada's highest rates of poverty and drug addiction. In Calgary, the numbers of homeless increased and shelters overflowed. The Calgary Homeless Foundation and other groups produced a ten-year plan to build affordable lodging and to provide services to treat persons dependent on drugs or who suffered from mental illness.

The situation on many First Nations reserves across Canada remains abysmal. Aboriginal youth face the highest rates of incarceration, drug and alcohol abuse, and suicide of any group in Canada. While life expectancy for registered Indians at birth continues to improve and to approach parity with the general Canadian population, in 2000 a gap of approximately 6.3 years remained between the registered Indian and Canadian population. Infant mortality rates among Aboriginal peoples stand at 1.5 times that of non-Aboriginals. The underfunding of child welfare services on reserves remains serious. This dilemma has contributed to a crisis to the point that, as of 2011, almost half of the 30,000 Canadian children in foster homes were Aboriginal. Indeed, there were more Aboriginals in foster homes than there had been students in residential schools at the high point of their existence in the mid-twentieth century. One out of ten Aboriginal children is in foster care, as against one in two hundred non-Aboriginal children.

Gays and Lesbians

Michael Stark, left, and Michael Leshner kiss after their wedding in Superior Court in Toronto on June 10, 2003. They became the first legally married same-sex couple in Canada.

Source: THE CANADIAN PRESS/Frank Gunn.

In the 1990s, gays and lesbians in Canada obtained legal protection from discrimination. In 1992 gays were allowed to serve openly in the military. Laws changed slowly, and opposition, particularly from conservative religious groups, was substantial. In 1999, a verdict of the Supreme Court of Canada compelled the last province, Alberta, to ban discrimination.

Gays and lesbians turned their attention to obtaining recognition for same-sex unions. In 1995 the Supreme Court of Canada ruled that the Charter of Rights and Freedoms prohibited discrimination against gays and lesbians. A series of court challenges established that gay couples possessed many of the rights and duties of married couples, and laws were rewritten to reflect this in such areas as spousal support, pension rights, adoption, and medical decision making. In 1997, British Columbia became the first province to amend laws to extend legal recognition to same-sex relationships.

Quebec extended full legal recognition to same-sex common-law unions in 2002, and a year later Ontario courts ruled that prohibiting gays and lesbians from marrying violated the equality provisions of the Charter of Rights and Freedoms. In 2005, the Liberal government passed Bill C-38, the Civil Marriage Act, changing the definition of marriage from a union between a man and a woman to one between two persons. This made Canada the fourth nation to officially sanction same-sex marriage. During the election campaign of 2006, the Conservative Party, most of whose candidates opposed same-sex marriage, promised to revisit the issue. When the Conservatives took power, they introduced a motion asking that the issue of same-sex marriage be reopened. But in a free vote, most MPs from all three opposition parties combined to defeat the motion, and the new definition of marriage prevailed.

Religious institutions were free to decide whether to perform marriage ceremonies for same-sex couples. The United Church of Canada authorized local congregations and clergy to choose whether to offer same-sex marriage services. The issue provoked heated debate within the Anglican Church, and the worldwide Anglican communion faced a schism over the question. Some liberal Jewish congregations also agreed to welcome same-sex unions. The Roman Catholic Church, Canada's largest Christian church, opposed the government's legislation.

Lesbian, gay, bisexual, and transgender (LGBT) political activism has centred most recently on support for youth and ensuring the rights of transgender Canada. Studies have shown that the Canadian public has become much more supportive of LGBT rights since the turn of the millennium.

Women and Gender Equality

As larger numbers of women took jobs outside the home, governments were called on to make day-care facilities more affordable and available. Quebec set up a system of publicly supported centres in which parents paid just $5 a day per child; the popular system proved costly for taxpayers, and waiting lists were long, although new places were added rapidly. Across Canada, there were far more families with preschool children than there were spaces in licensed day-care centres.

Pay Equity

The notion of equal pay for equal work, or pay equity, became the battleground of the 1990s, as women argued that they were generally paid less than men for jobs requiring similar skills, effort, responsibility, and educational levels, and entailing similar working conditions. Ottawa and some provinces instituted pay equity laws, but the NDP government of Premier Bob Rae in Ontario went further by forcing employers to compare the value of the work being done in their male- and female-dominated work categories and then to increase the wages of any women who, according to the results of the comparisons, were being underpaid. Reactions were predictable: the male-dominated business community expressed considerable hostility, while the 1 million members of the Equal Pay Coalition were disappointed that the measure did not cover casual workers and women working in small enterprises or in all-female establishments. Some provinces failed to bring in legislation to guarantee pay equity. The Supreme Court permitted the Newfoundland government to deny female public servants pay equity because of budgetary constraints.

The growing conservatism of the 1990s and early 2000s had implications for women and gender equality. In Ontario, for example, the Conservative government led by Mike Harris, which took office in 1995, repealed certain elements of the pay equity legislation adopted by the previous NDP government. Women argued that government budget cuts in health, welfare, and poverty-relief programs hit them disproportionately. The armed forces' plans to recruit, train, and keep a large percentage of women in their ranks failed. In the House of Commons, only 20 percent of members elected in 2006 were women. In other sectors, there was progress. Sixty percent of university students were women, and women outnumbered men in all undergraduate fields except engineering and math.

Women in Canada 2000, a report prepared by Statistics Canada, showed that the gap between higher men's pay and lower women's pay decreased substantially between 1985 and 1995. By 2000, women occupied about one-third of managerial positions, usually on lower rungs, but only 10 percent of corporate directors were women. Half of the doctors and dentists were women, and nearly half of the new lawyers and accountants. A gender-studies specialist commented, "Women have taken on men's roles, but men have not taken on to the same degree the roles of women." Not surprisingly, women experienced increased levels of stress and even depression as they attempted to hold down jobs while raising families.

Women play a much more prominent role in today's First Nations communities. Of the 633 communities represented by the Assembly of First Nations, over a hundred are led by female Aboriginal chiefs. Half a century ago there was only one woman chief in Canada; now 17 percent are female. Women are also very prominent in their communities as band councillors. In the non-political sector, many women work as teachers and social workers in their communities. One of the major issues facing First Nations women is violence. Activists had long condemned the Canadian police and legal systems for their inaction on the murder and disappearance of Aboriginal women, and in 2014 the RCMP released a report on 1200 Aboriginal women murdered or missing since 1980. In 2015, the Liberal government of Justin Trudeau announced the intention to set up a federal inquiry to examine the issue.

Challenges for Labour

The 1990s proved difficult for unionized workers. The elimination of positions by governments at all levels, as they tried to reduce expenditures and balance budgets, led to layoffs, wage freezes, and even wage cuts. In Ontario, Premier Mike Harris acted to reduce the number of public servants, hospital workers, and teachers. These cuts and others provoked "Days of Action" protests led by organized labour against "Mean Mike" and his policies. In Alberta, Ralph Klein, a former mayor of Calgary chosen as new Conservative Party leader and premier in 1992, instituted a policy of radical budget cuts to social spending and the civil service that produced a balanced budget by 1995.

Private-sector unions fared no better. Many high-paying manufacturing jobs disappeared as companies "rationalized" their operations, and union membership again declined. New contracts often imposed wage rollbacks, or pegged wages to profitability, or brought a reduced pay scale for new employees. The recession of the early 1990s undermined the bargaining power of unions and thus sharply reduced the number of work stoppages.

Recruitment again increased in the late 1990s, reversing a downward trend, due in part to an improving economy. By 2009, about one-third of Canadian workers were unionized. Quebec and Newfoundland at about 40 percent of workers were the most unionized provinces, Alberta and Ontario at about 25 percent of workers the least. In Ontario, many unionized jobs disappeared in the automobile industry, as General Motors and Ford announced plant closures, while non-unionized Toyota built new factories. Private-sector unions felt themselves under attack by the forces of globalization and cutthroat competition. Moreover most of these unions were still based in the United States and were often unresponsive to the needs of their Canadian membership. The "financial crisis" after 2008 again sent labour into a tailspin, particularly in southern Ontario where the automotive sector was severely hampered by the downturn in the United States and the collapse of the major automobile manufacturers.

Sports

Huge crowds cheered the Toronto Blue Jays on to their victories in the World Series in 1992 and 1993. From that summit, baseball in Canada went downhill. In Montreal, the Expos' hopes to reach the World Series evaporated as a strike ended the 1994 season prematurely. The team became a shadow of itself as, for financial reasons, it sold off its best players. Fans deserted, and the Expos finally moved to Washington, D.C., after the 2004 season. In 2015, the Blue Jays resurrected fans' hopes nationwide when they again made the playoffs, but they were defeated in the second round by the eventual World Series victors.

Haley Irwin (21) and Meghan Agosta (2) of Canada lie on the ice and celebrate with bubbly, beer, and a cigar following their team's 2–0 victory over the United States in women's hockey at the Vancouver 2010 Winter Olympics.

Source: Photo by Alex Livesey/Getty Images.

The Olympic Games created enthusiasm and fostered pride in Canadian athletes' prowess. Canada's performance in the summer games was uneven and occasionally even disappointing; in 2012, Canadian athletes won eighteen medals, but only one gold, the nation's lowest tally in almost forty years. However, Canada's performance in Winter Olympics has improved greatly in recent decades—particularly in women's sports, led by a hockey team that has won gold four successive times beginning in 2002. Overall, Canada climbed from winning the thirteenth-most medals of any country when Calgary hosted in 1998 to the fifth most when Turin, Italy, hosted in 2006.

As a result, expectations for Canadian athletes were exceptionally high when the Winter Olympic Games were held in Vancouver in 2010. Organizers vowed to "own the podium"—and athletes delivered, winning twenty-six medals, the most of any country. The highlight, as usual, was the performance of the nation's hockey teams. Both won gold but the nail-biting finish of the men's team in beating the Americans in overtime was undoubtedly the climax. It was the most-watched television broadcast in Canadian history, with three-quarters of the country witnessing superstar Sidney Crosby score the winning goal.

The result was a national euphoria similar to that caused by Paul Henderson's winning goal in 1972. Canada did almost as well at the Winter Olympics in Sochi, Russia, in 2014, ranking third among nations in terms of medals. Once again, both men's and women's hockey teams won gold.

Culture

Film

Canadian filmmakers have produced critically acclaimed and popular work in recent decades. James Cameron (*Titanic*), Paul Haggis (*Crash*), David Cronenberg (another *Crash*), Deepa Mehta (the *Elements* trilogy "Fire," "Earth," and "Water"), Atom Egoyan (*The Sweet Hereafter*), Sarah Polley (*Stories We Tell*), and Guy Maddin (*My Winnipeg*) are examples of Canadian directors who have thrived on the international stage. But English-language Canadian films captured barely 1 percent of Canadian box office receipts. The great majority of movies watched in Canadian theatres have been American-made. And most movies made in Canada were not Canadian movies at all: American major studios filmed many productions in Vancouver, Toronto, and Montreal, attracted by generous federal and provincial tax credits.

Canada was nominated for Best Foreign Language film at the Academy Awards three years in a row in the early 2010s—for *Incendies*, *Monsieur Lazhar*, and then *War Witch*—and it is telling that all three are Quebec films. Filmmakers in that province developed a highly distinctive voice and a successful movie-making industry to sustain them. The popularity of French-language films in Quebec means that the top-grossing Canadian films often hail from that province. Other than Oscar nominations, perhaps the greatest evidence of the accomplishment of Quebec cinema is that a number of its directors, such as Jean-Marc Vallée (*C.R.A.Z.Y.* and *Wild*) and Denis Villeneuve (*Incendies* and *Sicario*), have transitioned successfully to Hollywood.

Popular Music

Canadian Radio-television and Telecommunications Commission (CRTC) rules required 35 percent "CanCon"—Canadian content—on radio stations by the end of the 1990s. Perhaps this helped Alanis Morissette (*Jagged Little Pill*), Céline Dion (*The Colour of My Love*), Shania Twain (*The Woman in Me*), and Sarah McLachlan (*Fumbling Towards Ecstasy*) on the road to becoming four of music's biggest performers in that decade, or perhaps they would have succeeded on talent regardless. What was abundantly clear by the twenty-first century was that Canadian popular music was rarely Canadian in either style or subject matter. Put pessimistically, that meant it was not recognizably Canadian; put optimistically, that meant it was global in spirit and belonged everywhere. Singers from Michael Bublé (*It's Time*) to Drake (*Take Care*) achieved international stardom. Another artist, K'Naan, of Somali-Canadian descent, achieved worldwide acclaim for his 2010 release *Wavin' Flag*, which was chosen as the official anthem of the 2010 FIFA World Cup of Soccer. The meteoric rise of pop star Justin Bieber, from Stratford, Ontario, serves as another example of a highly successful Canadian artist.

Singer Justin Bieber performs on NBC's Today show at Rockefeller Plaza in New York City in 2015.

Source: Debby Wong/Shutterstock.com.

Literature

In recent decades, an increasing number of Canadian authors have found success internationally as well as nationally. In 2002, three of the finalists for the prestigious Booker Prize were Canadians Yann Martel (*Life of Pi*), Carol Shields (*Unless*), and Rohinton Mistry (*Family Matters*); Martel was awarded the prize. Margaret Atwood remained, book in and book out, one of the most respected writers on the planet, turning to speculative and science fiction with such novels as *Oryx and Crake* and *The Year of the Flood*. Some of the best and most important Canadian novels of recent memory—such as Joseph Boyden's *Through Black Spruce* and *The Orenda*, Lawrence Hill's *The Book of Negroes*, and Michael Crummey's *Galore*—have dealt with the nation's history, while other novelists, such as Mistry and Martel, do not necessarily write about Canada or Canadians at all. The high point for Canadian literature was Alice Munro's winning of the Nobel Prize for Literature in 2012.

The Environment

The chasm between Canadian attitudes toward the environment and Canada's actual environmental record grew wider in recent decades than ever before. On the one hand, membership in environmental groups steadily climbed; recycling became ubiquitous and alternative energy became less alternative; in federal elections roughly 5 percent of the electorate supported the Green Party, a party that cites ecological wisdom as a core value; and environmental groups had meaningful victories, such as managing logging at Clayoquot Sound, British Columbia. On the other hand, Canada's ecological footprint (the area of land and water needed to sustain a population), already one of the largest of any nation on the planet, continued to grow; and, with help from the Alberta oil sands, the country became one of the top global emitters of greenhouse gases.

At the core of this disconnect was that the Canadian way of life demanded a great many resources, and economic forces proved powerful detriments to political action. In the 1990s, provincial governments sought first to eliminate deficits and reduce taxes. They found it politically easier to cut environmental spending than health care. With lower budgets, governments often failed to apply their own environmental laws and to monitor compliance. The federal government, for example, was frequently accused of ignoring the Canadian Environmental Protection Act, which regulated toxic chemicals, and the Fisheries Act, which prohibited polluting oceans, rivers, and lakes. Although smog caused 5000 premature deaths every year, Ottawa's program for smog reduction, announced with great fanfare in 1990, remained a dead letter. Ultimately, the Harper governments muzzled federal scientists' ability to report their findings, to ensure the government line was toed and that Canadians were not informed about environmental matters.

COMMUNITY PORTRAIT

The "War in the Woods" at Clayoquot Sound

On May 5, 2000, Canadian political leaders met at Clayoquot Sound, on the west coast of Vancouver Island, to unveil a plaque designating this area of great natural beauty as a United Nations biosphere reserve. Henceforth, any logging in the area was to be carried out in an environmentally friendly manner that would ensure sustainable growth. Forestry specialists described the project as the most significant ecosystem management experiment in British Columbia's history, and perhaps Canada's.

Logging had been a major industry in British Columbia for over a century. After World War II, the provincial government awarded long-term licences to large companies, giving them the right to harvest timber. Modernized equipment and techniques such as caterpillar tractors and automatic grapples and yarders permitted increased production with fewer labourers. Harvest rates quadrupled between 1950 and 1980. Environmental values were of little concern: forests seemed inexhaustible. Priority went to short-term profit considerations.

Then, in the early 1980s, many people began to worry about the accelerating destruction of the earth's last remaining rainforests, both tropical and temperate. Environmentalists cited biologists who argued that old growth rainforests—forests with deep, multilayered canopies, standing dead trees, and centuries of accumulated deadfall on the ground—harboured an enormous diversity of species whose survival depended on preservation of their environment. Clearcut logging, the method preferred by the forest industry, could not be reconciled with biodiversity. Indeed, many clearcuts were so degraded with erosion and compacting that they remained permanently scarred.

Coastal British Columbia contained an important part of the world's last remaining temperate rainforests, but they were disappearing rapidly. In 1991 the federal government estimated that at current rates of logging, all substantial ancient forest on the Pacific coast would disappear within twenty years.

People who were convinced that British Columbia's forestry policies made it "the Brazil of the North" joined the forestry-focused environmental groups that sprang up. Among the groups interested in wilderness conservation were Greenpeace, the Sierra Club of Canada, the Western Canada Wilderness Committee, and the Canadian Parks and Wilderness Society. In the late 1980s and early 1990s, environmentalists actively promoted preservation. The campaign to save South Moresby on the Queen Charlotte Islands attracted nationwide attention, and in 1987, Ottawa and the provincial government signed an agreement to create a national park in the region.

Clayoquot, an area of some 260,000 hectares, was the last major unexploited watershed on Vancouver Island. In 1993, the provincial government, then MacMillan Bloedel's largest shareholder, gave the forestry giant permission to clearcut up to 70 percent of the area's rainforest. Angry environmentalists formed "Friends of Clayoquot Sound," which in the summer of 1993, waged a "war in the woods," a nonviolent campaign of civil disobedience to protest against the government's action and attract international attention. They set up camp in the Black Hole clearcut, an area logged in the 1970s, replanted unsuccessfully four times, and now badly eroded. Fearing that concessions would encourage environmentalists to seek to protect other areas from logging, MacMillan Bloedel obtained an injunction banning demonstrations on company work sites. The government had 900 protestors arrested at the blockades, charged with criminal contempt of court for defying the injunction, and jailed or fined. Friends of Clayoquot continued their campaign by targeting industrial consumers of British Columbia timber in Europe and threatening boycotts of their products if they did not cease their purchases. This tactic ensured that the battle at Clayoquot achieved international notoriety.

In October 1993, the British Columbia government appointed a Scientific Panel for Sustainable Forest Practices in Clayoquot Sound. It was composed of members of the region's First Nation, the Nuu-chah-nulth, and a team of scientists and technicians. The panel recommended an ecosystem approach that emphasized the maintenance of biological diversity, watershed integrity, and the protection of cultural, scenic, and recreational values. Clearcutting as a method of harvest was to be replaced by a method called "variable-retention," an alternative silvicultural system whereby trees and patches of forest were retained to protect a variety of values and ecosystem components. In 1995, the government announced that all of the panel's recommendations would be implemented. Premier Mike Harcourt wanted to make Clayoquot a showcase for progressive forest practices. MacMillan Bloedel, the largest company active in the area, suspended its clearcutting operations, and negotiated with First Nations and environmentalists to find a mutually acceptable approach to some continued logging.

After the Clayoquot campaign, environmentalists continued to work for preservation elsewhere. In 1994, the government set out a new Forest Practices Code that reduced the maximum size of clearcuts, mandated replanting of harvested areas, and tightened regulations and enforcement. British Columbia also moved to place 13 percent of its land base in protected areas, in recognition of its responsibilities in regard to the United Nations Convention on Biological Diversity, which Canada signed in 1992. Environmental critics asserted, however, that protected areas were often "rock and ice" where industry had no interest,

and that old-growth forests were underrepresented. Nor were there any guarantees that a future, more business-oriented government might not roll back environmental protection, or fail to monitor and enforce forest management rules. Indeed the Suzuki Foundation reported in 2003 that, on the basis of a survey of sites logged in 2001 and 2002, it was "business as usual," clearcutting being the method used.

The initiatives of the environmental movement generated substantial opposition. Plans for protecting areas of Vancouver Island led to massive demonstrations by loggers and their supporters in 1994. Compromise between preservationist and economic imperatives seemed impossible. The logging industry accused environmentalists of increasing its costs and diminishing its profits. Forestry workers argued that restrictions on logging would lead to job losses. Some rural communities feared for their very existence. At times, Native peoples and environmentalists differed in their attitudes toward nature. And governments wanted the attendant tax revenues and stumpage fees that the lumber industry provided.

Yet issues were undoubtedly more complex than they first appeared. Was it possible to assign a value in dollars to the maintenance of biodiversity? What would happen to jobs once all old-growth stands were cut? Was reforestation of areas already harvested not a wiser option to assure a sustainable forest industry? Could not other industries such as tourism and recreation offer new potential, thanks to wilderness preservation? The environmental movement's activities prompted all of those interested in British Columbia's forests, and in forests elsewhere in Canada, to ask these questions, and to seek answers.

A clearcut in the Temagami region in northeastern Ontario. The area was a focal point of environmental protests at the end of the 1980s. Today almost 90 percent of lumber harvesting in Ontario is still done by clearcut.

Source: Courtesy Canadian Parks and Wilderness Society - Wildlands League.

Environmentalists worked in a variety of sectors to show that the survival of humanity depended on the health of the environment. They argued that economic growth should proceed only if environmental safeguards were sufficient to ensure its sustainability.

FURTHER READING

Benjamin Cashore, George Hoberg, Michael Howlett, Jeremy Rayner, Jeremy Wilson, *In Search of Sustainability: British Columbia Forest Policy in the 1990s* (Vancouver: UBC Press, 2001).

Michael Howlett, ed., *Canadian Forest Policy: Adapting to Change* (Toronto: University of Toronto Press, 2001).

Ron MacIsaac and Anne Champagne, eds., *Clayoquot Mass Trials: Defending the Rainforest* (Philadelphia and Gabriola Island, BC: New Society Publishers, 1994).

Richard A. Rajala, *Clearcutting the Pacific Rain Forest: Production, Science, and Regulation* (Vancouver: UBC Press, 1998).

Jeremy Wilson, *Talk and Log: Wilderness Politics in British Columbia, 1965–96* (Vancouver: UBC Press, 1998).

Protected Places and Wildlife

As urbanization, agriculture, and resource exploitation occupied an ever-larger portion of the earth's surface, increasing numbers of wildlife species and plants faced the threat of extinction. Calling for immediate action, scientists warned that humans' actions were leading to the disappearance of life forms at a rate that the world had not seen since the age of the dinosaurs. In 1992, Canada played a key role at the Earth Summit in Rio de Janeiro and signed a convention on biological diversity by which it agreed to take measures to protect threatened species and their habitats. Yet Parliament adopted a Species at Risk Act only in 2002, after a decade during which the number of species on the endangered list increased markedly. Four years later, wildlife conservation groups called on NAFTA to launch an investigation into what they saw as Canada's failure to enforce endangered species laws.

Ottawa and several provinces did take action to set aside and protect habitat necessary for the survival of ecosystems. Since 1990, Parks Canada has created ten new national parks, three national park reserves (parks pending settlement of Aboriginal land claims), and three national marine conservation areas. All of the new parks and reserves are in the northern areas of the provinces or territories, in part to help Parks Canada achieve its ambitious goal of establishing at least one park in each of Canada's thirty-nine "natural regions"—and in part because such places can be more straightforward to acquire and restrict from development than places in southern Canada. Arguably Parks Canada's most important action has been to declare the management of parks' ecological integrity as its first priority.

Provinces also moved to create new protected areas and take better care of existing ones. In 2006, for example, Ontario adopted new legislation to protect the ecological integrity of its 600 provincial parks and conservation reserves. In British Columbia, the provincial government together with environmental organizations, Aboriginal communities, and the forest industry reached an agreement that protected from major logging the Great Bear Rainforest, a huge area on the province's north and central coasts that is rich in wildlife and flora. Yet many natural regions, particularly in heavily urbanized southern Canada, still have few or no protected areas.

Pollution

Modern society, in producing more desirable things, also produces more undesirable things that make their way into the land, the water, and the air. Waste disposal remained a serious issue in modern Canada. Torontonians were warned that they risked being buried beneath their own garbage if Michigan, northern Ontario, or Quebec refused to take it.

In 2005, *Maclean's* published a report on sewage entitled "From Sea to Stinking Sea" in which it exposed Canada's lack of sewage treatment standards. The city of Victoria, for example, continued to dump raw sewage into the Juan de Fuca Strait. When studies showed that the lands around sewage outfalls had high levels of toxic chemicals that made them contaminated sites, the provincial government directed Victoria to come up with a plan to upgrade its sewage treatment levels. In nearby Vancouver, environmental groups and the fishing industry prosecuted the city for discharging high levels of toxic chemicals into local waters. That Montrealers were aghast in 2015 to learn of the city's plan to divert billions of litres of sewage directly into the St. Lawrence River indicates that cities continued to treat waterways as the ultimate sink for dispensing waste and that many Canadians remain unaware of that fact.

The Great Lakes/St. Lawrence River waterway faced special challenges. The fundamental one was the difficulty of creating and enforcing environmental standards across the two provinces and eight states that bordered the waterway. Even as huge sums of money were spent attempting to clean up the lakes, industrial pollutants continued pouring in. In 1995, the Sierra Legal Defense Fund used the Freedom of Information Act to uncover that the Ontario government was aware of thousands of water quality violations by industry; Ontario's response was to stop publishing the reports altogether.

Air pollution is an example of how an environmental issue can simultaneously improve and worsen. Acid rain, caused by the sulphur dioxide produced in the burning of fuel, was a source of dispute between Canada and the United States in the 1980s. Since then, it has been greatly reduced, thanks to three rounds of air quality agreements between the two nations. But with the number of automobiles on Canadian roads more than doubling over the past three decades, and consumers' preference for heavier sport-utility vehicles, minivans, and light trucks, even much more efficient engines could not prevent carbon dioxide emissions from growing. The atmosphere continued to be used for free waste disposal by industry—and by governments, whose coal- and gas-fired power plants were some of the nation's biggest polluters. In 2014, Ontario closed its coal-burning plants to reduce pollution.

Alberta oil sands extraction and production held the dubious honour of being one of the worst causes of land, air, *and* water pollution in Canada. When the global price of oil began rising around the turn of the century, the oil sands became commercially viable, and by 2008, 1 million barrels of crude oil were being produced every day. The riches this brought Alberta, and indeed Canada, contributed significantly to the nation's prosperity even in the wake of the 2008 global financial crisis. But because bitumen is trapped in solid deposits, the oil extraction process is much more land-, water-, and energy-intensive than traditional oil drilling. Huge supplies of natural gas are required in extracting it from massive open-pit mines. Converting the deposits requires water—approximately three barrels of water (often, freshwater from the Athabasca River) to produce one barrel of bitumen. The solid and liquid wastes from the production process must be contained; the solid ones drift away. The results have included the destruction of local forests, waterways, and wildlife; a sharp rise in air pollution (while national levels have otherwise dropped); tailings ponds so vast they could be seen from space; and an industry that singlehandedly contributed an estimated 5 percent of Canada's total carbon dioxide emissions. And that was before the oil was actually used. Calls for a moratorium that would enable industry and governments to deal with economic, social, and environmental stresses caused by the aggressive pace of oil sands development went unheeded. Only a plummeting global price for oil, like the one that happened in 2015, would curb production.

Climate Change

On the heels of the 1987 Montreal Protocol, the international treaty that led to the elimination of pollutants causing ozone depletion, the 1988 Toronto "Our Changing Atmosphere" international conference brought global warming to the global policy agenda. In 1990, the United Nations established the Intergovernmental Panel on Climate Change (IPCC), a scientific body that has since produced periodic reports detailing that global temperatures are rising because of the buildup in the atmosphere of greenhouse gases (gases that absorb and hold heat), and that human activities, and in particular the burning of fossil fuels, is a principal cause.

Canada, like other industrialized nations, has sought to determine how to balance environmental considerations against economic development. Economies run on available and relatively affordable fossil fuels—the economies of oil-, gas-, and coal-producing nations such as Canada more than any. Nevertheless, when nations met in Japan in 1997, Canada signed the Kyoto Protocol, committing to a 6 percent reduction of its 1990 level of greenhouse gas emissions by 2012. The Chretien government that signed the accord ratified it in Parliament in 2002.

Canada implemented some measures to reduce greenhouse gas emissions, such as offering energy efficiency subsidies to homeowners. But otherwise Canada did little to meet even Kyoto's modest targets. One reason is that the nation's size means different regions have different energy regimes, making energy a potentially divisive regional issue. For example, a province such as Quebec, blessed with abundant sources of hydroelectricity, has been more open to reducing greenhouse gas emissions

Firefighters battle to control the fire that engulfed railway cars carrying crude oil when they derailed at Lac-Mégantic, Quebec, in July 2013. Forty-seven people died, making this the worst rail disaster since Confederation.

Source: THE CANADIAN PRESS/Paul Chiasson.

A protester on Parliament Hill demonstrates her opposition to oil sands extraction by being drenched in "oil" (actually, molasses) in September 2010.

Source: THE CANADIAN PRESS/Adrian Wyld.

than have oil-producing provinces such as Alberta. When the Harper government was elected to office in 2006, it dropped all pretence that Canada would meet its Kyoto targets, and opposed the principle that it should do so when developing nations such as China and India were exempt. In 2011, Canada withdrew from Kyoto altogether. Rather than Canada's greenhouse gas emissions falling 6 percent by 2012, they rose 24 percent, the most of any industrialized nation.

SUMMARY

Since 1867, Canada has evolved from an intermediate-sized country of 3.5 million people to a huge one of almost 35 million. The ethnic and cultural diversity of the nation has increased dramatically, with great waves of immigration in the early 1900s, after 1945, and since the 1990s. Material living conditions have improved greatly, but the gap between rich and poor has increased, too. Canadians have also come to realize that much of our wealth and security results from the fact that our relatively small population oversees a vast array of globally valued resources; we have developed a greater awareness of environmental degradation, and sustainability has become a new byword. The role of the state has increased greatly, especially after 1930, to the point that governments have come to play a role in virtually every aspect of life.

Although Canada has undergone immense change, many of the basic themes of the country's early history remain operative. In 1867, British and French were the two dominant ethnic groups, and First Nations made up close to 10 percent of the population. The easternmost provinces were small in population and power, Quebec was still defining its position within Confederation, Ontario was the largest and most populous province, and the West—and the idea of the West—beckoned.

Since then, not much has changed—and, of course, everything has. Canada in 1867 was a nation of regions, and despite modern transportation and the communications revolution, it remains so today—indeed, to such an extent that doubts have often abounded about the survival of existing political arrangements. By the late nineteenth century, federal–provincial affairs had become acrimonious; more than a century later, conflict continues to pervade intergovernmental contacts. French–English relations were the source of bitter controversy in the nineteenth century; intercultural relations continued to generate passionate debate in the twentieth. Relations with Indigenous peoples were an important preoccupation in the nineteenth century as European settlement expanded westward; during the second half of the twentieth century and into the twenty-first, Aboriginal rights have become a complex but ever-present public policy question. Canada was a nation of immigrants at its birth and is still one now, more than ever.

In 1867, British and American influences weighed heavily on the new nation; today, the impact of the United States on Canada—culturally, politically, and economically—is in many ways more evident. Finally, despite the coming of the welfare state, flagrant social inequalities still distinguish Canadians from one another, much as they did in the past. Constant change, but equally apparent continuity: these two themes reflect the past as Canada moves beyond a century and a half of existence as a nation.

NOTES

1. David Cameron and Richard Simeon, "Ontario in Confederation: The Not-So-Friendly Giant," in Graham White, *The Government and Politics of Ontario*, 5th ed. (Toronto: University of Toronto Press, 1997), p. 159.

2. Sydney Sharpe and Don Braid, *Storming Babylon: Preston Manning and the Rise of the Reform Party* (Toronto: Key Porter, 1992), p. 154.

3. Paul Wells, *Right Side Up: The Fall of Paul Martin and the Rise of Stephen Harper's New Conservatism* (Toronto: McClelland & Stewart, 2006), p. 315.

4. Stephen Clarkson, "Canada–U.S. Relations: No More Mr. Nice Guy," *The Globe and Mail*, November 10, 2000.

5. Thomas J. Courchene with Colin R. Telmer, *From Heartland to North American Region State: The Social, Fiscal and Federal Evolution of Ontario. An Interpretive Essay* (Toronto: Centre for Public Management, University of Toronto, 1998), pp. 268–96.

BIBLIOGRAPHY

For a critical study of Canadian–American economic relations, see Stephen Clarkson, *Uncle Sam and Us: Globalization, Neoconservatism, and the Canadian State* (Toronto: University of Toronto Press, 2002). Economist William Watson proposes a provocative critique of Canadian identity in *Globalization and the Meaning of Canadian Life* (Toronto: University of Toronto Press, 1998). For a look at free trade, see Martin A. Andresen, "The Effect of North American Trade Liberalization on the Nature of Canadian Trade, 1989–2002," *American Review of Canadian Studies*, 36(1) (2006): 283–312; and Martin A. Andersen, "Trade Specialization and Reciprocal Trading Relationships in Canada and the United States, 1989 and 2001," *Annals of the Association of American Geographers*, 99(1) (2009): 163–83. Peter C. Newman examines the influence of business magnates in *Titans: How the New Canadian Establishment Seized Power* (Toronto: Penguin Books, 1998). On one controversial business leader, see Richard Siklos, *Shades of Black: Conrad Black, His Rise and Fall* (Toronto: McClelland & Stewart, 2004).

Writings on the environment include Melody Hessing and Michael Howlett, *Canadian Natural Resource and Environmental Policy: Political Economy and Public Policy,* 2nd ed. (Vancouver: University of British Columbia Press, 2005); G. Bruce Doern, ed., *Canadian Energy Policy and the Struggle for Sustainable Development* (Toronto: University of Toronto Press, 2005); Judith I. McKenzie, *Environmental Politics in Canada: Managing the Commons into the Twenty-First Century* (Toronto: Oxford, 2002); Rodney White, *Climate Change in Canada* (Oxford: Oxford University Press, 2010); Karen Bakker, ed., *Eau Canada: The Future of Canada's Water* (Vancouver: UBC Press, 2006); and Dean Bavington, *Managed Annihilation: An Unnatural History of the Newfoundland Cod Collapse* (Vancouver: UBC Press, 2010).

Kim Campbell has written her memoirs, *Time and Chance: The Political Memoirs of Canada's First Woman Prime Minister* (Toronto: Doubleday Canada, 1996). Her disastrous election campaign in 1993 is recounted in David McLaughlin, *Poisoned Chalice: The Last Campaign of the Progressive Conservative Party?* (Toronto: Dundurn Press, 1994). For an analysis of the Mulroney years, see Raymond B. Blake, ed., *Transforming the Nation: Canada and Brian Mulroney* (Montreal/Kingston: McGill-Queen's University Press, 2007).

Studies of Jean Chrétien include Lois Harder and Steve Patten, eds., *The Chrétien Legacy: Politics and Public Policy in Canada* (Montreal/Kingston, McGill-Queen's University Press, 2006); Jeffrey Simpson, *The Friendly Dictatorship*, rev. ed. (Toronto: McClelland and Stewart, 2002); Stephen Clarkson, *The Big Red Machine: How the Liberal Party Dominates Canadian Politics* (Vancouver: UBC Press, 2006); and Lawrence Martin, *Iron Man: The Defiant Reign of Jean Chrétien*, vol. 2., rev. ed. (Toronto: Penguin Books Canada, 2003).

On the Reform Party, see Faron Ellis, *The Limits of Participation: Members and Leaders in Canada's Reform Party* (Calgary: University of Calgary Press, 2005); and Trevor Harrison, *Of Passionate Intensity: Right-Wing Populism and the Reform Party of Canada* (Toronto: University of Toronto Press, 1995). For a look at political polarization, see Richard Johnston, "Polarized Pluralism in the Canadian Party System," *Canadian Journal of Political Science*, 41(4) (2008): 815–34; and for an examination of leadership and representation, see Hans Michelmann et al., eds., *Political Leadership and Representation in Canada* (Toronto: University of Toronto Press, 2007). For a look at the rising influence of the Canadian west, see Gordon Pitts, *Stampede: The Rise of the West and Canada's New Power Elite* (Toronto: Key Porter Books, 2008), on the rise of a new western political elite; and Frederic Boily et al., "Portrait intellectual de l'ecole de Calgary: Definition et influence," *International Journal of Canadian Studies*, 32 (2005): 175–204, for a look at the ideas and influence of the "Calgary school" of political thought. Tom Flanagan has written about his years behind the scenes as campaign manager for Stephen Harper in *Harper's Team: Behind the Scenes in the Conservative Rise to Power* (Montreal/Kingston: McGill-Queen's University Press, 2007). The Bloc Québécois is discussed in Manon Cornellier, *The Bloc* (Toronto: James Lorimer, 1995).

Among works on the Canadian left, consult Ian McLeod, *Under Siege: The Federal NDP in the Nineties* (Toronto: James Lorimer, 1994); and James Laxer, *In Search of a New Left: Canadian Politics After the Neoconservative Assault* (Toronto: Penguin Books, 1996).

Recent journalistic accounts of Canadian politics include John Gray, *Paul Martin: In the Balance* (Toronto: Key Porter Books, 2004); Hugh Segal, *The Long Road Back: The Conservative Journey in Canada, 1993–2006* (Toronto: HarperCollins, 2006); Paul Wells, *Right Side Up: The Fall of Paul Martin and the Rise of Stephen Harper's New Conservatism* (Toronto: McClelland & Stewart, 2006); Bob Plamondon, *Full Circle: Death and Resurrection in Canadian Conservative Politics* (Toronto: Key Porter, 2006); William Johnson, *Stephen Harper and the Future of Canada*, rev. ed. (Toronto: McClelland & Stewart, 2006); and Chantal Hébert, *French Kiss: Stephen Harper's Blind Date with Quebec* (Toronto: Knopf Canada, 2007). For a scholarly debate about the nature of Canada's political history, see Jean-Francois Constant and Michel Ducharme, *Liberalism and Hegemony: Debating the Canadian Liberal Revolution* (Toronto: University of Toronto Press, 2008).

Different strands composing Canada's foreign relations are examined in Roy Rempel, *Dreamland: How Canada's Pretend Foreign Policy Has Undermined Sovereignty* (Montreal/Kingston: McGill-Queen's University Press, 2006); Rosalind Irwin, ed., *Ethics and Security in Canadian Foreign Policy* (Vancouver: UBC Press, 2001); and Thomas F. Keating, *Canada in World Order: The Multilateralist Tradition in Canadian Foreign Policy*, 2nd ed. (Toronto: Oxford University Press, 2001). Canada's role in the Gulf War of 1990 is examined in Richard Gimblett and Jean Morin, *Operation Friction: Canadian Forces in the Gulf War* (Toronto: Dundurn Press, 1996). On aspects of peacekeeping, see Nicolas Gammer, *From Peacekeeping to Peacemaking: Canada's Response to the Yugoslav Crisis* (Montreal/Kingston: McGill-Queen's University Press, 2001); and Sean M. Maloney, *Canada and UN Peacekeeping: Cold War by Other Means* (St. Catharines, ON: Vanwell, 2002).

For overviews of Canadian foreign policy, see Robert Bothwell and Jean Daudelin, eds., *Canada Among Nations, 2008: 100 Years of Canadian Foreign Policy* (Montreal/Kingston: McGill-Queen's University Press, 2008); Norman Hillmer and Adam Chapnick, eds., *Canadas of the Mind: The Making and Unmaking of Canadian Nationalisms in the Twentieth Century* (Montreal/Kingston: McGill-Queen's University Press, 2007); Evan Potter, *Branding Canada: Projecting Canada's Soft Power Through Public Diplomacy* (Montreal/Kingston: McGill-Queen's University Press, 2008); and James McCormick, "Democratizing Canadian Foreign Policy," *Canadian Foreign Policy*, 13(3) (2007): 113–32. Raymond Moriyama discusses the making of the new Canadian War Museum in *In Search of a Soul: Creating the New Canadian War Museum* (Vancouver: Douglas & McIntyre, 2006). For a look at the role of international law in Canadian lawmaking, see Andrew S. Thompson, "Uneasy Abolitionists: Canada, the Death Penalty, and the Importance of International Norms, 1962–2005," *Journal of Canadian Studies*, 42(3) (2008): 172–92.

Effects on Canada of the terrorist attacks of September 2001 are discussed in Ronald J. Daniels, Patricia Macklem, and Kent Roach, *The Security of Freedom: Essays on Canada's Anti-Terrorism Bill* (Toronto: University of Toronto Press, 2001); Kent Roach, *September 11: Consequences for Canada* (Montreal/Kingston: McGill-Queen's University Press, 2003); and Bruno Charbonneau and Wayne Cox, eds. *Locating Global Order: American Power and Canadian Security after 9/11* (Vancouver: UBC Press, 2010). See also J.L. Granatstein's (strongly opinionated) essay, *Whose War Is It? How Canada Can Survive in the Post-9/11 World* (Toronto: HarperCollins, 2007).

Relations between Ottawa and the provinces are discussed in Richard Simeon, *Federal–Provincial Diplomacy: The Making of Recent Policy in Canada* (Toronto: University of Toronto Press, 2006). For a more extended discussion of the Charter of Rights and Freedoms, see Michael Manley-Casimir and Kirsten Manley-Casimir, eds., *The Courts, the Charter, and the Schools: The Impact of the Charter of Rights and Freedoms on Educational Policy and Practice, 1982–2007* (Toronto: University of Toronto Press 2009). For a look at changing concepts of rights in Canada, see Dominique Clement, *Canada's Rights Revolution: Social Movements and Social Change* (Vancouver: UBC Press 2008). On the failed Charlottetown Accord, see Richard Johnston et al., *The Challenge of Direct Democracy: The 1992 Canadian Referendum* (Montreal/Kingston: McGill-Queen's University Press, 1996).

David R. Cameron and Janice Gross Stein, eds., *Street Protests and Fantasy Parks: Globalization, Culture and the State* (Vancouver: UBC Press, 2002), focuses on the cultural and social realities of globalization.

For a panorama of Canadian writing, W.H. New, ed., *Encyclopedia of Literature in Canada* (Toronto: University of Toronto Press, 2002) is the standard authority. Contemporary architecture is presented in Harold Kalman, *A Concise History of Canadian Architecture* (Toronto: Oxford University Press, 2000).

On sports history, consult Colin Howell, *Blood, Sweat, and Cheers: Sport and the Making of Modern Canada* (Toronto: University of Toronto Press, 2001); M. Ann Hall, *The Girl and the Game: A History of Women's Sport in Canada* (Peterborough, ON: Broadview Press, 2002); and Andrew C. Holman, ed., *Canada's Game: Hockey and Identity* (Montreal/Kingston: McGill-Queen's University Press, 2009). Pollster Michael Adams looks at the differences between Canadians and Americans in *Fire and Ice: The United States, Canada and the Myth of Converging Values* (Toronto: Penguin Canada, 2003).

Reginald W. Bibby examines contemporary religion in *Restless Gods: The Renaissance of Religion in Canada* (Toronto: Stoddart, 2002). Populist Christianity is discussed in Sam Reimer, *Evangelicals and the Continental Divide: The Conservative Protestant Subculture in Canada and the United States* (Montreal/Kingston, McGill-Queen's University Press, 2003); and G.A. Rawlyk, *Is Jesus Your Personal Saviour? In Search of Canadian Evangelicalism in the 1990s* (Montreal/Kingston: McGill-Queen's University Press, 1996).

Sylvain Larocque, *Gay Marriage: The Story of a Canadian Social Revolution* (Toronto: James Lorimer, 2006), deals with a major gay rights issue.

Critical studies of government welfare policies are Maude Barlow and Bruce Campbell, *Straight Through the Heart: How the Liberals Abandoned the Just Society* (Toronto: HarperCollins, 1995); and Gary Teeple, *Globalization and the Decline of Social Reform: Into the Twenty-First Century* (Toronto: Garamond, 2000). On poverty, see Jean Swanson, *Poor-Bashing: The Politics of Exclusion* (Toronto: Between the Lines Press, 2001). Health care issues are discussed in Colleen Fuller, *Caring for Profit: How Corporations Are Taking over Canada's Health Care System* (Vancouver: New Star, 1998). Child care is examined in Gordon Cleveland and Michael Krashinsky, eds., *Our Children's Future: Child Care Policy in Canada* (Toronto: University of Toronto Press, 2001).

An overview of the First Nations in present-day Canada, the United States, and Mexico appears in Alice B. Kehoe's Chapter 10, "First Nations of North America in the Contemporary World," in her *North American Indians: A Comprehensive Account*, 3rd ed. (Upper Saddle River, NJ: Pearson Prentice Hall, 2006), pp. 524–54. See also James S. Frideres, *First Nations in the Twenty-First Century* (Don Mills, ON: Oxford University Press, 2011).

Unfortunately, there are few historical studies of provincial policies toward Indigenous people. Three contributions are Paul Tennant, *Aboriginal Peoples and Politics: The Indian Land Question in British Columbia, 1849–1989* (Vancouver: University of British Columbia Press, 1990); F. Laurie Barron, *Walking in Indian Moccasins: The Native Policies of Tommy Douglas and the CCF* (Vancouver: University of British Columbia Press, 1997); and Laurie Meijer Drees, *The Indian Association of Alberta: A History of Political Action* (Vancouver: University of British Columbia Press, 2002). Other valuable introductory studies of the mid-twentieth century include Hugh Dempsey, *The Gentle Persuader: A Biography of James Gladstone, Indian Senator* (Saskatoon: Western Producer Prairie Books, 1986); Harold Cardinal, *The Unjust Society: The Tragedy of Canada's Indians* (Edmonton: Hurtig, 1969; Vancouver: Douglas and McIntyre, 1999), a Cree's indictment of Canadian Indian policy; and Edgar Dosman, *Indians: The Urban Dilemma* (Toronto: McClelland & Stewart, 1972). See also Yale D. Belanger and P. Whitney Lackenbauer, *Blockades or Breakthroughs?: Aboriginal People Confront the Canadian State* (Montreal/Kingston: McGill-Queen's University Press, 2015).

For an overview of First Nations social welfare issues, see Hugh Shewell, *"Enough to Keep Them Alive": Indian Welfare in Canada, 1873–1965* (Toronto: University of Toronto Press, 2004). An older study remains useful, namely Patrick Johnston, *Native Children and the Child Welfare System* (Toronto: James Lorimer, 1983). A regional study of health issues is T. Kue Young's *Health Care and Cultural Change: The Indian Experience in the Central Arctic* (Toronto: University of Toronto Press, 1988). Pat Sandiford Grygier provides a history of the tuberculosis epidemic among the Inuit in the mid-twentieth century in *A Long Way from Home* (Montreal/Kingston: McGill-Queen's University Press, 1994). Laurence J.

Kirmayer and Gail Guthrie Valaskakis address mental health in *Healing Traditions: The Mental Health of Aboriginal Peoples in Canada* (Vancouver: UBC Press 2008). For a look at alcohol regulation, see Robert A. Campbell, "Making Sober Citizens: The Legacy of Indigenous Alcohol Regulation in Canada, 1777–1985," *Journal of Canadian Studies*, 42(1) (2008): 105–26. Ryan Walker examines the social housing question in "Aboriginal Self-Determination and Social Housing in Urban Canada: A Story of Convergence and Divergence," *Urban Studies*, 45(1) (2008): 185–205.

For an understanding of residential schools, see The Truth and Reconciliation Commission of Canada, *Canada's Residential Schools: The History, Part I, Origins to 1939* and *Part 2, 1930 to 2000* (Montreal/Kingston: McGill-Queen's University Press, 2016); and J.R. Miller, *Shingwauk's Vision* (Toronto: University of Toronto Press, 1996)—the essential starting points. John S. Milloy examines the schools in *"A National Crime": The Canadian Government and the Residential School System, 1879 to 1986* (Winnipeg: University of Manitoba Press, 1999). Bernard Schissel and Terry Wotherspoon provide a sociological assessment in *The Legacy of School for Aboriginal People* (Don Mills: Oxford University Press, 2003).

Four recent studies provide good overviews of contemporary Indigenous issues in Canada: James S. Frideres and René R. Gadacz, *Aboriginal Peoples in Canada: Contemporary Conflicts*, 7th ed. (Toronto: Pearson Prentice-Hall, 2005); John Steckley and Bryan D. Cummins, eds., *Full Circle: Canada's First Nations*, 2nd ed. (Toronto: Pearson Prentice Hall, 2007); J.R. Miller, *Lethal Legacy: Current Native Controversies in Canada* (Toronto: McClelland and Stewart, 2004); and David R. Newhouse, Cora J. Voyageur, and Dan Beavon, eds., *Hidden in Plain Sight: Contributions of Aboriginal Peoples to Canadian Identity and Culture* (Toronto: University of Toronto Press, 2005). *Hidden in Plain Sight* is particularly valuable, as it covers treaties, arts and media, literature, justice, culture and identity, sports, and military. *Tapwe: Selected Columns of Doug Cuthand* (Penticton, BC: Theytus Books Ltd., 2005) includes a wide range of articles by a Plains Cree journalist on many contemporary Native issues.

Three treatments of contemporary Aboriginal and non-Aboriginal relations in Canada are Alan C. Cairns's *Citizens Plus: Aboriginal Peoples and the Canadian State* (Vancouver: UBC Press, 2000); Tom Flanagan's more controversial *First Nations? Second Thoughts* (Montreal/Kingston: McGill-Queen's University Press, 2000); and Dale Turner, *This Is Not a Peace Pipe: Towards a Critical Indigenous Philosophy* (Toronto: University of Toronto Press, 2006). An overview of First Nations land claims in Canada is Ken Coates, *Aboriginal Land Claims in Canada: A Regional Perspective* (Toronto: Copp Clark Pitman, 1992). See also J. Rick Ponting, *The Nisga'a Treaty: Polling Dynamics and Political Communication in Comparative Context* (Calgary: Broadview Press, 2006).

In *Native Literature in Canada: From the Oral Tradition to the Present* (Toronto: Oxford University Press, 1990), Penny Petrone reviews Aboriginal literature. Students should also consult her two edited collections *First People, First Voices* (Toronto: University of Toronto Press, 1983), and *Northern Voices: Inuit Writing in English* (Toronto: University of Toronto Press, 1988); and also Helmut Lutz, *Contemporary Challenges, Conversations with Canadian Native Authors* (Saskatoon: Fifth House, 1991). For contemporary Indigenous viewpoints on Aboriginal writing, see the section "Literature" in Newhouse et al., *Hidden in Plain Sight* (cited above), pp. 169–212.

D. Bruce Sealey and Antoine S. Lussier provide one of the few historical overviews of the Métis in the final chapters of their study *The Métis: Canada's Forgotten People* (Winnipeg: Manitoba Métis Federation Press, 1975), pp. 143–94. Olive P. Dickason provides a useful overview in "Aboriginals: Métis," in Paul Magocsi, ed., *Encyclopedia of Canada's Peoples* (Toronto: University of Toronto Press, 1999), pp. 70–79. A recent treatment is George and Terry Goulet, *The Métis: Memorable Events and Memorable Personalities* (Calgary: FabJob Inc., 2006). John Weinstein has written about the resurgence of Métis nationalism in *Quiet Revolution West: The Rebirth of Métis Nationalism* (Calgary: Fifth House Publishers 2007).

A short, well-illustrated overview of Northern history is William R. Morrison's *True North: The Yukon and Northwest Territories* (Toronto: Oxford University Press, 1998). Georges Blondin provides an interesting Dene view of the First Nations' history in the Mackenzie valley in *When the World Was New: Stories of the Sahtu Dene* (Yellowknife: Outcrop, 1990). Federal policy toward the Inuit is reviewed in Frank J. Tester and Peter Kulchyski, *Tammarniit (Mistakes): Inuit Relocation in the Eastern Arctic, 1939–63*

(Vancouver: University of British Columbia Press, 1994). John David Hamilton surveys post-World War II developments in the North in *Arctic Revolution: Social Change in the Northwest Territories, 1935–1994* (Toronto: Dundurn Press, 1994). Keith Brownsey and Michael Howlett, eds., *The Provincial State in Canada: Politics in the Provinces and Territories* (Peterborough, ON: Broadview Press, 2000), contains two articles on the Northwest Territories and Nunavut as follows: Peter Clancy, "The Northwest Territories: Old and New Class Politics on the Northern Frontier," pp. 335–68, and Jack Hicks and Graham White, "Nunavut: Inuit Self-Determination Through a Land Claim and Public Government?," pp. 389–439.

Students interested in Aboriginal politics in the past forty years should consult, as a starting point, Sally M. Weaver, *Making Canadian Indian Policy: The Hidden Agenda, 1968–1970* (Toronto: University of Toronto Press, 1981); and Michel Lavoie, "Politique sur commande: Les effets des commissions d'enquête sur la philosophie publique et la politique indienne au Canada, 1828–1996," *Recherches amérindiennes au Québec*, 37 (2007): 5–24. Studies of important First Nations leaders include: Peter McFarlane's *Brotherhood to Nationhood: George Manuel and the Making of the Modern Indian Movement* (Toronto: Between the Lines, 1993); Roy MacGregor, *Chief: The Fearless Vision of Billy Diamond* (Toronto: Penguin, 1989); and Pauline Comeau's *Elijah: No Ordinary Hero* (Vancouver: Douglas & McIntyre, 1993). Useful for an understanding of contemporary issues are John Bird, Lorraine Land, and Murray Macadam, eds., *Nation to Nation: Aboriginal Sovereignty and the Future of Canada* (Toronto: Irwin, 2002); and J.R. Miller, *Lethal Legacy: Current Native Controversies in Canada* (Toronto: McClelland and Stewart, 2004). For a look at Aboriginal anti-capitalism, see Peter Kulchyski, *The Red Indians: Aboriginal Resistance to Capitalism, Then and Now* (Winnipeg: Arbeiter Ring, 2006). For a look at the politics of hydroelectric development and First Nations communities, see Thibault Martin and Steven M. Hoffman, eds., *Power Struggle: Hydroelectric Development and First Nations in Manitoba and Quebec* (Winnipeg: University of Manitoba Press 2008); and Caroline Desbiens, *Power from the North: Territory, Identity, and the Culture of Hydroelectricity in Quebec* (Vancouver: UBC Press, 2013).

Interesting new studies on contemporary Aboriginal Canada include Blair Stonechild, *The New Buffalo: The Struggle for Aboriginal Post-Secondary Education in Canada* (Winnipeg: University of Manitoba Press, 2006); Yale D. Belanger, *Gambling with the Future: The Evolution of Aboriginal Gaming in Canada* (Saskatoon: Purich Publishing, 2006); Lorna Roth, *Something New in the Air: The Story of First Peoples Television Broadcasting in Canada* (Montreal/Kingston: McGill-Queen's University Press, 2005); Mary Jane Miller, *Outside Looking In: Viewing First Nations Peoples in Canadian Dramatic Television Series* (Montreal/Kingston: McGill-Queen's University Press, 2008); F. Laurie Barron and Joseph Garcea, eds., *Urban Reserves: Forging New Relationships in Saskatchewan* (Saskatoon: Purich Publishing Ltd., 1999); Annis May Timpton, ed., *First Nations, First Thoughts: The Impact of Indigenous Thought in Canada* (Vancouver: UBC Press 2009); Ian M. Thom, *Challenging Traditions: Contemporary First Nations Art of the Northwest Coast* (Vancouver: Douglas & McIntyre, 2009); Ted Binnema and Susan Neylan, eds., *New Histories for Old: Changing Perspectives on Canada's Native Pasts* (Vancouver: UBC Press 2007); Sam McKegney, *Magic Weapons: Aboriginal Writers Remaking Community After Residential School* (Winnipeg: University of Manitoba Press 2007); P. Whitney Lackenbauer, *Battle Grounds: The Canadian Military and Aboriginal Lands* (Vancouver: University of British Columbia Press, 2007); and Whitney P. Lackenbauer and Andrew E. Cooper, "The Achilles Heel of Canadian Good International Citizenship: Indigenous Diplomacies and State Responses in the Twentieth Century," *Canadian Foreign Policy*, 13(3) (2007): 99–120.

On the subject of Aboriginal rights, a plethora of publications have appeared in the past several years. See Hamara Foster et al., eds., *Let Right Be Done: Aboriginal Title, the Calder Case, and the Future of Indigenous Rights* (Vancouver: UBC Press 2007); Catherine Bell and Val Napoleon, eds., *First Nations Cultural Heritage and Law: Case Studies, Voices, and Perspectives* (Vancouver: UBC Press 2008); Catherine Bell and Robert K. Paterson, eds., *Protection of First Nations Cultural Heritage: Law, Policy, and Reform* (Vancouver: UBC Press 2008); Tom Flanagan, Christopher Alcantara, and Andre le Dressay, *Beyond the Indian Act: Restoring Aboriginal Property Rights* (Montreal/Kingston: McGill-Queen's University Press 2010); Paul Chartrand, "Aboriginal Identity and the Charter of Rights and Freedoms," *Canadian Issues* (Fall 2007): 109–12; Richard Boivin and Rene Morin, "La Commission royale sur les peuples autochtones (1991–1996) ou la longue marche des peuples autochtones du Canada vers la reconnaissance de leurs droits," *Recherches amérindiennes au Québec*, 37 (2007): 25–36; Jean-Francois Savard, "Intégration des recommandations de la Commission royale sur les peuples autochtones dans les politiques autochtones fédérales au Canada," *Recherches amérindiennes au Québec*, 37(8 1) (2007): 57–66; and Hugh Shewell, "Rassembler nos forces, ou recourir encore à l'aide sociale? La situation socio-économique des premières nations avant et après la Commission royale," *Recherches amérindiennes au Québec*, 37 (2007): 43–56. See also Cora Voyageur's *Fire-Keepers of the Twenty-First Century: First Nations Women Chiefs* (Montreal: McGill-Queen's Press, 2008).

Appendix

CANADIAN PRIME MINISTERS SINCE CONFEDERATION

Sir John Alexander Macdonald
Conservative
1867–73, 1878–91

Alexander Mackenzie
Liberal
1873–78

Sir John Abbott
Conservative
1891–92

Sir John Thompson
Conservative
1892–94

Sir Mackenzie Bowell
Conservative
1894–96

Sir Charles Tupper
Conservative
1896

Sir Wilfrid Laurier
Liberal
1896–1911

Sir Robert Borden
Conservative and Unionist
1911–20

Arthur Meighen
Conservative and Unionist
1920–21, 1926

William Lyon Mackenzie King
Liberal
1921–26, 1926–30, 1935–48

Richard Bedford Bennett
Conservative
1930–35

Louis St. Laurent
Liberal
1948–57

John Diefenbaker
Progressive Conservative
1957–63

Lester Bowles Pearson
Liberal
1963–68

Pierre Elliott Trudeau
Liberal
1968–79, 1980–84

Joe Clark
Progressive Conservative
1979–80

John Turner
Liberal
1984

Brian Mulroney
Progressive Conservative
1984–93

Kim Campbell
Progressive Conservative
1993

Jean Chrétien
Liberal
1993–2003

Paul Martin
Liberal
2003–06

Stephen Harper
Conservative
2006–15

Justin Trudeau
Liberal
2015–

Index

Note: References to tables and figures that appear in the text are indicated by a T or F following the page number.

debate over national policy, 68–69
evaluating Canada's multicultural policy, 509–10
gay and lesbian activism, 431–32
Indian residential schools, 563–65
industrial growth in Quebec, 158–59
Louis Riel and the Mêtis, 99–101
meaning of the BNA Act, 14–17
Quiet Revolution, 469–71
shifting historical paradigms: gender and women's history, 540–41
sports and culture, 232–33
treaties, 44–46
welfare state, 333–35
Winnipeg General Strike, 280–83
women and reform, 267–68
women and unions in postwar Canada, 409–11
Whitaker, Denis and Sheilagh, 367
White Paper of 1969, 520–21
White, Philip, 233
Whiteway, Sir William, 151
Whitney, James, 262
Whitson, David, 233
Whitton, Charlotte, 300, 320, 409
Wickett, Samuel, 198
wilderness and wildlife conservation, 199–202
Canada–United States Migratory Bird Convention Treaty, 200
Commission of Conservation, 200
Wilderness Area Act, Ontario, 390
Williams, Percy, 309
Wilson, Cairine, 326
Winnipeg General Strike, 279–80
where historians disagree, 280–83
Winnipeg Political Equality League, 205, 206F
Wireless Telegraph Company of Canada, 75
Wise, S.F., 369
Wohl, Robert, 173
Wolseley Expedition, 41–42
Wolseley, Garnet, 41–42
Woman's Christian Temperance Union (WCTU), 193, 202, 208
women
1860s, 23–24

1930s, 330–31
1960s, 433–34, 433F
after World War II, 392–93
status, 408–12
in the armed services, 355
changing roles, 538
clerical workers, 150, 148F
gender and history, where historians disagree, 540–41
and imperialism, 124
pay equity, 580–81
social reform and, 202–7
in the 1920s, 298–99, 299F
where historians disagree, 267–68
sports, 227–28, 227F, 309, 582
unions and, 182
in Postwar Canada, where historians disagree, 409–11
Women's Art Association, 216
in the workplace, 175–79, 179F, 408–9, 433–34
World War I, 257–58
World War II, 353–55, 354F, 373
Women's Art Association, 216
Women's Emergency Corps, 258
Women's Patriotic League, 257
women's suffrage movement, 205–6, 206F
reform in the 1920s, 297
World War I effects, 266
Wood, Henry Wise, 289
Woodcock, George, 100
Woodsworth, J.S., 194, 198, 280, 323
Worker's Unity league (WUL), 329
Workmen's Compensation Act, 194
World War I, 246–77
battles fought in Europe, 258–60
Canadian Expeditionary Force, 249–50
Canadian fatalities, 370T
conscription crisis, 263–64, 264F
demobilization, 272–73
enlistment/casualty rate, 1917, 259T
final year, 269–71
horrors of, 252–56, 253F
national disunity, 261–62
Ontario schools question, 262–63
prohibition and, 266
recruitment, 261
social reform and, 266–70

voice in Britain's war policy, 260–61
White Man's War, 252
women and, 257–58
women's suffrage and, 266
World War II, 344–85
1940–42, 349
Canada declares war, 347–50
Canadian fatalities, 370T
Canadian–American relations, 351–52
citizen inequality, 393
culture and the state, 357
economy during, 352–53
evaluation of Canadian participation, 365–66
where historians disagree, 367–69
federal–provincial tensions after, 399–400
First Nations and, 355–57
French Canada and, 359–60
the less advantaged, 391
national unity and, 357
plebiscite of 1942, 360–61, 361F
postwar prosperity, 389–91
prosperity and trade after, 395–96
regional and provincial developments after, 375–80
treatment of ethnic groups, 358–59
war effort intensifies, 362–70, 363F
war of limited liability, 348
women and the war effort, 353–55, 354F

Y
Yale-Toronto Conference on the North American Indian, 355–56
Young, George, 309
Young, Kevin, 233
Young, Sandy, 233
Young Men's Christian Association (YMCA), 272
Young Women's Christian Association (YWCA), 202, 228
youth protest, 424–29
Yukon Territory, 133–35

Z
Zouaves, 62, 62F